T0332453

Computational Models, Software Engineering, and Advanced Technologies in Air Transportation:
Next Generation Applications

Li Weigang
University of Brasilia, Brazil

Alexandre de Barros
University of Calgary, Canada

Ítalo Romani de Oliveira
Atech Tecnologias Críticas, Brazil

ENGINEERING SCIENCE REFERENCE

Hershey · New York

Director of Editorial Content:	Kristin Klinger
Senior Managing Editor:	Jamie Snavely
Assistant Managing Editor:	Michael Brehm
Publishing Assistant:	Sean Woznicki
Typesetter:	Sean Woznicki
Cover Design:	Lisa Tosheff
Printed at:	Yurchak Printing Inc.

Published in the United States of America by
Engineering Science Reference (an imprint of IGI Global)
701 E. Chocolate Avenue
Hershey PA 17033
Tel: 717-533-8845
Fax: 717-533-8661
E-mail: cust@igi-global.com
Web site: http://www.igi-global.com/reference

Library of Congress Cataloging-in-Publication Data

Computational models, software engineering, and advanced technologies in air transportation : next generation applications / Li Weigang, Alexandre de Barros and Italo Romani, editors.
    p. cm.
Includes bibliographical references and index.
Summary: "This book disseminates knowledge on modern information technology applications in air transportation useful to professionals, researchers, and academicians"--Provided by publisher.

ISBN 978-1-60566-800-0 (hbk.) -- ISBN 978-1-60566-801-7 (ebook) 1.
Aeronautics, Commercial--Information technology. 2. Aeronautics--Information
technology. 3. Air traffic control. 4. Airports--Traffic control. I. Li,
Weigang, 1958- II. Barros, Alexandre de. III. Romani, Italo.
TL552.C64 2010
387.70285--dc22
                        2009032821

British Cataloguing in Publication Data
A Cataloguing in Publication record for this book is available from the British Library.

All work contributed to this book is new, previously-unpublished material. The views expressed in this book are those of the authors, but not necessarily of the publisher.

Table of Contents

Section 1
Managing the Air Transportation Complexity

Chapter 1
Dave Young, EUROCONTROL, France
Nadine Pilon, EUROCONTROL, France
Lawrence Brom, EUROCONTROL, France

Chapter 2
Antonio Pedro Timoszczuk, Fundação Aplicações de Tecnologias Críticas – Atech, Brazil
Walter Nogueira Pizzo, Fundação Aplicações de Tecnologias Críticas – Atech, Brazil
Giacomo Feres Staniscia, Fundação Aplicações de Tecnologias Críticas – Atech, Brazil
Eno Siewerdt, Fundação Aplicações de Tecnologias Críticas – Atech, Brazil

Chapter 3
Bueno Borges de Souza, University of Brasília, Brazil
Li Weigang, University of Brasília, Brazil
Antonio Marcio Ferreira Crespo, CINDACTA I, Brazil
Victor Rafael Rezende Celestino, TRIP Linhas Aereas S/A, Brazil

Detailed Table of Contents

Section 1
Managing the Air Transportation Complexity

This section presents the problematic of multiple agents in the air transportation concurring for the same basic resources in their operations: airspace, airport surface, fuel and many others. The demand for flights increases apace as consequence of economic growth, but resource availability does not follow the same pace. Given the potential for enormous conflicts with these simultaneous demands, what can be done to make the air transportation system more efficient and safe for the user, as well as environmentally friendly, along the upcoming years, based on already proven improvements and on long term research and development activities on technological systems, policies and algorithms? This is what this section's chapters try to respond.

Chapter 1

    Dave Young, EUROCONTROL, France
    Nadine Pilon, EUROCONTROL, France
    Lawrence Brom, EUROCONTROL, France

Considering the continuing growth in air traffic volume and complexity, this chapter poses and discusses some important needs existing in the current European air transportation, in a systemic and evolutionary perspective, as well as the candidate solutions, and presents the directives to improve the air transport system, which are agreed among the main European air transport entities. Many of this chapter's contents are applicable to the other regions of the world.

Chapter 2

Antonio Pedro Timoszczuk, Fundação Aplicações de Tecnologias Críticas – Atech, Brazil
Walter Nogueira Pizzo, Fundação Aplicações de Tecnologias Críticas – Atech, Brazil
Giacomo Feres Staniscia, Fundação Aplicações de Tecnologias Críticas – Atech, Brazil
Eno Siewerdt, Fundação Aplicações de Tecnologias Críticas – Atech, Brazil

This chapter provides an overview of an important milestone achieved in the Brazilian Air Traffic Flow Management (ATFM). It begins laying down the ATFM-related background concepts and defining the different roles and responsibilities in this activity. Then an overview on the Brazilian Air Traffic Scenario is presented and, as a tool for improving air ATFM decision making, the SYNCROMAX product solution is explained in a reasonable level of detail.

Chapter 3

Bueno Borges de Souza, University of Brasília, Brazil
Li Weigang, University of Brasília, Brazil
Antonio Marcio Ferreira Crespo, CINDACTA I, Brazil
Victor Rafael Rezende Celestino, TRIP Linhas Aereas S/A, Brazil

This chapter is complimentary to the previous one, and describes a decision making support system which uses Graph Theory and Artificial Intelligence techniques to solve problems in Air Traffic Flow Management (ATFM). A prototype of the system was tested in some scenarios based on real input date, and the results were showed as satisfactory, however a discussion follows about how the results can be improved.

Chapter 4

Felipe Maia Galvão França, Universidade Federal do Rio de Janeiro, Brazil
Félix Mora-Camino, Ecole Nationale de l'Aviation Civile, France

In this chapter, the authors explain the problem of managing high levels of traffic in the airport surface, including aircraft and terrestrial vehicles. A mathematical model of this traffic is developed, allowing for uncertainty and perturbations. Assuming this traffic model, a multi-agent ground traffic control structure is laid, and algorithms of vehicles assignment for each aircraft movement are defined. Finally, some simulation results are reported and discussed.

Section 2
Improving Economic and Operational Performance

Each agent in air transportation has to be economically sustainable in order to continuously operate. This attribute is achieved with a combination of several important activities related to Information Technology, such as market research, enterprise resource planning, operations research, risk analysis, the use of decision support tools, etc. The following chapters present conceptual and mathematical models that can be embedded in computational tools aiming at improving return of investment, competitiveness, and operational performance of airports and airlines.

Chapter 5

Matthew G. Karlaftis, National Technical University of Athens, Greece

Given the importance of making proper dimensioning of airport facilities and proper airline network design, this chapter describes and critically analyzes several models which can support these tasks, taking as the main factor the demand forecast. The applicability of each model, and its relative strengths and weaknesses are discussed, helping the reader who is eventually interested in selecting and using them.

Chapter 6

Becky P. Y. Loo, The University of Hong Kong, China
H. W. Ho, The Hong Kong Polytechnic University, China
S. C. Wong, The University of Hong Kong, China
Peng Zhang, Shanghai University, China

This chapter unveils an innovative computational method to understand how passenger flows behave when competing airports are available in circumscribed a region. The Hong Kong-Pearl River Delta is used as a case study is used to demonstrate the effectiveness of the approach.

Chapter 7

Kasthurirangan Gopalakrishnan, Iowa State University, USA

This chapter reports a model to evaluate pavement elasticity parameters in real-time, therefore enabling more agility in decision-making depending on airport pavement conditions, which is very likely to have safety implications. The model and the evaluation technique, based on Artificial Neural Networks, is validated using actual field data.

Chapter 8

Félix Mora-Camino, French Civil Aviation Institute (ENAC), France
Luiz Gustavo Zelaya Cruz, Federal University of Rio de Janeiro, Brazil

This chapter presents a stochastic model and a computational method to forecast airline revenue based on ticket booking and cancelation events, and is divided in two main parts. The first part introduces the problem of updating the probability distribution of demand reservations, and the second part considers the design of a new Decision Support System for improving the reservation control process of airlines.

This chapter presents a comprehensive and systematic model for the process of operating commercial aircraft with Continued Airworthiness, which can help airline managers to better understand what is behind the commercially-available software they use, therefore enhancing their ability to see opportunities of process improvement.

Section 3
Improving Aircraft Performance

In order to improve the overall air transportation performance, we have to think of improving its principal artifact: the aircraft itself. This improvement, however, must come with two main strengths: the efficiency in its individual transportation requirements, such as fuel efficiency, flight safety, passenger comfort, etc.; and the aircraft integrability in a high throughput transportation system, because otherwise it would be of little use to operate very efficient aircraft, having to keep them tenths of miles separated from each other and, eventually, having them most of the time waiting on ground or flying in circles. The first two chapters of this section present studies on technological means that help to reduce separation requirements between aircraft and, therefore, optimize airspace usage. Besides, the third chapter relates the development of an extremely efficient algorithm to optimize aircraft trajectories to obtain a globally optimal solution in multi-aircraft mission.

This chapter deals with risk analysis in air traffic, considering technical advances coming into practice in the next years, such as Automatic Dependant Surveillance-Broadcast (ADS-B), and the Airborne Separation Assistance System (ASAS), presenting arguments showing that their correct exploitation can provide the skies with more safety.

Chapter 11

Henrique Moniz, University of Lisbon, Portugal
Alessandra Tedeschi, Deep Blue s.r.l., Rome, Italy
Nuno Ferreira Neves, University of Lisbon, Portugal
Miguel Correia, University of Lisbon, Portugal

The airborne separation management is also object of this chapter, which develops a technique called RAPTOR, to safely allow fully automatic aircraft self-separation, based on game theory and a stack of distributed protocols allowing robust and fault-tolerant aircraft agreement. Rigorous formal proofs are given to ensure the reliability of the protocols.

Chapter 12

S.P. Wilson, Numerical Optimisation Centre, University of Hertfordshire, UK
M.C. Bartholomew-Biggs, Numerical Optimisation Centre, University of Hertfordshire, UK
S.C. Parkhurst, Numerical Optimisation Centre, University of Hertfordshire, UK

This chapter describes the formulation and solution of a multi-aircraft routing problem which is posed as a global optimization calculation, considering a number of ways of decomposing the problem, with illustrative results are presented involving up to three aircraft. The presented algorithm is primarily developed for military aircraft operations, but is greatly adaptable to civil aviation.

Section 4
Improving Computer Software Effectiveness

Computer software is ubiquitous, and as such is in the core of air transportation operations. Considering the high criticality of air traffic management decisions and aircraft control computers, a bunch of special requirements are applicable to software in these applications. Having as background the assumption that software is a key factor for efficiency and safety, we created this section to accommodate the chapters that explore better ways to structure and produce software. The first chapter is concerned to software architectures to ensure that the right information of Air Traffic Management be in the right place, at the right time. The following two chapters present techniques to better ensure safety in aircraft onboard computers, such as for engine control and flight management. These techniques, however, are applicable in several fields outside air transportation.

This chapter explores the Service-Oriented Architecture (SOA) and the concept of System Wide Information Management (SWIM) in such a way to propose a system interoperation paradigm to ensure reliable Collaborative Decision Making (CDM) in air transportation operations, and various other benefits derived from efficient information sharing.

This chapter presents an overview of models and techniques for component-based software development, and develops a step-by-step case study on component modeling and verification for a specific function of a gas turbine controller, aiming at the achievement of high software reliability in a cost-effective way.

This chapter explores an accurate and effective technique to specify and verify multiprocessor hardware/software co-design for embedded systems. This technique is called Specification PEARL, which is based on a formally defined language, and uses also graphical elements to enhance the modeling power. At the end, an example of a Flight Guidance System is given.

Foreword

Recently, we have seen trillions of dollars from taxpayers being spent only to mitigate the contamination of financial institutions. If the country leaders could foresee what was going to happen, they would certainly have taken decisions to avoid the global financial tsunami. The problem is that, most of the time, we are pursuing short-term benefits, and not holistic and stable advancements in the activities we are doing. Fortunately, in Air Transportation many researchers are making efforts to provide safer, more secure, sustainable, reliable and environmentally-friendly systems. They are researchers from air transportation, operation research, computer science and other related areas. These people have not only sowed the seeds of a next generation for improving the air transportation continuously, the most significant results of which will be reaped in one or two decades. Despite knowing this, these researchers do not give up working with scarce or modest budgets in face of the huge challenges they will cope with. In view of the outbreak of epidemic and pandemic such as SARS and Human Swine Influenza, there is a need to strengthen the research in this area. If a financial amount, equivalent only to a negligible part of the crisis-curative money, could be available for extension of the research ideas in this book, it is believed that, in the near future, the human being will fly better and safer than birds and, more importantly, without taking them out of the sky.

After reading these chapters, I have been impressed on how the research work from researchers with different backgrounds and methodologies can be so unique and indispensable for the global air transportation system evolution. The topics explored in this book give to the readers an up-to-date and comprehensive understanding about how mathematical models and computer software can be developed and applied for improving the planning, design, operation and management of the air transportation systems. Their applications were demonstrated in numerical examples and practical cases, together with useful information and reliable references. I sincerely hope that this book will serve as a vehicle that stimulates novel research initiatives in air transportation studies.

William H.K. Lam
The Hong Kong Polytechnic University, Hong Kong

William H.K. Lam *has been actively involved in research and professional activities. Particularly in the last ten years (1998-2007), he has successfully received 10 earmarked research grants from the Hong Kong Research Grants Council. Recently, Prof. Lam has been granted of HK$ 100,000 from the Croucher Foundation for organizing the 18th International Symposium on Transportation and Traffic Theory (www.isttt18.org) in Hong Kong from 16th to 18th July 2009. Prof. Lam is currently the President of the Hong Kong Society for Transportation Studies (www.hksts.org) and the Chairman of the Civil Discipline Advisory Panel, the Hong Kong Institution of Engineers (www.hkie.org.hk). He is the Co-Editor-in-Chief of the SCI Journal of Advanced Transportation and the Editor-in-Chief of the SCI Journal – Transportmetrica.*

Preface

The air transportation system is a key element in the global economy. It makes people and goods move round the world and, for many geographical places for which the surface connections to the world are precarious, it may be the only economically feasible transportation. Where it competes with ground and water modals, it usually provides the shortest travelling time. Its success has been such that the demand for it has increased spectacularly in the past decades. However, the capacity to accommodate more and more aircraft in the airspace and in the airports has not met this demand growth. Infrastructure expansion is difficult and lengthy, mainly because land for airport runways and dependencies is increasingly scarce, among many other reasons. Besides, noise restrictions have brought limited operating times and more difficult flight profiles. Therefore, to accommodate the future demand pressure, the air transportation users need some breakthroughs, thus keeping the existing set of supporting technologies for the air transportation system is not an option.

To extract more capacity from the same basic resources, it is necessary to develop new technologies and, not surprisingly, to apply already existing ones, but in such a way that it keeps or improves safety levels, not to suddenly exclude less equipped or trained users, and that global interoperation continues to be harmonic. Several nations are promoting this evolution, but two modernization programs, with strong implications in most of the world's air traffic, are taking the lead: NextGen (*Next Generation Air Transportation System*), in the U.S., and SESAR (*Single European Sky Air traffic management Research*), in Europe. They are progressing at a fast pace and, because of them, in a few years, we will see quite a different picture in air transportation from the one we see today. Other countries, although not directly participating in these programs, are also seriously engaged with the evolution of their air transportation systems, and ambitious local programs have been laid out. In or around all these modernization programs, thousands of scientists, engineers, economists, pilots, air traffic controllers, business persons and many other sorts of professionals are producing knowledge and technologies to enable safer, more efficient and environmentally friendly air transportation.

In this context, it is very important to bring together renowned researchers and professionals from the industry, government and academia as contributors in a publication to disseminate and stimulate ideas to improve efficiency, safety and quality in air transportation. The background theme chosen for this book is Information Technology in Air Transportation, and along the chapters we have it inserted and exploited in several distinct contexts. The interdependence of subjects makes it difficult to categorize the chapters in distinct sections, but despite that we have arranged them in four sections, which we want to briefly comment to the reader.

The first section deals mostly with the Complexity of Air Transportation. The first chapter of which, "*Challenges Ahead for European Air Traffic*", poses and discusses some important needs existing in the current European air transportation, with a systemic and evolutive perspective, from authors who have unique roles in the SESAR program. Many of their challenges are applicable to the other regions of the world, and because of this, and of its systemic approach, we believe it to be a good opening for the book. After this, we have three interesting chapters presenting models and tools to deal with the complexity of managing and optimizing multiple flows of aircraft through airspace and airport resources with limited capacities. These chapters are *"The SYNCROMAX Solution for Air Traffic Flow Management in Brazil"*, *"Balance Modeling and Implementation of Flow Balance for Application in Air Traffic Management"*, and *"Cooperative Control for Ground Traffic at Airports"*, and together bring a powerful mix of software products and mathematical models.

The second section is devoted to improving the economic and operational performance of airports and airlines: for airport planning, *"Critical Review and Analysis of Air-Travel Demand: Forecasting Models"* describes and critically analyzes several models which can be handy for dimensioning airport facilities, with respect to the expected demands; *"Using the Continuum Equilibrium Approach to Solve Airport Competition Problems: Computational and Application Issues"* unveils an innovative computational method to understand how passenger flows behave when competing airports are available in a region; *"Real-Time Non-Destructive Evaluation of Airport Pavements Using Neural Network Based Models"* reports a smart model to evaluate pavement elasticity parameters in real-time, therefore enabling more agility in decision-making depending on airport pavement conditions, which is very likely to have safety implications. For the interest of airlines, *"Advances in Data Processing for Airlines Revenue Management"* presents a sophisticated model and a computational method to forecast airline revenue based on ticket booking and cancelation events; and finishing this group, we have *"Commercial Aircraft: A Holistic and Integrated Model of the Flux of Information Regarding the Operational Support"*, presenting a very comprehensive and systematic model for the process of operating commercial aircraft with Continued Airworthiness, which can help airline managers to better understand what is behind the commercially-available software they use, therefore enhancing their ability to see opportunities of process improvement.

After that, we have a section focused on safety and efficiency of aircraft operations. The first chapter of which deals with risk analysis in air traffic, considering technical advances coming into practice in the next years: *"A Case Study of Advanced Airborne Technology Impacting Air Traffic Management"*, with arguments showing that some key technological advances in airborne equipment, can provide the skies with more safety. A concept explored in this chapter, airborne separation management, is also in the core of the next chapter, *"A Distributed Systems Approach to Airborne Self-Separation"*, which develops a very elaborated technique to safely allow fully automatic aircraft self-separation. Afterwards, the reader will find an extremely efficient algorithm to find optimal aircraft trajectories: *"A Global Optimization Approach to Solve Multi-Aircraft Routing Problems"*, which is primarily focused on military aircraft missions, but is pretty adaptable to civil aircraft operation.

Up to this point, the chapters have presented computational and mathematical models to directly solve problems in the air transportation world. However, software has its own complexity, and it is often necessary to solve problems within the software, and for this we have the fourth and last section. *"Collaborative Decision Making and Information Sharing for Air Traffic Management Operations"* visits distributed software architectures to propose an interoperation paradigm to ensure that the right information is in the right place, at the right time, helping to make the right decision in air transportation operations. Next, one finds two chapters with a correlated aim, which is to formally define and use a method to specify and verify safety properties of embedded software, which turned out to be ubiquitous in aircraft control functions, often with highly critical roles. The chapter *"Component-Based Development of Aeronautical Software"* presents an overview of models and techniques for component-based software development, and develops a step-by-step case study on component modeling and verification for a specific function of a gas turbine controller; following this comes the chapter *"The Language Specification PEARL for Co-Designing Embedded Systems"*, which explores an accurate and effective technique to specify and verify multiprocessor hardware/software co-design for embedded systems, and an application example is given of a Flight Guidance System.

Acknowledgment

We acknowledge our authors, who dedicated their best efforts to produce this splendid book, which covered a large set of relevant topics in Air Transportation, some of them in more depth, some of them in less depth, depending on the approach adopted, but all being appropriate and brilliantly presented. They have met rigorous requirements from the reviewers, who also deserve an undeniable part of the merit of this book, by putting all their technical skills in helping authors and editors to improve the contents. Their participation was supported and strengthened by our Editorial Advisory Board, composed by Carlos Müller, Dave Young, Elton Fernandes, Félix Mora-Camino, João Batista Camargo Jr. and Maria Cristina Barbot Campos e Matos, to whom we feel very much obliged. Finally, we gratefully thank IGI Global for all the support, specially the Editorial Assistants Joel Gamon and Rebecca Beistline, by their patience and solicitude to make the book move forward.

Li Weigang, Alexandre de Barros, and Ítalo Romani de Oliveira
Editors

Section 1
Managing the Air Transportation Complexity

Chapter 1
Challenges Ahead for European Air Traffic

Dave Young
EUROCONTROL, France

Nadine Pilon
EUROCONTROL, France

Lawrence Brom
EUROCONTROL, France

ABSTRACT

The complexity and volumes of the projected future traffic require very demanding air traffic management systems and operations, and the perspective of continuing growth have triggered on both sides of the Atlantic initiatives to modernise the Air Traffic Management systems, namely NextGen in the USA and SESAR in Europe. The present European ATM infrastructure must be transformed. It must be propelled into the modern age, industrialised and developed into an integrated ATM Network facilitating the sustainable development of air transport, which will in turn contribute to a strong and sustainable growth of national economies, while enhancing safety and minimising environmental impact. This transformation requires the application of new operational concepts which fully exploit developments in information technology and airborne intelligence, integrated and implemented in a uniform and consistent manner. This chapter summarises the views of many European opinion leaders and actors of the industry captured in a recent study. It does not pretend to address these all in detail, but aims to provide the reader with insight into aspects where research is required, where issues must be confronted and resolved – where the industry's challenges lie. Whilst the chapter addresses these challenges with a distinct European flavour, it is quite possible that many aspects will find sympathy elsewhere around our increasingly interdependent globe.

INTRODUCTION

At the time of writing this chapter, Air Traffic growth in Europe was forecast to continue steadily to a level estimated at 2.4 more than its 2005 level by 2025 in terms of RPK (SESAR Consortium, 2006), stressing the airport and Air Traffic Management (ATM) infrastructure in Europe well beyond its current maximum capacity (EUROCONTROL,

DOI: 10.4018/978-1-60566-800-0.ch001

2008). Existing plans and identified improvements were expected to absorb or minimise the impact of increased demand until 2013 when delays would once again become significant. A recent study into the development of personal air transport means in Europe alone identified the potential for a further 40 million flights annually (EU FP6, 2008).

The current economic crisis has seriously impacted global air traffic growth, with previsionists now wringing their hands to come to grips with this unprecedented situation. In Europe, current forecasts do not foresee recovery to 2007 demand levels until at least 2011, when we once again enter into the spiralling growth patterns.

Not specifically the focus of the work presented here, it may be assumed that other regions of the world are suffering the same difficulties. The impressive 5% p. a. growth rates of recent years have been considerably reduced and are unlikely to be recovered for several years.

But recovery is expected and growth will once again become a major factor in decisions relating to infra-structural investments and research. Effectively, we now have an opportunity, a four year window, to take stock and lay solid foundations for ambitious developments, addressing the future of Air Transport. This four year window however should not be seen as a respite from the pressure created by the urgency of recent years, but as an opportunity to get in front of the demand curve.

The complexity and volumes of the projected future traffic require very demanding air traffic management systems and operations, and the perspective of continuing growth have triggered on both sides of the Atlantic initiatives to modernise the Air Traffic Management systems, namely NextGen in the USA and SESAR in Europe.

A number of external factors have a direct impact on the performance of today's ATM system, limiting the growth in capacity and inducing major additional costs for the users of the system. The average cost per year for European ATFM related delays are estimated at around €1bn since 2002 over and above the ~€6bn paid in route charges

(EUROCONTROL, 2008). These factors include the lack of a harmonised and integrated view on ATM evolution, the lack of a mandatory regulation and implementation process, the lack of implementation of new (existing) technologies and the fragmentation of service provision.

ATM is very much anchored in procedures which today rely on technologies of a past age where the human is central, and mostly unassisted, to assure the safe and secure transit of aircraft throughout the network, relying upon ingrained procedures and human natural creativity to resolve problems within the environment. This statement is by no means critical of the competences, professionalism and dedication to which the profession is renowned, but simply highlights that ATM remains at the level of craftsmanship – which whilst the quality is indisputable, has its price and productivity remains low.

Consequently, the present European ATM infrastructure must be transformed. It must be propelled into the modern age, industrialised and developed into an integrated ATM Network facilitating the sustainable development of air transport, which will in turn contribute to a strong and sustainable growth of national economies, while enhancing safety and minimising environmental impact. This transformation requires the application of new operational concepts which fully exploit developments in information technology and airborne intelligence, integrated and implemented in a uniform and consistent manner.

To achieve this modernised and fully integrated continuum of European Sky, there are major challenges ahead. This chapter summarises the views of many European opinion leaders and actors of the industry captured in a recent study (Brom & Pilon, 2008). It does not pretend to address these all in detail, but aims to provide the reader with insight into aspects where research is required, where issues must be confronted and resolved – where the industry's challenges lie.

Whilst the chapter addresses these challenges with a distinct European flavour, it is quite possible that many aspects will find sympathy elsewhere around our increasingly interdependent globe.

SETTING THE SCENE

It is accepted by many that European Air Traffic growth will hit a "capacity wall" at airports and in some of the densest airspace in Europe in the near future (2009-2010), causing the resurgence of major delays (EUROCONTROL, 2006).

Due to the 2008 global economic downturn, this dramatic situation has potentially been delayed by a number of years. Nevertheless, air transport is moving from the luxury of unlimited resources (runway, airspace, fuel, emissions, time…) to scarcity. The focus will no longer be upon increasing capacity, but more and more to manage scarce resources efficiently: to protect them from other users, to define, agree and implement rules for their optimal allocation within air transport, to optimise their use.

The saturation at airports is likely to be the constraining factor limiting growth: further capacity gains through the optimisation of existing infrastructure are limited; building new airports or augmenting infrastructure at saturated airports is almost impossible due to the unpopularity of such developments with the local residents and environmentalists and the lack of common policy at EU, national and local level. It would appear that the most realistic opportunity to find relief lies with the development and use of secondary airports, something that is already happening within the low costs segment of the market, but which raises additional challenges.

Today, congestion at the major European hub airports is costly to the airlines. From a global perspective, it is questionable whether hubs are optimal for the overall air transport system capacity. It is possible that in the future, more use of regional airports for point-to-point operations will co-exist with the hub and spoke model, thereby increasing the complexity of the airspace.

Runway capacity has physical limitations that even with more automation, ATM cannot overcome. Terminal Manoeuvring Areas (TMA) are a areas of extreme complexity confronted with high density of traffic either arriving or departing, making their management complex and environmentally inefficient. Many of the major European hubs are located within a relatively small area in core western Europe, adding additional complexity to the management of the TMAs. In order to reduce the environmental impacts of aviation, TMAs will be expanded to a point where potentially, the entire core area of Europe could become one enormous TMA with highly complex traffic.

The development of High Speed Trains (HST) and other connections between capitals and/or big metropolis in Europe may progressively make part of the short-haul connections by air redundant. Detrimental competition will be replaced by more co-operative approaches, such as airlines operating HST themselves, supporting the development of co-modal transport solutions for European citizens.

Airlines will adapt to their future customers for whom short haul transport will be a low cost commodity, whatever the mode of transport, which they will want to book directly through internet facilities. Long-haul air transport, where there is no competition with the train, will remain a luxury.

It can be foreseen that further consolidation of airlines will take place, leading to the concentration of three world-wide alliances with three major poles in Europe and a further three poles in the USA, structured around major long haul airlines. Business models of major and low cost airlines will progressively converge towards mid-cost transport.

The composition of the fleet at the 2030 horizon is already well documented by Airbus and Boeing market previsions. There may however be adaptations to fleet usage as airlines hub-and-spoke versus point-to-point operation business models evolve. Airlines may also evolve their strategies towards less frequency and larger aircraft.

The future fleet will see the emergence of more small aircraft operated by new airspace users competing for the same airspace: air Taxis, Business jets, Very Light Jets. The small aircraft market looks promising, as more and more people will be tempted by hassle-free travel and affordable air vehicles and/or air services.

The development of the Unmanned Air Vehicles (UAV) market segment, offering numerous applications in both civil and military areas, will also place additional requirements on the system, especially in the much contested area of radio spectrum.

The military needs will evolve with new technology, new types of threats and the reduction of military budgets in Europe. It can be expected that European Military operators will assume business-like cost aware behaviour, with operations better integrated within the global traffic.

The consequences of this evolution upon the air transport system include changes in the traffic patterns and complexity, risks on safety due to lesser trained pilots and to the need to integrate manned and unmanned vehicles in the same airspace. The air transport infrastructure modernisation with SESAR should bring technological solutions to these challenges.

Finally, the aviation manufacturing industry will see the emergence of new players from emerging economies. This will increase competition and also technical the complexity of system that need to become interoperable.

AIR TRANSPORT AND THE ECONOMY

Air transport is recognised as a safe, mature and irreplaceable method of transport which creates substantial added value for its customers and makes a significant contribution to World and European gross domestic products (GDPs). The European Air Transport industry is a major pillar in the European economy, contributing more than €220Bn to the European GDP and the employment of about 4 million people, facilitating mobility and business across borders (CERMAS, 2003; Cooper, 2005). By 2020 it is predicted that the industry will contribute some 14% of Europe's GDP. On average around 500 million passengers are transported every year by European airlines alone on more than 5,000 aircraft. It is estimated that 30% of exports from the EU are transported by air.

The European Air Transport Network will continue to contribute to the development of economic wealth to a much greater extent than in previous years. In particular this Air Transport Network will play a crucial role in supporting the integration of the new Member States into the European Union and the growing need for mobility of its citizens.

Underpinning this air transport network is the European Air Traffic Management (ATM) System. While its absolute economic value is small compared to the air transport industry at large (estimated 3% of employment), it plays a major role in assuring safe and efficient operations.

European Aviation in Global Economy

Economy and air transport are linked. Air traffic growth is generally accepted by the economists as an indicator of economic growth. In return, global geo-political and economy crises have a dramatic impact on air transport.

Today, the main macro-economic trend is the result of the exceptional growth encountered over the last 4 years. The World GDP increased by 4% annually. Air transport demand increased by 8% annually during the same period. From 2008 onwards, following the sub-prime crisis, it is expected that the world GDP growth will slow down slightly to stabilize around 3% for the next 5 years. This means potentially growth in worldwide air transport demand would remain at 6%, which historically has actually been the standard for the last 60 years.

It should be remembered though that, if air transport growth remains stable through economic stagnation and even recession, the economy may have a negative impact on it in special circumstances. Events that have had the greatest adverse effects are the unforeseen dramatic ones: oil crisis in the 70s, SARS, the first Gulf war, 9/11 etc, which have significantly depressed air transport growth over relatively short periods.

Forecast of traffic growth in air transport is the highest foreseen amongst all transportation means. It is sanctioned by the number of new aircraft sales and orders, which over the last two years were enormous. This trend is of course more visible in new member states than in the core area where high speed train developments have offered alternative means of transport for trips of up to 600kms.

One of the main challenges for European air transport is the globalisation of the economy. The impressive growth of emerging economic regions and the materialisation of new economic poles is a challenge for the European air transport industry. China and India face the problem of a major growth with the absolute necessity to develop their infrastructure. The 2008 Olympic Games have triggered an interest in China for Flow Management for instance. This very strong surge may well result in Europe being relegated to second league, well behind these regions in 10 to 15 years with regard to air transport and its supporting industries. It is unlikely that Africa will face any growth problems but will continue to be confronted mostly by problems related to safety.

Compared to Europe, emerging economies are less constrained, for example with regard to airport expansion. It is extremely interesting to examine closely the strategies employed by many of the Middle East nations who have embarked upon huge airport infrastructure developments, coupled with very large orders for new aircraft, clearly competing with EU aviation and their commercial hubs. This is a serious problem for Europe's economic competitiveness in the world.

Experts are of the opinion that this situation is reinforced by the attitude of European governments who do not act to promote air transport. Compared to other continents, air transport in Europe is only one of many transport modes. There are alternatives and it is very often seen as a luxury rather than a necessity. In other regions aviation is vital to the economy. Surface transport infrastructure, roads and railways, including the development of High Speed Trains are all but absent. Air transport becomes then the sole connectivity and, therefore, governments invest heavily in facilitating aviation development.

Air transport may be considered as an artery for the world economy through transport of goods and the mobility of citizens. If artificially constrained, the economy is damaged. This also applies to the EU, where constraints of a political nature may also be envisaged, ultimately initiating a vicious circle of recession.

Industrial Competition and USD / EURO Exchange Rate

The EU constitutional role in economy is weak and a general competitive approach is not adapted to aeronautics. Aviation involves only global players. Airbus has only one serious competitor. Even in Europe, there are only two major engine manufacturers. The European Commission may not favour any of them. In aeronautical industry, general rules of competition do not work. There should be a customised approach.

There is also an institutional question. The Airbus Power8 restructuring plan for instance has been established on the basis of a USD of 1.35 against the EURO. We are now far beyond that undermining certain aspects of the plan which are to be revised accordingly. It will take some time before a concern for industry due to EURO strength is assimilated and translated into some sort of flexible behaviour and action. Because European Institutions cannot or do not want to claim that it is a constitutional role to maintain the stability of prices within the Union, the position of EU industry is to ask European institutions to establish measures that will help industry help itself; e.g. how to facilitate intra-community transfers for instance?

Manufacturing industry is confronted to cycles of production which are heavily impacted by economic factors. The exchange rate between the US Dollar and the EURO is putting manufacturing industry under enormous pressure. European industry reacts through measures to re-localise in the dollar zone. Big companies are not immediately threatened, but to gain contracts in other parts of the world, they have to make attractive proposals by de-localising major activities, which in many cases is also accompanied by a technology transfer. Airbus, for instance, has announced that it will do this for an assembly line.

This has an effect on the supply chain. At the end of this chain are SMEs who are unable to take protective measures. Suppliers are replaced by suppliers in the dollar zone or elsewhere. De-localisation is very dangerous. A loss of 10 cents in the USD against the EURO may result in a Billion EURO losses for manufacturers and 100 millions EURO for the supply chain.

Currently, for Airbus, the magnitude of its order book acts as a buffer against the loss of margins; but it cannot continue. When the margin reduces, the company must react, seeking efficiency gains or cuts in non-critical activities. This may result in delocalisation, but in general the main threat is to cut or reduce research, which in turn poses major problems to its future competivity. Up to a certain level, this situation has incited the rationalisation and improvement of the industrial production at EU level. But this is judged to have reached its limits.

This situation is counter-productive with regards to the Lisbon Agenda. Industry is sensitive to economic cycles. This is not only true for civil aeronautics but even more for general aviation and helicopters. There is a overriding pessimism within the industry that we are entering into recession, where despite the increase in demand, orders are diminishing and investments are following a similar trend. For some, the deep recession starting now could last ten years. Low fare carriers have had a big effect on the air transport landscape, offering a lifeline to the manufacturing industry – but what now?

Fuel Price

Since its beginning air transport has been fuelled from oil derivatives. Profitability, reduced costs and return on investment are the key factors that govern organisations like Airbus, Boeing and airlines. For the economic well being of the commercial air transport operator, fuel cost is the represents the majority of its operating costs. Consequently, survival to a degree depends on fuel price and fuel burn and the ability to absorb the fluctuations.

Unexpectedly, 2007 and 2008 has seen the price of oil climb above 140 USD per barrel. As a reference, it is interesting to recall that the Single European Sky ATM Research Programme (SESAR) Business Case made in 2006 was based on the assumption that oil would remain close to 50 USD per oil barrel. Oil looks expensive today. But what are we comparing it to? In relative terms, in fact compared to 30 years ago, oil is probably less expensive.

Technological improvements in Aviation increasing engine efficiency are reaching the end of what is feasible today. Furthermore, no complete technology breakthrough can be expected within the next 20 years to dramatically improve or change this, with new solutions not envisaged much before 2050. Whilst alternatives to fossil fuel were known and tested some 20 to 30 years ago, for example with hydrogen and natural gas fuelled aircraft, these seem to have passed without notable impact upon the evolution of aviation, even if potentially more efficient than currently operated aircraft. The search for alternative fuel will probably affect other modes of transport before air transport.

Consequently, the demand and availability of oil will be important factors for air transport evolution as they drive fuel price. Oil price will continue to increase with demand, but it should be noted that this is not related to the scarcity of reserves. World oil reserves are probably more significant than estimated today and the demand from Air transport is small compared to other sectors, representing only 3% of the global fuel usage, which even if doubled still only represents 6% .

There is a general sentiment that while increasing oil price will force an increase in the cost of travel, it is not going to be a show-stopper. Without additional political intervention, it can be expected that higher fuel price will slow traffic growth. Air transport is probably the only fuel consumer that could afford buying its fuel at levels close to the 500 USD per barrel, placing air transport once again in the luxury product category.

Inevitably though, in this extreme case demand for air transport would be affected particularly in the leisure segment of the market. Initial cause/effect signs were already visible in spring 2008 where fuel surcharges incited a general fall in demand at London Heathrow, with the notable exception of long haul business travel where competition is low. In addition, strategically, in summer 2008, some major and low-fare airlines reduced capacity.

Ticket Price and Growth in Demand

Today air travel is at its lowest price ever. Competition between airlines is driving the ticket prices down which, in return, implies air transport growth. Airlines are becoming far more efficient in the way they operate their business, significantly reducing overhead and the ATM community is further contributing through the delivery of a more efficient service.

However it is likely that the fuel price and politically motivated increases in taxes will drive prices up again. Many within the industry feel that air ticket pricing has reached its trough and that it will never be as low again, although they are unable to predict the magnitude of price increases over the next 20 years.

Regarding air transport demand placed in this context, a quick economic analysis using the elasticity of demand to GDP and ticket price (that will increase because of oil) shows that even with very conservative assumptions, but taking into consideration the demography that plays an important role in the growth of air transport, a 2.5% growth per annum until 2025 may be expected.

SOCIETY'S INCREASING AWARENESS

Safety & Security

Air transport is recognised as a very safe transportation means as, even with constant traffic increase, the number of accidents doesn't rise significantly. However, society's increasing sensitivity to risks is putting it high on the agenda resulting in increased pressure on the actors within the air transportation sector. The role of the human in the system which is central to the design of automation is an important constituent of safety and a matter of debate within the profession.

The new ATM concept adopted by SESAR is driven by capacity issues. More (better) automation would be necessary to meet the target objective of 3 fold more traffic. A number of examples illustrate the benefits of automation for significant increase of capacity (high precision approaches, RVSM, road transport studies, metro).

The current role of the human in the system is questioned. Human-centred automation, very much the focus of SESAR, requires that human capabilities are taken into account and built into the design of automation from the outset. Human performance issues are now a central part of SESAR but some still adhere to the 'old automation philosophy' of selectively automating functions that constitute routine tasks and trying to automate these. However, this does not guarantee optimum total system performance as studies have shown.

In the long-term, the Air Traffic Controller's (ATCO) role will be subject to radical change. The human role in future ATM (after SESAR) will be more strategic for Flow and Trajectory management. This is anticipated to trigger resistance aiming at maintaining the status quo using safety as a justification, a movement which is likely to be led from the Unions and service providers who do not want to move towards automation.

Safety is a pre-requisite for air transport. It raises a number of challenges:

- Society will increasingly become less tolerant to risks and therefore could increasingly "criminalise" ATM professionals' deficiencies. In Italy, following the Linate accident in 2001, harsh court verdicts affected all organisational levels in ATM. One may wonder if this represents the start of a growing trend. If so, this would potentially influence the transparency required by the trade's safety culture (Cook, 2007).
- ATM professionals will have to accept that, more than causes of incidents, human errors are the consequence of constantly stressing the ultra-safe ATM system to its limits. Human errors are unavoidable, but recognition and acknowledgement of this situation are part of the change process that must be applied within the profession.
- The economic climate has a negative effect upon safety. Air Navigation Service Providers (ANSP) require a robust a Safety Culture to counter any effect resulting from downward trends in the economic cycle.

Robust regulatory structures are needed to maintain safety levels in all climates. The UK's Rail Track very poor safety record in recent years is an example of safety being compromised by commercial pressures. The safety culture was not robust enough to cope. It will be a challenge for EASA.

SESAR and NEXTGEN in the USA will face safety related challenges in system design, development, certification and regulation. As systems become more and more complex, equipment needs to be more and more reliable and safe, building in the necessary contingencies. Assuring safety within an automated system of systems, from design throughout its life time is an issue that the industry will have embrace and resolve. There is very little R&D world-wide today in this area. Standards do not exist nor do the processes which enable the certification of such complex systems.

Another challenge for air transport is Security. As already stated, the events that have had the greatest adverse effects on air transport are the unforeseen ones: oil crisis in the 70s, SARS, the first Gulf war, 9/11 etc have dramatically depressed air transport growth. It would probably take industry longer to recover from a future large scale attack such as 9/11 than it did in the past. Unfortunately it has been demonstrated that a commercial aircraft can be used as an arm against civilians or landmarks. As a result, some people still avoid US airlines for fear of attack. This creates inevitable emotional stress and the surge in hassle-free business travel.

ICAO has reacted by taking protective measures which significantly impact the traveller's comfort which in some cases further exacerbates his emotional stress. This tendency to over protect has risks associated which today are yet to be fully mastered. For example, there is a very large turnover of staff working in sensitive areas that are trained in critical procedures, thereby increasing the risk of violations. Security adds significant additional costs to the already struggling industry. The fare paying customer who seeks a certain quality of service now suffers hassle, abuse, delays and frequently has to forsake his dignity. The transmission of his personal information is now all but common practice raising major concerns over its protection and misuse.

One may consider today, that terrorism has become a fact of life and only international crises (Kosovo) or big sporting events (Olympic Games in China, World Cup in South Africa) will trigger major institutional changes in air transport.

Human Performance

ANS cost is an important component in the performance equation. The cost of the air navigation service, referred to and recovered as unit cost, is an important factor in the overall equation of ATM performance. ATM is very much anchored in procedures which today rely on technologies of a past age where the human is central to the safe and secure transit of aircraft throughout the network.

One of the main basic assumptions of the SESAR Operational vision is that "Humans will be central in the future European ATM system as managers and decision-makers". Consequently, it is therefore acknowledged that humans (with appropriate skills and competences) will constitute the core of the future European ATM System's operations. However, to accommodate the expected traffic increase, an advanced level of automation support for humans will be required, which will fundamentally change the manner and the content of his tasks.

Increased human performance and productivity remains the main driver to achieve reduction of ANS provision unit cost. It is expected that this will be achieved by introducing operational improvements aimed to relieve the human from many of the more tedious, repetitive tasks through advanced automation tools, increased awareness and an improved distribution of tasks between the actors in the system.

Recruitment, training, staffing and competence implications have to be identified and managed in order to support the change in the roles and responsibilities of all the actors within the ATM System up to a successful implementation of the ATM Target Concept.

Furthermore Social Factor and Change Management implications derived from the range of changes introduced by the future modus operandi are to be timely managed to overcome possible showstoppers on the path towards the full implementation of the envisaged future European ATM System.

While some core building blocks of the Human Performance Management System are currently understood, it is recognised that R&D will be necessary to address the size, scope and complexity of the SESAR Concept with regard to Human Performance issues.

Environmental Awareness

Politically, because of the shared awareness that Climate Change will dramatically modify our societies and their behaviours in the long term, there is a general agreement on the necessity to reduce (aviation) emissions. However, there is a debate on the range of reduction, between those who look for improvements to still allow traffic growth satisfying increasing demand, and those who consider that aviation growth should be capped.

Despite its relatively low impact upon the environment (2% of world-wide CO_2 emissions from fossil fuel use in 2007, which could reach 3% by 2050 (IPCC, 2007)), air transport is now singled out amongst the other polluters. Environment is a serious long term challenge for air transport growth, not only technically but also politically. The impacts upon the environment include noise and gaseous emissions, in the atmosphere and around airports' affecting local air quality. Air transport has very little understanding of its impact and is very immature in its communication.

Apart from one or two notable exceptions, the environmental discussion is still very much 'lip service' within the industry, whose main focus is upon efficiency and capacity considerations. There is increased awareness amongst the population but different behaviours have yet to adapt as a consequence.

There have been major improvements in technologies over the last decades which have increased the energy efficiency of the aircraft tremendously. Further technological improvements are being elaborated by industry, airlines, and regulators, but the magnitude of the efficiency gains is now reducing as the known technologies reach their limits. Kerosene will continue to be used even into the next generation of aircraft. Currently there is major research into the development and use of alternative fuels. Alas, at this point in time we are only able to dream about another type of energy as without a major breakthrough or discovery; this is far, far away. Of course, a solution could be nuclear energy which is "emissions-free" (apart from the waste issue). But even with our understanding today, experts predict that it could not be effectively introduced and run safely for at least another 100 years. There will be alternative fuels in between, but they will also produce emissions.

The ATM contribution, even if essential in cooperation with the other actors, can only bring marginal emissions reduction; i.e. 4 to 5%. The major areas where efficiency can be improved is within the Terminal Manoeuvring Area (TMA), which is the phase of flight transitioning the aircraft between its cruise and the airport. This will require EU regulation to harmonise airports procedures; i.e. a new domain of competence for the EU.

Unfortunately, despite popular belief that technology will improve air transport efficiency and reduce its environmental effects, it is not easy to find one solution that improves both emissions and noise impact. Therefore difficult trade-off decisions (between noise and emissions) will have to be made at all levels: airports, airlines,

manufacturing industries, regulators, and in ATM. It is essential that common policy be adopted at the European level in this regard, which whilst acknowledging sort term local issues, must offer long term perspectives for sustainable development of air transport.

At this time the solutions of lesser evil include voluntary agreements to environmental improvement measures and emissions trading, considered as a good economic tool to compensate for the inevitable growth in emissions.

There is strong and growing opposition to the liberal policies however, where opponents wish to reduce aviation emissions by artificially contracting travel demand through pricing, taxation or/ and individual emissions quota that would modify society values and behaviours. The potential impact of a drastic reduction in demand upon the manufacturing industry and consequently on the economy itself, reducing European industry's competitiveness in the global market place can only be cited as arguments against such radical measures.

The likelihood of such behavioural change in air travel is uncertain however. Air Transport is now considered as a commodity rather than a luxury and it must be said; politicians are sensitive to public opinion and are adverse in taking unpopular measures!

However, to avoid further deterioration of the air transport image in public opinion, the industry must redress the apparent lack of public awareness regarding the real impact of aviation (around 2.5%) and the measures the sector is taking. Failure to do so runs the risk of fertilising popular sympathy towards regulation limiting growth.

POLITICAL AND LEGISLATIVE CHALLENGES

The European Council of October 2003 highlighted the importance of accelerating the roll out of European transport networks and of increasing investment in human capital, perceived as crucial steps to boost growth, better integrate an enlarged Europe and improve the productivity and competitiveness of European businesses on global markets. Attention has been drawn to the ATM problems in the European Commission Transport White Paper (European Commission, 2001).

At the political level it was recognised that the current complexity and limitations of the European ATM environment requires a new approach to its development and operation, and has resulted in the adoption of the Single European Sky legislation in January 2004, considered as the first major milestone in the development process.

The Single European Sky legislation covers four major packages (European Commission, 2004, 2004b,c,d):

- Framework Regulation,
- Provision of Air Navigation Services,
- Organisation and Use of Airspace,
- Interoperability of Systems, Constituents and Procedures.

These four packages formulate a strong political and institutional impetus to change the paradigm in the way the overall Air Transport System functions today towards a more integrated, interoperable and less fragmented system, ensuring highest possible levels of safety, security and efficiency whilst minimising environmental impact.

Policy orientations for the European Transport network are driven by the Lisbon Agenda in which mobility of citizens and goods is an objective. The EU Transport policy supports air transport through CLEANSKY and SESAR, and fosters the complementarities between modes of transport for a sustainable transport in Europe (co-modality) by supporting industrial initiatives, even if a broader transport vision could be still reinforced in future steps.

The governance of the future European air transport infrastructure will progressively be fully in the hands of the EC as regulator, even for the non-EU Member States and for the civil-military coordination, and the European Parliament should have a stronger say to compensate for the industrial lobbying observed for instance in SESAR.

The model of regulation adapted to ATM is different from the usual EC market-led standardisation happening in other sectors. Applying economic efficiency rules to safety, public function, and control, doesn't work. ATM is a monopoly where policy orientation creates the market for industrial competition, as SESAR does for the ATM market in Europe.

The rationalisation and alignment of European and national regulations is essential for the full implementation of the Single European Sky. However, regulation should only be used where necessary in accordance with "better regulation" principles to reach agreements and to support enforcement of commitments across the diversity of Member States and stakeholder interests

In this regulatory context, the SESAR performance framework needs to be formally established within the regulatory framework in order to reach the required improvements in safety, efficiency, capacity, environmental sustainability and cost-effectiveness. The performance framework should be further supported by the establishment of a comprehensive, independent monitoring and reporting system.

From an institutional point of view, SESAR is a technological solution to foster institutional change. It is an industrial project against the technical fragmentation of ATM. It defines a standard stamped by EASA, and industry will produce SESAR-compliant components through call-for-tenders. Certification of ground and airborne automation needs to be addressed in SESAR (2020 concept to be certified).

Global air-ground standardisation is required: air transport is a global business, therefore products should be interoperable not only Europe and the USA but world-wide. Innovation in ATM has always been slow, because of the necessity to involve a majority of players for interoperability and for safety cases. As a result, the ground system may not take advantage of technological advances on-board. More regulation in ATM, comparable to the flight deck, is desirable and necessary to achieve high implementation rates of new concepts and systems. International standardisation takes time but is indispensable. It is a challenge for SESAR which will need to accelerate ICAO procedures.

Standardisation sourcing will become problematic. International standardisation bodies are producing more and more minimal standards that can be implemented by a majority of companies and that are not too expensive to maintain. Systems on the other hand are becoming more and more complex and industry is less willing to invest in making standards. The EU must strengthen the standardisation bodies.

In such a model, the technical expertise is a key. The identified need for the establishment of a single system design authority / network manager for future ATM System is potentially a role that EUROCONTROL, is able fulfil, technically supporting the regulator with its unique expertise mix and also with its ability to technically coordinate civil-military operations. Its tasks are seen to include both support of European standards in the international standardisation bodies and drafting of the EC mandates. But the need for the evolution of the EUROCONTROL statute and governance structure towards functioning as a European Agency is a prerequisite for acceptance in this role.

Sovereignty over the airspace is a matter of contention between States and the EC at the moment. The corner stone is the absence of EC competence over the military airspace and operations. Governments and populations are not keen to leave the airspace sovereignty to Europe, as there is no public outcry over the non-performance of the current ATM system.

However, from a purely operational viewpoint, sovereignty is not a blocking factor for Functional Airspace Blocks. State agreements can provide for seamless operations on a bi-lateral basis. In the future these will be replaced by a General Agreement in Europe. Regarding safety liability, on the long term (30 to 40 years), States will have freed themselves from it and it should be a global issue, not a national or European one.

The costs of the infrastructure investment (including SESAR) need to be shared between the users with equity (e.g. the payers should be the beneficiaries). The only mechanism to share the costs for the infrastructure is through the ATM Route Charges; the rest is own investment by the operators. The military will have enormous costs to achieve compliance with SESAR to share the same airspace; airlines will have to equip their fleet to fly in the SESAR airspace. Even for ANSP and States, the legacy systems will be very expensive to upgrade. The new small aircraft, with no legacy, might be the 'vehicles' to bring about new technology in the system.

SESAR, Addressing the Technological Challenges

The successful implementation of the Single European Sky in the complex European environment requires a comprehensive and integrated programme of accompanying technical activities covering the entire cycle from research, through development, implementation and finally into operation, assembling competences from all major actors of the air transport sector.

The SESAR project has been developed to support these objectives, federating the competences and capabilities of the supply industry, the Air Transport Users and Operators in a well-focused approach, receiving political support at the highest levels.

Consequently, SESAR is recognised today as the technological arm of the Single European Sky, aiming to achieve by 2020 a modernised, high-performance European air traffic management infrastructure which will enable the safe and environmentally sustainable development of air transport.

The SESAR project is composed of three phases: Definition, Development, and Deployment.

- The **Definition Phase** (2005-2007) which defined the different technological steps to be taken, the priorities in the modernisation programmes and the operational implementation plans. The main deliverables of this phase were the SESAR ATM Master Plan. The associated budget was 60 MEUR (co-funded by EC and EUROCONTROL). The contract was managed by EUROCONTROL with the 30-party consortium (including airspace users, ANSPs, manufacturing industry, airports). The project was successfully terminated in June 2008 with wide acknowledgement of the value of the work and a high degree of industry commitment to the shared implementation plan.
- The **Development Phase** (2008-2013) which will lead the development of the new equipments, systems or standards (which will ensure a convergence towards a fully interoperable ATM system in Europe) and prepare the Deployment Phase. For its governance, a Joint Undertaking (JU) – the SESAR Joint Undertaking has been established under Article 171 of the Treaty with a total budget of 2.1Bn Euro. The main task of the Joint Undertaking is to manage the research, development and validation activities of the SESAR project by combining public and private sector funding provided by its members and using external technical resources and in particular by using EUROCONTROL experience.
- The **Deployment Phase** (2014-2020) is envisaged as a large scale production and implementation of the new ATM infrastructure. The infrastructure should be

composed of fully harmonised and interoperable components which guarantee high performance air transport activities in Europe.

SESAR - A Performance Driven Approach to European ATM Development

In November 2005, on the occasion of the public announcement of the SESAR Definition Phase contract award, EC Vice-President Jacques Barrot highlighted the importance of the SESAR programme and of its objectives, which are to achieve a future European Air Traffic Management (ATM) System for 2020 and beyond which can, relative to today's performance:

- Enable a 3-fold increase in capacity which will also reduce delays, both on the ground and in the air;
- Improve the safety performance by a factor of 10;
- Enable a 10% reduction in the effects flights have on the environment and;
- Provide ATM services at a cost to the airspace user which is at least 50% lower.

To address this political vision, the SESAR Performance Framework has been developed, structured around the 11 ICAO Key Performance Areas (KPAs). The strategic performance objectives and targets represent the performance to be achieved in 2020. In a number of cases, intermediate (pre-2020) and long-term (post-2020) goals have also been defined. These are shown in Figure 1 below. It is important to note that the ATM System will further evolve after 2020 in order to sufficiently address the design goals.

Many of these targets in fact may be seen as contradictory. Safety at all costs? Maybe not, but certainly the target concept is already the result of a number of trade-off decisions performed amongst the principle actors within the future

Figure 1. European ATM performance targets

KPA	Key Performance Indicator (KPI)	Baseline		2020 Target	
		Year	Value	Absolute	Relative
Capacity	Annual IFR flights in Europe	2005	9.2 M	16 M	+ 73%
	Daily IFR flights in Europe	2005	29,000	50,000	+ 73%
	Best In Class (BIC) declared airport capacity in VMC (1 RWY), mov/hr	2008	50	60	+20%
	BIC declared airport capacity in VMC (2 parallel dependent RWYs), mov/hr	2008	90	90	+0%
	BIC declared airport capacity in VMC (2 parallel independent RWYs), mov/hr	2008	90	120	+25%
	BIC declared airport capacity in IMC (1 RWY), mov/hr	2008	25	48	+90%
	BIC declared airport capacity in IMC (2 parallel dependent RWYs), mov/hr	2008	45	72	+60%
	BIC declared airport capacity in IMC (2 parallel independent RWYs), mov/hr	2008	45	96	+110%
Cost Effectiveness	Total annual en-route and terminal ANS cost in Europe, €/flight	2004	800	400	-50%
Efficiency	Scheduled flights departing on time (as planned)			>98%	
	Avg delay of the remaining scheduled flights			<10 min	
	Flights with block-to-block time as planned			>95%	
	Avg. block-to-block time extension of the remaining flights			<10 min	
	Flights with fuel consumption as planned			>95%	
	Avg. additional fuel consumption of the remaining flights			<5%	
Flexibility	Accommodation of VFR-IFR change requests			>98%	
	Unscheduled flights departing on time (as requested)			>98%	
	Avg delay of the remaining unscheduled flights			<5 min	
	Scheduled flights with departure time as requested (after change request)			>98%	
	Avg delay of the remaining scheduled flights			<5 min	
Predictability	Coefficient of variation for actual block-to-block times: for repeatedly flown routes			<1.5%	
	Flights arriving on time (as planned)			>95%	
	Avg arrival delay of the remaining flights			<10 min	
	Total reactionary delay	2010			-50%
	Reactionary flight cancellation rate	2010			-50%
	Total service disruption delay	2010			-50%
	Percentage of diversions caused by service disruption	2010			-50%
Safety	Annual European-wide absolute number of ATM induced accidents and serious or risk bearing incidents	2005		No increase	
	Safety level (per flight)	2005			x 3
Environmental Sustainability	Avg. fuel savings per flight as a result of ATM improvements	2005			10%
	Avg. CO_2 emission per flight as a result of ATM improvements	2005			-10%
	Compliance with local environmental rules			100%	
	Number of proposed environmentally related ATM constraints subjected to a transparent assessment with an environment and socio-economic scope			100%	

system. Others will be greatly facilitated during its operation by the co-operative nature of decisions and the increasing role of automation and enabling technologies.

Orchestrating the Development and Deployment of the Technologies: The European ATM Master Plan

Initially heralded as the opportunity to change the operating paradigm of European ATM, SESAR has been confronted with the realities of the extremely long development and deployment cycles required to evolve the multitude of legacy systems which populate the landscape today. This has resulted in the identification of roadmaps which foresee the very conservative evolution of systems, initially through their federation and eventually, their integration into what should become an integrated system of systems.

The vehicle for this modernization process is the ATM Master Plan (see Figure 2), which addresses the future of ATM in Europe over the next decades (SESAR Consortium, 2008). It forms the basis for the work programme of SESAR including the implementation actions during the period 2008-2013. It will become a "rolling" plan that will be regularly updated in accordance with the results from the R&D activities starting under the responsibility of the SESAR Joint Undertaking (European Commission, 2007).

Master Plan is Coordinating the ATM Future of Europe

Clearly, due to the complex nature of the problem, it is important that the core components of the ATM Target Concept are implemented in a timely and consistent manner throughout the European ATM network to ensure the realization of the identified benefits. The ATM Master Plan establishes the R&D and deployment roadmaps for Operational Evolutions, the development their

technological "Enablers" and their deployment, including the necessary changes to regulations and standards.

ATM Target Concept: From Validation to Implementation

The Master Plan also links and aligns the individual stakeholder's programmes to meet the agreed performance requirements of the European ATM network. Continuous performance monitoring will be undertaken to ensure that the future ATM activities will be conducted to deliver the agreed benefits defined within an agreed performance framework.

The ATM Target Concept describes the main areas and directions of progress to be made. The specific and detailed changes (called "Operational Improvements [OI] steps") required to transition from today's system have been structured in a series of evolving ATM Service Levels (0-5) and organized in three Implementation Packages depending upon the date at which the corresponding capability can become operational (Initial Operational Capability (IOC) date):

- IP1 – Implementation Package 1 (short-term: IOC dates up to 2012) covering ATM Service Levels 0 and 1.
- IP2 – Implementation Package 2 (medium term: IOC dates in the period 2013-2019) covering ATM Service Levels 2 and 3.
- IP3 – Implementation Package 3 (long term: IOC dates from 2020 onwards), covering ATM Service Level 4 and 5.

The roadmaps included in the Master Plan show the R&D and deployment activities as foreseen in the current version of this plan.

They describe:

- How and by when the ATM Service Level of the European ATM system needs to be

Figure 2. SESAR ATM Master Plan

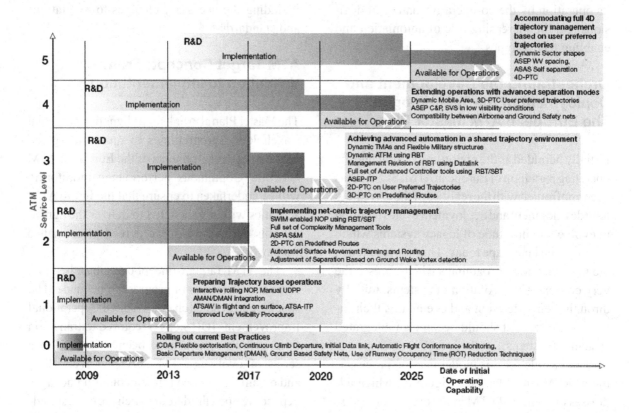

enhanced to respond to evolving performance needs while transitioning to the ATM Target Concept.

- What Stakeholders have to deploy and by when to realise a particular Capability Level. This is presented in the Stakeholder Plans.
- Which and by when Supporting Changes, including System Wide Information Management (SWIM) need to be implemented.

The objective of the Master Plan is to meet the performance targets and to deliver the expected benefits to the ATM stakeholders. Many of the technological challenges themselves are quite minor as for the most part, SESAR builds upon the results of successful or promising research, maximising the use of existing technologies.

Additional initiatives, external to the scope of the SESAR Programme but within the framework of the Single European Sky, are expected (and needed) in order to achieve the Cost Effectiveness target of €400/flight. These initiatives will be eased thanks to the technical ability of the ATM Target Concept to support the implementation of Functional Airspace Blocks aiming to reduce Air Traffic Service provision de-fragmentation.

The European ATM Master Plan was the much awaited main deliverable from the SESAR definition phase. Whilst it is agreed amongst the actors of the definition phase that the Master Plan and its revision processes are the fundamental tools to ensure coherent, European-wide development and deployment of the future ATM systems, it remains difficult to envisage commitment by all stakeholders prior to its endorsement at the highest political levels. In addition, there is a degree of reluctance to engage due to the ambiguity which shrouds the governance and leadership for the deployment of the operational improvements, an ambiguity which finds its roots in the ambitions of the various sectors of the industry itself.

The industry must be able to balance cost and benefits. To ensure in party this necessary commitment and engagement, an economic scheme needs to be developed which addresses the relationship between the required investments for all stakeholders and the commitment to achieve cost-effectiveness and quality of service targets from ANS Providers and Airport Operators. Additionally, the long lead times in some areas of the Master Plan may need specific measures to guarantee proper funding, where necessary through incentives, to assure timely deployment of the SESAR target solutions and decommissioning legacy systems.

The ATM Master Plan as a Vehicle to Mobilise and Consolidate Research Resources

The ATM Master Plan will be handed over to the SESAR Joint Undertaking, which is responsible for its execution and updates for the next 8 years. Engagement is sought from all stakeholders in Europe to adopt the proposals and recommendations in this Master Plan. Consequently, commitment is sought for the implementation of IP1 and towards the R&D plan in support of IP2 and IP3. The focus for all stakeholders must now be upon the timely deployment of the short-term solutions bringing early benefits (IP1), which form the foundation and assumptions upon which the R&D addressing IP2 can develop, ensuring the timely deployment of the 2020 System and consolidation of the roadmap for the implementation of the ATM Target Concept (IP3).

In recent years there has been a growing awareness that there needs to be structure introduced into the organisation and management of ATM research at a pan-European level to ensure a consistent and efficient approach to the challenges which are now identified. The importance of *"Establishing a European Area of Research and Innovation"* has been unambiguously affirmed by the Heads of State during the Lisbon Summit in Portugal (2000) (European Commission, 2002) .The European ATM Master Plan will contribute to this objective through the creation of a coherent and manageable research and implementation path toward a uniform, pan-European system and will ensure efficient use of scarce resources in its construction, to overcome the present fragmentation and duplication of research efforts in Europe.

Over the past 15 years, statistics taken from EUROCONTROL's ARDEP Green Book (EUROCONTROL 2005) show that Europe invests annually 200M - 220M EURO in ATM research and innovation. This has very much absorbed the capabilities of the research community, but seemingly has failed to deliver any major improvements. The European Commission, when initiating its Research and Technological Development Framework programme in Aeronautics and Air Transport, came up with the slogan "more money for research, more research for the money".

The major challenge and in fact what may actually be considered as the shift in paradigm for SESAR is the manner in which these European resources (2.1Bn over 8 years) are to be harnessed within a managed process ensuring that European ATM research capabilities are focussed upon recognised and agreed roadmaps for the development of the technologies – more money for research, more research for the money? Only time will tell, however it is already apparent that, much to the despair of the research community, innovation is all but absent and to a certain extent, not welcome in this industrialised production environment.

However, the European ATM Master Plan provides a sound basis upon which a cost efficient, "European research area" focused upon ATM is being established, stimulating the dynamism, excellence and productivity of European research. Acting as an internal market for research and

Figure 3. Lifecycle management

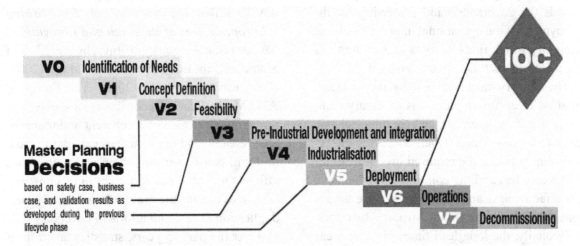

technology, as well as a space for the productive co-ordination of national and regional research activities and policies, it will facilitate the creation and mobilisation of critical masses of resources, strengthen the complementary character of national activities, and improve the coherence of public research agendas throughout Europe.

Through the adoption of a very simplistic "time to market" lifecycle, several phases have been identified covering research, development and implementation (see Figure 3). It is now fully recognised that these phases need to be consistently planned, with dependencies and milestones identified and the articulation between the phases managed. The steps facilitate the development and consolidation of resources, capabilities and expertises amongst the actors involved throughout the development process, clearly supporting decisions regarding investments, roles and responsibilities.

The ATM Master Plan as a Vehicle to Ensure the Integration of the Manufacturing Industry

A long recognised shortcoming in the evolution toward a harmonised and integrated European ATM environment has been the limited and dis-

parate involvement of the supply industry. With the consolidation of supply industry and the corporatisation of Air Traffic service provision, the conditions are created for the contribution of supply industry to be increased, thereby ensuring that the most adequate, cost-effective and worldwide interoperable solutions for the future ATM Network are proposed.

This participation is expected to:

- inject additional manufacturing industry expertise, processes and tools in ATM development from the outset;
- the leverage and articulation of R&D results with industrialisation and product developments;
- ensure the harmonisation of European ground, air and space industrial policies and ensure global inter-operability at an international level;
- introduce additional, proven programme management skills and processes acquired in complex objective driven, multi-disciplinary environments.

The European ATM Master Plan will allow Industry to take a more direct and early stake towards timely delivery of products suited to the planned applications in the operational field. This will in turn have a positive impact on the ability of both industry and its customers to identify and plan timely and efficient investments.

Innovation in ATM has always been slow because of the necessity to involve a majority of players for interoperability issues and for safety cases. As a result, the ground system may not easily take advantage of technological advances on-board. Concept improvements are not always easily implemented. It is a challenge for the next 5 to 10 years for civil air traffic services to make use of the airspace freed by the military: it's not yet the case, as pointed out by the PRC reports on inefficiencies.

One achievement of SESAR has been to gather together all stakeholders including government and industry with airlines and ANSP; and to obtain the buy-in for such a large development plan as SESAR is. SESAR has also a very large buy-in process adapted to the complexity of the European air transport sector. SESAR participants are convinced but gaining the buy-in of stakeholders which have not been involved in the definition phase remains a challenge

However the SESAR development might take more time than anticipated. Stakeholders' commitment may be a challenge and decision making for actual implementation by all stakeholders may require stronger arrangements than the simple ECIP process for the ANSP. For the manufacturing industry, for which ATM is a small market, and for airlines, for which SESAR might be too costly to invest, SESAR credibility is a challenge as it puts at risk the credibility of the current system as well.

The implementation of new concepts/systems may face the gaps in maturity levels between big and small, western and eastern ANSP in Europe that make it more difficult for less mature ANSP. SESAR will have to anticipate a potential lack of human resources for certification, regulation and operation of the new ATM system during the transition phase: there is a need for 20% more ATCO within the next 15 years for the day-to-day (increasing) operations whilst in parallel preparing for SESAR (R&D + training).

But Let's Not Forget Innovation

Air transport R&D management in Europe is in redefinition of its role, orientation and financing sources. Its role is seen as supporting policy decisions and technical regulations, in particular in ATM, with the two facets of strategic vision and technical validation, and the difficulty to measure the benefits of actual measures.

The need to reactivate up-stream research is recognised in complement to the current downstream research in SESAR and CLEANSKY. However there is a risk to future investments in R&D, as no new sources are identified. As can be seen already through SESAR, the place for innovation is questioned and consequently, there is a very strong risk that the topic will drop from the already sparse academic curriculum.

Arguments for a positive approach to long-term research and innovation are well understood in all branches of industry. But despite good intentions set out, for example, in the Lisbon Agenda, when it comes to ATM Europe's investment still lags way behind that of the United States, where it is estimated that some $40m are spent annually in innovation. It is vital that this type of research is given adequate priority and resources, without which Europe will be unprepared for the future not only in terms of technologies, but also in relevant expertise.

Construction needs to occur, supported by adequate financial resources to ensure that the Industry remains a major player in the global market place. The work should be done in partnership with the academic community, integrating capabilities, and developing a sustainable curriculum in Air Traffic Management.

In terms of R&D topics, foresight methods should be reinforced to better anticipate future evolution. Finally, a very strong technological research in aviation is called upon into alternative propulsion means -fuels, engines, even stratospheric transport-, with similar budget shares as in other transport modes.

New Vehicles, New Challenges

There should be no doubt that Unmanned Aerial Systems (UAS) represent a next major advance in aviation, necessitating access as legitimate airspace users to non-segregated airspace on a similar or equal basis to that of manned aviation. Assessment by EUROCONTROL of the evolving UAS market (civil and military) highlights the potential impact upon SESAR, whilst there is growing recognition of the necessity to accommodate their operations within the future NextGen system of the USA. Consequently, as legitimate airspace users, they will all require routine access to the present and any future European ATM system.

Whilst in their infancy today, presently lacking the regulations and technology to allow them to fly routinely outside segregated airspace, estimates on growth and usage must be considered as tentative only. Notwithstanding, current forecasts show the potential applications for some 4300 UAS of all kinds in Europe by 2015 with 100 medium to large civil and commercial UAS by 2017. The applications are substantial and it is expected that these numbers will increase rapidly thereafter.

In the USA, RTCA SC-203 (Radio Technical Commission for Aeronautics - Special Committee) has commissioned an OSED (Operational Services and Environment Definition) for UAS (latest draft dated 7 Aug 08) that examines future UAS operations in the National Airspace System (NAS).

The OSED confirms the difficulties in establishing appropriate regulatory and certification measures which will allow UAS flight in the NAS before 2020. However, thereafter, it predicts a slow but increasing growth in commercial UAS, until usage almost matches that of military UAS by 2030. State (surveillance, border control,

etc..) UAS usage will increase to 2015 and then remain steady.

On this basis, it is therefore evident that UAS will represent a very significant proportion of the airspace user community operating within overall SESAR concept, giving rise to a number of challenges and opportunities which alas, seem to have been underestimated by SESAR.

Today, military UAS make up 98% of UAS being produced, with operations being mainly visual line-of-sight. However, with the establishment of appropriate regulatory and certification frameworks and the development of the necessary supporting technology, such usage will soon extend to radio line-of-sight and beyond. This will entail flight in controlled airspace as UAS increasingly replace manned aircraft in a variety of roles, including, eventually, unmanned cargo flights.

Some UAS will replicate the tracks flown by manned aircraft, particularly when flying point-to-point (e.g. cargo flights) or transiting to distant operating areas. However, the very nature of UAS makes them well-suited to specific types of aerial work. This might be planned, and entail orbiting, surveillance or tracking flights via waypoints or it might be more ad hoc in nature, where the UAS cannot predict its intended flight path.

The specific technologies needed for UAS to ensure a transparent operation within controlled airspace, similar to a manned aircraft (e.g. dedicated high integrity UAV/operator command and control data links) fall outside SESAR. There is nonetheless some technologies that will be developed in the coming years by and for the UAS community that would greatly benefit the commercial, business and general aviation sectors, in particular sense and avoid technologies.

CONCLUSION

The successful evolution of the European Air Transport system is largely dependant upon the ability to assemble the correct balance of representative actors from all horizons and domains of activity directly concerned, generally referred to as the "stakeholders". Their needs, expectations and requirements are the drivers in establishing the European ATM Master Plan.

Wide stakeholder appropriation will ensure issues relating to convergence and transition, which are in many cases show stoppers or serious brakes to evolution, will be addressed in a timely and efficient manner. Transition planning, accompanied by a long term strategy targeting the rationalisation of infra-structure and service delivery, with particular attention paid to the social dimensions of the stepped change can only be constructed and appropriated by the active participation of the end customer.

Short term convergence of investment plans together with the identification and planning of longer term investment are essential elements of the European ATM Master Plan where customers will contribute directly, allowing the timely realisation of expected benefits.

Specific, focused performance and delivery driven research in accordance with the European ATM Master Plan will ensure the federation of the European research community around common goals, eliminating much of the inefficiencies generated through diverse national interests and programmes. The professional management of the Master Plan through the proposed central entity will ensure "more research for the money" and that the results are transformed into products.

The research community must remain attentive as the temptation will be to prioritise and redirect funding to short term, "quick win" elements as pressure builds upon the project to show early benefits. The preservation of resources directed towards creativity and innovation are essential to prepare for steps beyond the current vision horizon..., indeed, one may now ask whether NextGen in the USA and SESAR in Europe are sufficiently ambitious or innovative to support

continuations in demand growth. We now have an opportunity to take a closer look.

REFERENCES

Brom, L., & Pilon, N. (2008). *Challenges of Air Tranport 2030, survey of expert views*. EUROCONTROL Experimental Centre, Report n° 09/07/15-20.

CERMAS. (2003). *ACARE CERMAS Report*. Advisory Council for Aeronautic Research in Europe.

Cook, A. (2007). *European Air Traffic Management*. Aldershot, UK: Ashgate Publishing.

Cooper, A. *(2005)*. The Economic Catalytic Effects of Air Transport in Europe, EUROCONTROL Experimental Centre, EEC/SEE/2005/004.

EU FP6 (2008, February). *Potential transfer of passeenger demand to personal aviation by 2020*. European Personal Air Transportation System -D2.1.

EUROCONTROL (2005, September). ATM R&D Activities in Europe – Overview 2004. *Green Book 2004, R&D.ARDEP-2004*. Brussels, Belgium.

EUROCONTROL. (2006, May). *Performance Review Commission Performance Review Report* (PRR 2005). Brussels, Belgium.

EUROCONTROL. (2008). *Challenges of Growth 2008 Report*. Brussels, Belgium.

EUROCONTROL. (2008, May). *Performance Review Commission Performance Review Report* (PRR 2007). Brussels, Belgium.

European Commission (2001, September). *European transport policy for 2010: time to decide*. Brussels, Belgium.

European Commission. (2001b). *European Aeronautics - A Vision for 2020, Report of the Group of Personalities*. Brussels, Belgium.

European Commission. (2002). *STAR 21 - Strategic Aerospace Review for the 21st Century, July 2002*. Brussels, Belgium.

European Commission. (2004). *Regulation (EC) 549/2004, Single European Sky - The Framework Regulation*. Brussels, Belgium.

European Commission. (2004b). *Regulation (EC) 550/2004, Single European Sky - The provisions of Air Navigation Services*. Brussels, Belgium.

European Commission. (2004c). *Regulation (EC) 551/2004, Single European Sky - The Airspace Regulation*. Brussels, Belgium.

European Commission. (2004d). *Regulation (EC) 552/2004, Single European Sky - The Interoperability Regulation*. Brussels, Belgium.

European Commission. (2007). *Proposal for a council regulation on the establishment of a Joint Undertaking to develop the new generation European air traffic management system (SESAR)*. Brussels, Belgium.

IPCC (2007, May). *Aviation and the Global Atmosphere*. Report of the Intergovernmental Panel on Climate Change Working Groups III.

SESAR Consortium (2006, July). *Air Transport framework, the current situation, D1* (DLM-0606-001).

SESAR Consortium (2008, April). *SESAR Master Plan D5* (DLM-0710-001-02-00).

Chapter 2
The SYNCROMAX Solution for Air Traffic Flow Management in Brazil

Antonio Pedro Timoszczuk
Fundação Aplicações de Tecnologias Críticas – Atech, Brazil

Walter Nogueira Pizzo
Fundação Aplicações de Tecnologias Críticas – Atech, Brazil

Giacomo Feres Staniscia
Fundação Aplicações de Tecnologias Críticas – Atech, Brazil

Eno Siewerdt
Fundação Aplicações de Tecnologias Críticas – Atech, Brazil

ABSTRACT

This chapter charts Brazil's participation and strategy in dealing with Air Traffic Flow Management (ATFM). First a review of ATFM concepts is provided, where the demand and capacity balancing problem is defined. Afterwards the Brazilian air traffic scenario is laid out and a short history is presented. Finally, the SYNCROMAX system architecture is presented as defined for it's first implementation phase. Internal details to the system are given and finally current directions indicate a higher level of decision making tools required in the future, in order to face the growing air navigation requirements.

INTRODUCTION

At recent years, air traffic demand increased at double-digit figures at several Brazilian airports and as a consequence increased controller workload was observed at many Sectors of the Air Traffic Control Facilities, with clear indications that demand consistently surpassed the available capacity of airports and air traffic control units. Although determination of air traffic control capacity values is still a very subjective and controversial issue, with no proven and universally accepted method in place, there is no doubt that there are limits and operating at values above a certain "threshold" will impact the system's efficiency, and, ultimately, also it's safety.

"Demand" is defined as the number of aircraft requesting to use the Air Traffic Management system

DOI: 10.4018/978-1-60566-800-0.ch002

in a given time period, whilst "Capacity" stands for the maximum number of aircraft that can be accommodated in a given time period. Capacity is normally expressed as the maximum number of aircraft which can be accepted over a given period of time within the airspace or at the aerodrome concerned, and, in order to maintain a balance between demand and capacity, the National Aeronautical Authorities decided to establish the Air Traffic Flow Management service, as a centralized unit within the Brazilian Air Navigation Management Center (CGNA). From the very beginning it was clear that the management of air traffic flow would require acquisition and processing of huge amount of data and, therefore, the automated Traffic Flow Management System (SYNCROMAX) became a major enabler of the new service.

The automated Traffic Flow Management System presents a system-wide overview of actual and projected air traffic situations, offering flow managers with detailed information that supports the implementation of a broad range of measures, encompassing strategic, pre-tactical, and tactical scenarios. The variety of offerings assists in preventing imbalances between system and associated services capacity and demand on Air Traffic Control, airport and airspace systems. Ultimately, it contributes to reduce or eliminate restrictions to users and enhance operational safety. The system offers, through a set of user-friendly and intuitive graphical interfaces, secure and accurate decision support information.

This chapter starts focusing on some general aspects of Air Traffic Flow Management in Civil Aviation and its envisaged goals in terms of safe and efficient maximum use of limited capacity of airports and airspace, both in terminal areas and en route. Further, information is presented on the Brazilian Air Traffic scenario and more specific aspects of the SYNCROMAX System, it's overall architecture, the underlying principles for a phased implementation, and status of work being advanced in the Brazilian Air Navigation Management Center. Finally, trends in air traffic

flow management and technology are considered as guidelines to improve the system.

BACKGROUND

Air Traffic Flow Management

Air traffic flow management (ATFM) is a "service established with the objective of contributing to a safe, orderly and expeditious flow of air traffic by ensuring that ATC capacity is utilized to the maximum extent possible, and that the traffic volume is compatible with the capacities declared by the appropriate Air Traffic Services (ATS) authority" (ICAO, 2007). This document also establishes clear guidance about procedures applicable to shortfalls in capacity.

- Where traffic demand varies significantly on a daily or periodic basis, facilities and procedures should be implemented to vary the number of operational sectors or working positions to meet the prevailing and anticipated demand. Applicable procedures should be contained in local instructions.
- In case of particular events which have a negative impact on the declared capacity of an airspace or aerodrome, the capacity of the airspace or aerodrome concerned shall be reduced accordingly for the required time period. Whenever possible, the capacity pertaining to such events should be predetermined.
- To ensure that safety is not compromised whenever the traffic demand in an airspace or at an aerodrome is forecast to exceed the available ATC capacity, measures shall be implemented to regulate traffic volumes accordingly.

"Demand" has been defined as the number of aircraft requesting to use the Air Traffic Management system in a given time period, whilst

"Capacity" stands for the maximum number of aircraft that can be accommodated in a given time period by the system or one of its components (throughput).

The capacity of an Air Traffic Management system depends on many factors, including the Air Traffic Services (ATS) route structure, the navigation accuracy of the aircraft using the airspace, weather related factors, and controller workload. According to International Civil Aviation Organization (ICAO) Document on Procedures for Air Navigation Services – Air Traffic Management (ICAO, 2007), every effort should be made to provide sufficient capacity to cater to both normal and peak traffic levels; however, in implementing any measures to increase capacity, the responsible ATS authority shall ensure that safety levels are not jeopardized. In order to define the maximum number of flights that can be safely accommodated, the appropriate authority should assess and declare the Air Traffic Control (ATC) capacity for control areas, for control sectors within a control area and for aerodromes. The Air Traffic Controller, as an integral part of the ATC System, traditionally has been at the bottleneck of system capacity, due the fact that "Sector Capacity = Controller Capacity". Without proper planning provided by a systematic approach like ATFM, any problem can only be dealt with on a pure tactical way (like holding instructions or worse). The economic effect of this can be devastating and safety implications cannot be excluded.

Clearly, assessing capacity values, with all those factors that have to be taken into account, is a complex task, and there is still a lack of comprehensive guidelines on how to accomplish it. Nevertheless, there is at least one clear indicator that demand is surpassing capacity: delays. A certain amount of delays is acceptable, and might even be unavoidable when trying to achieve maximum utilization of available capacity (many readers may well be aware of initiatives, experienced in the past, like keeping a reservoir of aircraft, so as to always have at least one available to feed into busy airports). But, extreme caution is recommended, since growing delays may easily translate in higher number of incidents.

Just a glance at the demand-capacity equation on the ground brings up the old question about what can be done if airport capacity is less than demand. It's surely an old question, but with still the same answers:

- allow operations to grow and accept the increased cost from delay and pass it on to passengers through higher fares (eventually, risking incidents);
- restrict growth in flights (demand management, at the cost of losing business opportunities); and
- move flights to different times or airports (risking passenger disgust).

The Airline's strategies in response to airport capacity constraints are very restricted too, comprising actions like:

- schedule modifications, by moving flights to off-peak times and increasing night-time operations;
- aircraft size changes, by employing larger aircraft equipment;
- more geographically dispersed scheduling; and
- increase direct service to avoid congested hubs.

And administrators may rely on even less options:

- accommodate growth by increasing fares and rationing demand in the face of scarce capacity; and
- establish new hub airports to mitigate congestion at existing hubs.

There are no good options in this scenario, which is clearly a lose-lose one, as has been assessed in many locations. To overcome the shortcomings, an improved management system has to be established, as laid down in the Global Air Traffic Management Operational Concept (ICAO, 2004). Demand and Capacity Balancing is one of the major components of the Global ATM Concept and is an integral part of the solution to Air Traffic Flow Management.

Demand-Capacity Balancing

The ATM operational concept defines seven interdependent concept components that are integrated to form the future ATM system. They comprise Airspace Organization and Management, Aerodrome Operations, Demand and Capacity Balancing, Traffic Synchronization, Conflict Management, Airspace User Operations, and ATM Service Delivery Management. A well designed information management system will ensure that the information needs of ATM stakeholders — both within as well as outside the ATM network — will be satisfied.

Compared to current practices, there are some key conceptual changes in the Demand and Capacity balancing process, as has already been laid out in the ATM operational concept document. They include:

- through collaborative decision-making at the strategic stage, assets will be optimised to maximize throughput, thus providing a basis for predictable allocation and scheduling;
- through collaborative decision-making, when possible, at the pre-tactical stage, adjustments will be made to assets, resource allocations, projected trajectories, airspace organization, and allocation of entry/exit times for aerodromes and airspace volumes to mitigate any imbalance; and
- at the tactical stage, actions will include dynamic adjustments to the organization of airspace to balance capacity; dynamic

changes to the entry/exit times for aerodromes and airspace volumes; and adjustments to the schedule by the users.

Demand and capacity balancing at strategic, pre-tactical and tactical stages, deals with specific activities carried out in advance of the actual time of operations, as follows.

- **Strategic stage.** At the strategic stage, demand and capacity balancing will respond to the fluctuations in schedules and demands, including the increasing globalisation of traffic patterns, as well as the seasonal changes of weather and major weather phenomena. This stage will begin as soon as practicable. Through collaborative decision-making, assets will be optimised to maximize throughput, thus providing a basis for predictable scheduling. The strategic phase involves the long-term activities to produce a coordinated strategic plan of demand and capacity up to one year, or even more, in advance of the actual day of flight.
- **Pre-tactical stage.** At the pre-tactical stage, demand and capacity balancing will evaluate the current allocation of ATM service provider, airspace user and aerodrome operator assets and resources against the projected demands. Through collaborative decision-making, when possible, adjustments will be made to assets, resource allocations, projected trajectories, airspace organization and allocation of entry/exit times for aerodromes and airspace volumes to mitigate any imbalance. The pre-tactical stage, involving the modification of the coordinated strategic plan, typically encompasses a period of 48 hours before the actual time of flight.
- **Tactical stage.** At the tactical stage, demand and capacity balancing will focus more closely on demand management to

adjust imbalances. It will consider weather conditions, infrastructure status, resource allocations, and disruptions in schedules that would cause an imbalance to arise. Through collaborative decision making, these actions will include dynamic adjustments to the organization of airspace to balance capacity; dynamic changes to the entry/exit times for aerodromes and airspace volumes; and adjustments to the schedules by users. The tactical stage, involving final modifications to the plan, corresponds to the day of operations.

In any Air Traffic Management environment and, particularly, in the context of Air Traffic Flow Management, there will be intrinsic factors that impact the decision-making processes with respect to demand and capacity balancing.

- **Limitation of real-time operational decision-making.** In trying to balance demand and capacity, decisions will be made based on available information that may be constantly changing, often as decisions are being made.
- **Limited window of opportunity.** Decisions made in balancing demand with capacity will often be made quickly, as the opportunity to achieve a solution is usually associated with a brief window of opportunity.
- **Inaccuracy of prediction.** Decisions will be made regarding future states of the system that can only be estimated based on current data. For example, weather, which often reduces the capacity of airspace resources, cannot be accurately predicted, nor can its precise impact on airspace resources be known in advance.
- **Stochastic nature of air traffic patterns.** The pattern of air traffic is highly complex.

The effect of any one action on the overall flow of traffic cannot be modelled with certainty.

Therefore, decision-makers may have to take actions, the effects of which cannot always be precisely predicted. Demand and capacity balancing must take into account information about current and predicted airspace conditions and projected demand, as well as past performance. This involves handling a huge amount of information. Thus, availability of tools to strategically identify areas and times of higher density are increasingly becoming a requirement.

Demand and capacity balancing looks at system-wide traffic flows and aerodrome capacities to allow the airspace users to determine when, where and how they operate, while mitigating conflicting needs for airspace and aerodrome capacity. Demand and capacity balancing shall be capable of evaluating such system-wide traffic flows and capacities, weather and assets, in order to implement necessary actions in a timely manner.

Understanding the component of Demand and Capacity Balancing and it's relation regarding Air Traffic Flow Management, is vital to envisage what kind of technical solutions are perceived to be necessary in pursuit of meaningful implementation of the new services as required. According to the various stages in demand and capacity balancing, the collection, collation and analysis of data to produce an accurate picture of the demands and constraints that will affect any particular airspace volume will begin long before the day of operations. The degree of automation or sophistication required in the processes, including the support of advanced decision support systems, has to be carefully assessed in order to reflect the performance requirements or expectations applicable to a particular scenario.

ORGANIZATIONAL IMPACT OF ATFM

The implementation of air traffic flow management, as a centralized function, brought about several impacts on the actual workforce in air traffic control. For example, some controllers thought that the new function would be a second layer in conflict detection and aircraft separation. Of course, any organizational renaissance begins with people and the preparation of the controllers for the challenges of ATFM implementation implied the fostering of their intellectual curiosity and ability to learn, anticipate and adapt.

An important foundation for providing Air Traffic Flow Management service is the establishment of the aerodrome acceptance rate (AAR). Traffic managers require a numeric value for the arrival rate at key aerodromes in order to:

- measure the aircraft demand at the aerodrome against the available capacity;
- establish the traffic management initiatives required to balance demand and capacity; and
- evaluate the effectiveness of Air Traffic Flow Management (ATFM) measures.

ATFM implies a vast amount of strategic planning, and, as such, has to be based on a set of assumptions. Surprise may occur when core assumptions are proven wrong. To succeed, flow managers must continually validate the strategy across the ends, means, ways, and risk framework.

A centralized ATFM Entity would also be of little value, or even useless, if not supported by Flow Management Positions (FMP), at each major Air Traffic Control Unit. The FMP should perform a straight coordination with the centralized Flow Management Unit (FMU), and shall have the roles to supply the FMU about:

- information of air traffic demand;

- sector capacity of the ATC units;
- technical support, associated infra-structure; and
- meteorological phenomena that affect air navigation in its area of responsibility.

Responsibilities of a Flow Management Position

The flow management position involves several responsibilities, as listed in the following items.

- identify the situations of congestions and saturations of regulated elements localized in its area of responsibility;
- coordinate applicable ATFM measures with the ATC Units, users and airports;
- assess the operational status of relevant air navigation infrastructure and its impact on the air traffic flow;
- accomplish the coordination between the FMU and the ATC Units;
- assist the ATC supervisor, at the shift briefing;
- liaison with the Aerodrome Administration on ATFM subjects;
- planning of seasonal events;
- focal point, daily ATFM teleconferences;
- management, ATFM measures in case of special use airspaces activation that impact the air traffic flow;
- interface between local meteorological units and the FMU;
- maintenance of local ATFM data base;
- evaluation of the effects of ATFM measures and follow-up of the results; and
- elaborate statistical reports.

ATFM Automation

As laid down in the CAR/SAM regional ATFM Concept of Operations Document, the main objectives of a Centralized ATFM unit include:

- assist ATC in making the maximum use of its airspace and capacity;
- issue flow management initiatives, as required, in order to maintain a safe, orderly and expeditious flow of air traffic;
- ensure that air traffic volume is compatible with declared capacities;
- develop a description of the principles and functions of flow management units; and
- establish the requirements for equipping flow management and Centralized ATFM units.

Automation of Air Traffic Flow Management is a clear requirement and starts with the implementation of a common database, of high quality standards. As a minimum, the database shall include:

- the air navigation infrastructure, ATS units and registered aerodromes;
- pertinent ATC sector and airport capacity; and
- foreseen flight data.

The automated system shall be capable of displaying:

- a chart of foreseen air traffic demand;
- a comparison of demand and available capacity for pre-determined areas; and
- alerts and the time-frame of foreseen air traffic overloads.

Several automated ATFM systems have been developed and, although for different specific objectives, put into operational use, e.g., the FAA ETMS (nowadays TFMS), EUROCONTROL's ETFMS, BOBCAT (Southeast Asia – mainly designed for flow control of the Kabul FIR overflights and operated by AEROTHAI) and SYNCROMAX (Brazil).

AIR TRAFFIC SCENARIO IN BRAZIL

In the Brazilian air traffic scenario, conflicting needs for airspace and airport capacity, since the late years of the 20th century, have brought around the requirement for a fully established Air Traffic Flow Management service, designed to minimize constraints to traffic flows due to bottlenecks in capacity. Capacity shortfalls are a serious matter at just a small number of airports, and at some airspace sectors of Area Control Centers and certain Approach Control Centers. Notwithstanding, those airports showing a lack of capacity are located in areas generating high demand and under intense pressure to handle most of the Brazilian major traffic flows, thus impacting the air transport system efficiency as a whole. For example, aircraft movements at São Paulo-Congonhas domestic airport (see Figure 1), at São Paulo downtown, reached 950 operations daily back in 1998, and handling several million passengers with just a modest Passenger Terminal, by then, and two parallel runways not sufficiently spaced apart to allow for simultaneous operations.

Of course, air transport in Brazil also had it's year of decline in 2001, followed by two successive years of stagnation, but faced increased growth from 2004 onwards. In fact, numbers published by SNEA confirmed a domestic passenger traffic growth in Brazil of 5.9 per cent in the first trimester of 2004, compared to the same period of 2003. Shortly after, growth reached the 20% mark at some airports and traffic flows.

Whilst such figures are most welcomed and, indeed, are good news for everyone in the aviation business, they will most likely also start putting great pressure on airports, air navigation services providers, administrators, operators and regulatory bodies. If not adequately handled, typical capacity problems such as increased delays will quickly arise. At later stages, safety of operations may be compromised.

In Brazil, manual assessment of the situation on the basis of operational experience and of

Figure 1. São Paulo Congonhas airport (from DECEA – AISWeb - public)

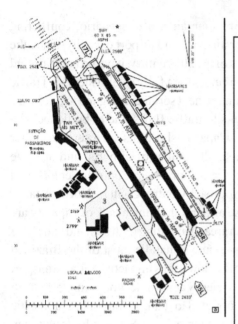

São Paulo TMA airspace is organized to serve three international airports, one major domestic airport, plus several relatively small airports for business and general aviation.

Congonhas remained the Nation's busiest airport in 2007, with 205.564 operations. Location is very convenient for business travel, but it is totally surrounded by urbanized areas and, therefore, is subject to a night curfew of operations. Although this airport has two parallel runways, most of the traffic is handled just on RWY 17R/35L, due to declared distances (reduced to cater for runway end safety areas, after a fatal A320 accident in July2007). See figure on the left.

The São Paulo Approach Control handled a total in excess of 510.000 aircraft movements in 2007.

historical analysis, due to the high volume and complexity of data to be processed could no longer be performed satisfactorily, and, thus, automated tools had to be brought in.

Ultimately, the automated ATFM tools were the key to recover the whole system after a major breakdown at the end of the first trimester of 2007, in a crisis that became known as the "aerial chaos", mainly originated by excessive demand on a weakened system, although other factors such as labor questions and improper fleet management also played a role.

Civil aviation, since the early 1950's, has increasingly become a significant contributor to the overall well-being and economic vitality of individual nations as well as to the world in general. One of the essential requirements of carrying out civil aviation activities is to ensure that a safe, secure, efficient, and environmentally sustainable air navigation system is available, at the global, regional and national levels. This requires the implementation of an air traffic management

(ATM) system, supported by proper communications, navigation and surveillance technologies. The current ATM system still has limitations that result in inefficient aircraft operations and significant improvement will only be achieved through enhanced automation, including, *inter alia*, increasingly sophisticated decision support systems, new display capabilities, conflict alert and resolution tools. These tools are expected to assist the controller to some degree with many demanding and time consuming tasks, like conflict prediction, detection, advisory and resolution, even in case of unexpected or unplanned events. Even so, any ATM system, no matter how sophisticated, will have some sort of limitation and, in such case, the systematic approach to deal with the shortcomings and alleviate the inadequate situation falls under the objectives of air traffic flow management.

Development of ATFM in Brazil

As the traffic numbers, the traffic complexity, and the user expectations all increased, the workload on air traffic controllers also increased. Traditionally, the means of alleviating this problem of potentially excessive workload has been to decrease the size of control sectors, and increase their numbers. The problem is that such measure is expensive on human and systems resources, is subject to the law of diminishing returns, and, moreover, greatly contributes in making the environment increasingly complex, thus providing room for worries, as has been well expressed by Professor Nancy Leveson's paradigm: "Complexity is the enemy of Safety".

Mainly at some airports comprised by the São Paulo Terminal Control Area, where demand surpassed capacity already in 1995, several restrictive, unilateral, measures were applied in order to maintain demand in balance with the declared capacity. The most challenging one was the decision to implement airport slots in order to cope with demand, but no other alternative could be identified as solutions for the short timeframe.

Simultaneously, work started to provide a centralized Air Traffic Flow Management Facility with Traffic Management Systems, i.e., tools designed to process all relevant data in order to allow for continuous monitoring of the airspace and airports, nationwide, with the responsibility for assessing situations where demand would exceed airspace and airport capacity and implementing timely flow management procedures to deal with the imbalances.

Such Traffic Management System eventually became known as SYNCROMAX (an acronym for Maximum Synchronization, in Portuguese language) and is a software package that displays arrival demand, airport acceptance rates, Air Traffic Control Sector Capacity, specific flight information, weather and other pertinent system information, such as equipment outages and mean-time-to-repair values. By having systematic access to such data, air traffic supervisors and flow managers are able to understand, and participate in, the traffic management decisions.

SYNCROMAX Architecture

SYNCROMAX is an Atech-developed solution that empowers ATFM Unit managers with decision support options that enable implementation of a broad range of measures, encompassing strategic, pre-tactical, tactical and operational scenarios. Such a variety of offerings assists in preventing imbalances between system and associated services capacity and demand on ATM, airport and airspace systems. Ultimately, it should be possible to reduce or eliminate restrictions to users and enhance operational safety.

SYNCROMAX offers, through a set of user-friendly and intuitive graphical interfaces (Figure 2), secure and accurate decision support information. System users have the ability to put into effect procedures and regulation measures most suited to a particular situation.

The Centralized Air Traffic Flow Management Unit in Brazil, firmly established under the umbrella of the Brazilian Air Navigation Management Center (CGNA) in the city of Rio de Janeiro (at the same site of the air Navigation Service Provider's Headquarters), already incorporates an advanced set of functionalities that enables it to provide strategic and tactical responses, based on:

- repetitive flight plan and intended flight data processing, for strategic planning purposes;
- ATS message (e.g., FPL, DEP, ARR, CHG, DLA) processing for current situation monitoring and intervention (tactical);
- Aeronautical Information and Meteorological Data reception and processing;
- indication of anticipated imbalances between capacity and demand, indicating affected airspace resources, flights and

Figure 2. SYNCROMAX interfaces. Left: Overview. Right: Airport demand

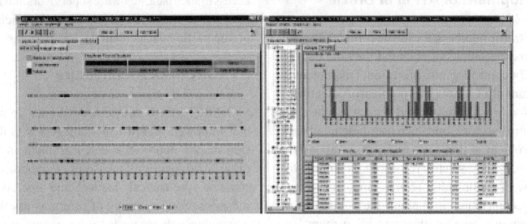

estimated schedules, displayed in graphical or table formats, based on demand calculations (airport, terminal area, control sector, etc.);

- screens and solutions that enable user to generate and maintain the airspace data base; and
- direct remote access to SYNCROMAX from flow management positions at ATC units, to retrieve latest flow information.

Currently, work is ongoing to provide the Brazilian Air Navigation Management Center with the capabilities required to take care of:

- centralized flight plan processing and distribution to ATC centers;
- reception and processing of graphical information for further enhancement of Aeronautical and Meteorological Information;
- aircraft user remote direct access for the flight plan information submission and retrieval, using web tools;
- new, more sophisticated teleconference means;
- continuous ATM system status and safety monitoring;
- statistical data generation for own use as well as for ATM system users; and

- enhanced flow management decision support tools, including Collaborative Decision Making (CDM) applications.

Atech's participation started in 1999, with the elaboration of the Operational Concepts Document (OCD) of the Air Navigation Management Center (CGNA) and System/Subsystem Specification (SSS) for the Air Traffic Flow Management Automated system. Since then, the CGNA is functionally organized in four units:

- Air Traffic Flow Management Unit - ATFMU,
- Air Space Management Unit - ASMU;
- Utilities Unit – UTILU; and
- System Operational Status Monitoring Unit - MOSU.

As seen on the Figure 3, the system interfaces with the several entities to exchange information, that includes, inter alia:

- ATC Centers - ACCs and APPs exchange tracks and flight plan information with the CGNA;
- Airport Reporting Office (ARO) - submit flight plans and get flight plan information from the CGNA;

Figure 3. SYNCROMAX system interfaces to exchange information

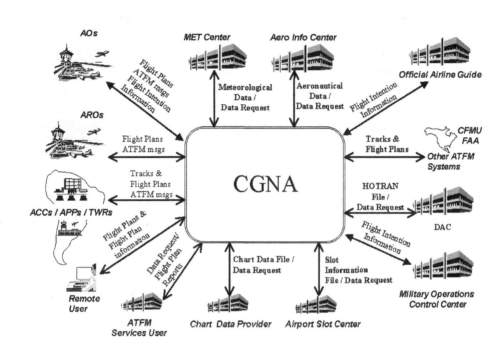

- Aircraft Operators (AO) - submit flight plans and get flight intention information from the CGNA;
- Aeronautical Information Center - provides aeronautical information to the CGNA;
- Meteorological Information Center - provides meteorological information, in text and graphical format to the CGNA;
- ANAC (CAA) - provides Flight Scheduling file to the CGNA;
- DECEA (ANSP) - gets reports and statistics from the CGNA;
- Slot Center - provides airport slot allocation files to the CGNA;
- ATFM Services User - gets reports and statistics from the CGNA;
- Remote User - submits flight plans to the system and gets flight plan information from the CGNA;

- Military Operations Control Center - exchange military flight intention information with the CGNA;
- Chart Data Provider - provides chart data to the CGNA;
- OAG - exchange flight intention information with the CGNA;
- Other ATFM centers - exchange tracks and flight plans with the system; and
- DCP/FMP - although physically distant from the Center, it can be considered an internal interface as well.

One fundamental aspect of the system is the capability to define elements for which the air traffic flow can be managed. An element can be one of the following: an aerodrome, a group of aerodromes, a fix or a waypoint, a sector, a group of sectors, and a segment of an airway. The element capacity and the Air Traffic Demand Correction Factor will be defined on an hourly basis for each day of the week. An aerodrome element may have more than one capacity curve, including the airport acceptance rate curve and different curves for each runway and different operational conditions.

The Flow Manager is able to set the capacity default values and the Air Traffic Demand Correction Factor default values for each aerodrome that can has to be managed.

SYNCROMAX presents, on a geo-referenced Air Situation Display, besides actual and projected aircraft tracks, the following elements:

- aerodromes;
- airways;
- corridors;
- fixes;
- SID;
- STAR;
- TMA boundaries;
- FIR boundaries;
- sector boundaries;
- SUA boundaries;
- waypoints;
- direct ways;
- alternate routes; and
- navigational aids.

SYNCROMAX also presents a Flight Plan Processing Subsystem that allows for creation, maintenance and presentation of an operational flight plan database. Such operations include:

- entry of flight plan data and pre-scheduled flight data;
- entry of flight plan update data and pre-scheduled flight data;
- read-out of flight plan data and pre-scheduled flight data; and
- cancellation of flight plan data and pre-scheduled flight data.

The Flight Plan Processing Subsystem is characterized not only as a flight plan processor, but also provides for "flight intentions processing", that, for future demand calculation purposes, corresponds to the sum of all filed flight plans (FPL + RPL) plus the flights pre-scheduled to occur (Operator Schedule Information, OAG, Slots).

The system provides functions that allow the Flow Manager to insert, modify, remove and have displayed data from Flight Plan Processing Subsystem files. Also, search filters are available online or offline, as well as online queries are feasible. Interface with the Flow Managers are very user-friendly, so that, flight plan data fields like: call sign, ADEP, EOBT, ADES, cruising speed, flight level, route, aircraft type, wake of turbulence will be displayed on the same screen to make it easier for the manager to visualize the whole set of data at a glance.

The system provides capabilities to the manger regarding visualization, printing, saving and sending the contents of the Flight Plan Processing Subsystem files. Regarding the flight plan processing, the FPS subsystem has two modes of operation:

- **Autonomous Mode**: the subsystem receives and processes flight plans and pre-scheduled flights, in order to get the information needed to perform its functions; and
- **Centralized Mode**: besides performing the same functions performed in the Autonomous Mode, in this mode, the subsystem centralizes the flight plan processing, validation and distribution to the ATC units. This phase is currently under development and, by end of 2009, will centralize the complete cycle of initial flight plan processing in Brazil. Main Flight Plan Processing will be done at CGNA in Rio de Janeiro, with a hot-standby Facility installed at the Institute of Airspace Control, in São José dos Campos.

Figure 4. Air traffic flow workstation at CGNA

SYNCROMAX displays the General Air Traffic Flow Status, presenting the status of each regulated element (sector, airport, fix and airway segment) and compares demand versus capacity. The status of an element type corresponds to the worst condition among all the elements of the given type.

The status of each element type shall be presented according to the following color code:

- Green - where the demand is less than 80% (VSP) of the capacity;
- Yellow - where the demand is between 80 and 100% of the capacity (congested); and
- Red - where the demand exceeds the capacity (saturated).

The flow manager has the capability to click on any of the element types and have all the elements of that type displayed in a graph (Figure 4), on the Air Situation Display, as horizontal bars, one bar for each element, varying in time with each period and colored according to the color code described above. He/she is also able to request a visualization of the demand versus capacity curve of a particular element, on the ASD, by clicking on the bar of the graph, that represents the element of interest.

The system is able to display to the flow manager, the demand versus capacity curve, calculated for a given period, in graph format for sector and route segment type elements and in histogram format for aerodromes and fix type elements.

The flow manager may save the demand versus capacity graph snapshot in electronic media and print or send the saved file to another flow manager, via e-mail.

The air traffic flow management system is also seen as the major factor to identify shortcomings and new requirements of the Air Traffic Control System. To this end, SYNCROMAX is undergoing a major change of it's architecture, designed with an open systems approach, highly flexible and with maximum portability. A schematic view of the new architecture is shown on the Figure 5.

Figure 5. Schematic view of SYNCROMAX architecture

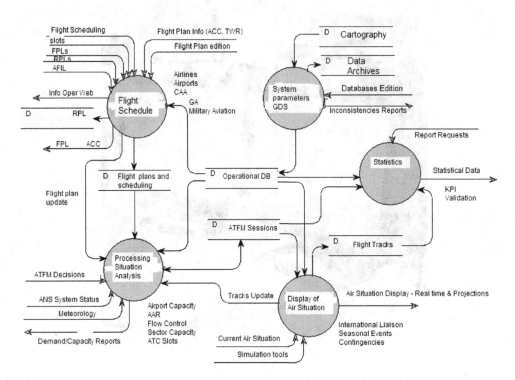

Air Traffic Flow Management implementation is not a choice, at the current aviation scenario, but a necessity. Aviation is a fast-changing industry that is fueling many of national economic success stories. Today's global crisis resulting from high oil prices and declining traffic is hitting all regions hard. Quick decisions, based on global standards in order to build a solid platform for future expansion of airport and air traffic sector capacity is required. To this end, a proven Air Traffic Flow Management system, tailored according to defined user requirements, will prove itself as a key element for success.

FUTURE DIRECTIONS

Compared to current practices of Air Traffic Flow Management, there are some key conceptual changes in the Demand and Capacity Balancing process, as has been laid out in the ATM operational concept document (ICAO, 2003). They include:

- through collaborative decision-making at the strategic stage, assets will be optimised to maximize throughput, thus providing a basis for predictable allocation and scheduling;
- through collaborative decision-making, when possible, at the pre-tactical stage, adjustments will be made to assets, resource allocations, projected trajectories, airspace organization, and allocation of entry/exit times for aerodromes and airspace volumes to mitigate any imbalance; and
- at the tactical stage, actions will include dynamic adjustments to the organization of airspace to balance capacity; dynamic changes to the entry/exit times for aerodromes and airspace volumes; and adjustments to the schedule by the users.

As presented previously, SYNCROMAX interfaces with many different systems to receive and send information. Nowadays a worldwide tendency is to integrate the information under the concept of System Wide Information Management (SWIM) and the first step is to standardize the format for information exchange. Underlying this standadization is the AIXM format and SYNCROMAX will have to implement such compatibility.

Therefore, the automated tools designed for ATFM purposes will have to undergo significant evolutions in order to keep abreast with the conceptual changes. Key areas of interest include the use of Intelligent Agents, further automation of routine air traffic control activities, like traffic synchronization and arrival and departure sequencing, and conflict detection and resolution.

CONCLUSION

This chapter presented some key concepts related to Air Traffic Flow Management and it's crucial Demand and Capacity Balancing function, as a component of the Air Traffic Management System. It should be possible to conclude on the implicit difficulties in achieving Demand and Capacity Balancing, since it involves forecasting future demand, handling enormous amounts of information, allocating resources, and taking complex decisions. SYNCROMAX, as a tailored system for the automation of Air Traffic Flow Management in Brazil, provides in a timely manner the infra-

structure that allows for nationwide Demand and Capacity Balancing, where necessary. Intelligent Multi-Agents are at the root of the evolutionary architecture. Despite the recent aviation market uncertainties and worries, there are reasonably clear indications that air traffic demand will continue to face a healthy growth in Brazil and in the South American Region, thus, ATFM will play an even more important role in fostering the so much needed efficiency of operations, required to assure that demand will not be shrunk due to a lack of capacity.

REFERENCES

Internatfional Civil Aviation Organization. (2003). *ATM Operational Concept Document (AN-Conf/11-WP/4 - Annex)*. International Civil Aviation Organization, Eleventh Air Navigation Conference, Montreal, Canadá. Quebec, Canada.

International Civil Aviation Organization. (2004). *Global Air Traffic Management Operational Concept [Doc 9854]*. Quebec, Canada.

International Civil Aviation Organization. (2007). *ATM – Air Traffic Management [Doc 4444]*. Quebec, Canada.

Chapter 3
Balance Modelling and Implementation of Flow Balance for Application in Air Traffic Management

Bueno Borges de Souza
University of Brasília, Brazil

Li Weigang
University of Brasília, Brazil

Antonio Marcio Ferreira Crespo
CINDACTA I, Brazil

Victor Rafael Rezende Celestino
TRIP Linhas Aereas S/A, Brazil

ABSTRACT

This work describes a decision making support system with Graph Theory and Artificial Intelligence methodologies applied to the Brazilian Air Traffic Flow Management. It consists of a flow management model based on graphs with heuristic adaptations for the dynamic regulation of the air traffic flow. The model lays the foundation of the architecture of the Flow Balancing Model (FBM) which integrates the Distributed Decision Support System applied to the Tactical Management of the Traffic Flow (SISCONFLUX), under development, and has the objective of improving the national airspace management. The FBM was proposed to give support to the system in operation at the First Air Defence and Air Traffic Control Integrated Centre (CINDACTA I), by providing additional information to the process applied by the controllers, in order to mitigate the workload and improve the results of their actions. Using flow maximization techniques adapted from Graph Theory, FBM was developed as a model of analysis which determines the separation time between departures from terminals integrating the Brasilia Flight Information Region (FIR-BS), and distributes the slack capacity along the controlled airspace, in order to prevent or reduce traffic congestion in various sectors of FIR-BS. The FBM gives support to traffic flow regulation, assisting the controllers and other units within the SISCONFLUX.

DOI: 10.4018/978-1-60566-800-0.ch003

INTRODUCTION

Both the FAA (Federal Aviation Administration) and the aviation industry had forecast a growth of air traffic from 150% to 250% along the next two decades (Swenson et al., 2006). With the airline companies crisis in the USA and fuel prices bump those estimates were reduced, but Airbus still forecasts an average growth of 4.9% all over the world. According to Rafael Alonso, vice-president of the European aircraft manufacturer Airbus, even with the financial crisis in the United States, this increase will not be seriously affected (EFE, 2008). Todd Benson and Chris Aspin (2008) highlight the development of the airlines in Latin America even with raising fuel prices.

In Brazil, even after two serious accidents together with an air traffic crisis in less than two years, the aviation market remains hot and foreign companies view Brazil as a good investment opportunity (Benson & Aspin, 2008). Foreign enterprises, such as Lufthansa (Germany), LAN (Peru), and TAP (Portugal) signed code share agreements with TAM, which is considered the main Brazilian airline company, and, similarly, KLM Royal Dutch Airlines and Air France made an agreement with GOL company. Besides, David Neeleman, founder of JetBlue Airways, is interested in opening a new low cost company in Brazil.

The hardships faced by North American airline companies contrast with the Brazilian reality. In the USA, Delta Air Lines and Northwest Airlines announced a joint loss of 10.5 billion dollars in the first quarter of 2008 on account of the fuel price raising. In Brazil, despite bankruptcy of BRA, as well as OceanAir and Varig financial constraints, TAM and GOL continue profiting.

Due to this increase in demand, Air Traffic Flow Management (ATFM) has become an even more critical activity. Ensuring the safety of aircraft in flight and, at the same time, controlling operational costs is a complex task which requires accurate and fast decisions to be made.

Existing ATFM service in Brazil provides visualization of data treated by fixed and transportable radars, visualization of multi-radar synthesis, and flight plans treatment. This kind of service allows information exchange among adjacent control centres, emission of air-to-ground and air-to-air collision alerts, visualization of meteorological images combined with video-maps, and electronic strips containing information about flight plans. This mass of data is under the responsibility of air traffic controllers (Dib, 2004; Crespo et al., 2007), who make proper decisions according to flight plans. The workload laid on these professionals is high and there are operational and legal directives regulating operators working conditions. Consequent restrictive measures concerning air traffic flow control are applied to prevent established limits from being exceeded.

One of the factors related to Brazilian air transport sector crisis is associated with the empirical manner with which air traffic flow techniques are conducted (Crespo et al., 2007). The selection of these techniques and the proportion of the associated restrictive measures are established according to the personal experience of controllers in the roles of operator and supervisor. The number of variables involved in this process renders the empirical decision partially ineffective. Therefore, there is room for improvement by means of efficiency increment of restrictive measures applied. The systematic selection of adequate measures may contribute to the increase of system effectiveness.

The Air Navigation Management Centre (CGNA) already posses tools to perform various analyses based on statistical studies and forecasts from the Air Traffic Flow Management System (SYNCROMAX). The SYNCROMAX solution, developed by Atech Technologies company, is in operation at the CGNA, in Rio de Janeiro (Staniscia & Filho, 2008). This system offers a set of useful information to assist operators' decision making process. Based on these pieces of information, it is possible to determine a comprehensive selection of measures to meet strategic, tactical and operational scenarios. These scenarios are built considering repetitive flight plans (RPLs) in a horizon of fifteen hours before takeoffs. SYNCROMAX offers the operator, by means of a friendly set of man-machine interfaces, safe and accurate information relative to the respective area, in graphical format, covering the analysis of unbalance between capacity and demand in the use of airspace; flight plans data for purposes of strategic planning; the centralization of RPLs planning and their further dissemination to the regional centres (ATECH, 2007).

Integration of meteorological conditions and aeronautical information data is envisaged, as well as real time data about airspace scenarios provided by radars and cooperative automatic surveillance (Automatic Dependent Surveillance – ADS) systems (ATECH, 2007). The integration of these pieces of information and their coherent and organized display to operators are fundamentally important for the treatment of air traffic flow management. However, decisions made with the assistance of SYNCROMAX are based on repetitive flight plans presented in the strategic phase and do not include events occurred after aircraft departures, thus, not considering the actual evolution of the traffic flow in the controlled airspace (Crespo et al., 2007).

Among tools presently used for air traffic control in Brazil, there is not a specific system aimed at the tactical management and flow synchronization. This shortage is made evident when there are scenarios that present a reduction of control resources or factors that cause significant alterations in the expected flow, such as: meteorological phenomena, aeronautical incidents and/or accidents. Such events may cause the saturation of control sectors, characterized by the simultaneous permanence of fourteen or more aircraft per sector (Crespo et al., 2007). Airspace is divided into control sectors, and there is a group of controllers (controller, assistant-controller and supervisor) who supervise the aircraft within these sectors; these ground personnel can control up to a limit number in each sector and, when this number is reached, it is said that the sector is saturated. The saturation of a sector may also be influenced by physical factors such as the dimensions of the sector and the geographical position of the sector, or may be stressed by factors such as the day of the week and the time of the day at which they occur.

Air Traffic Management (ATM) is an activity composed of various segments which develop specific cooperative simultaneous processes. The main objective of ATM is to ensure the realization of safe, regular and effective flights, balancing the needs of airspace users with the aeronautical and airport infrastructure capacity, taking into account the existing meteorological conditions and the operational limitations of the aircraft (Rolim et al., 2004). The Air Traffic Flow Management (ATFM) conducts studies that may indicate a possibility of infrastructure overload and, once the possibility is detected, procedures for flow adjustment are triggered.

ATM in Brazil is based on standards and procedures recommended by the International Civil Aviation Organization (ICAO), and is subdivided into: Airspace Management, Air Traffic Flow Management and Air Traffic Services (Rolim et al., 2004). The Airspace Management seeks the flexible use of airspaces with the objective of augmenting their capacity, their efficiency and the operational flexibility of aircraft. Controlled Airspace is a known environment subject to Air Traffic Control, having airways (AWY), control terminals (TMA) and control zones (CTR). In Figure 1, a simplified view of the airspace division in two dimensions is presented. This division also considers the altitude. In fact, other areas are also defined, such as the Upper Control Area (UTA), the Control Area (CTA) and the Aerodrome Control Zones (ATZ), which were suppressed in this representation. The areas named Sectors 1, 2 and 3 are subdivisions of the airspace into control sectors.

Figure 1. Simplification of controlled airspace

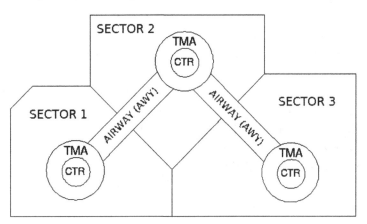

The Brazilian airspace is divided into four Flight Information Regions (FIR), each one under the responsibility of an Air Defense and Air Traffic Control Integrated Centre (CINDACTA). The Brasilia Area Control Centre (ACC-BS), located at CINDACTA I, is responsible for approximately fifty per cent of the air traffic flow in Brazil (CGNA 2005).

The Air Traffic Control (ATC) is a service provided on the ground by controllers who guide the aircraft both in the air and on the ground. The ATM management domain has peculiarities that have to be carefully explored. Specific legislation, regulating ATC rules in Brazil and abroad, defines a management process which must be followed. These rules must be included in all strategies chosen for the preparation of the environment in which agents participating in the management process will operate.

Air Traffic Controllers make use of rules and standards defined and approved by national and international aeronautical entities which regulate the air traffic circulation (DECEA 2006). The resolution of schedule conflicts occurs before and during the flight of each aircraft. This, in addition to being a risk factor for the users of air transportation, is also an overload factor for the controllers. The possibility of an anticipated, optimized and automated resolution of these conflicts, represents

a smaller probability for aircraft to be held up in flight (an action called "orbit") while awaiting landing clearance, less delay and more economy of resources available, such as fuel consumption and airspace occupation.

The restrictive measures applied in unexpected situations - based on flight plans schedule (after prior consultation of CGNA) and on an empirical analysis made by the controllers on duty - do not have their impact assessed in relation to the neighboring sectors by any computational means to support the decision making process. As a result, there is not an adequate level of predictability concerning the effects on the FIR-BS air traffic flow demand as a whole, and the best practices are not documented and stored to assist the decision making in similar situations. How should these measures be used in adequate proportions? What parameters must be considered? How should air traffic flow be adjusted so that certain terminal areas can be prioritized in the utilization of sectors capacity?

This chapter describes the implementation of the Flow Balancing Module (FBM), a subsystem developed with the objective of assisting controllers' decision making relative to the adjustment of the number of aircraft that should be allowed to enter a control region.

RELATED RESEARCHES

There are some works reported in the literature to improve ATFM in Brazil and around the world. These solutions present models using expert systems (Weigang et al., 1997); dynamic programming techniques (Zhang et al., 2005); integer linear programming techniques (Ball et al. 2003; Mukherjee 2004; Rizzi, 2003); distributed solution with the use of multi-agent techniques (Dib, 2004; Heymann et al., 2003); learning through reinforcement (Alves, 2006); among other techniques.

A mathematical model, developed to balance the air traffic demand based on the capacity of control sectors, was proposed by Rizzi (2003), focusing the optimization of this balance by using integer linear programming. Modeled to act up to twelve hours prior to the flight, it subdivides this period into one minute intervals. Flights are characterized by the sectors contained in flight plans and time intervals are planned for the occupation of these sectors. Sectors are characterized by the capacity indicating number of aircraft that can occupy the sector simultaneously.

The model seeks to balance *capacity vs demand* by means of the adjustment of departure schedules at the origin of the demand, that is, airports of origin. It is then defined for each flight a coefficient expressed in function of delays sustained by those flights and, over these coefficients, an objective function that will have to be minimized by the algorithm suggested in the model with a set of restrictions over this function. The computation of the solution depends on the specific technique chosen. In that case, *branch and bound* was suggested. The size of the space of possible solutions influenced negatively on the computation of the solution, as processing lasted about 30 minutes with the mean performance processors used at that time.

One of the most well known problems in the field is the so-called Ground Holding Problem (GHP), which consists in determining how much time an aircraft has to hold on the ground, before it takes off, so that it is not forced to hold in flight. Operational Research (OP) techniques are widely used by researchers to model solutions for the ATFM. Some variants include the association of OP with other techniques with the objective of reducing the space of solutions, increasing the efficiency and the model proximity with the real case. Ball et al. (2003) has proposed a dual net structure associated to OP to solve the Ground Holding Problem. Ma & Cheng (2004) proposed a model based on graphs where the air net was represented by interconnected arches and nodes. For each arch, a set of attributes was associated which restricted the flow through it and, finally, the objective function and the restrictive equations were established (Ma et al., 2004). The computation of the solution was also rather time consuming, and Zhang proposed a refinement to Ma's work by means of Dynamic Programming computing to speed up the obtention of a solution (Zhang et al., 2005).

Other proposed solutions suggested the use of Expert Systems (Weigang et al., 1997) and the use of multi-agent techniques (Dib, 2004). The researches with Expert Systems in this field did not attain great success. On the other hand, Distributed Artificial Intelligence techniques, in which multi-agent systems participate, appear as a great promise for critical applications such as ATFM. Dib proposed a multi-agent modeling where each airport was seen as an agent that negotiated with other agents the adjustment of the aircraft departure schedule, in accordance with the needs of the existing delays (Dib, 2004). This research innovated by the use of Grid Computing tools in the assembly of a net structure to manage the communication between airports. Later, Alves (2006) proposed a learning system based on Meta Control (Raja & Lesser, 2004), which would enhance the communication procedures between these agents.

Figure 2. Partial group sectors from FIR-BS

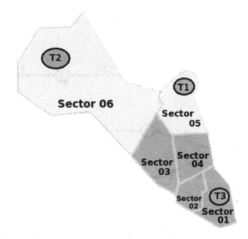

THE BALANCE METHODOLOGY

Differently from the earlier authors, this work does not focus on OP, but on the adaptation of basic algorithms from Graph Theory. A modeling was necessary to allow the use of these techniques and mainly the view of the multi-flow as a super-position of flows. A multi-flow is a kind of flow where the origins are also the destinations and vice-versa. The set of terminals interconnection possibilities, shown in Figure 2, compose the multi-flow depicted in Figure 3.

In a simplified manner, it is possible to iden-tify three flows in Figure 1 with origins at T1, T2 and T3. Supposing that F is the number of flows deriving from the multi-flow, in this case F=3. It is possible to build an equivalent graph (Cormen et al., 1998) which combines all these flows, associating a source node to a sink node, as shown in Figure 3.

Differently from Zhang et al. (2005), edges (arches) correspond to sectors, and a path in the graph corresponds to a possible path from an origin to a destination. Each edge has an as-sociated capacity, and nodes represent the point of transition between sectors. To illustrate the representation, consider again Figure 1, which shows a partial section of the FIR-BS with only three terminals.

Considering $C_{i,j}$ as the capacity of Sector i in the Flow j, and as legislation limits the capac-ity of each sector to a maximum value M, and also supposing a forecast occupation of Sector i of U_i, one has for the balancing a capacity slack equal to $L_i = M - U_i$. Subject to the condition $\sum_{j=1}^{F} C_{i,j} \leq L_i$, for every sector i, where F is the quantity of flows associated to the multi-flow, one wishes that the utilization of the flow be the highest possible, so it is possible to look for solutions where $\sum_{j=1}^{F} C_{i,j} = L_i$. Considering $k_{i,j}$ a fraction of the flow j associated to sector i, it is possible to rewrite the previous relationship as $\sum_{j=1}^{F} k_{i,j} \cdot L_i = L_i$ which results in $\sum_{j=1}^{F} k_{i,j} = 1$, always true on account of the very definition of $k_{i,j}$. The problem is then to determine $k_{i,j}$ so that the multi-flow has a balanced distribution.

The balancing is made by means of the utiliza-tion of the occupation forecast and a predefined distribution for $k_{i,j}$ according to good practices for specific situations. Applied to the context of air traffic, it is supposed a discretization of flows along the graph. In this case, there may be a sub utilization of some sectors, as there is a time delay between departures and the effective occupation of

Figure 3. Associate multi-flow

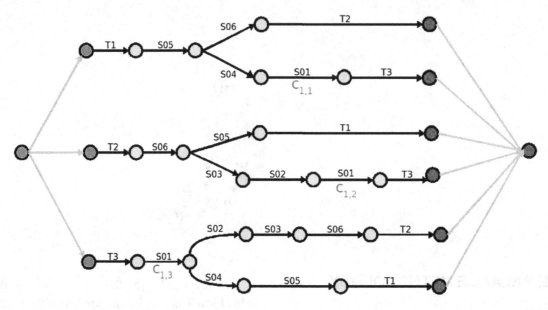

these sectors. When the departure rate is reduced to solve the problem of saturation of a sector *i* bound to get saturated, some of the intermediate sectors may work with a very low occupation rate in relation to their capacity. This aggravates when the sector is in the intersection of various paths (routes that share sectors). Besides, there is the need of adjusting the post-departure flow, that is, the saturation will occur with the aircraft that have already departed. In this case, measures of flow restriction become critical. It is necessary to control the internal flow between sectors. For that purpose, FBM makes a time analysis sector by sector, along a certain path, seeking the possibility of increasing sector residual capacity.

If average time to cross all sectors were the same, the solution would not have to consider this variant. From this perspective, the flow would be approximately continuous, and the model associated to the scenario forecast would be sufficient for the adjustments of ground holding. Unfortunately, there are variations relative to sectors size, variations in aircraft speed and various deviations

that change the amount of time to cross the sectors. A solution that intends to consider all these variants could result in an excessive processing time. Thus, the balancing was designed on the basis of estimates, considering: (1) There is an *average time* m_{s_i} to cross sector *i* with a superior limit m''_{s_i} and an inferior limit m'_{s_i} so that $m'_{s_i} \leq m_{s_i} \leq m''_{s_i}$. (2) the time elapsed for each aircraft in sector $b_{v_j s_i}$ is known and accessible (v_j is the flight *j* and s_i is the sector i). (3) The *time to exit* or the time the aircraft will take to leave the $a_{v_j s_i}$ can be calculated with a good accuracy by $a_{v_j s_i} = m_{s_i} - b_{v_j s_i}$. (4) The time to enter sector *i* is equal to the time to exit sector *i - 1*, sectors being along the same path.

Taking the sequenced list of flights (aircraft) in crescent order of exit times from sector *i* $(s_i) = a_{v_j, s_i} \leq a_{v_{j-1}, s_i} \leq a_{v_{j-2}, s_i} \cdots$, one makes the comparison between the exit time relative to the first element of the list (s_i) with the first element at (s_{i-1}), which represents the exit time from sector *(i-1)*. If the exit time from *i* is smaller or equal to the exit time from *(i–1)*, the aircraft will exit before the one immediately behind enters that sector (or at the same time), so the capacity of *i* may be increased by one. Repeating this same analysis for all other aircraft in the list until the exit time from *i* gets greater than the exit time from *(i – 1)*; in this case, the capacity does not change, as that aircraft will remain in the sector for the time period considered. Then, sectors *(i – 1)* and *(i – 2)* have to be processed in order to obtain the estimate capacity for these sectors. This procedure is named as the "ADJUST-OCCUPATION-BY-ROUTE" algorithm.

By means of the analysis of those lists, it is possible to calculate the time needed for en route holding, if *i* is saturated and the exit time from *(i – 1)* is too short. In this case, an en route holding may be suggested for one of the aircraft in the list (s_{i-1}), together with an estimate of the associated holding time.

After the adjustments of the forecast occupation in each sector, one performs the execution of EDMONDS-KARP algorithm for the calculation of departure rates within the terminal areas. Considering that the flow determined at the origin is *f*, that the average exit time from the terminal is Δt_1 and that the ground holding time is Δt_2, the entry rate into the flow *T* is calculated by $T = \dfrac{\Delta t_1 + \Delta t_2}{|f|}$. From this expression, it is observed that the increase of the allowed flow *f* results in a decrease of the interval between departures, that is, more airplanes will take off within a certain time interval. The increase of the ground holding time Δt_2 determines an increase of the interval between departures. The variable Δt_1 will be taken as a constant average along a route.

FLOW BALANCE MODULE

Once the scenario relative to the FIR-BS traffic flow is estimated, the Flow Balance Model (FBM) will make the analysis of evolving flights distribution, as well as the evolution intentions (repetitive and occasional flight plans, RPL and FPL), in the various controlled sectors.

If there is an occupation estimate with values close to congestion limits (80% of the sector capacity) or saturation (100% of the sector capacity) — such values are defined by Control Centres —, either associated or not to restrictive factors informed by the Evaluation and Decision Support Module (EDSM), FBM will begin the traffic flow balancing process by means of the analysis of a simplified model which will represent the aircraft distribution within the region of responsibility of CINDACTA I.

The FBM will seek to maintain the best fluidity, considering control sectors capacity restrictions and the adjustments of these capacities so that some flow can be prioritized. The selection of the congestion or saturation parameter will be determined by supervisors, considering technical and operational factors in force when the application of traffic flow restrictive measures is necessary. Once the deliberations are defined, the module will direct balance suggestions adjustments to EDSM.

Once the scenario is processed, FBM generates a set of graphs which will represent the scenario forecast in the memory, and will analyze them.

FBM is divided into sub modules, as shown in Figure 4. Its development includes two main sub modules and the sub module of data persistence. The latter has the role of communicating with other modules in order to allow system integration. This communication is made through a database connection. A summarized description of each FBM sub module functionality is presented as follows.

Figure 4. FBM's sub modules representation

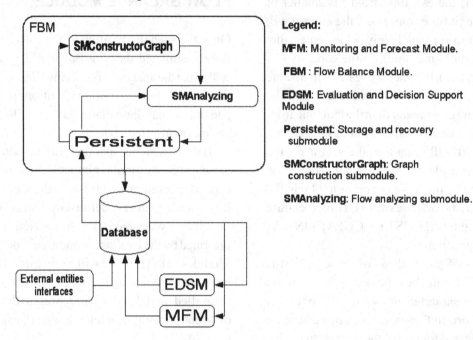

Legend:

MFM: Monitoring and Forecast Module.

FBM : Flow Balance Module.

EDSM: Evaluation and Decision Support Module

Persistent: Storage and recovery submodule

SMConstructorGraph: Graph construction submodule.

SMAnalyzing: Flow analyzing submodule.

MODELLING

The Flow Balance Module (FBM) is part of the Distributed Decision Support System applied to Tactical Management of Air Traffic Flow (SIS-CONFLUX) and functions in a constant interaction with the Scenario Monitoring and Forecast Module (MFM). It receives information from the Evaluation and Decision Support Module (EDSM) about modifications in the existing scenario not determined by aircraft movements and actions that could imply alterations in the traffic flow.

Once the scenario relative to FIR-BS traffic flow is estimated, FBM will make the analysis of evolving flights distribution, as well as the evolution intentions (RPL e FPL), in the various controlled sectors.

As previously stated, if there is an occupation estimate with values close to the limits of congestion (80% of the sector capacity) or saturation (100% of the sector capacity), either associated or not to restrictive factors informed by the EDSM, the FBM will begin the process of traffic flow balancing by means of the analysis of

the simplified model which will represent aircraft distribution within the region of responsibility of CINDACTA I.

FBM calculates restrictive measures that will have an effect for attaining flow balance with emphasis on keeping the aircraft on the ground until the possibility of congestion is no longer present in the scenario forecasts. FBM will seek the maintenance of the best possible fluidity, observing sectors capacities and the adjustment of these capacities. The selection of either the congestion or saturation parameter will be determined by supervisors considering technical and operational factors in force at the moment of application of traffic flow restrictive measures — these parameters relate to the maximum number of aircraft in each sector, and the number of sectors to be analyzed, among others. Once the deliberations are defined, the module directs the balance adjustments suggestions to the administrative module (EDSM). EDSM has the function of evaluating these suggestions, of informing the operational team about the recommended actions, and of executing the learning procedure which will allow the system to store a set of ideal previous decisions, favoring an adaptation of the system to the environment.

After the decision is made and submitted to EDSM, this module registers the scenario forecast associated to the set of actions that were taken. The actions are applied to the real scenario and the MFM forecasts a new scenario based on fresh pieces of information. This new scenario is, again, the entry for FBM which reprocesses the need for restrictive measures, if necessary.

FBM Architecture

As already mentioned, Flow Balance Model (FBM) is divided into sub modules, as shown in Figure 4. Its development includes two main sub modules and the module of data persistence. The proposed solution is based on the application of Graph Theory to an abstract representation of flights multi-flow within FIR-BS. The objective is, after scenario forecast and capacity distribution for each sector, to suggest flow restrictive measures favoring a more adequate utilization of available sector capacities.

Description of Sub Modules

A brief description of the functionality of each sub module that is part of FBM will be provided. It is pointed out that the subdivision of FBM into sub modules intends to distribute the tasks inherent to the system, favoring a better organization structure, facilitating global comprehension. In fact, a *top down* approach was utilized, where, from the core activity, custom designed specializations were defined for the performance of this activity.

Graph Construction Sub Module

This sub module has the function of constructing the Graph associated to the current sectors situation, starting from the routes included in the Table of Routes, and associating the attributes of the

active sectors in each route. Graphs construction is made in accordance with the following procedure: (1) Download valid routes from the database. (2) Separate routes according to the origin. (3) For each set from a distinct origin, number the sectors and terminals that are along the route so that each sector receives a unique number. Each number is considered a node (vertex) and the sectors are associated to the edges (arches) that interconnect the nodes. (4) Include the initial node labeled by zero. (5) Assemble a matrix of sectors, labeling each sector with its name and connecting the numbered nodes. (6) Construct the list of graph adjacency from the matrix associated to the set of routes.

Flow Analysis Sub Module

This sub module has the function of: computing the distribution of capacity slacks among various flows; adjusting the occupation of sectors according to aircraft en route average time; balancing flow and determining recommendable flow restrictions according to the balance solution obtained. The analysis of graphs is made according to the following sequence of analysis: (1) To distribute slacks in accordance with the policy determined by the administrative module. (2) To execute the "ADJUST-OCCUPATION-BY-ROUTE" algorithm (Graph f). (3) To execute EDMONDS-KARP(Graph f).

Algorithm: ADJUST-OCCUPATION-BY-ROUTE (Graph f).

```
1 Take all the routes in flow f
2 For each route in f do:
3 For each sector en route do:
4 retrieve list of flights in
sector.
5 order flights according to the
closest exit time.
6 For each current and previous
sector along the route, in the
inverse order, do:
```

```
7 For each flight v1 of the cur-
rent sector, do:
8 For each flight v2 of the pre-
vious sector, do:
9 If (exit from v1<exit from v2
- minimum separation)
10.  increase capacity slack of
sector where v1 is.
```

The minimum separation in line 9 refers to a constant that was created to add a safety margin to assure that one aircraft exits the sector before another aircraft enters.

Algorithm: EDMONDS-KARP(Graph f).

```
1 While there is a path in the
residual graph of f, do:
2 residue ← shortest capacity
slack of the path
3 for each route in the shortest
path, do:
4 flow in the sector ← previous
flow + residue
5 residual flow in the sector ←
- (flow in the sector)
6 Convert the computed flow to
the entry rate.
```

Data Persistence

This submodule has the function of receiving and/or searching and formatting data for the processing. The search is made via accessing a database, where system tables have been stored. The module utilizes a database generated by MySQL Manager.

IMPLEMENTATION

The prototype was implemented for the simulation of typical situations and the later comparison among actions really taken by air traffic control. For this implementation a Java platform was utilized (Sun Microsystems, version 1.5), aiming at the construction of a portable system compatible with the SYNCROMAX, system currently in operation at the CGNA, and MySQL 5.0.45 relational database. It can also be highlighted that the selection of the language was stimulated by the variety of resources made available by Java APIs.

Model Implementation

The prototype was built with the use of Object Oriented (OO) methodology. The classes were organized in packages, as shown in Figure 5. Each package stores a set of specific classes for the accomplishment of a certain task.

The beans package stores the classes representing objects integrating the model. These basic objects are: Sector, Route, Flight, Node, AverageTime, FlightSectorRoute and Queue-FlightSectorRoute. The bank package stores the classes with access functionalities to the database: ConnectionBank, PersistRoutes, PersistSectors, PersistAverageTime and PersistFlights.

The nucleus package has two internal packages: the Constructor and the Analyzer. Both of them work together for the construction of the representation and the analysis of the flow.

The constructor module has the following classes: SMConstructorGraph which coordinates the construction of the graph; GrafoTMA which stores the structure in the form of a graph of a specific TMA; GrafoEstendido which is the combination of various GrafoTMA's to assemble a complete graph that represents the multi-flow; and a class named FilaNodo which is an internal sub structure of the GrafoTMA for storing the nodes of the graph.

The Analyzer package aggregates intelligence to the module, as it contains algorithms for distribution and balancing. This package possesses the SMAnalyzing class which coordinates the actions of the other classes of the package. The OperadorGrafos class maintains all the algorithms

Figure 5. FBM's packages representation

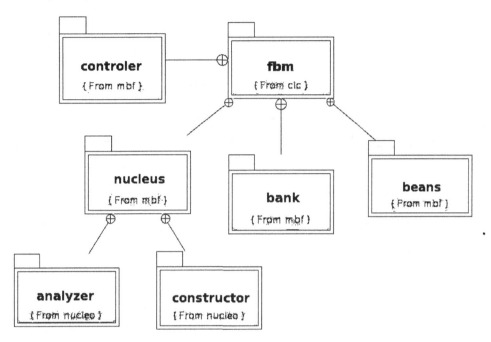

necessary for the conduction of the operations of handling, adjustment and balancing of graphs. The EstruturaReferencial class is the one that maintains an alternative structure of Access to the graph. This structure facilitates the access to sectors and organizes them, so that the access becomes fast and effective. The GrupoDeSetores class is part of the structure of the EstruturaDeControle class and accommodates the reference of various replicas of sectors in each flow. The Distribuidor-Folga classe has the responsibility of distributing capacity slacks of the sectors within the various replicas contained in the GrupoDeSetores. The AjustadorOcupacao class has the task of looking for, along the routes, the flights which will exit the sector before another one enters, and incrementing sector slack if this will occur.

The activity diagram shown in Figure 6 describes how the module works. Basically, the process starts with a request for a new balancing. This request originates in other modules. There are two main actions inside the module: the first one deals with the construction of the graph accord-

ing to the structure stored in the database, which describes a scenario as viewed by the scenario forecast. The module only searches the bank for the new graph representation, if it is up-to-date; if not, it passes directly to the analysis of the flow. Upon completion of the balancing, the information is included in the database, and the administrative module (EDSM) is advised. The diagram refers to MySQL as the bank manager, but any database manager will do it.

TESTS AND RESULTS

This case study is an evaluation of the compatibility between actions taken for the control of the air flow at CINDACTA 1 and the actions suggested by the flow balance model. A day with an intense flow and a day with a lower flow were analyzed. The data obtained were submitted to the balance module which then suggests the departure rate at the terminal sectors. Finally these rates are compared to the ones adopted by the ACC-BS. The

Figure 6. Activity diagram

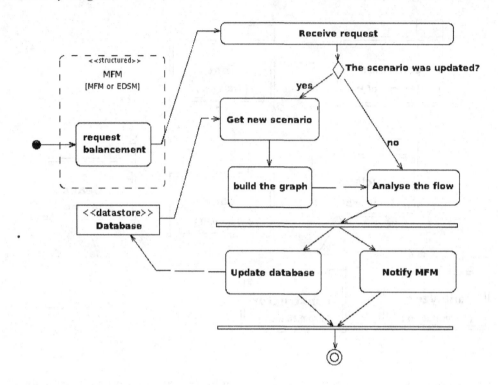

data were obtained directly from the CGNA and CINDACTA I. Two sources of data were analyzed: a set of graphs with repetitive air movements, and a set of registration of FPL and RPL flights (FPL are occasional flight plans, whereas RPL are repetitive flight plans), occurred on 30 April and 02 May 2008, with a total of 11,540 flights.

Case Study Planning

This case study had the following phases: (1) data collection on two predetermined days with basic differences regarding the occupation of the sectors (Wednesday and Friday). (2) Insertion of the data in the database for analysis in the prototype: these data represent the real situation of the aircraft traffic. (3) Definition of test policies: these policies represent the form of prioritization of certain flows in relation to the set of flows in the multi-flow. Since these policies depend on the time and on the day, this item is combined with the former

for the adjustment of the policy application. (4) Conduction of tests: it is the effective execution of the module over the database and computation of the suggested entry rates. (5) Comparison of the tests with the real situation: the actions taken in the real case and the computed actions are compared with the aid of the tables. (6) Analysis of the results: during this phase, an analysis of the results obtained is presented, comparing these results with the real data.

The data was updated with the use of a set of simulating class and the output was computed and analyzed by means of tables. A set of five periods was separated, in which flow restrictive measures were applied. The occupation of these sectors was simulated with classes of persistence, and aircraft dynamics was simulated by means of identification of flights occurred at intervals that correspond to the average time elapsed to cross each sector. There is a table for flow prioritization which relates "*flow ×sector × time*" so that it is possible to recover the percentage allocated for each flow that shares a sector in a specific period. Table 1 was used for the case of prioritization of flow originating from São Paulo (TMA_SP). Notice that lines represent flows starting from the origin indicated in the first label column. Null values are included when the sector is not part of the flow. For the tests, priority was given to flow starting from São Paulo (TMA_SP) and the remainder of the capacity slack was distributed in equal terms among other sectors of the group – the option for this egalitarian division was based on the experience of professionals who work in the area.

Case 1: Heavy Traffic Situation

This study refers to the day of intense air traffic in the FIR-BS. Basically, two policies of flow distribution were practiced: one was the egalitarian, and the other was the prioritized.

The balance policy based on an egalitarian distribution is founded on a just and egalitarian division among the flows in the network. With this policy, sectors slacks are equally divided among replicas of the same sectors, each replica pertaining to a distinct flow. This policy is the most simple, since it does not require the utilization of relationship tables, unlike the prioritized case.

The rates indicated in the tables are expressed in minutes per aircraft, that is, how many minutes elapsed between two aircraft within the terminal. In the case of Table 2, it is observed that the entry suggestion remained below the real frequency in almost all simulations. The time is expressed as Greenwich Mean Time (GMT), also known as Zulu time. The local time in Brazil corresponds to three hours earlier than the time presented. For all the forecasts, the simulation indicates the feasibility of a reduction of the applied restriction to a value between 6.5 and 7.5 minutes without exceeding the restrictions of sectors occupation.

The balance policy based on the distribution with prioritization of flows required a more com-

plex division. The division occurs according to the time at which a certain flow has to be prioritized over the flows in the network, bringing the need for the table "*flow × sector × time*" to simulate a distribution policy (This table is very long, and will not be presented here). It may be highlighted that the table was divided into two parts: the first relates "*flow × sector*", and indexes one of the coordinates of the second table with the time, thus obtaining the percentage of occupation related to the triple "*flow × sector × time*".

In Table 3, with prioritization of the flow originating from Sao Paulo, the separation suggested was shorter than in the case of the egalitarian distribution.

Case 2. Light Traffic Situation

This study refers to a day of light traffic. It involves the application of the same two balance policies, as in the previous case.

The policy of balance with egalitarian distribution is not sensitive to the prioritization of the flows. The division is egalitarian between the flows in the network. Again, this policy is the most simple, as it does not require the use of the table relating "*flow × sector × time*".

It can be observed in Table 4, that the rates utilized could also have been smaller in the majority of the cases; however, at 22:32h, it can be seen that the rate utilized was within the suggested interval. This indicates that the rate actually reached a limit, where an ideal rate was used for the maximization of the flow.

The policy of prioritized balance focuses, again, on the prioritization of the flows. The division occurs according to the time at which a certain flow has to be prioritized over the flows in the network, thus it is necessary to use the relation *flow × sector × time* to simulate updatings from the forecasting module (MFM).

In the prioritized case shown in Table 5, the rates are reduced due to the increase of the flow originating from Sao Paulo and, in this case, it

Table 1. Distribution of the slack between flows in the network for the prioritization of the flow originating at São Paulo (table listing. The complete time schedule has 154 entries and was omitted)

	S01	S02	S03	S04	S05	S06	S07	S08	S09	S10	S11	S12	S13	S14
AM	0	0	0,25	0	0	0,2	0,25	0,25	0	0,1	0	0	0	0
AN	0	0	0	0,1	0,1	0,2	0	0	0	0	0	0	0	0
BH	0,1	0	0	0	0	0	0,25	0,25	0,3	0,1	0,1	0,3	0	0,25
BS	0,2	0	0,25	0,1	0,1	0,2	0,25	0,25	0,4	0,1	0,1	0	0	0,25
CW	0	0,5	0,25	0,1	0,1	0,2	0,25	0	0	0,1	0,1	0	0	0,25
CY	0	0	0	0	0,1	0,2	0	0	0	0	0	0	0	0
RE	0,2	0,5	0	0,1	0	0	0	0,25	0	0,1	0,1	0,4	0	0
RJ	0	0	0	0	0	0	0	0	0,3	0	0,1	0	0,5	0,25
SP	0,5	0	0	0,5	0,5	0	0	0	0	0,5	0,5	0	0	0
VT	0	0	0	0	0	0	0	0	0	0	0	0,3	0,5	0
YS	0	0	0,25	0,1	0,1	0	0	0	0	0	0	0	0	0

Table 2. Table of egalitarian distribution and high flow frequency: TMA_SP

Hour	Origin	Minimum rate suggested	Maximum rate suggested	Minimum rate verified	Restrictive measure
13:25:00	TMA_SP	6.5	7.5	9.6	none
21:13:00	TMA_SP	9.2	10	9.6	none
21:45:00	TMA_SP	6.5	7.5	19.1	15 min separation
22:08:00	TMA_SP	6.5	7.5	9.6	5 min separation
22:32:00	TMA_SP	6.5	7.5	6.4	none

Table 3. Table of prioritized distribution and high frequency flow: TMA_SP

Time	Origin	Minimum Rate suggested	Maximum Rate suggested	Real minimum rate	Restrictive Measure
13:25:00	TMA_SP	3.2	3.8	9.6	none
21:13:00	TMA_SP	4.3	5	9.6	none
21:45:00	TMA_SP	4.3	5	19.1	15 min separation
22:08:00	TMA_SP	4.3	5	9.6	5 min separation
22:32:00	TMA_SP	3.2	3.8	6.4	none

would be possible to reduce the intervals between departures originating from this terminal, but this procedure would have an impact that might not be desired: the reduction of departure rates from terminals that share critical sectors with Sao Paulo terminal.

Based on data collected at CINDACTA I, which were processed by the prototype, results of Tables 2, 3, 4 and 5, relative to Sao Paulo terminal, were obtained. They show that the egalitarian distribution presents good results, with departure rates below the ones adopted by the ACC-BS.

Table 4. Table of egalitarian distribution and low frequency for the flow: TMA_SP

Time	Origin	Minimum rate suggested	Maximum rate suggested	Minimum rate occurred	Restrictive measure
13:25:00	TMA_SP	6.5	7.5	13.6	none
21:13:00	TMA_SP	6.5	7.5	10.6	none
21:45:00	TMA_SP	4.3	5	19.1	15 min separation
22:08:00	TMA_SP	6.5	7.5	10.6	5 min separation
22:32:00	TMA_SP	7	9	8.4	none

The policy of prioritization utilized showed that the simultaneous prioritization of various flows leads to results that are worse than those obtained by means of the egalitarian distribution, that is, if one wishes to prioritize a certain flow, one has to select one or two flows that do not interfere directly with one another. This may occur, for example, when flows present only one sector of intersection.

Model Validation

The tables show actual departure rates originating from TMA SP practiced on April 30 and May 2nd, 2008. These data come from CGNA database. Sector 1 flow was analyzed to determine an equivalent flow in a time interval considering the average time to cross the sector.

It can be observed that the model of egalitarian distribution presents satisfactory results, some of them close to real figures, while in others the model suggests values for the restrictive measures smaller than those effectively practiced. For ex-

ample, in the case of the flow at about 21:13hs in Table 5, the real data show a rate of 9.6, compared to rates suggested by the prototype, between 9.2 and 10.0 minutes per departure, in the egalitarian distribution, and between 4.3 and 5.0 minutes per departure, in the prioritized distribution, with flow originating from Sao Paulo being prioritized.

From these data, it can be stated that the model is indeed valid, and it may be very useful in real life flow regulation, once integrated to the SIS-CONFLUX system.

The results indicate that the departure rates currently adopted ensure a good margin of safety, but they could be adjusted to enhance air traffic flow, still maintaining acceptable occupation limits.

CONCLUSION

The prototype proved effective in the egalitarian balance, but in the prioritized balance it requires a more precise adjustment policy. The prioritization of a certain flow is bound to reduce other

Table 5. Table of prioritized distribution and low frequency for the flow: TMA_SP

Time	Origin	Minimum rate suggested	Maximum rate suggested	Minimum rate occurred	Restrictive measure
13:25:00	TMA_SP	3.2	3.8	13.6	none
21:13:00	TMA_SP	2.6	3	10.6	none
21:45:00	TMA_SP	2.2	2.5	19.5	15 min separation
22:08:00	TMA_SP	2.6	3	10.6	5 min separation
22:32:00	TMA_SP	4.3	5	8.4	none

flows and, thus, these policies must be operated with the application of criteria well defined by the aeronautical authority.

Basically, the Flow Balance Module (FBM) carries out the processing for the adjustment of the departure rates from the terminal which has a direct relation with the Ground Holding Problem (GHP). Once the departure rates from the terminals are defined, the air traffic organizations responsible for the respective terminals have to adapt themselves to the new rule, and this adaptation requires adjustments of flight schedules at the aerodromes.

This chapter has presented the implementation of the FBM, the results of the simulation of the prototype and the evaluation of the results. The experiments showed that the prototype is capable of making satisfactory adjustments and recommending departure rate restrictions less strict than those normally adopted, without compromising the capacities of the sectors and/or showing that, in some situations, the restrictions adopted were within the expected flow limits.

The use of the described methodologies to support the Brazilian Air Traffic Flow Management, with the utilization of adjustment techniques and flow balance, showed a good level of performance and reflected good results in the adjustment of the air traffic network internal flows. The FBM has been proposed to give operational support to the system in operation at CINDACTA I, with the objective of improving the management of the process applied by the controllers of this centre, by means of flow maximization techniques adapted from Graph Theory. Through the utilization of this system, air traffic controllers may improve their knowledge base to assist them in making better decisions.

The results can be improved by using as a selection parameter in the Edmonds-Karp algorithm the path with highest frequency of utilization. The use of the shortest path does not ensure that the flow adjustment in all sectors are good, it only assures that in the beginning of the flow the entry rate is the highest possible, considering the future configurations of the air traffic network.

It was not the intent of this work to determine restrictive measures of a critical nature, that is, measures which involve a higher risk such as aircraft orbits, speed decrease or increase, and so on. For the FBM to act in the determination of these measures, a set of parameters would be necessary for a more detailed analysis of each flight within the sectors.

The implementation of resources for the calculation of orbit time is pertinent to the problem, and possible. Aircraft in flight may be subject to speed restrictions or to holding patterns at some pre-established points. Based on the structure developed in this model, this type of adjustment can be implemented in the future. The analysis of the forecast time of aircraft permanence in sectors adjacent to the congested ones may suggest speed adjustments and/or adjustment of alternative routes through sectors with availability. Another possible contribution of the model is the suggestion of routes to alleviate the occupation of nearly saturated sectors by adjusting the flow in alternative routes.

As a future work, it is planned the execution of this prototype in a real environment, specifically at CINDACTA I, with the association between the FBM and other system modules, and its functioning in parallel with real operational procedures being conducted.

ACKNOWLEDGMENT

This work was partially supported by Brazilian National Council for Scientific and Technological Development – CNPq (Procs. 306065/04-5 and 485940/07-8) and Atech Tecnologias Críticas, Brazil. Thanks to Luiz Nelson Marcelino Dias for his editing.

REFERENCES

Alves, D. P. (2006). *Modelagem usando Apren-dizagem por Reforço em Sistemas Multi-agentes para um Ambiente Controlado em Nível Meta.* Master dissertation, Universidade de Brasília, Brasilia, DF.

ATECH. (2007). *Gerenciador de fluxo de tráfego aéreo - SYNCROMAX.* Retrieved December 2008 from http://www.atech.br/new/site/negocios/produtos.php?id=126

Ball, M. O., Hoffman, R., Odoni, A., & Rifkin, R. (2003). A stochastic integer program with dual network structure and its application to the ground holding problem. [INFORMS]. *Institute for Operations Research and the Management Sciences, 51,* 167–171.

Benson, T., & Aspin, C. (2008). *Latam airlines still buoyant even as fuel soars.* Retrieved April 2008 from http://uk.reuters.com/article/basicIndustries/idUKN2548662620080425.

CGNA. (2005). *Relatório Geral.* Departamento de Controle do Espaço Aéreo, Rio de Janeiro, RJ.

Cormen, T. H., Leiserson, C. E., & Rivest, R. L. (1998). *Introduction to Algorithms.* New York: McGraw-Hill Book Company.

Crespo, A. M. F., Aquino, C. V. D., Souza, B. B., Weigang, L., Melo, A. C. M. A., & Alves, D. P. (2007). Sistema Distribuído de Apoio a Decisão Aplicado ao Gerenciamento Tático do Fluxo de Tráfego: Caso CINDACTA I. In *VI Simpósio de Transporte Aéreo (VI SITRAER 2007),* (Vol. 1, pp. 317–327).

DECEA, Departamento de Controle de Espaço Aéreo, Divisão de Informações Aeronáuticas (2006). *Regras do ar e serviços de tráfego aéreo.* ICA 100-12.

Dib, M. V. P. (2004). *Sistema Multi-agentes para Sincronização e Gerenciamento de Fluxo de Tráfego Aéreo em Tempo Real.* Master dissertation, Universidade de Brasília, Brasilia, DF.

EFE. (2008). A crise nos EUA não reduzirá o tráfego aéreo de passageiros, diz AIRBUS. Retrieved April 2008 from http://www1.folha.uol.com.br/folha/dinheiro/ult91u394334.shtml

Gonzaga da Silva, A. M. (2001). *Sistema de simulação acelerado para análise de fluxo de tráfego aéreo.* Master dissertation, Instituto Nacional de Pesquisas Espaciais - INPE, São José dos Campos, SP.

Heymann, M., Meyer, G., & Resmerita, S. (2003). A framework for conflict resolution in air traffic management. *In Proceedings of 42nd IEEE Conference on Decision and Control,* (Vol. 2, pp. 2035–2040), Maui, Hawaii.

Ma, Z., Cui, D., & Cheng, P. (2004). Dynamic network flow model for short-term air traffic flow management. *IEEE Transactions on Systems, Man, and Cybernetics. Part A, Systems and Humans, 34*(3), 351–358. doi:10.1109/TSMCA.2003.822969

Mukherjee, A. (2004). *Dynamic Stochastic Optimization Models for Air Traffic Flow Management.* PhD thesis, University of California, Berkeley, CA.

Raja, A., & Lesser, V. (2004). Meta-level reasoning in deliberative agents. In *Proceedings of the Intelligent Agent Technology, IEEE/WIC/ACM International Conference on (IAT'04),* (Vol. 00, pp. 141–147).

Rizzi, J. A. (2003). *Um modelo matemático de auxílio para o problema de controle do tráfego aéreo.* Master dissertation, Instituto Tecnológico de Aeronáutica - ITA, São José dos Campos, SP.

Rolim, T. H. L., Portela, T. A. A., & Alves, T. R. A. (2004). *O controle do espaço aéreo*. Technical report, DECEA, Departamento de Controle do Espaço Aéreo.

Souza, B. B. (2008). *Modelo de Balanceamento com Multi-Fluxos para Aplicação em Gerenciamento de Tráfego Aéreo*. Master dissertation, Universidade de Brasilia, Brasilia, DF.

Souza, B. B., Weigang, L., Crespo, A. M. F., & Celestino, V. R. R. (2008). Flow balancing model for air traffic flow management. *In Proceedings of Twentieth International Conference on Software Engineering and Knowledge Engineering (SEKE'08)*, California, CA.

Staniscia, G. F., & Dalmolin Filho, L. (2008). ATM modernisation: Air traffic control facilities in brazil have undergone a huge modernization and increase in service capacity. *Air Traffic Technology International*, (pp. 74–76).

Swenson, H., Barhydt, R., & Landis, M. (2006). *Next Generation Air Transportation System (NGATS)*. Air Traffic Management (ATM) Airspace project. Technical report, National Aeronautics and Space Administration.

Weigang, L., Alves, C. J. P., & Omar, N. (1997). An expert system for Air Traffic Flow Management. *Journal of Advanced Transportation, 31*(3), 343–361.

Zhang, Z., Gao, W., & Wang, L. (2005). Short-term flow management based on dynamic flow programming network. *Journal of the Eastern Asia Society for Transportation Studies, 6*, 640–647.

Chapter 4
Cooperative Control for Ground Traffic at Airports

Felipe Maia Galvão França
Universidade Federal do Rio de Janeiro, Brazil

Félix Mora-Camino
Ecole Nationale de l'Aviation Civile, France

ABSTRACT

With the sustained increase in air transportation, resulting in increased operational costs, potential danger with conflictive traffic conditions and delays for passengers and airlines, ground traffic has become a critical issue for many airports. In this communication the ground traffic at an airport is considered to be composed of three dependent flows: aircraft, passenger vehicles and servicing vehicles. It is assumed in this study that each type of vehicles belongs to a common pool which attends every arriving or departing aircraft. The objective here is to propose a global control structure based on cooperation between the different agents responsible for the management of each fleet to reduce overall aircraft traffic delays at airside.

INTRODUCTION

With the sustained development of air transportation over the last decades, airport capacity has remained a permanent issue for airport planners and operators. Until recently, airport capacity was considered only through its two traditional bottlenecks: the runways system and the passenger's terminals. However, today, aircraft ground traffic at airports has become also a critical question with important influences on security and efficiency and new ground traffic management and control systems with a higher degree of automation have been introduced.

In this communication, a framework for modeling airside traffic at airport is proposed. This framework is useful since there exists many different ground operations organizations, often related with the geometry of each particular airport, and it is not possible to elaborate a common mathematical model of ground operations applicable to all airports. Then considering an airport where the airside includes near and remote parking positions for aircraft and two types of ground vehicles, a set of operational constraints guaranteeing feasibility is

DOI: 10.4018/978-1-60566-800-0.ch004

Figure 1. 3D theoretical airside capacity

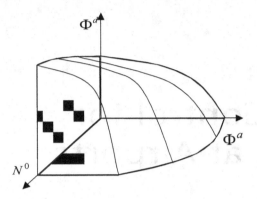

introduced. Then the formulation of an optimization problem for the management of airside traffic is considered. It appears that a global approach for the optimization of ground traffic management is too complex to be tackled in real time. Then a new approach based on multi agent systems is developed to provide a feasible solution to this problem. Simulation results are displayed and discussed.

AIRSIDE OPERATIONS AT AIRPORTS

Airside operations at airports are closely controlled and monitored by several systems, which are mainly operated by air navigation systems which make available detailed information about the progress and status of airside operations to each involved airport traffic decision maker. When incoming or departing flights are delayed, the airport decision makers are informed, and can thus adapt their operations, in order to integrate this delay. However, when considering airport ground traffic, until recently, there was in general no information available for ground operators in the airport, about the status and progress of aircraft ground traffic and of ground operations. Some airlines have already developed, for their own use, information systems which are able to provide information about ground operations on the apron. Also, some

systems have been developed, mainly in the case of freighters, for the monitoring and control of the different fleets of vehicles on the airport. But these systems, designed in general to attend the specific needs of each fleet manager, are not able to share information with other ground vehicle management systems and the other airport ground operators. This lack of coordination between the activities of the different airport ground actors (airport operations, ATC, airlines, luggage delivery system, catering systems, passengers boarding and disembarking resources, etc.) generates frequently unnecessary delays for aircraft and an inefficient use of the available fleets of ground service vehicles. This leads in the mean term to a diminution of the overall airside capacity of airports, since its ground component has been recognized recently (see figure 1 where Φ^a is the flow of arriving aircraft, Φ^d is the flow of departing aircraft and N^0 is the number of grounded aircraft) to have a relevant impact on it.

It also generates a large difficulty to anticipate delays and operations disruptions and to re-organize accordingly the different ground operations.

Different projects have been already realized to overcome these difficulties, providing in real time not only a global view of instant ground traffic at airports but also providing some degree of anticipation to compensate for predicted delays. Today these new information systems allow the development of improved ground traffic management systems. The resulting management structure should be composed of three levels:

- a planning level where ground vehicle fleets and workforce are dimensioned, fleet depots are localized and traffic ways are established;
- an operational level where resources (vehicles and staffs) are assigned on the short term to the different ground operations;
- a control level where vehicles are localized and controlled on line.

Figure 2. Ground operations and resources

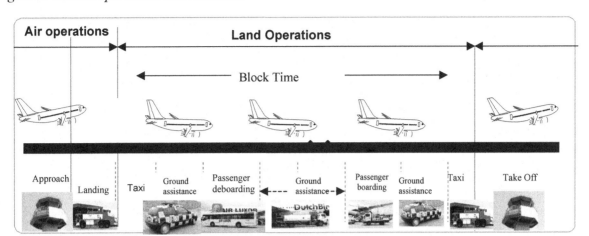

In this study, ground traffic at an airport is considered to be composed of three dependent flows: aircraft passengers vehicles and aircraft servicing vehicles. Figure 2 show a view of the different types of vehicles involved with aircraft traffic and operation at airside.

Aircraft, passenger vehicles and service vehicles move respectively along a network of taxiways and a network of service roads with some interactions such as crossings. Figure 3 displays the taxiway system at Roissy-Charles-de Gaulle airport.

The involved vehicles follow discrete dynamics where the discrete events corresponding to a transition between two operational states for a vehicle are triggered by other events. It is assumed in this study that all passenger vehicles and service vehicles belong to two common fleets which attend every arriving or departing aircraft attached to a remote parking position from their own fleet stations. Figure 4 displays possible discrete dynamics of passenger vehicles, while figure 5 displays possible discrete dynamics for service vehicles.

In both figures, states which correspond to activities which cannot be interrupted or split once they have been started are indicated by heavy lines.

MODELLING GROUND TRAFFIC OPERATIONS

Let I be the set of considered aircraft. For aircraft i, $i \in I$, $t_{ar}(i)$, and $t_{dp}(i)$ are respectively the planned arrival and departure times at the given airport., $t_{ar}(i)$ is the expected time of arrival of aircraft i at the entry of the taxiing system from a given runway and $t_{dp}(i)$ is the planned time for aircraft i to leave its parking stand for its departure flight, if any. Let $R(i)$ be the set of remote parking positions and $P(i)$ be the set of at gate parking positions, which could be assigned to aircraft i (these parking positions must be reserved by the airline owning aircraft i and their dimensions and static equipments must be compatible with the class of aircraft i) when the parking position is free at the requested instant for a sufficient time period. We have, since a unique parking position must be affected to aircraft i:

$$\sum_{j \in R(i) \cup P(i)} x_{ij} = 1 \quad i \in I \tag{1}$$

Then, the binary variables x_{ij} are such as:

$$x_{ij}\left((t_{ar}(i) + \delta_{ij}/V_i + \theta_{ij}^a) + T_{ij}^s - (t_{dp}(i) + \theta_{ij}^d)\right) \leq 0$$
$$i \in I, \quad j \in R(i) \cup P(i) \tag{2}$$

Figure 3. Runways, taxiways and aprons at Roissy-Charles-de-Gaulle airport in 2003

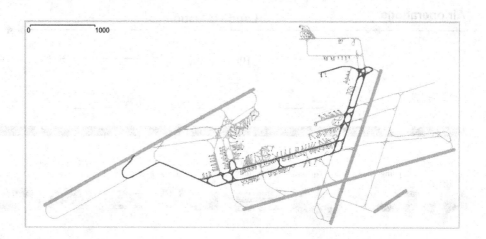

where δ_{ij} is the distance between taxiway entrance for aircraft i and parking position j, V_i is the mean taxiing speed of aircraft i, θ_{ij}^a and θ_{ij}^d are respectively the delays of aircraft i at arrival (delay until parking position j is available) and departure (delay until aircraft i is freed for departure from parking position j). T_{ij}^s is the servicing time of aircraft i at position j. The above restriction implies that departure time from parking position is allowed once all necessary servicing tasks have been executed.

Servicing Times at Parked Aircraft

The servicing time of aircraft i at position j is given by:

$$T_{ij}^s = T_{ij}^{ar} + T_{ij}^{sv} + T_{ij}^{dp} \tag{3}$$

Figure 4. Discrete states and transitions for passengers vehicles

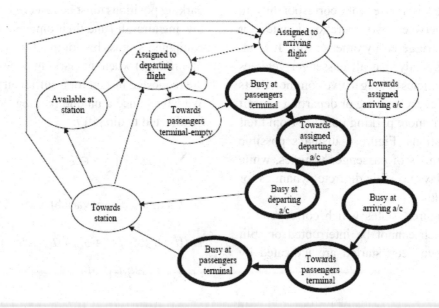

Figure 5. Discrete dynamics for service vehicles

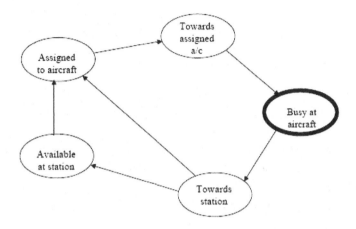

Let $t_{ij}^{park} = (t_{ar}(i) + \delta_{ij} / V_i + \theta_{ij}^a)$ if aircraft i is an arriving aircraft and $t_{ij}^{park} = t_{dp}(i) - \Theta_i$ if aircraft i was already parked at the start of the operations, where Θ_i is a given delay sufficient to perform aircraft servicing and boarding before departure.

Now, $t_{ij}^{park} + T_{ij}^{ar}$ is the instant of completion of disembark of passengers from aircraft i, $t_{ij}^{park} + T_{ij}^{ar} + T_{ij}^{sv}$ is the instant of completion of servicing at aircraft i, and $t_{ij}^{park} + T_{ij}^{ar} + T_{ij}^{sv} + T_{ij}^{dp}$ is the instant of completion of boarding the departure flight for aircraft i.

Two cases must be considered, depending if the parking position is a remote one or not.

Case 1: The parking position is at the gate ($j \in P(i)$):

In that case, it is supposed that every necessary equipment for boarding, disembark and servicing the aircraft are available at that position. Then:

$$t_{ij}^{park} + T_{ij}^{ar} = t_{ij}^{park} + \tau_{ij}^{deb} + \sigma_{ij}^{deb} \qquad (4\text{-}1)$$

$$t_{ij}^{park} + T_{ij}^{ar} + T_{ij}^{sv} = t_{ij}^{park} + T_{ij}^{ar} + \tau_{ij}^{sv} + \sigma_{ij}^{sv} \qquad (4\text{-}2)$$

$$t_{ij}^{park} + T_{ij}^{ar} + T_{ij}^{sv} + T_{ij}^{dp} = t_{ij}^{park} + T_{ij}^{ar} + T_{ij}^{sv} + \tau_{ij}^{brd} + \sigma_{ij}^{pd} \qquad (4\text{-}3)$$

where τ_{ij}^{deb} is the duration of disembark for arriving aircraft i at parking position j, τ_{ij}^{sv} is the duration of servicing aircraft i at position j, τ_{ij}^{brd} is the duration of boarding for aircraft i at position j, σ_{ij}^{deb}, σ_{ij}^{sv} and σ_{ij}^{pd} are respectively waiting times before starting disembark, servicing and boarding.

Case 2: The parking position is a remote one, $j \in R(i)$. In that case servicing the passengers and the aircraft makes use of vehicles between the aircraft and the passenger terminal. This case is quite complex and described in the next sub paragraph.

Traffic Constraints and Delays at Remote Parking Positions

To disembark passengers, the assigned passengers vehicle k can be previously in one of the three following situations:

• idle at the passenger vehicle depot, then:

$$y_{dik}^{da} = 1, \quad y_{dik}^{da} = 0 \quad otherwise \quad (5\text{-}1)$$

$$t_{ij}^{park} + T_{ij}^{ar} =$$

$$\max\left\{ t_{ij}^{park} + \tau_i^{deb}, t_k^{idpx} + \Delta_j^{depot} \big/ v_{pax} + \tau_{ij}^{deb} + \sigma_{ij}^{pa} \right\}$$
$$(5\text{-}2)$$

where t_k^{idpx} is the start time of passenger vehicle k from the depot (it is supposed that it will not return to depot until the end of operations), Δ_j^{depot} is the distance between depot and parking position j, v_{pax} is the mean speed of passenger vehicle, σ_{ij}^{pa} is a waiting time for the passenger vehicle if aircraft I at parking position j is not ready for disembark.

- Carrying passengers from arriving aircraft e at parking position f towards passengers terminal l. In that case:

$$y_{eik}^{aa} = 1, \quad y_{eik}^{aa} = 0 \quad otherwise \quad (6\text{-}1)$$

$$t_{ij}^{park} + T_{ij}^{ar} = \max\Big\{ t_{ij}^{park} + \tau_{ij}^{deb}, t_{ef}^{park} + T_{ef}^{ar} + \Delta_{fl}^{term}$$
$$\big/ v_{pax} + \sigma_{ef}^{db} + \tau_{ef}^{term} + \Delta_{lj}^{airc} \big/ v_{pax} + \tau_{ij}^{deb} + \sigma_{ij}^{pa} \Big\}$$
$$(6\text{-}2)$$

where Δ_{fl}^{term} is the distance between position f and terminal l, τ_{il}^{term} is the duration of disembarking from vehicle to the passenger terminal l, Δ_{lj}^{airc} is the distance between terminal l and parking position j.

- Carrying passengers towards departing aircraft e at parking position f, then:

$$y_{eik}^{dep} = 1, \quad y_{eik}^{dep} = 0 \quad otherwise \quad (7\text{-}1)$$

$$t_{ij}^{park} + T_{ij}^{ar} = \max\Big\{ t_{ij}^{park} + \tau_i^{deb}, t_{ef}^{park} + T_{ef}^{ar} + T_{ef}^{sv}$$
$$+ T_{ef}^{dp} + \Delta_{fj}^{park} \big/ v_{pax} + \tau_i^{deb} + \sigma_{ij}^{pa} \Big\}$$
$$(7\text{-}2)$$

where Δ_{fj}^{park} is the distance between parking positions f and j.

We have also the exclusion condition (only one passenger vehicle is assigned to an arriving aircraft):

$$\sum_k (y_{dik}^{da} + \sum_e (y_{eik}^{aa} + y_{eik}^{dep})) = 1 \qquad i \in I \quad (8)$$

If the assigned passenger vehicle is vehicle k, then:

$$\lambda_{ik}^{arv} = 1 \qquad \lambda_{ik}^{arv} = 0 \quad otherwise \quad (9)$$

To realize the servicing of departing aircraft, the assigned service vehicle h can be previously in one of the two following situations:

- idle at the service vehicle depot, then:

$$z_{dih}^{da} = 1, \quad z_{dih}^{da} = 0 \quad otherwise \quad (10\text{-}1)$$

$$t_{ij}^{park} + T_{ij}^{ar} + T_{ij}^{sv} =$$

$$\max\left\{ t_{ij}^{park} + T_{ij}^{ar} + \tau_{ij}^{sv}, t_k^{idsv} + \Delta_j^{desrv} \big/ v_{srv} + \tau_{ij}^{sv} + \sigma_{ij}^{sv} \right\}$$
$$(10\text{-}2)$$

where t_k^{idsv} is the start time of service vehicle k from the depot (it is supposed that it will not return to depot until the end of operations), Δ_j^{desrv} is the distance between service vehicle depot and parking position j, v_{srv} is the mean speed of service vehicle, τ_{ij}^{sv} is the duration of service for departing aircraft i at parking position j, σ_{ij}^{sv} is a waiting time for the service vehicle if aircraft i at parking position j is not ready for servicing.

- Servicing departing aircraft e at parking position f. In that case:

$$z_{eih}^{aa} = 1, \quad z_{eih}^{aa} = 0 \quad otherwise \quad (11\text{-}1)$$

$$t_{ij}^{park} + T_{ij}^{ar} + T_{ij}^{sv} =$$

$$\max\left\{t_{ij}^{park} + T_{ij}^{ar} + \tau_{ij}^{sv},\ t_{ef}^{park} + T_{ef}^{ar} + T_{ef}^{sv} + \Delta_{fj}^{park} / v_{srv} + \tau_{ij}^{sv} + \sigma_{ij}^{sv}\right\}$$

$$(11\text{-}2)$$

where Δ_{fj}^{park} is the distance between parking positions f and j.

We have also the exclusion condition:

$$\sum_h \left(z_{dih}^{da} + \sum_e (z_{eih}^{aa})\right) = 1 \qquad i \in I \qquad (12)$$

If the assigned vehicle is service vehicle h, then:

$$\mu_{ih}^{srv} = 1, \qquad \mu_{ih}^{srv} = 0 \quad otherwise \qquad (13)$$

To board passengers, the assigned passengers vehicle k can be previously in one of the three following situations:

- idle at the passenger vehicle depot, then:

$$w_{dik}^{da} = 1, \qquad w_{dik}^{da} = 0 \quad otherwise \qquad (14\text{-}1)$$

$$t_{ij}^{park} + T_{ij}^{ar} + T_{ij}^{sv} + T_{ij}^{dp} =$$

$$\max\left\{t_{ij}^{park} + T_{ij}^{ar} + T_{ij}^{sv} + \tau_{ij}^{brd},\ t_k^{idpx} + \Delta_j^{depot} / v_{pax} + \tau_{ij}^{brd} + \sigma_{ij}^{pd}\right\}$$

$$(14\text{-}2)$$

where t_k^{idpx} is the start time of passenger vehicle k from the depot (it is supposed that it will not return to depot until the end of operations), τ_{ij}^{brd} is the duration of boarding for departing aircraft i, σ_{ij}^{pd} is a waiting time for the passenger vehicle if aircraft i at parking position j is not ready for boarding.

- Carrying passengers from arriving aircraft e at parking position f towards passengers terminal l. In that case:

$$w_{eik}^{aa} = 1, \qquad w_{eik}^{aa} = 0 \quad otherwise \qquad (15\text{-}1)$$

$$t_{ij}^{park} + T_{ij}^{ar} + T_{ij}^{sv} + T_{ij}^{dp} = \max\left\{ t_{ij}^{park} + T_{ij}^{ar} + T_{ij}^{sv} + \tau_{ij}^{brd},\right.$$

$$\left. t_{ef}^{park} + T_{ef}^{ar} + \Delta_{fl}^{term} / v_{pax} + \tau_{ij}^{term} + \Delta_{lj}^{airc} / v_{pax} + \tau_{ij}^{brd} + \sigma_{ij}^{pd}\right\}$$

$$(15\text{-}2)$$

- Carrying passengers towards departing aircraft e at parking position f, then:

$$w_{eik}^{dep} = 1, \qquad w_{eik}^{dep} = 0 \quad otherwise \qquad (16\text{-}1)$$

$$t_{ij}^{park} + T_{ij}^{ar} + T_{ij}^{sv} + T_{ij}^{dp} = \max\left\{t_{ij}^{park} + T_{ij}^{ar} + T_{ij}^{sv} + \tau_{ij}^{brd},\right.$$

$$\left. t_{ef}^{park} + T_{ef}^{ar} + T_{ef}^{sv} + T_{ef}^{dp} + \Delta_{fj}^{park} / v_{pax} + \tau_{ij}^{brd} + \sigma_{ij}^{pd}\right\}$$

$$(16\text{-}2)$$

Here also, we have the exclusion condition:

$$\sum_k \left(w_{dik}^{da} + \sum_e (w_{eik}^{aa} + w_{eik}^{dep})\right) = 1 \qquad i \in I$$

$$(17)$$

If the assigned vehicle is passenger vehicle k, then:

$$\lambda_{ik}^{dep} = 1 \qquad \lambda_{ik}^{dep} = 0 \quad otherwise \qquad (18)$$

In the same way, many other constraints should be introduced here, among them runway occupancies by aircraft at landing or take-off are important ones since departing aircraft may queue up at their entrance.

Ground Vehicles Assignment Constraints

Of course, the same ground vehicle cannot be assigned to two overlapping operations, so we should have:

If $x_{ij}=1$ and $\lambda_{ik}^{arv} = 1$, then passenger vehicle k will be busy with arriving aircraft i during the span of time $[t_{ijk}^{\inf arv}, t_{ijk}^{\sup arv}]$ with:

$$t_{ijk}^{\inf arv} = y_{dik}^{da} t_k^{idpx} + \sum_e y_{eik}^{aa} (t_{ef}^{park} + T_{ef}^{ar} + \Delta_{fl}^{term} / v_{pax} + \sigma_{ef}^{db} + \tau_{ef}^{term})$$

$$+ \sum_e y_{eik}^{dep} (t_{ef}^{park} + T_{ef}^{ar} + T_{ef}^{sv} + T_{ef}^{dp})$$

$$(19\text{-}1)$$

and

$$t_{yjk}^{sup\,arv} = y_{dik}^{da}(t_k^{idpx} + \Delta_j^{depot} / v_{pax} + \tau_{ij}^{deb} + \sigma_{ij}^{pa})$$
$$+ \sum_e y_{eik}^{aa}(t_k^{idpx} + \Delta_j^{depot} / v_{pax} + \tau_{ij}^{deb} + \sigma_{ij}^{pa} + \Delta_{jl}^{term} / v_{pax} + \sigma_{il}^{db} + \tau_{il}^{term})$$
$$+ \sum_e y_{eik}^{dep}(t_{ef}^{park} + T_{ef}^{ar} + T_{ef}^{sv} + T_{ef}^{dp} + \Delta_{fi}^{park} / v_{pax} + \tau_i^{deb} + \sigma_{ij}^{pa})$$

$$(19\text{-}2)$$

Other similar time intervals where ground vehicles can be busy at departing aircraft must be also considered so that overlapping constraints are established.

Finally, each aircraft will be ready to depart from parking position j at time t_{ij}^{dep} given by:

$$t_{ij}^{dep} = \max\left\{ t_{dp}(i), t_{ij}^{park} + T_{ij}^s \right\} \qquad (20)$$

Observe that when connections between flights i (departing aircraft) and e (arriving aircraft) are present, the planned departure times obey to temporal constraints such as:

$$t_{dp}(i) \geq tar(e) + \theta_{ie}^{\min} \qquad (21\text{-}1)$$

where $\theta_{ie}^{\min}$ is a minimum delay between arrival and departure times with aircraft e and i respectively. When considering waiting times and ground operation times explicitly, we must have:

$$\sum_j (t_{ij}^{dep}\, x_{ij}) \geq \sum_j ((\sum_l (t_e^{park} + \theta_{ie}^{jl})\, x_{el})\, x_{ij}) \qquad (21\text{-}2)$$

where θ_{ie}^{jl} is a minimum delay between arrival and departure times while aircraft e and i are docked respectively at positions j and l.

If $t_{ij}^{dep} = t_{ij}^{park} + T_{ij}^s$, the departure delay will be such as: $\theta_{ij}^d \geq t_{ij}^{park} + T_{ij}^s - t_{dp}(i)$, $\theta_{ij}^d \geq 0$ otherwise.

Parking position j, will be available for aircraft i if:

$$[t_{ij}^{park}, t_{ij}^{dep}] \subset L(j, t_{ij}^{park}) \qquad (22\text{-}1)$$

where:

$$L(j, t) = [t, T] - \bigcup_{ij | t_{ij}^{park} \leq t \text{ and } [t_{ij}^{park}, t_{ij}^{dep}] \cap [t, +\infty[\neq \varnothing} (x_{ij}\, [t_{ij}^{park}, t_{ij}^{dep}]) \qquad (22\text{-}2)$$

Here, $L(j, t)$ represents the periods of time, starting at current time t, where parking position j is not busy.

Sources of Uncertainty and Perturbations

In the above formulation many parameters are subject to uncertainty:

- Arrival times $t_{ar}(i)$, $i \in I$, can suffer large variations, in general delays due to air traffic control, but information about these delays can be made available and these variations can be at the ground operations level reduced to few minutes.
- Boarding, disembark and other servicing times can suffer variations around a mean value.
- Transportation delays between runways and parking positions, between depots and parking positions, or between two parking positions can vary depending on traffic congestion and weather conditions.
- Technical problems (engine problems, door problems, complementary checking, etc) as well as security problems (delays due to a protection area around an abandonned luggage or due to an on-board passenger missing before departure, etc) may induce important perturbations in the airside traffic.
- Delayed operations may have a cascade effect on subsequent operations and the resulting delays are difficult to be predicted.

In general there are no relevant statistics about the majority of these events or phenomena and the construction of adequate scenarios appears useful to test the robustness of the different decision processes confronted with unexpected events.

A COOPERATIVE MANAGEMENT STRUCTURE

The proposed airside management structure is composed of three levels:

- a planning level where ground vehicle fleets and workforce are dimensioned, fleet depots are localized and traffic ways are established;
- an operational level where resources (vehicles and staffs) are assigned on the short term to the different ground operations;
- a control level where vehicles are localized and controlled on line by the airport authorities.

In the present work, it is supposed that resources have already been made available through an adequate planning process and that the control level is able to solve all local traffic conflicts and to prevent all dangerous traffic situations. So our aim is to propose decision schemes to manage in a coordinated way aircraft and ground vehicles traffic and activities. The traffic considered is highly complex since it is composed of very different vehicles with complementary tasks, and many different decision variables are involved with its management. Also, since different economic actors are involved with airside ground traffic operations, different criteria can be considered to assess the effectiveness of the operations management systems.

Decision Variables

Among the various variables introduced in the last section, some are true decision variables while others are a consequence of the decisions taken with respect to these true decision variables. This is a large difference with a mathematical programming approach where all these variables should be considered as a whole.

Here decision variables are of two main types: assignment variables and delay variables. The assignment variables are essentially logical variables while the delay variables take positive real values. These two types of decision variables are relevant in the case of the management of the grounded aircraft (examples are assignment decision of an arriving aircraft to a parking zone, delay decision for a departing aircraft at gate until the way to the runway is cleared). The decision variables related with the management of the ground vehicle fleets are also either assignment variables (example: which passenger vehicle is assigned to an arriving aircraft) or temporal variables (example: when starts a new task performed by a given vehicle). In that case, when delays happen, they are unwanted and the ground fleet managers have to find ways to minimize them through reassignment decisions.

Evaluation Criteria

With respect to airport authorities possible measures of merit are related with service quality to final users, the passengers, and to environmental considerations such as the amount of pollution generated by engines of aircraft and ground vehicles. Indirect evaluation of the first aspect can be done through the sum of total individual delays suffered by on board passengers. With respect to the second aspect, it can be evaluated through the total distance and the total engine running time per type of vehicles, either aircraft or ground vehicles.

From the point of view of airlines, they are mainly interested in diminishing their over costs due to working engines while aircraft remain still on the ground waiting for some clearance from the airport traffic control system (delayed aircraft on aprons, taxiways or at runway entries). So, their whole fleet operation can be optimized through effective aircraft routing over their operated network, as well as optimized delays at different stations. Two possible criteria, computed by each airline operating at that airport are given by:

$$\theta^a = \sum_{i \in I_s} \sum_{j \in P(i) \cup R(i)} x_{ij} \, \theta^a_{ij} \quad \text{and}$$

$$\theta^a = \sum_{i \in I_s} \sum_{j \in P(i) \cup R(i)} x_{ij} \, \theta^a_{ij}$$

$$T^d = \sum_{i \in I_s} \sum_{j \in P(i) \cup R(i)} x_{ij} \, T^d_{ij} \quad \text{and}$$

$$T^d = \sum_{i \in I_s} \sum_{j \in P(i) \cup R(i)} x_{ij} \, T^d_{ij} \tag{23}$$

where θ^a and T^d are respectively the total ground waiting times of arriving aircraft (at apron) and departing aircraft (at runway entries) with engines on.

From the point of view of ground traffic agents, what will be important is to fulfil their contractual activities with the airlines while minimizing their operational costs.

The Multi-Agent Management Approach

It appears that the objectives of the different agents involved with ground traffic management are here broadly convergent. So, a centralized approach adopting a global criterion as well as a multi-agent approach where each agent adopts a partial criterion of his own interest, should lead in both cases to acceptable performances for each of the agents. However, considering the operations constraints and relations relative to ground traffic, as displayed in section 3, a centralized approach should cope

with an excessively complex decision problem. So it appears natural to consider ground traffic management through a multi-agent approach as depicted in figure 6 where the whole problem is split in three interdependent sub problems.

The aircraft ground traffic manager takes its assignment decisions with respect to arriving or grounded aircraft considering the necessary resources (parking positions, gates, taxiways and ground vehicles). Aircraft assignment to parking positions takes into account their predicted availability, their distance from the runways and the estimated delays to dispose of adequate ground vehicles at parking positions. This information is obtained through requests to the vehicle ground traffic controllers. To provide this information, at their turn they have to solve another assignment problem where ground vehicles are assigned to docked aircraft processing tasks. In this case an on line accurate position knowledge is required for each vehicle.

Since many sources of perturbation are present, a pre-assignment of resources appears illusory and a first come first served philosophy combined with a look-ahead mechanism is adopted to process aircraft traffic requests.

Examples of such assignment procedures are displayed below:

- Passenger vehicle assignment at aircraft arrival.
- Passenger vehicle assignment at aircraft departure.

The two ground vehicles agents can divert vehicles from a first assignment, if it appears more convenient, depending on the relative positions of the different ground vehicles and of their operational state (Figure 9). Three operational states, $x(j, t) \in \{1, 2, 3\}$, are considered for each ground vehicle. This facility improves the reactivity of the fleet management systems to perturbations. When an unexpected delay appears at the level of the ground vehicles (increased travel time from

Figure 6. Multi-agent ground traffic control structure

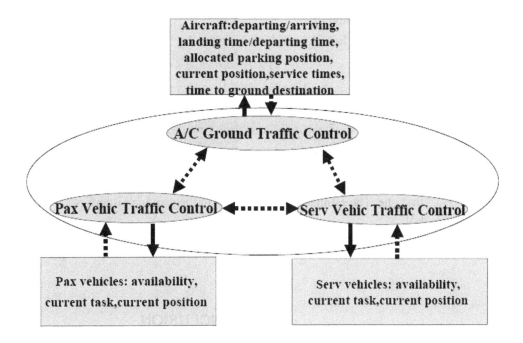

one assignment point to another, increased service time, etc), an estimate of this delay is sent to the related fleet manager.

A table of estimated delays to attend requests at parking positions or gates is generated on line to the grounded aircraft manager by each of the ground vehicle agents so that requests for ground vehicles can be done earlier than the estimated time to turn available the requested vehicle.

SIMULATION STUDY

To illustrate the proposed approach, a simulation study has been performed with a numerical simulator written in Java. Figure 10 displays the structure of the airport field considered. The main characteristics of the airside are: a single runway, a remote parking area without passenger terminal which should allow to operate in excess grounded aircraft situations, various bottlenecks in the taxiways, apron and service ways. It has

been supposed that the low level traffic control system provides priority to arriving aircraft with respect to departing ones, while other situations are treated in a first come first served basis.

Two main different traffic scenarios have been designed: one is relative to a low aircraft traffic demand, while the other is relative to a saturation situation where the runway operates near full capacity. In both cases the performance of the overall airside traffic management system has been considered with different levels of communication (availability of delays predictions and look-ahead mechanism) between the different agents. The first simulation results, show that aircraft arriving and departing delays are contained in saturation situations when a high level of communication is established between the aircraft traffic manager and the ground vehicle managers. In the case of low traffic levels, aircraft delays are not decreased noticeably but the ground vehicles appears to be much more efficiently managed since their total covered distances are clearly reduced.

Figure 7.

At time t_{ia} aircraft i is due to request a pax vehicle for arrival processing at position p_{ia}

The set of candidate pax vehicles is given by:

$$J_{ia}(t) = \left\{ j \in J \mid x(j,t) > 0 \ \textit{and} \ t + d_{jia} \leq t_{ia} \right\}$$

where d_{jia} is the delay for vehicle j to go from current position to position p_{ia}

$$\textit{if} \ J_{ia}(t) = \phi, \ J_{ia}(t) = \left\{ j \in J \mid x(j,t+k\Delta t) = 1 \ \textit{and} \ t + d_{jia} \leq t_{ia} + k\Delta t \right\}$$

where k is the minimum integer so that $J_{ia}(t) \neq \phi$

- Rank the available vehicles by increasing d_{jia} *and c*hoose the first one. The estimated delay applied to the arriving aircraft is $k\Delta t$.

Figure 8.

At time t_{id} aircraft i is due to request a pacs vehicle for departure processing at position p_{id}

The set of candidate pacs vehicles is given by:

$$J_{id}(t) = \left\{ j \in J \mid x(j,t) > 0 \ \textit{and} \ t + d_{jid} \leq t_{id} \right\}$$

where d_{jid} is the delay for vehicle j to go from current position to position p_{id}

$$\textit{if} \ J_{id}(t) = \phi, \ J_{id}(t) = \left\{ j \in J \mid x(j,t+k\Delta t) = 1 \ \textit{and} \ t + d_{jid} \leq t_{ia} + k\Delta t \right\}$$

where k is the minimum integer so that $J_{id}(t) \neq \phi$

- Rank the available vehicles by increasing d_{jid} *and c*hoose the first one. The estimated delay applied to the departing aircraft is $k\Delta t$.

CONCLUSION

With the sustained increase in air transportation, resulting in higher operational costs and delays for passengers and airlines, ground traffic has become a critical issue for many airports. In this communication the management of airside ground traffic has been considered. This large scale distributed problem is characterized by a vulnerability to many potential perturbations and it is expected from an efficient management system to present a high degree of reactivity in front of this

Figure 9. Assignability of ground vehicles

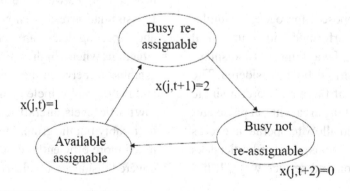

Figure 10. The simulated airside structure

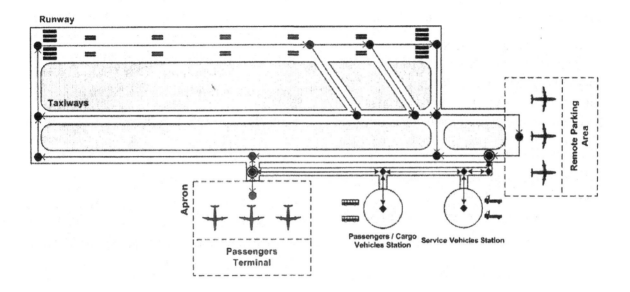

stochastic decision problem. The traffic of aircraft at airside and of ground passenger and service vehicles constitutes a case of dependent flows. Then, a global management structure for airside operations, based on cooperation between three different fleet manager agents, has been proposed while different levels of cooperation have been considered. From the first simulation results, it appears that this kind of cooperative control systems should contribute noticeably to airside capacity at airports and should reduce traffic induced damages to the airport environment.

REFERENCES

Andreatta, G., Brunetta, L., Odoni, A. R., Righi, L., Stamatopoulos, M. A., & Zografos, G. (1998). *A set of approximate and compatible models for airport strategic planning on airside and on landside.* 2nd USA/Europe ATM R&D Seminar, Orlando.

Andreatta, G., & Romanin-Jacur, G. (1987). Aircraft flow management under congestion. *Transportation Science, 21*, 249–253. doi:10.1287/trsc.21.4.249

Brunetta, L., Righi, L., & Andreatta, G. (1999). An operations research model for the evaluation of an airport terminal: SLAM (simple landside aggregate model). *Journal of Air Transport Management, 5*, 161–175. doi:10.1016/S0969-6997(99)00010-1

Carr, F. (2000). *Stochastic modelling and control of airport surface traffic.* SM Thesis Electrical Engineering and Computer Science, MIT, Cambridge, MA.

Dennis, F., Mathaisel, X., & Idris, H. (1998). Aircraft ground movement simulation. In G. Yu, (Ed.) *Operations research in the airline industry*, (pp. 189-227). Amsterdam: Kluwer.

Gilbo, E. P. (1993, September). Airport capacity: representation, estimation, optimisation. *IEEE Transactions on Control Systems Technology, 1*(3). doi:10.1109/87.251882

Lee, D., Nelson, C., & Shapiro, G. (1998). The aviation system analysis capability airport capacity and delay models. *NASA, C,* R-1998–R-207659.

Paulussen, T. O., Jennings, N. R., Decker, K. S., & Heinzl, A. (2003). Distributed patient scheduling in hospitals. In *IJCA-03* (pp. 1224-1232). San Francisco: Morgan Kaufman. Hallenborg K. (2007). *Decentralized scheduling of baggage handling using multi-agent technologies.* In E. Levner, (Ed.), *Multiprocessor Scheduling: Theory and Applications,* (pp.381-403). Vienna, Austria: I-Tech Education and Publishing.

Polak, F. R. (1996). *Airport modelling: capacity analysis of Schiphol airport in 2015.* 1st USA/Europe ATM R&D Seminar. Blondel, V.D., Hendrickx, J.H., Olshevsky A., & Tsitsiklis, J.N. (2005). *Convergence in multi-agent coordination, consensus and flocking.* 44th IEEE European Conference on Decision and Control-ECC.

Smith, D. E., Frank, J., & Jonsson, A. K. (2000). Bridging the gap between planning and scheduling. *The Knowledge Engineering Review, 15*(1), 47–83. doi:10.1017/S0269888900001089

Sultanik, E. A., Modi, P. J., & Regli, W. C. (2007). On modelling multi-agent task scheduling as a distributed constraint optimization problem. In *IJCAI,* (pp. 1531-1536).

Section 2
Improving Economic and Operational Performance

Chapter 5
Critical Review and Analysis of Air–Travel Demand:
Forecasting Models

Matthew G. Karlaftis
National Technical University of Athens, Greece

ABSTRACT

Demand forecasting may be the most critical factor in the development of airports and airline networks. This chapter reviews various approaches used to forecast air travel and airport demand forecasting. It classifies existing methods according to the modeling approach used to evaluate the available data; then, the forecasting approaches are viewed in relation to data requirements. Finally, a new matrix classification scheme is introduced that combines both the data available and the technique used to evaluate this data in a more concise and manner.

INTRODUCTION AND BACKGROUND

Air transportation is a mode in which demand increases continuously at a significant, yet highly variable rate. It is thus very hard to estimate the magnitude of demand at future points in time, no matter how critical this might be for a number of components of the air transportation industry. One of the most important components of the overall air transportation system is the airports. Airports have developed over the years to become huge and very costly projects that provide the basis for a country's financial development. It is estimated that the pas-senger terminal component of an airport can be as expensive as US $200 million, which was the cost of the new International Terminal Building (ITB) for Sydney, amounting to US $25 million per gate. It is obvious that the need for adequate forecasting in such a capital-intensive industry is of critical importance.

Besides the terminal area configuration a planner is required to provide valid forecasts for facilities on the airside of an airport (Figure 1). Such facilities are the gates, the aprons, and the runaways. Forecasts of this type are not based on passenger traffic, but rather on total aircraft movement for the airport. A combination of the previous two types of forecasts and a breakdown of these numbers will

DOI: 10.4018/978-1-60566-800-0.ch005

Figure 1. Airport demand forecasting and its effects on airport planning

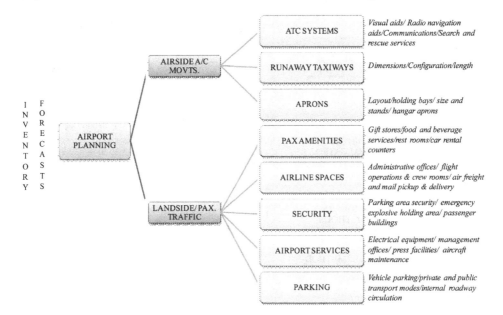

also be required to ensure an effective design of facilities such as the ground access system (rail, transit, highway), and the parking lots.

Forecasting is also very important for the economic development of the airlines, through the fleet development process. Airline fleets have grown significantly in the last few decades, and orders for commercial transport aircraft have reached an all time high, with delivery dates now backed up into the mid-1990's for some aircraft types. Economic implications and stringent environmental (noise) regulations for the subsonic jet aircraft has led airlines and aircraft manufacturers to search for new ways to develop their fleets in order to make them more competitive. Future fleet development has an important role in the design of terminals, since the aircraft size is critical to some geometric characteristics such as the main deck elevation and the lateral clearance at gates due o aircraft wing span.

Even though the maximum size of aircraft is not expected to grow much beyond 500-seats in the next decade, aircraft of smaller size such as jet aircraft of 50-70 seats are developed to serve some local markets. This down-sizing, combined with

the deregulation that provides for a larger number of airlines, will congest the air space more than even before. It is thus critical to be able to forecast the air traffic requirements in order to better plan and develop the new air traffic control system.

It is evident that the forecasting process can be the most critical factor in the development of the airport. Mistakes made in this phase of the process can be very costly and damaging for local economies. Underestimating demand can lead to increased congestion, delay, and lack of storage facilities, as it happened in Venezuela in 1974. The discovery of oil resulted in a dramatic and unforeseen increase of the freight volumes handled by the Caracas airport. The planned storage facilities were insufficient to handle this increased demand, and so the cargo was stored in areas where it was either destroyed or stolen. Overestimating demand could also create significant problems. Forecasts of passenger demand for the Newark airport were so high that the newly constructed airport remained empty for a number of years.

The purpose of this chapter is to review the various approaches used to forecast air travel and airport demand forecasting. The chapter begins

Figure 2. A classification of airport demand forecasting methods

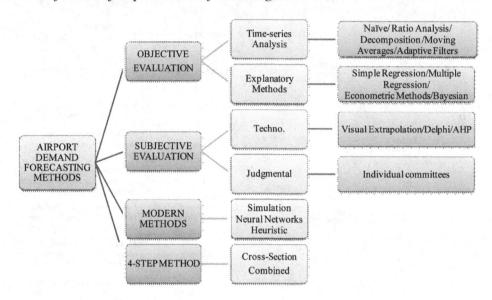

with the classification of the existing methods according to the modeling approach used to evaluate the available data. Then the forecasting approaches are viewed in relation to the data required for forecasting purposes rather than the technique used to evaluate it. Finally, a new matrix classification scheme is introduced that combines both the data available and the technique used to evaluate this data in a more concise manner.

FORECASTING CLASSIFICATION BASED ON MODELING APPROACH

The classification of forecasting methods based on the modeling approach used to evaluate the available data is a widely used approach that offers the forecaster a comprehensive look at the available techniques (Karlaftis et al., 1996). This type of classification is shown in Figure 2 and is consistent with the way many forecasters differentiate models; yet, it is by no means unique, but is rather heavily geared toward air travel demand approaches. The work done by both Taneja (1978) and Wheelwright and Makridakis (1987) has the same basic classification of models and

both their work has become the standard in the respective areas of airline traffic and managerial forecasting.

The classification scheme of Figure 2 categorizes the models in four different groups based on what technique they use to forecast air traffic and airport demand. The four basic categories are the *objective evaluation, subjective evaluation, modern methods*, and the *four step method*. In the following sections, a brief description of each category is done so that the reader can become familiar with the basic characteristics and underlying principles of each method.

Objective Evaluation Methods

The objective evaluation methods are statistical techniques that utilize historical data, of different kinds to predict the future. These methods can be further subdivided into two categories: the time-series analysis and the explanatory methods.

The *time-series* analysis methods, which are the most widely used methods for predicting air travel demand (Garvett & Taneja, 1974; Karlaftis et al., 1996), assume that history repeats itself and so the future will be some continuation of the past (Pack, 1987). The common characteristic and weakness of all time-series methods is that they ignore the determinants of demand such as fares and income, and do not attempt to explain the reason changes occur. Even though these methods lack the power of explanation they are rather accurate in producing short term forecasts such as monthly, weekly and hourly variations of passenger traffic at airports (Garvett & Taneja, 1974; Karlaftis et al., 1996). The techniques that are used to evaluate the historical data range from the rather simple and straightforward constant growth and ratio analysis methods, to the more sophisticated methods such as decomposition and adaptive filtering.

The constant growth method assumes t hat air traffic will grow at a constant rate during a given period of time. This method is simple and has been used extensively by aircraft manufacturers, yet it cannot deal with changes in patterns or relationships. To overcome this inflexibility of the constant growth method, a significant number of formulas exists that deal with time-series growth at varying rates. Each of the different formulas assumes that air travel grows with different types of trend (linear, quadratic. etc.) and with different growth rates (not necessarily constant). The most commonly used types of trend curves are: the linear, the exponential, the parabolic and the Gompertz curve. Their mathematical expressions are (Washington et al., 2003):

$$Y = a + bT \text{, for the linear curve} \quad (1)$$

$$Y = a(1 + b)^T \text{, for the exponential curve} \quad (2)$$

$$Y = a + bT + cT^2 \text{, for the parabolic curve} \quad (3)$$

$$Y = ab^{-c^T} \text{, for the Gompertz curve} \quad (4)$$

In all the relationships *a, b, c* are constants, the dependent variable *Y* is traffic and the independent variable *T* is time usually measured in years. The linear curve implies a constant annual increase in traffic levels, yet the rate of growth is declining. The exponential curve implies a constant annual rate of increase, while the parabolic implies a decreasing with time rate of growth, yet growth in absolute terms increases linearly with time. Finally, the Gompertz curve denotes high initial growth rates, yet when the curve approaches a saturation level *a* the rate decreases.

The ratio analysis is a quite common method of forecasting traffic at airports. The assumption is that traffic levels at a given airport vary according to national air traffic levels. Forecasts are done by extrapolating this historical ratio (Taneja, 1978). This type of forecast can be rather successful when an airports' traffic fluctuation has followed national levels and where this fluctuation is expected to continue. It should be noted that ratio analysis forecasts can be feasible alternatives to more complex methods when time, money or data restrictions exist.

The more sophisticated methods have also been used in airport forecasting, without always providing planners with more accurate projections (Cooper, 1973; Gillen & Hall, 2003). *De*composition is a technique by which data is "broken" down into trend, seasonality and randomness, and by which past patterns can be identified. Decomposition can be a very useful method in air traffic forecasting since identifying seasonality patterns is of great importance in terminal design (Goh & Law, 2002). Filtering is another advanced statistical technique that attempts to overcome the least-square technique's disadvantage of using coefficients that remain constant through time (Blake & Sinclair, 2003). Filtering has not been used extensively in air traffic forecasting, but new methods that utilize filtering in econometric modelling might prompt planners to do so (Huth & Eriksen, 1987; Lai & Lu, 2005; Sarris, 1973).

The air transportation industry faces continuous changes in the environment that make the forecasting process even more difficult than it would otherwise be. It might therefore be better to attempt to predict the future by understanding the factors that influence a variable of interest, than basing a forecast solely on the historical information for one variable. The *explanatory* methods try to determine causation or at least explanation when analyzing the relationship between certain data. In air travel and airport forecasting, explanatory methods are used extensively.

The most extensively used technique in the explanatory category is regression. Simple regression is a statistical tool that utilizes the relationship between two variables so that one variable (the dependent) can be predicted from the other (independent). Accordingly, multiple regression predicts one variable from more than one independent variables (Karlaftis et al. 1996; Neter, Wesserman & Kutner, 1989; Washington et al., 2003). Econometric models are systems of simultaneous equations that take into account the interdependence among variables (Levenbach & Schultz, 1987). In the context of air transportation, econometric methods are used for predicting, with regression, air travel (or another similar variable) based on socioeconomic indicators (Garvett & Taneja, 1974; Taneja, 1978; Washington et al., 2003).

Kanafani (1981), introduced the use of econometric models by formulating a simple multiplicative model that relates air travel in year t to demand and supply variables for that year. This model does not take into account any lagged time effects of changes in the variables, and can be written as:

$$T_t = C \prod_k D_{kt}^{\alpha_k} \prod_m S_{mt}^{\beta_k} \tag{5}$$

In this model, C is a constant term, and S, D are the values of supply and demand variables in year t. T_t denotes the volume in traffic in year t. a_k and β_k represent the elasticities of demand for the respective variables.

In the context of air transportation, demand variables are included in the models to account for the nature and level of socioeconomic activities that are likely to generate air travel. The most widely used demand variables are population, income, Gross National Product and personal consumption expenditures. The supply variables represent the attributes of the transport system that will affect the extent to which demand will materialize into actual air travel volumes. The most commonly used supply variable is that of price of travel. To facilitate the use linear regression techniques, Kanafani (1981) linearizes the general multiplicative form of the econometric model. The new model formulated is as follows:

$$T_t' = C' + \sum_k \alpha_k D_{kt}' + \sum_m \beta_m S_{mt}' \tag{6}$$

The prime (′) denotes the logarithmic form of the S and D, which are respectively supply and demand variables for air transportation.

This basic model has been further modified to reflect the assumption that changes in the levels of air travel take more than one time period to materialize when changes occur in one of the variables. This modification is called the *partial adjustment* model, and its hypothesis has been stated again by Kanafani (1981) as:

$$\frac{T_t}{T_{t-1}} = \left(\frac{T_t^*}{T_{t-1}} \right), \ 0 < \mu \le 1 \tag{7}$$

In this hypothesis T_t^* is the desired travel level. μ is the coefficient that measures the proportion of total adjustment that materializes in the travel T_t in year t.

By combining 6 and 7 *the* general form of the partial adjustment model in terms of observed traffic is derived:

$$T_t^{'} = \mu C^{'} + \sum_k \mu \alpha_k D_{kt}^{'} + \sum_m \mu \beta_m S_{mt}^{'} + (1-\mu)T_{t-1}^{'} \tag{8}$$

It should be noted that while a and β in model 6 represent the short run elasticities $\mu\alpha$ and $\mu\beta$ represent *the* long run elasticities.

There is one more model that was again formulated in Kanafani (1981), and which is called the permanent income model. The basis of this hypothesis is that a person's permanent income is a more appropriate, variable for inclusion in a forecasting model. This hypothesis can be written as follows:

$$I_t^{*} = \sum_\omega \omega_\theta I_{t-\theta} \tag{9}$$

In this formulation, I_t^{*} is the permanent income in year t, and ω_θ is the coefficient for the lagged income value $I_{t-\theta}$.

Again, combining 6 and 9 gives the general form for the permanent income model:

$$T_t^{'} = C^{'} + \sum_{k \neq 1} \alpha_k D_{kt}^{'} + \alpha_k I_t^{'*} + \sum_m \beta_m S_{mt}^{'} \tag{10}$$

Where, I is the income variable used, and D_{kt} $\forall\ k \neq 1$ are all other demand variables utilized in year t.

The three different models can now be combined into one, general, all inclusive model, given again in Kanafani (1981):

$$T_t^{'} = \mu C^{'} + \sum_{k \neq 1} \mu \alpha_k D_{kt}^{'} + \mu \alpha_I I_t^{'*} + \sum_m \mu \beta_m S_{mt}^{'} + (1-\mu)T_{t-1}^{'} \tag{11}$$

The above explanation of the three different hypotheses was a necessary one, since many air travel forecasting models refer and make use of them.

Bayesian forecasting is a very interesting and simple formula for conditional probability, used mainly for the updating process of objective forecasts (Martino, 1972). Besides the Bayesian method that has not been used in air travel forecasting, all other explanatory methods have been extensively used and will be further analyzed later in this chapter.

Subjective Evaluation Methods

The use of sophisticated statistical techniques in the forecasting process is a rather recent development when considering that people have been making predictions for the future, or forecasts, since ancient times. Those forecasts were subjective in nature, and although recent developments in statistics and computer technology make forecasting a more objective process, experts views can still play a major role in the area of air transportation forecasting (Cunningham & De Haan, 2006; Winkler, 1987). Subjective forecasts can be further subdivided into two groups: the judgmental and the technological forecasts.

Judgmental forecasts rely primarily on human judgment (Martino, 1972). These types of forecasts have been used in the past, yet they are being replaced by the technological forecasts that combine both expert judgment and a more structured approach. The judgmental forecasts occur in a panel form, where all the experts gather and exchange opinions, or brainstorm, on the state of air transportation and its future. The usual form of judgmental forecasts is the group approach, yet it can be done by individuals, who bring past experiences and inside knowledge to the forecasting process. The big drawback of judgmental forecasts is that they introduce bias in the group meetings or allow the individuals to be influenced from personal beliefs, and that their scope is too general to make specific forecasting conclusions (Wheelwright & Makridakis, 1987). Judgmental forecasts can be useful when assessing the general direction toward which a specific industry will head in the future.

Technological forecasts are concerned with the prediction of specific technological, social and economic characteristics in future technologies (Garvett & Taneja, 1974; Wheelwright & Makridakis, 1987). Using the technological forecasting process, an expert utilizes present analyses to access future conditions.

Visual extrapolation can be used in a variety of ways. First, it can he used to extend a demand pattern into some point in the future, and second it can be used in the "forecasting by analogy" process. In forecasting by analogy, a present developing technology can be compared with some similar technology's evolution in the past (Lenz, 1962). This method relies on the assumption that technical progress in one area lags another by a given length of time. This type of forecasts has been used in the area of air transportation. In 1961 Lenz found that the speed of commercial aircraft lagged the speed of military aircraft by six years in 1920. Furthermore, the growth of air transportation is compared at times with the S-curve derived by Gompertz' s law or to the evolution introduced by Pearl' s law of biological growth (Jantsch, 1972).

As mentioned previously, one of the significant disadvantages of panel forecasts is the bias that can occur by the persuasiveness of individual members and the lack of some scientific and statistical justification. To mitigate this bias, Olaf Helmer of the RAND corporation in Santa Monica, California, developed the Delphi technique (Garvett & Taneja, 1974). The goal of this method is to carefully design a number of successive questionnaires in order to obtain intuitive insights of experts, and then analyze the results statistically and make them converge. The underlying idea is that through successive trials, the forecasting spread is reduced. Highly qualified experts are requested to give their opinions separately as to when events will be realized in science and technology (McDonnell Douglas, 1972). A statistical analysis is then made of this

subjective data. The results of the analysis are then transmitted back to the experts who often choose to change their original forecasts and make new estimates. The new estimates are analyzed once again, and this process transforms subjective data into quasi-subjective data which converges to a stable point. The Delphi method has been used extensively in the fleet development process and in the aircraft manufacturing industry.

Another method worth mentioning is that of the Analytic Hierarchy Process (AHP). The AHP is a multicriiteria decision-making approach developed by mathematician Thomas Saaty, and is being used in such diverse areas as resource allocation, priority setting, and conflict resolution. The AHP uses an approach which employs a pairwise comparison procedure to arrive at a scale of preferences among sets of alternatives (Saaty, 1990). This process requires that a complex structure be broken down into components (variables). These variables are then assigned numerical values depending on their subjective importance. Finally wit h t he use of an eigenvalue computation of the matrix of pair wise comparisons the relative effect of the variables on a certain outcome is determined (Saaty & Vargas, 1991). The AHP is a promising method in the area of forecasting, due to its ability to model complex systems and determine how changes in different factors can influence future demand for air travel.

Modern Methods

The 'modern' forecasting methods have been used minimally in the area of air transportation forecasting. Their use though in other forecasting areas is increasing rapidly and it would be safe to assume that this trend will soon affect the area of air travel demand modelling. The most well known modern methods are those of simulation, neural networks, and fuzzy sets.

Simulation is the method that has been applied the most in the area of air transportation forecasting through a scenario examining process. With simulation, hypothesized relationships are used to reproduce the actions of a system through time.

All the potentially important variables and relationships that can affect the system are identified, and the actions are examined under alternative levels of demand, coming up with multiple forecasting scenarios. Simulation models permit a higher degree of flexibility in terms of accuracy and detail. Furthermore, simulation models are considered as having higher potential for accuracy than purely econometric techniques (Garvett & Taneja, 1974). Simulation models in forecasting still face limitations related to their data requirements and the interface with econometric methods (Washington et al., 2003).

Neural networks, which are algorithms for cognitive tasks such as learning and optimization, have not been used in air travel forecasting, but their pattern recognition ability, which can be utilized for example to recognize seasonality in travelling, gives them the ability to be involved in this type of forecasting (Widrow & Beaufays, 1992). Data is input (called the input pattern) in the neural network in a vector form which outputs a weighted combination of the components of this vector (Khadem, 1992). During the training process, the neural network is presented with patterns and corresponding output responses. At each training stage, an error signal is defined as the difference between the actual and the network's outputs. These errors are then used by a training algorithm to adjust the weights and make the input-output process as realistic as possible. In forecasting, the network could be 'trained' to recognize typical passenger traffic patterns and to produce forecasts for the following time period (Kikuchi, 1994). This forecasting method will be reviewed later in this chapter due to its potential applicability in air traffic forecasting.

The use of fuzzy sets in forecasting is a newly emerging area due to the ability of modelling a cause-effect relationship, such as air travel demand, that is inherently vague (Profillidis,

2003; Tanaka, 1980). The traditional methods, such as regression, assume that a deterministic relationship underlies the cause and the effect, such as increased fares reduce the demand for air transportation. Demand modelling deals with human and societal behaviours that can never be fully explained, that is they contain a degree of freedom that cannot he captured with traditional methods (Hutchinson, 1993). The ability to model this fuzzy relation between cause and effect could lead to the development of a new generation of travel demand forecasting models.

The 4-Step Method

The 4-step method in demand forecasting has been used extensively and for a long period of time in conventional modes of transport (i.e.: autos, transit). The conventional analysis follows a process of four consecutive steps:

> Trip Generation → Trip Distribution → Mode Choice → Route Assignment

The generation phase is concerned with the total number of trips that originate or terminate in a specific airport. The distribution phase calculates how many trips originate in one specific airport and terminate in another specific airport; it models trips as trip interchanges between a pair of airports. The modal choice phase splits the generated and distributed trips into specific modes of transport. The assignment phase models the specific routes taken by the individual traveller.

Hutchinson (1993) showed that in countries with a well-developed road system for trips of less than 300 km, automobile travel dominates approximately 90% of the transport market while air travel dominates intercontinental travel. This type of phenomenon, where the choice between auto and air travel is significantly influenced by the distance between the origin and. the destination of the trip, along with the hub-and-spoke system that the airlines prefer after deregulation, has helped combine the last two steps of the process with the first two steps. In the context of air transportation the four step model has decreased, for all practical purposes, to a two step process: the air trip generation and the air trip distribution phase (Ashford and Wright, 1984). The model calibration part of the distribution phase is very data intensive, yet it gives quite reliable results that can be used to give rather accurate forecasts. Interestingly, much recent research has concentrated on the question of modelling and predicting itinerary shares rather than mode choice; interested readers should refer to Coldren and Koppelman (2005) and Coldren et al. (2003) for an excellent exposition of the subject.

The most widely researched part of this process is the trip distribution phase, where models predict the level of trip interchange between a specific pair of airports. The most commonly encountered trip distribution model is similar to Newton's law of Gravity, and is thus named the gravity model. The use of this model in transportation is largely due to the social scientists, who utilize the gravity model when examining the interactions between human settlements (Ashford & Wright, 1984). In the context of transportation, the gravity model distributes trips between city or airport pairs proportionally to their population and inversely proportional to a power of the distance between the two airports. The gravity model can be written as follows:

$$T_{ij} = \frac{kP_iP_j}{d_{ij}^a}$$

(12)

where:

T_{ij} = Total number of passengers between cities i and j
P_i = Population of origin city i
P_j = Population of origin city j
d_{ij} = Distance between cities, i and j
k = Constant of proportionality

a = Constant that should be calibrated

The gravity model has been modified to include variables other than population and distance, and has also been combined with econometric models to provide for better forecasts. This combination of econometric variables evaluated with the 4-step method is a very interesting category, resulting in fairly complicated and accurate forecasting models. These types of models would be found in the "combination" category.

The forecasting classification that was introduced in Figure 2 and briefly described in the last few paragraphs was based on the modelling approach used to evaluate the data in order to make the forecasts. That is, a forecaster can choose the technique he prefers to use based on the characteristics of that technique. Unfortunately, in air transportation and probably in other modes of transport, the difficulty arises not in selecting the technique but, acquiring the data to *be* used in the analysis.

The short explanation of the preceding methods was done to help the reader become acquainted with some of the methods and the terminology that will be used in this thesis. For a more detailed analysis of the methods, Garvett and Taneja (1974), Taneja (1978), and Wheelwright and Makridakis (1987) provide a very good reference.

CLASSIFICATION OF DATA USED IN AIR TRAVEL DEMAND FORECASTING MODELS

Historical data needed to model demand is very difficult to acquire. Data shortcomings constitute the most important limitation in demand modeling and forecasting. Information on air transportation is available, yet many times it is given at a useless level of aggregation, it is inconsistent, unreliable and even unobtainable (Karlaftis et al., 1996; Moore, 1973). These problems force planners to adjust their forecasts based on the data available

Figure 3. Data used in airport demand forecasting

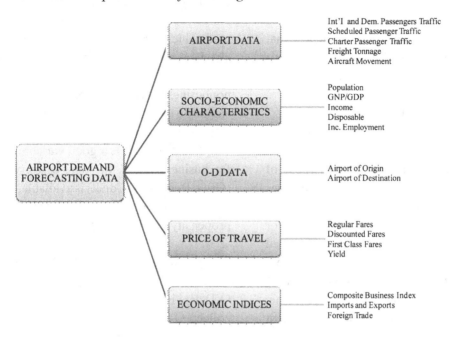

and not on the technique they wish to utilize. Figure 3 classifies the data available for forecasting in five main categories: airport data, socio-economic characteristics. Origin-Destination (O-D) data, price of travel and economic indexes.

Airport Passenger Data

Airport passenger data is related to the airport and the passengers, and it is ultimately the most useful and important type of data. It can be used to analyze and forecast both the total amount of air travelers for a given country or region, as well as the amount of a specific airport' s passengers. The historical data on passengers is the most critical component in modeling demand. For airport configuration purposes, the forecasts (and the passenger data needed to make the forecasts) need to be given at different level of aggregation. Total number of passengers is needed at first, but then the number of international and domestic passengers needs to be known so that planners can provide the necessary facilities to accom-

modate for the different kinds of needs such as floor space, immigration, security control, etc. Furthermore, it is very useful to have the amount of passengers stratified by scheduled passengers and nonscheduled, or charter, to provide for possibly different terminals and floor space. Airports do not only handle passengers, they also handle freight. The freight tonnage handled by an airport is an important piece of information, since storage requirements need to be planned. Finally, runway, apron and gate requirements will be planned based on the aircraft movement data, which also needs to be stratified by domestic and international flights (Kanafani, 1981).

Although from the previous discussion it becomes evident that the forecasting process depends on data availability, different authors (de Neufville, 1976; Karlaftis et al., 1996; Moore, 1973) have expressed the opinion that different airports collect and analyze the passenger data in different ways, and are not always willing to give out this information. Furthermore, aviation authorities collect their own kinds of data, which are not always usable for airport forecasting purposes. These types of inconsistencies make forecasting a very data dependent process, in the sencse that the forecasts have to be adjusted to the type of passenger data available.

Socioeconomic Data

The socioeconomic data is very important in the airport forecasting process. The purpose of including this kind of data is to find measures of an area's levels of socioeconomic activity that adequately describe the potential market for air travel. This data will also describe the need for a particular airport. There is a wide variety of variables that can be used. Among the most import ant measures are the Population, Income, Gross National Product (GNP), and Employment (Karlaftis et al., 1996).

Population usually mirrors the size of t he potential market for the airport. In many cases, when other variables are utilized in their per capita form, population becomes redundant. It is also possible to model population as a constant in the model for those areas where population changes steadily. It is usually considered that the larger the population, the larger the demand for the airport, and when included in a demand model population has an elasticity of approximately +2 (Kanafani, 1981).

Income is one of the most important variables since it represents a consumers purchasing power and habits, and is connected to traffic with an elasticity of about +2 to +3 (Kanafani, 1981). Income usually indicates a person's propensity to travel. Income can be used in different forms in the modelling process. Total income of the people in the region close to an airport is the most common form of utilization of this variable. Disposable income is a very useful form of income utilization. It is the income after taxes, and it can be argued that, income after taxes is a better indicator of a person's purchasing power. Income can also be used in its discretionary form. Discretionary

income reflects a person's recreational spending budget, and could be a good measure of pleasure, nonbusiness, travel. All types of income data can also be used in a per capita basis.

The income variable is a good measure of nonbusiness travel, yet a more appropriate variable should he used to account for business travel. The GNP shows a country's level of business activity and its wealth, and is a good variable to account for business travel. In some cases, when GRP (Gross Regional Product) is available, it might be more appropriate in showing a specific region's propensity for business travel.

Origin-Destination (O-D) Data

O-D data is also very useful, yet it is very hard to collect. O-D data signifies the amount of travel between specific pairs of cities or airports. This data can be used in the 4-step modelling process. This type of data has been used in the recently completed "Illinois-Indiana Regional Airport Study", and will be further reviewed later in this chapter (Ortuzar & Simonetti, 2008).

Price of Travel

Price of Travel can be used in two forms. The fares and the yield. Fare is most commonly used in its average fare form, and it is constructed by weighing traffic on the various routes in the system by the fares on these routes. Yield is another form of this variable. The yield represents the weighted average of the fares on all sectors of an airline's travel. The advantage of the yield is that it takes into consideration the effect of prorating tickets when airlines share segments of a certain route. Depending on what form the price of travel is taken into account in a model (i.e. constant value, real value, yield, fare), its elasticity can vary from -0.5 to -4 (Kanafani, 1981).

Table 1. Causal variables typically used in econometric forecasting

Size and spending ability of market	Population GNP or GDP for a country or region Personal Income Exports Imports	Passenger forecasts All types of forecasts International freight
Ethnic or linguistic ties between areas	Proportion of the population of one area born in the other area	Route forecasts
Price of air service	Published tariffs Yield	Route forecasts All types of forecasts
Quality of air service	Departure frequency Number of stops or connections Travel Time	Scheduled route forecasts Route forecasts
Access to air transport services	Number of destinations served Proportion of market within a certain distance from the airport	Regional forecasts Airport or route forecasts
Price and quality of competing service	Tariff of a competing air service, Departure frequency on a competing air service, Fares on a competing surface transport service, Travel time on competing surface transport	Route forecasts

Economic Indices

Economic indices are used to predict the level of economic activity in a certain region and the degree of interaction of the economic activity between regions (Chin et al., 1999). The *composite business index* is a measure of a community's confidence in the economic development and it account for the development of business travel. This index is a good measure for the traffic generated by a region, yet the foreign investment and trade are a better measure for the air travel demand in specific markets and routes.

This section provided a brief description of the variables and the data usually required for airport forecasting. Collecting and organizing data in different forms is for a tedious process, and a planner should be flexible enough to work around these data shortages. A very good source for further description and discussion on the variables utilized in air transportation is Kanafani (1981) (Table 1, Figure 3).

MATRIX CLASSIFICATION OF FORECASTING TECHNIQUES AND DATA

In the previous two sections of this chapter, the disadvantages of classifying forecasting methodologies by evaluation technique and available data were examined. Classifying methods by technique is acceptable in the academic world, but seems to be rather unfavourable with airport planners who usually have to face severe data shortages. Classifying methods based on data availability could cause problems when dealing with the manner of analyzing and evaluating the data available. A matrix classification seems to be able to combine both the data available and the technique used to evaluate this data in a concise manner, useful to both planners and academicians. Table 2 depicts this proposed matrix classification. The horizontal direction includes the most commonly used forecasting techniques. In the vertical direction are the categories of data usually available in the forecasting effort. Some of the techniques included in Figure 2 are not present in Table 2 because the matrix classification focuses more on the existing combination of techniques with data rather than

Table 2. Matrix classification of forecasting techniques and data

Forecasting Data	Objective				Subjective			
	Ratio Analysis	Regression	Filtering	Extrapolation	AHP	Delphi	Simulation	Neural Networks
Passenger Data	OPRA	OPRG	------------	SPEN	SAHP	SPDE	MPSM	MPNN
Socioeconomic Characteristics Price of Travel	------------	OPRG	------------	------------	SAHP	------------	MPSM	MPNN
O-D Data	ODRA	ODRG	ODFG	------------	------------	------------	------------	------------
Fuzzy Data	------------	OFRG	------------	------------	------------	SFDE	------------	------------

OPRA: Objective method with passenger data evaluated using ratio analysis
ODRA: Objective method with O-D data evaluated using ratio analysis
OPRG: Objective method with passenger and socio-economic data evaluated using regression
ODRG: Objective method with O-D data evaluated using regression
OFRG: Objective method with fuzzy data evaluated using regression
ODFG: Objective method with O-D data evaluated using filtering techniques
SPEN: Subjective method with passenger data evaluated using extrapolation
SAHP: Subjective method with passenger and socio-economic data evaluated using the AHP
SPDE: Subjective method with passenger data using the Delphi technique
SFDE: Subjective method with fuzzy data evaluated using the Delphi technique
MPSM: "Modern" method with passenger and socio-economic data evaluated using simulation
MPNN: "Modern" method with passenger and socio-economic data evaluated using neural networks

The models are named as follows: the first letter of the name denotes the forecasting category (S for subjective, O for objective. etc.), the second letter denotes the type of data used (P for passenger. S for socioeconomic, etc.), and finally the last two letters represent the specific technique utilized (CG for constant growth, RG for regression. etc.). In those cases where more than one kind of data are used in one model, then both cells will have the same name. Finally, when no data-technique combination was found in the literature, the cell is empty.

on a variety of individual techniques or data. This means that when a certain technique has been used interchangeably with another one, then the technique will be mentioned only once.

CONCLUSION

This chapter reviewed the literature related to air travel demand forecasting and traced its changes through time. Initially the classification of the existing forecasting methodologies was done based on the modeling approach used to prepare the forecasts. An alternate scheme that classifies the data used in air travel demand models was then examined. These two classifications were then combined in a single matrix classification that combines both the modeling approach and the available data. This matrix classification allows greater flexibility in selecting a model to be used in air travel demand forecasting.

Although a large number of categories was reviewed, the research interest has concentrated overwhelmingly on a small number of forecasting approaches primarily because of computational requirements and ease of use for specific approaches. The first category was the OPRA, where passenger and socioeconomic data were used to forecast passenger traffic using the ratio analysis approach. The ratio analysis is a useful *met*hod when the ratio of airport to national passenger volumes has remained relatively constant over the years. Using national forecasts and the ratio, airport forecasts are prepared. This simple method overlooks true factors that affect growth, and has been modified to allow the ratio to be adjusted for potential future changes in factors. This "evolved" form of ratio analysis is the "rates" or "shares" method and was used in the forecasting effort for a fourth international airport at the Chicago region. In this method, national historical data on market share and major factors affecting air travel demand are used to produce airport forecasts. This method is again rather simple to implement, but there is no evidence that the more sophisticated models that exist provide better forecasts.

Most forecasting models have been developed with passenger and socioeconomic data being evaluated with regression. These models belong in the OPRG and ODRG categories. A large number of different models that utilize an equally large number of independent (explanatory) variables exists. This type of models dominates the air travel forecasting industry because they have the ability to relate air travel to its influencing factors, and also because they are rather simple to calibrate. The same advantages that make these models popular can become disadvantages if good judgement and correct statistical analysis is not exercised. The most important error is one of judgement: variable correlation is mistaken for causality. Lack of judgement may easily lead to the 'peach blossom theory of polio' syndrome where we may notice some coincidence of events, as between peach blossoms and the onset of polio infections, and conclude that one causes the another. Thus it is with some statistical analyses: the process would have us believe that some factors affect travel merely because of some previous correlation.

The statistical calibration of these models although rather simple can be deceiving if not done carefully and correctly. It is also important to note that the majority of the models in the regression analysis category has R^2 values that indicate a very good fit of the data, yet the resulting forecasts are not equally good. This should be a warning sign against fully trusting such models and their usual criteria of fit. Conceivably the most important problem of these models is their reliance on forecasts of the independent variables.

While the models can be calibrated correctly the forecasting process will be done with forecasts of the independent variables, thus introducing uncertainty concerning the future model predictions. Due to the importance of this type of models in the area of air travel demand forecasting, they will be further examined in the fourth chapter of this thesis.

The third major category of models reviewed was different in that forecasts relied on subjective judgement. The two methods in this category were the Delphi technique and The Analytic Hierarchy Process (AHP). Both these methods combine expert judgement with a scientific approach of evaluating these judgements. The Delphi method, through a feedback and statistical analysis process, permits experts' predictions to converge to a commonly accepted forecast. This method does not require a large data base, and the experts' intuition concerning socioeconomic evolution is taken into account. The AHP is a promising method that evaluates in pairwise comparisons the importance of factors affecting air travel demand and the likelihood of forecasting scenarios in order to derive a best forecast. AHP's forecasts in areas such as the stock market and the oil prices give encouraging results concerning its potential use in airport forecasting.

From this literature review it is evident that different types of forecasting methods have different advantages and disadvantages. The critical issue is for a forecaster to be able to recognize the limitations imposed both by the developed demand models and by the very nature of forecasting. It has been said that there is no compelling evidence that the quality of forecasts involving multiple independent variables and complicated statistical analyses produce forecasts that are more accurate than simpler, straightforward methods. Many times, forecasters lose their judgement ability and common sense when dealing with a very large number of variables. The forecaster's critical ability is of extreme importance to avoid the "garbage-in, garbage-out" phenomenon that can occur when the influence of different factors is determined mechanically and not by using common sense and critical judgment.

REFERENCES

Ashford, N., & Wright, P. H. (1984). *Airport Engineering (3rd Ed.)*. New York: Wiley-Interscience.

Blake, A., & Sinclair, M. T. (2003). Tourism Crisis Management – US Response to September 11. *Annals of Tourism Research, 30*, 813–832. doi:10.1016/S0160-7383(03)00056-2

Chin, A., Hooper, P., & Oum, T. H. (1999). The Impacts of the Asian Economic Crises on Asian Airlines: Ahort-Run Responses and Long-Run Effects. *Journal of Air Transport Management, 5*, 87–96. doi:10.1016/S0969-6997(99)00003-4

Coldren, G. M., & Koppelman, F. S. (2005). Modeling the Competition Among Air-Travel Itinerary Shares: GEV Model Development. *Transportation Research Part A, Policy and Practice, 39*(4), 345–365.

Coldren, G. M., Koppelman, F. S., Kasturirangan, K., & Mukherjee, A. (2003). Modeling Aggregate Air Travel Itinerary Shares: Logit Model Development at a Major US Airline. *Journal of Air Transport Management, 9*(6), 361–369. doi:10.1016/S0969-6997(03)00042-5

Cooper, J. P. (1973). Time-varying regression coefficients: a mixed estimation approach and operational Limitations of general Markov structure. *Annuals of Economic and. Social Measurement, 2*, 525–530.

Cunningham, S. W., & De Haan, A. R. C. (2006). Long-Term Forecasting for Sustainable Development: Air Travel Demand Forecast for 2050. *International Journal of Environment and Sustainable Development, 5*(3), 297–314. doi:10.1504/IJESD.2006.010899

de Neufville, R. (1976). *Airport Systems Planning: A Critical Look at Methods and Experience*. Cambridge, MA: Macmillan and MIT Press.

Gillen, D., & Lall, A. (2003). International Transmission of Shocks in the Airline Industry. *Journal of Air Transport Management, 9*, 37–49. doi:10.1016/S0969-6997(02)00068-6

Goh, C., & Law, R. (2002). Modeling and Forecasting Tourism Demand for Arrivals with Stochastic Non-Stationary Seasonality and Intervention. *Tourism Management, 23*, 499–510. doi:10.1016/S0261-5177(02)00009-2

Hutchinson, B. G. (1993). Analyses of Canadian Air Travel Demands. *Journal of Transportation Engineering, 119*, 301–316. doi:10.1061/(ASCE)0733-947X(1993)119:2(301)

Huth, W. L., & Eriksen, S. E. (1987). Airline Traffic Forecasting Using Deterministic and Stochastic Time Series Decomposition. *Logistics and Transportation Review, 23*(4), 401–409.

Jantsch, E. (1972). *Technological planning and social features*. New York, NY: John Wiley and Sons.

Kanafani, A. (1974). *Demand Analysis for North Atlantic Air Travel* (Research Rep., Vol. 1). Berkeley, CA: Institute of Transportation Studies.

Kanafani, A. (1981). *Transportation Demand Analysis*. New York: John Wiley and Sons.

Karlaftis, M. G., Zografos, K. G., Papastavrou, J. D., & Charnes, J. D. (1996). Methodological Framework for Air Travel Demand Forecasting. *Journal of Transportation Engineering, 122*(2), 96–104. doi:10.1061/(ASCE)0733-947X(1996)122:2(96)

Khadem, M. (1992). Short-term load forecasting using Neural Networks. In Sobajic (Ed.), *1992 INNS Summer Workshop*.

Kikuchi, S., et al. (1994). *Estimation of trip generation using Fuzzy Regression Method.* Paper presented at 73rd Transportation Research Board Meeting in Washington, DC.

Lai, S. L., & Lu, S. L. (2005). Impact Analysis of September 11 on Air Travel Demand in the USA. *Journal of Air Transport Management, 11,* 455–458. doi:10.1016/j.jairtraman.2005.06.001

Lenz, R. C. (1962). *Technological Forecasting.* ASD-TDR-62-414. Ohio: Wright-Patterson AFB.

Levenbach, H., & Schultz, W. (1987). Econometric Methods for Managerial Applications. In Makridakis & Wheelwright (Eds.), *Handbook of forecasting.* New York: Wiley Intersience.

Martino, J. (1972). *Technological Forecasting for Decision Making.* New York: American Elsevier Publishing.

McDonnell-Douglas. (1972). *Measuring the Seventies.* Market Research Report CI-804-2752. Long Beach, California.

Moore, H. L., III. (1973). *Forecasting Demand at Airports.* Civil Engineering Thesis, Department of Civil Engineering, MIT.

Neter, Wesserman, & Kutner (1989). *Applied Linear Regression models (2nd Ed.).* Irwin, Homewood, III.

Ortuzar, J. D., & Simonetti, C. (2008). Modelling the Demand for Medium Distance Air Travel with Mixed Data Estimation Method. *Journal of Air Transport Management, 14,* 297–303. doi:10.1016/j.jairtraman.2008.08.002

Pack, J. (1987). A Practical Overview of Arima Models for Time Series Forecasting. In Makridakis & Wheelwright (Eds.), *Handbook of forecasting.* New York: Wiley Intersience.

Profillidis, V. A. (2000). Econometric and Fuzzy Models for the Forecast of Demand in the Airport of Rhodes. *Journal of Air Transport Management, 6,* 95–100. doi:10.1016/S0969-6997(99)00026-5

Saaty, T. L. (1990). *The Analytic Hierarchy Process.* Pittsburgh, PA: RWS Publications.

Saaty, T. L., & Vargas, L. G. (1991). *Prediction, Projection and Forecasting.* Boston, MA: Kluwer Academic Publishers.

Sarris, A. H. (1973). A Bayesian approach to estimation of time varying regression coefficients. *Annuals of Economic and Social Measurement, 2,* 501–523.

Tanaka, H. (1980). Fuzzy Linear Regression Model. *IEEE Transaction Systems, Man, Machine . Cybernetics, 10*(4), 2933–2938.

Taneja, N. K. (1978). *Airline Traffic Forecasting.* Lexington, MA: Lexington Books.

Washington, S. M., Karlaftis, M. G., & Mannering, F. L. (2003). *Statistical and Econometric Methods for Transportation Data Analysis.* Boca Raton, FL: Chapman & Hall / CRC Press.

Wheelwright, S. C., & Makridakis, S. (1987). Introduction to Management Forecasting. In Makridakis & Wheelwright (Eds.), *Handbook of Forecasting.* New York: Wiley Interscience.

Widrow, B., & Beaufays, F. (1992). Neural Control Systems. In Sobajic (Ed.), *1992 INNS Summer Workshop.*

Winkler, R. (1987). Judgmental and Bayesian Forecasting. In Makridakis & Wheelwright (Eds.), *Handbook of Forecasting.* New York: Wiley Interscience.

Chapter 6
Using the Continuum Equilibrium Approach to Solve Airport Competition Problems:
Computational and Application Issues

Becky P. Y. Loo
The University of Hong Kong, China

H. W. Ho
The Hong Kong Polytechnic University, China

S. C. Wong
The University of Hong Kong, China

Peng Zhang
Shanghai University, China

ABSTRACT

This chapter presents a computational method using the continuum equilibrium approach to solve airport competition problems. The mathematical formulation and solution algorithm are given. The Hong Kong-Pearl River Delta region is used as a case study to demonstrate the effectiveness of the approach in solving real-life large-scale airport competition problems. Behavioral choices of both international and domestic air travelers in the region are modeled. The results show the distinctive value of the continuum approach in understanding the spatial dynamics of air passenger flows in multi-airport regions.

INTRODUCTION

If one considers airports to be facilities providing services (rather than just intermediate stops), the delimitation of market areas of competitive airports becomes similar to the classical location problems of von Thunen's isolated states, Christaller's central place theory, and Hotelling's traveling salesman or retail locations. Airports constitute part of the movement space of air passengers (Borgstrom, 1974), and airport services generate utility to air passengers. When airports are viewed as service points, air passenger turnover is the result of aggregated personal decisions to use those facilities. On the demand side,

DOI: 10.4018/978-1-60566-800-0.ch006

the decision to choose a particular airport is no longer purely the (shortest) Euclidean distance between a passenger's home (or the origin of the freight) and the departure airport, or the distance between the final destination and the arrival airport. On the supply side, airports are differentiated by facility attributes including a set of primary level-of-service (LOS) factors, which are related to the price and frequency of flights, and a set of secondary LOS factors, which are related to the quality of airports and airlines. Secondary LOS factors tend to dominate in a multi-airport context where differences among primary LOS factors and distances among airports are not great (Bradley, 1998; Rubin & Fagan, 1976). In a multi-airport region (MAR), the choice of an airport facility is no longer peripheral to an individual's decision to travel, and services at different airports are differentiated products. Consequently, the delimitation of the market areas of airports becomes much more complicated than a simple case of nearest-center assignment (Bryan & O'Kelly, 1999). In the pioneer study of Ndoh et al. (1990), preference data were used to examine the choice of departing air travelers among four airports in central England: the East Midlands, Birmingham, Manchester and Liverpool airports. Specifically, Bradley (1998) found that the choice of air travelers among competitive departure airports in Europe was affected by at least twelve LOS factors. In light of these findings, there is a need to re-consider airport LOS attributes (rather than considering only an airport's physical location in relation to demand) to reflect real airport choices.

Apart from MARs in Europe, there has been a growing interest in airport competition in the southern part of China. In 1979, only two international airports operated in the Hong Kong and Pearl River Delta region (hereafter, the HK-PRD region). After two decades, four international airports were operating in this 48,000-sq.-km. region (Loo, 1999). Before 1997, the Hong Kong International Airport operated and thrived under British colonial rule. On the one hand, it faced

virtually no competition from airports across the border. On the other hand, few people and little freight from across the border passed through the airport facilities of the Hong Kong International Airport. Since 1997, the situation has gradually changed under the "one country, two systems" policy. The Hong Kong International Airport now faces competition from three other international airports in the region at Guangzhou, Shenzhen and Zhuhai. It is easy for Hong Kong people to use airport facilities in Mainland China and for Mainland Chinese people to use airport facilities in Hong Kong. Most importantly, the demand for air travel in a large part of the region has greatly expanded because of the rapid income growth. With these four international airports, the HK-PRD region represents an ideal case study for analyzing airport competition problems.

In the context of an MAR, traditional air traffic forecasting techniques based on national forecasts and local market shares are far from satisfactory because "it is unusual for airport service areas to overlap and even more unusual for an overlap to be considered in the forecasting process" (Rubin & Fagan, 1976, p. 1). Such forecasts are often made for single-airport regions with well-defined and fixed market areas. In reality, however, the simplified assumption of a single-airport region is unrealistic. The continuum equilibrium model offers an alternative in understanding air traffic distribution in MARs, where the market areas of airports are not well-defined and immutable. Taguchi and Iri (1982) were among the first to develop a promising numerical procedure to solve the problem of continuous transportation systems for a general city configuration. They used the finite element method (FEM) (Zienkiewicz & Taylor, 1989) to solve three continuum network problems: the maximum flow problem, shortest route problem and minimum-cost flow problem. For user equilibrium problems, a dual-based formulation was given by Sasaki et al. (1990), in which the user equilibrium problem in a continuous system was solved by minimizing an objective function with a set of constraints. To improve the numerical stability of the solution, Wong et al. (1998) developed a more robust algorithm that was based on the mixed finite element formulation. Wong and Yang (1999) and Yang and Wong (2000) developed continuum models for determining market areas of competitive facilities. For multi-commodity cases, Wong (1998) developed a multi-commodity traffic assignment formulation with a general city configuration to solve the problem of fixed and variable demand, and extended the formulation to deal with cases of combined distribution and assignment (Wong & Sun, 2001; Wong et al., 2004) and multi-class problems (Ho et al., 2004, 2006). It is envisaged that this continuum equilibrium approach can be used to examine airport competition.

Recently, a continuum equilibrium approach has been used to study the geography of air passenger flows in an MAR, but the solution algorithm was not discussed in details (Loo et al., 2005). In this paper, the computational method is presented. The rest of the paper is organized as follows. In Section 2, the continuum equilibrium model for solving the airport competition problem is formulated. Section 3 describes the finite element method using the continuum approach, and Section 4 reports the results of the case study to demonstrate the effectiveness of the methodology.

ISSUES, CONTROVERSIES, PROBLEMS

The Model

The model basically follows that of Wong and Yang (1999). Consider a study region in a two-dimensional plane with N competing airports. Air travelers are widely dispersed over the whole region and will travel from their demand locations through the continuum to patronize airports. Denote the study region as Ω, the boundary of the study region as Γ, and the location of the nth

airport as O_n. Air travel demand is assumed to be continuous over the region Ω and is represented by a nonnegative, heterogeneous density function $q(x,y)$, where $q(x,y)$ is the total demand per unit area, from location $(x,y) \in \Omega$. The local ground transportation cost in the region is assumed to be dependent on the local flow intensity and road configuration, but not upon direction (an isotopic case), $c(x,y,\mathbf{f}) = a(x,y) + b(x,y)|\mathbf{f}(x,y)|^{\gamma(x,y)}$, where $c(x,y,\mathbf{f})$ is the ground transportation cost of traveling a unit distance at coordinate $(x,y) \in \Omega$; $a(x,y)$, $b(x,y)$, and $\gamma(x,y)$ are strictly positive scalar functions; $\mathbf{f}(x,y) = (f_x(x,y), f_y(x,y))$ is a vector representing the flow state in the study region; $f_x(x,y)$ and $f_y(x,y)$ are the flow fluxes in the x and y directions, respectively; and $|\mathbf{f}(x,y)| = \sqrt{f_x(x,y)^2 + f_y(x,y)^2}$ is the norm of the flow vector at (x,y). The first term of the above transportation cost function represents the local uncongested (zero-flow) ground transportation cost per unit distance, and the second term reflects the effects of congestion. The explicit dependence of the cost function $c(x,y,\mathbf{f})$ on location (x,y) reflects the possibility that the density and capacity of the ground transportation system may vary over the two-dimensional space.

Inside region Ω, the flow vector and air travel demand must satisfy the flow conservation condition $\nabla \cdot \mathbf{f}(x,y) + q(x,y) = 0, \forall \quad (x,y) \in \Omega$. Assuming that no flow crosses the boundary of the study region, we have $\mathbf{f} = \mathbf{0}, \quad \forall \quad (x,y) \in \Gamma$. It is straightforward to extend the model to deal with the case of $\mathbf{f} \cdot \mathbf{n} = g(x,y)$ on the boundary Γ, where $\mathbf{n}$ is the normal vector on the boundary and g is a function representing the given demand distribution entering or leaving the study region. Each airport within the MAR is of a finite size enclosed by a clockwise boundary segment Γ_{cn}, $n = 1, 2, ..., N$. Denote Ω_n as the market area of airport n. The number of air travelers attracted to airport n becomes $Q_n = \iint_{\Omega_n} q(x,y) \, d\Omega, n = 1, 2, ..., N$. From the flow conservation principle at airport n, it can be shown that

$$\oint_{\Gamma_{cn}} \mathbf{f} \cdot \mathbf{n} \ \mathrm{d}\Gamma + Q_n = 0, \qquad n = 1, 2, \ldots, N.$$

Previous studies show that air travelers' choice of airports is based not only on ground transportation cost (Tam et al., 2008) but also airfare level, frequency of flights, airport conditions, safety and so forth (Bradley, 1998; Loo, 2008; Ndoh et al., 1990). Therefore, the generalized cost function to represent the total cost perceived by an air traveler to patronize an airport is modeled as a function of the relevant characteristics of the airport and ground transportation cost:

$$G\left[D(x,y),O_n\right] = \sum_{k=1}^{K} w_k p_k^n + c\left[D(x,y),O_n\right] = \bar{u}_n + c\left[D(x,y),O_n\right]$$

$$(1)$$

where $G\left[D(x,y),O_n\right]$ is the generalized cost for an air traveler at demand location $D(x,y)$ to patronize airport O_n ($n = 1, 2, \ldots, N$); $\bar{u}_n = \sum_{k=1}^{K} w_k p_k^n$ represents the total attribute measure of airport O_n, where K is the attribute measure with an associated weight of w_k; and $c\left[D(x,y),O_n\right]$ is the minimum ground transportation cost for traveling from demand location $D(x,y)$ to airport O_n. In our model, the weights and attribute measures are exogenous inputs to be calibrated from observed data, whereas the equilibrium ground transportation cost is determined by the user-equilibrium conditions.

The problem of an air traveler's spatial choice equilibrium is formulated as follows:

$$\underset{f}{\text{Minimize}} \qquad z(\mathbf{f}) = \sum_{n=1}^{N} \bar{u}_n Q_n + \iint_{\Omega} \left\{ a|\mathbf{f}| + \frac{b}{\gamma+1}|\mathbf{f}|^{\gamma+1} \right\} \mathrm{d}\Omega$$

$$(2a)$$

subject to

$$\nabla \cdot \mathbf{f} + q = 0, \qquad \forall (x,y) \in \Omega \qquad (2b)$$

$$\mathbf{f} = \mathbf{0}, \qquad \forall (x,y) \subset \Gamma, \qquad (2c)$$

$$\oint_{\Gamma_{cn}} \mathbf{f} \cdot \mathbf{n} \ \mathrm{d}\Gamma - Q_n = 0, \qquad \forall n = 1, 2, \ldots, N$$

$$(2d)$$

At the optimal point of the above minimization problem, the user-equilibrium path and airport choice of each air traveler can be determined. A detailed proof of this user-equilibrium condition is shown in the appendix.

Solution Algorithm

In this study, the finite element method (FEM) is used. The whole region first needs to be discretized into a finite element mesh, and the Lagrangian (equation A-1 in appendix) is modified as follows:

$$\Pi = \sum_{n=1}^{N} \sum_{e \in \Omega} \oint_{\partial\Omega \cap \Gamma_{cn}} \bar{u}_n \left(\mathbf{f} \cdot \mathbf{n}\right) \mathrm{d}\Gamma +$$

$$\sum_{i \in \Omega} \iint_{\Omega_i} a|\mathbf{f}| + \frac{b}{\gamma+1}|\mathbf{f}|^{\gamma+1} - \lambda\left(\nabla \cdot \mathbf{f} + q\right) \mathrm{d}\Omega$$

$$+ \sum_{e \in \Omega} \oint_{\partial\Omega \cap \Gamma} \mathbf{w} \cdot \mathbf{f} \, \mathrm{d}\Gamma + \sum_{n=1}^{N} \sum_{e \in \Omega} \oint_{\partial\Omega \cap \Gamma_{cn}} \sigma\left(\lambda - \bar{u}_n\right) \mathrm{d}\Gamma$$

$$(3)$$

where Ω_e is the subdomain of an element e, $\partial\Omega \cap \Gamma_{cn}$ and $\partial\Omega \cap \Gamma$ are the elements on airport boundaries and the outer bound of the HK-PRD region respectively; $\mathbf{w}$ and σ are the Lagrange multipliers along Γ and Γ_{cn} respectively. The solution of the minimization problem in equation (2) can be found by locating the stationary point of the Lagrangian in equation (3). As the first term of equation (3) represents the sum of the total cost to passengers of using each airport, it can be replaced by a simpler expression,

$$\sum_{n=1}^{N} \sum_{i=1}^{S_n} \bar{u}_n l_i \left(\frac{\mathbf{f}_j + \mathbf{f}_k}{2} \right) \cdot \mathbf{n}_i \qquad (4)$$

where S_n is the number of line segments on the boundary of airport n; l_i and n_i are the length and the unit normal vector of the line segment i around the boundary of airport O_n respectively; and $\mathbf{f}_j$ and $\mathbf{f}_k$ are the flow vectors of the initial and end nodes of the line segment i respectively. As there is no traffic flow across the regional boundary, the third term of equation (3) can be replaced by a stronger and more convenient expression,

$$\sum_{i=1}^{N_O} w_{xi} f_{xi} + w_{yi} f_{yi} \tag{5}$$

where N_O is the number of nodes along Γ; f_{xi} and f_{yi} are the flow fluxes in the x and y directions at node i respectively; and w_{xi} and w_{yi} are the corresponding Lagrange multipliers. The zero boundary flow condition can be guaranteed by forcing $f_{xi} = f_{yi} = 0$ for all nodes along Γ. Similarly, as it is proved that the cost potential at the boundary of the airport is equal to the total attribute measure of that airport (see appendix), the last term of equation (3) can be replaced by the following expression:

$$\sum_{n=1}^{N} \sum_{i=1}^{N_n} \sigma_i \left(\lambda_i - \bar{u}_n \right) \tag{6}$$

where N_n is the number of nodes on the boundary of airport O_n, λ_i is the cost potential of node i, and σ_i is its Lagrange multiplier at node i. The conditions of equation (6) can be ensured by forcing $\lambda_i - \bar{u}_n = 0$ for all nodes along the boundaries of airports. With all of the above modifications, equation (3) can be modified as follows:

$$\Pi = \sum_{n=1}^{N} \sum_{i=1}^{S_n} \bar{u}_n l_i \left(\frac{\mathbf{f}_j + \mathbf{f}_k}{2} \right) \cdot \mathbf{n}_i$$

$$+ \sum_{i=1}^{N_e} \iint_{\Omega_i} a |\mathbf{f}| + \frac{b}{\gamma+1} |\mathbf{f}|^{\gamma+1} - \lambda \left(\nabla \cdot \mathbf{f} + q \right) d\Omega$$

$$+ \sum_{i=1}^{N_O} \left(w_{xi} f_{xi} + w_{yi} f_{yi} \right) + \sum_{n=1}^{N} \sum_{i=1}^{N_n} \sigma_i \left(\lambda_i - \bar{u}_n \right) \tag{7}$$

The three-node linear triangular element is adopted for the approximation of variables over the solution space. The value of the flow vectors and the cost potential within the element are expressed as follows:

$$f_x(x,y) = N_i(x,y) f_{xi} + N_j(x,y) f_{xj} + N_k(x,y) f_{xk}, \tag{8}$$

$$f_y(x,y) = N_i(x,y) f_{yi} + N_j(x,y) f_{yj} + N_k(x,y) f_{yk}, \tag{9}$$

$$\lambda(x,y) = N_i(x,y) \lambda_i + N_j(x,y) \lambda_j + N_k(x,y) \lambda_k, \tag{10}$$

where subscripts i, j, and k represent the three nodes of the triangular element, and the variables with such subscripts denote their values at the nodal point. N_i, N_j, and N_k are the linear interpolation functions of the element, and they are expressed as:

$$N_i(x,y) = \frac{1}{2\Delta} (\alpha_i + \beta_i x + \xi_i y), \tag{11}$$

$$N_j(x,y) = \frac{1}{2\Delta} (\alpha_j + \beta_j x + \xi_j y), \tag{12}$$

$$N_k(x,y) = \frac{1}{2\Delta} (\alpha_k + \beta_k x + \xi_k y). \tag{13}$$

The values of α, β, ξ, and Δ are explicitly related to the nodal coordinates (x_i, y_i), (x_j, y_j), and (x_k, y_k) at nodes i, j, and k of the triangular element. The explicit forms of α, β, ξ, and Δ are $\alpha_i = x_j y_k - x_k y_j$, $\beta_i = y_j - y_k$, $\xi_i = x_k - x_j$ and $\Delta = (\beta_i \xi_j - \beta_j \xi_i)/2$ respectively.

With the FEM, variations of the flow vector and cost potential over the problem domain are expressed as nodal values of the generated triangular elements and interpolation functions. One can substitute equations (8) to (13) into equation (7) and denote

$$\Psi = \mathrm{Col}\left(\mathbf{f}, \lambda, \mathbf{w}, \sigma \right) \tag{14}$$

$$\mathbf{f} = \mathrm{Col}\left(f_{xi}, f_{yi}, i = 1, \dots N_N \right) \tag{15}$$

$$\lambda = \text{Col}\left(\lambda_i, i = 1, \dots N_N\right) \tag{16}$$

$$\mathbf{w} = \text{Col}\left(w_{xi}, w_{yi}, i = 1, \dots N_O\right) \tag{17}$$

$$\sigma = \text{Col}\left(\sigma_{ij}, f_{yi}, i = 1, \dots N_j, j = 1, \dots N_C\right) \tag{18}$$

where N_N is the total number of nodes within the problem domain. By expanding $\Pi(\Psi)$ by Taylor's expansion at Ψ^0 and neglecting the higher order terms, equation (7) becomes

$$\Pi(\Psi) \cong \Pi(\Psi^0) + \mathbf{R}^T(\Psi - \Psi^0) + \frac{1}{2}(\Psi - \Psi^0)^T \mathbf{J}(\Psi - \Psi^0) \tag{19}$$

where $\mathbf{R} = \nabla\Pi(\Psi^0)$ is the residual vector and $\mathbf{J} = \nabla^2\Pi(\Psi^0)$ is the Jacobian matrix of the Lagrangian. For a stationary point, the derivatives of all variables vanish (i.e., $\nabla\Pi(\Psi) = 0$). Hence,

$$\nabla\Pi(\Psi) = \mathbf{R} + \mathbf{J}(\Psi - \Psi^0). \tag{20}$$

After rearranging, the following iterative formula is obatined:

$$\Psi = \Psi^0 - \mathbf{J}^{-1}\mathbf{R}. \tag{21}$$

As the number of triangular elements generated for the HK-PRD region is quite large, the number of variables and the size of the Jacobian matrix are huge. To reduce the computational time, the quasi-Newtonian method is adopted. The iterative equation (21) is re-written as

$$\Psi_{i+1} = \Psi_i - \mathbf{J}_i^{-1}\mathbf{R}_i, \tag{22}$$

where subscript i denotes the ith iteration. Using the quasi-Newtonian method, the Jacobian matrix of the $(i+1)$th iteration can be updated from the results obtained from the ith iteration as follows:

$$\mathbf{J}_{i+1}^{-1} = \mathbf{J}_i^{-1} - \frac{[\mathbf{J}_i^{-1}(\mathbf{R}_i - \mathbf{R}_{i+1}) - (\Psi_i - \Psi_{i+1})](\Psi_i - \Psi_{i+1})^T}{(\Psi_i - \Psi_{i+1})^T \mathbf{J}_i^{-1}(\mathbf{R}_i - \mathbf{R}_{i+1})} \mathbf{J}_i^{-1} \tag{23}$$

Based on equation (22), let the following column vector be represented as

$$\mathbf{J}_i^{-1}\mathbf{A} = F(\mathbf{A}, \mathbf{R}_i, \mathbf{R}_{i-1}, \Psi_i, \Psi_{i-1}, \mathbf{J}_{i-1}^{-1})$$

$$= F(\mathbf{A}, \mathbf{R}_i, \mathbf{R}_{i-1}, \Psi_i, \Psi_{i-1},$$

$$F(\mathbf{A}, \mathbf{R}_{i-1}, \mathbf{R}_{i-2}, \Psi_{i-1}, \Psi_{i-2}, \mathbf{J}_{i-2}^{-1}))$$

$$\vdots$$

$$= F(\mathbf{A}, \mathbf{R}_i, \mathbf{R}_{i-1}, \Psi_i, \Psi_{i-1},$$

$$F(\mathbf{A}, \mathbf{R}_{i-1}, \mathbf{R}_{i-2}, \Psi_{i-1}, \Psi_{i-2}, \dots,$$

$$F(\mathbf{A}, \mathbf{R}_1, \mathbf{R}_0, \Psi_1, \Psi_0, , \mathbf{J}_0^{-1})\dots))$$

$$= F_i(\mathbf{A}, \{\mathbf{R}_j\}, \{\Psi_j\}, \mathbf{J}_0^{-1}) \tag{24}$$

where $\{\mathbf{R}_j\}$ and $\{\Psi_j\}$ correspond to the sets of the collection of $\mathbf{R}_j$ and Ψ_j vectors for all $i \geq j$ respectively.

In summary, the solution procedure is summarized as follows.

Step 1: Find an initial solution Ψ^0 and set $k = 0$;

Step 2: Evaluate the element residual vector $\mathbf{R}_e(\Psi^k)$ and assemble it to give the global $\mathbf{R}(\Psi^k)$;

Step 3: If $|\mathbf{R}(\Psi^k)| < \varepsilon$, an acceptable error, stop and take Ψ^k as the solution; otherwise, go to Step 4;

Step 4: Compute $\mathbf{J}^{-1}(\Psi^k)\mathbf{R}(\Psi^k)$

If $k = 3N$: Evaluate the integral element in the Jacobian matrix $\mathbf{J}_e(\Psi^k)$ and assemble it to give the global Jacobian matrix $\mathbf{J}(\Psi^k)$. Then, find the vector $\mathbf{V} = \mathbf{J}^{-1}(\Psi^k)\mathbf{R}(\Psi^k)$;

If $k \neq 3N$: Update the vector $\mathbf{V} = \mathbf{J}^{-1}(\Psi^k)\mathbf{R}(\Psi^k)$ using the quasi-Newtonian method;

Step 5: Update the solution vector by $\Psi^{k+1} = \Psi^k - \mathbf{V}$; and

Step 6: Replace Ψ^k by Ψ^{k+1}. Set $k = k + 1$ and go to Step 2.

In the above procedures, attention should be paid to the following cases.

Iteration 0

Equation (22) becomes $\Psi_1 = \Psi_0 - \mathbf{J}_0^{-1}\mathbf{R}_0$. For this particular iteration, an initial value of Ψ_0 is assumed; therefore, $\mathbf{J}_0^{-1}$, $\mathbf{R}_0$, and Ψ_1 can be evaluated directly. The vectors Ψ_1, Ψ_0, $\mathbf{R}_0$, and $\mathbf{V}_0 = \mathbf{J}_0^{-1}\mathbf{R}_0$ are stored for subsequent use.

Iteration i > 0

From equation (22), $\Psi_{i+1} = \Psi_i - \mathbf{J}_i^{-1}\mathbf{R}_i$. To find Ψ_{i+1}, the vector $\mathbf{J}_i^{-1}\mathbf{R}_i$ has to be evaluated, and it can be approximated by means of equation (23). Apart from the vectors obtained from the previous iterations, such as Ψ_i, Ψ_{i-1} and $\mathbf{J}_{i-1}^{-1}\mathbf{R}_{i-1}$, an additional vector $\mathbf{J}_{i-1}^{-1}\mathbf{R}_i$ has to be evaluated by means of equation (24). So, three additional vectors, Ψ_{i+1}, $\mathbf{J}_{i-1}^{-1}\mathbf{R}_i$, and $\mathbf{J}_i^{-1}\mathbf{R}_i$, are stored separately for use in the next iteration. To save storage space, the residual vector $\mathbf{R}_i$ can overwrite the same vector obtained from the previous iteration.

Regarding the quasi-Newtonian method, there are two additional issues. The first issue is the need to balance between the cost of storage and computational time. Allocating more space for storage helps save computational time to calculate the Jacobian from scratch every time. The second issue is the quality of the updated Jacobian, as the updating procedure in each iteration is only an approximation. This will affect the rate of convergence of the solution algorithm and the quality of the Jacobian matrix deteriorates with the number of iterations. Therefore, to ensure the quality of the Jacobian matrix and the rate of convergence, the Jacobian should be recalculated after certain iterations.

Descriptions of the Geographical Problem

In this study, the choices of passengers among airports within the HK-PRD region are modeled. As of 2002, the four major civilian airports in this region were the Hong Kong International Airport (HKG), Guangzhou Banyun International Airport (CAN), Shenzhen Huangtian International Airport (SZX) and Zhuhai International Airport (MFM) (Loo, 1999). The main aims of this study are to apply the continuum equilibrium approach to find out the market shares of these four international airports and to delimit their respective service areas under different scenarios. Both international and domestic flights are considered. Domestic flights are defined as flights for destinations within the People's Republic of China. Figure 1 shows the administrative divisions of the region. Altogether, there are 10 municipalities – Guangzhou, Shenzhen, Zhuhai, Dongguan, Foshan, Huizhou, Jiangmen, Qingyuan, Zhaoqing, and Zhongshan – in Mainland China's Pearl River Delta region (hereafter, the Mainland PRD). The boundaries of these 10 municipalities and the Hong Kong Special Administrative Region (HKSAR) are used to discretize the region into finite elements, as shown by the finite element mesh in Figure 2.

Following the continuum approach, air passengers located within the HK-PRD region, Ω, are assumed to travel from their demand locations (municipalities) through the continuum to patronize any one of these four airports (O_n, where $n = 1,\ldots, 4$). Furthermore, since it is assumed that there is no flow across the regional boundary ($\mathbf{f} = \mathbf{0}$, $\quad \forall \quad (x, y) \in \Gamma$), the current total demand for airport services in the HK-PRD region is the total air passenger turnover of the four airports. The international and domestic air

Figure 1. Administrative divisions of the HK-PRD region

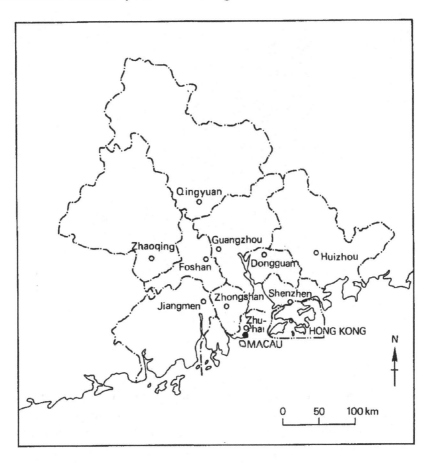

passenger turnovers of the Hong Kong International Airport were compiled and published by the Civil Aviation Department (CAD, 2002). For the three airports in the Mainland PRD, the corresponding international and domestic air passenger turnover data were obtained from Zhongguo jiaotong nianjian (Zhongguo jiaotong nianjianshe, 2000) and Chinainfobank (Chinainfobank, 2002).

Under the existing "one country, two systems" policy, a border still exists between the HKSAR and the Mainland PRD. In 2001, about 0.6 million Mainland PRD residents traveled across the border to take international flights from the Hong Kong International Airport (Information Services Department, 2002). During this period, about 0.43 million Hong Kong residents traveled across the

border to take domestic flights from the three airports in the Mainland PRD (Sing Dao Daily, May 9, 2002). When non-Hong Kong residents are considered, a conservative estimate of the additional cross-border flow was 1.05 million. Informal discussion with individuals working in travel agencies, major airlines, and the Airport Authority confirmed that most Mainland China tourists, including group and non-group tourists, coming from provinces outside Guangdong would use airports in the Mainland PRD (rather than Hong Kong) to return home. In estimating this additional flow, the data published by Guangdong tongjiju (2001), Hong Kong Tourism Board (2001), and Hong Kong Tourist Association (2001) were used. In 2000, 2.19 million visitors departed from Hong Kong to Mainland China by

Figure 2. Finite element mesh of the HK-PRD region

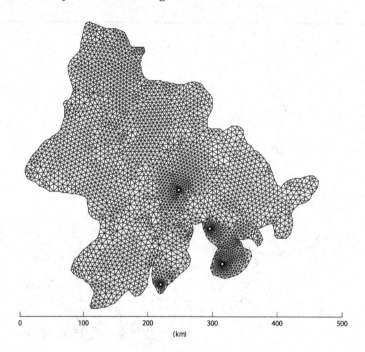

land. The number of visitors from Guangdong was estimated to be 0.87 million. Among them, 0.34 million (about 39%) visited Hong Kong as members of group tours (Hong Kong Tourism Board, 2001; Guangdong tongjiju, 2001). Among the rest of the visitors from outside Guangdong, it was estimated that about 80% took domestic flights from the Mainland PRD airports to return home. Therefore, the estimated flow of non-Hong Kong residents crossing the HKSAR border to take domestic flights from the Mainland PRD airports was estimated to be 1.05 million. By including the flow of Hong Kong residents, the total cross-border flow for domestic flights from the PRD airports was 1.48 million.

After taking into account these cross-border flows, the average propensity for international air travel in the Mainland PRD was estimated by taking the total international air passenger turnover of the three Mainland airports as a share of the total population (Guangdong sheng tongjiju, 2001). By multiplying this common average propensity for international travel and the different popula-

tion sizes of individual municipalities, the spatial distribution of international air travel demand was estimated for the Mainland PRD. Similarly, the demand surface of Hong Kong was obtained by using the latest sets of figures (CAD, 2002; Census and Statistics Department [CSD], 2001). Following the same computational steps, the spatial distribution of domestic air travel demand was calculated. Figure 3 shows the estimated annual demand for international and domestic flights in the HK-PRD MAR. It is noteworthy that the scale for the estimated annual demand for international and domestic flights in Hong Kong is different from the scales for the rest of region because the demand for the former was much higher. The estimated annual demand for international flights in the top three municipalities was 26.36 million in Hong Kong, 0.27 million in Guangzhou, and 0.16 million in Shenzhen. For domestic flights, the top three rankings were of the same order, with an estimated annual demand of 7.39 million in Hong Kong, 3.67 million in Guangzhou, and 2.22 million in Shenzhen.

Next, the generalized cost function, equation (1), representing the total cost perceived by an air traveler to patronize an airport in the HK-PRD region was estimated. Conceptually, this perceived total cost is a function of the airport's LOS attributes and ground transportation cost (O_n). First, the ground transportation cost was considered. To recall, the total travel cost defined in an airport competition problem, $c = a + b|\mathbf{f}|^{\gamma}$, comprises two terms that are represented by a, which reflects the zero-flow condition, and $b|\mathbf{f}|^{\gamma}$, which measures the effect of congestion. In view of the different ground transportation costs, two separate cost functions were necessary for Hong Kong and the Mainland PRD. Under uncongested conditions, the values of coefficient a for Hong Kong and the Mainland PRD were estimated by averaging the public transportation fares for traveling from downtown to the airports in Hong Kong and Guangzhou, respectively, in April 2002. For the congestion effect, coefficient b, as typical in any transport system, was considered to be the same for Hong Kong and the Mainland PRD. Estimation was based on the delay time and traffic flows of the three cross-harbor tunnels in Hong Kong. After calibration, the cost functions adopted in this model were $c = 2.042 + 1.178 \times 10^{-5}|\mathbf{f}|$ and $c = 2.363 + 1.178 \times 10^{-5}|\mathbf{f}|$ for the Mainland PRD and Hong Kong respectively.

The case of the whole HK-PRD region is more complex because it is also characterized by the HKSAR border. In the model, the border was represented by a fictitious cross-border zone to reflect the cross-border fare penalty and extra walking and waiting time experienced by passengers passing through customs. The cross-border fare penalty between Hong Kong and the Mainland PRD was defined as the difference in transport fare between traveling the same distance within Hong Kong and that of crossing the border. Based on the train fare differences in Hong Kong between alighting at the last train station before the border (Sheung Shui) and at the first station after the border (Lou Wu) and deducting this difference by the average traveling cost per km for the Hong Kong section, the cross-border fare penalty was estimated to be HKD23 (Kowloon-Canton Railway Corporation, 2002). The extra walking and waiting time at the fictitious cross-border zone was estimated based on actual cross-border flows (CSD, 2002). This customs delay was then multiplied by a value of time to convert it to a unit of dollar cost per km for passengers to travel in that zone. The additional cost was divided by the width of this fictitious zone to give the unit travel cost. Thus, for a passenger traveling across this fictitious zone, his/her ground transportation cost in that zone was the value of the time spent in walking and waiting plus the cross-border transport fare penalty. The estimated cost function for the fictitious cross-border zone was $c = 6.800 + 6.155 \times 10^{-3}|\mathbf{f}|$.

Next, the values of the total attribute measure, $\bar{u}_n$, of the four different airports were considered. In this paper, the attribute measure was considered to be captured by the primary airport LOS attribute of air ticket price. To obtain a realistic estimation of air ticket prices at the four airports, air ticket price quotations for departing from the four airports to various international and domestic destinations were obtained from the same sources and for the same period of travel during May 2002. The international air travel destinations included in this study were New York and San Francisco in North America, Paris and London in Europe, Sydney in Australia and Singapore in Asia. Quotations were obtained on the Internet from Trip.com Travel (2002). The domestic destinations included 17 common destinations of travelers departing from the four airports: Nanjing, Shanghai, Beijing, Chengdu, Kunming, Xian, Jinan, Harbin, Changchun, Shenyang, Fuzhou, Haikou, Hefei, Hangzhou, Wuhan, Changsha and Nanchang. Internet quotations were obtained from the China Aviation Administration of China (2002) and Wing On Travel (2002). In reality, passengers got discounts from their local travel

Figure 3. Spatial distribution of the estimated demand for international and domestic flights

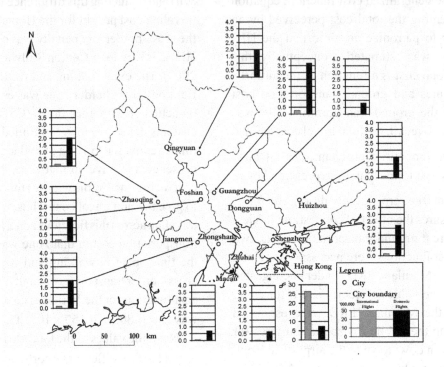

Figure 4. Average air ticket price at airports in the HK-PRD MAR, 2002

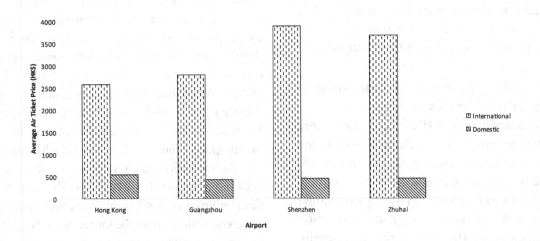

agencies or by joining group tours. After speaking with the management of the ticketing office of an airline and getting quotations from local travel agencies in Hong Kong and the Mainland PRD by phone, discount rates of 62% and 64% were considered appropriate for the international and domestic air ticket prices respectively. The discounted air ticket prices used for estimating the airport attribute measures are shown in Figure 4. It can be seen that Hong Kong's airport was the most attractive for international flights but the least attractive for domestic flights. For domestic flights, Guangzhou's airport was the most attractive. This scenario was highly consistent with the cross-border flows of Hong Kong residents to the Mainland PRD for domestic flights and the reverse flow of Mainland PRD residents to Hong Kong for international flights. Next, the data were substituted into the generalized cost functions for the market share analysis.

SOLUTIONS AND RECOMMENDATIONS

Using the parameters estimated in the previous section and the solution procedures elucidated earlier, the market share analysis for international and domestic air travel was conducted. Figure 5 shows the convergence curve for the domestic case. Due to the similarity of the curves, the convergence curve for the international case is not shown. The results of the market share analysis for international and domestic air travel in the PRD region are given in Figures 6 and 7 respectively. The 2000 air traffic turnover figures of the four airports are juxtaposed with the estimated market shares using the continuum approach of this paper. The flow patterns and cost functions for international and domestic air travelers are shown in Figures 8 to 11.

In comparing the estimations with the actual market shares of the four airports, the modeling results are found to be in good agreement with the actual situation (see Figures 6 and 7). The continuum approach has proven to be powerful in modeling the behavior of air passengers in the HK-PRD MAR. The degree of accuracy in estimating the market shares of international air travel was higher than that in estimating the market shares of domestic air travel. This difference could be attributed to the smaller air ticket price differentials for domestic air flights. Under such circumstances, other primary and secondary airport LOS attributes, such as the frequency of flights, efficiency of customs and availability of shopping facilities, could be more important in determining the choice of air travelers (Bradley,

Figure 5. Convergence curve for the domestic case

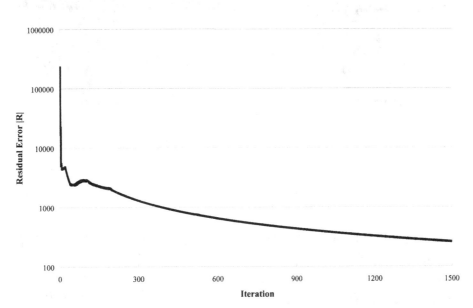

Figure 6. The international travel market share analysis

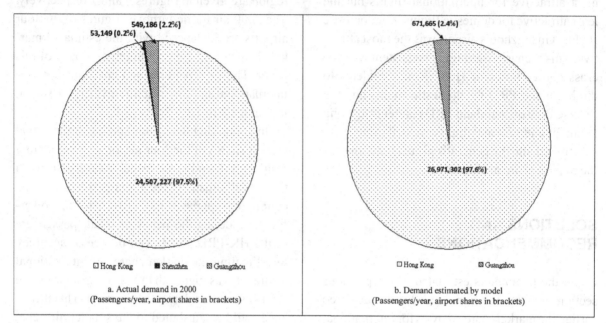

a. Actual demand in 2000
(Passengers/year, airport shares in brackets)

b. Demand estimated by model
(Passengers/year, airport shares in brackets)

Figure 7. The domestic travel market share analysis

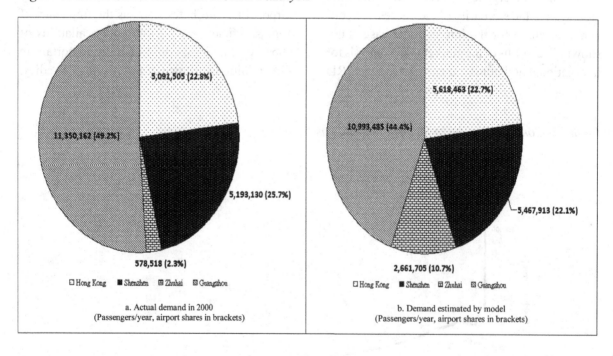

a. Actual demand in 2000
(Passengers/year, airport shares in brackets)

b. Demand estimated by model
(Passengers/year, airport shares in brackets)

1998; Loo, 2008; Rubin & Fagan, 1976). As mentioned earlier, the flexibility of our existing model (with $\bar{u}_n = \sum_{k=1}^{K} w_k p_k^n$) allows the inclusion of more airport attribute measures in future analysis.

The applications of the model for policy studies of the removal of the cross-border fare penalty, "one country, two systems" policy, sustained income growth in the Mainland PRD, and regional airport coordination have been reported in Loo

Figure 8. Flow pattern for international travel

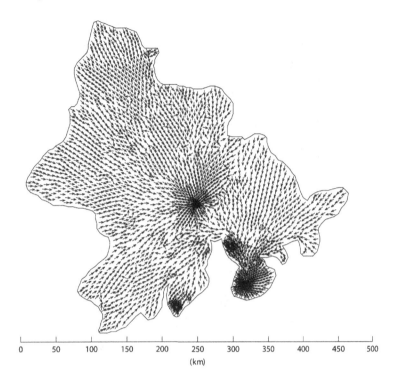

Figure 9. Cost function for international travel

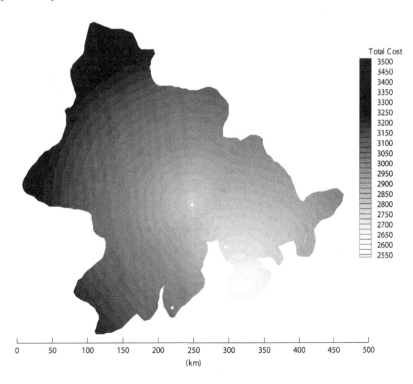

Figure 10. Flow pattern for domestic travel

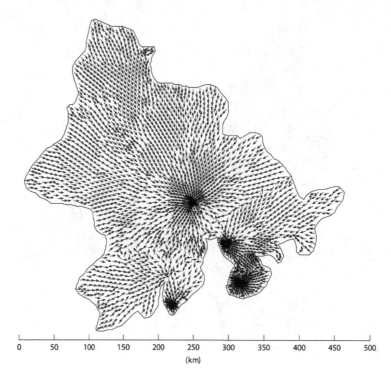

Figure 11. Cost function for domestic travel

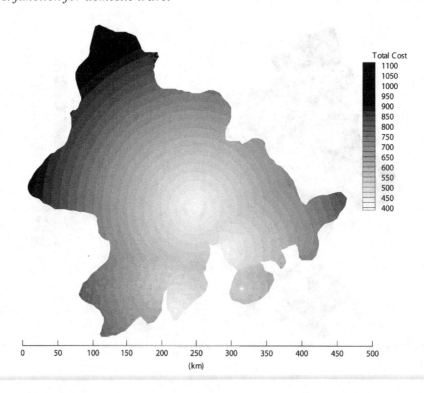

et al. (2005). Relevant policy implications were derived and extensively discussed. Interested readers may refer to that research paper.

FUTURE RESEARCH DIRECTIONS

Bowen (2000) observed that the international accessibility of a place "helps to define its access to global flows of goods, people, information, ideas, and capital" (p. 25). Accordingly, "an airport is perhaps the most important single piece of infrastructure in the battle between cities and nations for influence in, and the benefits of, growth and development" (O'Connor & Scott, 1992, p. 241). For a region, airport facilities are particularly important for supporting export-oriented industrialization (especially the electronics industries), tourism (especially international tourism), and international business services (including producer services such as finance, insurance and advertising, and regional headquarters functions) (Bowen, 2000; Butler & Kiernan, 1987). The analysis of Loo (2000) on the interrelationship between transportation and regional development shows that airport capacity was most highly related to the level of urbanization, value of industrial production and tertiary sector development, such as commerce and tourism, in the region. These developmental functions of airports are extremely important for regional development. Therefore, it is not surprising that airport development (including expansion) in the HK-PRD region had received active support from the national, provincial, and municipal governments throughout the 1990s. However, the environmental impact of air transportation, especially in comparison with the competing high-speed train operations, has caused growing concern (Givoni, 2007). This issue of inter-modal competition can also be studied by the continuum approach in future research.

CONCLUSION

In this paper, the continuum equilibrium approach is used to build a spatial model in solving the airport competition problem. The mathematical formulation and solution algorithm have been explained. A case study has been used to demonstrate the effectiveness of the methodology. The findings contribute to a better understanding of the geographical distribution of air traffic. Practically, the findings in this paper have significant policy implications for HK-PRD development.

ACKNOWLEDGMENT

Figures 1, 2, and 8 and some text extracts are reprinted from *Applied Geography*, 25, Becky P.Y. Loo, H.W. Ho, and S.C. Wong, An Application of the Continuous Equilibrium Modelling Approach in Understanding the Geography of Air Passenger Flows in a Multi-airport Region, 169-199, Copyright (2005), with permission from Elsevier. The work described in this paper was supported by the Outstanding Young Researcher Award of the first author and grants from the University of Hong Kong (10207394), National Natural Science Foundation of China (70629001), National Basic Research Program of China (2006CB705503) and Research Grants Council of the Hong Kong Special Administrative Region, China (HKU7183/08E).

REFERENCES

Borgstrom, R. E. (1974). Air travel: Toward a behavioral geography of discretionary travel. In M.E. Eliot-Hurst (Ed.), *Transportation geography: Comments and readings* (pp. 314-326). New York: McGraw-Hill.

Bowen, J. (2000). Airline hubs in Southeast Asia: National economic development and nodal accessibility. *Journal of Transport Geography*, 8, 25–41. doi:10.1016/S0966-6923(99)00030-7

Bradley, M. A. (1998). Behavioural models or airport choice and air route choice. In J. de Dios Ortuzar, D. Hensher, & S. Jara-Diaz (Eds.), *Travel behaviour research: Updating the state of play* (pp. 141-159). Amsterdam: Elsevier.

Bryan, D. L., & O'Kelly, M. E. (1999). Hub-and-spoke networks in air transportation: An analytical review. *Journal of Regional Science*, 39(2), 275–295. doi:10.1111/1467-9787.00134

Butler, S. E., & Kiernan, L. J. (1987). Measuring the regional transportation benefits and economic impacts of airports. In Transportation Research Board, National Research Council (Ed.), *Transportation economics: Issues and impacts* (pp. 63-69). Washington, DC: Transportation Research Board.

Census and Statistics Department (CSD), Hong Kong Special Administration Region (SAR) Government. (2001). *2001 population census: Basic tables for district council districts*. Hong Kong: Printing Department.

Census and Statistics Department (CSD), Hong Kong Special Administration Region (SAR) Government. (2002). *Hong Kong monthly digest of statistics*. Hong Kong: Printing Department.

Chinainfobank (2002). Retrieved April 19, 2002, from http://www.chinainfobank.com/IrisBin/ (in Chinese).

Civil Aviation Administration of China (CAAC). (2002). Retrieved April 19, 2002, from www.caac.cn.net.

Civil Aviation Department (CAD), Hong Kong Special Administration Region (SAR) Government. (2002). *CAD annual report 2000/2001*. Retrieved April 19, 2002, from http://www.info.gov.hk/cad/english/annualreport00.htm.

Givoni, M. (2007). Environmental benefits from mode substitution: Comparison of the environmental impact from aircraft and high-speed train operations. *International Journal of Sustainable Transportation*, 1(4), 209–230. doi:10.1080/15568310601060044

Guangdong tongjiju (Ed.) (2001). *Guangdong tonji nianian (Guangdong statistical yearbook)*. Guangzhou: Guangdong sheng tongjiju (in Chinese).

Ho, H. W., Wong, S. C., & Loo, B. P. Y. (2004). Sequential optimization approach for the multiclass user equilibrium problem in a continuous transportation system. *Journal of Advanced Transportation*, 38, 323–345.

Ho, H. W., Wong, S. C., & Loo, B. P. Y. (2006). Combined distribution and assignment model for a continuum traffic equilibrium problem with multiple user classes. *Transportation Research Part B: Methodological*, 40, 633–650. doi:10.1016/j.trb.2005.09.003

Hong Kong Tourism Board. (2001). *Visitor profile report 2000*. Hong Kong: Hong Kong Tourism Board.

Hong Kong Tourist Association. (2001). *Visitor departure statistics*. Hong Kong: Research Department, Hong Kong Tourist Association.

Information Services Department, Hong Kong SAR Government (2002). Press release on May 8, 2002.

Kowloon-Canton Railway Corporation. (2002). Retrieved April 20, 2002, from http://www.kcrc.com/eng/service/erdfc.html.

Loo, B. P. Y. (1999). Formation of a regional transport network: Some lessons from the Zhujiang Delta. *Journal of Transport Geography*, 7, 43–63. doi:10.1016/S0966-6923(98)00037-4

Loo, B. P. Y. (2000). An application of canonical correlation analysis in regional science: The interrelationships between transport and development in China's Zhujiang Delta. *Journal of Regional Science*, 40(1), 141–169. doi:10.1111/0022-4146.00168

Loo, B. P. Y. (2008). Passengers' airport choice within multi-airport regions (MARs): Some insights from a stated preference survey at Hong Kong International Airport. *Journal of Transport Geography*, 16, 117–125. doi:10.1016/j.jtrangeo.2007.05.003

Ndoh, N. N., Pitfieldand, D. E., & Caves, R. E. (1990). Air transportation passenger route choice: A nested multinomial logit analysis. In M. M. Fischer, P. Nijkamp, & Y. Y. Papageorgiou (Eds.), *Spatial choices and process* (pp. 349-365). Amsterdam: North-Holland.

O'Connor, K., & Scott, A. (1992). Airline services and metropolitan areas in the Asia-Pacific region 1970-1990. *Review of Urban and Regional Development Studies*, 4, 240 253. doi:10.1111/j.1467-940X.1992.tb00045.x

Rubin, D., & Fagan, L. N. (1976). Forecasting air passengers in a multiairport region. In Transportation Research Board, National Research Council (Ed.), *Airport and air transport planning* (pp. 1-5). Washington, DC: Transportation Research Board.

Sasaki, T., Iida, Y., & Yang, H. (1990). User equilibrium traffic assignment by continuum approximation of network flow. In *Proceedings of the 11th International Symposium on Transportation and Traffic Theory* (pp. 233-252). Japan, Yokohama.

Sing Dao Daily, (2002), May 9.

Taguchi, A., & Iri, M. (1982). Continuum approximation to dense networks and its application to the analysis of urban road networks. *Mathematical Programming Study*, 20, 178–217.

Tam, M. L., Lam, W. H. K., & Lo, H. P. (2008). Modeling air passenger travel behavior on airport ground access mode choices. *Transportmetrica*, 4(2), 135–153. doi:10.1080/18128600808685685

Trip.com Travel (2002). Retrieved April 22, 2002, from www.trip.com.

Wardrop, J. G. (1952). Some theoretical aspects of road traffic research. In *Proceedings of the Institute of Civil Engineers, Part II*, 1, (pp. 325-378).

Wing On Travel. (2002). Retrieved April 22, 2002, from http://202.181.172.71/v6/3tic/A_Ticket2.asp.

Wong, S. C. (1998). Multi-commodity traffic assignment by continuum approximation of network flow with variable demand. *Transportation Research Part B: Methodological*, 32, 567–581. doi:10.1016/S0191-2615(98)00018-6

Wong, S. C., Lee, C. K., & Tong, C. O. (1998). Finite element solution for the continuum traffic equilibrium problems. *International Journal for Numerical Methods in Engineering*, 43, 1253–1273. doi:10.1002/(SICI)1097-0207(19981215)43:7<1253::AID-NME468>3.0.CO;2-B

Wong, S. C., & Sun, S. H. (2001). A combined distribution and assignment model for continuous facility location problem. *The Annals of Regional Science*, 35, 267–281. doi:10.1007/s001680100042

Wong, S. C., & Yang, H. (1999). Determining market areas captured by competitive facilities: A continuous equilibrium modeling approach. *Journal of Regional Science*, 39, 51–72. doi:10.1111/1467-9787.00123

Wong, S. C., Zhou, C. W., Lo, H. K., & Yang, H. (2004). An improved solution algorithm for the multi-commodity continuous distribution and assignment model. *Journal of Urban Planning and Development*, *130*, 14–23. doi:10.1061/ (ASCE)0733-9488(2004)130:1(14)

Yang, H., & Wong, S. C. (2000). A continuous equilibrium model for estimating market areas by competitive facilities with elastic demand and market externality. *Transportation Science*, *34*, 216–227. doi:10.1287/trsc.34.2.216.12307

Zhongguo jiaotong nianjianshe (Ed.) (2000). *Zhongguo jiaotong nianjian 2000 (China transport yearbook)*. Beijing: Zhongguo jiaotong nianjianshe (in Chinese).

Zienkiewicz, O. C., & Taylor, R. L. (1989). *The finite element method*. New York: McGraw-Hill International Edition.

APPENDIX: PROOF OF THE USER EQUILIBRIUM CONDITION

Consider the Lagrangian function of minimization problem (2):

$$\Pi = \sum_{n=1}^{N}\left[\bar{u}_n Q_n + \pi_n\left(\oint_{\Gamma_{cn}} \mathbf{f}\cdot\mathbf{n}\,\mathrm{d}\Gamma - Q_n\right)\right] + \iint_{\Omega} a|\mathbf{f}| + \frac{b}{\gamma+1}|\mathbf{f}|^{\gamma+1} - \lambda\left(\nabla\cdot\mathbf{f} + q\right)\mathrm{d}\Omega + \oint_{\Gamma}\mathbf{w}\cdot\mathbf{f}\,\mathrm{d}\Gamma$$

(A-1)

where λ, $\mathbf{w} = (w_x, w_y)$, and π_n are the Lagrangian multipliers of equations (2b), (2c), and (2d), respectively. Apply the variational principle on the Lagrangian function and it can be shown that

$$'\Pi = \sum_{n=1}^{N}\left['\bar{u}_n Q_n + \bar{u}_n{'}Q_n + '\pi_n\left(\oint_{\Gamma_{cn}} \mathbf{f}\cdot\mathbf{n}\,\mathrm{d}\Gamma - Q_n\right) + \pi_n\left(\oint_{\Gamma_{cn}} '\mathbf{f}\cdot\mathbf{n}\,\mathrm{d}\Gamma - 'Q_n\right)\right] +$$
$$\iint_{\Omega}\frac{a}{|\mathbf{f}|}\mathbf{f}\cdot'\mathbf{f} + b|\mathbf{f}|^{\gamma-1}\mathbf{f}\cdot'\mathbf{f} - '\lambda\left(\nabla\cdot\mathbf{f} + q\right) - \lambda\left(\nabla\cdot'\mathbf{f} + 'q\right)\mathrm{d}\Omega + \oint_{\Gamma}'\mathbf{w}\cdot\mathbf{f} + \mathbf{w}\cdot'\mathbf{f}\,\mathrm{d}\Gamma$$

(A-2)

As $\nabla\cdot\left(\lambda'\mathbf{f}\right) = \lambda\nabla\cdot'\mathbf{f} + '\mathbf{f}\cdot\nabla\lambda$ and by divergence theorem

$$\iint_{\Omega}\nabla\cdot\left(\lambda'\mathbf{f}\right)\mathrm{d}\Omega = \int_{\Gamma}\lambda'\mathbf{f}\cdot\mathbf{n}\,\mathrm{d}\Gamma + \sum_{n=1}^{N}\int_{\Gamma_{cn}}\lambda'\mathbf{f}\cdot\mathbf{n}\,\mathrm{d}\Gamma$$

(A-3)

we have

$$'\Pi = \sum_{n=1}^{N}\left['\bar{u}_n Q_n + \left(\bar{u}_n - \pi_n\right)'Q_n + '\pi_n\left(\oint_{\Gamma_{cn}} \mathbf{f}\cdot\mathbf{n}\,\mathrm{d}\Gamma - Q_n\right) + \oint_{\Gamma_{cn}}\left(\pi_n - \lambda\right)'\mathbf{f}\cdot\mathbf{n}\,\mathrm{d}\Gamma\right] +$$
$$\iint_{\Omega}\left[\left(a + b|\mathbf{f}|^{\gamma}\right)\frac{\mathbf{f}}{|\mathbf{f}|} + \nabla\lambda\right]\cdot'\mathbf{f} - '\lambda\left(\nabla\cdot\mathbf{f} + q\right) - \lambda'q\,\mathrm{d}\Omega + \oint_{\Gamma}'\mathbf{w}\cdot\mathbf{f} + \left(\mathbf{w} - \lambda\mathbf{n}\right)\cdot'\mathbf{f}\,\mathrm{d}\Gamma$$

(A-4)

As $\delta\mathbf{f}$, $\delta\lambda$, δQ_n, and $\delta\pi_n$, $n = 1, 2,\ldots, N$ are arbitrary functions within Ω, $'\bar{u}_n$ and δq vanish because they are constant within Ω, and $\delta\mathbf{f}$ vanishes on the boundary Γ of the study region, the stationary point of the Lagrangian $\delta\Pi = 0$ requires that

$$\left(a + b|\mathbf{f}|^{\gamma}\right)\frac{\mathbf{f}}{|\mathbf{f}|} + \nabla\lambda = 0, \qquad \forall(x, y) \in \Omega$$

(A-5)

$$\nabla \cdot \mathbf{f} + q = 0, \qquad \forall (x,y) \in \Omega \tag{A-6}$$

$$\mathbf{f} = 0, \qquad \forall (x,y) \in \Gamma \tag{A-7}$$

$$\oint_{\Gamma_{cn}} \mathbf{f} \cdot \mathbf{n} \, \mathrm{d}\Gamma - Q_n = 0, \, n = 1, 2, \ldots, N \tag{A-8}$$

$$\bar{u}_n - \pi_n = 0, \, n = 1, 2, \ldots, N \tag{A-9}$$

$$\pi_n - \lambda = 0, \, n = 1, 2, \ldots, N \tag{A-10}$$

From equation (A-5), we have $\mathbf{f} \, // - \nabla\lambda$ (that is, the vector $\mathbf{f}$ is parallel with $-\nabla\lambda$), and

$$c = a + b|\mathbf{f}|^{\gamma} = |\nabla\lambda|. \tag{A-11}$$

Therefore, $|\nabla\lambda|$ can be interpreted as the ground transportation cost. Also, by equations (A-9) and (A-10), $\bar{u}_n = \lambda$ for all $n = 1, 2, \ldots, N$, which implies that the cost potential will have the same value as $\bar{u}_n$ at the airport O_n. This means that the total cost for a passenger, whose home is located at the periphery of the airport boundary, is equal to the total attribute measure of airport O_n only. In addition, for any used path p from demand location $D(x,y)$ to a selected airport O_n, the total generalized cost is

$$G_p\left[D(x,y), O_n\right] = \bar{u}_n + \int_p c \, \mathrm{d}s = \lambda(D) \tag{A-12}$$

whereas for any unused path $\bar{p}$ from D to O_n, the total generalized cost is

$$G_{\bar{p}}\left[D(x,y), O_n\right] = \bar{u}_n + \int_{\bar{p}} c \, \mathrm{d}s \geq \lambda(D) \tag{A-13}$$

where the function $\lambda(D)$ is the Lagrange multiplier associated with constraint (2b). Therefore, for any unused path the total cost is greater than or equal to that of the used path. Thus, the model guarantees that the air traveler will choose his/her transportation route to an airport in a user-equilibrium manner (Wardrop, 1952). Finally, it can also be shown that for any unchosen airport $O_{\bar{n}}$, the corresponding disutility $G_p\left[D(x,y), O_{\bar{n}}\right]$ along any path p from the demand location $D(x,y)$ to the airport will be greater than or equal to $\lambda(D)$, because no path from $D(x,y)$ to $O_{\bar{n}}$ is used and the cost integration along an unused path will result in a value higher than $\lambda(D)$. Consequently, the model gives rise to a spatial equilibrium choice pattern, and the Lagrange multiplier associated with the flow conservation constraint, $\lambda(D)$, can be interpreted as the total cost potential or disutility derived from patronizing a certain airport.

Chapter 7
Real–Time Non–Destructive Evaluation of Airport Pavements Using Neural Network Based Models

Kasthurirangan Gopalakrishnan
Iowa State University, USA

ABSTRACT

Nondestructive test (NDT) and evaluation methods are well-suited for characterizing materials and determining structural integrity of airfield pavement systems. The Heavy Weight Deflectometer (HWD) test is one of the most widely used NDT impulse device for assessing the structural condition of airport pavements in a non-destructive manner. Through inverse analysis of HWD deflection data (more commonly referred to as backcalculation), the structural stiffness parameters of the individual airport pavement layers are, in general, determined using iterative optimization routines. In recent years, Artificial Neural Networks (ANN) aided inverse analysis has emerged as a successful alternative for predicting pavement layer moduli from HWD deflection data in real time. Especially, the use of Finite Element (FE) based pavement modeling results for training the ANN aided inverse analysis is considered to be accurate in realistically characterizing the non-linear stress-sensitive response of underlying pavement layers. The development of an effective tool for real-time backcalculation of flexible airfield pavement layer moduli based on HWD test data is discussed in this Chapter. The ANN-based backcalculation tool is validated using actual field data acquired from a full-scale, state-of-the-art airport pavement test facility.

INTRODUCTION

Objective

The current study described in this Chapter focused on developing an effective tool for real-time backcal-

culation of flexible airfield pavement layer moduli based on Heavy Weight Deflectometer (HWD) test data. A multi-layer, feed-forward network which uses an error-backpropagation algorithm was trained to approximate the HWD backcalculation function. The developed ANN-models were used in backcalculating pavement layer moduli from actual HWD test data acquired at the National Airport

DOI: 10.4018/978-1-60566-800-0.ch007

Pavement Test Facility (NAPTF). The NAPTF was constructed to generate full-scale testing data to support the investigation of the performance of airport pavements subjected to new generation aircraft. The NAPTF test details are discussed under a separate section.

The results from this study were also compared with those obtained using a conventional ELP-based backcalculation program. It is noted that this was an initial study with limited scope specifically targeted towards the backcalculation of pavement layer moduli from HWD data acquired at the NAPTF. However, the results highlight the potential for extending this concept for developing generic ANN-based models which would be useful in the analysis of routine HWD test data collected at flexible airfield pavements. This could be accomplished by training the ANN models developed in this study over a broad range of input values.

Background

Much of the road infrastructure in both the United States and around the world are fast deteriorating due to age, increased demand on infrastructure systems, and inadequate investment. The problem concerns deterioration of an aging road infrastructure and how best to control it, taking into account the best interests and constraints of the economy and resources. A critical issue is the need to rapidly and cost-effectively evaluate the present condition of pavement infrastructure. Nondestructive test (NDT) and evaluation methods are well-suited for characterizing materials and determining structural integrity of pavement systems (Rix et al., 1995). Structural evaluation of pavements provides a wealth of information concerning the expected behavior of pavements (Haas et al., 1994).

The Falling Weight Deflectometer (FWD) test is one of the most widely used tests for assessing the structural integrity of roads in a non-destructive manner. In the case of airfields, a Heavy Weight

Deflectometer (HWD) test, which is similar to a FWD test, but using higher load levels, is used. In an FWD/HWD test, an impulse load is applied to the pavement surface by dropping a weight onto a circular metal plate and the resultant pavement surface deflections are measured directly beneath the plate and at several radial offsets. The deflection of a pavement represents an overall "system response" of the pavement layers to an applied load. A conventional Asphalt Concrete (AC) pavement is typically made up of three layers: a surface layer paved with AC mix, a granular base or/and subbase layer made up of crushed stone, and a subgrade layer made up of soil. When a wheel load is applied on an AC pavement, the pavement layers deflect nearly vertically to form a basin as illustrated in Figure 1. The FWD/HWD test tries to replicate the force history and deflection magnitudes of a moving truck tire/aircraft tire.

The deflected shape of the basin (Figure 2) is predominantly a function of the thickness of the pavement layers, the moduli of individual layers, and the magnitude of the load. *Backcalculation* is the accepted term used to identify a process whereby the elastic (Young's) moduli of individual pavement layers are estimated based upon measured FWD/HWD surface deflections. As there are no closed-form solutions to accomplish this task, a mathematical model of the pavement system (called a forward model) is constructed and used to compute theoretical surface deflections with assumed initial layer moduli values at the appropriate FWD/HWD loads. Through a series of iterations, the layer moduli are changed, and the calculated deflections are then compared to the measured deflections until a match is obtained within tolerance limits.

Used in combination with sampling and laboratory testing techniques, the FWD provides an effective and efficient means for evaluation of existing pavement structures, and for development of input parameters for design procedures. Typically, the FWD deflection measurements are used to backcalculate the *in-situ* elastic moduli of

Figure 1. Illustration of deflection surface caused by moving wheel loads

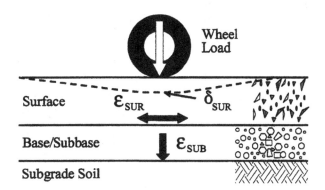

each pavement layer. The backcalculated moduli themselves provide an indication of layer condition. They are also used in an elastic layered or finite element program to predict the critical pavement responses (stresses, strains and deflections) under applied loads.

Many researchers have indicated that stiffness determined through FWD testing is a fundamental method of determining effective layer moduli (Rada et al., 1992; Rauhut & Jordahl, 1992; Thompson, 1992). As the use of deflection measurements to characterize pavement structural capacity and to determine the layer moduli of the separate layers increases, understanding and refining the backcalculation process becomes

increasingly important (Maestas & Mamlouk, 1992; Roque et al., 1992). At the project level, FWD testing is not only used for evaluation of structural condition of in-service pavements but also to characterize the pavement layer properties for use in mechanistic or mechanistic-empirical analysis and rehabilitation design procedures.

Numerous backcalculation techniques have been developed for the backcalculation of pavement layer moduli so far based on both static and dynamic analysis. The fundamental discrepancies among developed backcalculation models arise from the type of forward response model (linear or nonlinear; static or dynamic) and the optimization procedure (least squares, database search

Figure 2. Schematic of FWD configuration and deflection basin

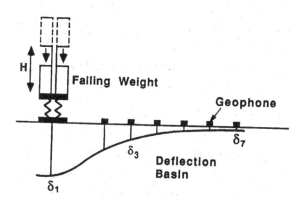

method, etc.) carried out for the determination of appropriate layer modulus values (Ullidtz, 2000; Goktepe et al., 2005). However, static, linear or quasi-nonlinear layered elastic model based backcalculation programs are still the most common among State Highway Agencies (SHA) for routine or production purposes interpretation of FWD data.

The process of static backcalculation of layer moduli from FWD data is not always robust enough to tolerate inherent measurement and modeling errors and often "judgment" is needed in interpreting the results. Undoubtedly this has negatively impacted the use of backcalculation to interpret FWD data and, in some cases, a decline in the use of FWD testing for structural evaluation of in-service pavements.

ARTIFICIAL NEURAL NETWORKS IN PAVEMENT MODULI BACKCALCULATION

Over the past 30 years, many research studies have addressed the interpretation of pavement deflection measurements as a tool to characterize pavement-subgrade systems, with many of the main findings appearing in American Society for Testing and Materials (ASTM) special technical publications, including those of Bush & Baladi (1989) and Tayabji & Lukanen (2000).

The Strategic Highway Research Program (SHRP) conducted a review of the features and capabilities of most of the then-available backcalculation programs, for the purpose of recommending which program or programs should be used in analysis of deflection data collected in the Long-Term Pavement Performance (LTPP) studies. Uzan (1994) presented a synthesis of different backcalculation procedures (both linear and nonlinear) and a discussion of their limitations. Johnson & Baus (1996) investigated a number of basin-matching backcalculation programs.

Recently, Stubstad et al. (2006) developed a new approach, called Forwardcalculation, to determine layered elastic moduli from in-situ FWD load-deflection data. This approach was used to conduct a comprehensive review and evaluation of Long-Term Pavement Performance (LTPP) backcalculation data. It was suggested that, although backcalculation is certainly rigorous and scientific, the user, however, must be aware of its limitations and assumptions, such as linear-elasticity, homogeneity, isotropic behavior, in addition to the assumption of being horizontally identical in stiffness for each structural layer beneath the width of the deflection basin, especially if a linear elastic model is chosen for backcalculation.

In the case of rigid pavements, researchers have developed many different methodologies for backcalculation of concrete pavement properties from FWD measurements, including the AREA method for rigid pavements (Ioannides et al., 1989; Ioannides, 1990; Barenberg & Petros, 1991), ILLI-BACK (Ioannides, 1994), graphical solution using IILI-SLAB (Foxworthy & Darter, 1989), use of regression analysis to solve AREA method for rigid pavements (Hall, 1992; Hall et al., 1996), and the use of best fit algorithm to find radius of relative stiffness (l) (Hall et al., 1996; Smith et al., 1996), among others. Crovetti (2002) proposed deflection-based analysis techniques including corrections for slab size, joint and crack load transfer, slab curling and loss of support for jointed concrete pavement systems.

Most of the conventional backcalculation programs currently in use (e.g. WESDEF, BISDEF) utilize an Elastic Layer Program (ELP) as the forward model to compute the surface deflections. For example, WESDEF uses WESLEA and BISDEF uses BISAR.

The ELPs consider the pavement as an elastic multi-layered media, and assume that pavement materials are linear-elastic, homogeneous and isotropic. However, in reality, it has been found that certain pavement materials do not show linear stress-strain relation under cyclic loading. The non-linearity or stress-dependency of resilient modulus for unbound granular materials and cohesive fine-grained subgrade soils is well documented in literature (Hicks, 1970; Thompson & Robnett, 1979). Unbound granular materials used in the base/subbase layer of an AC pavement show *stress-hardening* behavior (increase in resilient modulus with increasing hydrostatic stress) and cohesive subgrade soils show *stress-softening* behavior (reduction in resilient modulus with increasing deviator stress). Therefore, the layer modulus is no longer a constant value, but a function of the stress state. Also, the ELPs do not account for the available shear strength of these unbound materials and frequently predict tensile stresses at the bottom of unbound granular layers which exceeds the available strength. Thus, the pavement layer moduli values predicted using ELP-based backcalculation programs are not very realistic.

Advanced finite-element based pavement structural models such as ILLI-PAVE (Raad & Figueroa, 1980) and GT-PAVE (Tutumluer, 1995) can take into account nonlinear geomaterial characterization by incorporating stress-sensitive geomaterial models, Mohr-Coulomb failure criteria to limit material strength and material anisotropy behavior and as a result more realistically predict pavement responses needed for mechanistic based pavement design (Thompson, 1992; Garg et al., 1998; Tutumluer et al., 2003).

Literature review (Adeli, 2001; TRB, 1999) shows that NNs and other soft computing techniques like fuzzy mathematical programming and evolutionary computing (including genetic algorithms) are increasingly used instead of the traditional methods in civil and transportation applications (Flintsch, 2003). Meier & Rix (1993) trained backpropagation type ANNs as surrogates for elastic layered program analysis in a computer program for backcalculating pavement layer moduli and realized a 42 times increase in processing speed. Similar NN applications related to pavement, geotechnical and geomechanical

systems were also reported by Khazanovich & Roesler (1997), Ioannides et al. (1996), Kim & Kim (1998), Ghaboussi & Sidarta (1998), etc.

ILLI-PAVE is a two-dimensional axisymmetric pavement finite-element (FE) software developed at the University of Illinois at Urbana-Champaign (Raad & Figueroa, 1980). It incorporates stress-sensitive material models and it provides a more realistic representation of the pavement structure and its response to loading. The primary objective of this study was to develop a tool for backcalculating non-linear airfield flexible pavement layer moduli from HWD data using Artificial Neural Networks (ANN). The reason for using ANN to accomplish this task is that once trained, they offer mathematical solutions that can be easily calculated in real-time on even the basic personal computers, unlike conventional backcalculation programs. Also, ANN can learn a backcalculation function that is based on much more realistic models of pavement response (e.g., ILLI-PAVE) than are used in traditional-basin matching programs.

In recent years, ANNs are increasingly being used to solve pavement engineering problems which deal with highly non-linear functional approximations. In a study conducted at the University of Illinois, Ceylan (2002) employed ANNs in the analysis of concrete pavement systems and developed ANN-based design tools that incorporated the state-of-the-art finite element solutions into routine practical design at several orders of magnitude faster than those sophisticated finite element programs. Several other studies have reported the development of similar ANN applications (Meier & Rix, 1993; Gucunski & Kristic, 1996; Kim & Kim, 1997; etc.). In the development of the new mechanistic-empirical pavement design guide for the American Association of State Highway and Transportation Officials (AASHTO), ANNs have been recognized as nontraditional, yet very powerful computing techniques and were employed in preparing the concrete pavement analysis package of the design guide.

Figure 3. Cross-sectional views of NAPTF test sections

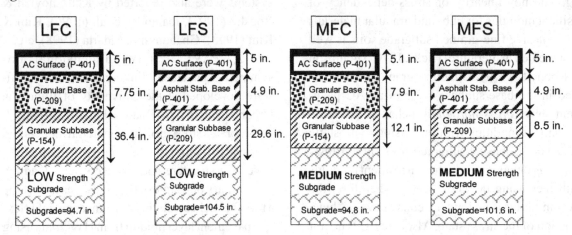

ANNs have been successfully used in the past for the backcalculation of flexible pavement moduli from FWD data (Meier & Rix, 1993). However, they did not account for realistic pavement layer properties as ELP-generated synthetic database was used to train the ANN. Recent studies at the Iowa State University and University of Illinois have focused on the development of ANN based models, trained using ILLI-PAVE generated synthetic database, to predict critical pavement responses and layer moduli from highway and airport pavement FWD data (Ceylan et al., 2004; Gopalakrishnan et al., 2006).

THE NATIONAL AIRPORT PAVEMENT TEST FACILITY

Pavement Test Sections

The NAPTF is located at the Federal Aviation Administration's (FAA's) William J. Hughes Technical Center, Atlantic City International Airport, New Jersey. The NAPTF test pavement area is 274-m (900-ft) long and 18.3-m (60-ft) wide. Four NAPTF flexible pavement test sections were considered in this study: (a) MFC – a conventional granular base flexible pavement resting over a medium-strength subgrade; (b) MFS – an asphalt-

stabilized base flexible pavement resting over a medium-strength subgrade; (c) LFC – a conventional granular base flexible pavement section built over a low-strength subgrade; and (d) LFS – an asphalt-stabilized base flexible pavement section built over a low-strength subgrade. Cross-sectional views of the as-constructed NAPTF flexible test sections are shown in Figure 3.

The items P-209, P-154 and P-401 are as per standard specifications detailed in the FAA Circular No. AC 150/5370-10A. A MH-CH soil classification (ASTM Unified Soil Classification System) material known as County Sand and Stone Clay (CSSC) was used for the low-strength subgrade while DuPont Clay (DPC) (CL-CH soil classification) was used for the medium-strength subgrade. Target strengths of the low-strength subgrade and medium-strength subgrade were 4 California Bearing Ratio (CBR) and 8 CBR, respectively. The naturally-occurring sandy-soil material (SW-SM soil classification) at the NAPTF site underlies each subgrade layer (20 CBR). The gradation information as well as the laboratory compaction properties for the subgrade soils, P-209 crushed stone base, and P-154 subbase (stone screenings) are presented elsewhere (Gopalakrishnan, 2004).

All of the test items conform to standard Federal Aviation Administration (FAA) airport pavement design practices except in closer control of the material properties than is normal. Construction of the subgrades was also carefully controlled to provide the desired strengths and to maintain uniformity within each lift. Selected properties of all of the materials used in the test item component layers were measured before, during, and after construction. The measured material properties were stored in a database which is a historical record of all of the testing conducted on the pavement materials and contains information about material properties of the component layers from quality control (QC), acceptance, and material characterization tests. The database is available for download or direct access on the FAA Airport Pavement Technology web site (Gopalakrishnan, 2004).

Traffic Testing

A six-wheel dual-tridem gear configuration with 1,372-mm (54-in.) dual spacing and 1,448-mm (57-in.) tandem spacing, representative of Boeing-777 (B777) landing gear, was loaded on the north side wheel track. The south side was loaded with a four-wheel Boeing-747 (B747) dual-tandem gear configuration having 1,118-mm (44-in.) dual spacing and 1,473-mm (58-in.) tandem spacing. The wheel loads were set to 20.4 tonnes (45,000 lbs) each and the tire pressure (cold) was 1,295 kPa (188 psi). In the LFC and LFS test sections, the wheel loads were increased from 20.4 tonnes (45,000-lbs) to 29.4 tonnes (65,000-lbs) after 20,000 initial load repetitions. Throughout the traffic test program, the traffic speed was 8 km/h (5 mph).

To realistically simulate transverse aircraft movements, a wander pattern consisting of a fixed sequence of 66 vehicle passes (33 traveling in the East direction and 33 traveling in the West direction), arranged in nine equally spaced wander positions (or tracks) at intervals of 260 mm (10.25 in), was used during traffic tests. This wander pattern simulates a normal distribution of aircraft traffic with a standard deviation (σ) of

775 mm (30.5 in) that is typical of multiple gear passes in airport taxiways.

According to the FAA, the primary objective of the NAPTF trafficking tests was to determine the number of load applications to cause shear failure in the subgrade. Per NAPTF failure criterion, this is reflected as 25.4-mm (1-in.) surface upheaval adjacent to the traffic lane. The low-strength sections (LFC and LFS) showed few signs of genuine distress even after 20,000 passes and therefore the wheel loading was increased from 20.4 tonnes to 29.4 tonnes.

Non-Destructive Testing

The FWD tests (Figure 4) are commonly used to assess the structural integrity of highway/airport pavements in a nondestructive manner. There are many advantages to using FWD tests, *in lieu* of, or supplement traditional destructive tests for pavement structural evaluation. Most important, is the capability to quickly gather data at several locations while keeping a runway, taxiway, or apron operational during these 2-minute to 3-minute tests, provided the testing is under close contact with Air Traffic Control. Without FWD, structural data must be obtained from numerous cores, borings, and excavation pits on an existing airport pavement. This can be very disruptive to airport operations. FWD tests are economical to perform and data can be collected at up to 250 locations per day. The FWD equipment measures pavement surface deflections from an applied dynamic load that simulates a moving wheel.

The deflection data that are collected with the FWD equipment can provide both qualitative and quantitative data about the strength of a pavement at the time of testing (FAA, 2004). Nondestructive tests using the FWD equipment were conducted on NAPTF flexible pavement test sections prior to traffic testing to verify the uniformity of pavement and subgrade construction and strength. For FWD testing, the Engineering & Research International (ERI) Inc. equipment

Figure 4. Falling Weight Deflectometer (FWD) NDT equipment attached to a van

was used. The ERI equipment is a FWD KUAB Model 150® with a segmented 30.5-cm (12-in) loading plate. A pulse width of 27-30 msec was used during the FWD tests.

The FWD tests were conducted on June 14, 1999 at nominal force amplitudes of 40-kN (9,000-lb), 60-kN (13,500-lb), 82.3-kN (18,500-lb), and 115.2-kN (25,900-lb). This study focused on the 40-kN (9,000-lb) FWD test results. Based on linear FWD load-deflection behaviors observed for both flexible and rigid airport pavements, McQueen et al. (2001) suggested that using NDT force amplitudes at prototypical aircraft loading may not be necessary to evaluate airport pavements. They further indicated that the amplitude of the FWD impulse load does not seem to be critical provided the generated deflections are within the limits of all deflection sensors.

During the NAPTF FWD tests, the deflections were measured at offsets of 0-mm (D_0), 305-mm (D_1), 610-mm (D_2), 914-mm (D_3), 1219-mm (D_4), and 1524-mm (D_5) intervals from the center of the load. A schematic of FWD/HWD test locations in each of the test sections is displayed in Figure 5. Note that during the NAPTF traffic testing, the

B777 test gear was centered on LANE 2 whereas the B747 test gear was centered on LANE 5.

The FWD load-deflection relationship for NAPTF medium-strength flexible test items is shown in Figure 6 for all six measured deflections. It appears that the load-deflection relationship is nearly linear. The non-linearity or stress-dependency of resilient modulus for unbound granular materials and cohesive fine-grained subgrade soils is well documented in literature (Brown & Pappin, 1981; Thompson & Elliot, 1985; Garg et al., 1998). Thus, if a granular material overlies a fine-grained subgrade, an increase in load level from the test load imposed on the pavement during non-destructive HWD testing will increase the base modulus and decrease the subgrade modulus. The net effect is that the surface deflections could be nearly linear with increasing load. Thus, even if the HWD load-to-deflection ratio is nearly linear (as seen in Figure 6), that fact alone is not sufficient to conclusively prove that the materials in the pavement layers are in their linear range (Chen & Hugo, 1998).

All test data referenced in this paper are available for download or direct access on the FAA

Figure 5. Schematic of FWD/HWD test locations in each NAPTF test section

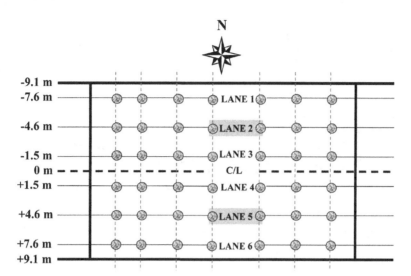

Airport Pavement Technology web site: www. airtech.tc.faa.gov/naptf/.

GENERATION OF ANN TRAINING AND TESTING DATABASE

The NAPTF flexible test sections were separately modeled as two-dimensional, axisymmetric FE structures using the as-constructed layer thicknesses. The individual pavement layers were characterized as follow.

The AC surface layer and the natural sand layer beneath the subgrade were characterized as a linear elastic material. Stress-dependent elastic models along with Mohr-Coulomb failure criteria were applied for the base, subbase and subgrade layers. The *stress-hardening* K-θ model was used for the base and subbase layers:

$$E_R = \frac{\sigma_D}{\varepsilon_R} = K\theta^n \qquad (1)$$

where E_R is resilient modulus (kPa), θ is bulk stress (kPa) and K and n are statistical parameters. It

has been shown that an inverse relationship exists between K and n (Rada & Witczak, 1970).

The fine-grained low-strength subgrade was modeled using the bi-linear model for characterizing the resilient modulus:

$$E_R = E_{Ri} + K_1(\sigma_d - \sigma_{di}) \quad for \ \sigma_d < \sigma_{di}$$
$$E_R = E_{Ri} + K_2(\sigma_d - \sigma_{di}) \quad for \ \sigma_d > \sigma_{di} \qquad (2)$$

where E_R is resilient modulus (kPa), σ_d is applied deviator stress (kPa), and K_1 and K_2 are statistically determined coefficients from laboratory tests.

The bi-linear model (Thompson & Elliot, 1985) is a commonly used resilient modulus model for subgrade soils. The value of the resilient modulus at the breakpoint in the bi-linear model, E_{Ri}, can be used to classify fine-grained soils as being soft, medium or stiff.

The effect of 160-kN (36,000-lb) HWD loading was simulated in ILLI-PAVE. A total of 5,000 datasets were generated for each test section by randomly varying the layer moduli parameters over typical ranges. During the initial phase, it was decided to use separate ANN models for each section. Of the total number of data sets, 3,750

Figure 6. FWD load-deflection relationship: (a) MFC; (b) MFS

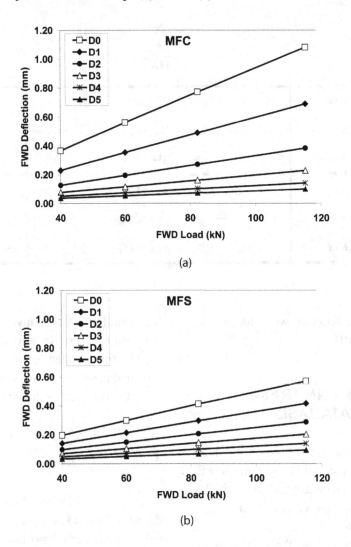

(a)

(b)

data vectors were used in training the ANN and the remaining 1,250 data vectors were utilized for the testing the network after the training was completed. The ranges of layer properties used in training the ANN are summarized in Table 1.

ANN ARCHITECTURE

A generalized n-layer feedforward artificial neural network which uses an error backpropagation (BP) training algorithm (Rumelhart et al., 1986) was implemented. The BP algorithm is based on

a gradient-descent optimization technique and is now described in many textbooks (Adeli & Hung, 1985). BP networks excel at data modeling with their superior function approximation capabilities (Haykin, 1999) and a great majority of civil engineering application of neural networks is based on the use of the BP algorithm primarily because of its simplicity (Adeli, 2001).

The BP model developed in this study can allow for a general number of inputs, hidden layers, hidden layer elements, and output layer elements. Two hidden layers were found to be sufficient in solving a problem of this size. Therefore the

Table 1. Range of layer properties

Pavement Layer	Thickness (mm)	Layer modulus (MPa)	Poisson's ratio
P-401 Asphalt Concrete (AC)	LFC - 127 LFS - 254	690 – 18,000	0.35
P-209 Base	LFC – 197	K: 11 – 140 n: 0.2 – 0.8	0.35
P-209 Subbase	LFC – 925 LFS – 752	K: 11 – 140 n: 0.2 – 0.8	0.35
Subgrade	LFC – 2,405 LFS – 2,654	11 – 140	0.45
Sand	3,660	310	0.4

architecture was reduced to a four-layer feedforward network.

A four-layer feedforward network consists of a set of sensory units (source nodes) that constitute the input layer, two hidden layer of computation nodes, and an output layer of computation nodes. The following notation is generally used to refer to a particular type of architecture that has two hidden layers: (# inputs)-(# hidden neurons)-(# hidden neurons)-(# outputs). For example, the notation 10-40-40-3 refers to an ANN architecture that takes in 10 inputs (features), has 2 hidden layers consisting of 40 neurons each, and produces 3 outputs.

An ANN-based backcalculation procedure was developed to approximate the FWD/HWD backcalculation function. Using the ILLI-PAVE synthetic database, the ANN was trained to learn the relation between the synthetic deflection basins (inputs) and the pavement layer moduli (outputs).

The first step in back-propagation learning is to initialize the network. It is recommended that the initialization of the synaptic weights of the network be uniformly distributed inside a small range. A range of (-0.2, +0.2) was used for random initialization of all synaptic weight vectors in the network for this study.

The model of each neuron in the hidden layer(s) and output layer of the network includes a *nonlinearity* at the output end. The presence of

a nonlinear activation function, $\varphi(.)$, is important because, otherwise, the input-output relation of the network could be reduced to that of a single-layer perceptron. The computation of the local gradient for each neuron of the multilayer perceptron requires that the function $\varphi(.)$ be continuous. In other words, differentiability is the only requirement that an activation function would have to satisfy.

For this problem, an *asymmetric hyperbolic tangent* function (tanh) was chosen for which the amplitude of the output lies inside the range $-1 \leq y_j \leq +1$. Since, the final outputs are real values instead of binary outputs, a *linear combiner* model was used for neurons in the output layer, thus omitting the nonlinear activation function.

In order to track the performance of the network, the Root Mean Squared Error (RMSE) at the end of each *epoch* was calculated. An epoch is defined as one full presentation of all the training vectors to the network. The RMSE at the end of each epoch defined as:

$$RMSE = \sqrt{\frac{\sum_{j=1}^{N}\left[d_j - Y(X_j)\right]^2}{N}} \qquad (3)$$

where d_j is the desired response for the input training vector X_j, $Y(X_j)$ is the computed output, and N is the total number of input vectors presented to the network for training. For the network to learn

Table 2. FWD/HWD deflection basin parameters

Deflection Basin Parameter (DBP)	Formula
AREA	$AREA = 6(D_0 + 2D_1 + 2D_2 + D_3)/D_0$
Area Under Pavement Profile (AUPP)	$AUPP = (5D_0 - 2D_1 - 2D_2 - D_3)/2$
Area Index	$AI_4 = (D_3 + D_4)/2D_0$
Base Curvature Index (BCI)	$BCI = D_2 - D_3$ $BCI2 = D_5 - D_4$
Base Damage Index (BDI)	$BDI = D_1 - D_2$
Deflection Ratio	$DR = D_1/D_0$

the problem smoothly, a monotonic decrease in the RMSE is expected with increase in the number of epochs. A smooth learning curve was achieved with a learning-rate parameter (η) of 0.001.

ANN INPUTS AND OUTPUTS

Deflection Basin Parameters (DBPs) derived from FWD/HWD deflection measurements are shown to be good indicators of selected pavement properties and conditions (Hossain & Zaniewski, 1991). Recently, Xu et al. (2001) used DBPs in developing new relationships between selected pavement layer condition indicators and FWD deflections by applying regression and ANN techniques. Apart from the six independent deflection measurements (D_0 to D_5), some of the commonly used DBPs were included as inputs for training the ANN (see Table 2).

Each DBP supposedly represents the condition of specific pavement layers. For example, AUPP is sensitive to the AC layer properties whereas BCI and AI_4 are expected to reflect the condition of subgrade. The desired outputs from the ANN are: AC modulus (E_{AC}), subgrade modulus (E_{Ri}), base modulus parameter (K_b or n_b) and subbase modulus parameter (K_s or n_s). Note that by predicting either K or n, the other parameter can be determined using the relation proposed by Rada & Witzcak (1970).

BEST PERFORMANCE NETWORKS

Separate ANN models were used for each desired output rather than using the same architecture to determine all the outputs together. The most effective set of input features for each ANN model were determined based on both engineering judgment and past experience gained through research studies conducted at the University of Illinois. Parametric analyses were performed by systematically varying the choice and number of inputs and number of hidden neurons to identify the best-performance networks (Gopalakrishnan et al., 2006). As it was found that the prediction accuracy of the network remained the same for hidden layers greater than or equal to two, the number of hidden layers was fixed at two for all runs.

The learning curve (RMSE Vs number of epochs) and the testing RMSE were studied in order to arrive at the best networks. It was found that the base and subbase moduli parameters (K and n) were the hardest to predict. Further research is needed to develop robust ANN models for predicting the non-linear base and subbase moduli parameters.

ANN Prediction of Pavement Moduli

A summary of the sensitivity analyses performed to select the best-performance networks for predicting AC modulus (E_{AC}) and subgrade modulus

Table 3. Best performance ANN prediction models

NAPTF Section	Output	Inputs	Network Architecture	Training RMSE	Testing RMSE
LFC	E_{AC}	D_0 to D_5	6-40-40-1	0.69 GPa	0.66 GPa
	E_{Ri}	D_0 to D_5, BCI, AI_4	8-40-40-1	8.9 MPa	8.1 MPa
LFS	E_{AC}	D_0 to D_5	6-40-40-1	0.62 GPa	0.62 GPa
	E_{Ri}	D_0 to D_5, BCI, AI_4	8-40-40-1	16 MPa	14.8 MPa

(E_{Ri}) in NAPTF test sections are shown in Table 3. Note that the ANN inputs are similar for both the test sections. In general, the testing RMSEs for the two output variables were slightly lower than the training ones. In Figures 7, 8, 9, and 10, the ANN-predicted pavement layer moduli values and the ILLI-PAVE target values are compared using the 1,250 test data vectors. Due to space constraints, results are displayed only for the LFC test section. Similar results were obtained for the LFS section. Average Absolute Errors (AAEs), calculated as sum of the individual absolute errors divided by the 1,250 independent testing patterns, are also reported in the figures. Excellent agreement is found between the predicted and target values for both E_{AC} and subgrade modulus E_{Ri}.

As mentioned previously, the base and subbase modulus parameters could not be predicted with reasonable accuracy.

One of the major reasons for developing this ANN-based moduli backcalculation procedure is to reliably evaluate the structural integrity of the NAPTF pavement test sections as they were subjected to traffic loading. The NAPTF test sections were subjected to trafficking until they exhibited failure (i.e., until they exhibited 25.4-mm surface upheaval adjacent to the traffic lane).

The LFC and LFS sections showed few signs of genuine distress even after 20,000 passes and therefore the wheel loading was increased from 20.4-ton (45,000-lb) to 29.4-ton (65,000-lb). The trafficking was terminated in the LFC and LFS test sections after 28,000 passes of 29.4-ton (65,000-lb) wheel load trafficking. The post-traffic trench studies revealed that the LFC and LFS sections

failed in the surface layers, signifying tire pressure or other upper layer failure effects, but not subgrade level failure (Gervais et al., 2003).

EFFECT OF TRAFFICKING ON AIRPORT PAVEMENT MODULI

To study the loss of stiffness in NAPTF flexible pavement sections resulting from trafficking, the AC and subgrade layer moduli values were backcalculated from the 160-kN (36-kip) HWD data acquired at the NAPTF using the ANN prediction models developed in this study.

The ANN predicted results were then compared with those obtained using a conventional modulus backcalculation program, BAKFAA which assumes the pavement materials to be linear elastic. The BAKFAA was developed under the sponsorship of the FAA Airport Technology Branch and is based on the LEAF layered elastic computation program (Hayhoe, 2002). In this program, the pavement layer moduli are adjusted to minimize the root mean square (rms) of the differences between FWD/HWD sensor measurements and the LEAF-computed deflection basin for a specified pavement structure. A standard multidimensional simplex optimization routine is then used to adjust the moduli values (Hayhoe, 2002). The detailed backcalculation results for NAPTF sections using the BAKFAA program are reported elsewhere (McQueen et al., 2001; Gopalakrishnan, 2004).

Note that the 160-kN (36-kip) HWD testing was performed at different stages during the traf-

Figure 7. ANN prediction of AC modulus (E_{AC})

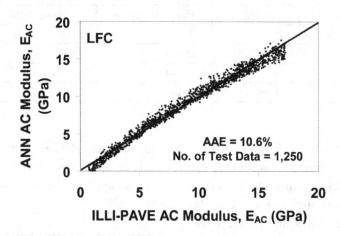

ficking on B777 traffic lane, B747 traffic lane and the untrafficked Centerline (C/L) of the test pavement (see Figure 5). It is reasonable to assume that the variation in moduli values in the C/L is mainly due to climatic effects. Thus, the changes in AC and subgrade moduli values in the traffic lanes can be compared to the corresponding C/L values and the degree of structural deterioration induced by B777 trafficking and B747 trafficking can be assessed.

The variations in ANN predicted AC moduli (E_{AC}) values with the number of traffic load repetitions (N) are displayed in Figure 11 and Figure 12

for LFC and LFS test sections, respectively. The gray arrow in the plots for LFC and LFS sections indicate where (20,000 load repetitions) the wheel load was increased from 20.4-ton (45,000-lb) to 29.4-ton (65,000-lb). Note that the changes in E_{AC} values in the untrafficked C/L are mainly due to the changes in the AC temperature. As expected, E_{AC} is significantly influenced by changes in AC temperature.

In the plots, the untrafficked centerline (C/L) AC modulus values (E_{AC}) and the trafficked lane values remain close to each other until 20,000 passes. Note that the wheel load magnitude was

Figure 8. ANN prediction of base modulus parameter (n_b)

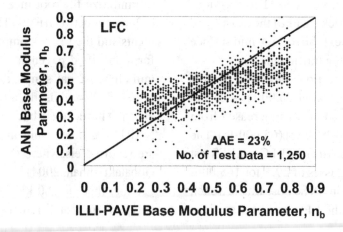

Figure 9. ANN prediction of subbase modulus parameter (n_s)

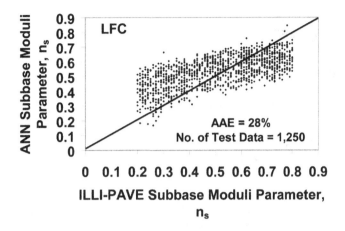

increased from 20.4 tonnes to 29.4 tonnes after 20,000 load repetitions in LFC and LFS sections. After 20000 passes the trafficked lane values show significant decrease compared to the C/L values. This is especially true in the LFC test section. At approximately 12,000 passes under the 20.4-ton (45-kip) wheel loading, the C/L E_{AC} value is 3.8 GPa while it is approximately 2.1 GPa (55% of C/L value) in the B777 traffic lane and is 3.0 GPa (79% of C/L value) in the B747 traffic lane. After 20,000 passes of 20.4-ton wheel loading and 12,000 passes of 29.4-ton (65-kip) wheel loading, the E_{AC} values are 7.8 GPa in the C/L, 0.6 GPa in the B777 traffic lane (8% of C/L

value) and 1.1 GPa in the B747 traffic lane (14% of C/L value).

The effect of trafficking on ANN backcalculated subgrade modulus values (E_{Ri}) is captured in Figure 13 and Figure 14 for LFC and LFS sections respectively. In the plots, the Y-axis is magnified as the subgrade moduli varied over a narrow range compared to the AC moduli. Compared to the C/L E_{Ri} values, the traffic lane E_{Ri} values show reduction in magnitude in the LFC and LFS sections as trafficking progresses.

The HWD tests were conducted in the center of the B777 and B747 traffic paths in addition to the tests on the pavement C/L. As trafficking

Figure 10. ANN prediction of subgrade modulus (E_{Ri})

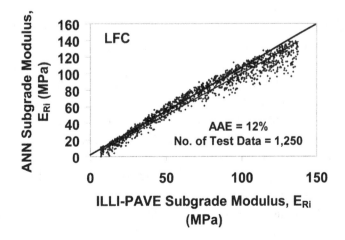

Figure 11. ANN predicted AC modulus versus N (LFC)

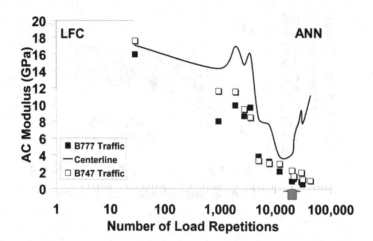

progressed, it is not known whether the HWD tests were conducted in the middle of the rutted area or towards the edges which showed surface upheaval. If the tests were conducted in the middle of the rutted areas (which were wide in extent) and not near the edge where subgrade shear occurred, a difference in backcalculated subgrade modulus may not result as a result of trafficking. In fact, a slight increase in subgrade modulus in the area tested may have occurred from compaction as seen in Figure 13 towards the end of traffic testing.

It is observed from figures 11 to 14 that, from an engineering standpoint, the effect of B777 trafficking on AC and subgrade moduli is not significantly different from that effected by B747 trafficking. Thus, the damaging effect of B777 and B747 traffic gears on flexible airfield pavements can be considered to be approximately equivalent based on the results from this study.

The comparison between the ANN predicted moduli values and BAKFAA backcalculated moduli values are presented in Figure 15 and Figure 16 for AC modulus and subgrade modulus, respectively. It should be noted that the rut depths in the NAPTF flexible test sections reached significant levels (76 mm to 102 mm) towards the end of traffic testing and therefore the HWD test results and hence the backcalculated moduli

values showed significant variability during the final stages of traffic testing.

It is seen that the ANN predicted AC moduli values agree well with the BAKFAA computed values for LFS section. In LFC section, the ANN predicted values are lower compared to the BAKFAA predicted values consistently. Similarly, there are variations between the ANN predicted subgrade modulus values and the BAKFAA computed values. Note that the ANN model predicts the stress-dependent subgrade breakpoint resilient modulus, E_{Ri}, whereas the subgrade modulus backcalculated by BAKFAA is based on the assumption that the subgrade soils are linear elastic. The differences in results between the two methodologies could also be attributed to the pavement structural model used in response computations. BAKFAA uses the LEAF multi-layered elastic analysis program whereas the ILLI-PAVE finite-element based program models the pavement as a 2D axisymmetric solid of revolution and employs nonlinear stress-dependent models and failure criteria for granular materials and fine-grained soils.

It is expected that the prediction of stress-dependent E_{Ri} would improve if multiple HWD load levels (53-kN, 107-kN, and 160-kN) are used in the generation of ILLI-PAVE synthetic database

Figure 12. ANN predicted AC modulus versus N (LFS)

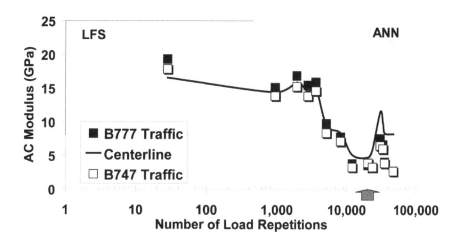

Figure 13. ANN predicted subgrade modulus versus N (LFC)

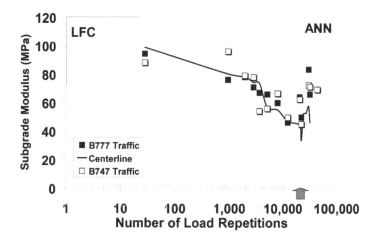

and in the development of the ANN algorithms. Further research is needed to develop robust ANN models for predicting base/subbase moduli parameters. It is proposed that by including the ANN-predicted E_{AC} and E_{Ri} values as inputs to the ANN, the chances of accurately predicting base/subbase moduli will increase. Also, the robustness of the ANN can be improved by including the field data sets in the training process, as they implicitly incorporate noise and errors seen typically in field measurements.

SUMMARY AND CONCLUSION

The Heavy Weight Deflectometer (HWD) test is one of the most widely used tests for assessing the structural integrity of airport pavements in a non-destructive manner. ANNs have been successfully used in the past for the backcalculation of flexible pavement moduli from FWD data. However, they did not account for realistic pavement layer properties as Elastic Layer Program (ELP)-generated synthetic database was used to train the ANN. Recent studies at the Iowa State University and University of Illinois have focused

Figure 14. ANN predicted subgrade modulus versus N (LFS)

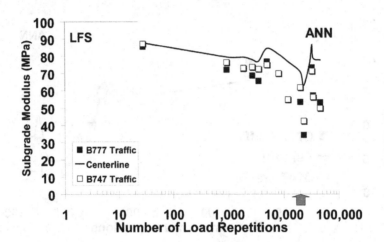

Figure 15. ANN AC moduli predictions compared with BAKFAA predictions

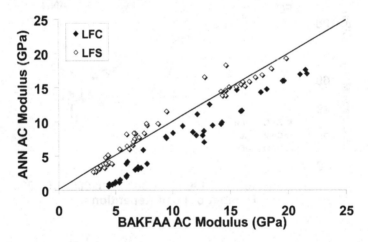

on the development of ANN based models, trained using ILLI-PAVE generated synthetic database, to predict critical pavement responses and layer moduli from highway pavement FWD data.

The primary objective of the study documented in this Chapter was to develop an effective tool for real-time backcalculation of airport flexible pavement non-linear layer moduli from HWD data using ANN, especially for airport flexible pavements serving the New-Generation Aircraft (NGA). The NAPTF sections were modeled in

ILLI-PAVE and synthetic database was generated for a range of moduli values. A multi-layer, feed-forward network which uses an error-back-propagation algorithm was successfully trained to approximate the HWD backcalculation function using the ILLI-PAVE database. The ILLI-PAVE solutions database was used in the ANN training to account for the typical stress-hardening behavior of unbound granular materials and stress-softening behavior of fine-grained subgrade soils.

ANN surrogate models were successfully

Figure 16. ANN subgrade moduli predictions compared with BAKFAA predictions

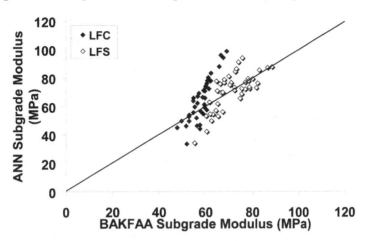

developed for predicting AC and non-linear sub-grade moduli from actual HWD field test data. However, the base/subbase moduli could not be predicted using ANN. Such ANN-based rapid solutions can enable analysis of a large number of HWD pavement deflection basins in real time, needed for routine airfield pavement structural evaluation.

ACKNOWLEDGMENT

The author gratefully acknowledges the financial assistance and support provided by Professor Marshall R. Thompson at the University of Illinois at Urbana-Champaign (UIUC) for conducting this research. The author is also grateful to Dr. Franco Gomez-Ramirez of EPSA-LABCO, Santa Domingo; Dr. Navneet Garg, Dr. Gordon Hayhoe, and Dr. David Brill of FAA for their valuable help and suggestions during the course of this research. The contents of this Chapter reflect the views of the author who is responsible for the facts and accuracy of the data presented within. The contents do not necessarily reflect the official views and policies of the Federal Aviation Administration. This paper does not constitute a standard, specification, or regulation.

REFERENCES

Adeli, H. (2001). Neural Networks in civil engineering: 1989-2000. *Computer-Aided Civil and Infrastructure Engineering*, *16*, 126–142. doi:10.1111/0885-9507.00219

Adeli, H., & Hung, S. L. (1995). *Machine learning: neural networks, genetic algorithms, and fuzzy systems*. New York: Wiley Inc.

Ahlvin, R. G., Ulery, H. H., Hutchinson, R. L., & Rice, J. L. (1971). *Multiple-Wheel Heavy Gear Load Pavement Tests, Vol. 1: Basic Report*. Technical Report No. AFWL-TR-70-113, U.S. Army Engineer Waterways Experiment Station, Vicksburg, MI.

Barenberg, E. J., & Petros, K. A. (1991). *Evaluation of Concrete Pavements Using NDT Results*. Project IHR-512, University of Illinois at Urbana-Champaign and Illinois Department of Transportation, Report No. UILU-ENG-91-2006.

Brown, S. F., & Pappin, J. W. (1981). Analysis of pavements with granular bases. *Transportation Research Record*, *810*, 17–23.

Bush, A. J. III, & Baladi, G. Y. (1989). Nondestructive testing of pavements and backcalculation of moduli. [STP]. *ASTM Special Technical Publication*, 1026.

Ceylan, H., Tutumluer, E., Thompson, M. R., & Gomez-Ramirez, F. (2004). Neural Network-Based Structural Models for Rapid Analysis of Flexible Pavements with Unbound Aggregate Layers. *Proceedings of the 6th International Symposium on Pavements Unbound (UNBAR6)*, Nottingham, UK.

Chen, D.-H., & Hugo, F. (1998). Full-Scale Accelerated Pavement Testing of Texas Mobile Load Simulator. *Journal of Transportation Engineering*, *124*(5), 479–490. doi:10.1061/(ASCE)0733-947X(1998)124:5(479)

Crovetti, J. A. (2002). Deflection-Based Analysis Techniques for Jointed Concrete Pavement Systems. *Transportation Research Record, 1809*, 3–11. doi:10.3141/1809-01

FAA. (2004). *Use of Nondestructive Testing in the Evaluation of Airport Pavements*. FAA Advisory Circular No. 150/5730-11A, Office of Airport Safety and Standards, Federal Aviation Administration, U.S. Department of Transportation, Washington, DC.

Flintsch, G. W. (2003). Soft Computing Applications in Pavement and Infrastructure Management: State-of-the-Art. *CD-ROM Proceedings of the 2003 Annual Meeting of the Transportation Research Board*, National Research Council, Washington DC.

Foxworthy, P. T., & Darter, M. I. (1989). ILLI-SLAB and FWD Deflection Basins for Characterization of Rigid Pavements. In A. J. Bush III & Y. Baladi (Eds.), *Nondestructive Testing of Pavements and Backcalculation of Moduli*, (pp. 368-386). West Conshohocken, PA: American Society for Testing and Materials.

Garg, N., & Marsey, W. H. (2002). *Comparison Between Falling Weight Deflectometer and Static Deflection Measurements on Flexible Pavement at the National Airport Pavement Facility (NAPTF)*. CD-ROM Proceedings of the 2002 Federal Aviation Administration Airport Technology Conference, Chicago, IL.

Garg, N., Tutumluer, E., & Thompson, M. R. (1998). Structural Modeling Concepts for the Design of Airport Pavements for Heavy Aircraft. *Proceedings of the Fifth International Conference on the Bearing Capacity of Roads and Airfields*, Trondheim, Norway.

Gervais, E. L., Hayhoe, G. F., & Garg, N. (2003). Towards a permanent ACN solution for 6-wheel landing gear aircraft. *Proceedings of the 2003 ASCE Airfield Pavement Specialty Conference*, Las Vegas, NV.

Gervais, E. L., Hayhoe, G. F., & Garg, N. (2003). Towards a Permanent Solution for 6-Wheel Landing Gear Aircraft. *Proceedings of the 2003 ASCE Airfield Specialty Conference*, Las Vegas, Nevada.

Ghaboussi, J., & Sidarta, D. E. (1998). New nested adaptive neural networks (NANN) for constitutive modeling. *Computers and Geotechnics*, *22*(1), 29–52. doi:10.1016/S0266-352X(97)00034-7

Goktepe, A. B., Agar, E., & Lav, A. H. (2005). Comparison of Multilayer Perceptron and Adaptive Neuro-Fuzzy System on Backcalculating the Mechanical Properties of Flexible Pavements. *ARI: The Bulletin of the Istanbul Technical University*, *54*(3), 1–6.

Gomez-Ramirez, F. M., & Thompson, M. R. (2002). *Characterizing Aircraft Multiple Wheel Load Interaction for Airport Flexible Pavement Design*. Civil Eng Studies, COE Report, University of Illinois at Urbana-Champaign, IL.

Gopalakrishnan, K., & Thompson, M. R. (2003). Rutting Study of NAPTF Flexible Pavement Test Sections. In *Proceedings of the 2003 ASCE Airfield Specialty Conference,* Las Vegas, NV, Sep. 21-24, 2003.

Gopalakrishnan, K., & Thompson, M. R. (2004). *Backcalculation of Airport Flexible Pavement Non-Linear Moduli Using Artificial Neural Networks.* CD-ROM Proceedings of the 17th International FLAIRS Conference, FLAIRS-2004, Florida Artificial Intelligence Research Symposium, Miami Beach, FL, May 17-19, 2004.

Gopalakrishnan, K., & Thompson, M. R. (2004). Comparative Effect of B777 and B747 Trafficking on Elastic Layer Moduli of NAPTF Flexible Pavements. In *Proceedings of the 2004 FAA Worldwide Airport Technology Transfer Conference,* Atlantic City, New Jersey, April, 2004.

Gopalakrishnan, K., Thompson, M. R., & Manik, A. (2006). Rapid Finite-Element Based Airport Pavement Moduli Solutions Using Neural Networks. *Int. J. of Computational Intelligence, 3*(1), 63–71.

Gucunski, N., & Kristic, V. (1996). Backcalculation of Pavement Profiles from Spectral Analysis of Surface Waves test Using Neural Networks using Individual Receiver Spacing Approach. *Transportation Research Record, 1526,* 6–13. doi:10.3141/1526-02

Haas, R., Hudson, R. W., & Zaniewski, J. P. (1994). *Modern Pavement Management.* Malabar, FL: Krieger Publishing Co.

Hall, K. T. (1992). *Backcalculation Solutions for Concrete Pavements.* Technical Memo Prepared for SHRP Contract P-020, Long-Term Pavement Performance Data Analysis.

Hall, K. T., Darter, M. I., Hoerner, T., & Khazanovich, L. (1996). *LTPP Data Analysis – Phase I: Validation of Guidelines for K Value Selection and Concrete Pavement Performance Prediction,* Interim Report prepared for FHWA, ERES Consultants, Champaign, IL.

Hayhoe, G. F. (2002). LEAF – A new layered elastic computational program for FAA pavement design and evaluation procedures. *CD-ROM Proceedings of the 2002 Federal Aviation Administration Technology Transfer Conference,* Chicago, IL.

Haykin, S. (1994). *Neural Networks: A Comprehensive Foundation.* New York: Macmillan College Publishing Company, Inc.

Haykin, S. (1999). *Neural networks: A comprehensive foundation.* Upper Saddle River, NJ: Prentice-Hall Inc.

Hicks, R. G. (1970). *Factors Influencing the Resilient Properties of Granular Materials.* Ph. D. dissertation, University of California, Berkeley.

Hossain, S. M., & Zaniewski, J. P. (1991). Characterization of Falling Weight Deflectometer Deflection Basin. *Transportation Research Record, 1293,* 1–11.

Ioannides, A. M. (1990). Dimensional Analysis in NDT Rigid Pavement Evaluation. *ASCE J. Transp. Engrg., 116*(1), 23–36. doi:10.1061/(ASCE)0733-947X(1990)116:1(23)

Ioannides, A. M. (1994). Concrete Pavement Backcalculation Using ILLI-BACK 3.0. In A. J. Bush III & Y. Baladi (Eds.), *Nondestructive Testing of Pavements and Backcalculation of Moduli,* (Vol. 2, pp. 103-124). West Conshohocken, PA: American Society for Testing and Materials.

Ioannides, A. M., Alexander, D. R., Hammons, M. I., & Davis, C. M. (1996). Application of artificial neural networks to concrete pavement joint evaluation. *Transportation Research Record, 1540*, 56–64. doi:10.3141/1540-08

Ioannides, A. M., Barenberg, E. J., & Lary, J. A. (1989). Interpretation of Falling Weight Deflectometer Results Using Principals of Dimensional Analysis. *Proceedings of the 4th International Conference on Concrete Pavement Design and Rehabilitation*, Purdue University, West Lafayette, IN.

Johnson, A. M., & Baus, R. L. (1993). Simplified direct calculation of subgrade modulus from nondestructive pavement deflection testing. *Transportation Research Record*, (1406): 133–141.

Khazanovich, L., & Roesler, J. (1997). DIPLOBACK: A neural networks-based backcalculation program for composite pavements. *CD-ROM Proceedings of the 1997 Annual Meeting of Transportation Research Board*, Washington, DC.

Kim, Y., & Kim, Y. R. (1998). Prediction of layer moduli from FWD and surface wave measurements using artificial neural network. *CD-ROM Proceedings of the 1998 Annual Meeting of Transportation Research Board*, Washington, DC.

Maestas, J. M., & Mamlouk, M. S. (1992). Comparison of pavement deflection analysis methods using overlay design. [Washington, DC: Transportation Research Board.]. *Transportation Research Record, 1377*, 17–25.

McQueen, R. D., Marsey, W., & Arze, J. M. (2001a). Analysis of Nondestructive Data on Flexible Pavement Acquired at the National Airport Pavement Test Facility. In *Proceedings of the 2001 Airfield Pavement Specialty Conference, ASCE*, Chicago, IL.

McQueen, R. D., Marsey, W., & Arze, J. M. (2001b). Analysis of nondestructive data on flexible pavement acquired at the national airport pavement test facility. In *Proceedings of the 2001 Airfield Pavement Specialty Conference*, ASCE, Chicago, IL.

NCHRP 1-26 (1990). *Calibrated Mechanistic Structural Analysis Procedures for Pavements*. Final Report, National Cooperative Highway Research Program Project 1-26, TRB. Washington, DC: National Research Council.

Raad, L., & Figueroa, J. L. (1980). Load response of transportation support systems. *ASCE J. Transp. Engrg., 106*(TE1), 111–128.

Rada, G., & Witczak, M. W. (1981). Comprehensive Evaluation of Laboratory Resilient Moduli Results for Granular Material. *Transportation Research Record, 810*, 23–33.

Rada, G. R., Richter, C. A., & Stephanos, P. J. (1992). Layer moduli from deflection measurements: software selection and development of Strategic Highway Research Program procedure for flexible pavements. *Transportation Research Record, 1377*, 77–87.

Rauhut, B. J., & Jordahl, P. R. (1992). Variability in measured deflections and backcalculated moduli for the Strategic Highway Research Program - Southern Region. *Transportation Research Record, 1377*, 45–56.

Rix, G. J., Baker, N. C., Jacobs, L. J., Vanegas, J., & Zureick, A. H. (1995). Infrastructure Assessment, Rehabilitation, and Reconstruction. *Proceedings of ASEE-IEEE Frontiers in Education Conference*, Atlanta, GA.

Roque, R., Romero, P., Shen, X., & Ruth, B. (1992). Prediction by asphalt pavement structural layer moduli using optimized FWD configuration. *J. Assoc. Asphalt Paving Technol., 64*, 278–305.

Rumelhart, D. E., Hinton, G. E., & Williams, R. J. (1986). Learning internal representation by error propogation. D.E. Rumelhart, (ed.), *Parallel Distributed Processing*, (pp. 318-362). Cambridge, MA: MIT Press.

Smith, K. D., Wade, M. J., Peshkin, D. G., Khazanovich, L., Yu, H. T., & Dater, M. I. (1996). *Performance of Concrete Pavements, Volume II – Evaluation of In-Service Concrete Pavements*, Report No. FHWA-RD-95-110, ERES Consultants, Champaign, IL.

Stubstad, R. N., Jiang, Y. J., Celvenson, M. L., & Lukanen, E. O. (2006). *Review of the Long-Term Pavement Performance Backcalculation Results – Final Report*. Report No. FHWA-HRT-05-150, Federal Highway Administration, McLean, VA, (p. 97).

Tayabji, S. D., & Lukanen, E. O. (2000). Nondestructive Testing of Pavements and Backcalculation of Moduli [STP]. *ASTM Special Technical Publication*, 1375.

The Asphalt Institute. (1982). *Research and Development of The Asphalt Institute's Thickness Design Manual (MS-1) Ninth Edition*. Research Report No. 82-2, The Asphalt Institute, College Park, MD, USA.

Thompson, M. R. (1992). Report on the discussion group on backcalculation limitations and further improvements. [Transportation Research Board, Washington, DC.]. *Transportation Research Record*, 1377.

Thompson, M. R., & Elliott, R. P. (1985). ILLI PAVE based response algorithms for design of conventional flexible pavements. *Transportation Research Record, 1043*, 50–57.

Thompson, M. R., & Robnett, Q. L. (1979). Resilient Properties of Subgrade Soils. *Transportation Engineering Journal, 105*(1), 71–89.

Thompson, M. R., Tutumlucr, E., & Bejarano, M. (1998). *Granular Material and Soil Moduli Review of the Literature*. Final Report, Center of Excellence for Airport Pavement Research COE Report No. 1, University of Illinois at Urbana-Champaign, February.

TRB. (1999). *Use of Artificial Neural Networks in Geomechanical and Pavement Systems*. Transportation Research Circular No. E-C012, TRB. Washington, DC: National Research Council.

Tutumluer, E., Little, D. N., & Kim, S.-H. (2003). Validated Model for Predicting Field Performance of Aggregate Base Courses. *Transportation Research Record, 1837*, 41–49. doi:10.3141/1837-05

Ullidtz, P. (2000). Will nonlinear backcalculation help? *NDT of Pavements and Backcalculation of Moduli*, ASTM STP 1375, PA.

US COE. (2001). *O & M: PAVER, Asphalt Surfaced Airfields Pavement Condition Index (PCI)*. Unified Facilities Criteria (UFC). UFC 3-270-06, U.S. Army Corps of Engineers (Preparing Activity), Naval Facilities Engineering Command, Air Force Civil Engineering Support Agency.

Uzan, J. (1994). Advanced backcalculation techniques. *NDT of Pavements and Backcalculation of Moduli*, ASTM STP 1198, PA.

Xu, B., Ranjithan, S. R., & Kim, Y. R. (2001). Development of Relationships between FWD Deflections and Asphalt Pavement Layer Condition Indicators. *CD-ROM Proceedings of the 81st Annual Meeting of the Transportation Research Board*, Washington, D.C.

Chapter 8
Advances in Data Processing for Airlines Revenue Management

Félix Mora-Camino
French Civil Aviation Institute (ENAC), France

Luiz Gustavo Zelaya Cruz
Federal University of Rio de Janeiro, Brazil

ABSTRACT

In this communication advances in data processing techniques applied to Airlines Revenue Management are displayed. The general introduction presents a brief review of Airlines Revenue Management. The first of the paper introduces the problem of updating the probability distributions of demand for reservations. This updating process, facing the stochastic nature of demand for travel, is a cornerstone for the design of an efficient on-line decision support system to control the reservation process for a flight by an airline. The considered problem is formulated as a dual geometric problem to which an unconstrained non-convex, primal geometric problem is associated. A genetic algorithm optimization approach is proposed to solve the primal geometric problem, and then the classical geometric primal-dual transformations provide the solution to the initial problem. Then, the second part of the paper considers the design of a new Decision Support System for improving the reservation control process of airlines. A new recursive Dynamic Programming model for maximum expected revenue evaluation is defined, which, contrarily to other approaches, takes explicitly into account daily booking request arrivals. A practical Backward Dynamic Programming algorithm is established, leading to the design of an on-line optimisation module for Revenue Management. In this study two cases are considered. The first one considers that fare classes are not physically confined and the obtained results are extended in the second case to cover the situations where confinement of fare classes (Business Class and Economy Class) is applied.

GENERAL INTRODUCTION

During the last forty years which followed the first publications about booking control, the passenger booking systems have known a large evolution as a result of the development of computer science and telecommunications technologies on one side and of demand and decision theories on the other side. This evolution has touched not only the level of basic inventory control but also the level of higher

DOI: 10.4018/978-1-60566-800-0.ch008

strategic decision making. Revenue Management appeared as a major matter for airlines with the Airline Deregulation act of 1978 in the United States of America. Since then, it has taken an increasing importance, especially in the context of the competitive market faced by airline companies. Born as a consequence of the Airline Deregulation Act of 1978 in the USA, called in its early days *Yield Management*, nowadays known as *Revenue Management* (McGill & van Ryzin, 1999), the new management technique which has revolutionized airline industry and many other perishable-asset industries is meant to maximize revenue on a company's network of flights, by finding the optimal passenger mix for each flight, given the demand forecasts for each of the different fare products offered to customers. In other words, the reservation process has to be controlled and implemented within a complex decision support environment which should be able to make, on-line, the right decision with respect to any booking request received by the Computer Reservation System (CRS) at any point in time during the booking horizon.

Today, the huge development of new communication devices, such as the Internet, which are used by more and more potential customers, contributes to make the flight/airline choice process more efficient in the context of a quasi-perfect information situation. Under these terms, the design of new decision support systems, providing optimal seat inventory control processes with real-time capabilities, becomes unavoidable to meet the harsh competition from concurrent transporters.

The first part of the communication is devoted to the problem of updating the probability distributions of demand for reservations. In fact, when considering Airlines' Revenue Management, demand forecasting is a prerequisite to establish booking limits and overbooking levels. Before the seventieth, almost all the research in this field was focused on the subject of overbooking con-

trol, but afterwards, many research works about detailed demand forecasting techniques applied to the number and the distribution of bookings, booking cancellations, no-shows and go-shows, were developed. The forecast of air transportation demand is a very difficult task since it has to take into account a multiplicity of complex factors such as distribution of fares and routes, seasonal effects, time schedules etc.

In order to take into account the highly stochastic nature of booking requests, forecasts should be updated with the latest information available to improve the efficiency of the Revenue Management decision process.

The second part of the paper is devoted to the design of a new Decision Support System for improving the reservation control process of airlines. Many design studies for on-line Revenue Management have been performed, some of them particularly towards the implementation of the Dynamic Programming technique. Here a step further is taken in this direction, by the proposal of a new recursive model for the maximum expected revenue evaluation which, contrarily to other approaches, takes explicitly into account daily booking requests arrivals. The optimisation module of the Revenue Management System works on-line. It gathers as input all the most recent updates provided by a demand forecasting function, as well as the present state of the reservations, to proceed with an optimisation algorithm in order to treat in an efficient way new requests. The temporal (daily) dimension of the reservation process in the airline industry has to be taken into account for a realistic implementation of any optimisation method. The Dynamic Programming technique, whose theoretical foundations were established in the early fifties, is used now in air transportation field with increased efficiency. Two main reasons can be quoted for that: first, the drastic increase in computational power of recent computers; second, the development of new forecasting methods which allow to estimate more accurately the probabilistic parameters describing the booking requests arrival process, which are needed by the Dynamic Programming (DP) algorithm.

PART I: UPDATING PROBABILITY DISTRIBUTIONS ESTIMATES OF AIR TRAVEL DEMAND FOR REVENUE MANAGEMENT

Formulation of the Updating Problem

Classical probabilistic distributions, such as Poisson distribution, binomial distribution or gamma distribution and variations or combinations of them have been proposed to model the dynamic process of booking, including cancellations, no-shows and go-shows. Data available in the records of past reservations which are used to provide a basis for demand forecasts are usually biased by the existence of booking limits for each fare class: in general booking requests exceeding the limits of these fare classes, are not recorded.

Once a prior probabilistic distribution of demand along the whole booking horizon is turned available, an on line adaptation process devoted to the updating, according to current data, of the temporal probability distributions of demand, should be started. This need leads to the formulation of a recurrent optimisation problem to be solved at each time step of the booking process.

To state for a given class the corresponding optimisation problem at time step n, the following notations are adopted:

- D is the initial global demand forecast (before starting the booking process) for a given fare class;
- N is the total number of decision periods in which the duration of the booking process is divided;
- $n=1$ is the first decision period, $n=N$ is the last decision period (just before departure time);

- d_n is the real demand recorded since the beginning of the booking process until the end of the nth decision period .
- δ_n denotes the global remaining demand estimated at the end of the $(n-1)^{th}$ decision period over the next $N-n$ decision periods.
- σ_n^2 is the estimated variance of the remaining demand estimated at the end of the same period.

In the simple case where demand suffers only temporal shifts, δ_n is given by

$$\delta_n = D - d_n$$

otherwise, complex estimation techniques, including qualitative reasoning to take advantage of expert knowledge, must be used to get an updated mean value of the remaining demand δ_n as well as of its variance σ_n^2. Consistency implies that the following relations hold

$$\delta_n - \sum_{k=n}^{N} \sum_{j=0}^{J} j \cdot p_{jk}^n = 0$$

$$\sigma_n^2 + \delta_n^2 - \left(\sum_{k=n}^{N} \sum_{j=0}^{J} j^2 \cdot p_{jk}^n \right) = 0$$

In the proposed approach, the a priori distribution probabilities have to be corrected at the beginning of each decision period n, over the remaining decision periods $k = n$ to N, taking into account the most recent available information (the expressed demand as well as other newly foreseen effects) obtained during the last decision period. To update the demand probability distribution, its potential changes (between the predicted and the real recorded demand) have to be spread over the remaining decision periods to meet the new consistency conditions (2) and (3). This leads to the minimization of the *information gain* criterion given in the following expression:

$$\min \sum_{k=n}^{N} \sum_{j=0}^{J} p_{jk}^{n} \cdot \log\left(\frac{p_{jk}^{n}}{p_{jk}^{n-1}}\right)$$

which corresponds also to the maximization of a relative entropy between a measure of the distance between the $(n-1)^{\text{th}}$ and the nth demand probability distributions estimations.

Here, p_{jk}^{n-1} denotes the previous probabilities computed at the beginning of the $(n-1)^{\text{th}}$ decision period, hence available for the nth decision period and the p_{jk}^{n} are the new probabilities to be obtained from the solution of the optimization problem whose set of constraints (2)-(3) is completed by:

$$\sum_{j=0}^{J} p_{jk}^{n} = 1 \text{, for all } k=n \text{ to } N \tag{5}$$

and $p_{jk}^{n} \geq 0$ for $j = 1$ to J and $k=n$ to N (6)

AN EQUIVALENT GEOMETRIC PROGRAMMING PROBLEM

The above optimization problem can be reformulated as a dual Geometric Programming problem.

Let $x_{jk}^{n} = \dfrac{p_{jk}^{n}}{N-n}$ for $j = 1$ to J and $k=n$ to N, then the objective function (3) can be rewritten as:

$$\min \cdot \sum_{k=n}^{N} \sum_{j=0}^{J} x_{jk}^{n} \cdot \log\left(\frac{x_{jk}^{n}}{x_{jk}^{n-1}}\right) \tag{7}$$

The normality constraints (5) are equivalent to the set of constraints:

$$\sum_{k=n}^{N} \sum_{j=0}^{J} x_{jk}^{n} = 1 \tag{8}$$

and

$$\sum_{j=0}^{J} x_{j\,n+1}^{n} - \sum_{j=0}^{J} x_{jk}^{n} = 0 \text{ for all } k=n \text{ to } N. \tag{9}$$

The first consistency relation (2) can be rewritten as:

$$\sum_{k=n}^{N} \sum_{j=0}^{J} \left((N-n)j - \delta_n\right) \cdot x_{jk}^{n} = 0 \tag{10}$$

while the second consistency relation (3) can be restated as:

$$\sum_{k=n}^{N} \sum_{j=0}^{J} \left((N-n)j^2 - (\sigma_n^2 + \delta_n^2)\right) \cdot x_{jk}^{n} = 0 \tag{11}$$

with $x_{jk}^{n} \geq 0$ for $j = 1$ to J and $k=n$ to N (12)

The optimization problem (7) to (12) can be identified as a Dual Geometric Programming problem where the x_{jk}^{n} are the dual geometric variables, relation (8) is the geometric normality condition and relations (9) and (10) represent geometric orthogonality conditions while relation (12) represents the geometric positivity conditions.

To this Dual Geometric Programming problem is associated a Primal Geometric problem given by:

$\min \varphi\left(\underline{\theta}, \underline{t}\right)$ with

$$\varphi(\underline{\theta}, \underline{t}) = \sum_{j=0}^{J} p_{jn}^{n-1} \cdot \theta_1^{(N-n)j-\delta_n} \cdot \theta_2^{(N-n)j^2 - (\sigma_n^2 + \delta_n^2)} \cdot \prod_{k=1}^{N-n-1} t_k$$
$$+ \sum_{k=1}^{N-n-1} \sum_{j=0}^{J} p_{j\,n+k}^{n-1} \cdot \theta_{n+1}^{(N-n)j-\delta_n} \cdot \theta_{n+2}^{(N-n)j^2 - (\sigma_n^2 + \delta_n^2)} \cdot t_k^{-1}$$

with $(N-n+1)$ primal variables θk and tk which are such that:

$$\theta_1 > 0,\ \theta_2 > 0 \text{ and } t_k > 0, \text{ for all } \theta_1\ \theta_2\ t_k > 0$$
$$k = 1 \ldots N - n - 1 > 0,\ \theta_2 > 0 \text{ and } t_k > 0, \text{ for}$$
$$\text{all } k = 1 \ldots N - n - 1. \tag{14}$$

and with $(N-n)\cdot(J+1)$ polynomials associated to the $(N-n)\cdot(J+1)$ dual geometric variables.

Observe that the rearrangement of relation (5) into relations (8) and (9) avoids the inclusion of additional constraints into the above Primal Geometric Program. This problem, which is not analytically constrained, is in general non convex and $\varphi(\underline{\theta},\underline{t})$ may present a large number of local minimums, invalidating classical minimization techniques.

Solution of the Probability Distribution Updating Problem

Since the following conditions are in general satisfied:

$$t_k > 0 \text{ and } (N-n)J^2 > \delta_n^2 + \sigma_n^2 \text{ for } t_k > 0$$
$$(N-n)J^2 > \delta_n^2 + \sigma_n^2 \; n = 0 \dots N-1 \text{ and}$$
$$(N-n)J^2 > \delta_n^2 + \sigma_n^2 \text{ for } n = 0 \dots N-1.$$
(15)

then the solutions of the successive Primal Geometric Programs indexed by n, are contained in a compact set of $(R^*)^{N-n+1}$. Writing the first order necessary optimality conditions, we get after some treatment two sets of conditions:one with respect to $\underline{t}$:

$$t_k^* = 1 \text{ for all } k=1 \text{ to } N-n-1$$
(16)

and then one with respect to θ_1 and θ_2 :

$$\begin{cases} \sum_{j=0}^{J}((N-n)j-\delta_n)\cdot\left(\sum_{k=n}^{N}p_{jk}^{n-1}\right)\cdot(\theta_1)^{(N-n)j}\cdot(\theta_2)^{(N-n)j^2}=0 \\ \sum_{j=0}^{J}((N-n)j^2-(\sigma_n^2+\delta_n^2))\cdot\left(\sum_{k=n}^{N}p_{jk}^{n-1}\right)\cdot(\theta_1)^{(N-n)j}\cdot(\theta_2)^{(N-n)j^2}=0 \end{cases}$$
(18)

Then θ_1 and θ_2 have to be taken within the set of positive solutions of equations (18). It is

possible to reduce the order of these equations by taking:

$$X_1 = (\theta_1)^{(N-n)} \text{ and } X_1 = (\theta_1)^{(N-n)}$$
$$X_2 = (\theta_2)^{(N-n)} \text{ and } X_2 = (\theta_2)^{(N-n)}$$
(19)

to get:

$$\begin{cases} E_1(X_1,X_2)=\sum_{j=0}^{J}((N-n)j-\delta_n)\cdot\left(\sum_{k=n}^{N}p_{jk}^{n-1}\right)\cdot(X_1)^j\cdot(X_2)^{j^2}=0 \\ E_2(X_1,X_2)=\sum_{j=0}^{J}((N-n)j^2-(\sigma_n^2+\delta_n^2))\cdot\left(\sum_{k=n}^{N}p_{jk}^{n-1}\right)\cdot(X_1)^j\cdot(X_2)^{j^2}=0 \end{cases}$$
(20)

The analysis of equations $E_i(X_1,X_2)$, $i=1,2$ with the help of *Cauchy* theorem for polynomials, shows that the positive real roots of these equations stay in an open domain Δ_X which is such that:

$$X_1 > 0, \; X_1 \; X_2 > 0, \; X_2 > 0$$
(21)

$$X_1(X_2)^{J_0^i+1} < X_1(X_2)^{J_0^i+1}$$
$$(1+J_0^i)\left(\max_{j=0 to J_0^i}\{|\alpha_j^i|\}\right)/(\alpha_{J_0^i+1}^i) <$$
$$(1+J_0^i)\left(\max_{j=0 to J_0^i}\{|\alpha_j^i|\}\right)/(\alpha_{J_0^i+1}^i) \text{ for } i=1,2$$
(22)

where

$$\alpha_j^1 = ((N-n)j-\delta_n)\left(\sum_{k=n}^{N}p_{jk}^{n-1}\right)$$
$$\alpha_j^2 = ((N-n)j^2-(\delta_n^2+\sigma_n^2))\left(\sum_{k=n}^{N}p_{jk}^{n-1}\right)$$

for $j = 0$ to J
(23)

and where J_0^i is such that:

$$\alpha_{J_0^i}^i \le 0 < \alpha_{J_0^i}^i \le 0 \;\; \alpha_{J_0^i+1}^i < \alpha_{J_0^i+1}^i \text{ for } i=1,2$$
(24)

Figure 1. The performance surface of the Primal Geometric Program

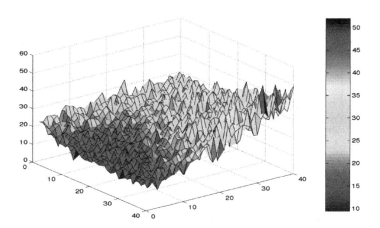

Using the non singular transformation over $(R^*)^2$ defined by relation (19), an open search domain Δ_θ can be easily defined for θ_1 and θ_2. Then many classical (gradient techniques and extensions) as well as more advanced (Genetic Algorithms) numerical techniques can be used to search for the global minimum of the following reduced minimization problem whose graphical representation is given in Figure 1:

$$\min_{\theta_1, \theta_2} \left\{ \sum_{k=0}^{N-n-1} \sum_{j=0}^{J} p_{j\,n+k}^{n-1} \cdot \theta_{n+1}^{(N-n)j-\delta_n} \cdot \theta_{n+2}^{(N-n)j^2-(\sigma_n^2+\delta_n^2)} \right\}$$

(25)

with $\left\{ \theta_1, \theta_2 \right\} \in \Delta_\theta$ (26)

where the neutral point *(1,1)* plays a central role for initialization of the search process.

Finally, the solution of the original Dual Geometric Program can be obtained using the primal-dual relationship relating primal and dual Geometric Program solutions. This leads to the expressions of the dual solution *for k = 0 to N-n-1* and *j = 0 to J*, shown in Equation (27), with $\omega_0 = \prod_{l=1}^{N-n-1} t_l^*$ and $\omega_0 = \prod_{l=1}^{N-n-1} t_l^* \; \omega_k = t_k^{*-1}$

and $\omega_k = t_k^{*-1}$ for *k = 1 to N-n-1*.

After simplification, we get the probability updating process at the beginning of the nth period:

$$p_{j(n+l)}^{n^*} = (N-n)\, \frac{p_{j(n+l)}^{n-1}\, \theta_1^{*(N-n)j}\, \theta_2^{*(N-n)j^2}}{\displaystyle\sum_{k=0}^{N-n-1} \sum_{j=0}^{J} p_{j\,n+k}^{n-1} \cdot \theta_1^{*(N-n)j}\, \theta_2^{*(N-n)j^2}}$$

for *l = 0 to N-n* and *j = 0 to J* (28)

Equation (27).

$$x_{j(n+k)}^{n^*} = (N-n) \cdot \frac{p_{j(n+k)}^{n-1}\, \theta_1^{*(N-n)j-\delta_n}\, \theta_2^{*(N-n)j^2-(\delta_n^2+\sigma_n^2)} \cdot \omega_k}{\displaystyle\sum_{j=0}^{J} p_{j(n)}^{n-1} \cdot \theta_1^{*(N-n)j-\delta_n}\, \theta_2^{*(N-n)j^2-(\delta_n^2+\sigma_n^2)} \prod_{l=1}^{N-n-1} t_l^* + \sum_{l=1}^{N-n-1} \sum_{j=0}^{J} p_{j\,n+l}^{n-1} \cdot \theta_1^{*(N-n)j-\delta_n}\, \theta_2^{*(N-n)j^2-(\delta_n^2+\sigma_n^2)} t_l^{*-1}}$$

Figure 2. The proposed structure for the dynamic RM process

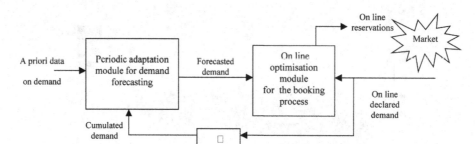

TOWARDS ON-LINE REVENUE MANAGEMENT

The above proposed approach presents two main contributions:

First, an on line probability distribution updating process is proposed so that Dynamic Programming approaches of Revenue Management Decision Making can be turned effective. Observe that this updating process could be also valuable for other fields of application related with the management of active stocks.

Second, the proposed solution approach takes advantage of an advanced Mathematical Programming technique, Geometric Programming, to include in the updating process new pieces of information and to simplify hugely the numerical difficulty of the resulting optimization problem.

Then, it is possible to propose a feedback structure such as the one displayed in figure 2 which confers to the decision system the needed reactivity.

PART II: AIRLINE RESERVATION CONTROL PROCESS USING DYNAMIC PROGRAMMING

The Probabilistic Demand Model

In this second part of the study, the whole decision period (the period during which bookings are open for a given flight) is divided in smaller decision periods (n) of duration of one day. Let I be the number of fare classes, K_i be the maximum number of demands for fare class i during decision period n. The probability $\wp^n_{i,k}$ to have during decision period n, a kth demand for fare class i is given by:

$$\wp^n_{i,k} = \left(\sum_{l=0}^{K-k} \sum_{m_1+m_2+\cdots+m_I=k+l} \prod_{i=1}^{I} p^n_{i,m_i} \right) \cdot \frac{\sum_{m=0}^{K} m \cdot p^n_{i,m}}{\sum_{i=1}^{I}\sum_{m=0}^{K} m \cdot p^n_{i,m}}$$

(29)

with $K = \sum_{i=1}^{I} K_i$.

This probability is the product between the probability to have at least k demands during decision period n and the probability to have a demand for class i.

This relation is based on the distribution of the $p^n_{i,m}$, which is the known probability to have m demands for the class i during the decision period n. This distribution can be made available by a demand forecasting module and can be updated daily, based on the latest information (newly registered bookings) available to the Revenue Management system. Based on these probabilities, in the following section a recursive model for the maximum expected revenue evaluation which takes into account daily booking requests arrivals is proposed.

The Proposed Dynamic Programming Approach

In the classical approach of dynamic programming models booking requests arrivals are treated with the following assumption: in each decision period there is *at most one booking request* and the considered length of the successive decision periods must be such that this assumption holds. This approach has been accepted until recently on theoretical grounds, but difficulties arise in the practical aspects of the decision period time length evaluation (and for the corresponding probability distributions forecasting).

Therefore, a modified dynamic backwards recursion algorithm is proposed, which treats a (more) practical aspect of the decision support system: supervising the decision making process on a daily basis, using decision periods corresponding to the natural daily time-frame of a booking process. The main idea behind this proposal is the assumption that the forecaster has a better capability to perform accurate predictions over relatively large and fixed length time intervals (i.e. 24 hours) rather than on variable decision periods.

Modelling Assumptions

- the demand probability distributions for the different fare classes are considered to be completely independent;
- only single leg flights are considered, cancellations and no-shows are not taken into account;
- go-shows are implicitly accounted for since bookings are permitted until the last moment before boarding closure; it is also implicitly considered that an estimate of the probability distributions for the "last day" demands (so, including the go-show probability distributions) are available;
- the whole capacity of the aircraft forms a pool of seats available for reservations in all the fare classes offered by the airliner

on a single leg flight (no physically confined classes);
- the dynamic booking limits (changing with time/decision period and remaining available capacity) for each fare class are made available by the solution of the expected revenue maximisation problem;
- a decision period n, $n \in \{N, N-1, ...,0\}$, lasts 24 hours (bookings by Internet can be performed at any time during the day);
- during each decision period n, a limited number of demand requests (min=0, max=K_i) for each of the fare classes, $i \in \{1, 2 ..., I\}$, can be received by the reservation system;
- a booking request can be either accepted or rejected; if rejected, it is considered lost for the company (no recapture possibility is integrated in the model, the probability of buy-up is not quantified);

Notations

- n=N denotes the "first booking day" (the first decision period) of booking process for a given scheduled flight;
- n=1 denotes the "last booking day", i.e. the day of departure, before boarding closure of a given scheduled flight;
- n=0 denotes the period following the boarding closure before the departure and during which no revenue can be achieved any more, regardless the number of seats still available. So the initial conditions for the recursive dynamic program will be indexed by n=0;

The Dynamic Programming Solution

The technique of Dynamic Programming has been established by Bellman (Bellman, 1957) to cope with sequential dynamic optimisation problems with applications in many different fields: Optimal Control (Bertsekas, 2000; Bertsekas, 2001),

Operations Research (Hillier & Lieberman, 1967; Winston, 1994), Management Sciences (Fabrycky & Torgersen, 1966). Some authors (Lee & Hersh, 1993; Subramanian, 1995; Talluri & van Ryzin, 1998) have already made use of this technique, in a limited way, as emphasised in the introduction, to cope with sequential decision process in Revenue Management.

Here a new approach for sequential decision making for airline Revenue Management, based on Dynamic Programming, is developed. The input data, as well as the decision criteria and the output of the process are described in this section.

Input data:

- the probability distribution of the $p_{i,k}^n$, where $p_{i,k}^n$ is the probability to have, during the decision period n, k booking requests for fare class i, is considered to be available;

Computed data:

- $\varphi_s^{n,k}$ = the maximum expected revenue to be obtained from the booking process when s seats are still available, when (K-k) requests have been already made during the nth decision period;

Output data:

- binary decision vectors (formed by the elements of each state: the amount of remaining available seats) for each stage (number of booking requests to come) of the decision period.

Examples of the set of binary decision vectors (1 = accept booking request, 0 = deny booking request), for one decision period (maximum number of booking requests to come, K, is 15), for an aircraft with three fare classes, are given in Figure 3 (F_1 = fare for class 1), Figure 4 (F_2 = fare for class 2) and Figure 5 (F_3 = fare for class 3), where the maximum number of seats available is 20 and $F_1 > F_2 > F_3$.

The recursive expressions of the formulation of the backward dynamic programming model are given by:

$$\phi_s^{n,k} = \left(1 - \sum_{l=0}^{K-k} \sum_{m_1+m_2+\cdots+m_I=k+l} \prod_{i=1}^{I} p_{i,m_i}^n \right) \phi_s^{n,k-1}$$

$$+ \sum_{i=1}^{I} \wp_{i,k}^n \max\left\{ F_i + \phi_{s-1}^{n,k-1}, \phi_s^{n,k-1} \right\}$$

$$\forall\, n \in \{N, N-1, ..., 1\} \text{ and } \forall\, s \in \{0, 1, ..., C\} \tag{30}$$

Figure 3. Example of binary decision vectors for fare class 1

	15	14	13	12	11	10	9	8	7	6	5	4	3	2	1	0
20:	1	1	1	1	1	1	1	1	1	1	1	1	1	1	1	0
19:	1	1	1	1	1	1	1	1	1	1	1	1	1	1	1	0
18:	1	1	1	1	1	1	1	1	1	1	1	1	1	1	1	0
17:	1	1	1	1	1	1	1	1	1	1	1	1	1	1	1	0
16:	1	1	1	1	1	1	1	1	1	1	1	1	1	1	1	0
15:	1	1	1	1	1	1	1	1	1	1	1	1	1	1	1	0
14:	1	1	1	1	1	1	1	1	1	1	1	1	1	1	1	0
13:	1	1	1	1	1	1	1	1	1	1	1	1	1	1	1	0
12:	1	1	1	1	1	1	1	1	1	1	1	1	1	1	1	0
11:	1	1	1	1	1	1	1	1	1	1	1	1	1	1	1	0
10:	1	1	1	1	1	1	1	1	1	1	1	1	1	1	1	0
9:	1	1	1	1	1	1	1	1	1	1	1	1	1	1	1	0
8:	1	1	1	1	1	1	1	1	1	1	1	1	1	1	1	0
7:	1	1	1	1	1	1	1	1	1	1	1	1	1	1	1	0
6:	1	1	1	1	1	1	1	1	1	1	1	1	1	1	1	0
5:	1	1	1	1	1	1	1	1	1	1	1	1	1	1	1	0
4:	1	1	1	1	1	1	1	1	1	1	1	1	1	1	1	0
3:	1	1	1	1	1	1	1	1	1	1	1	1	1	1	1	0
2:	1	1	1	1	1	1	1	1	1	1	1	1	1	1	1	0
1:	1	1	1	1	1	1	1	1	1	1	1	1	1	1	1	0

Figure 4. Example of binary decision vectors for fare class 2

```
           15  14  13  12  11  10   9   8   7   6   5   4   3   2   1   0
     20:    1   1   1   1   1   1   1   1   1   1   1   1   1   1   1   0
     19:    1   1   1   1   1   1   1   1   1   1   1   1   1   1   1   0
     18:    1   1   1   1   1   1   1   1   1   1   1   1   1   1   1   0
     17:    1   1   1   1   1   1   1   1   1   1   1   1   1   1   1   0
     16:    1   1   1   1   1   1   1   1   1   1   1   1   1   1   1   0
     15:    1   1   1   1   1   1   1   1   1   1   1   1   1   1   1   0
     14:    1   1   1   1   1   1   1   1   1   1   1   1   1   1   1   0
     13:    1   1   1   1   1   1   1   1   1   1   1   1   1   1   1   0
     12:    1   1   1   1   1   1   1   1   1   1   1   1   1   1   1   0
     11:    1   1   1   1   1   1   1   1   1   1   1   1   1   1   1   0
     10:    1   1   1   1   1   1   1   1   1   1   1   1   1   1   1   0
      9:    0   1   1   1   1   1   1   1   1   1   1   1   1   1   1   0
      8:    0   0   0   1   1   1   1   1   1   1   1   1   1   1   1   0
      7:    0   0   0   0   0   1   1   1   1   1   1   1   1   1   1   0
      6:    0   0   0   0   0   0   0   0   0   0   0   0   0   0   0   0
      5:    0   0   0   0   0   0   0   0   0   0   0   0   0   0   0   0
      4:    0   0   0   0   0   0   0   0   0   0   0   0   0   0   0   0
      3:    0   0   0   0   0   0   0   0   0   0   0   0   0   0   0   0
      2:    0   0   0   0   0   0   0   0   0   0   0   0   0   0   0   0
      1:    0   0   0   0   0   0   0   0   0   0   0   0   0   0   0   0
      0:    0   0   0   0   0   0   0   0   0   0   0   0   0   0   0   0
```

and

$$\phi_s^{n,0} = \phi_s^{n-1,K} \tag{31}$$

where k is the number of booking requests to the reservation system during a decision period, for all the fare classes i, with $k \in \{0, 1, ..., K\}$, and s is the number of seats still available for bookings, C being the aircraft capacity.

The decision criterion to accept or to reject an individual booking request is then given by:

$$F_i + \phi_{s-1}^{n,K-1} \geq \phi_s^{n,K-1} \tag{32}$$

In the case of group booking requests, this formula becomes:

$$q \cdot F_i + \phi_{s-q}^{n,k-q} \geq \phi_s^{n,k-q} \tag{33}$$

where q is the size of the group.

The initial conditions to compute the maximum expected revenue are such as:

$$\phi_s^{0,k} = 0 \quad , k \in \{1, ..., K\} \text{ and } s \in \{0, 1, ..., C\} \tag{34}$$

Case of Physically Confined Classes

The above approach is extended here to the case where the aircraft cabin is divided in two different spaces: Business Class and Economy Class spaces.

Additional Assumptions

The assumptions made in Section 3 are maintained here and additional ones are necessary:

- a booking request for a seat in the Business Class can be either accepted, if there are seats available in the Business Class, or rejected (a business passenger cannot be accommodated on an economy seat – a lower standing)
- a booking request for a seat in the Economy Class can be accepted in the Economy Class, if there are seats available and can be also accepted in the Business Class if there are seats available in this class and no seats available in the Economy Class, or rejected (an economy passenger can be accommodated on a business seat – a higher standing)

Figure 5. Example of binary decision vectors for fare class 3

	15	14	13	12	11	10	9	8	7	6	5	4	3	2	1	0
20:	1	1	1	1	1	1	1	1	1	1	1	1	1	1	1	0
19:	1	1	1	1	1	1	1	1	1	1	1	1	1	1	1	0
18:	1	1	1	1	1	1	1	1	1	1	1	1	1	1	1	0
17:	1	1	1	1	1	1	1	1	1	1	1	1	1	1	1	0
16:	1	1	1	1	1	1	1	1	1	1	1	1	1	1	1	0
15:	1	1	1	1	1	1	1	1	1	1	1	1	1	1	1	0
14:	0	1	1	1	1	1	1	1	1	1	1	1	1	1	1	0
13:	0	0	0	1	1	1	1	1	1	1	1	1	1	1	1	0
12:	0	0	0	0	1	1	1	1	1	1	1	1	1	1	1	0
11:	0	0	0	0	0	0	1	1	1	1	1	1	1	1	1	0
10:	0	0	0	0	0	0	0	0	0	0	0	0	0	0	0	0
9:	0	0	0	0	0	0	0	0	0	0	0	0	0	0	0	0
8:	0	0	0	0	0	0	0	0	0	0	0	0	0	0	0	0
7:	0	0	0	0	0	0	0	0	0	0	0	0	0	0	0	0
6:	0	0	0	0	0	0	0	0	0	0	0	0	0	0	0	0
5:	0	0	0	0	0	0	0	0	0	0	0	0	0	0	0	0
4:	0	0	0	0	0	0	0	0	0	0	0	0	0	0	0	0
3:	0	0	0	0	0	0	0	0	0	0	0	0	0	0	0	0
2:	0	0	0	0	0	0	0	0	0	0	0	0	0	0	0	0
1:	0	0	0	0	0	0	0	0	0	0	0	0	0	0	0	0

Additional Notations

- the Business Class has a total capacity of C_b seats;
- σ is the number of seats still available for booking in Business Class;
- the Economy Class has a total capacity of C_e seats;
- s is the number of seats still available for booking in Economy Class;
- the total capacity of the aircraft is $C = C_b + C_e$;
- the business fare classes are denoted by i, $i \in \{1, 2, ..., I_b\}$;
- the maximum number of booking requests that can arrive in Business Class during one decision period is given by:

$$K_b = \sum_{i=1}^{I_b} K_i \qquad (35)$$

- the economy fare classes are denoted by i, $i \in \{I_b+1, I_b+2, ..., I_b+I_e\}$;
- the maximum number of booking requests that can arrive in Economy Class during one decision period is given by:

$$K_e = \sum_{i=I_b+1}^{I_b+I_e} K_i \qquad (36)$$

- in total, there are $I = I_b + I_e$ fare classes offered on the aircraft.

The formulation of a decision process based on Dynamic Programming for booking control is in this case more complex, since passengers can be assigned to two different pulls of seats.

Let $\varphi_{s,\sigma}^{n,k,j}$ be the maximum expected revenue when s seats are still available in the Economy Class, σ seats are still available in the Business Class, when $(K_e - k)$ Economy Class booking requests and $(K_b - j)$ Business Class booking requests have been already made during the nth decision period.

The recursive expressions of the formulation of the backward dynamic program in this second case are given by:

$$\phi_{s,\sigma}^{n,k,j} = \left(1 - \sum_{l=0}^{K_e-k} \sum_{m_{I_b+1}+\cdots+m_{I_b+I_e}=k+l} \prod_{i=1}^{I_b+I_e} p_{i,m_i}^n \right)$$
$$\left(1 - \sum_{d=0}^{K_b-j} \sum_{m_1+\cdots+m_{I_b}=j+d} \prod_{i=1}^{I_b} p_{i,m_i}^n \right) \phi_{s,\sigma}^{n,k-1,j-1}$$
$$+ \sum_{i=I_b+1}^{I_b+I_e} \wp_{i,k+j}^n \max\left\{ F_i + \phi_{s-1,\sigma}^{n,k-1,j}, F_i + \phi_{s,\sigma-1}^{n,k-1,j}, \phi_{s,\sigma}^{n,k-1,j} \right\}$$

$$+\sum_{i=1}^{I_b} \wp_{i,k+j}^n \max\left\{F_i + \phi_{s,\sigma-1}^{n,k,j-1}, \phi_{s,\sigma}^{n,k,j-1}\right\}$$

$\forall\, n \in \{N, N\text{-}1, ..., 1\}, \forall\, s \in \{0, 1, ..., C_e\}, \forall$
$\sigma \in \{0, 1, ..., C_b\},$

$\forall\, k \in \{1, 2 ..., K_e\}, \forall\, j \in \{1, 2, ..., K_b\}$ (37)

and

$$\phi_{s,\sigma}^{n,0,0} = \phi_{s,\sigma}^{n-1,K_e,K_b} \tag{38}$$

The initial conditions, as in the previous case, are such as:

$$\phi_{s,\sigma}^{0,k,j} = 0 \tag{39}$$

For a booking request in the Economy Class, two cases must be now analysed:

- if there are still some seats available in the Economy Class, the accepting condition established in the previous section can be adapted for the pull of seats of the Economy Class (inequality 10); the $(K_e\text{-}k+1)^{\text{th}}$ booking request becomes an Economy Class reservation if:

$$F_i + \phi_{s-1,\sigma}^{n,k-1,j} \geq \phi_{s,\sigma}^{n,k-1,j} \tag{40}$$

- to cope with the case where all the seats of the Economy Class are already booked while seats remain available in the Business Class, the accepting condition for an Economy Passenger on a Business Seat can be adapted (inequality 11); then, the $(K_e\text{-}k+1)^{\text{th}}$ booking request becomes an Economy Class reservation if:

$$F_i + \phi_{s,\sigma-1}^{n,k-1,j} \geq \phi_{s,\sigma}^{n,k-1,j} \tag{41}$$

For a booking request in the Business Class, there is only one case that must be analysed, since these booking requests cannot be accommodated

elsewhere than in the pull of seats of the Business Class. If there are still some seats available in this class, the accepting condition established in the previous section can be adapted also for the pull of seats of the Business Class (inequality 12). The $(K_b\text{-}j+1)^{\text{th}}$ booking request becomes a Business Class reservation if:

$$F_i + \phi_{s,\sigma-1}^{n,k,j-1} \geq \phi_{s,\sigma}^{n,k,j-1} \tag{42}$$

Otherwise, booking requests (either in Economy Class of Business Class) which cannot be satisfied by applying these conditions will be denied.

Figure 6 compares, for a given case, the results obtained using the proposed dynamic programming approach with a first come first served policy.

GENERAL CONCLUSION

In this communication two advanced data processing techniques, Geometric Programming and Dynamic Programming, both based on the optimization concept, have been introduced to propose a reactive revenue management decision system. The new approach which has been proposed, based on Dynamic Programming, establishes an optimal airline booking control process. The proposed approach presents characteristics which turn it of real interest for practical utilisation by airlines. It is clear that the performance of the proposed control process depends on the quality of the available estimations of demand distributions. However, the recursiveness of the optimization method makes it fully compatible with the proposed on-line demand updating process, based on Geometric Programming, which takes into account the newest available information.

Figure 6. Comparison of performances using dynamic programming and FCFS policies

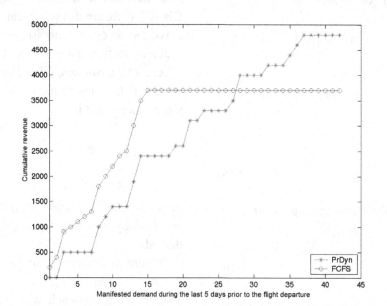

REFERENCES

Bellman, R. (1957). *Applied Dynamic Programming*. Princeton, NJ: Princeton University Press.

Bertsekas, D. P. (2000). *Dynamic Programming and Optimal Control,* (Vol. I, 2nd Ed.). Belmont, MA: Athena Scientific.

Bertsekas, D. P. (2001). *Dynamic Programming and Optimal Control,* (Vol. II, 2nd Ed.). Belmont, MA: Athena Scientific.

Bilegan, I. C. (2003). *Contribution à la conception de systèmes réactifs d'aide à la décision pour maximiser les recettes d'une compagnie aérienne*. PhD Thesis, Polytechnic National Institute in Toulouse and LARA/ENAC.

Bilegan, I. C., El Moudani, W., Achaibou, A., & Mora-Camino, F. (2001). A new approach to update probability distributions estimates of air travel demand. *Smart Engineering System Design*, *11*, 853–856.

Fabrycky, W. J., & Torgersen, P. E. (1966). *Operations Economy – Industrial Applications of Operations Research*. Englewood Cliffs, NJ: Prentice-Hall, Inc.

Goldberg, D.E. *Genetic Algorithms in Search, Optimization and Machine Learning*. Reading, MA: Addison-Wesley.

Hillier, F. S., & Lieberman, G. J. (1967). *Introduction to Operations Research*. San Francisco: Holden-Day, Inc.

Lee, T. C., & Hersh, M. (1993). A Model for Dynamic Airline Seat Inventory Control with Multiple Seat Bookings. *Transportation Science*, *27*, 252–265. doi:10.1287/trsc.27.3.252

McGill, J. I., & van Ryzin, G. J. (1999). Revenue Management: Research Overview and Prospects. *Transportation Science*, *33*(2), 233–256. doi:10.1287/trsc.33.2.233

Mora-Camino, F. (1978). *Introduction à la Programmation Géométrique*. Rio de Janeiro, Brazil: COPPE Edition.

Subramanian, J. (1995) *Airline Yield Management and Computer Memory Management via Dynamic Programming*. Ph.D. Dissertation, University of North Carolina, Dept. of Operations Research, Chapel Hill, NC.

Talluri, K., & van Ryzin, G. J. (1998). An Analysis of Bid-Price Controls for Network Revenue Management. *Management Science*, *44*, 1577–1593. doi:10.1287/mnsc.44.11.1577

Winston, W. L. (1994). *Operations Research – Applications and Algorithms,* (3rd Ed). Belmont, CA: Duxbury Press.

Chapter 9
Commercial Aircraft:
A Holistic and Integrated Model of the Flux of Information Regarding the Operational Support

José Lourenço da Saúde
State University of Beira Interior, Covilhã, Portugal

Jorge Miguel Reis Silva
State University of Beira Interior, Covilhã, Portugal

ABSTRACT

The Air Transportation is the type of activity that exhibits significant complexity mainly due to the fact that to take place a great number of interlinked services need to be made available, ranging from air traffic control and management to ground services as well as to maintenance. In this respect, the utilization of software is permanent, allowing the operators to perform, among various aspects, the relevant operational support of commercial aircraft essentially oriented to aircraft maintenance or in other words compliance with the applicable Continued Airworthiness Instructions. Despite the fact much commercial software is available, little literature exists describing conceptually the whole process. Starting from situation, this book chapter provides the reader and those involved in the development of software for aircraft support the structure and the type of information related thereto.

INTRODUCTION: OVERVIEW ON THE AIR TRANSPORTATION

Air Transport is commonly used by all categories and types of business. However it became particularly important for those categories engaged in what Button and Taylor (2000) call new economy activities, e.g., business categories requiring for those companies involved easy inter-personal contacts

only possible with high-quality transport services[1]. In this respect, those authors listed 125 activities that were organized into 11 groups:

The evaluation of the impact in the economy of those 11 groups of activities is not an easy task, (Harmatuck, 1996; Barros, 2008; Halpern and Pagliary, 2008; Tapiador *et al*, 2008) mainly for two reasons: services themselves may interact in several combinations, and territories themselves may react in several ways too according to its own endogenous characteristics, (Cole, 1998). Button

DOI: 10.4018/978-1-60566-800-0.ch009

Table. 1

• IT Software; • IT Services; • Telecom Services; • Advanced Materials; • Aerospace; • Biotechnology;	• Energy and Environment; • Electronics; • Transportation; • Management and Services; and • Technology Industrial Manufacturing.

and Taylor (2000) consider these *spatial* and *non-spatial* impacts in terms of four domains:

- Primary effects: direct and immediate benefits to a region for the creation of services and / or the expansion of others existing. The gains to the local economy are of short term and usually limited in their order of magnitude;
- Secondary effects: these are long term impacts. They are usually linked to local economic benefits of the air service operations mainly due to the employment involved in aircraft ground operations, such as, passengers, cargo and catering. The size of the secondary effects over the territories depends upon airport operations volume and nature;
- Tertiary effects: impacts over the local economy as the result of the air transport services available to individuals and companies;
- Perpetuity effects: these are the type of impacts assumed as being related with infra-structures, like concluded by Aschauer (1989, 1990)[2] who underlines that there are empirical evidences that infrastructure investment have an impact itself into the regional economy, by raising the activity level and stimulating the productivity, thus acting as a catalyst for higher economic growth.

In this respect, more recently despite the specific objectives and characteristics under which Low Cost Airlines (LCA) operate, they also became an

additional factor of economic and social progress for the Air Transportation mainly impacting regional airports and under utilised infra-structures most of them located in the suburban areas outside of large cities (see figure 1).

Given this multi-impact in the local and global economy, from a more specialised and detailed perspective, the Air Transportation involves a number of activities such as:

- Air Traffic Control/Management;
- Ground operations involving crews and passenger assistance, check in, load and unload aircraft;
- Aircraft servicing including loading, unloading and refuelling;
- Fleet management;
- Aircraft Operations Planning;
- Aircraft dispatch services;
- Flight crew management;
- Security services;
- Fire brigade services;
- Training services;
- Aircraft maintenance.

Parallel to the impact in the society and activities, specific organisations have also contribution to the Air Transportation influencing it direct or indirectly.

Those organisations include the civil National and International Aviation Authorities, such as, FAA and EASA, as well as civil International Aviation Associations/Organisations like ATA, IATA, ICAO and Eurocontrol. All of them share a common aspect, that is, they define rules and standards.

Figure 1. LCA general characteristics. Source: Adapted from York Aviation LLP (2007)

Features	Benefits
Direct (usually via Internet) ticket sales and no sales (directly) via travel agents	Direct relationship with customer, and reduced sales cost
Extras charged separately	Cost and price transparency (as reduced hold baggage and associated costs), and additional revenue (enabling lower fares)
Few or no on board frills	Reduced cost of on board services
Highly incentivised workforce	Higher employee productivity levels
Modern aircraft fleet usually with a single aircraft type	Lower aircraft maintenance and crew training costs, fuel efficiency, and better crew utilisation
Point to point services	Reduced complexity (no transfers)
Short turnaround times	Higher aircraft fleet utilisation
Simple ground facilities	No requirements for cost of premium terminal facilities (as air bridges)
Single class cabin	Reduced cabin crew costs, and higher seat density
Strong load factor management	Better fleet utilisation, and higher ancillary revenue
Use of secondary/regional airports	Lower airport charges, and less congestion in the air and on the ground

In the case of the Aviation Authorities the regulations have a legal configuration bonding the air transport stakeholders to the applicable laws, covering, among various aspects the aircraft maintenance and operation as well as crew and mechanics licensing.

The key role of these Aviation Authorities is inevitably the power to control and permit the air transportation to take place under strict airworthiness and safety procedures.

Likewise, the main purpose of the civil International Aviation Associations/Organisations is aimed to promoting safe, regular and economic air transport for the benefit of peoples of the world, as well as achieving recognition of the importance of a healthy Air transport Industry to worldwide, social and economical development, with high quality value for money and an industry providing products and services that meet the needs of the customers.

Finally, also important are the Aircraft and System Manufacturers, known as OEM.

These stakeholders of the Air Transportation play a major role by providing and maintaining the set of instructions for Continued Airworthiness enabling the operators to use the various airplanes.

Pursuant to Camelier *et al* (2008) this spectrum of activities associated with the Air Transportation can be expressed in a holistic manner as described in figure 2.

In the above picture the Air Transportation is organized under four components, that is, the Exploitation, the Operational Support and two Metasystems, i.e., the Context and the Enterprise.

The Exploitation is in fact the core of the Air Transportation, that provides development and the various types of impact above referred, represents the Operations or in practical terms the activity of regular flights or charters of passenger transportation or cargo, or a combination of both performed by airlines and airfreight carriers including Low Cost carriers.

Figure 2. Air transportation holistic structure – adapted from Camelier et al (2008)

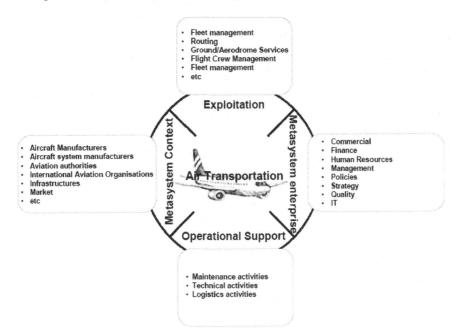

The lower element of the above concept includes the Operational Support. This component of the Air Transportation is crucial in the sense it encompasses on and off-aircraft support.

The main objective of this element is to ensure that the aircraft are airworthy and safe to fly.

The lateral elements of the holistic concept include two Metasystems, representing the Enterprise and the Context.

The meta-system Enterprise is the system in which the Air Transportation is residing. As such, this meta-system is important and includes the typical functions that can be observed in an organization/company, e.g., Finance, Commercial, Human Resources, Management, Quality, IT, Policies, etc..

The meta-system Context is the "external" element where the Air Transportation is evolving and where the various organisations (Aviation Authorities, International Associations and OEM) exist and interface with it. It is also the zone where we can find the global market.

THE COMMERCIAL AIRCRAFT OPERATIONAL SUPPORT

Mainly associated with the Secondary Effect above defined, among the various components of the holistic model used by this chapter to describe the Air Transportation, the Operational Support has been and will undoubtly continue to be a critical element, given the fact it is centred in ensuring aircraft airworthiness the safety, which are permanent concern of all those involved in the business, namely, Aircraft Operators and MRO companies, etc.

This type of support which tends to be related with aircraft maintenance, most of the times is approached under certain philosophies, such as, reliability-centred, human-centred, which in essence reflect specific management orientations valid for a certain period of time.

The reason to see maintenance as a synonym of support comes from the fact, that regardless the fleet size of an aircraft Operator, in order to maintain valid the respective *Air Operators Cer-*

tificate (in Europe) or the *Air Carrier Operating Certificate (in the USA)* that allows to perform the relevant air transport activities, a number of tasks have to be performed mainly aimed to ensure compliance with what it is formally known as the Continued Airworthiness Instructions.

This is in line with the aeronautical regulations (EASA PART M), (EASA PART 145), (FAA PART 145) (EASA OPS – ex JAR OPS) where 'Continuing Airworthiness' "*means all of the processes ensuring that, at any time in its operating life, the aircraft complies with the airworthiness requirements in force and is in a condition for safe operation*".

Such Continued Airworthiness Instructions are developed and maintained by the aircraft Manufacturer who submits them to the relevant Aviation Authority (e.g., FAA, EASA) at the time of aircraft certification in order to obtain the desired Type Certificate for a specific airplane - see EASA CS 25 for more details on this methodology, namely its Appendix H.

As prescribed in the aeronautical regulations codes, such as by the FAA PART 25 or by EASA CS 25, the Continued Airworthiness Instructions coincide with a number of aircraft publications that are prepared and kept duly updated by the Aircraft Manufacturer and made available to the Operators, thus enabling them to operate and maintain airworthy the airplanes. Those elements are in facts manuals, being among others at least:

- The Maintenance Manual;
- The Flight Manual;
- NDI manuals (X-rays, Ultrasonic, etc.);
- Manuals on Corrosion (Control and Prevention).

In this respect a number of publications from various authors exist, such as from King (1986) Hessburg (2000), Kinisson (2004), giving the reader a good insight about maintenance from an aircraft OEM perspective as well as from an MRO center.

Also other types of work have been done in specific domains of the aircraft support more specifically oriented to certain maintenance aspects like: Fisher (1983) who generated a mathematical model able to manage aircraft robbing (spares and rotables); Satishan (1989) who studied flight safety issues and their impact on maintenance indicators; Gopalan (1998) that developed a polynomial algorithm to optimise daily routing of aircraft to ensure that a certain aircraft maintenance center would be reached at the right moment (to allow aircraft to schedule maintenance); Mirghani (1996) who has studied costing elements associated with aircraft maintenance; Atkins (1998) that has identified various informational variables related to management of aeronautical systems; Iyer (1999) who has simulated the impact on the life cycle of aircraft as the result of certain maintenance factors, e.g., human resources, management policies; Adbdulkadir (2001) that minimized maintenance operational costs and their relation with the definition of aircraft maintenance routes towards MRO centres; Plumpton (2002) who analyzed the organizational aspects of the maintenance activities related to unscheduled tasks to improve competitive advantages; Samaranayake (2002) that has developed organization methodologies related to aircraft scheduled maintenance; finally, Garcia-Formieles (2003) that developed a heuristic work breakdown structure (WBS) to manage major aircraft modification.

Pursuant to the above situation, despite the fact aircraft publications exist enabling Operators to comply with Continued Airworthiness Instructions, there is still a need to have a management and holistic perspective regarding maintenance or in global terms the air transportation support.

THE NEED FOR SOFTWARE IN THE AIR TRANSPORTATION BUSINESS

Given the complexity of the Air Transportation above depicted in the holistic model, the software has becoming and is nowadays an important tool assisting many activities of the relevant stakeholders.

The software is present in almost all domains, ranging from ATC to ticket sales to passenger seat reservation including aircraft maintenance management and execution as well as fleet management.

The Air Transportation Operators, depending on their size of business, exercise option in terms of buying commercial software or create their own programmes, where the most complete packages are represented by ERP solutions which tend to cover *inter alia* finance, business planning, aircraft maintenance, logistics, quality, production and planning, fleet management, etc..

In terms of aircraft support namely for maintenance, a significant number of commercial products exist being made by Airlines and by software houses. Such type of software for airplane support includes at least the following capacities:

- aircraft configuration management;
- management of technical publications;
- planning of maintenance activities;
- modification embodiment;
- spares inventory control;
- reliability;
- management of Airworthiness Directives (AD) and other aviation regulations.

In this scenario of global market of aircraft support, it is indispensable to have reliable software products and if possible certified by aviation authorities.

This is for sure an important goal to be reached by anyone developing aircraft support-maintenance software instead on relying on products that do not hold any airworthiness certificate issued by an aviation authority.

Such type of software exists either developed by airlines, that made it available to the open market for other operators who take advantage of the developer's experience, or it is made by specific software houses.

However, there is no formal framework or regulation defining the criteria under which such type of software is to be developed; in terms of the requirements it should comply with or even the functionalities it should have thus enabling the Users to perform the relevant support activities.

This does not mean that the existent software is underdeveloped and/or has reduced quality. On the contrary, given the fact it is used by airlines and MRO which need to ensure at all time compliance with airworthiness regulations and thus maintain valid the applicable OAC, there is no option left in terms of using effective software. Otherwise the relevant business and/or flight safety could be put in cause.

Pursuant to this, and following Camelier *et al* (2008) work, which provides an integrated and detailed perspective about the support to commercial aircraft, this chapter offers to those involved in the design and development of such type of software, an important and complementary aspect, that is the Flux of Information among the various components of airplane operational support, under a specific model.

Moreover, the availability of that Flux of Information can also be seen as reference tool in terms of defining the activities and the various interdependencies among the aircraft support tasks or functionalities.

The background to this Flux of Information structure is in fact a consequence of the mentioned research project whose main objective was to develop, from a management perspective a sustainment model applicable to commercial aircraft[3].

COMMERCIAL AIRCRAFT OPERATIONAL SUPPORT COMPONENTS - MODEL

Understanding the aircraft support is essential to comprehend the Flux of Information namely its origin and how it combines with it.

Figure 3. Systemic model of commercial aircraft support

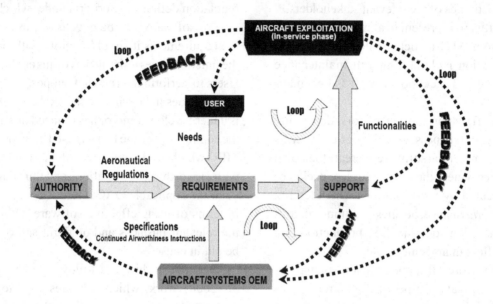

Generally speaking, the complexity of aircraft support software is two fold: it needs to cover all support components and it manages the immensity of data exchanged in the associated process.

In general terms the aircraft support can be defined as encompassing the following characteristics:

- has a systemic structure;
- includes a life cycle support;
- can be organised through a support breakdown structure.

The next paragraphs briefly describe these three elements of the aircraft support.

The Systemic Model of the Commercial Aircraft Support Structure

Figure 3 exhibits graphically the systemic model established to represent the support of commercial aircraft - see Camelier *et al* (2008). The systemic structure follows Senge (1990) approach, being

one of the main aspect the reinforcement (solid arrows) and the feedback lines (dotted arrows) involving the various Stakeholders related with the process, that is, the User (Operator), the Aviation Authority and the Aircraft OEM.

In general terms, the systemic model represents the way the aircraft support operates.

The element that triggers the whole mechanism is in fact the User, because he is the one that holds capacity upon the whole process.

The User establishes the requirements of the support taking in consideration his own needs but also the Aeronautical Regulations and the Continued Airworthiness Instructions prescribed by the OEM associated with the aircraft to be operated.

Once established the requirement of the aircraft support then the support is made available to aircraft exploitation through a number of functionalities. The support can be performed either by the User or by a third Party (a maintenance centre, known as MRO – Maintenance Repair and Overhaul).

This initial part of the systemic loop is closed by the dotted arrows that represent feedback informa-

Figure 4. Commercial aircraft support life cycle

Aircraft Support Life Cycle		
Phase In	**In Service Phase**	**Phase Out**

tion from operation. From exploitation important data (flying hours, cycles, malfunctions, incidents, etc.) is provided to the major Stakeholders, that is, to the Aviation Authority, to the User, to the OEM and to the Support itself.

This systemic model is made alive in accordance with the aircraft life cycle requirements that are discussed in the next paragraphs.

The Commercial Aircraft Support Life Cycle

The next element of the Operation Support model is the Life Cycle, an aspect that is also prescribed by ISO 15288.

From Senge (1990) associated with a systemic approach there is a Life Cycle. In this case, the aircraft support has a configuration represented in figure 4.

Such support Life Cycle, which may last up 30 years or more, has a simple configuration with three basic stages whose terminology is known in aeronautics, that is, Phase in, In service and Phase out.

"Phase in" represents the initial part of the whole process; varies from 1 to 3 years, depending on the type and the size of the fleet to integrate in the User.

The "In service" stage is the core of the whole process and accounts for 95% or more of the whole period.

"Phase out" has no predefined duration because that depends on the work to be done on the aircraft prior ending its exploitation. Most of the time, Phase Out includes modifications (cargo door, new painting, aircraft interior refurbishing/modification, etc.) when the aircraft to

phased out are to be returned to the Lesser under a predefined contractual configuration or when they are sold to a certain Operator that requires a specific configuration.

The Commercial Aircraft Operational Breakdown Support Structure

For the sake of completeness, it is provided to the reader a brief description of the Aircraft Operational Support Model. Details of such information on the aircraft support structure can be obtained in Camelier *et al* (2008).

The Commercial Aircraft Operational Breakdown Support Structure has a tree-type structure as observed in the Systems Engineering concept like described in NASA SP-610S (1995), a good example of how the development of systems can be adequately structured.

Figure 5 exhibits the cascade of the aircraft structure, which is line with the Commercial Aircraft Life Cycle, that is, it includes the 3 basic stages, Phase-in, In-service and Phase-out complemented by Management by an ad hoc stage Modifications/upgrade – Mod/Upd.

The above cascade has a top-down configuration where Management is included to ensure coherence with the whole breakdown structure and is in accordance with the model prescribed by Camelier *et al* (2008). The next section briefly describes each support element (a support functionality) of the above tree.

Phase In

It is an item dedicated to allow the setting up the support of aircraft and thus obtain from the

Figure 5. Aircraft breakdown support structure, based on Camelier et al (2008)

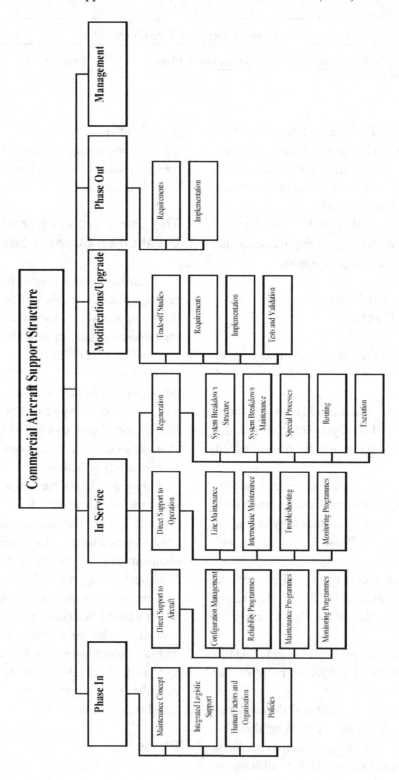

aeronautical authority permission to Operate. This goal is achieved by receiving from the Aviation Authority the relevant AOC and the indispensable maintenance rating related with the aircraft (to be) operated.

It includes 5 elements, that is: Maintenance Concept, Integrated Logistic Support, Human Factors and Organisation, Aircraft Certification Programme and Policies.

These five sub-elements exist to ensure the following set of activities:

- Maintenance Concept: ensures adjustment of the aircraft maintenance programme originally established by its manufacturer (the OEM and owner of the type certificate) thus enabling to prepare the aircraft maintenance programme to be submitted to the Aeronautical Authority for approval;
- Integrated Logistic Support: provides implementation of Infra-structures, Technical Publications, Equipment (Ground Support Equipment – GSE), Materials and qualified Human Resources essential to allow during the in-service phase performance of the Continued Airworthiness Instructions;
- Human factors and organisation: allows definition of organisation according to operational needs taking also into account human factors related to maintenance activities;
- Maintenance Programme Certification: encompasses the formal process to obtain from the relevant Aeronautical Authority approval for the maintenance programmes to enable aircraft operation;
- Policies: includes, in addition to the compulsory policies defined by the aeronautical regulations (namely Quality and Safety), definition of specific rules in terms of support, namely, logistics, maintenance and engineering related with support.

In Service Phase

Direct Support to Aircraft

This element includes off-aircraft tasks being organised in 4 levels whose scope is as follows:

- Configuration Management: controls the functional and physical configuration of the aircraft and of the associated systems to ensure aircraft airworthiness;
- Reliability programmes: organises and manages systems reliability data associated with operation to ensure compliance with the approved maintenance programmes and also control the efficiency of exploitation (readiness, costs, etc.);
- Maintenance Programmes: defines and schedules the implementation of aircraft maintenance programmes to ensure compliance with the Continued Airworthiness Instructions taking in consideration the aircraft exploitation needs;
- Monitoring Programmes: defines and manages the implementation of specific control activities related with specific needs, such as, MEL, engine trend Monitoring, vibrations.

Direct Support to Operations

It makes available on-aircraft tasks as follows:

- Line maintenance: encompasses Continued Airworthiness Instructions covering day-to-day activities, namely, pre and post flight maintenance inspections;
- Intermediate maintenance: performs the Continued Airworthiness Instructions that exceed line maintenance, e.g., embodiment of modifications, specific inspections and repairs, LRU, etc.;
- Troubleshooting: carries on problem identification and resolution associated with aircraft day-to-day operation;

- Monitoring: makes operational the monitoring activity.

Regeneration

This aircraft support element includes preparation and performance of the Base Maintenance related with airframe (other systems tend to be processed by third parties namely engines, landing gear, avionics and other accessories):

- Systems Structure - Engineering: organises, builds up and maintains the system breakdown structure (equivalent to the Product Breakdown Structure) in order to control configuration and allow description of the work including definition of the Bill of Material (BOM);
- Systems Structure - Maintenance: defines, organises and implements the operative structure associated with the base maintenance;
- Special Processes – item oriented to ensure quality certification, structures, manages and certifies the various special processes (e.g., electrolytic processes, painting, heat treatment) associated with maintenance;
- Routing – defines, structures and prepares all paper work indispensable to carry on the maintenance tasks;
- Execution – manages and performs the base maintenance activities.

Modifications/Upgrade

Like previously stated, it is an *ad hoc* item[4] covering the modifications/upgrade of aircraft that exceed the Continued Airworthiness Instructions prescribed by the aircraft OEM.

It is defined as including the following activities as a minimum:

- Trade off studies – defines, plans and performs alternative solutions and final solution;

- Requirements of the modification/upgrade: defines and establishes the specific conditions (technical, layout, systems, etc.) to be followed in carrying on the modification/upgrade process;
- Modification/upgrade programme: includes definition, planning, organisation, control, administration and implementation of the modification/upgrade tasks;
- Tests and validation: comprises definition, planning, organisation, control, administration and implementation to verify the conformity of the aircraft modification/upgrade in order to obtain the applicable certification;
- Certification: covers the submission of the necessary documentation to obtain the certification from the relevant aeronautical authority.

Phase Out

This support element covers the activities inherent to the last period of the operation cycle. It can be divided in the following manner:

- Requirements: covers the definition of the specific conditions under which the Phase Out is to be performed;
- Implementation: includes planning, control and execution of the Phase Out.

COMMERCIAL AIRCRAFT OPERATIONAL SUPPORT – FLUX OF INFORMATION

Background

As previously referred in this book chapter, the commercial aircraft support requires an intense utilization of software, mainly assisting the maintenance activities as well as all associated tasks, which in essence exist to ensure that the relevant

Figure 6. Distribution of the inquiry by world regions - see Camelier et al (2008)

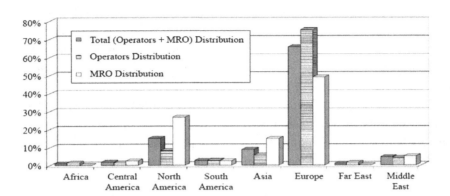

aircraft complies with the applicable Continued Airworthiness Instructions.

Notwithstanding the existence in the market of dedicated software, whose quality is obviously unquestionable, it makes sense to make available to Operators and to Software houses not only a support model (see figure 5 and associated description) covering what can be called the Support Functionalities but also the Flux of Information which is the backbone of all Support processes.

The Flux of Information can be seen as reference instrument but also, due to its holistic nature, allows the management and the various responsibles and organizations to integrate all elements and have a global perspective, essential to conduct a good, realistic and efficient management exercise.

The development of the Flux of Information was the result of a worldwide field survey conducted to capture heuristically aircraft support management practices including the associated activities.

The inquiry was sent to 114 companies from all over the world, directly addressed to senior managers responsible for aircraft operations or technical departments. Figure 6 depicts the worldwide by regions to which the inquiry was sent.

The actual results of the mentioned global inquiry involved collaboration of 21 regional, major national and private airlines and mainte-

nance centers (MRO) from Europe to America including from Middle and Far East as well as from Oceania – see Camelier *et al* (2008).

Starting from aforesaid field survey, a model was derived to establishing the commercial aircraft breakdown structure (described in section 4 above) and the flux of information exchanged between the various support elements. The result of that work was assessed by four national European airlines that provided important guidance elements for the formulation of the Aircraft Commercial Support Structure and the Flux of Information.

The questions associated with the field survey were defined using a System Engineering approach. As such, it was used information and method from specific publications, namely, NASA SP-610S and INCOSE-TP-2003-016-02. The result of this process led to the formulation of a questionnaire covering, among other aspects, the following elements:

- Life cycle phases of the management of support;
- Aircraft support activities;
- Management of aircraft support activities;
- Specific policies for the management of aircraft support activities; and
- Informational resources related to aircraft support activities.

The next paragraph describes the layout of the Flux of Information, how it is organized and must be read.

Overview of Flux of Information Layout

The main goal of the Flux of Information is to provide the reader with an understanding about the interdependencies among functionalities of the Commercial Aircraft Support Breakdown Structure as well as the type of information that circulates inside each support item during the various stages of the associated the support Life Cycle.

Figure 7 presents schematically the general structure of Flux of Information contained in figures 8 and 9, i.e., the Main Cycles and the Detailed Cycles, respectively.

The layout of the Flux of Information has 3 significant areas, that is:

- a zone designated "Commercial Aircraft Life Cycle" that encompasses all support items included in figure 5 (the support breakdown structure with all functionality boxes) and described in section 4;
- a zone with the 2 Meta-systems (Enterprise and Context) located in the left side of figure 2 with the associated boxes;
- and finally 2 rectangle areas underneath the functionalities of support with two sub-systems (Maintenance Operations and Logistics).

In these 2 *sub-systems* several boxes are included representing the typical tasks performed while carrying on "Operations in Maintenance" and "Logistics". Such types of activities are part of standard commercial ERP solutions, like those provided by SAP or Oracle products and by other vendors selling applications for aeronautics.

The *Logistic Sub-System* tends to be defined by modern commercial software normally by

Warehouse Management Tools, duly linked to specific Meta-System Enterprise activities, like Finance, Suppliers and Reporting modules. As a consequence, it is not a priority nor an intention of this section to treat it in general or in detail, because it is not specifically a concern of aircraft support software – except in the aspects that are related with material forecast which are highly dependant upon aircraft configuration and exploitation plans (fleet utilization plans in a certain period of time).

As the result of this perspective, only the "main boxes" describing the logistic activities are kept inside that sub-system. This means that the reader is encouraged to approach warehouse management tools associated to ERP solutions, if wants to have deeper knowledge about it.

Likewise, in what concerns the *Sub-System Maintenance Operations*, it can also be considered part of a standard Operations Management module available in commercial ERP solutions involving aeronautics features.

Due this aspect, only a general representation is provided in terms of the associated activities, in order to be coherent with the whole process and thus allow the reader to integrate it in the global structure whilst providing adequate links to the above aircraft support elements.

Adjacent to the sub-systems Maintenance Operations there are also depicted 5 types of Working Documents that output from it, which are as follows:

- Job Cards regarding the Aircraft Basic Inspection (B/I) (also known as routine cards for specific airplane checks such aircraft A, B, C and D-Checks, etc.);
- Repair Cards (findings resulting from B/I);
- Service Bulletins and Airworthiness Directives (AD) job cards;
- Additional Tasks (e.g., engine removal, aircraft painting, etc); and
- Special Routine tasks (e.g., monitoring, reliability, etc.).

Figure 7. Flux of information layout

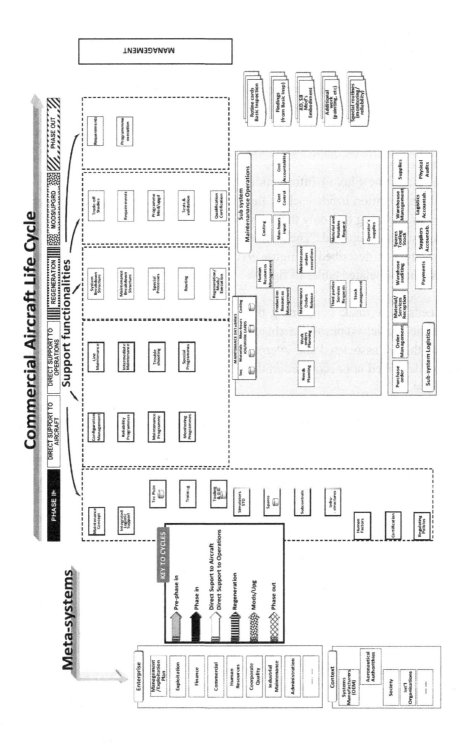

The identification of type of each cycle is included in the rectangle area labeled "key to cycles". Each cycle is described using a solid arrow. The starting and ending points of each cycle can be easily identified in figure 8.

The various solid arrows represent the paths of information associated with the support elements. For the sake of coherence with the Commercial Aircraft Breakdown Structure, depicted in figure 5, all paths of the Flux of Information cycles start at the Management box.

The Main Cycle of the Flux of Information does not provide information inside each of the five support cycles, meaning that only the entry and the exit arrows are depicted. The inside circuit of information is described in figure 9 (detailed cycles) and associated tables of figures 10 to 12.

A remark needs to be made concerning the Management element which is considered a black box. This means that all associated and internal activities are not described nor accounted in the present description.

Pursuant to the above, in addition to the basic aeronautical knowledge and indispensable experience that the reader should have in terms of the concept and how the support of commercial aircraft can be performed, reading of the Flux of Information is done by combining the Main Information Flux lines (figure 8), the Detailed Cycle (figure 9) and the type of data exchanged (see tables included in figures 10, 11 and 12).

The next two sections describe the Main Lines and the Detailed Lines of the Flux of Information.

Flux of Information: Main Cycles

In practical terms, the main Flux of Information provides the way the information circulates inside the Commercial Aircraft Breakdown Structure shown in figure 5.

This allows, during the process of software development to establish the dependency and the origin of the relevant data.

Based on figure 5 and associated description (see section 4), figure 8 depicts schematically the sequences of the Main Flux of Information of the commercial aircraft support.

In this respect, five cycles of information exist, named after the System Breakdown Structure exhibited in figure 5, that is:

- Cycle Phase In;
- Cycle Direct Support to Aircraft and Direct Support to Operation;
- Cycle Regeneration;
- Cycle Modifications/Upgrade;
- Cycle Phase Out.

Before describing the sequence of the 5 cycles, a remark needs to be made regarding a cycle designated "Pre-Phase in".

"Pre-Phase in" is not exactly a Commercial Aircraft Life Cycle Support stage, however it exists because it triggers the whole process that starts at the Meta-System Enterprise.

In concrete, "Pre-Phase in" makes available the applicable Master Plan of activities and milestones (constructed by the Stakeholder User), to enable the execution of the "Phase in" cycle. That information, in a format specifically defined by the User, is transferred to the Management Area.

The next part of this section describes the various aspects related with each one of the 5 support cycles abovementioned, described in figure 8.

Cycle Phase In

It is a cycle that enters in the "Maintenance Concept" and in "Integrated Logistic Support" box activities.

Like referred, the "Phase in" cycle is launched taking in consideration the information provided by the management area, that normally takes into account the timeframe (contractual or other) stipulated for the entrance into service of a new fleet or aircraft as well as the deadlines defined in the aeronautical regulations, related with the

Figure 8. Aircraft breakdown support structure - main cycles of information

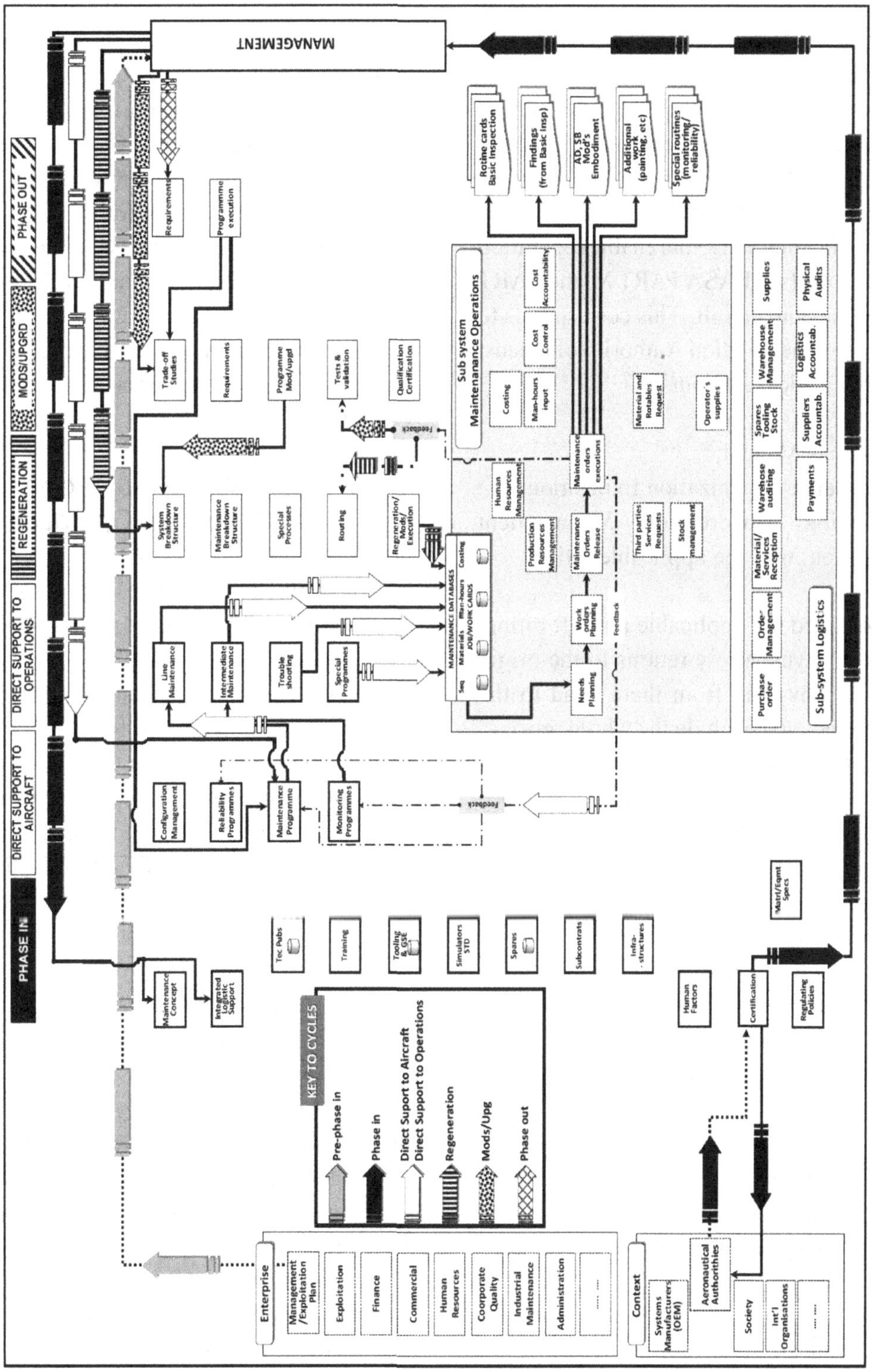

application and issuance by the Authority of the relevant approvals.

The scope of each "Phase in "support box is defined in section 4.

As shown in figure 8, the path of the "Phase in" cycle has a link with the Metasystem Context, namely with the Aviation Authority to allow to submit the necessary documentation in order to obtain the applicable rating, that enables operation and maintenance (see EASA PART M and PART 145) of the relevant aircraft. This corresponds to the approval by the Aviation Authority of at least the following critical elements:

- Operations Manual;
- Maintenance Organization Exposition;
- Continuing Airworthiness Management Exposition, with the applicable rating.

Once obtained the applicable aircraft rating, the "Phase in" cycle arrow returns to the origin (Certification box) and from there head to the management box to conclude the whole process. The User is then in condition to start the aircraft operation thus carries on the applicable support.

Although not depicted in figure 8, "Phase in" cycle has an important link to the "Sub-system Logistics".

This zone is responsible for making available a predefined number of items whose nature is fundamental in terms of aircraft support to operation (and essential to obtain from the Authority aforesaid approvals). In practical terms, "Sub-System Logistics" must ensure the supply of:

- Aircraft Ground Support Equipment and Specific Aircraft Tooling;
- Aircraft Spares, Accessories, Consumables and Products;
- Aircraft Documentation (the Continued Airworthiness Instructions);
- Training duly qualified to perform aircraft support;

- Simulators (if applicable).

Requirements (nomenclature and quantities) concerning abovementioned items are identified inside the "Phase in" cycle and passed to the "Sub-System Logistics" area in order to conduct the supply of aforesaid items; or to allow to contract to third parties the responsibility for the supply of services that provide the same items.

Once closed the "Phase in" cycle, the aircraft can be operated / exploited and thus permit the support to enter in the next step, i.e., "Cycle Direct Support to Aircraft and Direct Support to Operation".

Cycle Direct Support to Aircraft and Direct Support to Operation

This combined cycle represents the core of the commercial aircraft support thus allowing to take place the "In Service phase".

As previously stated, it starts after "Phase in" has been concluded which formally occurs after the User has received from the Aviation Authority the relevant approvals, expressed through the approval of a number of expositions/manual with the applicable aircraft rating, that is, the Operations Manual, the Maintenance Exposition and the Airworthiness Management Exposition.

The present combined cycle starts at the Management box entering the arrow directly in the "Direct Support to Aircraft" in the "Maintenance Programme" element.

The reason for this entry option, comes from the fact the aircraft "Maintenance Programme" (previously approved by the Aviation Authority in the "Phase in") is the support element that regulates the whole process, due to the fact it drives the calendar of aircraft intervention in terms of scheduled maintenance, in the various levels (line, intermediate and base).

Once entered the "Maintenance Programme" the path of the flux of information moves then into the "Direct Support to Operation" (in the corresponding maintenance level). Then it enters in the "Sub-system Maintenance Operation" to enable the maintenance activity to effectively take place.

The result of this process is depicted in figure 8 through the issuance of a set of 5 working type of documents previously identified, that is:

- Job cards relative to aircraft Scheduled Inspection (routine cards);
- Repair Cards to correct findings resulting from Scheduled Inspection and from aircraft logbooks/on-board maintenance/maintenance reports (failures, malfunctions, etc.);
- Job cards to embody Service Bulletins and Airworthiness Directives;
- Job cards regarding Additional Tasks;
- Job cards to implement Special Routine tasks.

In order to issue the working, a set of databases of information need to exist in the "Sub-System Maintenance Operation", covering namely, the sequence of tasks, the man-hours assigned to tasks, the quantity of products and material, the type of equipment and tool indispensable to allow work to be done by the maintenance department.

The present support cycle is concluded by providing feedback data (dash dotted lines) that re-enter in the various life cycle support boxes of this flux of information.

The feedback information is essential because it permits at least the following:

- to eventually adjust the maintenance programmes and promote adequate scheduled and unscheduled tasks;
- to obtain information regarding maintenance deferred tasks;
- to identify premature removals of components;

- to conduct effective reliability programmes (as prescribed by the Aviation Authority);
- to compile and treat information regarding aircraft and systems operating conditions;
- to report to the OEM about specific needs regarding improvement of aircraft systems;
- to capture data regarding actual progress of maintenance work on the shop floor versus programmed;
- to know the consumed spares, products and materials vs their predicted values.

This cycle of support is maintained by the User in a permanent loop until the aircraft is/are phased out.

Regeneration Cycle

Regeneration is the support element that exceeds line and intermediate maintenance, that is, it corresponds to Base Maintenance performed at MRO duly certified, e.g., under EASA PART 145, FAR PART 145 or equivalent. From an airframe perspective it covers specific heavy maintenance programmes, such as, A, B, C and D checks whose nature is defined by the owner of the aircraft type certificate.

Important remark needs to be made concerning this support element in case the aircraft Operator does not hold capacity to perform it. In these circumstances, the Regeneration element must be detached from the layout of the Flux of information.

In any case, for the sake of the integrity of the global model, the reader should consider the Regeneration an element of the present support item.

Notwithstanding any specific regeneration intervention resulting from unexpected situations (e.g., incidents, failures, malfunction, lost of performance) this cycle element represents scheduled maintenance governed by calendar, operating hours, operating cycles or a combination.

From a Flux of Information standpoint, the final purpose of this item is to make available the set of documents that allows the performance of applicable tasks.

This means, that like the "Direct Support to Operation" the associated lines of the flux of information also enter in the "sub-system maintenance operation" to permit the issuance of the type of documents already identified.

Like in the previous support element, this cycle is concluded by providing feedback data (dash dotted lines) whose objective is in essence similar to the aspects already referred.

Despite the fact the common purpose of the present support element *vis a vis* the objective of the "Direct Support to Operation" the complexity among them is not equal.

In fact, Regeneration involves more complexity and volume of work to be done due to the fact the level of maintenance tasks are more intense and require deeper intervention in the aircraft and its systems.

As in the previous cycle, this element of support is maintained by the User in a permanent loop until the aircraft are/is phased out.

Modification/Upgrade Cycle

The Flux of Information of this *ad hoc* element, whose purpose is described in section 4, has an important link with the Regeneration.

The reason for this connection comes from the fact that the effective implementation of modification/upgrade of aircraft is a complex process that needs to be duly organized, programmed and financed. As such it exceeds the day-to-day routine of support.

Due to these aspects, the aircraft Operators tend to establish an adequate timing to embody the relevant modification-upgrade normally coinciding it with the ground time required to carry on the scheduled heavy maintenance.

Unlike the previous support elements, the final objective of this support cycle only aims to one type of document output, that is, Job Cards related with the execution of the modification/upgrade.

The closing loop of this cycle includes feed back lines that enter in the "test and validation" element. The reason for this option results from the fact that the conclusion of any modification needs validation prior approval.

Phase Out Cycle

The last element of the Flux of Information can also be considered ad hoc element, whose purpose is described in section 4.

Due to the variable nature of the work to be accomplished at Phase out, the only reference that can be done in terms of the flux of information suggests a similar approach to the modification/upgrade cycle that is, a link with the Regeneration support item.

Flux of Information: Detailed Cycles

Pursuant to the description of the main cycles of the Flux of Information, figure 9 exhibits the detailed path of the information inside the commercial aircraft support structure, namely the various lines of information entering and leaving each box.

As such, the main goal of this section is to provide the reader with the nature of data associated with the tasks, as well as where that is generated and where that is needed.

In this respect, figures 10, 11, and 12 include six tables describing for each line of the output/input data duly numbered.

Reading of the several paths of the detailed of flux of information is done combining figures 9 through 12.

Due to its relevance, the Flux of Information inside the "Sub-system maintenance operations" is also provided to the reader thus enabling to see of what happens inside the maintenance sub-system whose management techniques typically includes as a minimum Capacity Resources

Figure 9. Aircraft breakdown support structure – detailed flux of information

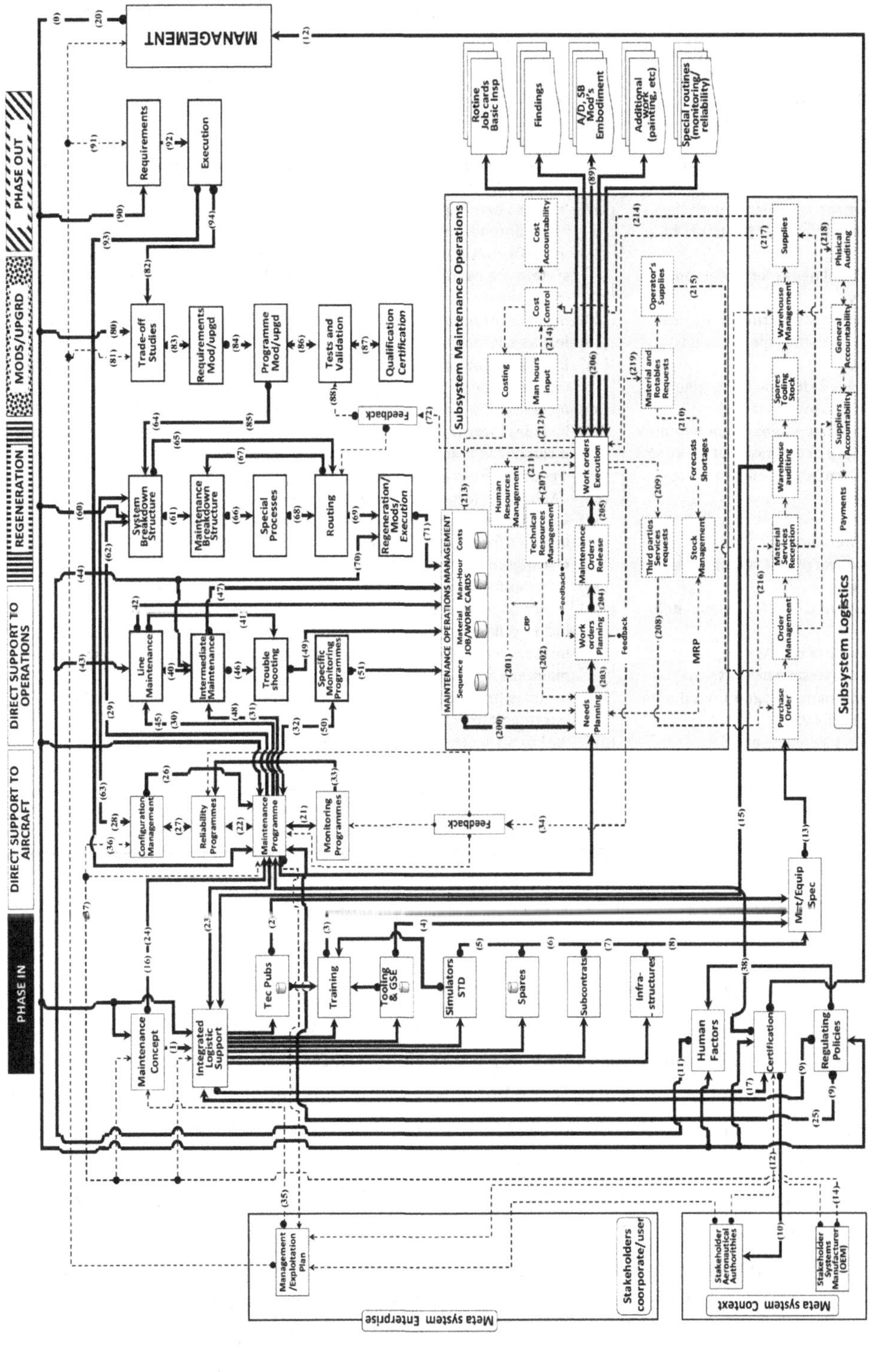

Figure 10. Data exchange on phase in, direct support to aircraft and to operations

PHASE IN	DIRECT SUPPORT TO AIRCRAFT	DIRECT SUPPORT TO OPERATIONS
(0) - Master calendar of activities .	(20) –Management/Master calendar of activities.	
(1) - Aircraft Maintenance adjusment.	(21) -Defines monitorization needs – gets feedback to adjust maintenance;	
(2) - Tech Pubs specifications (Continued Airworthiness Instructions - CAI).	(22) -Defines reliable programmes needs – gets feedback to adjust maintenance.	
(3) - Personel training specifications.	(23) -ILS allows maintenance programme .	
(4) - Aircraft equipment specifications to ensure compliance with the CAI.	(24) -Release of maintenance programme approved by Aviation Authority.	
(5) - Specifications of Simulators for training.	(25) -Includes specific orientations for the aircraft maintenance programme.	
(6) - Material needs for maintenance tasks.	(26) -Includes Aircraft Configuration data essencial maintenance programme.	
(7) - Subcontract specifications needs.	(27) -Includes exchange of configuration data for reliability programmes including for Maintenance Significant Item (see MSG3).	
(8) - Infra-strcuture specifications needs;	(28) -Includes exachange of data regarding aircraft configuration data and the system breawkdown structure (Nomenclature, P/N, S/N) related with base maintenance.	
(9) - Policies definition for engineering, logistics, maintenance).	(29) -Includes information on CAI regarding the performance of base maintenance.	
(10) - Aircraft maintenance programme delivery to Aviation Authority to obtain AOC and maintenance rating.	(30) -Includes information on CAI regarding the performance of line maintenance.	
	(31) -Includes information on CAI regarding the performance of intermediate maintenance.	
(11) - Human resources specification for maintenance.	(32) -Includes information on CAI regarding the performance of monitoring.	
(12) - Approval of AOC and maintenance rating	(33) -Includes information regarding monitorization needs in terms of realibity.	
(13) - Integrated logistic Support items supply	(34) -Includes feedback from maintenance activities.	
(14) - OEM data on CAI	(35) - Feedback from aircraft maintenance plan to exploitation.	
(15) - Allows to start aircraft maintenance programmes due to ILS availaility.	(36) -CAI from OEM regarding configuration of systems.	
	(37) -CAI from OEM regarding aircraft maintenance programmes.	
(16) - Makes available aircraft maintenance programme.	(38) -Includes from phase initial information regarding aircraft programme maintenance.	
(17) – ILS informs "certification" that all ILS items are available	(40) -Includes maintenance needs not resolved by line maintenance.	
	(41) -Includes specific requests on "troubleshooting".	
	(42) -Includes line maintenance description of work to be done by operations.	
	(43) -Includes from phase in specific requirements on human aspects for line maintenance.	
	(44) -Includes from phase in specific requirements on human aspects for intermediate maintenance.	
	(45) - CAI to be accomplished by line maintenance.	
	(46) - Includes specific requests on "troubleshooting".	
	(47) - Includes intermediate maintenance description of work to be done	
	(48) - CAI to be accomplished by intermediate maintenance.	
	(49) - Includes troubleshooting activities to be done by operations.	
	(50) - CAI instructions regarding monitoring programmes (reliability, MSI, etc).	
	(51) - Includes monitoring description of work to be done by operations.	

Planning (CRP) and Material Resources Planning (MRP I) tools.

CRP and MRP are well known methods associated with Operations Management that can be perfectly extrapolated and utilized in the management of aircraft maintenance. However, sometimes those features are not easy to determine and not optimized for aeronautics.

In this respect, we provide general comments on how CRP and MRP are determined in terms of aircraft support.

In what concerns aircraft maintenance operations, (see path lines (201) and (202)) the calculation of CRP in the base maintenance (at MRO)

is in fact the most complex situation, because it involves various types of resources including specialized technicians (e.g., airframe mechanics, engine mechanics, electro-avionics mechanics, etc.) as well as various type of industrial equipment (grinding, heat furnaces, etc.) to perform the repair work. Determination of CRP takes in consideration the resources (human and industrial equipment) assigned to the job cards established for a certain type of aircraft inspection.

In relation to MRP process, this aspect applies to material and products required to perform aircraft maintenance (regardless the level) and to materiel needs, namely, engine, accessories

Figure 11. Data exchange on regeneration, mod/upd and phase out

REGENERATION	MODS/UPGRD	PHASE OUT
(60) -Master calendar of activities to establish base maintenance.	(80) -Master calendar of activities to establish modifications.	(90) -Master calendar of activities of Phase out.
(61) -System breakdown Structure.	(81) -Exploitation requirements regarding the modifications programme.	(91) -Exploitation requirements regarding phase out.
(62) -Base maintenance programme needs.	(82) -Phase out requirements regarding modifications.	(92) -Phase out requirements.
(63) -Exchanges system configuration data.	(83) -Trade-off studies.	(93)-Maintenance requiremsnts affecting phase out.
(64) -Applicable to modification programmes: incldes data on systems to modify.	(84) -Modifications requirements.	(94)- Phase out requiremnst requsiting modifications (if applicable).
(65) -Includes the System breakdown Structure to allow base maintenance tasks;	(85) -Modifications requirements to be done at base maintenance.	
(66) -Include information on the production configuration: layout, human resources, equipament, special processes (shotpeening, heat treatments, electroplating, NDT, painting).	(86) -Testing and and validation requirements.	
(67) -Feedback on production man-hours imput.	(87) -Testing and validation results for qualification and certification.	
(68) -Special processes approved.	(88) -Feedback on testing and validation	
(69) -Includes data regarding the work, the sequence and manhours related with the work maintenance.		
(70) -Human factors to be taken in account for maintenance.		
(71) -Data package covering all aspects related with work to be done (tasks, sequence, equipment, toolds, materials, man-hours, quality),		
(72) -Feed on maintenance done (findings, actual man-hours, materials, sequence)		

and components which are controlled under the "configuration management" process in terms of operating hours, cycles, calendar or a combination.

This means that the calculation of MRP takes in consideration:

a) The maintenance concept (such as hard time, life limited, on-condition and condition monitoring) applicable every aircraft element;

b) The actual consumption of calendar, flying hours and cycles and the exploitation forecast for a certain period of time;

c) Warehouse management at the level of stock (actual and forecast consumptions);

d) Items under acquisition.

As such, MRP calculation (in aircraft support) is the combination of all these aspects with the management of warehouse stocks that determines the MRP output at a certain moment in time – see path dashed line labeled "CRP" and dashed line (210).

The next sections highlight the data elements that are significant for the understanding of the Flux of Information and the methodology related thereto.

Figure 12. Sub-systems (operations and logistics) - data exchange

SUB-SYSTEM MAINTENANCE OPERATIONS	SUB-SYSTEM LOGISTICS

(200) - Includes needs in terms of material, manpower, equipment, tooling, components, spares, rotables.
(201) - Includes exchange of human resources availability for planing and maintenance operations.
(202) - Includes exchange of technical resources availability for planing.
(203) - Provides planning of needs material, equipment, manpower, spares.
(204) - Provides detailed programming of work .
(205) - Issues maintenance orders.
(206) - Executes maintenance orders.
(207) - Includes feedbacl to technical resources management form operations.
(208) - Includes performance of external services.
(209) - Includes request of external services.
(210) - Includes request of rotables.
(211) - Includes feedback from operations to human resources management
(212) - Includes feedback regarding manhours actual input from operations;
(213) - Includes information for costing.
(214) - Includes feedback to cost control.
(215) - Includes request of material.
(216) - Includes supply of material from operator.
(217) - Includes supply of material from warehouse to maintenance.
(218) - includes feedback from hwarehouse management to audits.
(219) - Includes material request to operator.

Detailed Cycle "Phase In"

In accordance with the timeframe of activities predefined in the management box, this support element encompasses the execution of all tasks of each associated support box.

From (0) to (16) all significant elements of data are identified in figure 10 (left column). Despite the fact most of the data are self-explanatory, the relevant information in the process relates with ILS and the "Maintenance Concept" as follows:

- The Integrated Logistic Support uses lines of information (2), (3), (4), (5), (6), (7) and (8). All these items enter in the "sub-systems logistics" to enable the indispensable acquisition to be performed inside of it.

Once concluded the acquisition programme (normally simultaneously done with the acquisition of the aircraft under Phase in), that information is fed back using element (15). Then using line (17) the ILS informs the "Certification" that the acquisition process applicable to the items below described has been finished:

- Aircraft Ground Support Equipment and Specific Aircraft Tooling;
- Aircraft Spares, Accessories, Consumable and Products;
- Aircraft Documentation (the Continued Airworthiness Instructions);
- Training duly qualified to perform aircraft support;
- Simulators (if applicable).

This allows the "Certification" box through line (10) to submit the application process to the Aviation Authority to obtain the required authorizations/certification to conduct operation. That information is fed back using line (12) – in fact that information is formally passed to the meta-system Enterprise to the Accountable Manager (see dotted lines) to allow the company to start to exploit the commercial aircraft.

- The "Maintenance Concept" is important in the sense it provides, after analysis of the aircraft data, the maintenance programme to be used during the "in-service phase", by feeding with line (16) the "Direct Support to Aircraft".

In concrete, from associated work of this "Phase in" support element for each aircraft item, i.e., fuselage, engine, accessories, components, a database is generated compiling the applicable maintenance criteria/concept for each aircraft item to be controlled in terms of Configuration Management, i.e., identification is made in terms of the maintenance concept applicable, e.g., life limited parts, hard time, on condition and condition-monitoring elements.

It also includes identification of any aircraft Maintenance Significant Items associated to the MSG-3 methodology (if required/applicable by the Continued Airworthiness Instructions).

Cycle Direct Support to Aircraft and Direct Support to Operation

As previously stated, this is a combined cycle and the core of the aircraft support. Both support segments are inter-linked and mutually allow the aircraft to be operated. Notwithstanding the individual contribution of each of the support element, the central support aspects are in fact "Configuration Management" and the "Maintenance Programme" because they dictate the implementation of the "Continued Airworthiness Instructions" upon the aircraft under exploitation.

It is also important to refer that the feedback information line (34) is critical. This information includes the result of maintenance activities (important for reliability) as well as data regarding operation (flying hours, cycles, deferred tasks, unscheduled removal, etc.) that enable to establish the status of aircraft configuration and control the execution of the maintenance programmes.

This feedback information is complemented by the operating hours, cycles and calendar (as well as failures, malfunction and other aspects reported in the aircraft logbooks and/or onboard systems) provided by the exploitation (see dashed line from meta-system enterprise entering the "direct Support to aircraft" in the Maintenance Programmes box.

Without prejudice for the specific contribution of each of 8 elements that form the present block of Support Elements, the essential lines of information are represented by the sequence (21), (22), (26), (27), (30), (31), (32), (42), (47), (49) and (51). This sequence of data elements allows the Direct Support to Operations to take place in the "sub-system maintenance operations".

In this sub-system area the main sequence of support information is provided by (200), (203), (204), (205) and (206) whose final goal is the issuance of the set of 5 working documents already described – see section 5.3 b).

The main support feedback data is provided by line (34) with the elements and the scope previously referred (see section 5.3).

Double arrow lines of information, e.g., (22), (27) and (21) mean that data are exchanged between each other.

In concrete, those elements of the flux of information establish the requirements (scheduled inspections to be performed, unscheduled activities and repairs) in terms of the line and intermediate maintenance as well as the needs to perform monitoring programmes taking in consideration what is defined in the aircraft maintenance manuals.

Finally, a remark needs to be made about line path (29). This represents the link between "Direct Support to Aircraft " to "Regeneration". In practical terms, this datum item defines the calendar and maintenance requirements for the scheduled and unscheduled Base Maintenance activities (C, D and other types of Checks). It also takes in consideration the data coming from maintenance operations which have a direct interface with aircraft exploitation, through the adequate aircraft documents (logbooks) and/or to aircraft onboard computer maintenance systems.

Cycle Regeneration

The table that contains the data items is in figure 11, being the essential path from (61) to (71). The loop of data is closed by item (72) entering in the "routing" element. The reason for the feedback approach comes from the fact that the initial set of information provided by (71) includes reference data (namely, task sequence, man-hours, material, products, tooling and equipment) that enable "sub-system maintenance operations" to take place.

Once maintenance operations have been effectively conducted the shop floor needs to feed back the whole set of information actually gathered to permit the relevant adjustment in the whole process thus converging forecast to real.

This means that path (72) is to provide real consumption of material and products duly indexed to a certain task and aircraft (or system), actual man-hours spent. Path (72) also provides findings from aircraft inspection regarding material condition and unscheduled removals.

After analysis, usually performed by the Engineering Department, this feedback process will led to the issuance of new and revised maintenance works through (71).

Cycle Modifications/Upgrade

This is a simple sequence of information (83), (84), (85), (86) and (87). The relevant aspect is the link to "Regeneration" (85) given the fact the stakeholder Operator tends to decide to implement the modification at the time of major base maintenance tasks.

Item (85) is to define the type of activities required from the "Regeneration" to enable successful completion of the modification/upgrade programme.

Due to its nature and eventually complexity, this *ad-hoc* support information item, pertaining to this part of the Life Cycle, has a specific configuration, very similar to project management because (as previously stated) it deals with situations outside the normal continued airworthiness instructions prescribed for a certain type of aircraft.

Hence the Operator (or someone contracted for that purpose) shall prepare and organize a dedicated project involving the execution of a certain type of aircraft modification/upgrade.

To this end, there is a number of management techniques available, namely, for the Book of Knowledge-(BoK), of the System Engineering, see INCOSE-TP-2003-016-02 (2004) or equivalent.

The critical aspect of this support element is in fact the "Test and Validation" that we assume it captures data from the "sub-system maintenance operation" – see feedback line 88. The feedback line provides the results from the field tests that were pre-defined in the "Requirements Mod/upg" and by "Programme Mod/upg" activity boxes.

The duration of this aircraft support item obviously depends upon the complexity of the modification/upgrade programme that in certain cases may require a Supplemental Type Certificate" approval by a specific Aviation Authority.

Cycle Phase Out

This final element of aircraft support in terms of execution is very similar to the "modification / upgrade" meaning that the path of information leads to the "Regeneration" because, as previously stated the operators tend to implement phase out activities during the associated aircraft ground time.

FUTURE RESEARCH DIRECTIONS

Having described the conceptual model related to aircraft support two aspects emerge in relation to the application of software:

- the need to generate what can be called a BoK acting as a reference structure for aircraft support;
- the need to integrate aircraft support software with the remaining areas of the holistic model described in figure 2.

The existence of a BoK like suggested is an essential goal to consolidate the software processes that permit to carry on the aircraft support. By doing so, the functionalities of aircraft support could be assessed and eventually approved using a neutral tool that could normalise the whole process.

To reach this goal, specific software would have to be developed acting as benchmark tool regarding aircraft support. That could serve to detect the weak and strong aspects of the commercial software and eventually allow determining the level of quality.

The second part of the suggestion represents the full integration of all air transportation support processes. This is in line with what normally ERP solutions tend to ensure.

Although not explicitly referred in this chapter, the model of the operational support described, namely its flux of information, has few links with both meta-systems whilst it is known the positive/negative influence that certain elements of the Enterprise and Context could have on the aircraft support.

These type of interdependences need to be studied and a more sophisticated model should be developed establishing the main cycle and the type of information exchanged.

In fact, more and more the influence of mentioned meta-systems exist upon the aircraft support, namely, the finance, the exploitation plans that reflect the commercial success of a certain operator or the high costs of fuel.

The full integration in a model of all these aspects represents a major challenge that could leverage simulation processes in terms of aircraft support in its multiple domains and variables.

CONCLUSION

This book chapter starts with a brief description about the complex environment where the Air Transportation is evolving. The positive impact on the local and global economy and the various activities and services that are associated represent such level of complexity.

In this respect, it is fundamental to have an aircraft support that meets the Continued Airworthiness Instructions and allows airplane to fly safely.

In this respect, commercial software exists, either developed by airlines or by software houses. Notwithstanding the inherent quality and functionalities of the existent software it is fundamental to have an aircraft support model acting as reference structure for such type of software.

This book chapter starts from an existent model applicable to commercial aircraft that encompasses a support breakdown structure with an associated life cycle and complements that with the flux of information.

The support breakdown structure is the dorsal spine of the aircraft support and is devoted to ensure performance of all tasks from "Phase in" to "Phase out" being oriented to comply with the applicable Airworthiness Instructions.

The flux of information is the active portion of the aircraft support and provides the type of data exchanged inside the support breakdown structure.

The availability of both elements that represent the support of commercial aircraft is realistic and permits Aircraft Operators and software houses to have a reference model for their own processes.

It represents a holistic and integrated approach that leverages the management processes related with the support of commercial aircraft.

REFERENCES

Abdulkadir, S. (2001). *Daily Operational Aircraft Maintenance Routing Problem*. PhD Thesis. State University of New York at Buffalo, Buffalo, NY.

Aschauer, D. (1989). Is Public Expenditure Productive? *Journal of Monetary Economics, 23*, 177–200. doi:10.1016/0304-3932(89)90047-0

Aschauer, D. (1990). Why Infrastructure is Important? In A. Munnell (ed), *Is there a Shortfall in Public Capital Investment? Conference Series No 34*, Boston, Federal Reserve Bank of Boston.

Atkins, S. (1998). *A Unified Methodology for the Management of Time-Dependent Information in Aeronautical Systems*. PhD Thesis, Massachusetts Institute of Technology, Cambridge, MA.

Barros, C. (2008). Technical Efficiency of UK Airports. *Journal of Air Transport Management, 14*, 175–178. doi:10.1016/j.jairtraman.2008.04.002

Button, K., & Taylor, S. (2000). International Air Transportation and Economic Development. *Journal of Air Transport Management, 6*, 209–222. doi:10.1016/S0969-6997(00)00015-6

Camelier, I., Lourenço, L., & da Saúde, J. (2008). Aircraft Sustaining: A Holistic And Systemic Approach Establishing The Various Support Components. *Aircraft Engineering and Aerospace Technology, 55*, 3.

Cole, S. (1998). Applied Transport Economics. In *Policy Management and Decision Making* (2nd Edition). London: Kogan Page Limited.

EASA CS 25. (2003) *European Aviation Safety Agency*. Decision nr 2003/2/RM, October 17.

EASA OPS. (2006). *Commission Regulation (EC) No 1899/2006 of the European Parliament and of the Council*, Annex I.

EASA PART 145, (2003). *Commission Regulation (EC) No 2042/2003 of November 20*, Annex II.

EASA PART M. (2003). *Commission Regulation (EC) No 2042/2003 of 20 November*, Annex I.

FAA PART 25. (n.d.) *Airworthiness standards: transport category airplanes*. Federal Aviation Administration. Code of Federal Regulations.

FAR PART 145. (n.d.) *Repair Stations. Federal Aviation Administration. Code of Federal Regulations*.

Fisher, W. (1983). *Cannibalisation Policies In An Aircraft Maintenance System With Spares, Repair And Resources Constraint*. PhD Thesis. The University of Texas Austin, USA.

Garcia-Formieles, J. (2003). A Work Breakdown Structure that Integrates Different View in Aircraft Modification Projects. *Concurrent Engineering-Research And Applications, 11*, 47–54. doi:10.1177/1063293X03011001005

Gopalan, R. (1998). The Aircraft Maintenance Routing Problem. *Operations Research, 46*(2). doi:10.1287/opre.46.2.260

Gramlich, E. (1994). Infrastructure Investment: a Review Essay. *Journal of Economic Literature, 32*, 1176–1196.

Halpern, N., & Pagliary, R. (2007). Governance Structures and the Market Orientation of Airports in Europe's Peripheral Areas. *Journal of Air Transport Management, 13*, 376–382. doi:10.1016/j.jairtraman.2007.07.003

Harmatuck, D. (1996). The influence of Transportation Infrastructure on Economic Development. *Logistics and Transportation Review, 32*, 63–76.

Hessburg, J. (2000). *Air Carrier MRO Handbook*. New York: McGraw-Hill.

INCOSE-TP-2003-016-02 (2004). *Systems Engineering Handbook, Version 2a*. International Council on Systems Engineering, Bristol.

ISO 15288. (n.d.). *Systems Life Cycle Processes*. International Standard Organisation.

Iyer, P. (1999). *The Effect of Maintenance Policy on System Maintenance and Life Cycle Cost*. MSc Thesis, Faculty of the Virginia Polytechnic Institute and State University, USA.

Izquicrdo, R. (1997). *Gestión y Financiación de las Infraestructuras del Transporte Terrestre*. Madrid: Asociación Española de la Carretera.

Izquierdo, R. (2003). *Economic Impacts of Infrastructure Investment: the Spanish Infrastructure Plan 2000-2001*. In ECMT (ed), 16th International Symposium on Theory and Practice in Transport Economics. Budapest, ECMT.

JAA JAR-OPS Part 1 (2005). *Commercial Air Transportation (Aeroplanes) Amendment 9*, September.

King, F. (1986). *Aviation Maintenance Management*. Carbondale, IL: Southern Illinois University Press.

Kinnisson, H. (2004). *Aviation Maintenance Management*. New York: McGraw-Hill.

Mirghani, M. (1996). Aircraft Maintcnancc Budgetary and Costing Systems at the Saudi Arabian Airlines: An Integrated Business Approach. *Journal of Quality in Maintenance Engineering*, *2*, 4. doi:10.1108/13552519610153580

Munnell, A. (1992). Infrastructure Investment and Economic Growth. *The Journal of Economic Perspectives*, *6*, 189–198.

NASA SP-610S (1995). *Systems Engineering Handbook*. Washington, DC: National Aeronautics and Space Administration.

Plumpton, D. (2002) *Planning to Maintain an Advantage: an Aircraft View. An Industry Research Document to Effectively Plan Aircraft Maintenance*. MBA thesis, University of Bath, England.

Samaranayake, P. (2002). Development to Engineering Structures for Scheduling and Control ff Aircraft Maintenance. *International Journal of Operations & Production Management*, *22*, 8. doi:10.1108/01443570210436172

Satishan, S. (1989). *Airline Safety Posture: A Study ff Aircraft Maintenance-Related Indicators*. PhD Thesis, University of California-Berkeley, USA.

Senge, P. (1990) *The Fifth Discipline*. Currency Press.

Tapiador, F., Mateos, A., & Martí-Henneberg, J. (2008). The Geographical Efficiency of Spain's Regional Airports: a Quantitative Analysis. *Journal of Air Transport Management*, *14*, 205–212. doi:10.1016/j.jairtraman.2008.04.007

TRB. (1997). *Macroeconomic Analysis of the Linkages between Transportations Investments and Economic Performance*. NCHRP Report No 389. Washington DC: National Academy Press.

Vickerman, R. (1996). Location, Accessibility and Regional Development: the Appraisal of Trans-European Networks. *Transport Policy*, *2*(4), 225–234. doi:10.1016/S0967-070X(95)00013-G

Vickerman, R. (2000). Transport and Economic Growth. *In Regional Science Association International (ed), 6th World Congress of the RSAI*. Lugano, Switzerland: RSAI.

York Aviation, L. P. P. (2007). *Social Benefits of Low Fares Airlines in Europe*. Leeds: York Aviation.

ENDNOTES

[1] Simat, Helliesen and Eichner Inc. - cited for Button and Taylor (2000:213), estimated "(…) that those employed in the new economy sectors fly over 1.6 times as much as those in traditional industries".

[2] And also Munnell (1992), Gramlich (1994), Vickerman (1996, 2000), TRB (1997) and Izquierdo (1997, 2003).

[3] The model is applicable to commercial aircraft because the defence sector has different

stakeholders namely in terms of Aviation Authority as well as the Regulations are specific to Operators.

[4] The management circumstances determine its implementation.

APPENDIX

Acronyms:

ACOC: Air Carrier Operating Certificate
AD: Airworthiness Directive
AOC: Air Operator Certificate
ATA: Air Transport Association
ATC: Air Traffic Control
B/I: Basic Inspection
BoK: Book of Knowledge
BOM: Bill of Materials
CAI: Continued Airworthiness Instructions
CRP: Capacity Requirements Planning
EASA: European Aviation Safety Agency
ERP: Enterprise Resources Planning
FAA: Federal Aviation Administration
FAR: Federal Aviation Regulation
GSE: Ground Support Equipment
IATA: International Air Transport Association
ICAO: International Civil Aviation Organization
ILS: Integrated Logistic Support
INCOSE: International Council on Systems Engineering
IT: Information Technologies
JAA: Joint Airworthiness Authority
LCA: Low Cost Airlines
LRU: Line Replacing Unit
MEL: Minimum Equipment List
MRO: Maintenance Repair and Overhaul
MRP: Materials Requirements Planning
MSG: Maintenance Steering Group
MSI: Maintenance Significant Item
NASA: National Aeronautics and Space Administration
NDI: Non Destructive Inspection
NDT: Non Destructive Inspection
OEM: Original Equipment Manufacturer
P/N: Part number
S/N: Serial number
UAV: Unamaned Air Vehicle
WBS: Work Breakdown Structure

Section 3
Improving Aircraft Performance

Chapter 10
A Case Study of Advanced Airborne Technology Impacting Air Traffic Management

Ítalo R. de Oliveira
Atech Tecnologias Críticas, Brazil

Lúcio F. Vismari
Safety Analysis Group (GAS), University of São Paulo (Poli-USP), Brazil

Paulo S. Cugnasca
Safety Analysis Group (GAS), University of São Paulo (Poli-USP), Brazil

João B. Camargo Jr.
Safety Analysis Group (GAS), University of São Paulo (Poli-USP), Brazil

Bert (G.J.) Bakker
Air Transport Safety Institute, National Aerospace Laboratory NLR, The Netherlands

Henk A.P. Blom
Air Transport Safety Institute, National Aerospace Laboratory NLR, The Netherlands

ABSTRACT

Great advance is expected from the CNS/ATM (Communication, Navigation, Surveillance / Air Traffic Management) paradigm. It provides significant support of a seamless global air traffic management system. Its key technical elements are the Global Navigation Satellite System (GNSS), and the Aeronautical Telecommunication Network (ATN), which will support digital applications such as the Automatic Dependent Surveillance Broadcast (ADS-B) and the Airborne Separation Assistance System (ASAS). ADS-B will greatly increase surveillance precision and availability, and ASAS is aimed to increase traffic efficiency. This chapter provides an overview of the CNS/ATM infrastructure, the specific airborne technologies, and details of an example advanced air traffic management concept. For this example advanced concept, the chapter applies an advanced approach in dynamical safety risk modeling and Monte Carlo

DOI: 10.4018/978-1-60566-800-0.ch010

simulation based mid air collision risk estimation. The dynamical model covers the advanced airborne technologies and the cognitive contributions by the pilots and controllers involved. These initial results show the value of advanced airborne technologies for future air traffic management.

INTRODUCTION

The advent of ubiquitous distributed computing, communication and sensing systems has created an environment in which we have ability to access, process and communicate huge amounts of data. This environment could be mentioned as the major enabler for new applications of control for large-scale, complex systems (Murray et al, 2003). Currently, energy and water distribution and manufacturing processes are some application areas that use the integration of distributed computing and communication in supervision and control systems to optimize their processes performance and to increase their service capacity.

This phenomenon can be noticed in one of the key services upon which our global society is build: air transportation. As a way to increase the air transportation capacity, changes in the air traffic management paradigm are agreed by the International Civil Aviation Organization (ICAO) to critically depend on joint international improvements at many levels of Communication, Navigation, Surveillance and Air Traffic Management (CNS/ATM). More specifically, CNS/ATM has been defined as follows: "*Communications, Navigation, and Surveillance systems, employing digital technologies, including satellite systems together with various levels of automation, applied in support of a seamless global air traffic management system*" (ICAO, 2000). Compared to conventional CNS/ATM approach, the key improvements cover the following elements of CNS/ATM:

- *Communication*: increasing the coverage, accessibility, capacity, integrity, performance and security of aeronautical communication systems, in accordance with future ATM requirements;
- *Navigation*: increasing the coverage and capacity of air operations in any weather conditions and airspace types, including approaches and landings, while maintaining or increasing the levels of integrity, accuracy and performance, in accordance with future ATM requirements;
- *Surveillance*: expansion in the effective coverage over oceans and remote areas, and the increment of situational awareness levels for pilots, in accordance with future ATM requirements.

In order to achieve these desired improvements for each of these three system elements, ICAO has developed the following evolution plan for the technologies applied to the elements of Communication, Navigation and Surveillance of the air traffic system, as shown in Figure 1, based on (Vismari, 2007).

The framework of technology enhancements, pictured in Figure 1, aims to provide, in a systematic way, higher levels of automation and accuracy to the air transportation system, and minimizes the current restrictions to air capacity growth. It will contribute to the completion of the CNS/ATM main mission, which is to develop a comprehensive and unified system to Air Traffic Services (ATS) that comply with the demand growth for this modal of transportation, and with improvements in the levels of safety, efficiency and regularity of air traffic, providing the use of the routes desired by users and minimizing the differences in use of equipment currently seen different regions of the planet.

Figure 1. Technological Evolution Plan to CNS elements (an example). The meaning of all terms and acronyms is given at the end of the chapter.

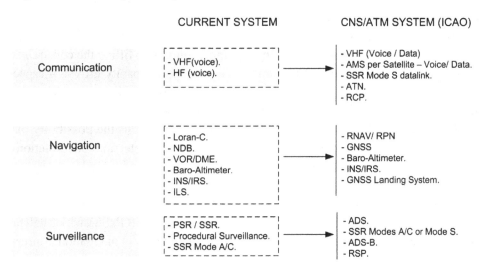

The application of these digital technologies to air transportation infrastructure as a way to improve communication, surveillance, navigation, and air traffic management service capabilities will transform current air traffic management, which is based on voice communications and human-centered terrain control, in a large-scale distributed digital network. On the one hand, if this new system paradigm makes some applications feasible, on the other hand they bring new challenges and problems to be solved. Most of the challenges occur when this new paradigm is applied to safety-critical applications in air transportation, where failures could result in life losses, significant damage to property or to the environment (Knight, 2002). One of the main challenges to applying this paradigm on safety-critical applications is their complexity. Besides, complexity introduces an unknown number of new failure modes; the huge number of distributed and functional elements interacting through a communication network makes the future system behavior different from its current behavior.

Another challenge comes from the interdisciplinary characteristic of the paradigm change, which implies changes in concepts of control,

computer sciences and communication disciplines. As a consequence, all changes must be considered together, for which new points-of-view must be considered into the systems lifecycle. As an example, concepts of time delays, data transfer rates and packet length (from communication discipline); stability (from control discipline), security and real-time computing (from computing discipline) must be considered systemically in all system lifecycle stages. The last challenge mentioned here is the lack of well-established methods to assess safety-critical applications related to the new paradigm, which is a need, considering all the new paradigm characteristics and the relationship between supervision and control system and the application process (in our case, related to safety requirements).

We can see that the CNS/ATM paradigm is a way in moving the constraints to a safe growth of air transportation, because technological developments on the elements CNS directly affect the characteristics of air traffic management and, consequently, their ability to manage, effectively, the distances of separation between aircraft, especially with regard to increasing the accuracy of surveillance data, its coverage area and the reduction of congestion in the communication channels, besides the possibility of improving techniques for the detection and resolution of conflicts because of higher levels of system automation.

However, this paradigm change, based on distributed computing and communication in supervision and control systems, when used in safety-critical applications, brings together new challenges and needs. Considering the air transportation services, it is necessary to assess in which conditions CNS/ATM will promote the increase in the traffic system capacity without compromising its current safety levels. I.e., if risks introduced by CNS/ATM in this safety-critical system are socially acceptable and worth the benefits brought by it.

The aim of this chapter is to present some of the most important concepts contained by advanced CNS/ATM:

- "*Automatic Dependent Surveillance by Broadcast*" (ADS-B) ; and
- "*Airborne Separation Assistance System*" (ASAS).

An additional aim of this chapter is to demonstrate the value of the operational use of these two advanced airborne technologies through explaining the approach and results of an in-depth analysis of the possible capacity and safety improvements for a specific advanced CNS/ATM operational concept that makes use of ADS-B and ASAS technologies.

This chapter is structured as follows. Section 2 presents what are the ADS-B and ASAS concepts, their main characteristics, structures and expected operational scenarios. Section 3 presents a case study where the risks related to ASAS are assessed. Finally, Section 4 contains the conclusions and some remarks about follow-up work.

ADS-B AND ASAS: WHAT ARE THEY?

ICAO's CNS/ATM advancements aim at providing a solution to lifting the constraints of current air transport capacity growth – especially those regarding to surveillance data accuracy, its coverage area and the communication channels congestion – and it opens the possibility of improving techniques for detection and resolution of conflicts (regarding to the higher levels of automation in air traffic systems). The CNS/ATM key elements are based on the existence of a Global Navigation Satellite System (GNSS), which will provide both the functionality of navigation to aircrafts and the surveillance information to Air Traffic Controllers (ATCo), and an Aeronautical Telecommunications Network (ATN), which will enable the exchange of all aeronautical information between the various system users in a safely and efficiently way.

The Aeronautical Telecommunication Network (ATN) is the element responsible for transforming the current air transportation system in a large-scale distributed digital network. As defined by ICAO (1999a), ATN comprises *application entities* and *communication services*, which make the ground elements, the air-ground networks and the airborne data networks interoperate through the adoption of protocols and services interface based on common reference model of 7 layers ISO/OSI (International Organization for Standardization (ISO) open System interconnection (OSI) reference model). Figure 2 illustrates the conceptual model to ATN proposed, and is based on (ICAO, 1999a).

ATN is a communication network applied to exchange data between *End Systems* (ES) containing the 7 layers of the model ISO / OSI and one or more Application Process (AP) to each one. An AP is a set of resources, within a real open system, which can be used to perform a specific information processing activity. An Application Entity (AE) is part of an AP related to communication within the 7 layer ISO/OSI environment. The

Figure 2. ATN conceptual model.

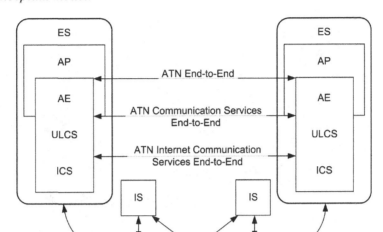

Internet Communications Service (ICS) allows the ground elements, the air-ground networks and the airborne data networks interoperate adopting a common interface based on the OSI model. The Intermediate Systems (IS) is responsible to message routing, corresponding to layers 1 through 3 of the ISO/OSI model (physical, link and network layers).

The Sub-Networks (SN) represents the data communication networks that implement homogeneous protocols and addressing plans and are under the control of a single authority. In the case of CNS/ATM, the SN to Air-Ground Communication, named Datalinks (DL), are the means (channels) through which aircrafts communicate with the ground elements. ICAO has normalized the following types of Datalinks (DL) within the context ATN (ICAO, 1999b):

- *Aeronautical Mobile Satellite Service* (AMSS), using satellites for communication, both geostationary and non-geostationary satellites, allowing communication by voice and data on a global range.
- *VHF Datalink* (VDL), using techniques of data communication in VHF bands. It was defined 4 different VDL modes: Mode 1, Mode 2, Mode 3 and Mode 4, differentiated by their characteristics of modulation, control for access to the physical environment and, especially, transfer rates.
- Secondary Surveillance Radar (SSR) - Mode S, using the Mode S SSR ability to communicate data in a bidirectional way between air and ground elements with nominal rates of 4Mbits/s (uplink) and 1Mbits/s (downlink) (ICAO, 1998).
- HF Datalink (HFDL): the HFDL is the union between the characteristics of long-range electromagnetic propagation in HF spectrum and digital data modulation, providing data communication in remote areas.

Figure 3 presents a CNS/ATM communication environment example, representing the relationship between Datalinks (DL) and End Systems (ES) (Vismari, 2007).

In the ATN environment, the Application Entity (AE) presented in Figure 2 represents, in other words, the 7th layer (application layer) of the ISO/OSI Reference Model. Thus, the AE are

Figure 3. CNS/ATM communication environment.

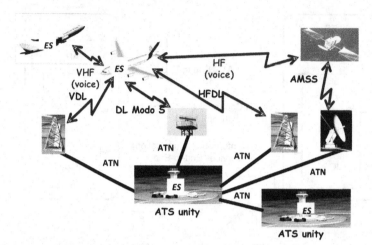

the applications (functionalities) of the Aeronautical Telecommunication Network (ATN) used by End Systems (ES) in the air traffic system. ICAO (1999a) distinguishes two AE categories:

- *Air-Ground AE*, whose are the ATN functionalities applied to communication between End Systems in ground (ATS unities) and in the air (aircrafts). The AE defined to this category are the *Context Management* (CM), which provides the ability to establish connection (log) between two points; the *Automatic Dependent Surveillance* (ADS), which provides to end users (specially ground systems), in an automatic way, position and other pertinent information contained at end users (specially that information contained in the airborne flight management system); the *Controller-Pilot Data Link Communication* (CPDLC), which provides the ability to establish a peer-to-peer message communication between pilots and air traffic controllers; and the *Flight Information Services* (FIS), which allows pilots to request and receive flight information services.

- *Ground-Ground AE*, whose are the ATN functionalities applied to communication applications between End Systems in ground (ATS unities). The AE in this category are the *ATS Message Handling Service* (ATSMHS), which proves communicate messages between ATS end users; and the *Inter-Communication Center* (ICC), which provides message communication between ATS centers for notification, coordination, transfer of control activities, among others.

Automatic Dependent Surveillance (ADS), mentioned above as one of the most important concepts contained in the CNS/ATM paradigm, is one of the Application Entities defined to the ATN. This application allows the distribution of surveillance information between properly equipped air and ground End Systems. And even if ADS application has the surveillance functionality to air traffic system, it is structurally defined in the context of communication for the air traffic system. That is, ADS is strongly dependent from both CNS/ATM key elements: from the ATN, where its definition is contained; and from the Global

Navigation Satellite System (GNSS), where the surveillance data (mainly position) are obtained. Thus, an ADS concept has both surveillance requirements - such as coverage volume, accuracy and scan rate - and data communication requirements - such as quality of service requirements (QoS – bit error rate, delay), message format, message handling and priorities.

ADS is one of the principal concepts in the CNS/ATM paradigm, given that it is the enabler to the main technological improvements to the Air Traffic Management (ATM), such as the "*Airborne Separation Assistance System*" (ASAS). Then, a description of Automatic Dependent Surveillance (ADS) is given, more specifically its broadcast category (ADS-B), and an overview of its application to air traffic.

Automatic Dependent Surveillance: Broadcast (ADS-B)

As explained before, Automatic Dependent Surveillance (ADS) is an ATN application that provides "ADS reports" – containing aircraft state (position, speed, etc.) and flight intention information (next waypoints and levels) to ATN end systems (ES). There are two ADS implementations types: ADS by Contract (ADS-C) and ADS by Broadcast (ADB-B).

In the first case (ADS-C), the exchange of ADS messages is provided through a contract between two addresses: an aircraft and an end system in the ground. Therefore, this form of ADS is also known as addressable (ADS-A), and implement, in the network domain, a peer-to-peer connection-oriented communication.

In the latter case (ADS-B), an aircraft (or another properly equipped end user) transmits ADS messages periodically and in a broadcast way (as a radio station). This broadcast transmission provides that any end user properly equipped and within its coverage range can receive ADS messages. In resume, end user cannot establish contracts and thus the transmitter end user does

not need to know which elements are receiving their messages.

Based on the distinction made above, ADS-C could be defined as a cooperative surveillance, because the aircraft (or any other end user) cooperate with the surveillance process, responding for contract establishment requests from air traffic controller (ATS unity) and providing them with ADS messages. Already ADS-B is included in the category of dependent surveillance, because the process of tracking elements depends on the messages sent by the own tracked element, and regardless of requisition by the control system. The minimum content of a message, in the case of ADS-B, must be composed of:

- *Emitter Category*, defining characteristics of emitter end user. As examples of categories, there are light, medium and heavy aircrafts, helicopters, unmanned aerial vehicles (UAV), balloons, land vehicles, obstacles and so on.
- *Emitter Identifier*, corresponding to the network sender address (24-bit) in aeronautical telecommunications network.
- *Latitude, Longitude and Flight Level*, corresponding to the 3D position of emitter end user.
- Aircraft Identification, corresponding to the alphanumeric code to identify the aircraft (Squaw Code).
- *Figure of Merit* (FOM), corresponding to the information integrity level provided by emitter end user.

Because ADS-B is one of the Application Entities defined to the ATN, there are some requirements defined to it and related to communication domain (ICAO, 1999a):

- With regard to message handling, messages must be delivered at an appropriate rate dependent on the phase of flight, besides they being generated, transmitted and delivered to the receiver end user in an orderly manner over time. Related to the maximum time to update the messages, it was defined times of 10s for en-route flights, 5s and 1s terminals for areas to the surface of airports, where their update likelihood is 98%.

- Regarding to the message priority, ADS-B messages applied to surveillance must have *"normal priority flight safety"* over the ATN.

- Regarding to the Quality of Service (QoS), the datalink must respect a loss of message probability lower than 10^{-6} per message, a latency lower than 2s (or, according to Shorthose et al (2004), between 0.4 s and 1.2s), an integrity lower than 10^{-7} and reliability, availability and continuity of 99.996%.

ADS-B Supporting Technologies

The requirements presented to the ADS-B are related to the adopted datalink between end systems. In the 11th Air Navigation Conference promoted by ICAO in 2003, three potential ADS-B datalink candidates were presented (ICAO, 2003): the SSR Mode S Extended Squitter (1090ES), the Universal Access Transceiver (UAT) and VHF Data Link Mode 4 (VDL4). It was defined that 1090ES would be the best option for international flights, leaving the UAT and the VDL4 as regional solutions (ICAO, 2003b). In this way, Federal Aviation Administration (FAA) adopted, for the North American territory, the 1090ES in high performance aviation and the UAT for general aviation (FAA, 2002). Already Europe, Asia and Pacific regions adopted only the 1090ES in their operations, not setting (so far) a second option for their datalinks (ICAO, 2003b).

The SSR Mode S Extended Squitter (1090ES) takes the present characteristics of the Secondary Surveillance Radar Mode S transponder, which transmits (squitter) through the Mode S reply channel (1090 MHz) – by broadcast and once per second – a 56-bit message containing the transponder address (ICAO, 2004). This mechanism is used in onboard systems to prevent collision (ACAS) (ICAO, 2006b), and allows that an aircraft, upon receiving the message, ask to the message originator and get information from surveillance through a message of 112 bits. In the case of ADS-B, the format of "extended" (extended) uses "squitter" messages of 112 bits, leaving 56 bits for the ADS-B message content.

A 1090ES receiver, with an omnidirectional antenna, is able to cover an area of more than 200nm containing up to 120 aircraft, considering updating rates of 5s in 99.5% of times (5s@99.5%). Thus, the ADS-B surveillance coverage using the 1090ES datalink needs relatively simple equipment, becoming an economically viable solution to its adoption. As an example, Australia has expanded the coverage of ADS-B in its territory installing 1090ES ground receivers. Figure 4 illustrates the evolution of ADS-B and Radar levels of coverage in Australian territory, as indicated by Summer (2007) and Dunstone (2004).

ADS-B is planned to be applied as a primary surveillance system for Air Traffic Services in areas where installing Radar equipments is unfeasible (e.g. ocean); besides, ADS-B will complement surveillance capabilities where Radar service is available. To reach this objective, ADS-B is composed by a transmitter (for generation and transmission of the message), by datalink and by the receiver (that receives the message, processes and displays the message information to the end system). Thus, ADS-B is part of the process of communication in the surveillance system, and it is needed to be clear that the sources of information to the transmitter and the application of the information obtained by ADS-B receiver do not take part of the ADS-B system (CASA, 2007). Therefore, the *ADS-B out* (ADS-B transmission element) must be supplied with information from onboard navigational equipment, and the use given to ADS-B information contained in the message

Figure 4. ADS-B surveillance coverage in Australian airspace. It is noticed that radar surveillance coverage is maintained the same along the time (only new ADS-B sites are being installed in Australia territory).

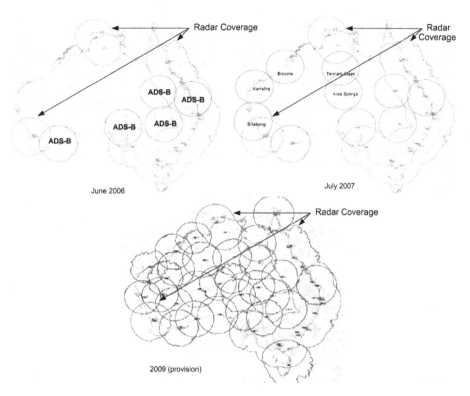

is out of the ADS-B system. Figure 5 (adapted from ICAO (2003c)) illustrates ADS-B system boundaries, showing the functional relationship between it and the other systems.

Beyond ADS-B can be applied as a primary surveillance system for Air Traffic Services, it can be applied in several air traffic management functional levels, such as in airborne situational awareness systems, in automatic conflict detection and resolution systems or even in meteorological systems (ICAO, 1999a). In resume, others automated systems can take advantage of surveillance information provided by ADS-B (illustrated as "Application" in Figure 5), which will enable great strides to the air traffic management, such as one of main technological improvements planned to the Air Traffic Management: he "*Airborne Separation Assistance System*" (ASAS), and which will

be described in details in a specific section ahead in this chapter.

ADS-B and Air Transport Safety

Because of this high potential to improve the air traffic system as a whole, ADS-B is considered by the ICAO as "*...an enabler of the global ATM operational concept bringing substantial safety and capacity benefits ...*" (ICAO, 2006). However, ADS-B changes significantly the navigation and the surveillance concepts as we know today, introducing a strong interdependence between these elements. In the current air traffic system, there is a clear independence between these domains, because the technologies used for surveillance (Radar) and Navigation (VOR, DME and NDB) are independent of each other. Under advanced

Figure 5. ADS-B system boundaries.

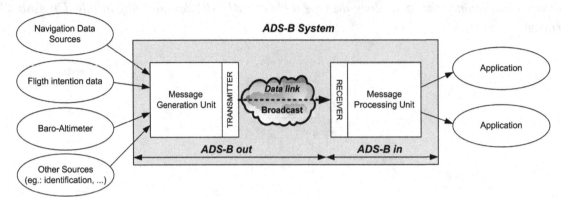

CNS/ATM, surveillance will be based on ADS, which will be fully dependent on the technologies used in the field of navigation as the GNSS. In addition to the interdependence between the navigation and surveillance created by ADS-B, other systemic parameters suffer significant conceptual changes. For example, the deterministic and synchronous nature of today's surveillance (given the characteristics of radar systems), may change for more randomness and asynchronism, typical in digital communications networks (in this case, the ATN).

Therefore, it is necessary to consider these new characteristics and assess in which conditions ADS-B will promote benefits without compromising current air traffic system safety levels. In this way, Vismari and Camargo Jr. (2008) have assessed the impact caused by Automatic Dependent Surveillance - Broadcast (ADS-B) concept over the safety levels of the Air Traffic Control (ATC) system. Considering that specific environment, it was concluded that:

... ADS-B is a viable application, considering its safety aspects, to substitute the current surveillance (Radar) in the ATC system despite the fact that the ADS-B shows strong interdependence between the ATC navigation and the surveillance elements as well as promotes an asynchronous and stochastic surveillance data sample process.

Moreover, the coupled behavior of surveillance and communication (and of navigation and surveillance) characteristics has demonstrated that it is possible to compensate the degradation in the GNSS position accuracy (caused by, e.g. atmospheric phenomena) by the increment of the ADS-B message sending rate (the ADS-B scan rate). Therefore, this complementary behavior of the ADS-B can improve the resilience of the air traffic surveillance system, especially to surveillance services. ... (Vismari, Camargo Jr., 2008).

We presented the ADS-B concept and the conclusion that it is safe considering its surveillance application to the ATC system. Now, we present one of main technological improvements planned to the Air Traffic Management and enabled by ADS-B: the *"Airborne Separation Assistance System"* (ASAS). An in-depth analysis of the risks associated with ASAS is presented either, providing valuable information for regulating the implementation and use of this important ATM improvement.

Airborne Separation Assistance System – ASAS

In the current ATM philosophy, flight crews are in charge of safe and efficient control and navigation of their individual aircraft, and air traffic controllers are responsible for maintaining aircraft separation. Only when some exceptional situation occurs, the flight crew receives separation support from the Airborne Collision Avoidance System (ACAS), as an emergency device. The current situation, however, is that air traffic controllers frequently are overloaded and, therefore, prone to errors. A new task allocation between air traffic controller and flight crew is envisaged as a possible option to improve ATM performance and safety. This different task allocation is expected to increase controller availability, which could lead to improved safety, enable better quality of service and more airspace capacity. Also, flight crews are expected to gain in situation awareness and anticipation by taking an active part in the management of their situation with respect to a designated aircraft.

This concept of operation relies on a set of applications enabled by ASAS (Airborne Separation Assurance System), a concept first formalized in 1994 at CENA (Centre *d'Etude de la Navigation Aérienne*, France). Under this paradigm, the task of maintaining a safe distance between aircraft may be delegated to pilots, which will be supported by new devices and algorithms. With ASAS, currently in experimental phase, pilots become aware of the surrounding air traffic risks with up to 15 minutes in advance, without the help of air traffic controllers on the ground. This antecedence is much greater than the one provided by the current Traffic Collision Avoidance System (TCAS): an ACAS implementation that relies on Mode-C transponder and is broadly used in the current civil aviation for collision avoidance purposes. The ASAS communication, instead, is based on ADS-B (Automatic Dependent Surveillance – Broadcast), and applications of both (ASAS and ADS-B) are being intensively developed in Eurocontrol and in other initiatives in the United States of America. The use of ASAS for civil air traffic purposes can occur in some different modes of operation, basically distinguished for Conflict Detection and Resolution, and for Maintaining

Spacing. Each of these operation modes will be described in this chapter.

The Air Traffic Control Loop and ASAS

Hansman et al. (1997) very well describes the *Air Traffic Control Loop,* which is a control network which includes airborne and ground-based systems, and the human operators such as pilot and ATCo. In figure 6, we present this control network, but now with ASAS inserted, and with a few other modifications.

Beginning by the right-top corner of this figure, we have the Surveillance means, using Radar and ADS equipment, to provide up-to-date aircraft position and speed. This information is processed by the Automation Tools, which have the primary function of synthesize raw information and, depending on the automation level, may have a decision-support role. The Flight Progress Strips contain basic information about each ongoing flight. In modern systems, they exist as data entities in the automation system, and are transferred successively in the chain of air traffic controllers along all the flight phases. The AOC (Airline Operations Center) provides to the aircraft the flight plan approved by the aeronautical authority, previously to the flight and, during the flight, may send commands to the pilot, regarding eventual flight alterations, and receive flight information from the aircraft, via Datalink or voice communication.

The ATCo – Air Traffic Controller – becomes aware of the air traffic situation by means of a Graphical Interface, and may exert influence in the aircraft trajectory, through Vectors, which are horizontal direction alterations, through Flight Plan Amendments, which may involve localized altitude changes, new reference points, etc., or through Flight Plan Changes, which consist in greater trajectory changes, such as a whole different airway or an alternate destination airport.

The pilot controls the aircraft in four different levels. At the navigation programming level, this

Figure 6. ASAS included into the Air Traffic Control Loop of Hansman (1997).

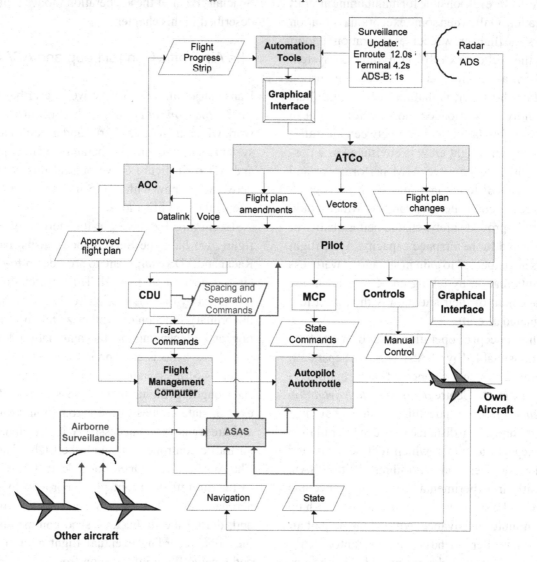

is done by means of a CDU – Control and Display Unit –, which is a graphical interface that is linked to the Flight Management Computer. The next control level has to do with the behavior relative to other aircraft, and is done with ASAS, through Spacing and Separation Commands. This control level is the location of the innovative concept studied in this research work.

The next aircraft control level is the state control level, where pilots issue State Commands such as "maintain a given altitude", or "maintain a given speed", and this is done through the MCP – Mode Control Panel, with knobs, switches and buttons, which determine the behavior of the Autopilot and the Autothrottle. Finally, the last control level allow the pilot to operate more directly the engine and actuators, through the throttle lever and the control wheel or sticks, moving the aerodynamic control surfaces.

All the control computing units receive the feedback Navigation and State data from the aircraft navigation and state sensors, and ASAS receive information from other aircraft from the Airborne Surveillance devices (primarily ADS-B).

Finally, the pilot receives feedback of all these systems through the cockpit gauges and Graphical Interfaces.

Description of the ASAS Time-Based Spacing Operation

The present study considered ASAS Time-Based Spacing (TBS) application in TMA. ASAS TBS aims to delegate to the flight crew some tasks necessary to maintain a precise spacing between aircraft in converging or coincident arrival flows. It is expected that TBS application can provide more accurate spacing between arriving aircraft, minimize the idle runway time without violating the separation minima and increase the possibility for TMA to handle more aircraft (Grimaud et al., 2005; Ivanescu et al., 2005). The study of Cloarec et al. (2004) shows that there is a potential increase between 12% and 15% in the terminal airspace capacity when using ASAS TBS operations, due to the Air Traffic Controller workload reduction per flight.

The TBS procedure in this report focuses on the airspace before the final approach (Grimaud et al., 2005). It is assumed that TBS procedure may start between the Extended-TMA entry point (assumed here to be 60 nautical miles from the airport, after the top of descent) and the Final Approach Fix (FAF). In this phase of the flight, as in other phases, the flight crew must be aware of the surrounding traffic through the ASAS traffic synthesis provided in the Cockpit Display of Traffic Information (CDTI), which is often integrated with the CDU. It is also assumed that ASAS system will be working in Airborne Spacing mode (that is one of the available modes), and the conflict detection is a task of the ATCo.

To have an idea of how it works, the following example of (RFG, 2005) is shown in Figure 7. In this example, the controller builds the sequence of aircraft early in the sector by assigning a target aircraft to each aircraft in the sequence (i.e. E is a target for F, D is a target for E, etc). Sequencing

and merging instructions are then given to ensure the appropriate spacing is achieved by the merging waypoint (WPT). Having built the sequence, and having given the aircraft instructions to maintain the sequence (by maintaining the spacing), the controller must now monitor the aircraft for compliance, as C spaces itself from its target B, and B spaces itself from its target A.

The example shows that the TBS operation involves two steps. In a first step, an ATCo instructs the flight crew to select a neighboring aircraft as a target on the CDTI (Ivanescu et al., 2005), which will present a screen similar to Figure 8. Aware of the required target, the flight crew must identify and select it in the ASAS system, and report the target identification to the ATCo.

In the second step, after the target identification read-back of the target identification instruction, ATCo instructs flight crew with one of the following options, depending on the trajectories of the flights involved:

(a) **Merge behind**: the flight crew is instructed to merge the own flight trajectory behind the trajectory of the target aircraft, in a chosen waypoint, maintaining at a given time spacing to the target aircraft. This is the case when the aircraft involved are executing converging approach routes. In Figure 9, AFR123 is the target and DLH456 is instructed to merge behind, maintaining the spacing D.

(b) **Direct-to then merge behind**: the merge operation described above is executed, but preceded by a horizontal-path change, which consists in turning to the direction of the merging waypoint when the aircraft reaches the required spacing (this position is called *resume point*). This instruction is used when the follower aircraft has to achieve the desired spacing, then it follows a divergent path of the target aircraft to achieve a desired spacing, and when the spacing is achieved, the pilot must turn to the cleared merge waypoint. In Figure 10, AFR123 is

Figure 7. Airborne Spacing operational example.

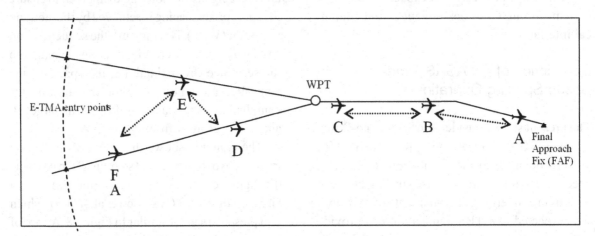

the target and DLH456 is instructed to go directly to the merge waypoint, merging behind AFR123 with spacing D.

(c) **Remain behind**: the flight crew is instructed to achieve and maintain a given time spacing behind the trajectory of the target, in a chosen waypoint, maintaining at this point a given time spacing to the target aircraft. This third option is applied when the own aircraft is already flying on the same trajectory of the target aircraft, like in Figure 11.

After selecting one of the options (a), (b) or (c), the flight crew of the follower aircraft will

Figure 8. CDTI screen for Airborne Spacing application.

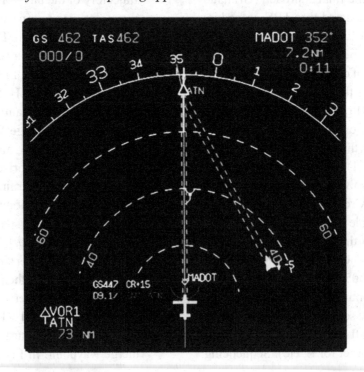

Figure 9. "Merge behind" (a) schema.

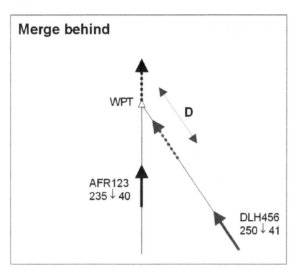

monitor the evolution of the spacing to check if it tends to the desired spacing. Normally, the speed adjustments of the follower aircraft are done automatically, since the aircraft are equipped with the ASAS speed director, which automatically inputs the ASAS suggested speed in the Autopilot System. As an exception, in case of doing training or happening some equipment failure, the flight crew may have to manually apply speed adjustments suggested by the ASAS system.

The aircraft which is applying TBS is denominated the "follower" aircraft, in order to

Figure 10. "Direct-to then merge" (b) schema.

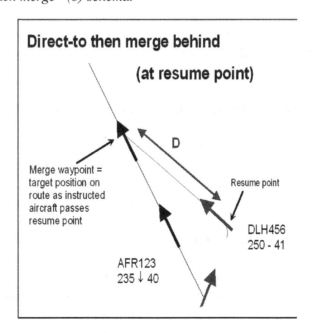

Figure 11. "Remain behind" (c) schema.

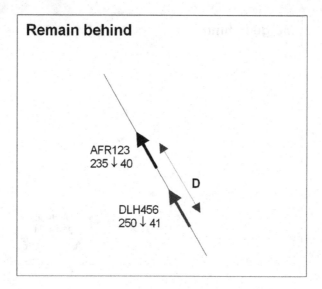

distinguish from the "target" aircraft, which is supposed to land in the same airport as the follower aircraft, but earlier. While monitoring the TBS procedure, flight crew will monitor the execution of the flight plan, and this execution must have RNP-1 (Required Navigation Performance Level 1) property.

The Air Traffic Controller will have graphical system tools for aiding the task of mounting and monitoring chains of airborne spacing aircraft. The interface developed in (CoSpace, 2006) is shown in Figure 12. In this figure, the aircraft selected as target by someone are indicated by the small circumferences, and the aircraft performing airborne spacing are indicated by the greater circumferences. The links between aircraft indicate which the target of the other one is.

The TBS procedure may normally finish after passing the Final Approach Fix, or eventually be interrupted, due to some failure in the ASAS system, or to some hazard detected by the flight crew or the ATCo. In cases of abnormal termination, the ATCo will execute conventional procedures for separating and sequencing aircraft. In this paper, only one single flow of arriving aircraft will be considered, with no other surrounding traffic.

Considerations about Pilot Workload

ASAS operation introduces new tasks to the pilots and thus has a potential to increase pilot workload. However, several studies, such as of Ruigrok et al. (2005), Ruigrok & Hoekstra (2007) and CoSpace (2006), agree that that the workload increase is comfortably tolerable and is compensated by the greater situational awareness (the pilots feel safer) and the decrease in the communication with ATCos.

CASE STUDY: DYNAMIC RISK MODEL OF ASAS-TBS OPERATION

Vismari and Camargo Jr. (2008) explain that ADS-B has raised certain expectations regarding potential improvements on safety and capacity of advanced CNS/ATM. The question then is whether the proposed ASAS-TBS operation actually will deliver such capacity and safety improvements. In order to answer this question, we have to develop a dynamic safety risk model of the ASAS-TBS operation, which can subsequently be used to assess the potential safety and capacity improvements.

Figure 12. ATCo graphical interface for airborne spacing.

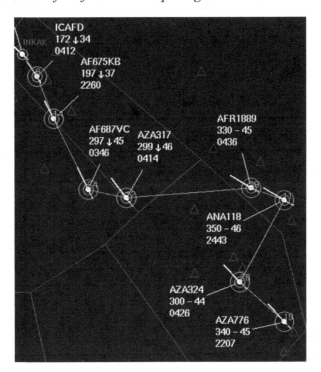

Safety is acknowledged as a key property when designing advanced ATM concepts. Although ATM engineers try to obtain improvements in capacity and efficiency, the target levels of safety (TLS) of the new applications are intended to be "equal or better" as compared to the current practice. Therefore, civil aviation official regulators require that all significant operational changes undergo rigorous safety assessment before becoming standards.

Safety assessments can be qualitative, quantitative, or both. Qualitative safety assessments are good for identifying local concept inconsistencies against the safety requirements, and depend on the elaboration of a set of pre-defined and understandable scenarios. These elements can also support basic quantitative analysis. However, when the complexity of the set of scenarios is high, dynamic safety risk modeling and probabilistic analyses is the direction to go. Quantitative risk analysis is mainly probabilistic and tries to put

the several ATM applications in a continuous risk scale, enabling objective comparison and definition of minimum acceptable levels. This chapter will present fundamental safety considerations about ASAS, and will dedicate a great extent to a quantitative risk assessment based on dynamical model-based probabilistic simulation of ASAS, in order to provide support for regulators about some possible constraints of the CNS/ATM applications.

Historically, for low density air traffic, researchers in the civil aviation community have developed a mathematical model to estimate mid-air collision risk levels as a function of spacing (ICAO, 2001). This model is known as the Reich collision model (Reich, 1964). In this model one assumes that the physical shape of each aircraft is a box, having a fixed x,y,z orientation, and the collision risk between two boxes is obtained by integrating the incrossing rate over the time period in which these boxes may be close to each other

(Hsu, 1981). Hence, it is more precise to speak of incrossing integral rather than collision risk (Blom et al., 2003). Another limitation of the Reich model is that it does not adequately cover busy continental situations with tactical interventions by air traffic controllers, because it does not allow discrete mode transitions, which happen when an air traffic controller asks an aircraft to deviate from route.

Therefore, a more sophisticated approach is needed in order to model the accident risk under the influence of human behavior, technical systems behavior, communications environment, flight procedures, etc. The approach taken in this paper is to develop a stochastic hybrid model of the air traffic operation considered, and subsequently to evaluate this model through conducting stochastic analysis and Monte Carlo simulations (Blom et al., 2001b, 2006c). More specifically, this approach has been introduced under the acronym TOPAZ, which stands for Traffic Organization and Perturbation AnalyZer. In the sequel of this chapter we illustrate how the quantitative part of this approach works for the ASAS-TBS operation considered.

Estimation of Incident and Accident Probabilities

Air transportation is a safety-critical system, where abnormal, out-of-requirements operation could lead to fatalities, human life injury or environmental harm. In this way, the conditions that contribute to the occurrence of these "safety-related events" must be minimized to levels considered acceptable.

In aeronautical context, as defined by ICAO in its Annex 13, the occurrence of fatalities, human injuries, severe structural damage or aircraft missing during an its operation is considered an "accident". In the same way, an occurrence other than an accident that affects or could affect the operational safety is considered an "incident".

Accidents and incidents must be evaluated in a risk assessment context: conditions (scenarios, sequence of events) could lead to an accident ("occurrence of fatalities ...") must be identified, their severities (e.g. number of fatalities produced) must be determined and, mainly, the occurrence probabilities of these scenarios must be calculated. Only after obtaining the 3-tuple {*Condition, Severity, Probability*} it is possible to evaluate the accident risk and, consequently, proceed to minimize to social acceptable levels their occurrences rates.

According to De Oliveira (2007), the inherent aircraft operational risks (or possible scenarios could lead to an accident) are related both to the isolate actions of each aircraft – such as fire risk, the depressurization risk and the impact against the ground – and to the interaction between different aircraft – such as mid-air collision risk or the risk of aircraft destabilization by wake turbulence. According to Profit (1995), mid-air collision is the most significant aviation safety-related event due to its huge social impact. Therefore, our accident risk model for ASAS-TBS considers the event "mid-air collision risk" as the main event to be investigated in the Risk Assessment process.

So, in this risk assessment context, we need to estimate the probability p of occurrence of a mid-air collision event. There are two problems in doing so. Typically, we formalize an estimation problem as one to evaluate the expected value of a random quantity such as

$$p := \mathbf{E}_f \left[\mathcal{N} \left(Z \right) \right] \tag{1}$$

where $Z = \left(z_1, ..., z_m \right) \in \mathbf{R}^m$ is a realization of a random vector with joint probability density function (pdf) $f(Z)$, and N is a real-valued mapping on $\mathbf{R}^m$. When f and N are analytically known in a closed formula, this may be used to deduce p, however typically this is not the case for advanced ATM operations. Another problem is that for level crossing events like mid-air collisions, there does not even exist an exact characterization of the form in (1). Fortunately, there is a relative simple way in solving both problems, and that is running Monte Carlo simulations with the stochastic hybrid model of the ASAS-TBS operation.

The Monte Carlo simulation method refers to a class of algorithms very commonly used for obtaining numerical approximations of complex functions. This method involves the generation of some implicit probability distribution and the use of the obtained sample to approximate the function of interest.

The basic idea of the Monte Carlo method is quite straightforward. It consists in randomly drawing a great number of observations from a sampling space, and counting how many of them fall into a particular set. The rate of the number of observations falling into that set over the total number of observations gives the estimated quantity. In the particular case of estimating the collision probability per a single ASAS TBS operation, define N_s as the number of observed simulated operations, and Z_i the collision indicator for the observation i, i.e.:

$$Z_i = \begin{cases} 0 & \text{if observation } i \text{ does not collide} \\ 1 & \text{if observation } i \text{ collides} \end{cases}$$

(2)

If all observed operations have the same weight, then the estimated probability of collision p is

$$p = \frac{1}{N_s} \sum_{i=1}^{N_s} Z_i$$

(3)

Accidents such as mid-air collisions are supposed to occur with a very small probability, and so one could spend nearly infinite computing resources in order to obtain a reasonable precision for an estimate of the collision probability. Suppose that p is expected to be as low as 10exp-9,

for example, then the number of simulated observations necessary for the Monte Carlo returning a valid result, i.e., a non-zero result, would be expected to be around 10exp9. Assuming that that the simulated scenario in each observation takes half a second to be executed, then the number of hours necessary to calculate p would be in the order of 2.8×10exp5, or equivalently about 15 years. Therefore, some additional technique has to be used on top of the basic Monte Carlo principle, and this will be explained in the section "Monte Carlo Speed Up". But before that, we will present the mathematical model for the ASAS TBS operation.

Development of Stochastic Hybrid Model of ASAS-TBS Operation

A prerequisite for running Monte Carlo simulations is to develop an appropriate mathematical model of the operation considered. Hence, as part of the evaluation of the expected number of aircraft accidents per flight hour in airborne spacing operation, a stochastic model is built that describes this accident risk under the influence of human behaviour, technical systems behaviour, communications environment, flight procedures, etc. In the context of the TOPAZ methodology, such a model is in the form of a Stochastically and Dynamically Coloured Petri Net (SDCPN) (Everdij & Blom, 2005, 2006). This model is a stochastic hybrid system, which enables to evaluate the collision risk by means of Monte Carlo simulation. Because straightforward Monte Carlo simulation would be far too much time-consuming, we make use of importance sampling based acceleration methods that have recently been developed (Cérou et al., 2002, 2005; Krystul & Blom, 2005; Blom et al., 2006, 2006b).

For the ASAS TBS operation considered in this chapter, a complete model in terms of the SDCPN language has been developed in (De Oliveira et al., 2006), which describes the situations "Remain Behind" and "Merge Behind" for small angles (less than 45 degrees). The SDCPN languaged model of the ASAS-TBS operation is developed using the compositional specification approach of (Everdij et al., 2006c) towards another ASAS and ADS-B based advanced ATM operation. First the relevant agents that play a role in the operation are identified. Next, each agent is modeled through a collection of agent specific Local Petri Nets (LPNs), where each LPN is a Petri net describing an agent specific process. Finally, the connections between LPNs within the same agent and between LPNs of different agents are being specified (De Oliveira et al., 2006). In this Section, the main characteristics of the resulting stochastic hybrid model for ASAS TBS operation are summarized.

General Definition of SDCPN

The formal definition of a Stochastically and Dynamically Coloured Petri Net follows Everdij and Blom (2005, 2006), and the graphical representation of its elements are shown in Figure 13.

The state of a SDCPN is determined by where the tokens are placed, and by the colors of the tokens. A token stays in one place until some transition connected to this place through an outgoing arc fires. This transition will consume at least one token from the input place, and may put tokens to the output place. Figure 14 shows

an example of SDCPN representing aircraft radio telecommunication equipment availability. At any moment, the Aircraft R/T system may be either in the state Working, i.e., working normally, or in the state Not working, i.e., in failure, with no possibility of performing communication. In this example, the transitions are of the Delay type, identified with a D. In this type of transition, the instant of transition is determined by an exponential distribution with a given parameter, defined and validated with experts in the field, as reported (De Oliveira et al., 2006).

SDCPN's are very adequate to mathematically model ATM applications. The use of continuous variables called colors, in the SDCPN, enables the use of differential equations, as for example the aircraft physical behavior and control law presented in Subsection "Aircraft Guidance Behavior LPN". However, because of the complexity of the model, the formalism of SDCPN is extended to allow hierarchical grouping of its basic elements in agents and LPNs.

Instantiation of the SDCPN Model for ASAS-TBS Operation

Agents

An agent is defined as an entity that maintains some kind of situation awareness (Blom & Stroeve, 2004) and may play a role in the operation

Figure 13. Graphical representation of the SDCPN elements.

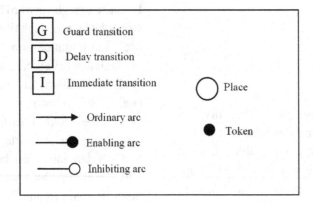

considered. For this particular application, in order to assess the accident risk, the following agents are adopted in the SDCPN model of the TBS operation (De Oliveira et al., 2006):

- Aircraft;
- Aircraft Guidance, Navigation and Communication Systems (GNC), including Guidance Systems, Own Positioning System, and Communication Systems;

- ASAS System;
- Pilot Flying (PF);
- Pilot Not Flying (PNF);
- Air Traffic Services (ATS) System, including Ground Radio Telecommunication, Navigation Systems Global / GNSS (Global Navigation Satellite System), and ATS Surveillance System;
- Tactical Air Traffic Controller (ATCo).

Figure 14. Example of two different states of a LPN.

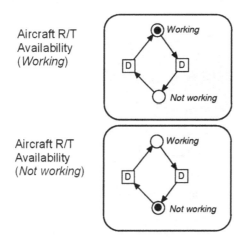

Figure 15. Relations between Petri nets at agent level.

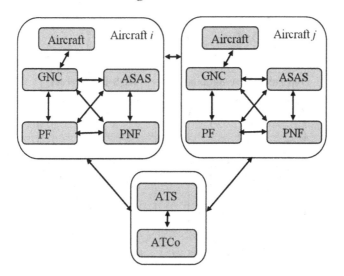

A high level representation of the relations between agents is shown for two aircraft in Figure 15.

Each of the agents present in Figure 15 is internally composed by LPNs.

Local Petri Nets (LPNs)

Each agent is modelled with multiple Local Petri Nets (LPN), which are mutually connected forming the complete SDCPN. The resulting SDCPN specified model developed for ASAS TBS operation consists of 43 LPNs (De Oliveira et al., 2006). The ones that deviate a lot from those for conventional ATM are shortly explained in the sequel of this paper.

In general, the hybrid state of the LPN is determined by the place in which the token remains, and by the color that is attached to the combination of token and place. Some LPNs are shown in Figure 16, representing some aircraft communication components. At any moment, one of these systems may be either in the state Working, i.e., working normally, or in the state Not working, i.e., in failure, not performing its communication functions. In these LPNs, the token switches between places through the delay transitions, as explained in Section. "General Definition of SDCPN". For sake of simplicity, exactly one token is assumed to be in each LPN.

Figure 16. Aircraft communication LPNs.

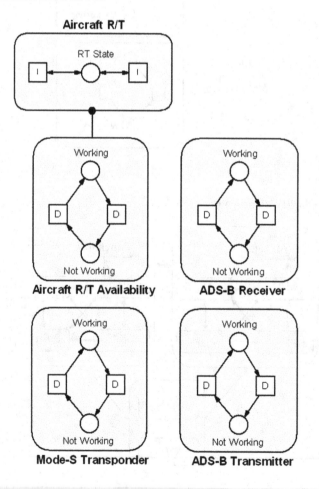

Aircraft Guidance Behavior LPN

The LPN describing the aircraft physical dynamics is shown in Figure 17. The possible places for the aircraft state are Level, when the aircraft is trying to keep a constant altitude, Climb/Desc. standard vertical speed, when the aircraft is changing the altitude, or Evasion, when the aircraft is leaving the approach route. The immediate transitions (indicated by I in Figure 17) are triggered by tokens in other places (not shown in the figure) that represent commands input by the pilot in the aircraft guidance system. The aircraft equations in all the places of this LPN follow the model described by Van der Geest (2002). In this model, the basic aircraft dynamics is described by the following differential equation system:

where:

- $y \in \Re^6$ and $[y_1, y_2, y_3]^T$ is the aircraft 3-D position, y_4 is the aircraft true airspeed, y_5 is the heading angle and y_6 is the vertical path angle;

- $u \in \Re^3$ is the control input vector, with u_1 being the engine thrust, u_2 the angle of attack and u_3 the bank angle; these variables are evaluated using the control laws described by van der Geest (2002);

- $w \in \Re^3$ is the wind vector;

- m is the aircraft mass, g is the gravity acceleration;

- $D : \Re^3 \mapsto \Re$ is the aircraft drag function;

- $L : \Re^3 \mapsto \Re$ is the aircraft lift function.

ASAS Agent LPNs

The LPNs composing the ASAS Agent are shown in Figure 18. The ASAS Surveillance LPN has a token whose colour contains state information of all aircraft inside the range of the ADS-B receiver, plus the own aircraft state information.

The ASAS System Mode LPN has the places Working, which represents the nominal ASAS working state, Failure, where ASAS is not executing its functions, and Corrupted, where ASAS is working with some non-detectable fault. The enabling arc between the place Working and the ASAS Spacing LPN makes that the transitions between the places of ASAS Spacing occur only if there is a token in the Working place, i.e., if ASAS is correctly working.

Figure 17. Aircraft guidance behavior LPN.

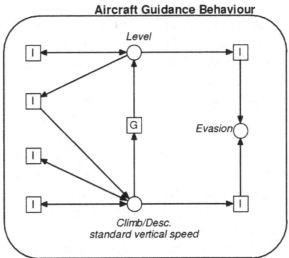

Aircraft Guidance Behaviour

Figure 18. ASAS agent LPNs.

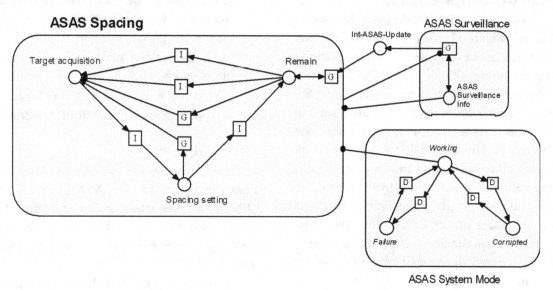

The token ASAS Surveillance LPN has a color containing state information of all aircraft inside the range of the ADS-B receiver, plus the own aircraft state information. The ASAS Spacing LPN determines the phase of execution of the ASAS spacing function. Target Acquisition is the initial phase, where the Pilot Not-Flying can select an aircraft as target through the CDTI. After this selection, the token moves to the Spacing Setting place, when the Pilot Not-Flying can give a spacing value to ASAS. Finished this phase, the token moves to the Remain place, where ASAS constantly calculates a required speed to maintain the required spacing. The calculation of this speed depends on the information in the ASAS Surveillance LPN, and is done in accordance with the feedback control design model of Van der Geest (2002).

LPNs of Human Operators

The Pilot Flying, the Pilot Not-Flying and the ATCo are the most complex agents in the model. Following the approach developed in (Blom et al., 2001), and earlier applied to another ASAS application (Everdij et al., 2006c; Blom et al., 2007), the Petri Net model of the Pilot Flying Agent

has been adapted (De Oliveira et al., 2006). The resulting LPNs are jointly presented in Figure 19. The LPN named Task Performance PF presents a pattern of stages for the human operator task execution. Each stage is represented by one place of this LPN:

(T1) *Monitoring*: stage where the pilot gathers and integrates information about the current goal. For example, this stage may consist in reading the altimeter or the speed indicator.

(T2) *Monitoring and Decision*: in this stage, using information provided by the instrumentation systems and, possibly, by other human operators, and based in his situational awareness, the pilot makes decisions about: (a) If he needs to query some other human operator and, if it is, what is the query to be done; (b) If a particular action is required and, in case it is, what are the parameter values for its concrete application.

(T3) *Coordination*: stage where the pilot coordinates with other human operators, communicating, questioning and answering, and checking the consistency of his decisions.

Figure 19. Pilot flying task performance LPN.

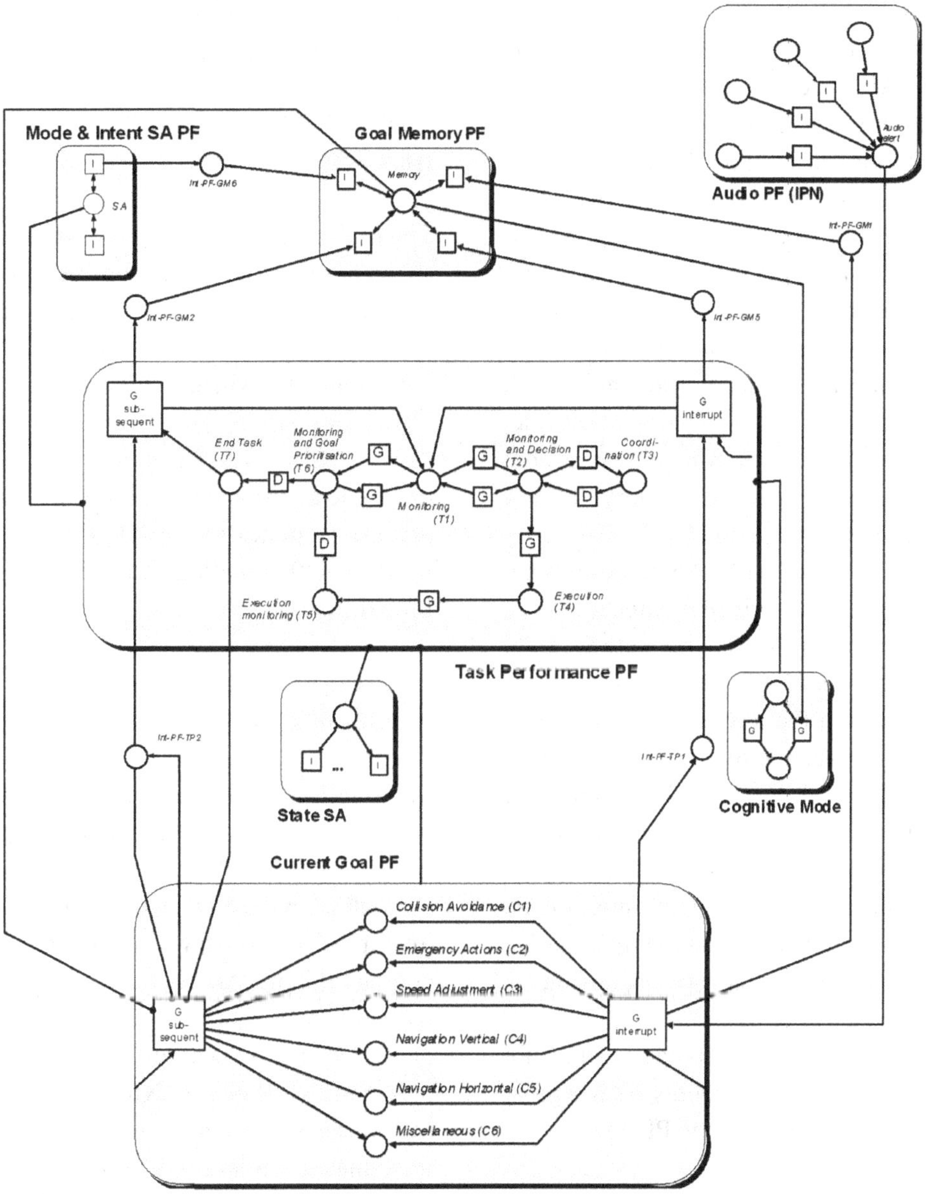

(T4) *Execution*: stage where the pilot is effectively operating the aircraft control, activating functions by means of the aircraft control devices.

(T5) *Execution Monitoring*: stage on which the pilot observes the events resulting from the executed action.

(T6) *Monitoring and Goal Prioritization*: stage in which the pilot gathers information and

decides which of his goals most require attention in the following instant.

In this model, it is assumed that the pilot performs exclusively one of the stages T1-T6 per time. This is a simplification of the reality, because it is known that the human being is able to perform some mechanical, repetitive or even cognitive tasks simultaneously with decision-making tasks. However, the current design tries to keep the model simple.

Another LPN of the Pilot Flying Agent is Current Goal PF, which determines the goal assumed by the PF in a given instant. The Current Goal token may be moved in two different ways. By one side, through the "interrupt" transition, which is fired by audio alerts coming from the interaction place *Audio alert*. In this case, the next goal is decided based on the audio message received. By the other side, the Current Goal token may move through the transition "subsequent", which is enabled at the end of a task performance cycle, and so the pilot must decide which the next goal is. The goals stored in the Goal Memory PF LPN are then taken in consideration.

The Mode & Intent SA PF LPN represents the aircraft desired state at a given moment (such as altitude and speed), by the PF. The State SA LPN models the knowledge of the currently active failure indicators in the aircraft, and Cognitive Mode is a simpler version of the contextual control mode model of Hollnagel (1993). When the pilot has few tasks to perform, the token stays in the Tactical mode, and this means that the pilot has a small probability of error or omission. In the opposite, when the pilot has too many tasks, the token goes to Opportunistic mode, raising his probability of error or omission.

The architecture of Petri Net models of the Pilot Not-Flying and of the ATCo agents are in a great extent similar to the LPNs of the PF agent.

Other Hazardous States in the LPNs

The set of LPNs in the model also includes several possible failure components in the system state, such as engine failure, noise in the aircraft instrumentation, failure in the ATC systems, etc. With the entire Petri net model, it is possible to simulate the execution of an ASAS TBS operation and check if a collision has occurred or not. Since the ASAS TBS operation is designed to be as safe as possible, a low probability of collision is expected, i.e., a significant number of collisions

only occurs amongst a very large number of Monte Carlo simulated flight hours The next section explains how this has been accomplished.

Monte Carlo Simulation of ASAS-TBS Model

The probability of collision between two aircraft subject to airborne spacing operation is estimated over the SDCPN model and, as we cannot build closed analytic formulae to describe the model behaviour, we will use the principle of Monte Carlo simulation. However, as mid-air collision is expected to be rare events, we have to use some additional technique to get reasonably precise estimates in feasible time, as explained in Section "Estimation of Incident and Accident Probabilities".

Challenge of Rare Event Probability Estimation

Many techniques have been developed over the years to provide estimates better than basic Monte Carlo, in the sense that the variance of the resulting estimates is reduced and, therefore, can achieve a given precision with fewer observations, in a shorter computing time. An overview of classic variance reduction techniques can be found in (Bratley et al., 1983), and we will just cite a few of them.

Common Random Numbers (CRN), Control Variates and Antithetic Variates techniques introduce correlation among observations to reduce variance. CRN and Antithetic Variates need a reference model to be simulated parallely and be compared with the model of interest, and such a model, similar to the SDCPN model here presented, we do not have. Antithetic Variates requires one to explore antithetic behaviors of the model, what could be done in this study, but in a complex model like ours this could take long time to be properly tuned.

Other important variance reduction technique is called Importance Sampling (IS), which uses a different distribution, rather than the distribution of interest, to generate samples. Suppose we need to estimate some quantity from the distribution of interest f. With importance sampling, we chose a distribution g which has the same support as of f, but is more efficient to generate samples. At the end, we need to use the relation f/g to correct the final estimation. However, in our case of the SDCPN model, which determines f, we cannot find an adequate g to use this technique. More recently, Rubinstein (1993) created a variant of IS which starts in a basic IS, then allows for choosing an optimal g from a given sample, and then use the new g in the next iteration, repeating the process in several iterations, until one achieves an adequate precision. This technique was named Cross-Entropy and can produce great achievements on rare event simulation, and more details on it can be found in (De Boer et al., 2004). However, the Cross-Entropy present the same impediments of IS to be applied to our model. So, we remain with few alternatives to perform variance reduction.

We begin to see a way through these restrictions when we study the principles of the Stratification technique (Bratley et al., 1983), which uses weighted sampling based on a priori qualitative or quantitative information. Then, *a posteriori*, an unweighting correction is applied to eliminate bias. Stratification embodies the precept that recasting an estimation problem, so that random variables are replaced by their expected values, whenever known, often is a good idea. When valid, this replacement reduces variance without injecting bias. This idea is exploited in a powerful technique called Conditional Monte Carlo, which in turn is the basis for the variance reduction technique applied in this research work to accelerate the collision probability estimation. Among the variations in the conditional Monte Carlo techniques, the specific acceleration technique used in this research work is explained in the following section.

Monte Carlo Speed Up

The optimization technique used in this work to speed up the Monte Carlo simulation essentially is the Interacting Particle System (IPS) approach of Cérou et al. (2002, 2005) for the estimation of rare events in strong Markov processes. This IPS approach has been adapted to hybrid state strong Markov processes by Krystul and Blom (2005). Everdij & Blom (2005, 2006) have proven that by using the SDCPN modelling language, one is guaranteed to end up with a simulation model which generates samples of a hybrid state strong Markov process. This ensures that the IPS approach can be applied as a valid speed-up mechanism to the ASAS-TBS model developed. In order to get the details of the IPS approach right for a specific ATM application, we follow the approach that has been developed by Blom et al. (2006, 2006b).

The IPS denominates a hybrid state sample of an air traffic situation as a particle, and takes benefit of certain predictability in the state of each particle, i.e., the probability that an aircraft collides in the interval $[t, T_{max}]$ is higher for aircraft that have smaller separation distance at (present) time t. A filter selects only the particles with smaller distances between aircraft and stops them. In the beginning of the next prediction level, all particles are replications of the selected particles. The particles evolve separately and then a smaller separation distance is used to select particles and the process is repeated, until the aircraft dimensions are reached, meaning the occurrence of a collision event. This filtering process of IPS is depicted in Figures 20 and 21. The first one shows the initial position of particles as small circles, and the number of sampled particles starting from that position, in each filtering level. Figure 21 shows the final collision probability as the product of all the intermediate conditional evaluated probabilities.

For the ASAS TBS operation, one IPS run of 50 thousand particles and 11 filtering levels, with the software written in Java, and running in the

Figure 20. Example of three levels of particle filtering (showing relative aircraft distances along time).

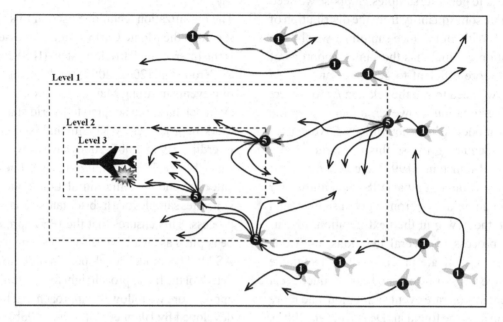

Figure 21. Schematic of Interacting Particle System algorithm.

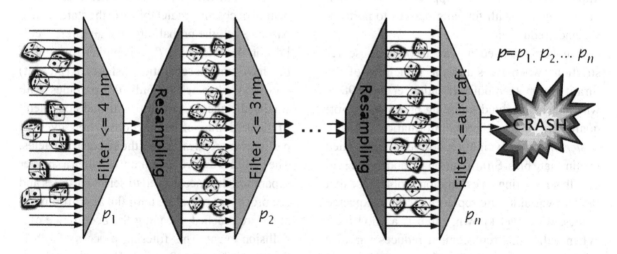

$$p = p_1 . p_2 . \cdots p_n$$

Java Virtual Machine, takes around 5.5 hours in an Intel Xeon 64 bits, 3 GHz dual processor machine, with a memory load of 2.7 GB. Some parallelism is used to take benefit of using multiple processors. In each level, the evolution of each particle can be computed simultaneously to the evolution of other particles in each processor.

Collision Probability Estimation Results

The set of Monte Carlo/IPS executions produced the results shown in Figure 22. These results were obtained for an average flight time of 11 minutes and 7.2 seconds, in the approach airspace considered. These results suggest that the operation of

Figure 22. Collision probabilities.

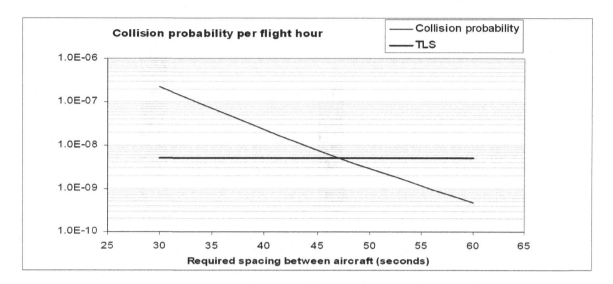

airborne spacing in the ASAS TBS paradigm is, for a spacing period greater than 47s, compliant with a Target Level of Safety (TLS) of 5x10exp-9 (ICAO, 2001), that is the current ICAO TLS considered for the risk in each one of the three possible collision geometries, and when TCAS is not taken into account.

Consideration about Bias and Uncertainty

The model used to calculate the collision probabilities uses several simplifying assumptions, and so there will be bias and uncertainty in the result. Bias is a systematic deviation of the results estimated through the Monte Carlo method from the real collision probabilities; uncertainty is a spread around each estimated result that has to be assumed. Both bias and uncertainty exist due to structural assumptions, parameter value assumptions in the model, and also because of numerical assumptions. Bias and uncertainty assessment involves the estimation of parameter sensitivities (Everdij et al., 2006b). The evaluation of bias and uncertainty remains to be done.

Analysis of the Collision Cases

The occurrence of a collision between aircraft, as observed in the simulations, is caused by a combination of several factors. In order to find clues of these factors from the Monte Carlo simulations performed, our software stored some data about each scenario's history. The data presented in this section refer only to the scenarios where a collision occurred, and include information such as altitude, speed and instant of collision, from which we try to find possible correlations.

With the samples obtained, a separate dataset has to be analyzed for each point of interest of the graph in Figure 22. We begin by the dataset where the required spacing between aircraft, denoted by the symbol $t_{spacing}^{default}$, has the value of 60 seconds. The sample size was of 20.000 scenarios with collision.

In Figure 23, one can see the joint distribution of the collision speed v_{follow} of the follower aircraft, with the collision altitude h_{col}. An abnormal situation was observed, for the dynamics of the flight operation defined in the SDCPN model. The nominal situation is that, when an aircraft receives the instruction to descend from 9,000

Figure 23. Joint histogram of speeds and altitudes of collision, for $t_{\text{spacing}}^{\text{default}} = 60\,s.$

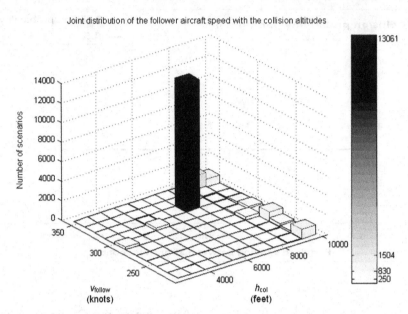

Figure 24. Histogram of instants of collision, for $t_{\text{spacing}}^{\text{default}} = 60\,s.$

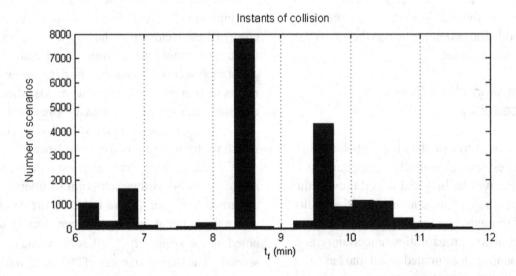

to 7,000 feet, it also receives the instruction to reduce the speed to 250 knots. Instead, what we note in Figure 23 is that the aircraft which are at 7,500 feet have speed around 320 knots, indicating that the speed instruction from the ATC has not been given or has not been accomplished. In any case, the descent from 9,000 to 7,000 feet may contribute to that the speed of the follower aircraft be above an adequate speed to maintain a safe spacing relative to the leader aircraft (the aircraft ahead in the sequence).

Other figures which allow a better comprehension of the collision cases are present below. In Figure 24, the distribution of instants of collision is

Figure 25. Joint histogram of speeds and instants of collision, for $t_{\text{spacing}}^{\text{default}} = 60\,s$.

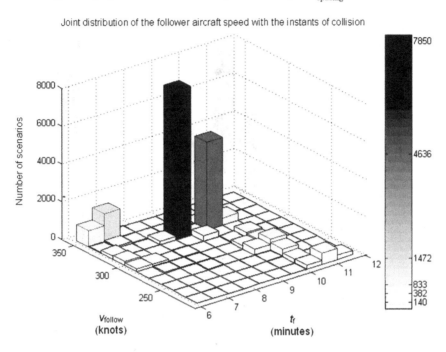

Joint distribution of the follower aircraft speed with the instants of collision

presented, expressed in minutes since the entrance of the leader aircraft in the sector; these instants have a distribution whose average is 8 minutes and 50 seconds.

If we plot the instants of collision of Figure 24 together with the speeds, we obtain Figure 25. One can observe that the group of final speeds around 320 kt is more disperse along time than along altitudes (considering Figure 23, concentrated around 7,500 feet), showing two concentration regions of t_f, one on the neighborhood of 8.5 minutes, and other around 10 minutes. However, given the great concentration observed in Figure 23, we believe that both concentration regions of Figure 24 contain scenarios of collision occurred close to 7,500 feet of altitude.

Similarly to the above analysis, we make a similar one to the scenarios where $t_{\text{spacing}}^{\text{default}} = 45$ seconds. The distributions present some differences from the ones of 60 seconds. Figure 26 illustrates the correlation of speeds and altitudes of collision. In there, we observed that the most

frequent cases are that ones where neither the speed nor the altitudes were decreased in relation to the initial values and, thus, the trend of follower aircraft acceleration cannot be attributed to altitude descent. Being so, the only reason, inside the SDCPN model, which explains the speed increase, is the instrumentation errors of the aircraft sensors.

The next distribution of interest is of the instants of collision t_f, presented in Figure 27. Excepting the value concentration in the neighborhood of 9.5 minutes, the shape of this distribution is similar to some standard distributions such as lognormal, Rayleigh or gamma, whose densities grow abruptly in the least values of the random variable, reach a peak, and decrease slowly in a long tail. The average of the t_f values in the sample is 6 minutes and 6 seconds, and the standard deviation 1 minute and 24 seconds. One can note scenarios where the collision occurred in advanced instants, close to 9.5 minutes, meaning that these aircraft were closer to the airport.

Figure 26. Joint histogram of speeds and altitudes of collision, for $t_{\text{spacing}}^{\text{default}} = 45\,s$.

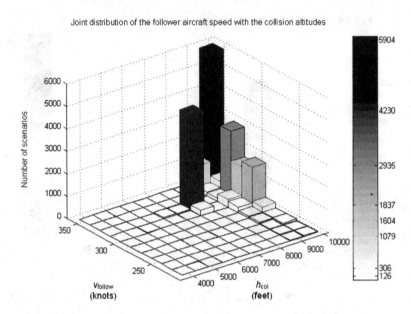

Now we analyze Figure 28, showing the joint distribution of the follower aircraft with the instant of collision t_f. Differently from Figure 25, where we had $t_{\text{spacing}}^{\text{default}} = 60$ seconds, we observe less concentration of the speed values.

Furthermore, if we compare Figure 25 with Figure 28, we can note that, when $t_{\text{spacing}}^{\text{default}} = 45$ seconds, the collision speed is clearly concentrated at higher values, and the collision instants at smaller values. This can be understood as, when the initial separation between aircraft is smaller, the ATCo has less time to detect and correct the unsafe situation, therefore he cannot issue speed reduction or route deviation instructions, so resulting in higher collision probability.

CONCLUSION AND FINAL REMARKS

This chapter has presented some of the most important technology advances in the air traffic management, ADS-B and ASAS, part of the advanced CNS/ATM (Communication, Navigation, Surveillance / Air Traffic Management) paradigm,

aimed to provide a seamless air traffic system. They are founded on the Global Navigation Satellite System (GNSS) and the Aeronautical Telecommunication Network (ATN), although traditional means such as ground based navigation aids, primary radars and analog radio voice channels will be available for undefined time in many airspaces around the world, for safety and availability reasons.

ADS-B will be the primary surveillance system where installing Radar equipment is too much costly or unfeasible, such as oceans and deserts, and will greatly increase surveillance accuracy and availability in areas already covered by Radar, helping to increase the aircraft density with new routes. Other automated systems can take advantage of the high update rate of surveillance information provided by ADS-B, which can also be forwarded through the ATN, taking the air traffic management to a higher quality level. In this way, ICAO considers ADS-B as "...an enabler of the global ATM operational concept bringing substantial safety and capacity benefits ..." (ICAO, 2006). One of the most important applications

Figure 27. Histogram of instants of collision for $t_{\text{spacing}}^{\text{default}} = 45\,s$.

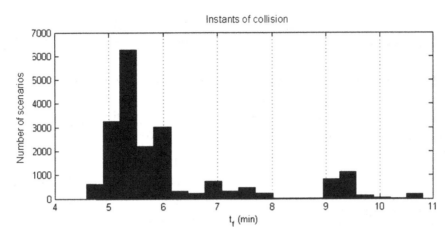

based on ADS-B is the Airborne Separation Assistance System (ASAS), which cause a paradigm shift in Air Traffic Management, transferring part of the responsibility for aircraft separation from the Air Traffic Controller to the flight crew. This will help to decrease the Air Traffic Controller workload without overloading the pilots, thus reducing the probability of human errors. Also, flight crews are expected to gain in situation awareness and anticipation by taking an active part in the management of their situation with respect to surrounding traffic.

The case study here presented, about a specific application among the ASAS functionalities, as-

Figure 28. Joint histogram of speeds and instants of collision, for $t_{\text{spacing}}^{\text{default}} = 45\,s$.

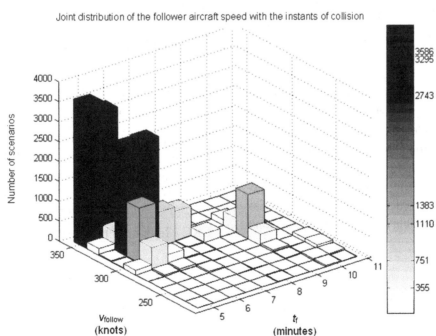

sessed the risk of aircraft sequencing using ASAS to maintain a fixed spacing between aircraft, in an operation coordinated by an Air Traffic Controller on ground, but with extra responsibility attributed to the flight crews. The Monte Carlo simulations allowed us to affirm that, using ASAS time-based spacing, it is possible to use reduced spacing between aircraft, such as 60 seconds, with no visibility conditions, without infringing the applicable ICAO Target Level of Safety, considering several potential failures in the operation, thus demonstrating that ASAS can increase air traffic efficiency without loosing safety. In addition to this founding, in the cases when there is no need to use such a reduced spacing, it has been demonstrated, in documents cited, that ASAS helps to reduce the Air Traffic Controller workload, and to increase the pilot situational awareness, thus contributing to decrease the human error rate.

There are several issues of interest for follow-up research, such as:

- The further improvement of the IPS approach in accelerating Monte Carlo simulations of rare events,
- Conducting parameter sensitivity studies and assessing the bias and uncertainty in the estimated collision probabilities,
- Identifying and using other computer programming language than Java, with high performance, optimal use of huge amounts of memory, and task parallelization;
- Wake turbulence modelling;
- The inclusion of ACAS in the model;
- Modelling and simulating chains with many aircraft in more complex route geometries, in order to better assess the risk of other possible encounter configurations.

REFERENCES

Blom, H. A. P., Bakker, G. J., Blanker, P. J. G., Daams, J., Everdij, M. H. C., & Klompstra, M. B. (2001b). Accident risk assessment for advanced ATM. In G.L. Donohue & A.G. Zellweger, (eds.), *Air Transportation Systems Engineering*, (Progress in Astronautics and Aeronautics, Vol. 193, pp. 463-480).

Blom, H. A. P., Bakker, G. J., Everdij, M. H. C., & van der Park, M. N. J. (2003, September). Collision risk modelling of air traffic. In *Proc. European Control Conf. 2003* (ECC03), Cambridge, UK.

Blom, H. A. P., Bakker, G. J., Klein Obbink, B., & Klompstra, M. B. (2006, June). Free flight safety risk modelling and simulation. In J.V.Doorn, V. Tosic (Ed.), *Proc. Int. Conf. on Research in Air Transport – ICRAT,* Belgrade, Serbia.

Blom, H. A. P., Daams, J., & Nijhuis, H. B. (2001). Human cognition modelling in air traffic management safety assessment. In G.L. Donohue & A.G. Zellweger (Ed.), *Air Transportation Systems Engineering* (Vol.193, pp. 481-511). Reston, VA: American Institute of Aeronautics and Astronautics.

Blom, H.A.P., Krystul, J., & Bakker, G.J. (2006b). A particle filter system for safety verification of free flight in air traffic. In P. Misra (Ed.), *Proc. 45th IEEE Conf. on Decision and Control.* San Diego: IEEE Society.

Blom, H. A. P., Krystul, J., Bakker, G. J., & Klein Obbink, B. (2007). Free flight collision risk estimation by sequential Monte Carlo simulation, In G.G. Cassandras, J. Lygeros, (Eds.), *Stochastic Hybrid Systems*, (pp. 249-281). Boca Raton, FL: CRC / Taylor & Francis.

Blom, H. A. P., & Stroeve, S. II. (2004). Multi-agent situation awareness error evolution in air traffic. In E.J. Bonano (Ed.), *Proceedings of Probabilistic Safety Assessment and Management Conference – PSAM 6* (pp. 272-277). Berlin: ASME Press.

Blom, H. A. P., Stroeve, S. H., & De Jong, H. H. (2006c, February). Safety risk assessment by Monte Carlo simulation of complex safety-critical operations. In F. Redmill & T. Anderson (eds.), *Proc. 14th Safety-critical Systems Symposium*, Bristol, UK. London: Springer.

Bratley, P., Fox, B., & Schrage, L. (1983). *A Guide to Simulation*, (2nd Ed.). Berlin: Springer.

CASA (2007). *Airworthiness Approval of Airborne Automatic Dependent Surveillance Broadcast Equipment* (Draft (March 2007) - AC 21-45(0)). Australia: Civil Aviation Safety Authority (CASA).

Cérou, F., Del Moral, P., Le Gland, F., & Lezaud, P. (2005). *Limit theorems for the multilevel splitting algorithms in the simulation of rare events*. Proc. Winter Simulation Conference, Orlando, USA, 2005.

Cérou, F., Del Moral, P., LeGland, F., & Lezaud, P. (2002). *Genetic genealogical models in rare event analysis*. Toulouse, France: Institut de Mathématiques, Laboratoire de Statistiques et Probabilites.

Cloarec, D., Purves, K., & Vergne, F. (2004). *CoSpace 2003 Controller Model Based Study Assessment of Airborne Spacing Tasks in the Extended TMA* (EEC Report no. 392). Brétigny-sur-Orge, France: Eurocontrol Experimental Centre. *CoSpace website*, (n.d.). Retrieved July 10, 2006 from http://www.eurocontrol.int/eec/public/standard_page/SSP_CoSpace_home.html

De Boer, P.-T., Kroese, D. P., Mannor, S., & Rubinstein, R. Y. (2004). A Tutorial on the Cross-Entropy Method. *Annals of Operations Research, 134*(1), 19–67. doi:10.1007/s10479-005-5724-z

De Oliveira, I. R. (2007). *Análise de Risco da Operação de Espaçamento Temporal Aerotransportado por meio de um Modelo em rede de Petri Estocástica e Dinamicamente Colorida*. PhD Thesis, School of Engineering, University of São Paulo, Brazil.

De Oliveira, I. R., Bakker, G. H. J., & Blom, H. A. P. (2006). *Accident Risk Assessment Model for ASAS Time Based Spacing Operation in ATM* (Draft Report). The Netherlands: NLR.

De Oliveira, I. R., Cugnasca, P. S., Blom, H. A. P., & Bakker, G. J. (2007, July). *Modelling and estimation of separation criteria for airborne time-based spacing operation*. Proc. 7th USA/Europe Air Traffic Management R&D Seminar (ATM2007), Barcelona, Spain.

De Oliveira, I. R., Cugnasca, P. S., Blom, H. A. P., & Bakker, G. J. (2007b, June). *Estimation of collision risk in time-based spacing air traffic by sequential Monte Carlo simulation*. Proc. World Congress on Traffic Research, Berkeley, CA.

Dunstone, G. (Ed.). (2004). *Required ADS-B Performance Radar-like Services*. Presented at the Second Meeting of Automatic Surveillance - Broadcast (ADS-B) Study and Implementation Task Force (ICAO). Bangkok, Thailand.

Everdij, M. H. C., & Blom, H. A. P. (2005). Piecewise deterministic Markov processes represented by dynamically coloured Petri nets. *Stochastics, 77*, 1–29. doi:10.1080/17442500512331341040

Everdij, M. H. C., & Blom, H. A. P. (2006). Hybrid Petri nets with diffusion that have into-mappings with generalized stochastic hybrid processes. In H.A.P. Blom & J. Lygeros (Ed.), *Stochastic hybrid systems: Theory and safety-critical applications* (pp. 31-63). Berlin: Springer Verlag.

Everdij, M. H. C., Blom, H. A. P., & Bakker, G. J. (2007). Modelling lateral spacing and separation for airborne separation assurance using Petri nets. *Simulation, 83*(5), 401–414. doi:10.1177/0037549706063820

Everdij, M. H. C., Blom, H. A. P., & Stroeve, S. H. (2006b). Structured assessment of bias and uncertainty in Monte Carlo simulated accident risk. In M.G. Stamatelatos, H.S. Blackman (Ed.), *Proc. 8th Int. Conf. on Probabilistic Safety Assessment and Management – PSAM 8*. New Orleans, LA: ASME Press.

Everdij, M. H. C., Klompstra, M. B., Blom, H. A. P., & Klein Obbink, B. (2006c). Compositional specification of a multi-agent system by stochastically and dynamically coloured Petri nets. In H.A.P. Blom, & J. Lygeros (eds.), *Stochastic hybrid systems: Theory and safety-critical applications*, (pp. 325-350). Berlin: Springer

FAA. (2002). *Overview of the FAA Data link Decision*. Retrieved June 7, 2002, from http://www.faa.gov/asd/ads-b/06-07-02_ADS-B-Overview.pdf

Grimaud, I., Hoffman, E., Rognin, L., & Zeghal, K. (2005). Spacing Instructions in Approach: A Stepwise Design Approach. *Air Traffic Control Quarterly, 13*(2), 127–153.

Hansman, R. J., et al. (1997, June). *Integrated Human Centered Systems Approach to the Development of Advanced Air Traffic Management Systems*. Paper presented at the Air Traffic Management Research & Development Seminar, Saclay, France.

Hollnagel, E. (1993). *Human reliability analysis, context and control*. London, UK: Academic Press. London.

Hsu, D. A. (1981). The evaluation of aircraft collision probabilities at intersecting air routes. *Journal of Navigation, 34*, 78–102.

ICAO. (1998): *Air Traffic Services Planning Manual* (Doc.9426). Montreal, Canada: International Civil Aviation Organization (ICAO).

ICAO. (1999a). *Manual of Technical Provisions for the Aeronautical Telecommunication Network* (Doc.9705/AN956). Montreal, Canada: International Civil Aviation Organization (ICAO).

ICAO (Ed.). (1999b). *Status of Air-Ground Data link Standardization* (Information Paper 4). Presented at the 3rd Meeting of CAR/SAM (ICAO). Buenos Aires, Argentina.

ICAO. (2000). *Global Air Navigation Plan for CNS/ATM Systems* (Doc.9750). Montreal: International Civil Aviation Organization (ICAO).

ICAO. (2001). *International Standards and Recommended Practices – Air Traffic Services* (Annex 11), (13th Ed.). Montreal, Canada: International Civil Aviation Organization (ICAO).

ICAO (Ed.). (2003). *Comparative Analysis of ADS-B Data links* (Information Paper 12). Presented at the 11th Air Navigation Conference (ICAO). Montreal, Canada: International Civil Aviation Organization (ICAO).

ICAO (Ed.). (2003b). *ADS-B Study and Implementation Task Force* (Working Paper 8). Presented at the CNS/MET-ATM (ICAO). Bangkok, Thailand.

ICAO (Ed.). (2003c). *ADS-B Concept of Use* (Working Paper 6 - Appendix). Presented at the 11TH Air Navigation Conference (ICAO). Montreal, Canada.

ICAO. (2004). *Manual on the Secondary Surveillance Radar (SSR) Systems* (Doc.9684), 3rd edition. Montreal, Canada: International Civil Aviation Organization (ICAO).

ICAO. (2004). *Airborne Collision Avoidance System (ACAS) Manual* (Doc.9863), (1st Ed.). Montreal, Canada: International Civil Aviation Organization (ICAO).

ICAO (Ed.). (2006). *A Regional Approach to Accelerate ADS-B Implementation* (Information Paper 10). Presented at the 5th Meeting ALLPIRG / Advisory Group (ICAO). Montreal, Canada.

Ivanescu, D., Shaw, C., Hoffman, E., & Zeghal, K. (2005). A Pilot Decision Support Tool for Merging Behind a Lead Aircraft. In *Proc. 44th IEEE Conf. on Decision and Control, and the European Control Conference*. Seville, Spain: IEEE Society.

Knight, J. C. (2002). Safety-critical Systems: Challenges and Directions. In *Proceedings of the 24rd International Conference on Software Engineering* (pp. 547-550). Toronto, Canada: IEEE Press.

Krystul, J., & Blom, H. A. P. (2005). Sequential Monte Carlo simulation of rare event probability in stochastic hybrid systems. In *Proc. 16th IFAC World Congress (Paper Th-E07-TO)*. Prague: Elsevier Science.

Murray, R. M. (2003). Future Directions in Control in an Information-Rich World. *IEEE Control Systems Magazine, 23*(2), 20–33. doi:10.1109/MCS.2003.1188769

Profit, R. (1995). *Systematic Safety Management in the Air Traffic Services*. London: Euromoney Publications.

Reich., P.G. (1964). *A theory of safe separation standards for Air Traffic Control* (Technical Report 64041). UK: Royal Aircraft Establishment.

RFG (2005). *SPR SG: Package I – Enhanced Sequencing and Merging Operations (ASPA-S&M) Application Description*. International: Requirement Focus Group.

Rubinstein, R. Y., & Shapiro, A. (1983). *Discrete Event Systems: Sensitivity Analysis and Stochastic Optimization via de score function method*. Hoboken, NJ: Wiley.

Ruigrok, R. C. J., de Gelder, N., Abma, H. J., Klein Obbink, B., & Scholte, J. J. (2005). Pilot Perspective of ASAS Self-Separation in Challenging Environments. Presented at the *6th USA/Europe ATM R&D Seminar*, Baltimore, USA.

Ruigrok, R. C. J., & Hoekstra, J. M. (2007). Human factors evaluations of Free Flight: Issues solved and issues remaining. *Applied Ergonomics, 38*(4), 437–455. doi:10.1016/j.apergo.2007.01.006

Shorthose, M., Schielmann, P., Basker, S., & Brooker, P. (2004). *Separations Standards in an ADS-B Environment* (Tech. Final Report). London: Helios Technology and Eurocontrol.

Summer, S. (2007). *Upper Airpace Program Operacional Update* (Information Paper 4). Presented at the 10th ADS-B Implementation Team (ABIT) Meeting. Camberra, Australia.

Van der Geest, P. J. (2002). *The AMAAI Modelling Toolset for the Analysis of In-Trail Following Dynamics* (NLR-CR-2002-112). AMAAI Deliverable D2: Description and User Guide. The Netherlands: NLR.

Vismari, L. F. (2007). *Vigilância Dependente Automática no Controle de Tráfego Aéreo: avaliação de risco baseada em Redes de Petri Fluidas e Estocásticas*. Master in Engineering Degree Dissertation, School of Engineering, University of São Paulo, Brazil.

Vismari, L. F., & Camargo Junior, J. B. (2008). An Absolute-Relative Risk Assessment Methodology Approach to Current Safety-critical Systems and its Application to the ADS-B based Air Traffic Control System. In L. Romano (Ed.), *Proceedings of the 27th IEEE International Symposium on Reliable Distributed Systems* (pp. 95-104). Naples, Italy: IEEE Computer Society.

ACRONYMS

ACAS: Airborne Collision Avoidance System

ADS-B: Automatic Dependant Surveillance Broadcast

AMSS: Aeronautical Mobile Satellite Service

AOC: Airline Operations Center

AE: Application Entity

ASAS: Airborne Separation Assistance (or Assurance) System

ATCo: Air Traffic Controller

ATN: Aeronautical Telecommunication Network

ATS: Air Traffic Services

ATM: Air Traffic Management

ATN: Aeronautical Telecommunications Network

CDTI: Cockpit Display of Traffic Information

CDU: Control and Display Unit

CNS: Communication, Navigation and Surveillance

CRN: Common Random Numbers

DL: Datalink

ES: End System

FAF: Final Approach Fix

GNC: Guidance Navigation and Communication Systems

GNSS: Global Navigation Satellite System

ICAO: International Civil Aviation Organization

ILS: Instrument Landing System

INS/IRS: Inertial Navigation System / Inertial Reference System

IPS: Interacting Particle System

LPN: Local Petri Net

MCP: Mode Control Panel

NDB: Non-Directional Beacon

PF: Pilot Flying

PNF: Pilot Not Flying

PSR: Primary Surveillance Radar

RCP: Required Communication Performance

RNAV: Area Navigation

RNP: Required Navigation Performance

RSP: Required Surveillance Performance

R/T: Radio Telecommunication

SDCPN: Stochastic and Dynamically Colored Petri Net

SSR: Secondary Surveillance Radar

TBS: Time-Based Spacing

TLS: Target Level of Safety

TCAS: Traffic Collision Avoidance System

TMA: Terminal Movement (or Maneuverings) Area

VDL: VHF Datalink

VOR/DME: VHF Ominidirectional Range / Distance Measure Equipment

Chapter 11
A Distributed Systems Approach to Airborne Self-Separation

Henrique Moniz
University of Lisbon, Portugal

Alessandra Tedeschi
Deep Blue s.r.l., Rome, Italy

Nuno Ferreira Neves
University of Lisbon, Portugal

Miguel Correia
University of Lisbon, Portugal

ABSTRACT

This chapter introduces the reader to the benefits of distributed computing in air transportation. It presents a solution to airborne self-separation based on RAPTOR, a stack of distributed protocols that allows aircraft to reach different types of agreement in the presence of faults, both of accidental and malicious nature. These protocols are used as primitives to implement specific services for airborne self-separation, which are created within the context of a conflict resolution algorithm based on game theory.

INTRODUCTION

Air Traffic Management (ATM) is concerned with the management of air traffic flow in a safe and efficient manner. In its current form, ATM is based on rigid off-line flight planning and ground-based air traffic controllers (ATCOs). The airspace is divided into sectors, and each sector is assigned an ATCO team, which becomes its central authority. The ACTOs are responsible for maintaining horizontal and vertical separation among aircraft, while ensuring an orderly and expeditious air traffic flow.

This task is performed by issuing directions to aircraft and by providing flight context information to pilots, such as routes to waypoints and weather conditions.

The current controller-based approach to ATM relies heavily on controllers' skills, with little or no autonomy for pilots and companies. Moreover, it does not scale up to cope with the increasing volume of future air traffic, which is expected to grow at a rate of 5 to 6 percent per year (Eurocontrol, 1999).

DOI: 10.4018/978-1-60566-800-0.ch011

Several alternative solutions and complementary approaches to overcome the limits of current ATM are actively under investigation. Recent advances in technologies are making possible a new concept of ATM, namely *airborne self-separation* (FAA/ Eurocontrol, 2001). It represents a concept in which the responsibility for aircraft separation is shifted from the ground to the air and where pilots are allowed to select their flight paths without any external intervention by air traffic controllers (Nordwall, 1995; Perry, 1997). In a future self-separation environment, pilots will have more responsibility for the safe and efficient conduction of the flight and they should be supported by an automated decision-support system that processes all available information, thus assisting the pilot in optimizing the aircraft trajectory while maintaining separation among aircraft.

In general terms, the economic advantages of airborne self-separation will manifest in two ways. First, it should lead to reduced costs. Self-optimization by the airlines could be more effective than any global optimization that can be performed by a human controller (RTCA Task Force 3, 1995). This is because different airlines might give higher priority to different parameters. One airline might prefer to optimize fuel consumption, while other might prefer to optimize flight delays. These preferences depend on company strategy or other factors only known to the airline and crew. Second, the global expansion in capacity of air traffic volume, due to the departure from the centralized and human-centric approach, will allow airlines to meet an increasing demand for air transportation.

This new approach, however, will not emerge without its share of technical issues. As a major paradigm shift, the deployment of airborne self-separation will also unveil a whole new domain of threats to the safety of air transportation. The consequent automation brought in by self-separation unveils a class of attacks that target these navigational systems in increasingly inconspicuous ways. Aircraft will need to rely on information provided by other aircraft in their vicinity to ensure proper coordination. Thus, it becomes imperative that this information is exchanged in a reliable and secure manner. Unfortunately, wireless communication is inherently unreliable, and the presence of a single malicious aircraft with the ability to transmit incoherent information or jam communication brings unpredictable and potentially catastrophic consequences for the safety of aircraft. Techniques must be adopted that allow aircraft to coordinate their maneuvering even if communication among them is subject failures, regardless of their nature - accidental or malicious.

This chapter presents an approach to airborne self-separation, taken from the discipline of distributed computing, that systematically addresses the problem of fault-tolerant decentralized coordination. In a distributed system, at the core of any kind of coordinated activity lies the need for some sort of agreement among the processes that compose the system (Guerraoui & Schiper, 1997; Turek & Shasha, 1992). Reaching agreement in the presence of faults is a fundamental and non-trivial problem in the distributed systems literature - a topic subject of countless papers. See (Cristian, 1991; Correia, Verissimo, & Neves, 2006; Fischer, 1983) for surveys. Within the context of this work, the distributed system represents the airborne self-separation environment, and the processes correspond to the aircraft.

The main thrust of this chapter is divided in two parts. The first part describes Satisficing Game Theory (SGT), introduced in (Johnson, Hill, Archibald, Frost, & Stirling, 2005), which is an approach for conflict resolution that can be applied to airborne self-separation where agents (i.e., aircraft) collaboratively exchange information to reach a solution for the group. SGT is offered as a case study that is representative of the limitations commonly present in current approaches, which do not take into account the potential hostility of the environment. In particular, this part identifies common gaps between the assumptions and the environment that lead to the need for mechanisms to provide consistent information in the presence of faults.

The second part of our contribution introduces one of such mechanisms. It presents a set of agreement protocols, organized into a stack called RAPTOR, which allows processes of a distributed system to reach different types of agreement. These agreement protocols are particularly adapted to wireless communications and operate correctly even if message transmissions are unreliable and some aircraft purposely exchange wrongful or inconsistent information. The protocols are designed within the context of a system model that appropriately captures the airborne self-separation environment. A rigorous correctness proof is also provided with each protocol to show that the properties of the protocol are met for the given model.

The agreement protocols, depicted in Figure 1, are *binary consensus*, *multi-valued consensus*, and *terminating reliable broadcast*. Binary consensus is the most basic protocol and it allows processes to agree on a common binary value. This form of agreement is mostly used as a building block to construct other agreement protocols, but it can also be used to implement useful services. Imagine that a group of aircraft needs to perform some sort of maneuver where either all do the maneuver or none does. They can execute an instance of the binary consensus protocol. If the result is 1, then they all commit to the maneuver. If the result is 0, then none commits to the maneuver.

Figure 1. RAPTOR protocol stack.

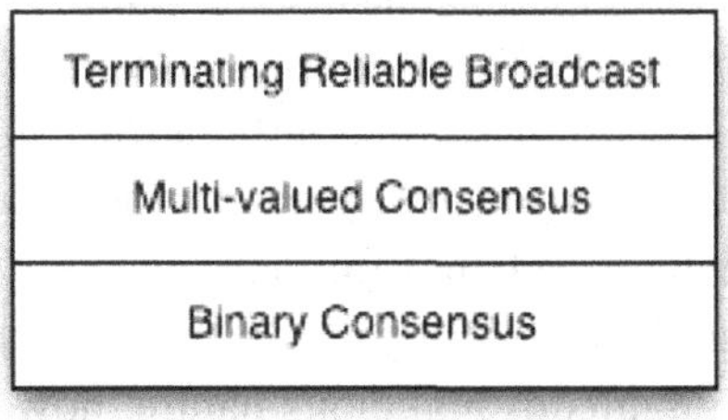

Terminating Reliable Broadcast
Multi-valued Consensus
Binary Consensus

Above binary consensus is multi-valued consensus. This protocol uses binary consensus as a primitive and lets processes reach agreement on a value from an arbitrary domain. One example of the usefulness of this protocol is shown by the rank consistency service, described later in this chapter. The service resorts to multi-valued consensus to ensure that aircraft agree on a common ranking of the aircraft within a group. This ranking then determines how aircraft maneuver in order to avoid collisions.

Finally, terminating reliable broadcast allows a process to broadcast a message, giving both sender and receivers the guarantee that the message is uniformly delivered at all processes. For example, this protocol can be employed by an aircraft that wishes to disseminate some information to every aircraft within a certain radius. The view augmentation service, also described later in the chapter, implements a similar functionality.

As hinted above, the protocols of RAPTOR are used as primitives to implement specific services for airborne self-separation, namely *group membership*, *rank consistency*, and *view augmentation*. These services ensure that any complex coordination algorithm (e.g., SGT) is executed upon information consistent amongst all aircraft, which leads to a deterministic and safe maneuvering in the airspace. Additionally, since the RAPTOR protocols can tolerate both accidental and malicious faults, the correct operation of the services is guaranteed even in adverse conditions.

The remainder of the chapter is organized as follows. Section 2 provides some background. The SGT approach to airborne-self separation is analyzed in Section 3. The RAPTOR protocols and related services are presented in Section 4. The future trends are discussed in Section 5. Finally, Section 6 concludes the chapter.

BACKGROUND

In the past decades, several feasibility studies about the airborne self-separation operational concept have been carried out (FAA/Eurocontrol, 2001; Wing, 2005). This research led to the proposal of a variety of interesting and effective techniques for the detection and resolution of conflicts in a self-separation environment. Most of them are described in two, very exhaustive, surveys (Kuchar & Yang, 2000; Dimarogonas & Kyriakopoulos, 2002). No approach, however, is found in the literature that applies the principles of fault-tolerant distributed systems to airborne self-separation.

The protocols of RAPTOR descend from a lineage of randomized consensus protocols that were proposed in 1983 by Ben-Or and Rabin (Ben-Or, 1983; Rabin, 1983). The consensus problem is the most typical form of agreement in distributed systems. Basically it can be described as follows. Each process starts with a private value that is used as a proposal value for consensus, and then, when a conclusion is reached, all processes obtain the same decision, usually on one of the proposed values. Behind this simple definition, consensus and other agreement problems in general end up being fairly complex, particularly when one starts to consider potential system errors. In fact, consensus has been proven to be deterministically impossible to solve in certain types of systems. The FLP impossibility result, named after its authors' last names, states that consensus is impossible to solve in asynchronous systems (i.e., systems that make no assumptions on the processes' computation and communication delays) if only one process can fail by crashing (Fischer, Lynch, & Paterson, 1985). A similar result exists for synchronous systems (i.e., systems with known bounds for the processes' computation and communication delays) if the transmissions associated with just one process can fail (Santoro & Widmeyer, 1989). The aforementioned protocols of Ben-Or and Rabin, however, circumvent the FLP impossibility result. Instead of trying to solve consensus deterministically, which is impossible, they utilize a technique called *randomization* to reach agreement in a probabilistic way.

The RAPTOR protocols are bound by the impossibility result of (Santoro & Widmeyer, 1989) for synchronous systems with transmission faults. The result is circumvented also by employing randomization at the level of the binary consensus protocol. This is the only protocol that actually needs to be randomized because all other protocols are built on top of this one. Previous to RAPTOR, some of the authors designed a stack of agreement protocols named RITAS, but this stack was designed for asynchronous systems and not with wireless communications in mind (Correia, Neves, & Verissimo, 2006; Moniz, Neves, Correia, & Veríssimo, 2006). RITAS was evaluated in a car-to-car communication scenario and, although the results were feasible for that particular application, it was clear that the protocols were not specially fit for wireless communications (Moniz, Neves, Casimiro, & Veríssimo, 2007). This was due to the fact that RITAS relies on a reliable point-to-point communication model, which forces the implementation of end-to-end message delivery mechanisms (e.g., TCP) that significantly increase the medium access contention.

Fault-tolerant agreement protocols for wireless networks represent a relatively recent research within the scientific community. Chockler et al. propose consensus algorithms for systems where nodes fail only by crashing and messages are lost due to collisions (Chockler, Demirbas, Gilbert, Newport, & Nolte, 2005). They resort to a specialized failure detector, which determines when message collisions occur and allows nodes to take some recovery actions. Koo et al. focus on a weaker problem, reliable broadcast, in multi-hop radio networks where each node adheres to a pre-determined transmission schedule (Koo, Bhandari, Katz, & Vaidya, 2006). Their algorithm tolerates faults of malicious nature, however, it also relies on collision-detection information to solve the problem and assumes that messages are only lost due to collisions. Finally, Drabkin et al. present a reliable broadcast protocol for wireless ad-hoc networks in asynchronous systems (Drabkin, Friedman, & Segal, 2005). Their protocol extends the system model with three types of failure detectors (mute, verbose, and trust) that detect messages sent too often, messages not sent, and incorrect nodes. The broadcast protocol is then built by combining together these failure detectors along with the use of digital signatures and gossiping.

CASE STUDY: SATISFICING GAME THEORY

A particular approach for airborne self-separation is presented as a case study in order to exemplify the limitations of current solutions and how they can be dealt with the protocols of RAPTOR. The approach resides on a decision-making algorithm that aims to provide adequate separation between aircraft by deciding how aircraft should maneuver to avoid potential conflicts. It is based on the framework of game theory for multi-agent systems where there is no centralized control and there is a clear global objective function that needs to be optimized.

Usually, the main difficulty in applying game theory to multi-agent systems is that it is hard to define the global objective function in terms of what is best for each agent. SGT tries to overcome such limit by seeking an adequate solution for the multi-agent system, rather than the optimal solution (Stirling, 2005). Basically, SGT defines the objective function by means of two utility functions, selectability and rejectability, which represent benefits (selectability) and costs (rejectability) for the choices of each agent. There may exist dependence between utility functions of different agents. In order to specify and analyze such system, utility functions can be conveniently viewed as marginal of a multivariate global probability function, in which dependences are expressed as conditional probabilities between variables. This way, a directed graph can be used to specify the system, and a solution can be obtained through standard Bayesian analysis.

In airborne self-separation, SGT can be applied as described in (Johnson, Hill, Archibald, Frost, & Stirling, 2005). Selectability and rejectability of each aircraft represent the benefits and costs of the aircraft's maneuvering choices. Benefits are essentially proportional to the optimality of the possible route. Costs, on the other hand, are proportional to the risk of collision with another aircraft. Correctly defining dependence between utility functions is the most important design factor because dependencies that are not necessary lead to unsatisfactory solutions. Thus, first of all, influence flows between aircraft are created. Influence flows are basically oriented graphs where nodes represent aircraft and edges represent relation between directional choices of aircraft. In order to create influence flows, at each time step, every aircraft exchanges information with all other aircrafts within a certain radius. This information is then used to rank the aircraft according to a certain policy. The information may include current position, destination, actual heading, and all the characteristics of the flight that can be considered useful for the ranking of the aircraft and the creation of influence flows. Then, the selectability of any particular aircraft is conditioned upon the selectability of all higher-ranked aircraft that are within a certain proximity range. Rejectability of agents is unconditioned: each aircraft responds to threats with exclusive self-interest. SGT scales well to high number of aircraft, since two important simplification can be safely applied: indirect influences between selectability functions can be discarded, and each aircraft can represent all viewable aircraft as a single entity that summarizes their maneuvering choices.

SGT Limitations

SGT has several shortcomings when applied to real-world scenarios. It makes two implicit assumptions about the information used to compute aircraft maneuvering: (1) information is complete and homogeneous, and (2) information is fresh. Homogeneous means that aircraft have no contradictory or incomplete information about any other aircraft. Fresh means that it always reflects the current state of other aircraft. For the SGT algorithm to function under these assumptions with a mere information exchange (i.e., every aircraft broadcasts its individual information), the system must be synchronous (i.e., information exchange can happen only at fixed time steps) and communication links must be reliable (i.e., no message can be lost at each time step). While the synchrony assumption is reasonable since on-board GPS units can provide very accurate clock synchronization, the reliability assumption is not.

Regrettably, in a real environment, the wireless communication medium is inherently unreliable. For instance, if messages are transmitted within overlapping time intervals, then a message collision occurs leading to message losses. This may create failure scenarios that can disrupt SGT operation. For instance, if two aircraft in conflicting courses have inconsistent or outdated information about each other, it is possible for each of them to derive maneuvering decisions that may further put them into a conflict. Additionally, if one of the communication subsystems fails, even if temporarily, then an incident can happen because both aircraft might be convinced that it is the responsibility of the other aircraft to maneuver around. There is also the threat of malicious activity, where aircraft can send wrong or incomplete information or no information at all. This can be performed in a calculated way as to maximize the chances of forcing an incident between two aircraft.

These failures can occur in the real world, but even if rare, they can lead to catastrophic consequences. Thus, it becomes imperative that they are dealt with in some way. The following section presents a set of protocols to support the exchange of information in a consistent manner, even in the presence of unreliable communications and malicious attacks.

RAPTOR

This section describes RAPTOR, a stack of agreement protocols particularly fit for wireless communication environments such as airborne self-separation. RAPTOR represents a bridge between the limitations identified in SGT and the actual conditions of the airborne self-separation environment. The protocols are distributed algorithms that are concurrently run by a set of n processes (i.e., aircraft). A number of message exchanges are performed as part of the execution of the algorithms. Each process executes an instance of a particular algorithm, and each instance outputs the same value, allowing them to reach various sorts of agreement. The protocols are also resilient to arbitrary communication failures (i.e., the communication links of the processes are allowed to fail). The only restriction is that no more than f processes may simultaneously experience failures in their outgoing links, with f being no more than a third of the total number of processes. In other words, the total number of processes must be $n \geq 3f + 1$.

Section 4.1 describes the distributed system model, containing the assumptions that properly model the airborne self-separation environment.

The protocols are then described in their own respective sections. Section 4.2, 4.3, and 4.4 present binary consensus, multi-valued consensus, and terminating reliable broadcast, respectively. These sections adhere to the same structure. Each one starts with an informal discussion of the protocol, followed by the formal properties and a step-by-step description of the protocol. The protocol is illustrated in an accompanying figure. Next, it is outlined a hypothetical run of the protocol to help the reader better understand how it works in practice. Finally, each section ends with a rigorous mathematical proof showing that the algorithm satisfies the formal properties of the protocol. Each property is addressed individually and some lemmas are constructed and proved in order to support other proofs.

Section 4.5 wraps up this section. It bridges the theoretical protocols with specific services for SGT and airborne self-separation in general – group membership, rank consistency, and view augmentation. It informally discusses how easily the protocols of RAPTOR can be applied to implement these services.

System Model

The airborne self-separation environment is modeled as a set of processes (i.e., the aircraft) that exchange information through wireless communication. The system is composed by a static set[1] of n processes $\Pi = \{p_1, p_2, ..., p_n\}$ that exchange messages through two communication primitives: *broadcast* and *receive*. The primitive broadcast(t, Π, m) transmits a message m to all processes in set Π at step t. The primitive receive(t, Π) returns a set with the messages that arrived due to invocations of *broadcast* from the processes in Π at step t. In some circumstances, the receive primitive can also be invoked as receive(t, S), where S is an arbitrary subset of Π. In this case, the process only receives the messages broadcasted by the processes in S.

The system is synchronous, meaning that both the processing times of processes and the communications delays are bound by known constants. Communication between processes occurs at synchronous steps. At each step t, every process $p_i \in \Pi$ executes the following actions: (1) invokes broadcast(t, Π, m), (2) invokes receive(t, Π), and (3) performs a state transition based on its current state and the set of values in the received messages. These values are stored by each process p_i

in a local set V_i. Additionally, the protocols make extensive use of a function $\#_v(V_i)$ that returns the number of occurrences of value v in the set V_i.

The failure model follows closely the *communication failure model* introduced in (Santoro & Widmeyer, 1989), in which the communication links are subject to transmission failures. A message transmission is defined as a pair (α, β), where α is the message value sent by the source process, if any, and β is the value received by the destination process, if any. A transmission of a message amongst a source process p_i and a destination process p_j is faulty if one of the following occurs:

- Omission. The message sent by p_i is not received by p_j.
- Addition. A message is received by p_j when no such message was sent.
- Corruption. The message sent by p_i is received by p_j with different content.

A broadcast by a source process p_i originates n transmissions, one for each process in Π, and faults can non-uniformly occur at any of these transmissions. The system can exhibit any type of transmission fault with the restriction that faults cannot affect more than f source processes per step, where $n \geq 3f + 1$ is the total number of processes. A fault is said to affect a source process p_i if it occurs at a transmission made by p_i.

The particularity of this model is that processes are modeled as not to exhibit faulty behavior, i.e., they correctly follow the protocols until termination. The notion of a faulty process is instead captured by the assumption of faulty message transmissions. This is because the effect of a crashed or malicious process is always reflected in message omissions or corruptions. For example, a process p_i whose communication systems are malfunctioning is captured by omission faults originating at p_i. Similarly, a malicious process p_i that sends messages with different content to every other process is captured by corruption faults originating at p_i. In order to properly capture the malicious behavior of processes into the model, it is also assumed that integrity-checking mechanisms cannot detect this kind of message corruption. Otherwise, corruption faults could be easily converted into omission faults.

Finally, each process has access to a local random bit generator through a function coin_flip() that returns unbiased bits. This is required since one of the protocols (i.e., binary consensus) requires processes to propose random values in certain situations.

Binary Consensus

The binary consensus represents the most basic form of agreement (i.e., on a single bit of information) and it is used as a building block for the other protocols provided by RAPTOR. In the protocol, each process p_i proposes a bit value x_i and all processes decide on the same result $d \in \{0,1\}$. Additionally, if all processes propose the same initial value v, then the decision has necessarily to be v.

Properties

Formally, the properties of the protocol are defined as follows:

- **BC1 (Validity).** If all processes propose the same value v, then any process that decides, decides v.
- **BC2 (Agreement).** No two processes decide differently.
- **BC3 (Termination).** Every process decides within r rounds with a probability P that approaches 1 with the number of rounds: $\lim_{r \to \infty} P = 1$.

The termination property (BC3) is formulated in a probabilistic way. This is done by defining a probability P for the processes to reach a decision that approaches 1 as the number of rounds increases (consensus algorithms are usually round-based). This basically states, in probabilistic terms, that the processes eventually reach a decision. The probabilistic definition of the termination property is required because there is an impossibility result for the communication failure model, which states that any form of deterministic agreement is unattainable if there can be $n-1$ or more transmission failures at any particular step. Adjusting the termination property in probabilistic terms allows this result to be circumvented using, for instance, *randomization* techniques. This approach has been used in the past to circumvent a similar impossibility result (Fischer, Lynch, & Paterson, 1985) with great success in terms of real world performance of the algorithms (Moniz, Neves, Correia, & Veríssimo, 2006). This happens because the fault pattern required to significantly delay the execution of the algorithm is very improbable to happen in practice and difficult to force by a malicious adversary.

Description

The protocol presented in Algorithm 1 (see Figure 2) proceeds in rounds of two steps each and takes as input the proposal value x_i. Every process $p_i \in \Pi$ starts the protocol by initializing the round number r_i to 0, the decision result d to an undefined value $\perp$ indicating that no decision has been made yet, and the variable $stop_i$ to an undefined value $\perp$. Variable $stop_i$ will keep the round number where the algorithm should halt its execution.

Each process p_i then enters step 1 of the protocol (lines 5-11). It broadcasts x_i and saves the received messages in V_i (lines 5-6). If there are $2f + 1$ messages with the same value v in V_i, then x_i is set to v to indicate the preference value of p_i. Otherwise, x_i is set to $\perp$ (lines 7-11).

Processes then proceed to step 2 (lines 12-28). Each process p_i broadcasts x_i and saves the arriving messages in V_i (lines 12-13). If there are $2f + 1$ messages with the same value v in V_i, then p_i sets the decision value d to v and sets the variable $stop_i$ to indicate the algorithm should stop its execution at the next round (lines 14-18). Additionally, the proposal value x_i is updated to v (line 19). If there are not $2f + 1$ messages with v, but at least $f + 1$, then the only action taken is to update the proposal value x_i to v (lines 20-21). Otherwise, if none of the thresholds are observed, then x_i is set to a random value 1 or 0, each with probability 50% (lines 22-23). Finally, the algorithm checks if it should stop the execution by

comparing the current round number r_i with the $stop_i$ variable (line 25). If the numbers match, the algorithm halts (line 26), otherwise it increments the current round number (line 28) and continues for another round.

The algorithm completes the execution exactly one round after making a decision. This means that an efficient implementation must not wait until the end of the protocol execution to output its decision value. It should output the decision value immediately when one is available and then continue the execution for an extra round.

Figure 2. Algorithm 1

Algorithm 1: Binary Consensus Algorithm

Input: Set of Processes Π
Input: Initial Proposal Value x_i
Output: Decision Value d_i

```
1   d_i ← ⊥;                          // decision value;
2   r_i ← 0;                          // round number;
3   stop_i ← ⊥;      // round number where execution halts;
4   while do
5       broadcast (2r + 1, Π, x_i);                   // step 1;
6       V_i ← receive (2r + 1, Π);
7       if ∃_{v≠⊥} : #_v(V_i) ≥ 2f + 1 then
8           x_i ← v;
9       else
10          x_i ← ⊥;
11      end

12      broadcast (2r + 2, Π, x_i);                   // step 2;
13      V_i ← receive (2r + 2, Π);
14      if ∃_{v≠⊥} : #_v(V_i) ≥ 2f + 1 then
15          if d_i = ⊥ then
16              d_i ← v;
17              stop_i ← r_i + 1;
18          end
19          x_i ← v;
20      else if ∃_{v≠⊥} : #_v(V_i) ≥ f + 1 then
21          x_i ← v;
22      else
23          x_i ← coin_flip();
24      end

25      if r_i = stop_i then
26          halt();                               // stop execution;
27      end
28      r_i ← r_i + 1;
29  end
```

Example Execution

Table 1 outlines a hypothetical execution of binary consensus with four processes. For every step the following information is provided (for each process): the value broadcasted, the values received, and the value computed (to be broadcast in the following step). The received values are presented in the form $< v_1, v_2, v_3, v_4 >$, where v_1 is the value received from process p_1, v_2 is the value received from process p_2, and so on. An asterisk (*) indicates a faulty message transmission. For example, the representation $< v_1, *, v_3, v_4^* >$ indicates the message transmission from process p_2 had an omission fault - an asterisk is present instead of a particular value - and the message from process p_4 had a corruption fault – an asterisk follows the value.

The execution comprises two rounds until a decision is reached. The fault pattern in this example captures malicious behavior from process p_4 and an omission from process p_2. On step 1 of round $r_i = 0$, all processes except for p_3 propose value 1, however some of the transmissions from process p_4 result in corruptions. This can be seen as a deliberate attempt from p_4 to disrupt the correct operation of the protocol. As a result, only processes p_1 and p_2 propose value 1 in step 2. Processes p_3 and p_4 propose $\perp$ which indicates that they have no preference. In the transmissions carried out in this step, only process p_3 experiences a (omission) fault on the reception of a message from p_2. Since processes p_1, p_2, and p_4 receive $f + 1$ messages with value 1, they compute 1 to be proposed for the next step. Process p_3, on the other hand, has to flip to coin to decide which value to broadcast the following step. This value turns out to be 1.

For the second round, every process proposes 1 as the initial value, however every transmission from p_4 results in a corruption fault, effectively changing the value from 1 to 0. Nevertheless, every process receives $2f + 1$ messages with value 1, which result in every process proposing

1 to the next step. In step 2, again, every process receives $2f + 1$ messages with value 1 despite every transmission from p_4 has a corruption fault. This is enough for every process to perform a decision on value 1.

Correctness Proof

This section shows that the above protocol ensures the three properties from Section 4.2.1. The proof is supported by Lemmas 1 and 2, which in essence demonstrate that the messages processes receive at each step can differ from one another in a limited way. Lemmas 3 and 4 are specific to prove the termination property (BC3).

Definition 1. Let Ω be the set of messages broadcast by all processes in $\prod$ at some step t, with $|\Omega| = n$.

Definition 2. Let V_i be the set of messages received by a process p_i at some step t, with $n - f \leq |V_i| \leq n$.

Lemma 1. At any communication step t, $|\Omega \cap V_i| \geq n - f$ is true.

Proof: If no transmission failures occur, then $\Omega = V_i$, i.e., the set of broadcasted messages is equal to the set of received messages. Since, according to the system model, transmission failures can originate at most from f processes per step, then at most f messages in V_i are subject to transmission failures (i.e., not received or received with different content). Therefore, the sets Ω and V_i have to contain at least $n - f$ messages in common: $|\Omega \cap V_i| \geq n - f$.

Corollary 1. Set V_i has at most f elements not contained in set Ω: $|V_i \setminus \Omega| \leq f$.

Lemma 2. Let V_i and V_j be the sets of messages received at any communication step by processes p_i and p_j, respectively, with $i \neq j$. Then, $|V_i \cap V_j| \geq n - f$.

Proof: According to the system model, transmission failures can originate at most from the same f processes per step. Therefore, any two sets

Table 1.

	p_1	p_2	p_3	p_4
Round $r_i = 0$, step 1 (lines 4-11)				
Broadcast	1	1	0	1
Receive	$< 1, 1, 0, 1 >$	$< 1, 1, 0, 1 >$	$< 1, 1, 0, 0^* >$	$< 1, 1, 0, 0^* >$
Compute	$x_i = 1$ (line 8)	$x_i = 1$ (line 8)	$x_i = \perp$ (line 10)	$x_i = \perp$ (line 10)
Round $r_i = 0$, step 2 (lines 12-24)				
Broadcast	1	1	$\perp$	$\perp$
Receive	$< 1, 1, \perp, \perp >$	$< 1, 1, \perp, \perp >$	$< 1, *, \perp, 0 >$	$< 1, 1, \perp, \perp >$
Compute	$x_i = 1$ (line 21)	$x_i = 1$ (line 21)	$x_i = 1$ (line 23)	$x_i = 1$ (line 21)
Round $r_i = 1$, step 1 (lines 4-11)				
Broadcast	1	1	1	1
Receive	$< 1, 1, 1, 0^* >$	$< 1, 1, 1, 0^* >$	$< 1, 1, 1, 0^* >$	$< 1, 1, 1, 0^* >$
Compute	$x_i = 1$ (line 8)	$x_i = 1$ (line 8)	$x_i = 1$ (line 8)	$x_i = 1$ (line 8)
Round $r_i = 1$, step 2 (lines 12-24)				
Broadcast	1	1	1	1
Receive	$< 1, 1, 1, \perp * >$	$< 1, 1, 1, \perp * >$	$< 1, 1, 1, \perp * >$	$< 1, 1, 1, \perp * >$
Compute	$d_i = 1$ (line 16)	$d_i = 1$ (line 16)	$d_i = 1$ (line 16)	$d_i = 1$ (line 16)

V_i and V_j have to include at least the same $n - f$ elements, i.e., the messages not subject to transmission failures. It follows that $\left| V_i \cap V_j \right| \geq n - f$ must be true.

Corollary 2. Set V_j has at most f elements not contained in set V_i: $\left| V_j \setminus V_i \right| \leq f$.

BC1 (Validity). If all processes propose the same value v, then any process that decides, decides v.

Proof: Let V_i be the set of messages received by a process p_i in step 1. Since all processes propose the same value v, then, by definition, all messages in Ω have the same value v. According to Lemma 1, at least $n - f$ messages in Ω are also in V_i. Therefore, V_i includes at least $n - f$ messages with value v, and $\#_v(V_i) \geq n - f$. This means that all processes execute line 8 of the algorithm, setting $x_i = v$. A trivial inspection of the protocol shows that a similar reasoning applies to step 2. Here, if

a process receives at least $n - f = 2f + 1$ messages with the same value v, then it decides v.

Lemma 3. If a process p_i decides v at round r, then no process broadcasts the value $v' \neq v \neq \perp$ at step 2 of round r.

Proof. For a process p_i to decide on a value v at round r, it means that it must have received at least $2f + 1$ messages with value $v \neq \perp$ at step 2 of round r (lines 14-19). This implies that some processes broadcasted the value $v \neq \perp$ at step 2 (line 12), and, hence, they must have set their proposal value to v at step 1 of round r (line 8). For a process p_i to set its proposal value to $v \neq \perp$ at step 1, it must receive at least $2f + 1$ messages with v at step 1 (lines 6-8). Consequently, no other process can receive more than $2f$ messages with value $v' \neq v$ at step 1 (see Corollary 2). It follows that no process at step 1 sets its proposal value to $v' \neq v \neq \perp$. Thus, no process broadcasts the value $v' \neq v \neq \perp$ at step 2 of round r.

BC2 (Agreement). No two processes decide differently.

Proof: The proof assumes that some process p_i decides on a value v at round r, and proceeds to show that no other process can decide on a value $v' \neq v$. A process p_i decides on a value $v \neq \perp$ if it receives at least $2f+1$ messages with v at step 2 of round r (lines 14-16). By Corollary 2, every other process receives at least $f+1$ messages with value v at step 2 of the same round. By Lemma 3, since p_i decides at round r (line 16), then no process broadcasts $v' \neq v \neq \perp$ at step 2 of this round (line 12). This implies, by Corollary 1, that no process receives more than f messages with value $v' \neq v \neq \perp$ at step 2 of round r (line 13). Consequently, the only value for which every process receives $f+1$ or more messages is v. Therefore, every process at step 2 of round r sets its proposal value to v (either at line 19 or 21). On round $r+1$, every process proposes the same value v at the beginning of step 1. According to BC1, any remaining process that needs to decide will also chose v. Thus, no two processes decide differently.

Lemma 4. At step 2 of any round r, if a process p_i sets its proposal value to v without resorting to a coin flip (line 23), then no other process sets its proposal value to $v' \neq v$ unless it resorts to a coin flip.

Proof: At step 1, a process p_i sets its proposal value to $v \neq \perp$ if it receives $2f+1$ messages with v (lines 7-11). Thus, according to Corollary 2, no process receives more than $2f$ messages with $v' \neq v$. Therefore, no other process sets its proposal value to $v' \neq v$. This implies that for step 2 every process broadcasts the same value v or $\perp$ (line 12) and, based on Corollary 1, no process receives more than f messages with a value $v' \neq v \neq \perp$. Thus, no process sets its proposal value at step 2 to $v' \neq v$ unless it resorts to a coin flip (line 23) since at least $f+1$ messages with a value v' are required to be received at step 2.

Lemma 5. If every process proposes the same value v at the beginning of any round r, then every process decides v by the end of round r.

Proof: Since all processes propose the same value v at the beginning of round r, then, by Lemma 1, all processes receive at least $n-f=2f+1$ messages with v at step 1. Therefore, all processes propose v for step 2 since they all executed line 8. This implies that, again by Lemma 1, all processes receive at least $n-f=2f+1$ messages with v at step 2. Consequently, all processes decide v at line 16.

BC3 (Termination). Every process decides within r rounds with a probability P that approaches 1 with the number of rounds: $\lim_{r \to \infty} P = 1$.

Proof: According to Lemma 5, if all processes propose the same value v at the beginning of a round, then all processes decide v at that round. The proof consists of showing that eventually all processes propose the same value v.

At step 2 of any round r, processes set their proposal values to be broadcasted at the beginning of round $r+1$. This value can be set deterministically (lines 14-19, 20-21) or randomly (lines 22-23). Let D be the set of processes that set their value deterministically and R the set of processes that set their value randomly. By Lemma 4, all processes in D set their proposal to the same value v. Therefore, with probability $2^{-|R|}$, all processes in R set their proposal value to v at the beginning of round $r+1$.

In a worst-case scenario, where $|R| = n$, the probability of the processes not proposing the same value at the beginning of a round is $1-2^{-n}$. Thus, the probability P that all processes in R set their proposal to the same value v within r rounds is at worst $P = 1 - (1 - 2^{-n})^r$. Thus, $\lim_{r \to \infty} P = 1$, meaning that eventually all processes propose the same value v at the beginning of a round.

Multi-Valued Consensus

The multi-valued consensus protocol allows processes to agree on a value v from an arbitrary domain V. The advantage of this protocol with respect to the binary consensus protocol is that it allows the proposed and agreed value to be anything, not just 1 or 0. Each process proposes a value $x_i \in V$ and they all decide on a value v proposed by some process or on a default value $\perp \notin V$. The protocol also ensures that if all processes propose the same value v, then the decision value is v. Additionally, if a decision is made on a value $v \neq \perp$, then v was proposed by at least one process whose transmissions were not faulty. This is important to prevent decisions on values that are only proposed by malicious processes. The protocol resorts to binary consensus as an underlying primitive.

Properties

The protocol is defined formally by the following properties:

- **MVC1 (Validity 1).** If all processes propose the same value v, then any process that decides, decides v.
- **MVC2 (Validity 2).** If a process decides v, then v was proposed by at least $f + 1$ processes or $v = \perp$.
- **MVC3 (Agreement).** No two processes decide differently.
- **MVC4 (Termination).** Every process eventually decides.

Multi-valued consensus provides the pivotal service of RAPTOR: agreement on arbitrary information despite transmission failures. It can be used, for example, to ensure that aircraft maneuvering is based on information that is consistent amongst all aircraft. This way, the possibility of conflicts is eliminated as long as the assumptions of the system model hold.

Description

The protocol presented in Algorithm 2 (see Figure 3) is divided in three steps. Step 1 begins with

every process p_i broadcasting the initial proposal value x_i and saving in V_i the received messages (lines 1-2). If a process p_i receives $2f + 1$ or more messages with the same value v, then the proposal value x_i is set to v, otherwise it is set to a default value $\perp$ (lines 3-7). Next, at step 2, every process p_i broadcasts the updated proposal value x_i and saves the received messages in V_i (lines 8-9). If p_i receives $2f + 1$ or more messages with a value $v \neq \perp$, then it sets its binary consensus proposal value b_i to 1, otherwise it sets it to 0 (lines 10-14). Finally, at step 3, a binary consensus instance is initiated using b_i as the proposal value and if its decision value is 1, then p_i decides on the value v that appears at least $f + 1$ times in V_i (see Lemma 6). Otherwise, if the binary consensus decision value is 0, then p_i decides on the default value $\perp$ (lines 15-20).

Example Execution

Table 2 presents a hypothetical execution of multi-valued consensus with four processes. The representation follows the one described in section 4.2.3. Again, the fault pattern captures malicious behavior from process p_4.

The execution starts with processes p_1, p_2, and p_4 proposing the value A, and process p_3 proposing the value B. Since the transmission from p_4 to p_3 results in a corruption fault, only processes p_1, p_2, and p_4 propose the value A to step 2. Again, in this step, some of the transmissions from p_4 result in corruption faults. This allows only p_1 and p_2 to propose 1 to the binary consensus execution, which means that the result could be a decision of either 1 or 0. In this case, it is 1. The processes finally decide on A because it is the only value for which they have received $f + 1$ messages in step 2.

Rigorous Proof

The proof is relatively straightforward. It only resorts to one lemma (Lemma 6). The lemma is similar, in essence, to Lemmas 1 and 2 from binary

Figure 3. Algorithm 2

Algorithm 2: Multi-Valued Consensus Algorithm

Input: Initial proposal value x_i
Output: Decision value d_i

```
1  broadcast (1, Π, x_i);                          // step 1;
2  V_i ← receive (1, Π);
3  if ∃_v : #_v(V_i) ≥ 2f + 1 then
4  |   x_i ← v;
5  else
6  |   x_i ← ⊥;
7  end

8  broadcast (2, Π, x_i);                          // step 2;
9  V_i ← receive (2, Π);
10 if ∃_{v≠⊥} : #_v(V_i) ≥ 2f + 1 then
11 |   b_i ← 1;
12 else
13 |   b_i ← 0;
14 end
15 c_i ← binary_consensus (b_i);                   // step 3;
16 if c_i = 1 then
17 |   d_i ← v : #_{v≠⊥}(V_i) ≥ f + 1;
18 else
19 |   d_i ← ⊥;
20 end
```

---

consensus. It states that processes can only receive a limited amount of contradictory messages and it serves to support the proof of the agreement property (MVC3). Additionally, the proof makes use of Lemmas 1 and 2 defined previously. These lemmas are also useful for multi-valued consensus because they are general lemmas that essentially state how much the sets of messages received by the processes overlap with each other and with the set of broadcasted messages.

MVC1 (Validity 1). If all processes propose the same value v, then any process that decides, decides v.

Proof: At step 1, if all processes propose the same initial value v, then by Lemma 1, every process receives at least $n - f = 2f + 1$ messages with v (lines 1-7). This implies that every process proposes v at step 2 (line 8). For a process to decide on a value $v' \neq v$ it has to receive at least $f + 1$ messages with v' at step 2 (lines 16-17). However, according to Lemma 1, this is impossible because at most f messages can have a value $v' \neq v$.

MVC2 (Validity 2). If a process decides v, then v was proposed by $f + 1$ processes or $v = \perp$.

Proof: For a process to decide on $v = \perp$ (lines 16-17) some process must have seen $2f + 1$ messages with v at step 2 (line 10). Otherwise, no process proposes 1 to the binary consensus protocol and the decision would have to be 0 (by BC1). By Lemma 1, for this threshold to be observable, at least $f + 1$ processes have to propose v.

Lemma 6. If, at step 2, a process p_i receives at least $f + 1$ messages with value v, then no process receives more than f messages with value $v' \neq v \neq \perp$.

Proof: By Lemma 1, at step 2, a process p_i receives at least $f + 1$ messages with value v, if and only if some process broadcasts a message with value v (lines 8-9). If a process broadcasts a message with value v at step 2, then it is because it received at least $2f + 1$ messages with value v at step 1 (lines 2-4). By Lemma 2, this implies that no process could have received more than $2f$ messages with value $v' \neq v$ at

Table 2.

	p_1	p_2	p_3	p_4
step 1 (lines 1-7)				
Broadcast	A	A	B	A
Receive	$< A, A, B, A >$	$< A, A, B, A >$	$< A, A, B, B^* >$	$< A, A, B, A >$
Compute	$x_i = A$ (line 4)	$x_i = A$ (line 4)	$x_i = \perp$ (line 6)	$x_i = A$ (line 4)
step 2 (lines 8-14)				
Broadcast	A	A	$\perp$	A
Receive	$< A, A, \perp, A >$	$< A, A, \perp, A >$	$< A, A, \perp, \perp^* >$	$< A, A, \perp, \perp^* >$
Compute	$b_i = 1$ (line 11)	$b_i = 1$ (line 11)	$b_i = 0$ (line 13)	$b_i = 0$ (line 13)
step 3 (lines 15-20)				
Propose	1	1	0	0
Decide (binary)	$c_i = 1$ (line 15)	$c_i = 1$ (line 15)	$c_i = 1$ (line 15)	$c_i = 1$ (line 15)

step 1 and, consequently, no process could have set its proposal value at step 1 to $v' \neq v \neq \perp$. Therefore, no process proposes $v' \neq v$ at step 2. This, according to Lemma 1, implies that no process receives more than f messages with value $v' \neq v \neq \perp$ at step 2.

MVC3 Agreement. No two processes decide differently.

Proof: Processes either decide on a value $v \neq \perp$ or decide $\perp$. These two cases are treated separately in the proof.

For the first case, a process p_i decides on a value $v \neq \perp$ if it gets 1 from the binary consensus protocol. According to the binary consensus properties (BC1, BC2, BC3), if p_i decides 1, then all processes decide 1. Hence, all processes decide on a value $v \neq \perp$ that is received at least $f + 1$ times at step 2 (line 17). This value v is necessarily the same for all processes. This happens because for processes to get 1 from binary consensus, then some process had to propose 1; otherwise the decision value would had to be 0 (see BC1). A process proposes 1 to binary consensus if and only if it receives at least $2f + 1$ messages with

value $v \neq \perp$ at step 2 (lines 10-14). By Corollary 2, every other process has to receive at least $f + 1$ messages with value $v \neq \perp$. Furthermore, according to Lemma 6, if p_i receives at least $f + 1$ messages with $v \neq \perp$ at step 2, then no processes receives more than f messages with $v' \neq \perp$. Thus, if some process gets 1 from the binary consensus, every process decides on the same value $v \neq \perp$.

For the second case, a process p_i decides $\perp$ if it decides 0 on the binary consensus protocol. According to the binary consensus properties (BC1, BC2, BC3), if p_i decides 0, then all processes decide 0. Therefore, if p_i decides $\perp$, then all processes decide $\perp$.

MVC4 Termination. Every process eventually decides.

Proof: The proof is obtained from a trivial inspection of the protocol.

Terminating Reliable Broadcast: The terminating reliable broadcast protocol is an information dissemination protocol that provides strong properties. It allows a sender process to transmit a message with value m that is delivered uniformly at all processes: every process is either delivered *m* or delivered a default value ⊥. In both cases, processes are always delivered a message even if the sending process is affected by transmission failures. In this situation, processes end up getting a message ⊥ not actually broadcast by the sending process.

Properties

The formal properties of the protocol are defined as follows:

- **TRB1 (Termination).** Every process is delivered exactly one message.
- **TRB2 (Validity).** If a sender process p_i broadcasts a message with value *m* and no transmissions of p_i are faulty, then p_i is delivered *m*.
- **TRB3 (Agreement).** If a process is delivered a message *m*, then all processes are delivered the same message *m*.
- **TRB4 (Integrity).** If a process is delivered a message *m*, then the message was broadcasted from the sender process p_i or *m* = ⊥.

Description

The protocol, presented in Algorithm 3 (see Figure 4) is rather simple. The sender broadcasts a message *m* and every process p_i saves the delivered message, if any, in x_i. In case no message is delivered, then $x_i = \perp$. Every process p_i then proposes x_i to a multi-valued consensus execution and the decision value *d* is the message that p_i consistently delivers.

Example Execution

Table 3 presents an execution of the terminating reliable broadcast protocol with four processes.

Rigorous Proof

The proof is quite straightforward because the underlying multi-valued consensus ensures that all processes deliver the same message.

TRB1 (Termination). Every process delivers exactly one message.

Proof: The proof is obtained by a trivial inspection of the protocol.

TRB2 (Validity). If a process p_i broadcasts a message with value *m* and no transmissions of p_i are faulty, then p_i delivers *m*.

Proof: If no transmissions of p_i are faulty then every process delivers the value $x_i = m$ (line 4). Consequently, every process proposes *m* to the multi-valued consensus protocol and, by MVC1 and MVC4, every process decides *d* = *m* (line 4).

TRB3 (Agreement). If a process is delivered a message *m*, then all processes are delivered the same message *m*.

Proof: A process p_i delivers the message obtained from the execution of the multi-valued consensus protocol (line 5). Since this protocol ensures that every process decides on the same value, then if a process delivers *d* = *m*, all processes deliver *m*.

TRB4 (Integrity). If a process is delivered a message *m*, then the message was broadcasted from the sender process p_i or *m* = ⊥.

Proof: If p_i does not broadcast a message *m*, then no process proposes *m* to the multi-valued consensus protocol. Only up to *f* addition faults may initiate a multi-valued consensus execution, however, by MVC2, this can only result in a decision being made on ⊥. Thus, either the value delivered is broadcast by the sender p_i or *m* = ⊥.

Services for Airborne Self-Separation

This section is concerned with the applicability of the RAPTOR protocols to airborne self-separation.

Figure 4.

Algorithm 3: Terminating Reliable Broadcast Algorithm

    Input: Sender Process ID sid

    Input: Message to be Broadcast m `// if sender process;`

    Output: Delivered Message d

1 **if** $p_i = sid$ **then**

2 | `broadcast`$(1, \Pi, m)$;

3 **end**

4 $x_i \leftarrow$ `receive`$(1, \{sid\})$;

5 $d_i \leftarrow$ `multivalued_consensus`(x_i);

Table 3.

	p_1	p_2	p_3	p_4
Broadcast	m	-	-	-
Receive	m	m	m	m
Propose	$x_i = m$	$x_i = m$	$x_i = m$	$x_i = m$
Decide/Deliver	m	m	m	m

To illustrate how RAPTOR can be used in practical situations, three services for airborne self-separation and SGT in particular are presented. Each service is directly based on one of the protocols and, for the most part, its implementation is relatively simple because most of the complexity is abstracted by the respective RAPTOR protocol. These services inherit the capabilities of RAPTOR, which means that the correct operation of the services is guaranteed even in the presence of arbitrary transmission faults as long as, at any particular communication step, they originate at less of one third of the processes.

The first service is an extension to RAPTOR that makes it more suitable for the dynamic environment of airborne self-separation. It deals with the fixed group assumption identified in Section 4.1. The solution resides on a group membership service, which allows an aircraft to continuously and reliably update the set of aircraft surrounding it and, consequently, the group(s) it belongs to.

The second service represents an SGT-specific service: rank consistency. It bridges that gap between the implicit SGT assumptions (i.e., timely and reliable exchange of information) and the environment (i.e., unreliable communication and potentially malicious aircraft) by providing aircraft within a group with consistent SGT rankings.

Finally, the third service is the view augmentation service. It enhances the basic SGT functionality, or any other conflict resolution algorithm, by expanding an aircraft's awareness beyond what its communication capabilities can directly provide.

Group Membership

The protocols of RAPTOR are group communication protocols. They operate under the assumption that aircraft have knowledge about the group, i.e., they are aware of the surrounding set of aircraft within the communication range of each other. It is only when aircraft know of the groups they belong to that the protocols can be properly executed.

Unfortunately, in an airborne self-separation environment, from the perspective of any one aircraft, the set of surrounding aircraft within communication range is constantly changing. The *a priori* group knowledge assumption is a safe one when aircraft are in vicinity of airports where the ground-based infrastructure can provide reliable group information to nearby aircraft - both grounded and airborne. Nevertheless, as aircraft takeoff and fly away, this infrastructural support eventually becomes unavailable. The aircraft require some way to update the group information in a decentralized fashion.

This section informally describes a solution to this problem. It presents an extension to RAPTOR that allows the system to handle the dynamism of the environment. Interestingly, the presented solution resorts to the RAPTOR protocols themselves and does not require any additional assumptions, except for each aircraft to be equipped with an unreliable aircraft detector. This is a module that detects the presence of nearby aircraft in a possibly incomplete manner (i.e., it may fail to detect some aircraft at some instants). It represents a type of abstraction thoroughly used in the distributed systems literature (Chandra & Toueg, 1996; Vora, Nesterenko, Tixeuil, & Delaet, 2008). Commercial aircraft are usually able to provide this sort of support using mechanisms like ADS-B (Hicok & Lee, 1998).

The solution resides on an algorithm that is executed at pre-determined time intervals. It allows any existing group of aircraft to agree on a set of aircraft that is within a certain distance of any one of them and, based on this set, update their group information. The algorithm assumes that aircraft are bootstrapped with some initial group information. This can be easily achieved since aircraft begin their operation in an airport and, as stated before, the latter can support the former with this information. Updating the group

information can mean partitioning the group, add new members to the group, dismantling the group altogether, etc. It all depends on the criteria used to form groups (any particular solution can be applied), which should usually be based on the geographical distribution of the aircraft. Thus, the protocol for group membership is as follows:

1) Each aircraft TRB-broadcasts[2] the information provided by its local aircraft detector module (i.e., the set of aircraft that were observable to it since the last time the algorithm was run) to the aircraft in its group.

2) Each aircraft receives the information that was TRB-broadcast by every other aircraft in its group.

3) This information is consolidated in a set DA that contains every aircraft that was observable by the aircraft of group Π. This set is consistent amongst all aircraft in the group because of the properties of terminating reliable broadcast. Note that DA may contain aircraft inside and outside Π.

4) The set DA is passed as an argument to an algorithm that forms one or more groups according to the geographical positioning of aircraft in DA. Note that RAPTOR requires that processes within a group to be within communication distance of each other defined by some distance D. Depending on the criteria used to form the groups, it may be desirable for any particular aircraft to be included in more than one group.

5) The information about the new groups is broadcast to the aircraft in DA that are not part of Π.

6) Finally, all aircraft (both those in Π and those in DA that are not in Π) update their group information to reflect the newly formed groups and their communication proceeds accordingly.

The previous algorithm is just a proof-of-concept and has room to be considerably optimized.

For example, it is possible to use a regular broadcast instead of the more expensive terminating reliable broadcast followed by a vector consensus execution[3] (Correia, Neves, & Verissimo, 2006). Nevertheless, it serves to show how to use the RAPTOR protocols in a dynamic system.

Rank Consistency

As described in Section 3, individual maneuvering decisions are taken based on a ranking of the aircraft performed by the SGT algorithm. The ranking is built based on the information exchanged among the aircraft in a given area. If this information is not consistent across all of them, it is possible for aircraft to build contradictory rankings leading to further conflict. This can happen when messages are lost, corrupted, or purposely contradictory.

The rank consistency service ensures that all aircraft build the same ranking despite some failures. To achieve this, it resorts to the multi-valued consensus protocol, thus ensuring rank consistency even if failures originate at up to f out of $n = 3f + 1$ aircraft. The service is rather simple: aircraft run a multi-valued consensus execution where the proposal value of each aircraft p_i is the ranking rkg_i obtained via the SGT message exchange. If the value returned by the multi-valued consensus is a ranking $R \neq \perp$, then every aircraft uses R as the ranking for SGT decisions (R is guaranteed to be the same for all aircraft). Otherwise if the value is a ranking $R = \perp$, then every aircraft resorts to its own individual ranking rkg_i, which may be inconsistent with some other aircraft.

View Augmentation

As discussed in Section 4.5.1, any particular aircraft p_i may belong to more than one group at any given moment. This depends on the geographical distribution of aircraft around it. While, by definition, every aircraft known by p_i is within communication range of p_i, not all of those aircraft are necessarily within communication range of each other. This forces these aircraft to be partitioned into more than one group. The view augmentation service has the potential to expand the awareness of a particular group to the groups adjacent to it (two groups are adjacent if they contain the same aircraft p_i as a member). From an airborne self-separation perspective, this information may be useful in case it is desirable to include a larger set of aircraft in any conflict resolution or optimization calculation such as the ones performed by SGT.

View augmentation of a particular group $\prod$ is performed by having any of its members to transmit the information about any other groups they might belong to $\prod$. This is achieved by resorting to the terminating reliable broadcast protocol. It ensures that every member of $\prod$ has the same information about the other groups, thus guaranteeing that every member of $\prod$ performs the calculations based on the same consistent information leading to compatible actions.

FUTURE TRENDS

Distributed systems, and the disciplines that come hand in hand with it, such as fault-tolerance and security, provide a readily and extremely valuable body of knowledge to be applied in the design of efficient and safe solutions for air transportation. It is expected that the fields of avionics and distributed systems further intersect in the near future. In particular, intrusion-tolerance seems very promising in bringing the desired qualities for such a critical industry like air transportation. Intrusion tolerance is concerned with building systems that are capable of delivering a correct service despite accidental faults or malicious attacks, of which critical environments such as air transportation are subject due to their complexity and exposure.

CONCLUSION

With the steady increase of air traffic volume, the demand for automated decision-support systems for ATM will grow. Decisions that are fundamentally based on human interaction will have to be progressively replaced by more efficient forms of control without adversely affecting safety. This chapter presents a dependable solution to ATM based on a distributed systems approach that, through proper modeling, introduces a set of agreement protocols to support a game theory algorithm for decentralized conflict-resolution and traffic optimization in an airborne self-separation environment. The services that arise from the application of the protocols to specific problems bridge a gap that exists between the assumptions of the game theory algorithm and the actual conditions provided by its operating environment. The overall robustness of the system is improved, increasing its resilience to deteriorating environmental conditions.

REFERENCES

Ben-Or, M. (1983). Another Advantage of Free Choice: Completely Asynchronous Agreement Protocols. In *Proceedings of the 2nd ACM Symposium on Principles of Distributed Computing*, (pp. 27-30).

Chandra, T. D., & Toueg, S. (1996). Unreliable Failure Detectors for Reliable Distributed Systems. *Journal of the ACM, 43*(2), 225–267. doi:10.1145/226643.226647

Chockler, G., Demirbas, M., Gilbert, S., Newport, C., & Nolte, T. (2005). Consensus and Collision Detectors in Wireless Ad-hoc Networks. In *Proceedings of the Twenty-fourth Annual ACM Symposium on Principles of Distributed Computing*, (pp. 197-206).

Correia, M., Neves, N. F., & Verissimo, P. (2006). From Consensus to Atomic Broadcast: Time-Free Byzantine-Resistant Protocols without Signatures. *The Computer Journal, 49*(1), 82–96. doi:10.1093/comjnl/bxh145

Correia, M., Verissimo, P., & Neves, N. F. (2006). Byzantine Consensus in Asynchronous Message-Passing Systems: a Survey. In *Resilience-building Technologies: State of Knowledge, RESIST Network of Excellence Deliverable D12*.

Cristian, F. (1991). Understanding Fault-Tolerant Distributed Systems. *Communications of the ACM, 34*(2), 56–78. doi:10.1145/102792.102801

Dimarogonas, D. V., & Kyriakopoulos, K. J. (2002). Inventory of Decentralized Conflict Detection and Resolution System in Air Traffic. *Technical Report HYBRIDGE, Deliverable D6.1*.

Drabkin, V., Friedman, R., & Segal, M. (2005). Efficient Byzantine Broadcast in Wireless Ad-hoc Networks. In *Proceedings of the 35th IEEE/IFIP International Conference on Dependable Systems and Networks*, (pp. 160-169).

Eurocontrol. (1999). *1999 Annual Report*.

FAA/Eurocontrol. (2001). Principles of Operation for the use of ASAS. *FAA/EUROCONTROL Cooperative R&D Report for Action Plan 1*.

Fischer, M. J. (1983). The Consensus Problem in Unreliable Distributed Systems (A Brief Survey). In *Proceedings of the International FCT-Conference on Fundamentals of Computation Theory*, (pp. 127-140).

Fischer, M. J., Lynch, N. A., & Paterson, M. S. (1985). Impossibility of Distributed Consensus with One Faulty Process. *Journal of the ACM, 32*(2), 374–382. doi:10.1145/3149.214121

Guerraoui, R., & Schiper, A. (1997). Consensus: The Big Misunderstanding. In *Proceedings of the 6th IEEE Workshop on Future Trends of Distributed Computing Systems*, (pp. 183-188).

Hicok, D. S., & Lee, D. (1998). Application of ADS-B for airport surface surveillance. In *Proceedings of the AIAA/IEEE/SAE 17th Digital Avionics Systems Conference, 2*, 34/1-34/8.

Johnson, F., Hill, J., Archibald, J., Frost, R., & Stirling, W. (2005). A Satisficing Approach to Free Flight. In *Proceedings of the 2005 IEEE International Conference on Networking, Sensing and Control*, (pp. 123-128).

Koo, C.-Y., Bhandari, V., Katz, J., & Vaidya, N. (2006). Reliable Broadcast in Radio Networks: the Bounded Collision Case. In *Proceedings of the Twenty-fifth Annual ACM Symposium on Principles of Distributed Computing*, (pp. 258-264).

Kuchar, L., & Yang, L. (2000). A Review of Conflict Detection and Resolution Modeling Methods. *IEEE Transactions on Intelligent Transportation Systems, 1*(4), 179–189. doi:10.1109/6979.898217

Moniz, H., Neves, N. F., Casimiro, A., & Veríssimo, P. (2007). Intrusion-Tolerance in Wireless Environments: An Experimental Evaluation. In *Proceedings of the 13th IEEE Pacific Rim International Symposium on Dependable Computing*, (pp. 357-364).

Moniz, H., Neves, N. F., Correia, M., & Veríssimo, P. (2006). Randomized Intrusion-Tolerant Asynchronous Services. In *Proceedings of the 36th IEEE/IFIP International Conference on Dependable Systems and Networks*, (pp. 568-577).

Nordwall, B. D. (1995, July 31). Free Flight: ATC Model for the next 50 years. *Aviation Week & Space Technology, 143*(5), 38–39.

Perry, T. S. (1997, August). In Search of the Future of Air Traffic Control. *IEEE Spectrum, 34*(8), 18–35. doi:10.1109/6.609472

Rabin, M. O. (1983). Randomized Byzantine Generals. In *Proceedings of the 24th Annual IEEE Symposium on Foundations of Computer Science*, (pp. 403-409).

RTCA Task Force 3. (1995). *Final Report.*

Santoro, N., & Widmeyer, P. (1989). Time is not a Healer. In *Proceedings of the 6th Annual Symposium on Theoretical Aspects of Computer Science, 349*, 304-313.

Stirling, W. (2005). Social Utility Functions - Part I: Theory. *IEEE Transactions on Systems, Man and Cybernetics. Part C, Applications and Reviews, 35*(4), 522–532. doi:10.1109/TSMCC.2004.843198

Turek, J., & Shasha, D. (1992). The Many Faces of Consensus in Distributed Systems. *Computer, 25*(6), 8–17. doi:10.1109/2.153253

Vora, A., Nesterenko, M., Tixeuil, S., & Delaet, S. (2008). Universe Detectors for Sybil Defense in Ad Hoc Networks. *INRIA Technical Report* (6529).

Wing, D. J. (2005). A Potentially Useful Role for Airborne Separation in 4D-Trajectory ATM Operations. In *Proceedings of AIAA 5th Aviation, Technology, Integration, and Operations Conference.*

ENDNOTES

[1] The assumption of a fixed group of processes does not model the environment in a complete way. In reality, the groups are dynamic due to the aircraft being moving constantly. The fixed group assumption is present for the sake of simplicity because it allows a much clearer understanding of the protocols. Nevertheless, at Section 4.5.1 we informally describe a protocol that allows the creation of dynamic groups and, consequently, the

practical applicability of the protocols.

2   It uses the terminating reliable broadcast protocol.

3   Vector consensus allows processes to agree on a vector composed by a subset of the

proposed values. Although not defined as part of RAPTOR, vector consensus can be easily constructed from a multi-valued consensus primitive.

Chapter 12
A Global Optimization Approach to Solve Multi-Aircraft Routing Problems

S.P. Wilson
Numerical Optimisation Centre, University of Hertfordshire, UK

M.C. Bartholomew-Biggs
Numerical Optimisation Centre, University of Hertfordshire, UK

S.C. Parkhurst
Numerical Optimisation Centre, University of Hertfordshire, UK

ABSTRACT

This chapter describes the formulation and solution of a multi-aircraft routing problem which is posed as a global optimization calculation. The chapter extends previous work (involving a single aircraft using two dimensions) which established that the algorithm DIRECT is a suitable solution technique. The present work considers a number of ways of dealing with multiple routes using different problem decompositions. A further enhancement is the introduction of altitude to the problems so that full three-dimensional routes can be produced. Illustrative numerical results are presented involving up to three aircraft and including examples which feature routes over real-life terrain data.

INTRODUCTION

The aircraft routing problem involves finding paths (in two or three dimensions) from a specified start point to a specified destination (possibly also passing through some rendezvous points on the way). Routes are composed of straight line segments joining intermediate "waypoints" and the problem is to position these waypoints so that the resulting

path avoids certain "hard" constraints (such as geographical features and "no-fly zones") and has low exposure to "soft" constraints (such as risks from military missile threats or low fuel reserves). The *optimality* of a route is based on minimizing a "cost" composed of a weighted sum of penalties for constraint violations together with similar penalties for lateness at rendezvous points, flying excessive distances, using extreme manoeuvres et cetera. More discussion about operational aspects of aircraft routing can be found in (Hewitt & Broatch,

DOI: 10.4018/978-1-60566-800-0.ch012

1992) and (Hewitt & Martin, 1998) which also describe a heuristic routing algorithm.

Other papers which discuss different versions of the aircraft routing problem include (Carlyle et al., 2007; Chen et al., 1995; Karczewski, 2007; Zabarankin et al., 2006).

This chapter is an extension of earlier work (Bartholomew-Biggs, Parkhurst & Wilson, 2003, both papers) in which the aircraft routing problem was tackled using a number of global optimization direct search techniques applied to a basic two-dimensional problem which we shall refer to as the Simplified Route Model (SRM). It was found that the deterministic DIRECT algorithm (Jones, Perttunen & Stuckman, 1993) appeared better suited to this problem than the random-sampling and tabu-search techniques of TSHJ (Al-Sultan & Al-Fawzan, 1997) and ECTS (Chelouah & Siarry, 2000).

Our previous work has been concerned with finding routes for a single aircraft. This chapter extends the SRM cost function both to handle multiple routes and also to introduce altitude to the problem so that full three-dimensional routes can be produced. We present results using both the SRM and also a Realistic Route Model (RRM) (Wilson, 2003), involving actual terrain data.

The SRM test results given in this chapter were obtained from a Pentium 3 (500Mhz) PC running on a Linux platform. Hardware details for the RRM model cannot be disclosed. All of the software was implemented in C/C++.

THE SIMPLIFIED ROUTE MODEL (SRM) ROUTE COST FUNCTION

We first summarise the main features of the Simplified Route Model; more details can be found in (Wilson, 2003). In the two-dimensional case we can attempt to find the ground plan of a route, avoiding a number of obstacles that we shall henceforth call "threats". A route will be defined by its (given) start and end points and by a number of intermediate waypoints. The co-ordinates of these waypoints will be optimization variables; and we assume that the flight path follows straight lines between them. We shall now describe a Simplified Route Model (SRM) route cost calculation.

Suppose that the distance flown is to be as short as possible, subject to suitable avoidance of the threats. Then, for any choice of waypoints, we first calculate the Euclidean length of the corresponding route, denoted by L, say. We can write $L = \sum l_j$ where l_j is the length of the "leg" between the j-th and (j+1)-th waypoint. We then determine how much of the route passes through threats. If the route passes through the i-th threat for a distance L_i then the "cost" of the route C can be expressed as

$$C = L + \sum_i \rho_i L_i^p \tag{1}$$

where ρ_i is a penalty *parameter* associated with the i-th threat and p is an integer exponent to be discussed below. Our aim will be to choose the waypoint co-ordinates so as to minimize C. The balance between flight path length and threat penetration will depend upon the choice of the parameters ρ_i. If the i-th threat is a physical obstacle then ρ_i must be large to ensure that the solution does not attempt to pass through it; but if threat i represents some risky but not impossible region then a more moderate value of ρ_i may be appropriate because it will allow a shorter route which makes an acceptably brief incursion into some danger area. Hence, in (1), the length of leg j that lies inside threat i is defined as $L_i = \sum l_{ji}$.

In the SRM examples used in this chapter we shall use circular threats; but in general we may need to deal with no-fly zones and geographical obstacles with irregular boundaries. Therefore we must calculate threat violations using a sampling process along each leg of a route. We suppose that it is possible to determine whether a point (x, y) is inside or outside a threat but that no explicit expression is available for the threat boundary. (For example, if a threat is simply an area of high ground then a database which provides terrain height for given latitude and longitude will enable us to determine whether some constant-altitude flight-path is feasible or not). Then, using a sampling and linear interpolation process (Bartholomew-Biggs et al., 2003; Wilson, 2003) we can calculate a value for l_{ji}.

In practice we wish to avoid routes which involve sharp turns and short distances between waypoints. Therefore we can add further penalty terms to the cost function to reflect these issues. Let ϕ_j denote the angle between legs j and $j + 1$; if ϕ_{max} is the limiting turn angle then we define

$$\psi_j = \begin{cases} 0 & \text{if } \varphi_j \leq \varphi_{max} \\ \varphi_j - \varphi_{max} & \text{otherwise} \end{cases}$$

If l_{min} denotes the least acceptable leg-length then we can also define

$$\bar{l}_j = \begin{cases} 0 & \text{if } l_j \geq l_{min} \\ l_{min} - l_j & \text{otherwise} \end{cases}$$

Taking the above ideas into account, the route cost function that we use for a problem with n stages and m threats is slightly different from (1) in that it individually penalises stage lengths lying inside threats. The function is

$$C = \sum_{j=1}^{n+1} (l_j + \mu \bar{l}_j^{-2} + \sum_{i=1}^{m} \rho_i l_{ji}^3) + \sum_{j=1}^{n} \nu \psi_j^2 \qquad (2)$$

where μ and ν are penalty parameters. We have chosen the threat penalty exponent as $p = 3$ because it is shown by Wilson (2003) that, provided $p \geq 3$, C retains continuous first derivatives as changes in waypoint position cause a leg to move from being wholly outside a threat to being partly inside it . The usual quadratic penalty for the

other constraints ensures that C is differentiable at boundaries of the feasible region.

THE REALISTIC ROUTE MODEL (RRM) ROUTE COST FUNCTION

The Realistic Route Model (RRM) cost function uses real geographical data to define physical obstacles and also involves more types of constraint than the SRM. These include no-go areas, weather, exposure to military threats and fuel limitations. Evaluation of a route cost depends upon reference to a database of terrain information in order to evaluate penalties associated with flying too close to obstacles or with over-exposure to threats such as radar detection. The precise details of this route cost function (the relative weights attached to different constraints and the ways in which these constraints are measured) may not be disclosed. However, they can be assumed to reflect considerable operational experience within the aerospace industry. We shall be using this route cost evaluation as a "black box" in examples discussed in later sections.

GLOBAL OPTIMIZATION APPROACH AND THE DIRECT ALGORITHM

It is a feature of both the SRM and RRM route cost functions that they often have several local minima. This is easily understood if we consider two possible routes that pass either side of some obstacle: there may be a locally "best" route for each of the alternative branches but these will be separated by routes which have a high value of the cost function. In practice we want to find the best of all the locally optimal routes, i.e., the global optimum.

We now give a brief description of the global optimization algorithm DIRECT (Jones et al., 1993). This is a deterministic rather than random approach which works by repeatedly dividing the region of search into smaller and smaller hyperboxes.

When applied to a function *f(x)*, DIRECT begins with a given "hyperbox" defined by upper and lower bounds on the optimization variables. At the beginning of the first iteration we have the value of the objective function at a centre point, i.e., $f_0 = f(c_0)$. The initial region is then systematically split into smaller hyperboxes on subsequent iterations. For each hyperbox *j* (*j* = 1,...,*J*) we have a centre point c_j (where the function value is f_j). Hyperboxes are grouped according to a size parameter δ_j, which is the distance from its centre to any corner.

At each iteration of DIRECT, some of the current hyperboxes *j* = 1,...,*J* are selected for further subdivision. The aim is to explore the whole region efficiently by only computing extra function values in regions which can be termed "potentially optimal". Potentially optimal hyperboxes are chosen via a procedure given below. We shall suppose that among the *J* hyperboxes there are only $K_j \le J$ different size values. We note first of all, however, that we need only examine K_j of the hyperboxes – i.e. for each of the different δ_j-sized candidates, we need only consider the one whose centre has the least function value. Subdivision of a hyperbox involves trisecting it along the longest edge. (If several edges have the same "longest" length, then the trisection process is repeated for each of them

We now explain the process of selecting hyperboxes which are worth further exploration. If Ω is a Lipschitz constant for *f* then a lower bound upon *f* inside the hyperbox *j* is given by $f_{\_j} = f_j - \Omega \delta_j$. Hence, the most promising box would be the one for which $f_{\_j}$ is smallest. Since a valid Lipschitz constant will not usually be known, DIRECT is based on considering whether there exists any Lipschitz constant such that box *j could* contain a lower function value than any other box. Thus

box *j* is potentially better than box *k* if there exists a Lipschitz constant Ω such that

$$f_j - \Omega \delta_j \le f_k - \Omega \delta_k.$$

(No such Ω exists if $\delta_j = \delta_k$ and $f_j \ge f_k$ and hence, as already mentioned, we need only test the potential optimality of boxes having the smallest *f* value for any size parameter δ.)

If $\delta_j > \delta_k$, then box *j* can only be potentially optimal for

$$\Omega \ge \Omega_{\min_k} = \frac{f_j - f_k}{\delta_j - \delta_k}$$

while if $\delta_j < \delta_k$ then box *j* can only be potentially optimal for

$$\Omega \le \Omega_{\max_k} = \frac{f_j - f_k}{\delta_j - \delta_k}.$$

Thus, for a box to be potentially optimal, the following condition must be met:

$$\Omega_{\min} \le \Omega \le \Omega_{\max} \quad \text{where} \quad \Omega_{\min} = \max(\Omega_{\min_k})$$
and $\Omega_{\max} = \min(\Omega_{\max_k})$.

Hence, there can only be a suitable Ω if $\Omega_{\max} > \Omega_{\min}$ and $\Omega_{\max} > 0$. If these conditions do not hold, then box *j* cannot be potentially optimal.

To reduce the number of boxes to be subdivided, a further filter is applied. We only treat box *j* as potentially optimal if

$$f_j - \Omega_{\max} \delta_j < f_{\min} - \varepsilon |f_{\min}|.$$

If this inequality fails then box *j* is not judged to be worth further subdivision. In the original version of DIRECT, ε is the only user-choice to be made. In the examples which follow, we have typically used $\varepsilon=0.01$ as suggested by Jones et al., (1993). No automatic convergence test is proposed by the authors; instead it is suggested that the algorithm should be simply run for a fixed number of iterations.

Refinements to DIRECT

In applying DIRECT to routing problems we make use of various improvements to the algorithm outlined above (Bartholomew-Biggs et al., 2003; He et al., 2002; Jones, 2001; Watson & Baker, 2001).

Stopping Criteria

One form of stopping rule is based on terminating the algorithm when the objective function does not decrease sufficiently over a specified number of iterations. However, employing such a criterion carries a risk of premature termination. It can be quite common for DIRECT not to decrease the objective function for a significant number of steps while it explores a region round a local optimum. It may take many iterations before potentially optimal hyperboxes are identified in a new area (which could contain the global solution).

Another stopping criterion proposed by He et al. (2002) is to stop DIRECT when boxes become sufficiently small. This idea can be used to save wasteful function evaluations by preventing subdivisions from occurring when box j has $\delta_j < \delta_{min}$ where δ_{min} is a user-defined parameter.

Single Box Subdivisions

As proposed by Jones (2001), performing only one subdivision of each potentially optimal hyperbox can improve the economy of the algorithm. In high dimensional problems where the original hyperbox has several edges the same length, the original version of DIRECT may subdivide potentially optimal hyperboxes many times on each iteration which increases the number of function evaluations. Because not all potentially optimal hyperboxes will actually be worth exploring, this may produce a lot of redundant evaluations. Performing single hyperbox subdivisions will mean that regions that are really promising will be eventually identified; in the meantime, the number of new boxes and function evaluations will not grow quite so rapidly. This will give a saving in both memory and computational workload.

Aggressive Searches

Another possible change to DIRECT (Watson et al, 2001) is to perform periodic "aggressive searches" in which *all* the candidate hyperboxes are subdivided without using the filter on potential optimality. The aim is obviously to cause exploration of the neighbourhood of the global optimum to start after fewer iterations. Any benefits will, however, come at the cost of creating a bigger set of new boxes at each aggressive iteration, leading to an increase in the computational workload and storage requirements.

Use of Restarts

It has been noted that in certain computational tests it is often beneficial to use DIRECT in "restart" mode (Bartholomew-Biggs et al., 2003; Wilson, 2003). That is, instead of performing m iterations from one initial centre point and within one initial hyperbox, we can stop after, say, $m/2$ iterations and begin a new DIRECT exploration in a hyperbox centred on the best point found so far. It is often the case that performing *2*m/2* (or perhaps *4*m/4*) iterations in this way will yield a better point (and at lower computational cost) than what would be obtained by m straight iterations of DIRECT. Possible reasons for this are discussed by Wilson (2003).

DIRECT Versions

In some of the examples below, we quote results from DIRECT-1, which is an implementation of DIRECT including the minimum box size stopping criteria (with $\delta_{min} = 0.001$) and also using aggressive searches. An aggressive search is applied if no significant decrease in f_{min} occurs after $100n$ function evaluations. At most, two aggressive searches are allowed and thereafter the algorithm stops if no reduction is observed in f_{min} after $100n$ function evaluations.

A second implementation, DIRECT-2, is also included in some of our tests. It uses all the features of DIRECT-1 but performs a single subdivision of each potentially optimal box. DIRECT-2 is therefore less expensive per iteration than DIRECT-1 (and because of this we will allow it to perform more iterations).

USING DIRECT FOR MULTI-AIRCRAFT OUT-AND-HOME PROBLEMS

Additions to the SRM Route Model

The examples in this section are all based on the two-dimensional SRM cost function. In order to deal with multiple aircraft we form a cost function for each route and then consider the minimization of the sum of these functions. However, we must also add a penalty term that ensures that the aircraft do not come too close together. To do this, we need to consider the speed of each aircraft (which is assumed to remain constant throughout a mission). It is then possible to calculate the position of the aircraft along their respective paths after t seconds and the distance between them can be checked to ensure that it exceeds the minimum allowable value.

In the examples presented in this chapter, we assume that the aircraft are together at time $t = 0$

and we use an "exclusion zone" near the start of the mission within which there is no penalty for aircraft being too close together. In practice the aircraft could be started at different times (probably with the faster aircraft leaving later). For the purposes of the investigation in this chapter we shall not deal with such operational decisions.

Approaches to Solving Multi-Route Problems

In our experiments – described fully by Wilson (2003) – we have chiefly been interested in planning missions involving both outward and return phases. These have generally proved to be more challenging than "one-way" routing; and three different approaches have been tried.

Approach 1 solves for all routes simultaneously and regards the waypoints for all n routes as variables in one optimization problem. This approach seems adequate for problems with small numbers of waypoints (e.g. those involving "one-way" rather than "round trip" routes). However, as the number of waypoints increased many DIRECT iterations were required before acceptable routes were found. This in turn led to very large computational costs.

Approach 2 involves dealing with outbound and return (multi-aircraft) routes separately. This approach has not worked well because the separate computation of out-and-home routes does not take account of the "whole picture". When DIRECT is optimizing the outbound routes it will aim to find the best possible routes between the start and target. These optimum outbound routes, however, may not be well positioned to permit good return paths.

Approach 3 (the most successful one) is to solve the whole out-and-return problem separately for each aircraft. This was motivated by our difficulties with approach one. Considering one route at a time will make the problem size smaller than if we were optimizing several routes at the same time. Our experiments (Wilson, 2003) showed that approach three produces much better routes than the others and the computational cost is smaller.

In all the following examples, therefore, we use the approach of solving whole out-and-return problems separately. The route separation constraints are implemented as follows. The first route is computed by DIRECT with the separation constraints disabled. Once the first route has been generated, the waypoint positions are stored. The second route is then computed by DIRECT (using the same starting guess as the preceding route) but this time with the separation constraints enabled. Every time a route cost is requested, the stored waypoints from the previously computed route (or routes) are used to determine any separation penalties.

Solving Multi-Route Out-and-Home Problems

In this section we give results obtained by DIRECT on various multi-aircraft SRM problems. The penalty factors appearing in a cost function like (2) for all the problems in this section are: Threat penalty:10; Turn angle penalty: 5; Leg length penalty:1; Route separation penalty:10. (The turn angle penalty factor is relatively high to prevent unacceptable turn angles at the target point during transition from outbound to homebound route.) The separation penalty exclusion zone has radius 1km.

All problems involve aircraft flying at equal speeds since this is more challenging for the separation constraint. The initial guess used for all the problems places waypoints at equal intervals along a straight line from start to target. The initial box sizes for each waypoint coordinate was ±10km which allows DIRECT ample freedom to move the waypoints into optimal positions. For all the problems, we have run DIRECT in restart mode (see section 4).

Test 5.1: Solving a Five-Threat Problem Involving Two Aircraft

We start by considering a five-threat problem in which eight waypoints are used for each route. We allow 4*128 DIRECT iterations to be performed for each route computation. The routes found are shown in the Figure 1.

Two very good routes have been found. Both routes initially diverge because of separation constraints and converge towards the end of the return route because, by then, one aircraft has fallen behind the other. The total number of evaluations used was 166792 and each restart took eight minutes. This compares very well with the simultaneous route-finding approach 1 which did nearly twice as much work and gave routes that were significantly poorer than those in Figure 1.

Test 5.2: Solving a Ten-Threat Problem Involving Two Aircraft

We next consider a ten-threat problem using twelve waypoints for each route. We again allow 4*128 DIRECT iterations for each route computation. Figure 2 shows that both the routes found avoid all the threats. As with the previous test, both routes have remained fairly close to each other throughout the entire mission.

A total of 288434 evaluations were used to obtain the solution shown in Figure 2 and the time taken for DIRECT to run each restart was approximately twenty minutes. This is once again a significant improvement over approach 1 which produced worse routes and took 543026 evaluations.

In Tests 5.1 and 5.2 the aircraft have remained fairly close throughout the mission. Because the same starting guesses are used for each route, the initial subdivisions of the hyper-boxes surrounding the waypoints are identical and so the same areas are searched for each route calculation. This tends to mean that the routes will only move

Figure 1.

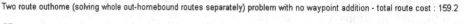

Two route outhome (solving whole out-homebound routes separately) problem with no waypoint addition - total route cost : 159.2

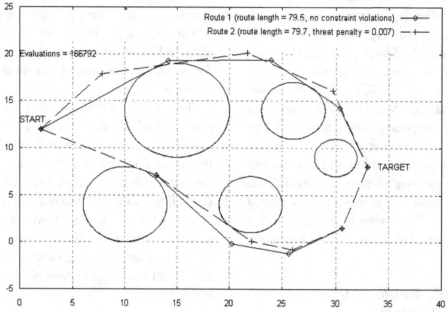

apart if the minimum separation constraint forces them to do so.

In other tests – not detailed here - we also introduced a *maximum* separation constraint to the problem to prevent routes from separating too much. Keeping aircraft reasonably close to one another can be quite an important mission requirement since it allows mutual protection from attacks by enemy fighters and provides more personnel to monitor any ground or air threats. We had some partial success with this maximum separation constraint. In particular, we found that where routes would normally separate and fly around different sides of a threat, the constraint forced the routes together so that they passed on the same side. However, little difference was made to routes that took similar directions around threats. In such cases, the maximum separation constraint sometimes forced the routes to be slightly shorter. More detailed information on the maximum separation constraints can be found in (Wilson, 2003). It is worth commenting here, however,

that careless imposition of both maximum and minimum separation constraints can result in a problem having no feasible solution!

Using Automatic Waypoint Additions

In the previous examples we assumed that we knew in advance how many waypoints would be "enough" to enable a route to negotiate the threats and obstacles. We now describe an automatic strategy for adding extra waypoints during a solution. This involves examining the routes obtained by DIRECT at the end of a restart cycle and adding an extra waypoint at the midpoint of any leg that passes through a threat. The enclosing box of this new waypoint has the same size as that for the old waypoints. (New waypoints are only added to route legs whose length is greater than $2l_{min}$.)

Extensive experimentation with the use of automatic waypoint additions has shown that good routes can be produced with low computational cost when we start off with a small number of

Figure 2.

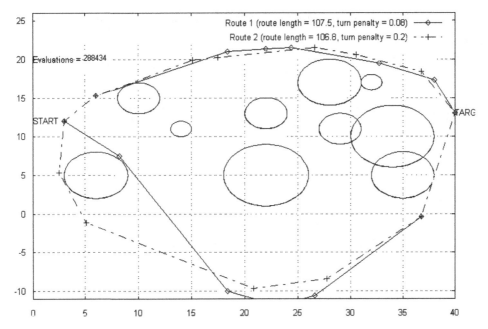

waypoints and only allow additions to occur on alternate restarts of DIRECT. This strategy enables DIRECT to conduct a more thorough search with a current set of waypoint variables before any new ones are added. We now give an example of the waypoint additions strategy.

Test 5.3: Solving a Five-Threat Problem Using Waypoint Additions

This is the same problem as Test 5.1, but the DIRECT solution is now started with just three waypoints placed at equal intervals along the straight line between the start and destination. The routes found by DIRECT are shown in Figure 3; Table 1 compares these results with those from Test 5.1.

Compared with Test 5.1, Test 5.3 needed two more restarts of DIRECT, along with an extra call to the automatic waypoint addition procedure, before route 2 became feasible. An improvement is seen in the length of route 1 when compared to

Test 5.1 but this has resulted in slight violations to the constraints. Route 2 however, is not as good as route 2 in Test 5.1. It should be understood, however, that such differences between individual routes may be rather accidental, since DIRECT is seeking to minimize the *total* route cost: and Table 1 shows that the sum of the route lengths is quite similar for Test 5.1 and Test 5.3. Nevertheless, we can still regard the waypoint-addition approach as successful because, by starting off with fewer waypoints, we have solved Test 5.3 more cheaply than Test 5.1.

Test 5.4: Solving a Ten-Threat Problem Using Waypoint Additions

We next consider the ten-ten threat problem from Test 5.2. Starting with four waypoints (equally spaced along the straight line between the start and destination) and allowing waypoint additions after every other restart of DIRECT we obtained the routes shown in Figure 4. A comparison be-

Figure 3.

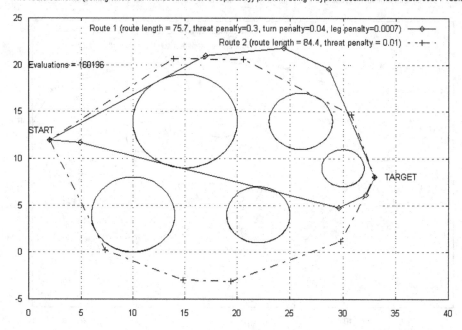

Two route outhome (solving whole out-homebound routes separately) problem using waypoint additions - total route cost : 160.8

tween the solutions to Tests 5.2 and 5.4 appears as Table 2.

In this case, use of the waypoint addition strategy has produced much better routes than those obtained with a fixed number of waypoints. Moreover, Test 5.4 incurs far less computing cost than Test 5.2 both because it uses half the number of function evaluations and also because it involves fewer waypoints and so each DIRECT iteration will be less expensive. The only drawback in the

solution to test 5.4 is that Route 1 has incurred some minor turn penalties.

MULTI-AIRCRAFT PROBLEMS INVOLVING THE RRM COST FUNCTION

In this section we present some multi-aircraft routes obtained when DIRECT is applied to the

Table 1. Comparing results of tests 5.1 and 5.3

Test	Route number	length	Threat	Turn	leg	Total evaluations
5.1 Using 8 waypoints with no way-point additions	1	79.5	0	0	0	166792
	2	79.7	0.007	0	0	
5.3 Starting with 3 waypoints and using waypoint additions	1	75.7(4)	0.3	0.04	0	160196
	2	84.8(5)	0.01	0	0	

*The value in parenthesis shows the number of added waypoints

Figure 4.

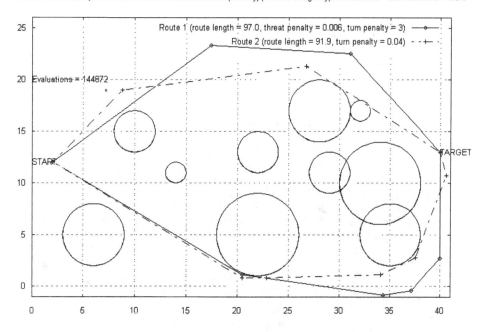

Two route outhome (solved whole out-homebound routes separately) problem using waypoint additions - total route cost : 192.3

RRM cost function using the one-route-at-a-time strategy. In this section we make use of the modified versions of DIRECT, introduced at the end of section 4, and known as DIRECT-1 and DIRECT-2.

We consider the three scenarios all using the same terrain, threats and no-fly zones but characterised by different start and finish points. For each scenario, we compute outbound only routes for three aircraft flying at equal speeds. For all tests we set the minimum separation to 200 metres

(allowing a separation penalty exclusion zone of 1km near the start). For each scenario, initial guessed waypoints equi-spaced along the straight line joining the start and target.

Scenario 1

We start by running the three versions of DIRECT using Scenario 1. For this problem, a box size equivalent to about 63km north-south and 40km east-west is used. We allow DIRECT and

Table 2. Comparing results of Tests 5.2 and 5.4

Test	Route number	length	Threat	Turn	leg	Total evaluations
5.2 Using 12 waypoints with no waypoint additions	1	107.5	0	0.08	0	288434
	2	106.8	0	0.2	0	
5.4 Starting with 4 waypoints and using waypoint additions	1	97.0(3)	0.006	3	0	144872
	2	91.9(4)	0	0.04	0	

*The value in parenthesis shows the number of added waypoints

Table 3. Performance of DIRECT for RRM cost function on Scenario 1

Route	DIRECT		DIRECT-1		DIRECT-2	
	Route cost	Evals	Route cost	Evals	Route cost	Evals
1	445.6	57952	383.6	64634	457.3	31130
2	387.7		453.0		460.5	
3	374.2		392.8		559.9	

Figure 5. Routes produced by DIRECT on Scenario 1

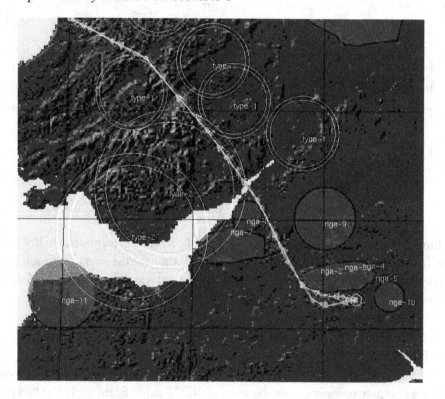

DIRECT-1 to run for 4*32 iterations per route and DIRECT-2 for 4*128 iterations per route. Although 4*32 iterations seems a small number, our experience indicates that this is adequate to find good routes on this scenario. Results are summarised in Table 3.

Of the three variants, the basic version of DIRECT has performed best although the total route cost is only about 0.2% less than that found by DIRECT-1. The routes produced (see Figure 5) are obtained at smaller computational cost. DIRECT-2 was the cheapest variant and found routes which – although visually similar to those found by DIRECT and DIRECT-1 – had route costs about 2% higher. We can see from Figure 5 that all three routes follow very similar paths to the target and appear to make sense in terms of avoidance of threats

Scenario 2

For this problem we use a box approximately 120km north-south and 80km east-west and allow DIRECT and DIRECT-1 to run for 8*32 itera-

Table 4. Performance of DIRECT for RRM cost function on Scenario 2

	DIRECT		DIRECT-1		DIRECT-2	
Route	Route cost	Evals	Route cost	Evals	Route cost	Evals
1	3234.3	49446	1245.6	54306	5333.3	41260
2	1151.5		1234.2		4213.4	
3	1128.3		1163.4		4626.7	

Figure 6. Routes produced by DIRECT-1 on Scenario 2

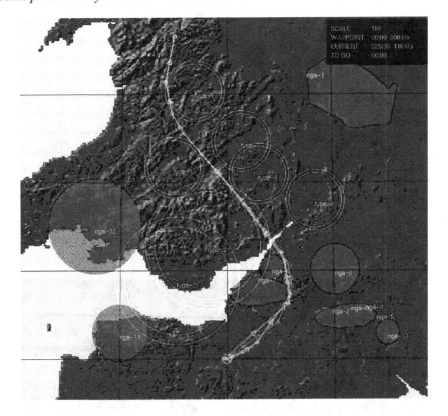

tions and DIRECT-2 to run for 8*128 iterations. The routes found by each variant are shown in Table 4.

For this scenario, DIRECT-1 has produced much better solutions (see Figure 6). DIRECT found good solutions for routes 2 and 3 but did not do so well for route 1. DIRECT-2 has performed the worst by finding routes that are not at all competitive with the other two versions.

As with the previous case, all three routes appear visually sensible and follow very similar paths to the target. The initial separation of the routes will mean that they can follow in line at the later stages.

Scenario 3

For this problem we use the same box–size as scenario 1 and allow DIRECT and DIRECT-1 to perform 4*64 iterations per route and DIRECT-2, 4*128 iterations per route. The solutions found are given in Table 5. On this scenario DIRECT has performed best (see Figure 7). DIRECT-1 produces similar routes, with the exception of route 1, which has a much higher cost. DIRECT-2 has again performed worst but used far fewer evaluations than the other versions. A further test was performed on this scenario in which DIRECT-2 was run for 4*256 iterations. The solutions produced were much improved and competitive with those found by DIRECT and the number of evaluations used was 105896.

DIRECT appears to have found routes that are only locally optimal since the global optimum lies in the middle valley between the threats (the position of the global optimum had been previously determined through numerical experiments). The initial legs of route 1 pass between the two no-go areas whilst the initial legs of routes 2 and 3 are forced around the outside of the small no-go area (at the bottom of the figure) to satisfy the separation constraint.

Table 5. Performance of DIRECT for RRM cost function on Scenario 3

	DIRECT		DIRECT-1		DIRECT-2	
Route	Route cost	Evals	Route cost	Evals	Route cost	Evals
1	1609.8	115486	2756.6	134850	2586.2	55308
2	2551.8		2273.4		2574.6	
3	2522.3		2537.3		3856.2	

Figure 7. Routes produced by DIRECT on Scenario 3

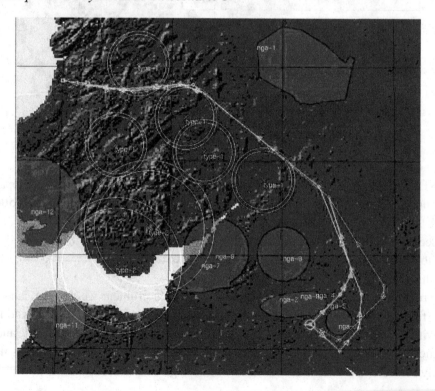

EXTENDING MULTI-AIRCRAFT ROUTING TO THREE-DIMENSIONS

In this section, we extend the routing problem to three space dimensions and investigate the performance of DIRECT (and its variants) on SRM problems involving altitude. Routes are now composed of straight line segments between waypoints expressed as (x,y,z) coordinates.

Adding an Altitude Dimension to Threats

To account for the extra dimension, some threats are represented by ellipsoids. This allows for modelling geographical obstacles like hills or mountains of varying height. Threats such as missile sites can be made spherical and no-fly zones could be modelled using infinite cylinders.

Threats are now defined by centres $c_i = (c_{ix}, c_{iy}, c_{iz})$ and radii $r_i = (r_{ix}, r_{iy}, r_{iz})$. Thus, a point (x, y, z) on the path is inside a threat if

$$\frac{(x - c_{ix})^2}{r_{ix}^2} + \frac{(y - c_{iy})^2}{r_{iy}^2} + \frac{(z - c_{iz})^2}{r_{iz}^2} - 1 < 0$$

$$i = 1, ..., m$$

where m is the number of threats. The calculation of threat intersections within a leg is similar to that outlined in section 2. The route cost function is also extended to include a penalty term for excessive climb and descent angles, similar to that already used for turning angles.

A minimum altitude penalty can also be added to the cost function (2) for the three-dimensional model. This is of the form $(z_{min} - z)^2 * \omega$ where ω is a penalty parameter. When using DIRECT, the *initial* box sizes and waypoint selection can be made to exclude the possibility that z is negative. However, if DIRECT is run in restart mode, then, after the first cycle, it may be possible for a waypoint to be placed below the minimum height.

Inclusion of a minimum altitude constraint guards against such an occurrence.

Tests with Three–Dimensional Routes

The parameter settings used in all of the following tests are given below.

- Maximum climb/descent angle = 50°; Maximum turn angle = 42.5°;
- Minimum route separation distance = 200 metres;
- Minimum waypoint altitude = 500 metres; Minimum leg length = 2km;
- Threat penalty factors = 10; Turn penalty factors = 5;
- Climb/descent angle penalty factor = 5; Minimum altitude penalty factor = 1000
- Minimum route separation penalty factor = 10

The starting guesses given to DIRECT are straight-line solutions with all waypoints being given the minimum altitude setting of 500 metres.

In the first example, DIRECT is given the same initial box dimensions for altitude as for the horizontal directions. Subsequently, we examine the more realistic case where the box size in the x, y plane are greater than for the z axis.

In all the following tests we use the approach of obtaining routes for each aircraft separately. Where the waypoint addition procedure is used, we always start with a small number of waypoints and allow additions after every other restart.

Test 7.1

For this problem, which involves 18 threats, we compute routes for three aircraft, flying at the same speed. Each route uses three waypoints (initially placed equidistant along the straight line between the start and destination). The results found after running DIRECT for 2*64 iterations are shown in Figure 8.

We can see that all three routes fly around the edge of the two large hills rather than flying directly over the peak. All three routes are distinct. Route 1 is the shortest (due to it being lower than others) and routes 2 and 3 are equal in length. A total of 27472 evaluations was used to find the above routes which took a little over five minutes.

In the above test, DIRECT was started with hyperbox edges that were the same in the vertical and horizontal directions and hence the solution routes are often flown at quite high altitudes. On real-life missions this may not be acceptable and the range for the *z*-component of the waypoint may then be smaller than that for the *x*- and *y*-components. In other words the waypoints could be given a freedom of say ± 15km horizontally but only ± 1km vertically.

The fact that the co-ordinates of each waypoint are now represented using two contrasting values (i.e. horizontal and vertical distance) will have implications for DIRECT. The reason for this is as follows. When any particular hyperbox has been selected for subdivision, it is the longest edge that is identified and trisected. Therefore, the horizontal waypoint coordinate dimensions will tend to be subdivided much more often than the vertical one. In order to prevent this, we consider an approach

Figure 8.

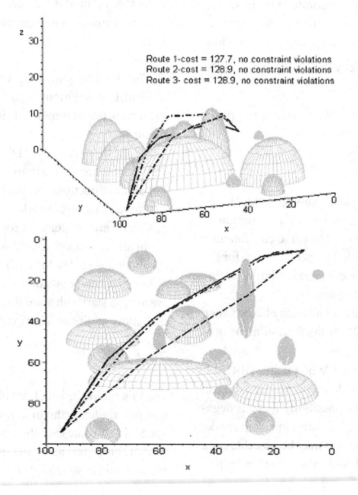

which was recommended by Jones et al. (1993). The aim is to transform and scale the problem so that all the optimization variables are centred on zero and have initial box side lengths of ± 1. This will mean that all the box dimensions will be equal in length and hence DIRECT should not pay too much attention to any particular variable(s). When passed in to the SRM cost function, the variables are then scaled up to their actual size and a route cost obtained in the usual way.

For the next example we make use of this *unit-box* size idea and also re-introduce the algorithm variants DIRECT-1 and DIRECT-2.

Test 7.2 (Using Unit-Box Scaling)

In this test we run the three forms of DIRECT on the same eighteen-threat problem as in Test 7.1. The initial box surrounding each waypoint has edges of ± 50km in the horizontal directions and ± 2km in the vertical direction. Restricting the z-dimension may mean that routes can no longer simply fly above high terrain and so we have used large horizontal side lengths to allow for a wider area of freedom of movement in the *(x,y)*-plane.

We allow DIRECT and DIRECT-1 to run for 4*64 iterations and DIRECT-2 to run for 4*192 iterations. The three waypoints are initially placed equidistant along the straight line joining the start and target points. The results are presented in Table 6.

DIRECT-2 has overall produced the better routes in the fewest evaluations. DIRECT and DIRECT-1 have generally produced similar routes

with DIRECT-1 being slightly more expensive due to the periodic aggressive searches. The routes found by DIRECT-2 are shown below.

We can see from Figure 9 that the routes are flown much lower than those in Figure 8 and have therefore been forced to perform more horizontal manoeuvres. All three routes follow similar trajectories and fly over the small threat between the higher obstacles. As all three routes approach the target, sharp turns are made which has resulted in turn constraint penalties.

Test 7.3 (Using Waypoint Additions)

We now run the three forms of DIRECT on the same problem, but using the waypoint-addition procedure. Each route starts off with two waypoints with the opportunity to add waypoints at the end of the first and third re-start. The results from this test are presented in Table 7.

DIRECT-1 has found the best routes (shown in Figure 10) which improve on those found with a fixed number of waypoints. DIRECT-1 is again the most expensive variant whilst DIRECT-2 produces quite good routes and is the cheapest method.

Test 7.4

We now consider some out-and-home routes over the same terrain and threats as used for tests 7.1 – 7.3. We start with a two-aircraft problem and allow both routes to use eight waypoints (including the fixed target point). We let DIRECT and DIRECT-1 run for 4*128 iterations and DIRECT-2

Table 6. Solutions to Test 7.2

Route	DIRECT		DIRECT-1		DIRECT-2	
	Route cost	Evaluations	Route cost	Evaluations	Route cost	Evaluations
1	163.0	52664	160.7	54360	172.3	37048
2	216.5		165.0		148.2	
3	169.5		216.4		152.1	

Figure 9.

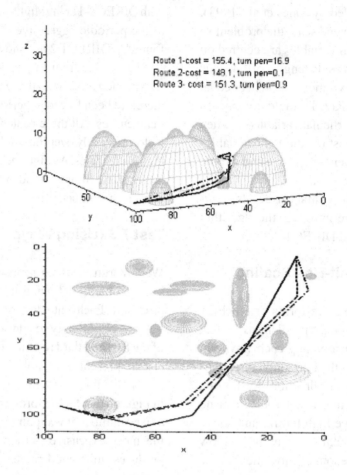

Table 7. Solutions to Test 7.3

Route	DIRECT		DIRECT-1		DIRECT-2	
	Route cost	Evaluations	Route cost	Evaluations	Route cost	Evaluations
1	135.8 (2)	43778	135.0 (2)	50670	179.3 (0)	33656
2	206.6 (0)		159.1 (1)		139.5 (1)	
3	482.4 (0)		163.0 (1)		460.1 (3)	

* The values in parenthesis show the number of added waypoints

for 4*382 iterations. Due to the added complexity of the out-and-home problem, we relax the restriction on height by increasing the box size for altitude to ±4km. The results from this test are presented in Table 8.

In this case DIRECT-1 has produced the best routes (see Figure 11) but is again the more expensive variant (although not much worse than DIRECT). The routes found by DIRECT-2 are similar to those found by DIRECT-1 but the cost is higher because the turn constraints are violated more heavily, though a significant saving in the

Figure 10.

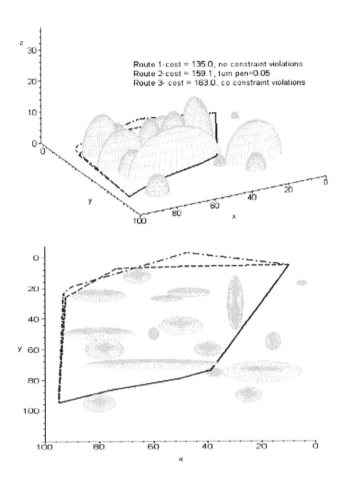

Table 8. Solutions to Test 7.4

Route	DIRECT		DIRECT-1		DIRECT-2	
	Route cost	Evaluations	Route cost	Evaluations	Route cost	Evaluations
1	6762.5	223276	1684.7	227366	6670.2	56384
2	8435.7		1575.2		6663.6	

number of evaluations is observed. DIRECT found the worst routes and was only slightly more economical than DIRECT-1.

Both the outbound and return legs of each route follow the tight valley through the high terrain. The turn angle penalties occur near the transition from outbound to return route.

Test 7.5 (Using Waypoint Additions)

For this test we apply the automatic waypoint addition procedure to the same problem as in Test 7.4. Each route starts off with three waypoints (including the fixed target points). We allow 4*128 iterations per route with the opportunity to add waypoints occurring at the end of the first

Figure 11.

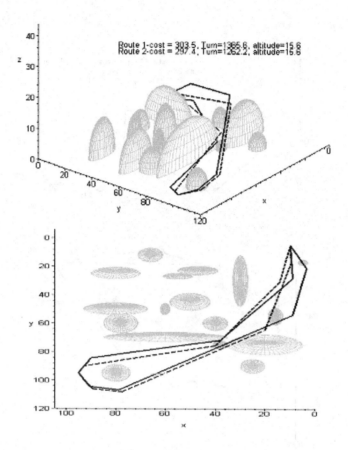

Table 9. Solutions to test 7.5

Route	DIRECT		DIRECT-1		DIRECT-2	
	Route cost	Evaluations	Route cost	Evaluations	Route cost	Evaluations
1	8254.4 (2)	118528	10455.1 (3)	113948	8878.9 (1)	35694
2	3204.7 (4)		321.8 (4)		9534.5 (1)	

*The values in parenthesis show the number of added waypoints

and third re-start. The routes produced are shown in Table 9. In some cases we have obtained better solutions than when a fixed number of waypoints was used. DIRECT-2 and DIRECT-1 have found routes with fewer constraint violations with the former producing shorter routes in considerably fewer evaluations (though only a single waypoint was added to each route). DIRECT on this occasion is the most expensive version but produced poorer routes that violated threat and altitude constraint violations. Figure 12 shows the routes computed by DIRECT-2.

Both routes follow similar paths (unlike those computed by DIRECT and DIRECT-1). The

Figure 12.

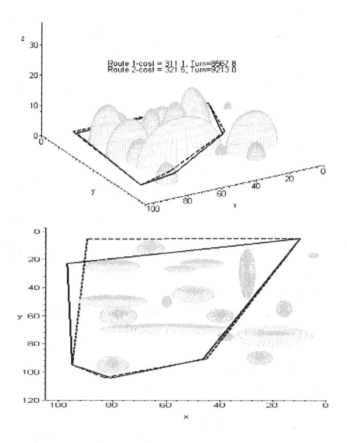

outbound route legs fly around the outside of the threats and terrain on the left-hand side and the return legs cut through the valley between the high terrain.

CONCLUSION

The extension of the aircraft routing problem to handle several routes in both two and three dimensions has generally been handled well by DIRECT and its variants.

The problem of computing multiple routes was tackled in several different ways. We started by solving for all the routes simultaneously; but we found that posing the problem in this way meant that a large number of variables were used (particularly for out-and-home problems) and this made

obtaining routes very expensive because many iterations were needed to ensure that a sufficiently refined search was performed. Jones (2001) remarks that DIRECT is at its best for problems in less than about 20 variables. We have sometimes dealt with routing problems where the number of waypoint coordinates exceeds thirty.

A second approach was to calculate outbound and return routes separately. We found that this approach delivered very poor solutions and, although it worked well on single-aircraft problems, it seemed unsuitable for multiple aircraft.

Our third approach was to solve for each route separately. This became the preferred strategy since good solutions were generally obtained more cheaply than with the other two approaches. Based on our experience so far, we have found that decomposing the problem into smaller ones improves both the accuracy and computational costs of the DIRECT algorithm. Currently we are investigating an extension to approach 3 which aims to break the problem down even further.

We have also experimented with a strategy that allows waypoints to be added "on the fly" during a solution. We found that starting with a small number of waypoints and adopting a rather cautious strategy for adding new ones could be both effective and economical. A strategy of only allowing waypoints to be added at specified intervals ensures that the problem size does not grow too rapidly.

We have found that periodic restarts of the DIRECT algorithm can often improve solutions, reduce computational costs and help convergence to a global optimum. These benefits may be due to the fact that, after a restart, waypoints will be centred upon "good" points and so in the subsequent iterations fewer boxes will be found potentially optimal. Therefore, fewer boxes will be selected for subdivision which in turn means that fewer boxes will have to be stored. This prevents evaluations from being wasted on large numbers of "bad" boxes which will help accelerate convergence to the global optimum and reduce the total number of evaluations used. There is scope for further investigation on how best to choose the re-start frequency.

Changes were also made within the framework of the DIRECT method. Two modified algorithms were tested (DIRECT-1 and DIRECT-2). The former uses periodic "aggressive searches" whereby the best box of every size is subdivided after a predefined number of evaluations have passed without improvement to the route cost. It also incorporates stopping criteria which terminate the algorithm once the smallest box is less than a predefined value. DIRECT-2 has the same features as DIRECT-1 except that it performs only *one* subdivision of each potentially optimal hyperbox. Our experience has shown that DIRECT-1 often produces similar results to DIRECT although there were occasions when the aggressive searches led to

significant improvements in solutions. DIRECT-2 was by far the most economical version and was often competitive with DIRECT and DIRECT-1. However, disappointingly it has performed less well when used with the RRM cost function. This is a matter for further investigation.

Three-dimensional routing problems where waypoints are expressed as (x, y, z) coordinates require the use of "unit boxes" in DIRECT. DIRECT only trisects along the longest edges; and since altitude coordinates will typically have smaller ranges than those in the x, y plane, it was observed that DIRECT did not explore these variables so thoroughly. A transformation of variables so that a unit box can be used around each waypoint removes any bias towards the longer box edges.

The ideas outlined in this chapter are a contribution to the development of a complete routing solution system. Such a system should also automate, as far as possible, the selection of initial guessed solutions and the choice of box-size for each waypoint variable.

ACKNOWLEDGMENT

This work was supported by BAE SYSTEMS, Rochester, England.

REFERENCES

Al-Sultan, K. S., & Al-Fawzan, M. A. (1997). A Tabu Search Hooke and Jeeves Algorithm for Unconstrained Optimization. *European Journal of Operational Research, 103*, 198–208. doi:10.1016/S0377-2217(96)00282-2

Bartholomew-Biggs, M. C., Parkhurst, S. C., & Wilson, S. P. (2003). Global optimization approaches to an aircraft routing problem. *European Journal of Operational Research, 146*, 417–431. doi:10.1016/S0377-2217(02)00229-1

Bartholomew-Biggs, M. C., Parkhurst, S. C., & Wilson, S. P. (2003). Using DIRECT to Solve an Aircraft Routing Problem. *Computational Optimization and Applications*, *21*, 311–323. doi:10.1023/A:1013729320435

Carlyle, W. M., Royset, J. O., & Wood, R. K. (2007). Routing military aircraft with a constrained shortest-path algorithm. Retrieved from http://www.nps.navy.mil/orfacpag/resumePages/papers/woodrkpa/CarlyleRoysetWoodAircraftRouting.pdf

Chelouah, R., & Siarry, P. (2000). Tabu Search applied to global optimization. *European Journal of Operational Research*, *123*, 256–270. doi:10.1016/S0377-2217(99)00255-6

He, J., Watson, L. T., Ramakrishnan, N., Shaffer, C. A., Verstak, A., & Jiang, J. (2002). Dynamic Data Structures for a Direct Search Algorithm. *Computational Optimization and Applications*, *23*(1), 5–25. doi:10.1023/A:1019992822938

Hewitt, C., & Broatch, S. A. (1992). *A Tactical Navigation and Routeing System for Low Level Flight.* [Tech. Rep]. Rochester, UK: BAE SYSTEMS Avionics Ltd.

Hewitt, C., & Martin, P. (1998). *Advanced Mission Management.* [Tech. Rep]. Rochester, UK: BAE SYSTEMS Avionics Ltd. Chen, Z., Holle, A.T., Moret, B.M.E., Saia, J. & Boroujerdi, A. (1995). Network routing models applied to aircraft routing problems. *Simulation Conference Proceedings, Winter,* 1200-1206

Jones, D. R. (2001). The DIRECT Global Optimization Algorithm. *Encyclopedia of Optimization,* (vol. 1, pp. 431-440).

Jones, D. R., Perttunen, C. D., & Stuckman, B. E. (1993). Lipschitzian Optimization without the Lipschitz Constant. *Journal of Optimization Theory and Applications*, *79*, 157–181. doi:10.1007/BF00941892

Karczewski, N. J., III. (2007). Optimal Aircraft Routing in a Constrained Path-Dependent Environment. Master's thesis, Naval Postgraduate School, Monterey, CA.

Watson, L. T., & Baker, C. A. (2001). A fully distributed parallel global search algorithm. *Engineering Computations*, *18*, 155–169. doi:10.1108/02644400110365851

Wilson, S. P. (2003). *Aircraft Routing Using Nonlinear Global Optimization.* Unpublished PhD thesis, University of Hertfordshire.

Zabarankin, M., Uryasev, S., & Murphey, R. (2006). Aircraft Routing under the risk of detection. *Naval Research Logistics*, *53*(8), 728–747. doi:10.1002/nav.20165

Section 4
Improving Computer Software Effectiveness

Chapter 13
Collaborative Decision Making and Information Sharing for Air Traffic Management Operations

Osvandre Alves Martins
Aeronautics Institute of Technology (Instituto Tecnológico de Aeronáutica – ITA), Brazil

Denis Silva Loubach
Aeronautics Institute of Technology (Instituto Tecnológico de Aeronáutica – ITA), Brazil

Giovani Volnei Meinerz
Aeronautics Institute of Technology (Instituto Tecnológico de Aeronáutica – ITA), Brazil

Adilson Marques da Cunha
Aeronautics Institute of Technology (Instituto Tecnológico de Aeronáutica – ITA), Brazil

ABSTRACT

One of the most notable concepts related to the future cooperative Air Traffic Management (ATM) is the Collaborative Decision Making (CDM). This new management philosophy of using collaborative technologies and procedures to enable ATM partners drives efforts towards the common goals of sharing and exchanging information. To support the implementation of CDM, a likely solution was found in the context of System of Systems (SoS), system integration, and interoperability. Service-Oriented Architecture (SOA) principles and technologies were recognized as one of the best alternatives to allow this implementation. Within this architecture, the System Wide Information Management (SWIM) has been developed on the last decade, and SWIM applications will be accessible to all ATM partners on the next decade by providing full airspace information, updated in real-time by all involved partners. This chapter presents an overview of key elements in information sharing for ATM and explains how SOA, SWIM, Aeronautical Information Management (AIM) and CDM support each other development.

INTRODUCTION

As a complex global system, the Air Transportation comprises many public and private partners.

Today's Air Traffic Management (ATM) is reaching its capacity limits. This means it will not be able to sustain demands already in a near future. On this context, some problems need attention and solution, such as the following presented by the European

DOI: 10.4018/978-1-60566-800-0.ch013

Organization for the Safety of Air Navigation (EUROCONTROL) (2004):

- Inefficient use of available airport and airspace capacity;
- Awareness lack of airspace real-time status;
- Limited coordination between Airspace Management Cells (AMC), Flight Management Positions (FMP), and Central Flow Management Unit (CFMU);
- Limited information sharing between Air Traffic Control (ATC), Aircraft Operators, CFMU, Ground Handlers, and Airport Operators;
- Different demands from predicted and actual traffic flow;
- Static route structure and lack of flexibility in use of airspace; and
- Limited interface between airports and the air network.

An alternative way of addressing these issues is to apply the Collaborative Decision Making (CDM) by using collaborative technologies and procedures to get benefits associated with flight and strategic planning.

Applications of CDM and information sharing represent two key elements for the future cooperative ATM concept. They are enabled by the Information Management and Services principle which deals with: logistics of Information Management; information sharing in a scattered environment of information suppliers; and consumers allowing the ATM community to conduct its business in a safe and efficient manner.

Within the ATM Operational Concept, the application of CDM aims to improve Air Traffic Flow and Capacity Management (ATFCM) in the airport and airspace context.

Therefore, this chapter aims to present information about concepts and technologies supporting the CDM functionalities development such as System Wide Information Management (SWIM).

The Service-Oriented Architecture (SOA) is considered as the basis for SWIM. Behind it is the concept of Software as a Service (SaaS) from where the main ideas of software functionality disclosures including information retrieval, computation, and storage came from. Then, in order to become more effective SaaS needs SOA.

SWIM is still being developed. It is a concept on which current ATM software systems will be adapted and new ones will be developed accordingly, becoming the so-called SWIM-enabled software applications.

Therefore, considering ATM scenarios, this chapter focuses only on Airport CDM, SOA, Aeronautical Information Management (AIM) and SWIM. At the end, it tackles some future research directions, trends and perspectives, and conclusions.

BACKGROUND

As stated by (Ky & Miaillier, 2006), air transportation is considered a global industry. Europe and the USA, the two densest air traffic regions, face the same challenges for transforming their ATM systems.

In Europe, the EUROCONTROL through the Single European Sky ATM Research (SESAR) program aims to significantly increase safety, security, capacity, efficiency, and environmental compatibility of air transportation. This is to be done to restructure European airspace, adjust air traffic flow, create extra capacity, and increase the overall efficiency of the European ATM system. In USA, the Federal Aviation Administration (FAA) through the Next Generation Air Transportation System (NextGen) program aims the same. They both represent ATFCM modernization initiatives around the world looking for more effective ways of using the Air Transportation system thus improving the air safety.

NextGen and SESAR are similar initiatives which have been coordinated to make sure that ideal definitions and technology implementations are harmonized and coordinated across oceans. In order to allow this, FAA and EUROCONTROL have been working in a framework of a Memorandum of Cooperation (MoC). This framework of MoC states that their cooperation represents a joint Action Plan, which has already made a significant contribution to define a future globally interoperable ATM system (Ky & Miaillier, 2006).

Therefore, several Research and Development (R&D) projects have been started in USA and Europe considering various issues for future cooperative ATM systems. In order to carry out their harmonization and synchronization objectives a wide number of joint efforts have been performed under the International Civil Aviation Organization (ICAO) control and standardization.

Some examples of addressed issues are CDM, SOA, AIM and SWIM applications for ATM. These philosophies and concepts by themselves or all together can be applied under another major concepts such as the so called Cooperative Air Traffic Management (C-ATM) presented by the C-ATM Consortium (2005).

Nowadays, a wide number of software system products from different suppliers can be applied to support ATM operations. Each one of them based on or built from specific technologies.

To achieve information sharing and system integration for cooperative work, the refactoring of these software products, intending to produce a large and unique one, may be expensive, needing significant coordinated efforts.

The overall objective is that a large and unique system could integrate the existing ones. A possible and applicable solution for these issues is the application of the concept of SaaS on ATM environments. The main idea behind this is to disclose functionalities from existing and new systems, in a standardized way, propitiating information retrieval, and computation and storage through software interfaces. Information about that is provided by systems owners and published in

a catalog which can be accessed from public or private sources. Interested users can access this catalog and gain enough information to implement others to use previous ones.

In order to be implemented, the SaaS concept needs the SOA and related technologies. This implementation offers a framework for better-integrated software systems that meets business needs. SOA is a conceptual business architecture where its functionality or application logic is made available to SOA users or consumers as shared and reusable services. It is implemented and performed on Information Technology Networks. The term "Service" from SOA means businesses modules or software application functionalities with exposed interfaces invoked by messages.

Lately, the value of SaaS has been increasing on the context of system software development and integration. One meaningful example is its selection as basis for the SWIM implementation, a proposed and adopted solution for information sharing and ATM systems integration on both, the USA and Europe. The SWIM operational concept was first depictured looking for aeronautical information, flight data, traffic flow management, surveillance, and weather information. However, it can be applied also to several other knowledge domains besides ATM.

Since information sharing for CDM has been fulfilled based on SWIM, significant further improvements can be achieved for instance by implementing some CDM concept elements. This can be achieved by improving the decision making process. By using the SWIM technology one can share up-to-date relevant information and consider preferences, available resources, and needs of those involved at the airport, by tracking the progress of a flight from early planning up to take off, and so on.

Next section provides information about the so called Airport CDM, an European concept based on CDM philosophy. Following, SOA and SWIM are presented depicting how one can support the development of the other and why the SWIM has enough tools to provide information sharing and system integration on the ATM context.

AIRPORT COLLABORATIVE DECISION MAKING

In fact, the air traffic all over the world is growing quickly (ICAO, 2005; Frangolho & Zerkowitz, 2006). If improvements are not provided by air transportation resources, such as airports, the air traffic will not keep up with demands. As stated by Arbuckle, et al. (2006) and Ky & Miaillier (2006), an alternative way of providing such improvements is by applying the CDM concept and using collaborative technologies and procedures to achieve benefits associated with flight planning.

The term CDM has first officially been used in April, 1995. Actually, it was the given name for a program, named Rules of Engagement adopted by FAA. The CDM comprises a kind of new philosophy in order to manage the air traffic (Wanbsganss, 2001).

The CDM concept was generated within the FAA Airlines Data Exchange (FADE) (Ball, et al. 2001). The FADE project and CDM initial operation implementation has been aimed at the development of new operational procedures and decision support tools for implementing and managing ground delay programs. Nevertheless, it became clear that CDM philosophy and principles might be applied also to a wider problem class regarding traffic management.

According to EUROCONTROL (2004) and the Joint Planning & Development Office (JPDO) (2007), the main CDM objective is to increase airspace and control capacity to improve flight operations by increasing the involvement of aircraft operators in the ATM process and maintaining a high level of safety efficiency. This is achieved by developing information management systems and procedures, and implementing functions, which take into account specific priorities of aircraft operators and airport operations, during all flying phases using full data available.

Airport CDM is a concept, defined by European ATM community, which aims the improvement of: the ATFCM at airports, by reducing delays; the predictability of events; and the optimization of resources utilizations (EUROCONTROL 2006).

Most initiatives on this area improves performance of only individual partners at airports, but most recently, the focus of attention has been on the team performance, mainly because success depends on interaction amongst several elements working together, as a team, properly coordinating their decisions and activities by sharing their information and resources.

Main Airport CDM Partners and Their Benefits

Airport CDM aims to allow partners to synchronize their activities by sharing experience; monitoring the coordination, and communicating; and providing feedback and backup assistance when needed. The challenge is to move from individual partners with specific role assignments and tasks to a team where interaction, coordination, and collaborative procedures and decisions are required to achieve common goals and outcomes (EUROCONTROL, 2008b).

The main Airport CDM partners in the ATM system are:

- ATC;
- Flow Management Centers;
- Airport Operators;
- Ground Handlers;
- Aircraft Operators;
- De-icing Companies; and
- Support Services (e.g. Police, Customs and Immigration, Security Companies and Meteorological Services).

The application of CDM at airports improves the way of how all involved partners use to work. It tries to replace the current central planning paradigm with a collaborative process by sharing individual partner information among all in a useful wide system.

Investigations have shown considerable benefits for all involved partners in terms of more efficient operations, better use of resources, and increased punctuality. This has been making Airport CDM a very beneficial and attractive concept.

By applying Airport CDM concept the main benefits that can be achieved by partners are (EUROCONTROL, 2006):

- For ATC:
  - Accurate planning information,
  - Optimum use of airport infrastructure,
  - Flexible pre-departure planning,
  - Situational awareness enhancement, during disruption times and delays, and
  - Congestions reduction;
- For Flow Management Centers:
  - Optimum use of ATFM slots,
  - Enhancement use of leading en route and airport capacity,
  - Accurate departure estimates enabling improved demand calculation,
  - The growth of airports implementing CDM,
  - Accurate demand calculation by improving flow and capacity management, and
  - Enhancement of ATFM slot by reducing the number of wasted slots;
- For Airport Operators:
  - Enhancement of departures and arrivals punctuality,
  - Enhancement of the existing infrastructure use (stands, gates, terminals, and others),

- Airport slot compliance, and
- Enhancement of operational recovery disruption times and delays;
- For Ground Handlers:
  - Enhancement of departures and turn-round times punctuality,
  - Optimum use of resources,
  - Reduction amount of ground activities,
  - Enhancement predictability by enabling better planning, and
  - Maximization of operational efficiency;
- For Aircraft Operators:
  - One schedule flight operations program,
  - Situational awareness improvement,
  - Enhancement of predictability and punctuality,
  - Improvement of operational efficiency and reduction of delays, and
  - Reduction of ground movement costs; and
- For De-icing Companies:
  - Precise knowledge of demand, and
  - Enhancement of resources use.

All these partners are deliverers and users of data at the same time.

Airport CDM Application Approach

Airport CDM represents mainly a new culture that emphasizes the importance of global collaboration in planning and managing air traffic enabling the partners to make the right decision with other partners (Spies, et al. 2008). Although its implementation needs a phased bottom-up approach, according to EUROCONTROL (2006) and Kazda (2007), the approach may be executed in an iterative and incremental way, each divided in four levels with one or more so-called concept elements, as follows:

- **Level 1** – The Airport CDM Information Sharing and CDM Turn-round Process;
- **Level 2** – Collaborative Management of Flight Updates, and Variable Taxi Time Calculation;
- **Level 3** – Collaborative Pre-departure Sequence, and CDM in Adverse Conditions; and
- **Level 4** – Advanced Concept Elements.

The aim of **Level 1** is to achieve a Common Situational Awareness (CSA), facilitating the information exchange among various partners. This will improve the decision making process and the efficiency of operations by using the best available information. As mentioned by Arbuckle, et al. (2006) and Ball, et al. (2001), decision makers have the ability to request information when they need it, to publish information as appropriate, and to use subscription services for automatically receiving desired information. Information environments enable more timely access to information and increased situational awareness while providing information consistency among decision makers, as well as enable the implementation of CDM procedures among all the Airport CDM partners, having positive effects on the entire ATM network. As stated by ICAO (2005), some specific objectives for creating a CSA are:

- To distribute timely and accurate information in the right format;
- To record data for post-operation retrieval and analysis; and
- To optimize the use of all resources for all involved partners.

The general objective of CSA is to provide the foundation of the traffic network, which is essential for the system planning improvement. The two main concept elements in Level 1 are (Kazda, 2007):

- The Airport CDM Information Sharing; and
- The CDM Turn-round Process.

Airport CDM Information Sharing can be implemented by a logical and distributed data repository from and to the involved partners. It does not necessarily introduce radically new systems or procedures and its benefits may come from enhancing and improving existing systems and processes.

The CDM Turn-round Process defines key events during the planning or progress of a flight describing and enabling the estimation of the future progress of it. The information will be shared by all involved partners. They will have a better understanding of the traffic management in progress through increased operator situational awareness of air and ground movements. This understanding of the traffic by the pilot might allow him to adapt the maneuvering to suit a timely and smooth flow.

The **Level 2** of the Airport CDM Application Approach aims to increase the punctuality of the required data for the ATM system with the emphasis on managing the balance between traffic demand and capacity, maintaining an overall ATM perspective to maximize the use of available resources and to coordinate adequate responses (ICAO, 2005). The two main concept elements of this level are (Kazda, 2007):

- The Collaborative Management of Flight Updates; and
- The Variable Taxi Time Calculation.

The Collaborative Management of Flight Updates tries to obtain a view of the complete ATM network in order to identify bottlenecks and predicted air traffic based on filed flight plans. Its efficiency depends largely on the quality of the traffic prediction, which on its turn is highly influenced by the quality of the flight plan data.

Its inaccuracy is a major source for uncertainty in the overall traffic prediction and this lack of predictability leads to inefficient uses of existing en route capacity. The objective of this element is to bring further improvements to the flexibility of aircraft and airport operations by:

- Ensuring information completeness between en route and airport operations;
- Improving ground operations predictability; and
- Improving estimates of take off times for all flights.

The Variable Taxi Time Calculation element has the general objective to provide an accurate and automated taxi time calculation for each flight, resulting in an enhanced predictability of in block and take off times (EUROCONTROL, 2006). One specific objective of this concept element in this second level is to allow ATC and Ground Handlers, through more accurate calculations, make more efficient use of existing facilities and resources, and optimizing en route capacity.

The **Level 3** of the Airport CDM Application Approach aims the flexibility enhancement of requirements described in (ICAO, 2005). It claims the ability to react to constraints in such a way that decisions are made at the most appropriate points. From the service provider side, this may involve issuing advisories and allocating limited resources in a more efficient way. From the operator side, it involves a set of rules and procedures to facilitate and make more flexible deals with constraints.

The two main elements of this level are (EUROCONTROL, 2006):

- The Collaborative Pre-departure Sequence; and
- The CDM in Adverse Conditions.

The Collaborative Pre-departure Sequence applies the same principle as a general rule, the "first come first served". To enhance the flexibility, aircraft operators and ground handlers will be able to indicate their preferences and ATC will take these into account together with other operational constraints. This allows ATC to arrange Target Off Block Times (TOBT) provided by the CDM Turn-Round Process, so that flights can leave their stands in the optimum order based on operational situation. Efficient Pre-departure sequencing is possible if and only if all other CDM concept elements, except CDM in Adverse Conditions, have been implemented (EUROCONTROL, 2006).

The CDM in Adverse Conditions carried out by a large number of partners, and all aiming for maximum efficiency in their particular activity. Adverse conditions are part of the life of any airport and most of the various airport partners have developed methods of dealing with them. The problem is, not all such methods are equally effective and many are applied inconsistently and without coordination with other partners.

The operation of CDM in Adverse Conditions requires that other CDM concept elements, more specifically CDM Information Sharing, Turn-Round Process, and Pre-departure Sequence, are available at the concerned airport (EUROCONTROL, 2006).

New technologies have been introduced in daily operations to enhance decision support for safety systems. Some examples are advanced ATC tools from Europe like Arrival Manager (AMAM), Departure Manager (DMAN) and Advanced Surface Movement Guidance and Control System (A-SMGCS). In this case, according to EUROCONTROL (2008b), they cooperate with the Airport CDM concept by sharing information, and optimizing arrivals, departures and ground movement.

The integration by using advanced technologies and linking Airport CDM Elements with those advanced tools will enhance and extend CSA and increase collaboration between airport partners. This integration belongs to the **Level 4** of the Airport CDM Application Approach, representing one of the so-called Advanced Concept Elements.

The C-ATM Consortium (2005) states that, from a generic point of view, a CDM application for ATM follows principles like:

- Sharing information among partners through a common platform, improving efficiency and operational decision making;
- Improving data quality and predictability; and
- Achieving CSA for all partners.

It is essential to achieve users CSA by making full use of agreed responsibilities and procedures. Therefore, by creating the foundation to enable information sharing and exchange is one of the first and most important tasks to perform.

Information sharing is fundamental for the future cooperative ATM concept and represents the basis for the CDM concept implementation (Ky & Miaillier, 2006).

SOA represents the basis for the implementation of a concept called SWIM which the main idea is not to construct a new big system, but transform current systems in a kind of System of Systems (SoS) by means of its application SOA.

SERVICE-ORIENTED ARCHITECTURE FOR SYSTEM SOFTWARE

Air Navigation Services Providers (ANSP) is one group in ATM using system products from a wide number of suppliers to support its operations. As previously mentioned, the architectural and technological basis of these products is not so common among them.

Therefore, to achieve information sharing and integration for cooperative work, the refactoring of these products, intending to produce just one big system, may be expensive and needs coordinated efforts.

On the context of possible and applied solutions for this issue, SaaS is emerging. The main idea behind it is to expose, functionalities or software application logic including information retrieval, computation and storage through an Information Technology Network using software interfaces invoked by messages. Information about interfaces as for example "what are" and "how to use them" are provided by system owners and published in public or private registers.

In order to work properly, SaaS needs to take into account SOA concepts in the software design, implementation, and deployment. Lately, the SaaS added value has been increasing on the context of software systems development and integration. The following section describes it.

The Growth and Importance of Software as a Service (SaaS)

The term service has been present in the commercial computing arena for a longtime and has been used in many different ways (Krafzig, et al. 2004).

Today, the concept of services is increasing in a noticeable rate. More and more one has to use some service provided by someone else.

This reality is alive also when the subject is software. Therefore, the idea of SaaS is getting stronger day after day all over the world. If a person types the subject "Software as a service" on Internet search tools, he or she will get more than 90,000,000 results, showing how significant SaaS is becoming today.

According to Sun *et. al.* (2007), SaaS is represented by software applications and can be considered a software delivery model. Applications are hosted on it as a service provided to clients across a network, as for example Internet, Intranet, Local Area Network (LAN) or even Virtual Private Network (VPN).

There is no need to install or run an application on the customers' side. Instead of doing so, SaaS aims to cut off customers' software maintenance, continuing operation, and support. Conversely, they resign control over software versions or changing requirements.

Using SaaS also can conceivably reduce expenses of buying software less costly at on-demand pricing.

SaaS has provided stronger protection of its intellectual property setting up a constant revenue stream. SaaS seller may host the application on its own web server. On the other hand, this role may be handled by a third-party Application Service Provider (ASP). As a spin-off, end users may reduce their investment also on hardware. Considering this context, the pay-off goes to both sides: suppliers and customers.

SaaS is commonly referred as an ASP model. It has been announced as a new wave in application software distribution.

In sum, SaaS consumers may rent an application from a central provider. Business models may vary according to a level of which the software is streamlined, to lower the price and increase the efficiency, or add value to customize further improved digitized business.

As stated before, SaaS needs SOA to become more effective. This idea offers a framework for better-integrated systems that meets business needs.

Next section presents SOA Key ideas in order to SaaS became effective used and implemented.

SOA Key Concepts

First off all, the term software architecture ought to be defined. According to (Krafzig, et al. 2004, p. 76), software architecture is a set of statements describing software components and assigning system functionality to these components. It describes the technical structure, constraints, components characteristics, and interfaces among them. The architecture is the scheme for the system and therefore the implicit high-level plan for its construction.

SOA is also considered a method for both development and integration. Hence, functionalities are grouped around business and packaged as interoperable services.

Moreover, SOA describes Information Technology (IT) which allows different applications to exchange data with one another as they join into the business. The aim is to provide a service loose coupling regarding operating systems, programming languages, and other related technologies, which underlie applications (Newcomer & Lomow, 2005). SOA allows the separation roles into distinct units, or services (Bell, 2008), which are made accessible over a network. These services communicate with one another through parameters exchange from one service to another or also coordinating activities between them (Erl, 2005). SOA ideas may be seen as built on and changing from older ideas of distributed computing (Bell, 2008; Erl, 2005) and modular programming.

SOA depends on a business expert in order to both link and sequence services in a process known as orchestration, thus meeting a new or existing business system requirement.

SOA is also considered as a business approach and methodology as much as a technological approach and a method. This could be pointed out as one of its most important characteristics. It also enables businesses to make business decisions supported by technology instead of just making some business decisions determined or constrained by technology.

According to Durvasula, et al. (2006), SOA basically has as its foundation the three following main parts:

- **Business architecture** – describes the business strategy, objectives, priorities, and processes to be supported by SOA, which is successful only if it delivers on the business architecture. Some of the best practices for developing the business architecture include to:

Collaborative Decision Making and Information Sharing

○ Review the current specification and the underlying technologies;

○ Map these to the business strategy to identify gaps;

○ Review the horizontal (business) and vertical (role-based view) needs;

○ Prioritize the application (services) portfolio to provide these capacities;

○ Standardize the user experience across applications; and

○ Define business policies on key such as application and data access and regulatory compliances;

- **Infrastructure architecture** – is the engine that enables SOA. It addresses all the aspects of the scalable infrastructure from networks, enterprise servers, data centers, and firewalls, to application, security, monitoring, and middleware; and

- **Data and information architecture** – the data portion which copes with the logical and physical modeling of the data, as well as data manipulation and quality. SOA reference architecture covers each of these areas at length by providing approaches, needs, and design patterns wherever possible. The information portion models key ideas and events for a given business. The business represents any business entities needing to be exchanged by or for applications that support the enterprise.

The efficient SOA use shall be in compliance with requirements like interoperability among different systems and programming languages to provide the basis for integration between applications on different platforms through a communication protocol.

The following guiding principles define the ground rules for the development, maintenance, and use of the SOA (Balzer, 2004):

- Reuse, granularity, modularity, composition, componentization, portability, and interoperability;

- Compliance to standards (both common and industry-specific); and

- Services identification and classification, provisioning and delivery, and noting and tracking.

When defining a SOA implementation, it should be considered the efficient use of resources; service maturity and performance; and enterprise application integration reasons.

The term Web Services (WS) represents a possible way, so it can be used to set up an SOA. It makes the SaaS happens. The purpose of WS is to make functional building blocks accessible through standard Internet protocols like Hypertext Transfer Protocol (HTTP) or Transmission Control Protocol/Internet Protocol (TCP/IP) which are independent from platforms and programming languages. These services can be new applications or even modified in order to make them able to operate in a network.

Each SOA building block can play one or more of the following roles:

- **Service Provider** – it may create WS and possibly publish its boundary and access information to the **Service Registry**. Each provider decides which services declare, how to cope with security and availability, price issues, how to exploit them for other values, and so forth. Providers also have to choose on which category a service should be listed in. Moreover, it registers which services are available within it. It lists all the potential service requesters. The broker's implementer determines about its scope. Public ones are available over Internet, while private are limited; and

- **Service Consumer** – the service requester or even a WS client finds registers in the **Service Registry** by using a set of find operations. Then, it binds to the service provider to invoke one of its WS. These Brokers will look for services. Any

Figure 1. Web services architectural layers

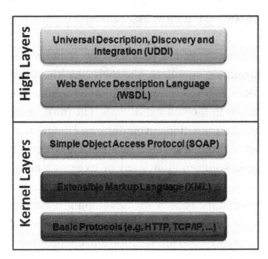

service they need they have to take into the Brokers, then bind with respective service and finally use it. A WS may provide multiple services.

SOA is commonly built using WS' standards (for example, by using Simple Object Access Protocol – SOAP for communication). These standards also referred to as WS specifications provide greater interoperability.

To make the WS usage possible, both Providers and Consumers must know which services are available and theirs getting process. Therefore, Extensible Markup Language (XML) documents are created. They are named Web Service Description Language (WSDL). Those documents aim to standardize the WS presentation structure, hence its features can be identified by others.

Fortunately, SOAP is also based on XML. That fact contributes to software interoperability via WS, since SOAP is open-source. This eases interpretations from different platforms. Figure 1 shows layers distribution of WS technologies. Also based on XML there is the Universal Description, Discovery and Integration (UDDI) protocol as one of the highest layers in the WS Architectural Layers. It was approved as a standard by the Organization for the Advancement of Structured

Information Standards (OASIS) and it specifies how Service Registries are implemented in order to support publishing and discovering operations in SOA.

SOA is becoming the mainstream for enterprise applications. The key to any successful SOA environment is the framework on which it is built. The most resilient framework is based on market-leading open standards representing a good alternative for the basis of next generation software applications.

In fact, without robustness in standards based platforms, directly focused on interoperability, it is impossible to build new composite applications using services. Most SOA industry standards are defined in XML frameworks, and there are emerging XML-based specifications addressing aspects concerning SOA security. Most of these specifications become part of the so-called Web Services specifications stack (GEIA, 2008).

By recognizing the SOA benefits, the USA and European ATM communities have selected it as the architectural base for a solution which intends to be the main responsible mechanism for information sharing and integration powers on future ATM systems, transforming them into a big system comprised of small ones. This solution was called SWIM.

SYSTEM WIDE INFORMATION MANAGEMENT (SWIM)

Today's ATM systems in the most countries comprise a wide number of systems developed overtime for specific purposes. These systems are connected discretely to support decision making needs and their interfaces are custom designed, developed, managed, and individually maintained at a significant cost to their maintainers. The EUROCONTROL by Frangolho & Zerkowitz (2006) named this approach as product-centric. It represents the traditional provision method of Aeronautical Information that needs multiple point-to-point and custom interfaces.

NextGen and SESAR rely on a new decision which brings more data, systems, customers, and service providers into the air transportation process. Data will be needed at more places, for more purposes, in a timely way, and in common formats and structures to ensure consistent use of ATM systems in the future.

Based on these information needs, and generalizing shortfalls highlighted in FAA, (2007), the following are being considered:

- Costs to develop, test, deploy, and support new interfaces and applications for ATM systems are too high. Costs of developing and maintaining custom point-to-point interfaces limits connectivity;
- Current ATM systems are not agile. They are difficult to dynamically adapt to special events, disruptions, and changing user business models;
- Data sharing in current ATM systems is labor-intensive. Agility needs rapid, widespread, and cost-effective spread of information. The infrastructure of these systems make this cost prohibitive;
- Timely access to common data is lacking in the ATM systems. A lack of shared situational awareness limits visibility into the current state of the ATM systems for their users and their customers; and
- The underlying tools to support for becoming a performance–based organization are currently lacking. The information needed to measure and oversee ATM systems performance is often not available. This limits the ability of administrators such as FAA and EUROCONTROL to meet their goals to become performance-based organizations.

Future ATM Systems as a System of Systems (SoS)

Considering needs for changes, lots of aeronautical information suppliers, and their specific systems EUROCONTROL and FAA have found a likely solution in the context of SoS. The purpose is to make the transition, on medium and longer terms, from a product-centric to a data and network-centric solution composed of existing and new systems by interacting through software services. The primary reason for developing a network-centric solution is to gain the ability to rapidly collect and share information and create information superiority. In this new scenario, as said by Arbuckle, et al. (2006), aircraft will become mobile "nodes" integrated to this information network, not only using and providing information, but also routing messages or information being sent from other aircrafts or ground sources.

Five principal characteristics, presented by Maier (2006), are useful to explain why SoS context is being considered in transforming current ATM systems to the future:

- **Operational Independence of the Elements** – SoS is disassembled into its component systems and they must be able to usefully operate independently. The SoS is composed of systems which are independent and useful in their own right;
- **Managerial Independence of the Elements** – component systems not only can operate independently, but also they do operate independently. The component systems are separately acquired and integrated but preserve a continuing operational existence independent of the SoS;
- **Evolutionary Development** – the SoS does not appear fully formed. Its development and existence is evolutionary with functions and purposes added, removed, and changed with experience;

- **Emergent Behavior** – the system performs roles and carries out purposes that do not stay in any component system. These behaviors are emergent properties of the entire SoS and cannot be localized by any component system. The main purposes of the SoS are fulfilled by these behaviors; and
- **Geographic Distribution** – the geographic extent of the component systems is large. Large is an unclear and relative concept as communication capabilities increase, but at a minimum it means that the components can readily exchange only information and not substantial quantities of mass or energy.

In the context of SoS applied to support Airport CDM functionalities, for example, information management and information sharing represent fundamental elements which need to be fully coordinated, evolutionary harmonized, and flexible.

Aeronautical Information Management – Steps toward Digital Aeronautical Information

The term Aeronautical Information Management (AIM) is presented by Frangolho & Zerkowitz (2006). It is applied to the globally interoperable provision of aeronautical data. That intends to provide the needed data quality, covering the needs of present and future ATM system for all phases of flight, in a data oriented and holistic approach. Its role is to watch and control the quality of shared data and to provide mechanisms that support the ATM community in setting up and managing information sharing in a collective effort of all suppliers of data.

The AIM strategy was defined aiming the interoperability among systems. It is based on the networking of various ATM databases, and intends to cover all phases of flight, including:

- The planning (Strategic Planning, Pre-Tactical Planning and Tactical Planning);
- The execution (Departure, En-route and Arrival); and
- The post flight activities.

According to Stricht (2008), AIM aims to make possible the so-called Global Interoperable Data Exchange based on data standardization content and meaning through data modeling, and the standardization of interfaces. Then, it is possible to provide well-defined means to access data and enable seamless interoperation, considering the following main characteristics of interoperability:

- **Temporal** – rich temporality to support timely information filtering and decision making;
- **Open** – based on documented standards to simplify community adoption;
- **Geospatial** – rich georeferencing to support location based and decision making;
- **Global** – worldwide participation and applicability; and
- **Standards** – based on leveraged standards to reduce costs.

Global Interoperability Standards are being adopted. They are presented in Table 1.

According to information from (EUROCONTROL, 2008a), the Digital AIM is a project related to AIM which has the following key aspects and expected effects:

- Key aspects:
  ○ Digital provision of quality information,
  ○ Information sharing and exchange following EC 552/2004 interoperability regulation,
  ○ Enabling ATM with location and time based information filtering in support

Table 1. Global Interoperability Standards adopted by AIM.

Standard	Purpose and Description
Global AIM Data Models	To promote the interchange of aeronautical information. Involve exchange models, such as: • Aeronautical Information Exchange Model (AIXM); • Aerodrome Mapping Exchange Model (AMXM); • Weather Exchange Model (WXXM); • Airport Operations Information Exchange Model (ANXM); and • Terrain Information Exchange Model (TIXM).
Ground-to-Air Data Link Standards	For information sharing and exchange between ground based systems and users in airborne side, such as airline and general aviation pilots. The communication is possible through data links recognized and standardized by ICAO, that is Very High Frequency Digital Link(VDL) Mode 2, VDL Mode 4 or Universal Access Transceiver (UAT).
Geomatics Standards	To provide implementing geospatial functionalities in ATM systems. Some standards considered are, for example: • The ISO 19100 geographic series of standards; • The Geography Markup Language (GML) specification; • Implementation specifications for the geospatial industry including location based services such as Web Feature Services and Web Map Services.
World Wide Web Consortium (W3C)	Provide interoperable technologies (specifications, guidelines, software, and tools) to lead the Web to its full potential (e.g. XML and XML Schemas).
The OASIS.	Who is driving the development, convergence and adoption of open standards for the global information society. Its work includes SOA and Web Services.

of future 4D trajectory management and decision making,

○ Based on SOA concepts aligned with SESAR and trends towards Network-centric Operations, and

○ Leveraging existing global and open interoperability standards into the current system based on Enterprise Architecture (EA) best practices; and

• Expected effects:

○ Information On-demand,

○ Information filtering based on location and time (4D),

○ Static and dynamic information fusion,

○ Seamless information sharing and open solutions,

○ Innovative digital services and products, and

○ Improved situational awareness and CDM.

Besides that, and also according to EURO-CONTROL (2008a), the following represents AIM Domain activities related to the implementation of AIM and specific data models intended to structure and organize data:

• **Aeronautical Lexicon** – aims the definition of terms used to describe the meaning of a data model which will serve at improving the quality of the information and the interoperability between systems;

• **Aeronautical Information exchange (AIXM)** – is focused in the development of a specification designed to enable the encoding and the distribution in digital format of the aeronautical information;

• **Airport Network Information Management (ANIM)** – represents a major component of EUROCONTROL AIM Strategy which consists on the cooperative development, with the European Aeronautical Information Systems (AIS) and airport communities, of a paperless mechanism for airport information sharing. It is responsible for the ANXM development;

- **Aerodrome Mapping Database (AMDB)** – a data standardization activity based on the EUROCAE/RTCA and ISO/OGC foundation;
- **Digital AIM (D-AIM) Projects** – a proof-of-concept for AIM intended to create new digital means for exchanging geo-temporal aeronautical information in a seamless manner to multiple networked users;
- **Digital NOTAM (xNOTAM)** – a project to provide standards, the framework, resources, and a supported proof-of-concept for the full European Civil Aviation Conference(ECAC)-wide implementation of the digital NOTAM concept;
- **Electronic AIP (eAIP)** – this project develops, preserves, and further improves Electronic Aeronautical Information Publication (eAIP) specifications designed to replace the current paper-based elements of the Integrated Aeronautical Information Package (IAIP); and
- **Terrain and Obstacle Data (TOD)** – an activity to aid States in harmonized and coordinated implementation of the ICAO Amendment 33 from Annex 15.

EUROCONTROL and LFV Group (www.lfv.se) are responsible for D-AIM Projects implementing AIM concepts in Europe. They embed open AIM standards in an operational environment intending to share findings, promote interoperable data exchange, and leverage global geospatial interoperability standards into the ATM world.

Seamless information sharing between originators, integrators, publishers, and information consumers is a key aspect of the transition to a network-centric system. By using Open AIM standards it will be possible to create customer oriented digital information services, empowering

users and systems with the right and updated information. Interoperable information exchange will trigger innovation and stimulate automation.

Initiatives like AIM development represent steps toward to digitalize Aeronautical Information and meet requirements of information sharing and system interoperability, as planned for ATM Systems in the future. The implementation of network-centric operations using SOA, in the context of D-AIM Projects, is presented in details by Li (2007). More specific information about D-AIM Projects can be found in its Web site (http://www.d-aim.aero).

A Wide ATM System for the Future

The application of concepts such as SoS, SaaS, and AIM transforms future ATM systems in a kind of "wide system". By doing so, as stated by Meserole & Moore (2006), they start having the ability to support information domains such as flight data, surveillance, weather, aeronautical information, airspace infrastructure status, and other flight domains such as surface, terminal, en-route, and oceanic or remote. In order to achieve such a competence both should controllably endure and evolve and some standards must be developed for and/or adapted to them. The implemented architecture (including data architecture) must be compliant as well as the applicable standards for information assurance (including information security). Significant benefits both from nonrecurring development and in life cycle maintenance arise from a single system-wide implementation of mandated functions and from standards such as information security and data descriptions.

The SWIM idea emerges from concepts of SoS, and SOA, for instance. SWIM represents a modern information infrastructure able to simplify information management and sharing within attendant quality and security levels to support world's airspace operations. Therefore, researches and developments in AIM are being considered within SWIM development and vice-versa.

According to FAA (2007), the operational concept for SWIM is to provide open, flexible, modular, manageable, and secure information management and sharing architecture. This concept has being applied in the USA and Europe airspace systems' operational data under the agreement and standards of ICAO. It includes, but it is not limited to aeronautical information, flight data, traffic flow management, surveillance, and weather information.

The application of the SWIM concept represents migrating system applications in the context of ATM towards a loosely coupled, open distributed processing environment focused on information sharing. By the term loosely coupled, it means that systems tend to be highly scalable, robust, and agile. Open architecture principles provide added value by reducing the number of needed interfaces, costs, and risks, and by enabling new services, and extending value to existing ones.

The aim of SWIM is to combine forces of all suppliers of ATM information so as to assemble the best possible integrated picture of the past, present and (planned) future state of the ATM situation. It is like providing the basis for improved decision making by all ATM partners. That includes military, during their strategic, pre-tactical and tactical planning processes, as well as real-time operations and post-flight activities. The system will be accessible by all partners, providing full airspace information to users and it will be updated in real time by civil and military organizations. Information about the past, present and future status of airspace including those from on routes, associated scenarios as well as sectors and area relationships will no longer be kept as separate as inconsistent pieces, but rather as different data elements of the same logical set of information which could be operated from different systems nodes, as convenient. The management of data will be responsibility coming from the appropriate level of Airspace Management, depending on their roles for information maintenance regarding the dynamism required for its use (EUROCONTROL, 2004).

At the USA, there is FAA SWIM Program, and at Europe the work is being performed under SESAR SWIM Program. The future ATM systems of these two regions do not intend to be completely identical by the application of the SWIM concept. Those countries are considering the differences between their regions (e.g. the USA is just one country and Europe is represented by a group of countries). However, as stated by Miaillier (2007), the harmonization is necessary to: ensure aircrafts can take off in one region, fly and land into another; ensure common standards are available in time; minimize costs by sharing efforts and results; and enable manufacturers to compete and supply all markets.

SWIM-Suit, shorthand for SWIM-Supported by Innovative Technologies is a research project supported by the European Commission Directorate General Transport and Energy within the 6th Framework Program. It includes 20 partners as well as a user group which provide inputs in terms of requirements and review of the SWIM related deliverables in Europe. In the USA, FAA performs similar tasks producing requirements and considering its standards and peculiarities.

According to Sodano, et al. (2008), SWIM can be considered as a multifaceted and multidisciplinary subject, consisting of the following constituents to achieve the goal of a fully integrated seamless European ATM System (EATMS):

- A physical SWIM network;
- A SWIM Infrastructure consisting of common and standardized IT technical products;
- Standardized domain-level interfaces, guaranteeing interoperability, for accessing SWIM ATM;
- Data and ATM functionality (derived from an EATMS-wide enterprise architecture model, that defines a common view on ATM business processes, the logical and the physical system architecture that perform these business processes);

- Agreed system and data standards for performance, quality, safety, security and interoperability;
- Standardized and agreed rules, roles and responsibilities; and
- A suitable governance framework.

SESAR SWIM environment as well as FAA SWIM environment intend to support the sharing and exchange of data about flight, surveillance, aeronautical, weather, capacity and demand, and ATFCM.

The SWIM concept was defined few years ago and its implementation is being performed as described in the following section.

Some SWIM Development Background and Planning

The first SWIM concept was presented by EUROCONTROL to FAA in 1997 and was adopted by ICAO in 2002. In the meantime a similar concept called Common Information Network (CIN) was developed by Boeing and Radio Technical Commission for Aeronautics (RTCA) incorporating other so-called National Airspace System (NAS) Wide Information Service (NWIS) (Sayadian & Weill, 2003). Harmonization efforts were conducted by EUROCONTROL, FAA, Boeing and others until 2005, resulting in the real SWIM concept. From 2005 until the middle of 2008 the SWIM development was planned and major requirements were named. Deployments in both schedules, from the USA and Europe, are planned, in average, for years 2013, 2016, 2020 and 2025.

SWIM has being developed iteratively and incrementally, until 2025, based upon the needs of various data communities, maturity of concepts of use, and segments that are right-sized to fit reasonable cost, schedule, and risk thresholds.

The FAA SWIM is planned to be fulfilled in segments each one lasting about four years. In this case SWIM system engineers collaborate with partners. They are called Communities of Interest (COIs). They possess the expertise to accurately describe how information is currently being used in the NAS, predict future NAS information needs, and discern how to best fulfill those needs using a network-centric solution.

Wolfowity (2004) describes COIs as a "collaborative group of users that must exchange information in pursuit of its shared goals, interests, missions or business processes and therefore must have shared vocabulary for the information it exchange".

There are three main segments planned as follow:

- Segment 1 – planned for 2009-2013;
- Segment 2 – likely to start in 2012; and
- Segment 3 – follows the Segment 2 implementation in approximately 2015.

Segment 1 will provide nine main capabilities, associated with three active COIs, whose applications can be exposed conforming to SWIM standards. This is summarized in the Table 2.

Each COI comprises a number of SWIM Implementing Programs (SIPs). In the Segment 1 there are the following SIPs:

- En Route Automation Modernization (ERAM);
- Terminal Data Distribution System (TDDS);
- Traffic Flow Management System (TFMS);
- Airspace/Aeronautical Information Management (AIM);
- Corridor Integrated Weather System (CIWS);
- Weather Message Switching Center Replacement (WMSCR); and
- Integrated Terminal Weather System (ITWS).

Table 2. FAA SWIM Segment 1 description

COI Name	Focus	Capabilities
Flight and Flow Management (F&FM)	The exchange of flight data information.	1. Flight Data Publication; 2. Terminal Data Distribution; 3. Flow Information Publication; 4. Runaway Visual Range (RVR) Publication; and 5. Re-Route Data Exchange.
Aeronautical Information Management (AIM)	The dissemination of Special Use Airspace (SUA) information.	6. Special Use Airspace (SUA) Data Exchange
Weather (Meteo)	The exchange of weather information.	7. Corridor Integrated Weather Service (CIWS) Publication 8. Integrated Terminal Weather Service (ITWS) Publication 9. Pilot Report (PIREP) Data Publication.

These SIPs will provide the hardware to host the Government Furnished Equipment (GFE) Core Capabilities software and the configuration management, life cycle support, safety, and security for the SWIM GFE Core Capabilities as part of their planned releases (FAA, 2007).

The Segment 2 intends to consider the Surveillance COI and refine and improve implementations about Segment 1. The Segment 3 and their respective needs are still very preliminary. Others segments might be defined during the SWIM evolution.

The arrangement in segments is not considered by the European community but the content and objectives in phases of SESAR SWIM development schedule consider a near scope.

The schedule for SWIM development was created considering the necessity to provide early all infrastructure comprising hardware and common software services to support ATM partners provide and consume services in the two phases of SWIM Services Lifecycle (Design-time and Run-time). These phases also define distinct environments: Design-time Environment which comprises proposal, specification, analysis, design, implementation, test and deployment of services considering Providers and Consumers; and Run-time Environment which comprises the execution in ATM operations.

The desired harmonization and full integration of several partners and their specific business and system require a common operational process under governance and regulation. Next section presents an overview of these concepts within SWIM.

SWIM Governance, Regulation and Common Support Services

As previously mentioned, SOA is one of the architectural basis for SWIM implementation. The application of SOA in the SWIM context represents that information sharing is provided mainly by software services from providers, controlled registries of services offered, and consumers, as depicted in Figure 2. SWIM Service Providers represent maintainers of any information source like databases and applications. They can expose functionalities as services, publishing information about them in the Registry using WSDL. The Registry, a kind of catalog like "Yellow Pages" if public, can be accessed by SWIM Service Consumers, any ATM partner who needs to retrieve, to perform computations and to publish

Figure 2. Providers and consumers interaction model in SWIM context.

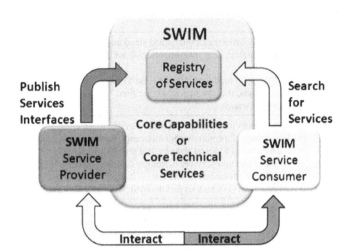

data according to its business needs. The Registry provides functionalities based on UDDI enabling searches, e.g. by service description, type, and category. Therefore, SWIM Service Consumers can obtain information (also in WSDL format) about interfaces of the services offered by Providers, making possible for them to develop software applications functionalities which interact via network, using SOAP, with software applications from them.

A key instrument for the success of SWIM is the presence of a strong governance structure (Sodano, et al. 2008). Based on information in (FAA, 2007) this governance defines, in summary, the following:

- Activities to architect, design, develop, test and implement services;
- Methods employed to perform activities, roles and responsibilities;
- Metrics to characterize success and adherence to policies; and
- The content for Interface Control Documentation (ICD) that depicts physical, functional, and test interface characteristics between the service consumer and the service provider.

According to SWIM-Suit Program (Sodano, et al. 2008) the governance structure will be federated, covering the topics presented in Table 3.

Besides governance, some regulations considering areas like safety, security and interoperability are being produced to provide the same situational awareness for all involved partners (ATC, Flow Management Centers, Ground Handlers, Airports and Aircraft Operators, ANSP, and others) and their customized needs within the common environment of SWIM.

Common support services such as network connectivity, security, Quality of Services (QoS), among others, guarantee the accomplishment of interoperability requirements.

In the SWIM context, common support services are known as Core Capabilities (by FAA point of view) and Core Technical Services (by European point of view). In the whole SWIM context, common support services are standardized. The search functionality of the Registry is one example of them.

The aim of the Core Capabilities is to isolate IT from business concerns, allowing developers to focus on applying service oriented principles to developing services without being distracted by IT issues. It also promotes re-use of exist-

Table 3. SWIM governance topics.

Topic	Subjects
Policy and Strategy	• Governance processes, policies and standards definition. • Business strategy (e.g. investments, roll-out plan, linkage of business & investment plans, and trade-offs). • SWIM System road-map definition (services prioritization – what and when). • Goals, targets, success measures definition. • Technical Strategy.
Design time governance	• Right services for SWIM users needs design. • Maintenance of a common data dictionary, service specifications and a meta-data repository. • Maintenance of a logical and physical architecture model. • Guarantee that new services definition complies with SWIM design principles and policies. • Architecture advice and assistance. • Agreement on QoS metrics and detailed Service Level Agreements (SLAs).
Implementation governance	• Ensure implementation principles are respected. • Ensure the service is tested sufficiently and given a validation certificate before entering into operation.
Runtime governance	• Versioning, Configuration Management, Deployment • Ensure the service respects its contractual SLA. • Monitoring system security and stability. • Co-ordinate 1st and 2nd levels support of the entire SWIM system. • Crisis management in event of partial system failures. • Identification of root cause of failure.

ing services and the encapsulated infrastructure (FAA, 2007).

The main types of Core Technical Services offered by SWIM are:

- **Messaging** – offers supports for multiple application transport protocols; allows location independent invocation of services; and supports message conversion between Local Services and Enterprise Services;
- **Security** – provides authentication, authorization, and access control;
- **Interface Management** – allows consumers to find published services; and
- **Enterprise Service Management** – monitors QoS, exceptions, security, and availability.

In the design-time the SWIM Service is developed by Service Developers who act normally as both Providers and Consumers, since they may use third-part services to develop their own. Each service developer must develop services ac-cording to SWIM Policy and Guidelines. When development of a SWIM Service is completed, it is deployed and monitored according to the governance and regulation in the run-time environment. The SWIM Service is first published only for the governance which performs verification and validation with standards and regulations. If approved, it is turned public to some partners, according to security configurations.

During service execution, it is monitored using SWIM provided GFE software which includes the monitoring of messages exchanged between the Service Provider and Service Consumer to capture and report any service execution anomalies (FAA, 2007).

SWIM Main Expected Benefits

By aiming information sharing the SWIM will be able to supply flexibility and agility, and to support the essential data sharing for future ATM systems (Government Electronics and Information Technology Association [GEIA], 2008).

SWIM will also provide a common network infrastructure with reduced number and types of interfaces, systems, and potentially facilities compared to current ATM systems. This will reduce infrastructure, operation and maintenance costs. Development costs of new systems also will be reduced mainly because they will interface with SWIM consuming approved services.

Information sharing and information quality improvement will be also provided by SWIM. This added with benefits from the common network infrastructure contributes to meeting future ATM system objectives such as:

- Expansion of system capacity;
- Reduction of costs for the aviation;
- Predictability improvement;
- Common or shared situational awareness; and
- CDM.

In sum, the following improvements, presented by FAA (2007) will be provided by SWIM:

- It will enable:
  - Reusable, loosely coupled interfaces versus many point-to-point interfaces,
  - Reduced time and complexity for building new applications and interfacing existing applications, and
  - Common shared services for information management replacing costly redundancies;
- It facilitates:
  - Greater independence of geographical facilities and operations,
  - Easier and quicker system failure recover,
  - Special events planning and implementation, and
  - Automation and platform convergence consistent with the so-called NAS Enterprise Architecture;

- It provides the conduit so that shared data can be published once and be distributed electronically several times;
- It makes published data available to all authorized users; and
- It provides a mechanism so that published data can be mined according to appropriate metrics.

FUTURE RESEARCH DIRECTIONS

In the future, CDM activity will trust on implementation and benefits evaluation, continuously improving service and data quality, developing new collaborative procedures where flexibility would be the main concept, establishing corresponding service level agreements, implementing potential enablers, and increased cooperation with Flow Management Centers.

Weather is a major limiting factor today (Arbuckle, et al. 2006). For the future, it has to increase the capacity concept being able to accommodate safe and efficient travel under all weather conditions across surface, terminal area, and en route domains. The main identified CDM benefits are (EUROCONTROL, 2006; JPDO, 2007):

- **Flexible traffic management around weather constraints** – jet routes have to be described how it can be redefined in real time;
- **Weather and traffic predictions** – algorithms have to look ahead of aircraft and estimate the amount of time needed for weather avoidance; and
- **Shared situation awareness through coordination, collaboration, and fused weather and traffic information** – decision makers should be able to identify types of interfaces, roles, responsibilities, and procedures to support effective decision-making during weather impacted conditions.

Decision support tools provide controllers with surface routing and guidance information integrated with arrival and departure planning management. Such information can be transmitted by controllers to pilots via data link. Advanced Dependent Surveillance (ADS) and Electronic Flight Bag (EFB) research and development activities, like the presented by Theunissen, E. *et. al.* (2005, August), represent good examples of steps toward this direction.

It is possible to realize the software process importance in the CDM and SWIM contexts. Software service has been present in commercial computing for a longtime and has been used in many different ways. Software service already represents a reasonable part of all work done so far.

SaaS is a good candidate to help information sharing and exchange. SOA takes place to do the design, implementation and the deployment of software as a service. It is considered a method for both systems development and integration. It also describes IT infrastructure which allows different applications to exchange data with one another, as they take part in business.

SOA is becoming the mainstream for enterprise applications. From now on, by recognizing the SOA benefits, the USA and European ATM communities have selected it as the an architectural basis for the idea of SWIM which intends to be the main responsible for information sharing and integration powers on future ATM systems by turning them into a big one comprised of small systems.

Then, research efforts towards this direction should be considered and are also welcomed. Indeed, information sharing and exchange need a new way of thinking.

ATM systems transformation into SWIM-enabled applications represents a big challenge. The wide number of heterogeneous systems considered in the intended integration requires many technical and research efforts in several different areas.

The harmonization and regulation considering all partners and their own businesses, applications and technologies require continuous improvements and maintenance. Then, research on development and application of standards represent important issues.

As aircrafts are being considered possible nodes of the intended big network, providing and consuming SWIM services, the development of avionics, communication systems and networks points to new challenges including embedded and real-time software, data links and protocols, among others.

EUROCONTROL and FAA spent considerable resources for SWIM definition and specification. The adoption of SWIM by other regions is possible. Those definitions and specifications represent good basis for even new investigations about the feasibility of its adoption, and advanced starting points for newer SWIM users.

CONCLUSION

Both the USA and Europe are concentrating efforts aiming to improve safety, security, capacity, efficiency, and environmental compatibility of air transportation. The USA is concentrating its efforts with the Federal Aviation Administration (FAA) through the Next Generation Air Transportation System (NextGen) program. Europe is doing the same with the European Organization for the Safety of Air Navigation (EUROCONTROL) through the Single European Sky ATM Research (SESAR) program. These programs represent the main two Air Traffic Flow and Capacity Management (ATFCM) modernization initiatives around the world looking for more efficient use of airspace to increase air safety.

Since the mid nineties, several Research and Development (R&D) projects were started on these regions. They had considered a set of issues on future Air Traffic Management (ATM) systems. Collaborative Decision Making (CDM) applications for ATM and System Wide Information Management (SWIM) concepts are just some of them.

To support this context, this chapter had introduced the four main topics of: Collaborative Decision Making (CDM), Service-Oriented Architecture (SOA), Aeronautical Information Management (AIM) and System Wide Information Management (SWIM).

CDM comprises a new philosophy to manage the air traffic. It represents a new management manner of using collaborative technologies and procedures enabling ATM partners to drive their efforts towards a common goal by sharing and exchange information.

In order to support the CDM concept implementation, SOA was found as a likely solution supporting System of Systems (SoS), system integration, and interoperability. Its principles and technologies were recognized as one of the best alternatives to propitiate the CDM concept implementation.

SOA can be considered a method for both systems development and integration. On it, functionalities are grouped around business processes and packaged as interoperable services. It describes Information Technology (IT) infrastructure which allows different applications to exchange data with one another as they engage in business. The aim behind that is a loose coupling of services with operating systems, programming languages, and other technologies which underlie applications. SOA is needed by Software as a Service (SaaS) to become effective. Behind SOA is the concept of SaaS, from where the main ideas of software functionality disclosures came, including information retrieval, computation, and storage.

Nowadays, SaaS is emerging. It is a model of software use. On it, an application is hosted as a service provided to clients across networks such as Internet, Intranet, Local Area Network (LAN), or Virtual Private Network (VPN), so clients may rent an application from a central provider. This idea offers a framework for better-integrated systems that meets business needs.

Over SOA it is being developed the so called SWIM. It will be accessible by all ATM partners to provide full airspace information to them, updated in real time by both civil and military entities.

Since Airport CDM Information Sharing has been implemented based on SWIM, significant further improvements can be achieved, for example, by carrying out the Airport CDM Turn-Round Process with a specific focus on the aircraft turn-round procedures. This is achieved by improving the decision making process. It shares up-to-date relevant information and considers preferences, available resources, and needs of those involved at the airport, tracking the progress of a flight from the first planning up to take off, and so on.

The authors of this chapter believe that with the effective employment of technologies and ideas like AIM, SWIM, SaaS, and SOA, the CDM environment will work as necessary. In fact, information needs a new way of thinking to be shared for more effective future cooperative ATM systems. SWIM and SOA are both key elements belonging to the ATM domain. But its successful implementation depends on intensifying collaborative and coordinated efforts, rather than individual ones.

ACKNOWLEDGMENT

The authors would like to thank Brazilian Federal Agency for Support and Evaluation of Graduate Education (CAPES), the German Academic Exchange Service (DAAD), together with the Brazilian Aeronautics Institute of Technology (ITA) and the Technical University of Berlin (TU-Berlin) for their important support provided to the accomplishment of research activities which were fundamental for the development and conclusion of this chapter.

REFERENCES

Arbuckle, D., et al. (2006). U.S. Vision for 2025 Air Transportation. *ATCA Journal of Air Traffic Control, January-March 2006 quarterly issue.* Retrieved July 12, 2008, from http://www.jpdo. gov/library/vision_2025_air_trans.pdf

Ball, M. O., Chen, C., & Hoffman, R. (2001). New Concepts and Methods in Air Traffic Management. In Lucio Bianco (Ed.), *Collaborative Decision Making in Air Traffic Management: Current and Future Research Directions* (pp. 17-30). Berlin: Transportation Analysis.

Balzer, Y. (2004). *Improve your SOA project plans: Strong governance principles ensure a successful outcome.* Retrieved September 22, 2008, from http://www.ibm.com/developerworks/library/ws-improvesoa.

Bell, M. (2008). *Service-Oriented Modeling: Service Analysis, Design, and Architecture.* Hoboken, NJ: Wiley.

C-ATM Consortium. (2005). *Cooperative Air Traffic Management - Phase 1: C-ATM High-Level Operational Concept: Deployable from 2012* (Tech. Rep). Retrieved July 13, 2008, from http://www.eurocontrol.fr/Newsletter/2005/March/SVC/CATM_HLOC.doc

Durvasula, S., Guttmann, M., Kumar, A., Lamb, J., Mitchell, T., Oral, B., et al. (2006). *SOA Practitioners' Guide Part 2: SOA Reference Architecture* (Tech. Rep.). Retrieved July, 14 from http://www.soablueprint.com/practitioners_guide.

Erl, T. (2005). *Service-oriented Architecture: Concepts, Technology, and Design.* Upper Saddle River, NJ: Prentice Hall PTR.

European Organization for the Safety of Air Navigation. (2004). *EUROCONTROL Operational Concept Document (OCD) Volume 1 (The Vision)* (Tech. Rep. FCO.ET1.ST07.DEL01). Retrieved July 12, 2008, from http://www.eurocontrol.int/oca/gallery/content/public/docs/op_concept/OCD_2_1_Released.pdf

European Organization for the Safety of Air Navigation. (2006). *Airport CDM Operational Concept Document, 3th ed.* (Tech. Rep. 05/04/05-1). Retrieved June 23, 2008, from http://www.euro-cdm.org/library/cdm_ocd.pdf

European Organization for the Safety of Air Navigation. (2008a). *Digital AIM.* Retrieved September 10, 2008, from http://www.eurocontrol.int/aim/public/standard_page/interoperability.html

European Organization for the Safety of Air Navigation. (2008b). *Airport CDM Implementation: The Manual* (rev. 3). Retrieved January 13, 2009, from http://www.euro-cdm.org/library/cdm_implementation_manual.pdf

Frangolho, A. P., & Zerkowitz, E. (2006). *Aeronautical Information Management Strategy* (Tech. Rep. 4th ed.). Retrieved September 10, 2008 from http://www.eurocontrol.int/aim/gallery/content/public/pdf/aim_strategy_vol1_ed4.pdf

Government Electronics and Information Technology Association. (2008). *FAA SWIM Program: SOA Best Practices – Industry Input* (Doc. Version 7). Retrieved September 9, 2008 from U.S. FAA website http://www.faa.gov/about/office_org/headquarters_offices/ato/service_units/techops/atc_comms_services/swim/documentation/media/best_practices/ATC FAA SWIM Program SOA Best Practices.pdf

International Civil Aviation Organization. (2005). *Global Air Traffic Management Operational Concept.* (Doc 9854-AN/458, 1st Ed.). Montreal, Canada: ICAO.

Joint Planning & Development Office. (2007). *Concept of Operations for the Next Generation Air Transportation System* (Tech. Rep.). Retrieved September 10, 2008 from http://www.jpdo.gov/library.asp

Kazda, A., & Caves, R. E. (2007). *Airport Design and Operation* (2nd. ed., pp. 188-190). Oxford, UK: Elsevier.

Krafzig, D., Banke, K., & Slama, D. (2004). *Enterprise SOA: Service-Oriented Architecture Best Practices.* Upper Saddle River, NJ: Prentice Hall PTR.

Ky, P., & Miaillier, B. (2006). SESAR: Towards the New Generation of Air Traffic Management Systems in Europe. *ATCA Journal of Air Traffic Control.*

Li, R. (2007). *D-AIM Deliverable 2: D-AIM Architecture Description,* (Tech. Rep. D-LFV 2006-37208). Retrieved December 20, 2008, from http://www.d-aim.aero//output/D-AIM Deliverable 2_D-AIM Architecture Description.pdf

Maier, M. W. (2006). *Architecting Principles for Systems-of-Systems.* Retrieved September 06, 2008, from http://www.infoed.com/Open/PAPERS/systems.htm

Meserole, J. S., & Moore, J. W. (2006). What is System Wide Information Management (SWIM)? In *25th Digital Avionics Systems Conference.* Retrieved September 08, 2008, from http://ieeexplore.ieee.org/iel5/4106227/4106228/04106233.pdf

Miaillier, B. (2007). *The SESAR Vision* [PowerPoint slides]. Retrieved September 07, 2008, from 26th DASC – Digital Avionics Systems Conference, Plenary Session Presentation http://www.dasconline.org/26dasc/plenary/bm.pps

Newcomer, E., & Lomow, G. (2005). *Understanding SOA with Web Services.* Upper Saddle River, NJ: Addison Wesley Professional.

Sayadian, L., & Weill, E. (2003). *System-Wide Information Management (SWIM) Concept in the ATN Architecture* (Tech. Rep. WGN02-WP05). Retrieved September 22, 2008 from ICAO http://www.icao.int/anb/panels/acp/wg/n/wgn2/wgn02-wp05.doc

Sodano, M., et al. (2008). *SWIM-SUIT: System Wide Information Management Supported by Innovative Solutions - Overall SWIM Users Requirements version 01* (Tech. Rep. D1.5.1). Retrieved August 13, 2008 from http://www.swim-suit.aero/swimsuit/projdoc.php

Spies, G., et al. (2008). *Operational Concept for an AirPort Operations Center to enable Total Airport Management.* Paper presented at ICAS 2008 - 26th Congress of International Council of the Aeronautical Sciences, Anchorage, Alaska, USA.

Stricht, S. V. (2008). *Digital Aeronautical Information Management (D-AIM).* Retrieved October 10, 2008, from EUROCONTROL, http://www.eurocontrol.int/aim/public/standard_page/daim_principles.html

Sun, W., Zhang, K., Chen, S., Zhang, X., & Liang, H. (2007). Service-Oriented Computing – ICSOC 2007. In *Software as a Service: An Integration Perspective* (pp. 558-569). Berlin: Springer.

Theunissen, E., Koeners, G. J. M., Roefs, F. D., Rademaker, R. M., & Bleeker, O. F. (2005, August). *Evaluation of an EFB Airport Map with Integrated Routing in a Distributed Simulation Environment.* Paper presented at the AIAA Modeling and Simulation Technologies Conference and Exhibit, San Francisco, CA.

U.S. Federal Aviation Administration. (2007). *System Wide Information Management (SWIM) - Final Program Requirements - Segment 1* (Tech. Rep. rev. ed. 7.3). Retrieved September 5, 2008 from http://www.faa.gov/about/office_org/headquarters_offices/ato/service_units/techops/atc_comms_services/swim/documentation/media/requirements/20070523_swim_fpr.pdf

Wambsganss, M. C. (2001). New Concepts and Methods in Air Traffic Management. In L. Bianco (Ed.), *Collaborative Decision Making in Air Traffic Management* (pp. 1-16). Berlin: Transportation Analysis.

Wolfowitz, P. (2004). *Guidance for Implementing Net-Centric Data Sharing* (DoD Directive 8320.2-G). Retrieved August 15, 2008, from http://www.dtic.mil/whs/directives/corres/pdf/832002p.pdf

Chapter 14
Component–Based Development of Aeronautical Software

Ítalo Romani de Oliveira
Atech Tecnologias Críticas, Brazil

Ricardo Alexandre Veiga Gimenes
Safety Analysis Group (GAS), University of São Paulo (Poli-USP), Brazil

Jorge Rady de Almeida Jr.
Safety Analysis Group (GAS), University of São Paulo (Poli-USP), Brazil

ABSTRACT

Modern aircraft heavily relies on software to fly and operate, which lessens pilot workload, increases flight stability and fuel efficiency, and provides several other benefits. However, the more automated an aircraft is, the more prone to complexity its software modules are, raising special safety issues to be considered in the project. This chapter presents an overview of the Verification and Validation requirements for safety-critical software in aeronautics and, given the high costs to meet them, explains in detail a component-based methodology which can contribute to reduce the overall costs of software development and, at the same time, provide enhanced safety.

INTRODUCTION

Modern Air Transportation demands a great amount of software, with a wide variety of purposes, from airline ticket reservation to aircraft engine control. Higher levels of system integration on transport aircraft systems and equipment have created new safety and certification challenges, making the aviation industry and the regulatory authorities elaborate technical guidance, gathering their mutual objectives and responsibilities in the system safety area. A great part of the software systems in aviation is considered safety-critical, as is the case of many aircraft control systems, in which failures can lead to catastrophic events, as happened to the Airbus A320 in Habsheim, France, 1988, just to mention a classical example. This accident was attributed to a software design error related to the complexity introduced by the once innovative computerized flight control. The failure showed the crew that the

DOI: 10.4018/978-1-60566-800-0.ch014

plane was flying at 100 ft above ground. When the captain increased throttle to level off at 100 ft, the engines and the completely computerized throttle control did not respond. The gear was only 30 ft above ground when the aircraft was passing over the runway (Walters, 2000), and a few seconds later the aircraft crashed into the bush. Due to the high social impact related to flight safety, there is a paramount need of requiring strict verification processes and tests on critical aeronautical software, defined and supervised by governmental authorities.

Software Verification and Validation (V&V)

The way to improve the verification and validation of software is still a theme of several scientific studies. However, there are recommendations and methodologies in which many researches converge, helping to improve the software reliability .

The objectives of the software verification activities are to demonstrate the following properties (Howden, 1986; Powell, 1986):

a. Correctness: the extent to which the product is fault free;
b. Consistency: the extent to which the product is consistent within itself and with other products;
c. Necessity: the extent to which everything in the product is necessary;
d. Sufficiency: the extent to which the product is complete;
e. Performance: the extent to which the product satisfies its performance requirements.

Verification activities come together with validation activities, which aim at ensuring that the project deliverables are in accordance with the expectations of the project stakeholders. Since verification and validation activities complement each other and are often overlapped, in software engineering they are treated in the same bucket called V&V.

Types of Software Verification

Software verification can be performed by testing and by formal techniques. Testing consists in defining a set of conditions for the software inputs, and requiring the outputs to provide the expected results in each case. It cannot demonstrate absolute absence of errors, except for the cases tested. Frequently, however, the algorithmic complexity and the dependency on hardware events turn exhaustive testing very hard, and formal techniques must be applied. These formal techniques consist in automatically exploring all the software execution paths, in which case it is called model-checking, or using rules of propositional calculus to automatically prove that some required property is valid, given the system axioms, in which case the technique is called theorem proving.

The possibility of performing automatic verification sounds very interesting; however, in practice, model-checking techniques suffer from combinatorial explosion, and automatic theorem proving requires extremely disciplined and time-consuming logical creativity; besides, both formal techniques are incompatible with the continuum hypothesis (i.e., to work with continuous number intervals in the real domain), which is an essential support for elaborating closed-loop control systems. Nevertheless, the perception in the Computer Science community is that automatic formal verification can be very helpful if carefully used. The use of formal verification techniques can help to increase the verification effectiveness and, sometimes, dispense testing.

Verification and Validation of Aeronautical Software

Critical software for civil aviation can be categorized in two major groups: Avionics and Air Traffic Management (ATM). The former one is embedded in the aircraft, more precisely in every computer module related to the aircraft flight mission; the latter involves every piece of software outside the aircraft and dedicated to ATM functions, such as air traffic control consoles, telecommunication, navigation, surveillance, tactical and real-time decision support tools. This chapter focuses on avionics software, more specifically for civil aircraft.

A civil aircraft is authorized to operate only when it receives a certificate from the aeronautical authority, such as the FAA for the United States of America, EASA for Europe, ANAC for Brazil, etc. In order to receive such a certificate, there must be evidence that its project has been developed and tested in accordance with specific regulations. As the aircraft design is normally developed to operate globally, the different local aviation authorities make agreements on the applicable regulations, and because of that, it can be said that the locally required certification processes are highly similar or acknowledge the one established by the Federal Aviation Administration (FAA) from the US, that serves as the main reference for the certification process in this document.

According to this process, the certificate to operate an aircraft, denominated *Type Certificate* or TC, is granted for the aircraft as a whole, and not for its individual parts. On the other hand, the FAA establishes a list of standardized equipment, for which the certification process may be reused for an arbitrary number of times to obtain a TC. These items are proven to meet a specific set of performance requirements, determined in the *Technical Standard Orders* (TSO) (FAA, 2008), avoiding that most of their V&V effort be re-made. However, the TSO concept is not applicable to isolated software components and, according to this logic, any software item which is not contained in a TSO equipment must be completely re-assessed, *ab initio*, for each new aircraft model to be released. Such was the situation until December 2004, when the FAA released advisory circular AC 20-148 (FAA, 2004), regulating reusable software components.

In addition, in the last years, civil and military researches have often promised widespread use of Unmanned Aerial Vehicles (UAVs) in the global market. UAVs are aircraft in which the functionalities are high dependent on software systems. Regulations, which guide the safe software design for the UAV system operation, still have to be defined so as to ensure their safety objective is met (Clothier & Walker, 2006).

Main Goals of This Research

Software for civil aircraft has to succeed in a very demanding Verification and Validation (V&V) process, which often causes a 100% increase in the cost of avionics products.

As the added cost of V&V for avionic software is significant, there is great interest in minimizing it, and one of the most promising approaches is to reuse the certification effort spent on previous projects, by means of reusable components. However, reuse is not a trivial task, as will be shown in the next sections. The technical contribution of this research work is to show an analysis of a real case study, with both quantitative and qualitative criteria, of how the reuse of component verification evidence can improve the verification of composite software modules.

Therefore, the purpose of this chapter is to present a component-basedmethodology which can help to decrease the software V&V costs, while increasing the product reliability and safety. The Component-based methodology presented in this chapter is based on using automated tools which are described in detail in section 3.

The paper is organized as follows: after this Introduction, Section 2 provides a background on reuse of software components, with an intuitive notion of component, stressing the specificities of avionics software; Section 3 develops an unambiguous definition of software component and commercial tools available for a Compositional approach; Section 4 presents an analysis of our case study for reuse of verification evidence using two of the commercial tools presented in section 3, and Section 5 provides the final remarks.

REUSE OF SOFTWARE COMPONENTS

Following Adolph (1999), *"if you ask five programmers what reuse is, you get eight answers"*. In his article, Adolph tries to reinforce the idea that, in order to make a proper software reuse, it is necessary for the software to have been designed to be reused from the very beginning, stating that *"reuse is different from salvage"*. According to Sodhi & Sodhi (1999), software reuse is the process of implementing and updating software systems using existing software artifacts. Such artifacts may be defined as components, objects, requirement analysis models, domain architecture, database schemas, code, documentation, manuals, standards, test scenarios and plans.

Independently of the precise definition of the term *software reuse*, the basic goal behind this concept is to use software artifacts developed in previous projects to their maximum extent, so as to reduce costs and risks associated to the development of software from scratch.

Some Risks Associated with Software Reuse

It has been empirically observed that software reuse is not always a safe option. The explosion of the Ariane V rocket in 1996 is a classical example of a catastrophic event resulting from improper software reuse. Most of that software had been inherited from Ariane IV, and worked perfectly in that rocket. However, there were differences between the two rockets that had not been adequately considered, eventually leading to the accident. Mao & Lu (2005) argue that just catching the fatal exception could have saved the

mission. Some other examples of serious accidents caused by improper software reuse can be found in (Leveson, 1995), one of which referring to an avionics software that, developed for aircraft in the northern hemisphere and operating above sea level, caused problems for aircraft in the southern hemisphere, or operating in airports below sea level. Besides these classical examples, any experienced programmer can recall situations in which erroneous use of software artifacts was made, and happy are the ones who timely detected and corrected the problem.

Another risk related to software reuse is associated to the system maintenance and update. In case the documentation of the reused software is deficient, it is hard for new developers to perform alterations and to fix the software problem, and even for the very person who made the first development; generally speaking, if the reused software is not adequately structured for maintenance, alterations which seem to be very localized and simple may introduce very spread and complex problems throughout the software and, most likely, will cause failures during the system operation.

The use of automatic tools is an effective way to verify the complexity of a software and, consequently, to validate it. Through these tools, it is possible and important to control to the quality of the software while it is being developed, as it is possible to discover problems at the development time, which is highly recommendable for critical application software.

In order to mitigate the risks related to software reuse, Rierson (2000) proposes some approaches, such as Reuse Planning, Domain Engineering, Object Orientation, Portability, Commercial-Off-The-Shelf (COTS) items, Service History and Software Components. The Verification and Validation of Software Components is the main topic of this paper.

The Commercial-off-the-Shelf Software Components (COTS)

The use of Commercial-Off-The-Shelf Software Components, no matter how they were made or in what language, is more and more an irreplaceable asset. In order to do this, all these software blocks must be efficiently and carefully managed, in order to avoid execution loss and corruption problems, due either to latent failures, natural disasters or even manmade activities such as terrorist strikes, in which software security weaknesses may be exploited. This is extremely important in aeronautics, where the applications are safety-related. The design of such blocks should consider all of the more recent techniques in order to avoid inconsistent states. These states can present erroneous data, disturbing inputs acquisition and interpretation. Their inputs and outputs must be very accurate, thoroughly updated and their availability must be as high as possible. Such a requirement is more and more present in the civil aviation industry.

When designing software which includes off-the-shelf components, one must make sure that such elements meet the system reliability requirements. Meanwhile, required safety for a given system is in direct proportion to society's demands and expectations about it.

COTS Software is acquired with no regard to its source code. For large system software using complex transactional processes, the use of COTS software is mandatory, since it is unpractical to develop an entire required infrastructure from scratch. Some strategies are here presented to enhance system safety and reliability of software components without inspecting their source code. Another result arising from this research is that one may safely develop COTS software-based solutions for critical applications, as long as a few extra cautionary measures are taken, such as the use of proper Verification and Validation techniques for every software module. Inspections of these modules contribute to further clarify requirements and rationales for projects using COTS software elements, such as implementing a system reliability enhancing features.

Software Criticality Levels

It is important to observe that each software module or component may have a distinct criticality level. For instance, a failure in an autopilot is supposed to be more critical than a failure in the airline message exchanging system (ACARS) and thus the rigor levels for V&V in these modules must be different.

The DO-178B (RTCA, 1992) standard establishes five distinct criticality levels, officially named *assurance levels*, based on the module contribution for potential failure conditions, to be determined in an initial safety assessment of the project. The assurance level will require a certain amount of effort to demonstrate compliance with the certification requirements. Such assurance levels are:

Level A: software the anomalous behavior of which, as demonstrated in the system safety assessment process, would cause or contribute to a catastrophic failure for the aircraft;
Level B: software the anomalous behavior of which would cause or contribute to a failure of major severity for the aircraft;
Level C: software the anomalous behavior of which would cause or contribute to a severe failure for the aircraft;
Level D: software the anomalous behavior of which would cause or contribute to a failure of minor severity for the aircraft;
Level E: software the anomalous behavior of which does not influence the aircraft operational capability or the pilot workload; in this case, the DO-178B process is not required.

There is some guidance for determining the assurance level in the DO-178B itself, but they are far from exhaustive and, because of that, another guidance document is used, named "Guidelines and Methods for Conducting the Safety Assessment Process on Civil Airborne Systems and Equipment" (SAE, 1996b). Additionally, the document SAE ARP 4754, "Certification Considerations for Highly-Integrated or Complex Systems" (SAE, 1996a), presents the systems engineering process and the interfaces with the certification process. The guidance explains the requirements allocation and capture process with emphasis on requirements validation and verification. The safety assessment process is also described at a high level and references ARP 4761 for detailed descriptions of the various safety assessment tools (Portwood, 1998). The document recommends that a Preliminary System Safety Assessment (PSSA) be made, based on a Functional Hazard Assessment (FHA) that, in turn, must account for the elaboration of a fault tree for the hazards identified.

The Development Environment of the Software Component

Since the increase in complexity raises the difficulty in testing and understanding software, complexity is directly related to reliability. From this perspective, the complexity allows qualitatively measuring the effort necessary to reach a definite level of reliability. Given a fixed effort level, as a typical example in projects, the complexity offers a measure of the reliability itself. The list of challenges to produce a reliable software involves a very large range of considerations such as:

- Different systems and software engineering organizations have different needs. They may produce a large range of deliverables, such as software or an integrated hardware-software environment.

- Different systems and software engineering using a same software component have different goals and needs.

- Aerospace systems usually demand some distinctive best practices. These include independent testing teams, extensive system modeling period of time and expensive really destructible tests. These practices are driven by a combination of engineering, risk-management, and contractual considerations.

In a set of factors, a safety-critical software has to consider safety concerns not just over the source code but also over the language used to develop it. The language relies on its compiler which has to assemble an object code able to be run over a specific hardware platform. Considering the Operating System, there are two moments when it can be critical: the environment in which the compiler will be hosted and the environment in which the safety-critical software will be hosted (the run-time environment). It is very common for these two Operating Systems to be different.

Safety-critical software can be understood as software a failure of which can result in losses of human lives or physical damages. Therefore, tests of verification and validation of safety-critical software require special attention for its development team. Some of them are presented below to allow a complete vision of the development of this sort of software.

Static Analysis searches for problems such as buffer overflow through the code verification, informing the programmer about possible invalid states, even if, in normal conditions, the code is correct.

Safe languages are those possessing rules that foresee possible compiling inconsistencies. These languages seek to be similar to the existing commercial languages, despite having limitations such as memory access restrictions. A disadvantage of these languages is their high programming cost, frequently requiring to convert an original source code into this safe language through another software, or even manually. Compilers which introduce programming limitations provide good safety solutions for buffer overflow, where all vector indexes are verified to guarantee that the software will not read from or write to an improper place.

Hardware and Operating System design tries to construct barriers in order to make them resistant to imperfections and vulnerabilities. Safe Operating Systems divide the memory into at least two areas: code segment and data segment. The code segment is marked as read-only. This prevents a program from being able to modify the code which is loaded in these segments, unless this program has an explicit writing permission. Permissions like this must be denied in safety-critical systems. In the same way, to define the stack as an area of not executable memory prevents overflow problems and blocks invalid execution of codes on it.

The computing community has been studying standards for safety-critical software for at least a quarter of a century, and uncertainty is always present in the development of software-intensive systems. Naturally, all techniques to improve software safety and reliability have to be considered, and the Component-Based Verification proposed in this chapter is one of them. For a thorough vision of software component reuse, the reader may study Almeida et al. (2007). In this chapter, though, the focus is on critical applications and formal methods. In order to properly present this verification approach, we need to use an unambiguous definition for software component.

SOFTWARE COMPONENT DEFINITION

Firstly, the definitions of component from two important normative references on avionics software are taken:

From ARP 4754 (SAE, 1996a): *"Any self-contained part, combination of parts, subassem-*

blies or units, which perform a distinct function necessary to the operation of the system."

From DO-178B (RTCA, 1992): *"A self-contained part, combination of parts, subassemblies or units, which performs a distinct function of a system."*

Note that ARP 4754 and DO-178B definitions are applicable to system components, while this chapter specifically approaches software components, which are a subclass of the general component concept.

Apparently, the notion of "performing a distinct function" of ARP 4754 and DO-178B, to a great extent, expresses the idea of segregating functionality. This does not necessarily mean that a component is associated to only one function, or that a function must be in only one component. The expected characteristic is the *functional cohesion*, which is present when a component has a number of distinct functions, but all of them with a common purpose. Additionally, the term "part", found in both definitions above, makes explicit that the component is not justifiable alone, but rather as part of a greater entity.

This said, the following definition of *reusable software component* is proposed:

A **reusable software component** *is a software component with an interaction contract, the compliance with which guarantees proper behavior throughout reuse.*

In this definition, the term "interaction" was preferred to "interface", because the interaction between the component and its environment may occur through several distinct interfaces. The idea of the interaction contract is that, for each desirable component behavioral property, there are some constraints for the way in which the environment interacts with the component. These constraints may be defined as input and output data constraints and operation sequences expressed by means of temporal logic propositions.

The component attributes and interaction contract are explored in the next sections.

Software Component Representation

Following the basic component definition, it is necessary to to allow proper reuse of the component lifecycle artifacts. A lifecycle artifact of a software component is any artifact related with its definition, design, operation and maintenance, as for example, requirements, UML diagrams, code, manuals, test cases and results, installation instructions, error logs, etc. For certification purposes, it is very important to reuse artifacts with evidences found in the V&V process and the component representation should therefore facilitate that. This representation should be applicable both for forward and reverse component design, i.e., both for creating new components and for extracting component design from existing pieces of software.

Notion of interaction between a software component and its environment: A component can be understood as a software part with passive and active behavior and, in this sense, it provides a set of operations to the environment and requires another set of operations from it. A provided operation is implemented within a particular component and executed when some entity of the environment invokes it; a required operation is defined elsewhere in the environment (e.g. in another component) and executed when a particular component invokes it.

The idea of *operation* is considered here to be more essential to the concept of software component than the ideas of *port* and *interface*, given that a port is an instrument for assigning an operation or set of operations to a communication means, and an interface serves as a bundle of operations.

The component interaction may include hardware devices, and in this case they could be seen as a special type of component. The particularities that should be taken into account when representing hardware components in the environment remain to be studied.

For the sake of simplicity, from this point on, the term *component* must be understood as *software component*. The specification of the elements of interaction between the component and the environment is given in the *component signature*.

Component Signature

A component signature has:

- A component identifier;
- A set of provided operations;
- A set of required operations.

Each operation of a component is specified by an operation identifier and a set of typed data input and/or output operations. Each data input or output operation may be associated, as part of the component interaction contract, to data constraints.

Operation activation can be implemented by procedure call, by interruption, by messaging or by other means of inter-process communication, and this is defined in the implementation architecture. What is most important to know, when designing components, is which component encapsulates the implementation of an operation (*provides* the operation), and which components activate this operation (*requires* the operation). If a component activates some of its own operations within the same instance, this is considered internal behavior and must not appear to the environment.

Interaction rules between a software component and its environment are specified in the *component interaction contract*.

Component Interaction Contract

A component interaction contract includes:

- *A set of component vectors*: the rationale behind requiring this is to guarantee behavioral consistency and completeness throughout composition (Moschoyannis & Shields, 2004; Moschoyannis et al., 2005);

- *A set of data constraints per operation*: necessary when operations require or provide data values within certain data interval or combination of intervals;
- *Environment behavior clauses*: Environment behavior clauses are a set of assertions in some kind of temporal logics (to be defined), which specify, for each desired property in the component behavior, the environment behavior constraints that must hold in order to guarantee that component property. This is crucial for the re-use of verification evidence.

The notion of component interaction contract used here excludes the invariant as defined by Bertrand Meyer for the Eiffel language, because these invariants are related with the internal states of a component, and the aim here is to encapsulate the internal component behavior.

Every communication of the component with the external environment, including reading and writing to global/shared variables, is considered here to have to be explicitly defined as an operation, otherwise this would be against the idea of "encapsulation" or "self-containment". A global variable could ultimately be considered as a component with trivial and mutually-exclusive read and write operations.

Even though components are entities that interact in some environment, the notion of component is different of the notion of *agent*, because the latter is an autonomous entity, the existence of which in an environment is self-justified, whereas components have their existence justified only when interconnected with other components.

Tools Available for the Compositional Approach

Some frameworks for component modelling, which are integrated with some sort of automatic verification and requirements traceability method, are currently available for embedded systems, and some of them, combining some degree of compositional capability with a certain maturity level, have been assessed in this research work, and are briefly described in the next subsections.

AADL

AADL (Architecture Analysis Description Language) is a well-established framework in the avionics community, with powerful modelling capabilities and having many successful cases of application (Hudak & Feiler, 2007), with the natural advantage of having emerged within the avionics design community.

AADL allows analyzing system architectures, giving better guarantees that requirements, including real-time, will be met at an early stage, avoiding the high cost of late fixes. However, in practice, the main available tool for AADL, namely MetaH, considerably constrains the language power, and forces some implementation schemes incompatible with several architectures employed in the industry.

Nonetheless, recently an open source environment for AADL has arisen from a SEI initiative, called OSATE (Open Source AADL Tool Environment) (OSATE, 2008). It provides syntax and semantics checking for textual AADL and text file project organisation, as an Eclipse plugin. Another integrated plugin is Topcased, which allows graphical object modelling and translation to AADL textual representation. There are also integrated plugins for architecture consistency checks, but fault and reliability analysis has no ready tool support for the time being, and this must be made by means of tools that translate OSATE files into MetaH. It can thus be said that AADL supported by OSATE is promising, but it may take some time for all the necessary tools to become available and reliable.

CoConES

CoConES stands for Components and Contracts for Embedded Software, presented in (Berbers et al., 2005), and provides a tool for component modelling, starting at graphical representation of static model, allowing diagramming sequences of events to define component behaviours, and also component composition. This tool is called CCOM (Component and Contract-Oriented Modelling), which makes the verification of behaviour consistency in component composition over contracts that have to be established for the components. Another tool, called DRACO (Distrinet Reliable and Adaptive Components), is provided in this framework for running the components at runtime, on Java Virtual Machines.

Although CoConES provides tools for a good level of automation in component modelling and verification, there are some obstacles to its utilisation. The first is that CCOM code generation works only to generate Java code, the second is that CCOM contracts do not specify functional requirements and data requirements.

Koala

Koala (van Ommering, 1998) is a component model aimed at consumer electronic products with several of the usual component concepts, such as ports, interfaces and events. Besides that, it allows defining diversity interfaces which manage different component behaviours depending on the context in which it is working. This is thought in the sense of using the same component in several different products in a product family, and configuration means, including dynamic binding.

The applicability problems of Koala arise mainly from the fact that the automatic verification is conducted only at the architectural level, not treating functional component properties. Other issues are that its textual specification language and graphical representation tend to be very specific. The tools available generate C code only.

OMEGA

Omega was a FP5 European project which aimed at defining a development framework in UML for embedded and real-time systems based on formal techniques (Omega, 2008). It defined a UML subset appropriate for real-time embedded systems, and established links to requirements analysis and to methods and tools for formal specification and verification, with several tools specifically developed for Omega. Some of these tools help in refining and using the UML models into formal verification, with the help of some previous techniques such as PVS (Proof Verification System) and LSC (Live Sequence Charts).

An interesting feature of the Omega framework is that it allows the UML modelling to be performed in commercial front-ends such as Rhapsody or Rational Rose, and translates the UML representation to an intermediate representation that can be used by the various Omega tools. The applicability of Omega has been demonstrated by some case studies described in (Omega, 2008). Despite Omega having foundations for formal component approaches, no special attention in it was given to verification reuse.

MOCHA

MOCHA (Model-Checking for ATL (Alur et al., 2001)) is based on the theory of reactive modules and allows models to be checked against properties expressed in *Alternating Temporal Logic* (ATL). It comprises representation of both synchronous and asynchronous behaviour. The most interesting characteristic of MOCHA is the importance given to exploit the hierarchical model structure in order to leverage the formal verification. The hierarchy is exploited by the tool in three ways. First, verification tasks such as refinement checking can be decomposed into sub-goals using assume-guarantee rules. Second, instead of traditional temporal logics such as CTL, it uses ATL, a game-based temporal logic designed to specify collaborative as well as adversarial interactions between different components (Alur et al., 1997). Third, the MOCHA algorithms incorporate optimizations based on the hierarchical reduction of sequences of internal transitions (Alur & Wang, 1999).

For the time being, a detailed evaluation of MOCHA usability in MOSAIC has not been performed. However, a preliminary assessment, based on the sources cited in this section, allows us to say that MOCHA has some useful graphical tools that make it more user-friendly, but it still requires learning its particular textual language to build and verify models. Moreover, the model-checker is not completely integrated with the graphical tool, which makes the formal analysis more difficult. It is somewhat strange that a project with great ambitions such as MOCHA, supported by powerful theoretical framework, having started in 1997-1998 and achieved a considerable toolset in 2000 and, after all this, one hardly finds references about its application cases. Pasareanu & Giannakopolou (2006) suggest that the discontinuation of MOCHA is due to the need of high developed skill to generate useful environmental assumptions to form the basis of the verification process.

Rhapsody

Rhapsody is a suite of professional tools commercially provided by Telelogic (now part of IBM). It comprises UML 2.1 and SysML modelling, requirements analysis, code generation, test generation and on-the-fly model-checking. Besides this, it has Domain-Specific Modelling Capabilities (DSL) which enables customised modelling. Another important strength of Rhapsody is to have elements supporting DO-178B certification and DoDAF compliance. A great advantage of using Rhapsody is to consistently keep almost all the software lifecycle in one integrated tool. Because

of this, it has often been used by companies that produce embedded software subject to intensive certification.

On the other hand, Rhapsody is an expensive tool and, in order to repay its investment, it has to be used all throughout the software development process, consistently to its automatic code generation functionality (which, in turn, requires more licenses to more engineers and so may become even more expensive). Sometimes the overhead of adapting a successful software development process to Rhapsody is just not worth it.

SCADE

SCADE (Safety-Critical Application Development Environment) is a tool suite for the development of real-time embedded software. It provides a programming language called SCADE, a simulation environment, automatic code generation, and formal verification (Dajani-Brown et al., 2004). It offers a graphical deterministic, declarative and structured data-flow programming environment based on the Lustre language. The SCADE semantics is synchronous and implements a cycle-based and reactive computational model.

The SCADE Design Verifier is a model-checker of safety properties which is the formal verification module of SCADE. It is not capable of using CTL expressions, but works with instantaneous properties and some temporal reasoning. The core algorithms are based on Stalmarck's SAT-solving algorithm for dealing with Boolean formulae, surrounded by induction schemes to deal with temporal behaviour and state space search. The Design Verifier allows for restriction of the state space while verifying a property through a notion of assertions. A SCADE assertion on an input or output variable prunes the search space only to those instances in which the assertion holds true. The potential of these assertions for component-based verification reuse remains to be assessed.

Simulink Design Verifier Toolbox

The Simulink Design Verifier Toolbox (Mathworks, 2008) is used for Simulink and Stateflow models. It is designed to enable V&V early in the development process, helping to decrease the cost of fixing model errors and inconsistencies. The tasks which can be performed with this Toolbox are:

- Automatic Test Generation: generation of unit tests and model test harnesses directly from models.
- Proving user-defined properties, using design verification blocks, and generation of violation examples.
- Simulation with entire parameter state-space exploration.
- Monte Carlo Simulation for large system state-spaces.
- Requirements tracing, by means of the Requirements Management Interface.
- Writing custom checks, using the Model Advisor.
- Model Coverage Evaluation: the Design Verifier can evaluate how much of the model has been covered by the tests and simulations executed so far.
- Formal verification, with analysis of all possible execution paths allowed by the model. It also performs code correctness verification and identifies model elements that represent dead code.

The results of these tasks are automatically documented.

These characteristics make this toolbox extremely useful for V&V of Simulink-based software. The potential for verification evidence reuse lies in exploring user-defined verification blocks associated to components throughout reuse, and, in a lesser extent, defining custom checks to improve consistency of component reuse, and reusing violation examples. However, some restrictions must be respected: low-complexity models to avoid state-space explosion, which also compromises with the simulation time step length; no use of user-defined functional blocks (S-functions); and other types of blocks already highlighted in the official documentation (Mathworks, 2008).

Spark

Spark is a language associated with a tool suite, which enables high-integrity software development with the approach 'correctness by construction'. This approach has been applied with success for years in avionics and railway signaling (Barnes, 2003), improving program correctness and decreasing development costs. Besides, it uses a safe subset of the Ada programming language, which is widely used in the high-integrity systems industry.

Instead of working with temporal logic formulae and performing full-state space model-checking, Spark uses code annotations to perform flow analysis, and to impose and verify local conditions over variables. It has been observed (Ambühl, 2007) that around 90% of the verification proofs needed for a Spark program are performed automatically by the Simplifier tool, and the remaining ones need specialist user knowledge to be proved, which can be done with the Proof Checker interactive tool. If, on the one hand, this process is not fully automated, the code annotations are reused every time the source code is reused. The lack of a graphical user interface is a disadvantage for Spark.

SPIN Model-Checker

Spin (Holzmann, 2006) is a popular open-source software tool that can be used for the formal verification of distributed software systems. The tool was developed at Bell Labs in the original UNIX group of the Computing Sciences Research Center, starting in 1980. The software has been available freely since 1991, and continues to evolve to keep pace with new developments in the field.

The tool supports a high level language to specify systems descriptions, called PROMELA (a PROcess MEta LAnguage). Spin has been used to trace logical design errors in distributed systems design, such as operating systems, data communications protocols, switching systems, concurrent algorithms, railway signalling protocols, etc. The tool checks the logical consistency of a specification. It reports on deadlocks, unspecified receptions, flags incompleteness, race conditions, and unwarranted assumptions about the relative speeds of processes.

It was observed that SPIN is more appropriate to verify behavioural properties of distributed systems rather than code correctness itself, because SPIN constructs an abstract model of the code and, besides, does not have floating point types. As stated by (Holzmann, 2006), the purpose of the language is to encourage abstraction from the computational aspects of a distributed application while focusing on the verification of process interaction, synchronization and coordination.

One possibility of exploring the potential for verification evidence reuse in SPIN is establishing a systematic way to generate different codes which correspond to the same abstraction, thus the higher level verification would be reused when creating new components or assembling existing components.

Considerations about the Existing Tools

Although the theoretical background supporting compositional reuse of verification evidence is very sound, there is currently no tool that fully explores its advantages for industrial safety-critical software applications.

Besides the available tools presented in section 3, two of them have been analyzed during this research work, representing two different development approaches: Spark, the user interface of which is completely textual, and the verification is performed per local portions of code, and the Simulink Design Verifier, the primary interface

of which is graphical, and allows automatic check of every model execution path.

Both tools are compatible with the necessary theoretical background, and each has advantages and disadvantages over one another: Spark, with its recently incorporated Ravenscar profile, has more potential for dealing with concurrent tasks, yet it cannot perform full-state searches, as provided by the Simulink Design Verifier; another interesting comparison is that Spark allows more freedom to use complex iterative algorithms, while this is not allowed when performing full state-space verification with the Simulink Design Verifier (S-Functions, which contain programmatic logic, are not allowed).

Nevertheless, the Simulink Design Verifier seems to be more versatile, if one considers that it is more user-friendly, and that it is capable of performing fully automatic model-checking. Simulink models represent well-behaved and componentized sequential programs and, as such, compatible with our proposed uniform component representation, for which the benefits of assume-guarantee reasoning (Alur & Henzinger, 1996) are achievable. The case study presented in the next sections helps to assess the potential of Simulink Design Verifier for verifying evidence reuse.

A REAL COMPONENT-BASED V&V: CASE STUDY

This section shows the use of Simulink Design Verifier (SDV) for automatic verification of some components of a Thrust Reverser Controller, presenting and comparing some strategies with and without use of verification evidence. A thrust reverser is a mechanism present in most commercial jet aircraft to cause deceleration, by reversing the exhaust air flow from the turbines. In most cases, this mechanism has pivotable doors that remain stowed when forward thrust is required, and open, or technically *deployed*, when reverse thrust is needed. The pilot controls

Figure 1. Thrust Reverser Controller, component diagram at top level. Component Inputs and Outputs

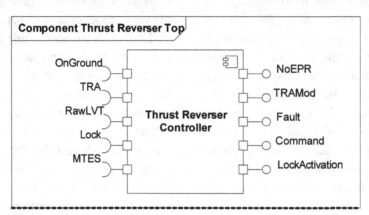

the mechanism on the throttle lever: when the lever is positioned behind a backward threshold, the thrust reverser will deploy doors and cause reverse thrust. There are considerable physical limitations for the achievable reverse thrust, thus the computerized engine controller limits the engine rotation to an idle level when thrust reverser doors are deployed.

Section 4.1 presents the architecture of the thrust reverse controller, and Section 4.2 presents the distinct component verification strategies, with (Section 4.2.3) and without (Sections 4.2.5 and 4.2.4) reuse of verification evidence, finishing with a comparison among these strategies (Section 4.2.6).

Thrust Reverser Controller Architecture

The Thrust Reverser Controller is an ensemble of software components running in a FADEC – Full Authority Digital Engine Controller, an autonomous avionics module physically attached to the engine, and responsible for its control and monitoring. The component model presented here is hypothetical, but not far from the actual FADEC components, and it is structured in four hierarchical levels. The model will not be shown in full details, but just enough to illustrate the compositional software approach here proposed.

UML Component Diagram – Top Level

In this section, the Thrust Reverser Controller is presented as a whole component, as shown in Figure 1.

The Inputs of the Thrust Reverser Controller component are:

1. OnGround: Boolean signal indicating whether the aircraft is on ground.
2. TRA (Thrust Resolver Angle): validated pilot lever angle indicating the pilot lever position; its nominal values vary in the interval $[TRA_{min}, TRA_{max}]$.
3. RawLVT: voltage measuring the position of the thrust reverser doors; its nominal values vary in the interval $[RAW\_LVT\_INPUT_{min}, RAW\_LVT\_INPUT_{max}]$.
4. Lock: Boolean thrust reverser lock switch indicator; when active, the thrust reverser doors are prevented from moving.
5. MTES: Maintenance Test Enabler Switch, Boolean signal which indicates that the thrust reverser may be operated in maintenance mode.

And the outputs are:

1. NoEPR: Boolean signal indicating that the Engine Pressure Ratio (EPR) must not be

Figure 2. Thrust Reverser Controller, component diagram at second hierarchical level.

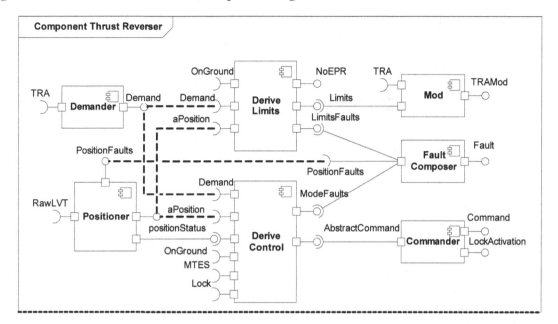

used for thrust control;

2. TRAMod: modulated thrust demand; nominal values vary in the interval [0%,100%];

3. Fault: several fault indication signals, to be defined;

4. Command: signal which commands the thrust reverser door actuators; it can be one of the following values: {HOLD, DEPLOY, RESTOW};

5. LockActivation: Boolean signal which commands the thrust reverser door locks.

UML Component Diagram – Second Hierarchical Level

This section presents the first breakdown of the Thrust Reverser Controller, as shown in Figure 2 and is explained in the next sections.

• **Demander**: this component reads the validated pilot lever angle (TRA) and provides an abstract thrust direction demand as output, which can be FORWARD or REVERSE.

• **Positioner**: reads the thrust reverser position signals (RawLVT voltage values), validates them and provides the abstract position number (aPosition), the position status and indication of position faults.

• **Derive Control**: it is responsible for controlling the thrust reverse doors so that thrust is deflected according to pilot demands, and for providing mode fault messages. It reads the thrust demand, the abstract door position, the position status, the OnGround indication, the maintenance test enabler switch (MTES), and the lock switch, and derives the following outputs: the abstract command for the thrust reverser actuators and the mode faults messages.

• **Derive Limits**: reads the OnGround indicator, the validated thrust demand, and the abstract control inputs (aPosition), and provides the following outputs: NoEPR, a Boolean signal indicating that the EPR must not be used for thrust control, Limits as the thrust limits, and LimitsFaults as indications that some limits fault has been detected.

Figure 3. Positioner component diagram.

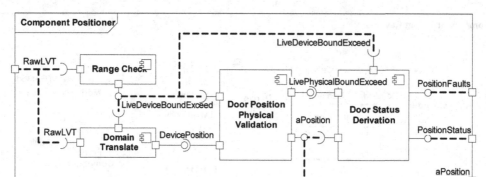

- **Mod**: reads the validated TRA value and the thrust limits, and provides the modulated thrust demand, which is a continuous percentage value.
- **Fault Composer**: integrates fault information and provides validated fault data.
- **Commander**: reads the abstract command (for the thrust reverser doors) and provides the command for the thrust reverser door actuators and lock activation to command thrust reverser lock.

These components must still be further broken down to study the benefits of the compositional approach proposed in this chapter.

UML Component Diagrams –Third Hierarchical Level

Only some of the components presented in the last section will be described in detail, since the purpose of this study is only to analyze some strategies for using the Simulink Design Verifier tool, and not verifying a whole module in industrial scale. This section presents the breakdown of the components Positioner and Derive Control.

Positioner Component Breakdown

The internal design of the component Positioner is shown in Figure 3, and the description of each component is presented in the paragraphs that follow.

- **Range Check**: this component is responsible for comparing the door position input characteristics against device-specific limits.
- **Domain Translate**: this component is responsible for converting from the device-specific inputs domain to that of abstract position. It has an FFV (Failure Fallback Value) set half-way along the position range.
- **Door Position Physical Validation:** this component is responsible for assessing the door position according to physical constraints arising from the configuration of the door mechanisms.
- **Door Status Derivation**: This component is responsible for extracting and validating stow, deploy and in-transit indicators.

Component Verification Strategies

This section presents the verification strategies for a component presented in the previous sec-

Figure 4. Door position physical validation high level component diagram.

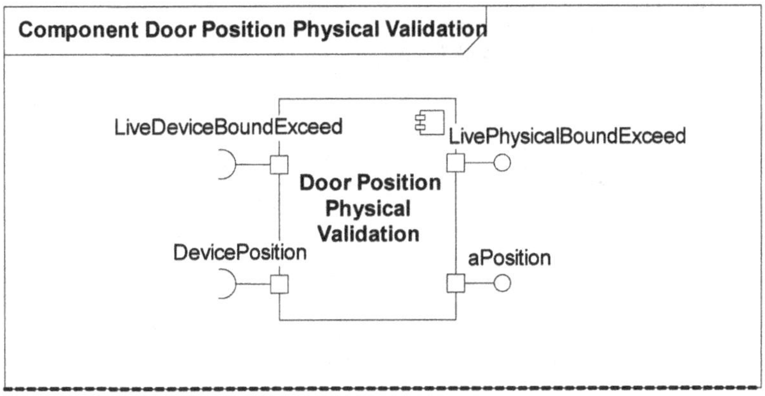

tion. However, before that, the types of verification allowed in Simulink Design Verifier are described.

Types of Verification in Simulink Design Verifier

Basically, the Simulink Design Verifier toolbox performs two types of model verification:

A. *Coverage test generation and execution*: given a Simulink model with any kind of logic that will result in Boolean outputs or conditional branching in the target code, the Design Verifier generates tests to check if every piece of the Boolean expressions and the branching logic is *meaningful* in the model. In order to accomplish this task, three subtypes of coverage tests are available:

- *Decision coverage*: checks if both outcomes of a conditional (true of false) are reachable;
- *Condition coverage*: checks if both outcomes of every subcondition (true or false) of a conditional are reachable;
- *MCDC (Modified Condition/Decision Coverage)*: given that a subcondition may change the entire outcome of a conditional from true to false or vice versa, checks whether this change is reachable.

Required by the DO-178B assurance level A.

Once the coverage tests have been generated, the Design Verifier toolbox generates a test harness to run these tests and to obtain numeric data about model coverage, and to help the user to observe the model behavior in the presence of the inputs generated for these tests.

B. *Property proving*: the user defines specific model assumptions and properties to be proved. The Simulink Proof Checker will use model-checking techniques to verify if that property holds for every possible dynamic combination of inputs and, if any counter-example is found, this is presented to the user.

The next sections present the concrete components to be verified, the verification strategies and their corresponding results.

Detailed Component Description

Let us consider the component *Door Position Physical Validation*, firstly presented in Subsection 4.1.3. Taking it separately, we see it as in Figure 4.

This component is responsible for assessing the thrust reverser door position according to physical constraints arising from the configuration of the door mechanisms.

Figure 5. Door position physical validation low level component diagram.

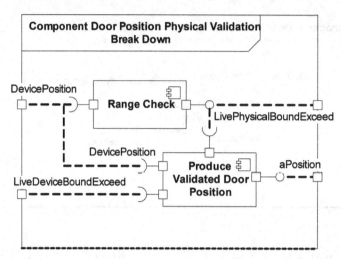

The typed input variables are:

- LiveDeviceBoundExceed, Boolean: the current sensed position of the door mechanism is out of the nominal interval;
- DevicePosition, Double: the current sensed position of the door mechanism.
- And the typed output variables are:
- LivePhysicalBoundExceed, Boolean: the current door position is detected to be out of the nominal interval;
- DoorPosition, [DOOR_POSITION$_{min}$, DOOR_POSITION$_{max}$]: the validated door position presented by the system.

In this document, two different designs for this component are considered: compositional and monolithic.

Compositional Design

In the compositional design, the Door Position Physical Validation is broken down into two sub-components, Range Check and Produce Validated Door Position, as depicted in the figure below. Its input and output variables are the same as for the outer level component above, except that **LivePhysicalBoundExceed** output is also an internal input of the **Produce Validated Door Position** component.

Each component functionality is described by defining its output values as a function of its input values.

Range Check Component Functionality

This component is responsible for checking whether the DevicePosition is in its valid value range. Table 1 specifies its functionality.

Table 1. Range check functionality.

Input	*Output*
DevicePosition	LivePhysicalBoundExceed
IN [DOOR_POSITION$_{min}$, DOOR_POSITION$_{max}$]	False
OUT [DOOR_POSITION$_{min}$, DOOR_POSITION$_{max}$]	True

Table 2. Produce validated door position functionality.

Input			Output
Live Physical Bound Exceed	Live Device Bound Exceed	Device Position	aPosition
F	F	X	= Device Position
F	T	X	DOOR_POSITION_FFV
T	F	X	DOOR_POSITION_FFV
T	T	X	DOOR_POSITION_FFV

Figure 6. Range check low-level Simulink design.

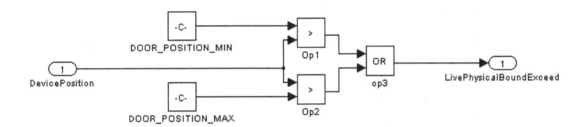

This functionality led to the following low-level design in Simulink, shown in Figure 6.

Produce Validated Door Position Component Functionality

This component is responsible for producing the validated door position. If LivePhysicalBoundExceed is true, or DevicePosition is out of the nominal interval, then a constant failure fallback value, DOOR_POSITION_FFV, is used as output. Table 2 specifies its functionality more precisely.

This functionality led to the following low-level design in Simulink (Figure 7).

This monolithic design alternative was developed to compare the verification effort with

Figure 7. Produce validated door position low-level Simulink design. Monolithic design

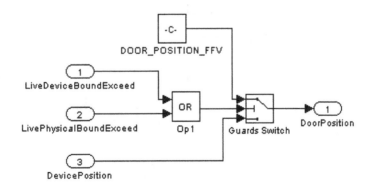

Table 3. Door position physical validation monolithic functionality.

Inputs		Outputs	
Live Device Bound Exceed	DevicePosition	Live Physical Bound Exceed	aPosition
F	IN [DOOR_POSITION$_{min}$, DOOR_POSITION$_{max}$]	F	= DevicePosition
T	IN [DOOR_POSITION$_{min}$, DOOR_POSITION$_{max}$]	F	DOOR_POSITION_FFV
F	OUT [DOOR_POSITION$_{min}$, DOOR_POSITION$_{max}$]	T	DOOR_POSITION_FFV
T	OUT [DOOR_POSITION$_{min}$, DOOR_POSITION$_{max}$]	T	DOOR_POSITION_FFV

the previous compositional development. Tables 1 and 2 were merged to serve as the basis of the low-level design.

According to Table 3, the following low-level Simulink design was obtained (Figure 8). To obtain this design, one pretends that the compositional design of the previous section never existed, and builds the logic by obtaining each output separately as a straightforward function of the inputs.

Note that the monolithic design has 7 operation blocks (excluding constants and input/output blocks), compared to the total 5 of the compositional

design. This is already an indication that monolithic design tends to present more complexity.

Compositional Verification Strategy

This verification strategy means to separately model-check each of the two components of the compositional design and reusing the evidence obtained to verify the behavior of the composite module. The Simulink Design Verifier tool was used to perform the model-checking, as explained in the following.

Figure 8. Door position physical validation monolithic low-level design.

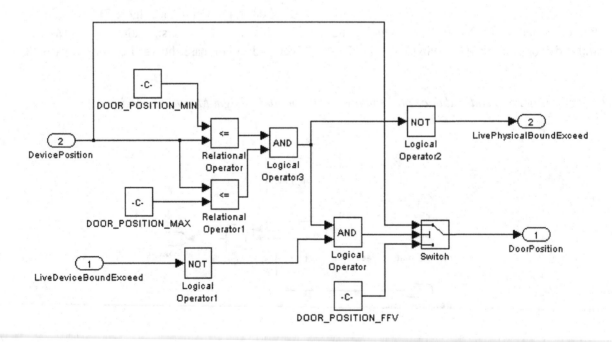

Figure 9. Range check verification model.

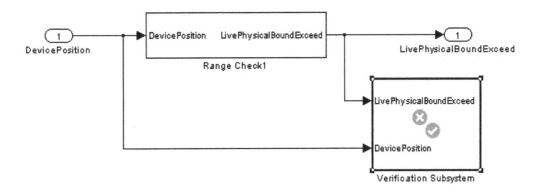

Range Check Component Verification

A model file was prepared to isolatedly verify this component. The overall aspect of this model is shown in Figure 9.

The verification subsystem is presented in Figure 10.

It is required that a verification subsystem be constructed independently of the internal design of the component to be tested, otherwise errors in the component design could be transported to the verification subsystem. This first verification subsystem was obtained from Table 1, assuming that this very table stands as the only external functional verification objective for the component **Range Check**. Indeed, one factor that influences

this decision is that Table 1 covers all possible input values for this component.

The Proof Objective block in this case is depicted as the gray round block marked with a big **P** in Figure 10, and means that the invariant value **true** must always be present in its input. The Design Verifier generates all combinations of values of the free variables (in this case, only DevicePosition, which is an input of the component being checked) and checks if any of these combinations falsify the proof objective. The result obtained in this first verification was that the proof objective is valid for every input and thus the external functionality of the component **Range Check** is compliant with its verification objective.

Figure 10. Range check verification subsystem.

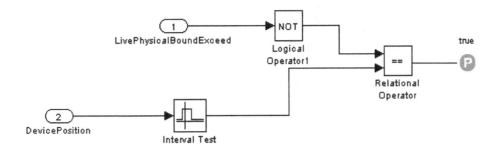

Figure 11. Produce validated door position verification model.

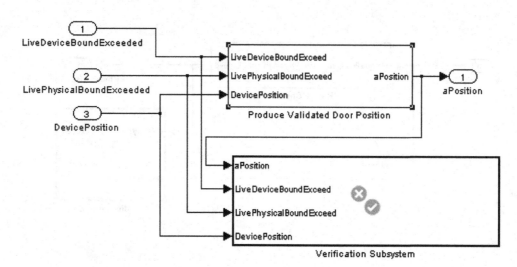

Produce Validated Door Position Component Verification

Another model file was prepared to isolatedly verify this component. The overall aspect of this model is shown in Figure 11.

And the verification subsystem is built as shown in Figure 12.

Similarly to the verification subsystem of the previous component, this verification subsystem was obtained from Table 2. The result of checking the proof objective was that the objective is valid for every input and so the external functionality of this component complies with the verification objectives.

The next section explores what can be deduced from the evidence obtained from the verification of the two components verified so far.

Figure 12. Produce validated door position verification subsystem.

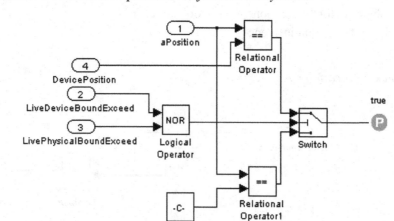

Figure 13. Door Position Physical Validation verification model.

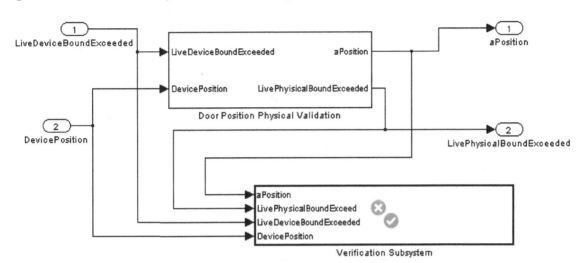

Composite Module Verification

Evidence that individual components meet their verification objectives is not necessarily evidence that the composite module or system meets the system verification objectives. Nevertheless, if properly used, the component-wise evidences can help to obtain evidence about the composite module behavior. In the case of the two components above, **Range Check** and **Produce Validated Door Position**, the composite module resulting from their composition is the component **Door Position Physical Validation**. Tables 1 and 2 are proven to hold and respectively correspond to the external behavior of each of those components; besides, only the variables in these tables are sufficient to determine the interaction between **Range Check** and **Produce Validated Door Position**.

It is important to observe that, when one integrates components in the Simulink Environment, it is important to have a well-established and disciplined routine to verify if every connection between blocks is correct. It is very easy to make a mistake when connecting two blocks, mainly when they are graphically distant, the signal names are similar or there is some cluttering in the diagram.

Tables 1 and 2 can be merged to obtain Table 3 which, in turn, suffices to determine the external behavior of the composite module **Door Position Physical Validation**. Actually, the component and composite tables cover all the possible input values for the components and the composite module (the most general environment), the components behavior is normal, their interfaces are compatible and thus assume-guarantee reasoning, which allows deducing that the composite module will behave as determined by Table 3, and no further verification is necessary.

Unified Verification Strategy

This strategy consists in building only one verification subsystem for the composite module **Door Position Physical Validation**. The verification model is shown in Figure 13.

The **Door Position Physical Validation** is internally built compositionally, as shown in Figure 5, but the Verification Subsystem is built monolithically from Table 3, as shown in Figure 14. Therefore, here there is no reuse of verification evidence.

Note that there are two proof objectives, the uppermost to check the output LivePhysical-

Figure 14. Door position physical validation verification subsystem.

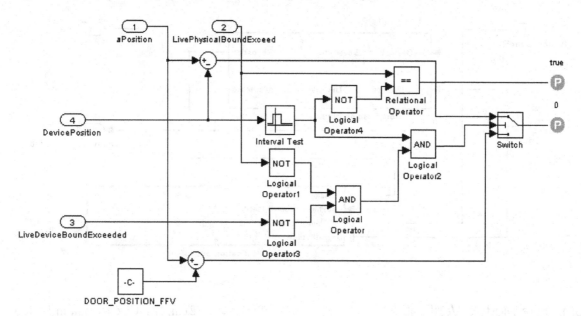

BoundExceed, and the lowermost to check the output aPosition. As already mentioned, the invariant values of the proof objectives must always be present in their inputs, which are chosen to determine conditions about the component inputs and outputs.

The two proof objectives were proven valid and, therefore, the composite module really behaves as defined in Table 3, reassuring the statements of Section 4.2.2. However, as built here, this verification strategy is more likely to be used as an integration verification, rather than a unit verification, if one assumes that only Tables 1 and 2 are part of the components specification. The next section presents a more sound verification strategy regarding this aspect.

Monolithic Verification Strategy

In this section, it is assumed that the only component specification provided is the monolithic one in Section 4.2.2, so the verification objective is checking whether Table 3 always holds. The verification model here built has the overall

aspect exactly as in Figure 13, but the internal design of the component **Door Position Physical Validation** is not compositional, but monolithic, as shown in Figure 8. The verification subsystem used is exactly as in Figure 14, therefore without reuse of verification evidence. The two proof objectives were proven valid and, therefore, the monolithic component really behaves as defined in Table 3.

Comparison of the Verification Strategies

This comparison focuses on the complexity aspects of the two strategies, both quantitative and qualitative ones. The quantitative aspects are:

- Number of Simulink operation blocks used, including functional and verification subsystems;
- Total time spent on automatic verification;
- Number of Test Objectives generated by the Simulink Design Verifier Test Generator;
- Number of verification units.

Table 4. Comparison of the verification strategies.

Aspect	Compositional	Unified	Monolithic
Reuse of verification evidence	Yes	No	No
Number of Simulink operation blocks	13	16	18
Total time spent on automatic verification	0.11 sec	0.10 sec	0.10 sec
Number of Test Objectives generated	18	18	22
Number of verification units	2	1	1
Requirements traceability	Good	Poor	Adequate
Ease of Understanding	Good	Poor	Adequate/Poor

And the qualitative aspects to be compared are:

- Requirements traceability;
- Ease of understanding.

The comparison is shown in Table 4.

On the quantitative aspects, it can be seen that the Compositional strategy has less internal complexity (less Simulink operation blocks), which will result in less code lines, although the computing time spent on automatic verification was a little higher. It is believed that this higher time is due to the overhead of instantiating and deallocating the verification tool twice, one time per component. Nonetheless, the components are very simple, even the composite module is relatively simple, and the reported computing time does not seem to be a very significant criterion in these cases.

About the number of Test Objectives generated, this aspect is important when one considers code coverage test for certification purposes. The Test Objectives generated by the Design Verifier aim to cover every possible internal condition in the internal logic of the components under test, being the lowest level test and often being required for certification purposes such as for DO-178B. Thus, this is an indicator of the test effort required, and it will be higher for the Monolithic strategy.

The only aspect that really seems to be a drawback of the Compositional strategy is the number of verification units. For this strategy, there are two verification units, one per component, instead of one verification unit for the other strategies. This means that there will be more artifacts to document and keep track of in the verification process. However, this aspect results from the underlying "divide-to-conquer" idea of the Compositional strategy, which provides advantages in the qualitative aspects.

It can be observed that, for smaller components, the requirements are simpler and, therefore, the verification objectives are easier to deduce and to relate with the requirements. Complex requirements of greater modules are more likely to be coupled and overlapped, and so the relation between verification objectives and requirements can be less clear. The Poor mark attributed to the Unified strategy is due to the fact that the verification objectives used in this strategy are poorly connected with the previous artifacts of the development process.

Finally, it is possible to note that the greater the number of blocks within a component, the more difficult the understanding of its functionality and the error identification will be, and in this aspect the Compositional strategy has advantages over the other strategies. The Adequate mark attributed to the Monolithic approach is because, sometimes, certain non-trivial functionality is better understood as performed by an atomic unit rather than performed by a combination of components. The Poor mark attributed to the Unified strategy in this aspect is due to the fact that the verification process works with entities that are not entirely defined in the component model.

FINAL REMARKS ABOUT THIS CHAPTER

The last section presented the elaboration of three different component verification strategies, their results, and the comparison of several of their aspects. The overall outcome is that the Compositional strategy, in which the verification is performed per component, and later reused for integration verification, is the best one when the components are designed from the most reasonably early stages of the development process, as was the case for the Compositional strategy here studied. The definition of component functionality and, consequently, component size, is highly dependent on domain expert knowledge, and will impact the complexity of the verification effort in the size of the code generated, as observed when comparing the Compositional and the Monolithic strategies.

Proven functional tables that define the component functionality can be reused as verification evidence for Simulink blocks, as Tables 1 and 2 were used to deduce Table 3 and later used as a guarantee on composite behavior. However, the components behavior in this case study are extremely simple, which is not always the case in real-life systems, and state-machine behavior requires more complex evidences than functional tables. The definition and application of compositional verification strategies in more complex components is being developed and will be published soon. One of them could be defining component safety interfaces using user-defined verification blocks, with monitoring state machines and exploring property violation examples, found by the Design Verifier, throughout composition.

The component verification strategies involve coverage tests and property verification, and rely on the SDV formal verification engine that can provide good results but, frequently, find undecidable cases. A very useful side effect of the coverage test generation is that it enables a reasonably easy and reliable process to eliminate dead code.

In theory, a software unit that was positively verified with a consistent model-checker, as has been done in Section 4.2, against all the relevant safety properties, has a very strong argument to be considered safe, because model-checkers visit all possible execution paths in the entire state space. On the other hand, many functional aspects cannot be checked this way, simply because the underlying formalism cannot express them (e.g. signal processing in the complex domain). Owing to this and to other considerations, certification standards such as DO-178B require testing every single code line, although the new release of this standard, DO-178C, currently being elaborated, will provide more support to formal verification. In any case, automatic formal verification, within a compositional software approach, may be a strong safety evidence and drastically reduces the need of defensive programming, improving software performance, reducing software complexity and, consequently, minimizing the effort for certification.

REFERENCES

Adolph, S. (1999). Whatever Happened to Software Reuse? *Software Development*. Retrieved in July, 2008, from http://steveadolph.com/articles%20and%20papers/articles%20and%20papers.htm

Almeida, E. S., Alvaro, A., Garcia, V. C., Mascena, J. C. C. P., Burégio, V. A. A., Nascimento, L. M., et al. (2007). *C.R.U.I.S.E. – Component Reuse in Software Engineering*. C.E.S.A.R e-books Brazil. Retrieved March, 2009, from http://cruise.cesar.org.br/.

Alur, R., de Alfaro, L., Grosuz, R., Henzinger, T. A., Kangy, M., Majumdar, R., et al. (2001). MOCHA: A Model Checking Tool that Exploits Design Structure. *23rd International Conference on Software Engineering*, (pp. 835-836).

Alur, R., & Henzinger, T. A. (1996). Reactive Modules. In *Logic in Computer Science, 1996, LICS '96, Proceedings Eleventh Annual IEEE Symposium* (pp.207-218), New Brunswick, NJ.

Alur, R., Henzinger, T. A., & Kupferman, O. (1997). Alternating-time temporal logic. *Proceedings of the 38th Annual Symposium on Foundations of Computer Science*, (pp.100-109).

Alur, R., & Wang, B.-Y. (1999). "Next" heuristic for on-the-fly model checking. In *Proceedings 10th CONCUR*, (LNCS 1664, pp. 98–113). Berlin: Springer.

Ambühl, C. (2007). *Introduction to Spark. Seminar of the Complexity Theory and Algorithmics Group*, University of Liverpool. Retrieved in March 01, 2009, from http://www.csc.liv.ac.uk/~ctag/

Barnes, J. (2003). *High Integrity Software: The Spark Approach to Safety and Security*. Reading, MA: Addison-Wesley.

Berbers, Y., Rigole, P., Vandewoude, Y., & Van Baelen, S. (2005). COCONES: An Approach for Components and Contracts in Embedded Systems. In *Component-Based Software Development of Embedded Systems*, (LNCS 3778). Berlin: Springer.

Cheng-Ying, M., & Yan-Sheng, L. (2005) Improving the Robustness and Reliability of Object-Oriented Programs through Exception Analysis and Testing. In *Proceedings 10th IEEE International Conference on Engineering of Complex Computer Systems, (ICECCS 2005)*.

Clothier, R. A., & Walker, R. A. (2006). Determination and Evaluation of UAV Safety Objectives. *In Proceedings 21st International Unmanned Air Vehicle Systems Conference*, (pp. 18.1-18.16), Bristol, United Kingdom.

Dajani-Brown, S., Cofer, D., & Bouali, A. (2004). *Formal Verification of an Avionics Sensor Voter Using SCADE*. (LNCS 3253). Berlin: Springer.

FAA. (2004). *Reusable Software Components*. Advisory Circular (AC) 20-148.

FAA. (2008). *Current TSOs by Number*. Retrieved July, 2008, from http://www.airweb.faa.gov/Regulatory_and_Guidance_Library/rgTSO.nsf/MainFrame?OpenFrameSet

Holzmann, G. J. (2006). *The SPIN Model-Checker: Primer and Reference Manual*. Boston: Addison-Welsey.

Howden, W. E. (1986). A Functional Approach to Program Testing and Analysis. *IEEE Transactions on Software Engineering, SE-12*(10), 997–1005.

Hudak, J., & Feiler, P. (2007). *Developing AADL Models for Control Systems: A Practitioner's Guide*. Technical Report. CMU/SEI-2007-TR-014, ESC-TR-2007-014.

Leveson, N. (1995). *Safeware: System Safety and Computers*. Boston: Addison-Wesley.

Mathworks. (2008). Verification, Validation (V and V) and Test in Model-Based Design. *The Mathworks website*. Retrieved in June, 2008 from http://www.mathworks.com/products/featured/vv/.

Moschoyiannis, S., & Shields, M. W. (2004). A Set-Theoretic Framework for Component Composition. *Fundamenta Informaticae, 59*(1), 1–24.

Moschoyiannis, S., Shields, M. W., & Krause, P. J. (2005). Modelling Component Behaviour with Concurrent Automata. *Electronic Notes in Theoretical Computer Science, 141*, 199–220. doi:10.1016/j.entcs.2005.04.035

Omega. (2008). Definition of a development methodology in UML for embedded and real-time systems based on formal techniques. *Correct Development of Real-Time Embedded Systems*. Retrieved in June, 2008, from http://www-omega.imag.fr/.

OSATE. (2008). *Open Source AADL Tool Environment.* Retrieved in July, 2008, from http://la.sei.cmu.edu.

Pasareanu, C., & Giannakopolou, D. (2006). *Towards a Compositional SPIN* (LNCS 3925). Berlin: Springer.

Portwood, B. E. (1998). Current government and industry developments in the area of system safety assessment. *Proceedings of the 17th DASC Digital Avionics Systems Conference,* (vol.1, pp.B31-1-6). The AIAA/IEEE/SAE.

Rierson, L. (2000). *Software Reuse in Safety-Critical Systems*. Master's Thesis, Rochester Institute of Technology.

RTCA Incorporated (1992). Software Considerations in Airborne Systems and Equipment Certification. *RTCA document number RTCA/DO-178B.*

SAE. (1996a). Certification Considerations for Highly Integrated or Complex Aircraft Systems, Aerospace. *Recommended Practice (ARP) 4754.*

SAE. (1996b). Guidelines and Methods for Conducting the Safety Assessment Process on Civil Airborne Systems and Equipment, Aerospace. *Recommended Practice (ARP), 4761*(12).

Sodhi, J., & Sodhi, P. (1999). *Software Reuse: Domain Analysis and Design Process*. New York: McGraw-Hill.

van Ommering, R. (1998). *Koala, a Component Model for Consumer Electronics Product Software* (LNCS 1429). Berlin: Springer.

Walters, J. M., & Sumwalt, R. L. (2000). *Aircraft Accident Analysis: Final Reports, an Aviation Week Book*. New York: McGraw-Hill Professional Book Group.

Chapter 15
The Language Specification PEARL for Co-Designing Embedded Systems

Roman Gumzej
University of Maribor, Slovenia

Wolfgang A. Halang
Fernuniversität, Germany

ABSTRACT

The Specification PEARL language and methodology for hardware/software co-design of embedded control systems is presented. The Specification PEARL language has its origins in standard Multiprocessor PEARL, and was enhanced as foreseen by the standard to model layered and asymmetrical multiprocessor system architectures. Its constructs were extended by additional parameters for model verification and validation by schedulability analysis. Graphical symbols were introduced for Specification PEARL constructs to enable graphical modeling while maintaining their semantic background. Originally, Specification PEARL was intended as a superlayer for normal PEARL programs, implementing the Multiprocessor PEARL specification. Later on, however, it evolved to a methodology to specify and co-design applications for other target programming languages, such as C and C++, based on the superior programming model of PEARL. To supplement structural modeling by a behavioural model, Timed State Transition Diagrams were defined to model program tasks. A system model is verified for coherence by model checking as well as for temporal feasibility with co-simulation. The resulting information is used to correct and fine-tune a current model. To enhance availability and safety as well as to support maintainability, dynamic re-configuration planning is included in the software-to-hardware mapping specifications. Since UML has become the de facto standard also for designing embedded control systems, a UML profile for the methodology was defined using UML's extension mechanisms.

DOI: 10.4018/978-1-60566-800-0.ch015

INTRODUCTION

Since embedded real-time systems depend on both – hardware and software – in order to fulfill their duties safely and efficiently, they should be designed in a holistic way taking both aspects into consideration. This chapter presents the results of a project whose purpose was to devise a language, methodology, and development environment to achieve this – Specification PEARL (Gumzej, 2004).

The Specification PEARL (S-PEARL) language is based on the notation of standard Multiprocessor PEARL (DIN 66253-3, 1989), which was extended in the manner foreseen by the standard by the following features:

- enhanced constructs to describe hardware configurations,
- enhanced constructs to describe software configurations,
- construct properties endowed with timing information (where applicable),
- graphical representation of constructs to enable graphical modeling,
- constructs to specify communication and its characteristics (peripheral and process connections, physical and logical connections, transmission protocols), as well as
- constructs to specify both conditions and methods of carrying out dynamic reconfigurations.

The Specification PEARL co-design methodology enables to construct a conceptual system model, whereby its hardware and software architectures may be described in parallel. It supports a project's lifecycle as shown in Fig. 1. After a system model is built from its hardware and software specifications within the co-design environment, it is checked for consistency, and its temporal feasibility is analysed with the associated co-simulation environment (Gumzej, 2004). These steps may be repeated multiple times while introducing changes to the software/hardware designs in order to correct/improve the system model. Once the designer is satisfied with the model, a target platform model can be produced from the design environment for cross-compilation to the target platform.

The project evolution process from specification of system architectures, via software design, verification and validation, to deployment of the system model is straightforward and based on the waterfall model, leaving the designer with no semantic gap between specification and design formalisms as well as implementation and verification of models produced. The resulting feasible models retain their validity even after enhancement to fully functional applications in case their timing limitations are not violated.

The main benefits of using the Specification PEARL methodology to co-design embedded control applications are the abilities to:

- reason on system integration at an early stage,
- introduce timing constraints wherever applicable into a design, and
- check the temporal feasibility of a design before implementation.

BACKGROUND

Designing real-time systems has always been a challenge. Only recently, however, adequate methodical tools have formally been introduced. Naturally, they were present from the beginning. But due to the large diversity of the areas in which embedded systems are deployed, special formalisms have been developed and used in, e.g., telecommunications, industrial control, aerospace, or mechatronics. Embedded systems constitute a large subset of real-time systems and, hence, these two terms are often used interchangeably. Owing to the increase in complexity of information systems and applications in general, as well

Figure 1. Specification PEARL project lifecycle

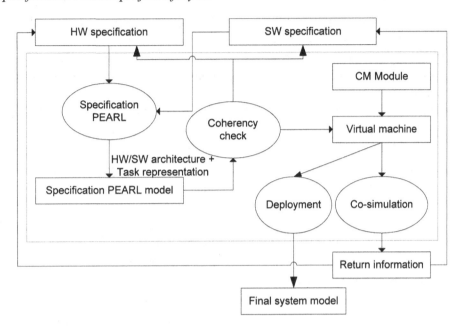

as real-time criteria becoming part of them, the need to integrate real-time specific formalisms became a necessity.

The paradigm shift to object orientation in programming languages and the associated quite complex formal background caused the merge of the mentioned formalisms not to be as straightforward as desired. This is the main reason for the relatively late introduction of real-time concepts into object-oriented design, which started with, e.g., ROOM (Selić, Gullekson, & Ward, 1994), was developed further in the RT extensions of UML (Douglass, 2002, Selić, & Rumbaugh, 1998), and took its final form with the new UML 2 specification and associated profiles, cp. (OMG, 2005).

Here, a different approach to real-time systems design and development is described. The real-time programming language PEARL, which became a DIN industry standard (DIN 66253-2, 1998), was developed especially to program real-time applications introducing a wide variety of constructs and concepts used in industry. It was enhanced by a library of hardware devices from

Siemens, ABB, AEG and Telefunken (c.p. (Kappatsch, Mittendorf, & Rieder, 1979)) in order to be able to directly address them in high-level language programs, which should eliminate the need for low-level assembly language programming of appropriate device drivers. Later, it evolved into a language to program (distributed) multiprocessor systems – Multiprocessor PEARL (DIN 66253-3, 1989). Enhancements of it evolved addressing safety (cp. (Halang, Pereira, & Frigeri, 2002)) and object orientation (cp. (Verber, 1999)). Originally being an imperative language, however, these additions were not widely accepted and remained without support by appropriate system tools such as PEARL operating systems. Industry preferred to use C, because it is more widespread and easier to upgrade and integrate into C++ projects, being used to program contemporary object-oriented applications.

The Specification PEARL language and design methodology (Gumzej, 1999) was developed in order to ease design and development of applications based on concepts found in the language

Multiprocessor PEARL. In the final version of the related co-design environment (Gumzej, 2004), besides native S-PEARL language code also the construction of C/C++ target applications from S-PEARL models was enabled with PEARL-specific system calls to support the PEARL process model. Finally, an S-PEARL real-time profile was devised for UML also enabling PEARL-oriented real-time systems design in UML (Gumzej & Lu, 2007). The S-PEARL language builds upon the strengths of its foundations in PEARL and Multiprocessor PEARL, viz.,

- the rigid textual syntax of PEARL and its extensions, and an
- own Real-Time Operating System (RTOS), which has been tailored for optimum support of the programming language's features.

The S-PEARL design methodology also profits from both, because models can be stored in native language format, which is human- and machine-readable, and their deterministic execution is supported by its well defined semantics and the PEARL process model. As for the constructs of S-PEARL and its UML profile, their attributes were selected from device properties and RTOS parameters in a natural way. A database of standard devices is a feature, which should find greater acceptance in programming languages used to develop embedded applications. Lessons learnt in consistent design of real-time systems oriented at their Quality of Service (QoS) are discussed throughout this chapter together with appropriate concepts and constructs from S-PEARL.

SPECIFICATION PEARL (S-PEARL)

System Model

In S-PEARL, system models are composed of hardware and software models, as well as of system libraries which provide software models with the underlying semantics of the methodology.

A hardware model consists of STATIONs, being the processing nodes of a system. Stations themselves are compositions of hardware components such as processors, memories, or interfaces. These components, on one hand, determine their structure and connection points for their interconnections with other stations. On the other hand, they also represent their resources and provide the necessary timing information for schedulability analysis.

A software model is composed of COLLEC-TIONs, which are mapped to the STATIONs of the hardware model and invoked selectively, depending on their state information. They consist of MODULEs of TASKs that carry out their activities. At any time, there is exactly one collection assigned to run on a station. Thus, the collection is also the unit of dynamic re-configuration.

To administer collections, a dynamic re-Configuration Manager (CM) is required, which forms a middleware layer between the real-time operating system, if any, and the applications. Its role is to function as (1) a hardware abstraction layer, (2) a hardware/software interface, and (3) as an inter-collection co-operation agent. In order to form executable units, the configuration manager is joined with the application model and compiled for the target platform, or additionally joined with the co-simulation environment for temporal feasibility checking (as shown in Figure 1).

Station

A station is a top-layer hardware-architectural component and represents a processing node – a system on chip (SoC) or an integrated circuit consisting of a processor, bus, memory, and peripheral devices (see Figure 2). The components of the station are introduced and described on its respective component sublayer.

Stations can be of different types, depending on their role in a system:

Figure 2. Station properties

Attributes:
- name,
- type (BASIC, TASK, KERNEL, COMPOSITE),
- states (e.g.: INITIAL, NORMAL, CRITICAL,…),
- PART OF attribute,

additional KERNEL station attributes:
- real-time clock resolution,
- scheduling strategy,
- maximum number of tasks, semaphores, monitored events (timing, interrupts, signals,…), events in a queue, scheduled events,

additional TASK station attribute:
- supervisor (KERNEL) station reference.

Icons:

BASIC

TASK

KERNEL

COMPOSITE

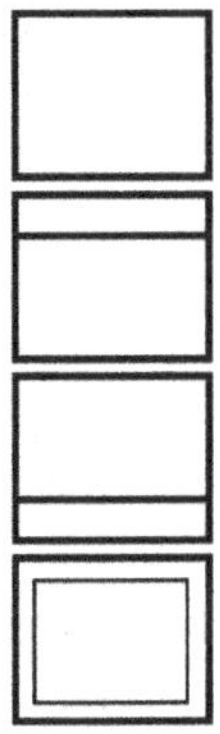

- KERNEL stations – representing master/control stations to their dependent TASK stations, usually running an operating system;
- TASK stations – representing slave/application stations, which may be co-ordinated by a KERNEL station; and
- COMPOSITE stations – representing compositions of stations, e.g., processing nodes composed of multiple KERNEL/TASK stations, sharing the same physical location and possibly interconnections with other stations.

Considering the type of a station, it may own additional parameters. The KERNEL station has attributes for the parameterisation of the RTOS: scheduling strategy ID, maximum number of tasks, synchronisers, external events, and events in the event queue, real-time clock resolution, etc. On the other side, the TASK stations have their associated KERNEL station specified, too. To be able to describe hierarchical architectures, a COM-

POSITE station was introduced as a superstation consisting of one or more stations. Its substations are characterised by specifying their superstation in their PART OF attribute. Hence, multiprocessor nodes are introduced rather by composition of single-processor nodes than by introducing more than one processor in a station.

Proctype

Processors (PROCTYPE) are station sublayer components. They are assigned a speed description (clock frequency). It is possible to have multiple processors in a single station, whereas a separate station should preferably be introduced for each of them, especially if the second processor is not connected to the same bus. In this case a multiprocessor node is better represented by two interconnected stations within a superstation (Figure 3).

Workstore

Memories (WORKSTORE) are station sublayer components. The working storage (WORK-STORE) is described by the size and allocation of

Figure 3. Proctype properties

Attributes:
- name,
- processor speed (in MHz).

Icon:

PROCTYPE

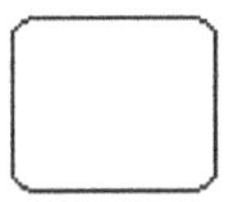

Figure 4. Workstore properties

Attributes:
- name,
- attributes (RAM, ROM, XOM, SHARED),
- access time.

Icons (WORKSTORE):

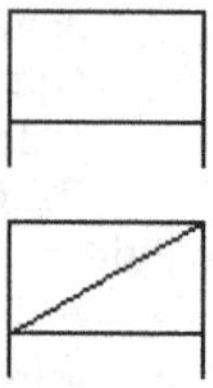

RAM

ROM

individual memory areas. It is possible to specify the access time to these areas and their type (on-chip RAM, RAM, ROM usually have different access times). This information can be used by the compiler to assign memory space correctly to programs and data accordingly, and to optimise the access times. The RAM and ROM memory areas can be modeled separately, since they usually have different purposes. One can specify more than one memory area for each, but their address spaces shall not overlap (Figure 4).

Device/Interface

I/O devices (INTERFACEs) are station sublayer components. The specification of integrated devices' attributes (DEVICE) is primarily meant to parameterise their drivers, since they mainly represent memory-mapped devices. One can specify the address or the name of a driver. Since most devices represent connection points of I/O lines, INTERFACEs have been introduced beside general devices. Here, one can also parameterise a driver by specifying the address and control

registers, transfer kind (package or DMA) and speed. Otherwise, due to the great diversity of these devices, it does not make sense to describe them in great detail. In case of "standard devices", whose properties may be obtained from a database, only their unique name or ID may be specified (Figure 5).

Bus

Buses are station sublayer components. For completeness reasons the bandwidth of a BUS must be specified for each station. It is foreseen that all station components are attached to a bus (Figure 6).

Collection

A collection is a top-layer software-architectural component. The biggest program part, which can be associated with a station, is the COLLECTION. It is composed of MODULEs of TASKs. For their intercommunication PORTs are used. PORTs are global with respect to the COLLECTION, and are

Figure 5. Device/interface properties

Attributes:
- name,
- device type (generic, interface),
additional attributes for an INTERFACE:
- driver ID or start address of the driver,
- single transfer unit (smallest item being transferred in a packet) or DMA,
- address and control registers,
- transfer speed.

Icons:

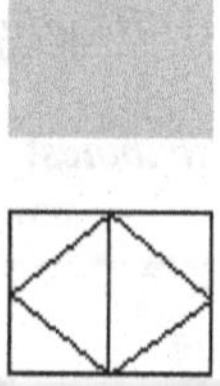

DEVICE

INTERFACE

Figure 6. Bus properties

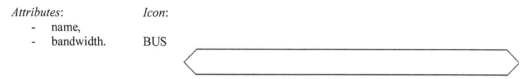

Attributes:
- name,
- bandwidth.

Icon:

BUS

visible from the outside. They are addressed by a combination of the COLLECTION's and the PORT's names (Figure 7).

COLLECTIONs are loaded to a specified STATION. It is possible to define the state of a station that is associated with a COLLECTION. The collections, which are loaded to the same station, and the conditions under which they are/become active form its configuration. These conditions refer to the state of their STATION and inform its configuration management program (CM) on how to perform the dynamic re-configuration operations.

The associations of states with collections may have different purposes and depend on the application. They can be considered phases of a complex procedure, where the individual operations can safely be separated by their time of occurrence. The states can also represent the global state of the system or its parts, where the initial state represents the start-up operations on each node, after which the station is transferred to the operating state, in which it remains until an exceptional event changes its state. Based on the cause of a state change and provided one can foresee it, a corresponding reaction (dedicated

COLLECTION) can be assigned the task to handle the situation and bring the station into operating or safe shut-down state.

The PORTS of a collection are described by the direction of data flow and the attributes of the connection. In case hardware connections (specified in the NET division) are meant, the described hardware connection, which serves the communication among ports, can be specified by the VIA connection specification. If there are more possibilities, the preferred connection can be specified by the PREFER attribute (then it is up to the CM to chose the first available connection line). Each PORT, physical or logical, can be assigned a protocol, which is used for communication, and any additional signals may be specified. The protocols *No-Wait-Send, Blocking-Send,* and *Send-Reply* are predefined

In standard Multiprocessor PEARL, some common signals representing expected communication errors were defined. They have been adopted in S-PEARL:

- CONNECT_ERROR: If, upon entering the TRANSMIT or RECEIVE operations, the corresponding PORT-to-PORT connection

Figure 7. Collection properties

Attributes:
- name,
- station name (residence),
- state (associated with a station's state).

Assignment of logical names to connections between COLLECTIONs (PORTs) and STATIONs (INTERFACEs).

Icon:

COLLECTION

Figure 8. Module properties

Attributes:
- name,
- imports,
- exports.

Icon:

MODULE

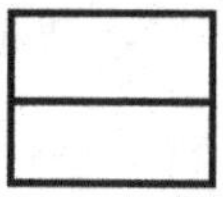

is non-existent, this signal is raised and the operation is aborted.

- BUFFER_ERROR: If, on using the No-Wait-Send protocol, some message could not be transferred as the buffer was full, this signal is raised, and the TRANSMIT operation is aborted. The recipient is also informed – if this error occurs before the end of the RECEIVE operation, this signal is raised and the operation is aborted.
- TRANSMISSION_ERROR: Transmission errors (noise or time frame delays, etc.) raise this signal. It is raised in both – the sender and recipient – sides, and the corresponding transfer operations are aborted. The current message is considered to be not transferred.
- REPLY_ERROR: On an error upon receiving the answer with the Send-Reply protocol (noise or time frame delay, etc.) this signal is raised. It is raised in both – the sender and recipient – sides, and the corresponding transfer operations are aborted. The current message is considered to be not transferred.
- TRANSFER_OK: An additional signal, which denotes a successful message transmission, has been added.

Module

A module is a collection sublayer component. The MODULEs which encapsulate TASKs are described by their names and interfaces (IMPORT, EXPORT definitions. See Figure 8).

Task

A task is a module sublayer component. TASKs are defined by specifying their response times. They are additionally defined by two attributes: (1) initial, which denotes an initial task – the task which starts the execution of the collection and activates or schedules any additional tasks – and (2) keep, which denotes a "critical" task – a task, which is not pre-empted even in the case of an overload situation. Their semantics and trigger conditions are defined by their associated timed state transition diagrams (Figure 9).

Task Model

According to Mok (1991), the computational model of most applications running in the real-time mode can be written in the form of the following "equation":

Real-time program model = Dataflow model + State automaton + Timing limitations

The tasks of an application represent the (computational) processes in a running system. They are mainly characterised by activation conditions and timing limitations as well as by being part of certain COLLECTIONs. This information is sufficient to build a coarse program model, but it is not enough to determine its feasibility. Therefore, timed state transition diagrams are introduced to represent the execution behaviour of tasks. Their synchronisation and intercommunication are realised by calls to the configuration manager and/or the real-time operating system of the station executing the tasks' collection.

Figure 9. Task properties

Attributes:
- name,
- trigger condition (on demand, timer, interrupt),
- priority or response time,
- maximum execution time,
- alternative task ID (scheduled instead, if schedule becomes infeasible).

Icon:

TASK

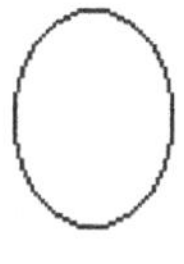

Task State Transition Diagrams (TSTD) are hierarchical finite-state automata consisting of what is shown in Figure 10.

Any state contains the following properties:

- state type (start-, working-/super- or final state),
- pre-condition for the state's execution (activation condition in case of a start state),
- time frame (shortest and maximum execution times),
- timeout action (the action executed in case a state exceeds its time frame),
- connection(s) to the next state(s) in case the execution continues successfully, and
- actions carried out within the state, i.e., program code with PEARL system calls.

The connections between states represent the progress of tasks in time. All connections are uni-directional and local (i.e., bound to the states of one task). Intertask co-operation is modeled by system calls to the operating system or the configuration manager. Usually they also trigger the continuation pre-conditions of subsequent states. Trigger conditions differ slightly depending on the state type. Only start states have the possibility of explicit (on-demand) activation. Other state types rely on the following types of pre-conditions:

- external events (*int(number)*), representing interrupts,
- internal events (*sig(number)*), representing signals,
- timers (*timer(at,every,during)*), representing timing signals,

Figure 10. Task TSTD properties

- *start states*, introducing task activation conditions and initialisation actions,

  Icon:

- *working states*, containing atomic activities with predictable duration,

  Icon:

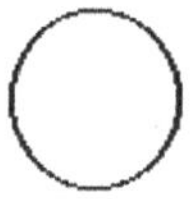

- *superstates*, representing non-atomic activities – hierarchical composition of working states, and

  Icon:

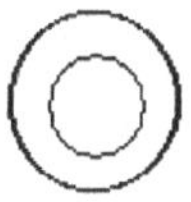

- *final states*, representing finalisation actions.

  Icon:

- general conditions (*cd(expression)*), i.e., expressions returning Boolean results from the evaluation of internal system/program states or data structures of the operating system.

The real-time operating system and configuration manager are accessible through their system calls (API), and are parameterised by the system architecture configuration.

CONFIGURATION MANAGEMENT AND RTOS SUPPORT

To support the tasking model of PEARL and to be able to service the same rich set of system calls supporting real-time operation, a real-time operating system was built and is used when building simulation and target platform models expressed in S-PEARL. The RTOS supports the deadline-driven scheduling strategy (later enhancements for other strategies, e.g., "rate monotonic" and similar are also foreseen). Since this RTOS (cp. (Gumzej, 1999)) is not off-the-shelf, but rather a part of the designed system model, its source code, written in C, can be compiled with appropriate adjustments for any hardware platform with a C cross-compiler. Its resources are determined (e.g., number of tasks, synchronisers, signals, events, or queued events) by the parameter-setup of a KERNEL STATION.

The configuration manager represents a dynamic re-configuration management and communication agent as well as a hardware abstraction layer as configured by the hardware architecture model. The execution at each processing node (station) starts by initiating the configuration manager. It loads the collections, and activates the initial collection by triggering the latter's initialisation task. In stations without a real-time operating system, the main task of the collection is started and delegated control to by the CM, whereas otherwise the CM acts as a front-end to the operating system functions, and uses appropriate system calls and system ports to transfer system requests to/from RTOS-enabled nodes to schedule the collection's tasks. Besides local execution, the CM also handles interstation communication. Hence, it must establish port-to-port connections through the stations' interfaces. A dedicated system service port is used when transferring operating system requests between KERNEL stations and TASK stations.

The application programming interface (API) of the CM has the following functions:(Re-) Configuration:

- Cm_Init(S) – to initialise the station S and to load the initial software configuration, and
- Cm_Reset(S) – to restart the station with the initial software/hardware configuration.

Station state monitoring:

- Cm_Getstate(S) – to retrieve the current state of station S, and
- Cm_Setstate(S, state) – to change the current state of station S to "state".

Interstation communication:

- Cm_Transmit(TCBi, portID, msg_buff[]) – message transmission through a connection,
- Cm_Reply(TCBi, portID, msg_buff[]) – response message transmission through a connection, and
- Cm_Receive(TCBi, portID, msg_buff[]) – message receipt through a connection, where TCBi denotes the index of the task's control block (TCB), portID the name of the port, and msg_buff[] the buffer for the message.

Connections among collections are established through ports of the software architecture and associated devices of the hardware architecture. The attributes of ports represent the communication parameters (smallest package, protocol, etc.) and routing parameters (VIA/PREFER). Routing affects the way hardware communication devices are used. The attribute VIA determines the exact line to be used, while PREFER is usually assigned to the most trusted line in a list. Lines represent connections between hardware architecture devices (e.g., interfaces).

In asymmetrical architectures, calls to real-time operating system services are passed as messages among KERNEL/TASK stations. To generate them, substitute RTOS-API functions are invoked. The messages are then transferred through the CM system service ports of the KERNEL/TASK stations. The parameters of system requests are extracted from the transferred messages in concordance with a pre-defined coding scheme also used in the construction of the parameter set. To enable uniform handling of system requests, the RTOS-API has been designed in a way enabling the transformation of system calls to parameter strings, which can be routed to the RTOS input queue, or sent to the KERNEL station for handling. Two additional internal functions have been introduced in the CM interface for this reason:

- Cm_SysRequest(S, sys_par[]) – send system call parameters for processing to the RTOS, and
- Cm_SysResult(S) – store result from the RTOS (result of the system call and possible context switch request for the local dispatcher routine of the CM (CM_System(S)).

EXAMPLE

To demonstrate the use of Specification PEARL concepts here we present a practical example based on a research version of an avionics system (Miller, 1998). namely, its autopilot. In particular,

the operation of the mode control logic of a Flight Guidance System (FGS) for a General Aviation (GA) class aircraft is considered. Being a part of the Flight Management System, an autopilot is usually composed of several (e.g., five) interconnected motherboards, running at least two processes of each task on separate boards and issuing results by voting. In our simplified example only three processors are being used, two performing the FGS functions and one acting as voter.

The FGS compares the measured state of an aircraft (present position, speed, and attitude) to the desired state and generates pitch and roll guidance commands in order to minimise the difference between the measured and desired states. Any FGS can be broken down into the mode control logic and the flight control laws. In our example, we focus on the mode control logic.

FGS accepts instructions from the pilots, the Flight Management System (FMS), and information about the current state of the aircraft to determine which system modes are active. The active modes determine which flight control laws are used to generate the pitch and roll guidance commands. When engaged, the autopilot translates these commands into directions for movements of the aircraft's control surfaces. When disengaged, these commands originate from the crew and are input to the flight control logic directly.

From the Software Cost Reduction (SCR) specification of the mentioned example, we developed a Specification PEARL model to help demonstrate how operation scenarios are switched safely and transparently. Our operating scenario is two-fold: with the autopilot "ON", the flight control commands are issued by the autopilot with respect to minor corrections from the flight crew; this represents the FGS's "NORMAL" operating mode. In "MANUAL" state, entered upon malfunction of the autopilot or on demand by the crew, the flight control logic is controlled solely by manual controls handled by the crew.

In the sequel, first the textual architecture description in S-PEARL is given for the example. The

"!" sign denotes a comment. In Figure 11 below these main system components are presented.

ARCHITECTURE:

```
STATIONS: ! processing node descriptions
   NAME: S1; ! avionics node
    PROCTYPE: p AT 10 MHz;
    STATEID: (NORMAL, MANUAL);
    STATIONTYPE: BASIC;
    INTERFACE Line
         DRIVER: IO
         TRANSFER: INOUT
         TRANSFERRATE: 20971520 BPS;
    INTERFACE Line2
         DRIVER: IO2
         TRANSFER: INOUT
         TRANSFERRATE: 10485760 BPS;
   ! any additional avionics nodes…
   NAME: S2; ! voter/controller node
    PROCTYPE: p AT 10 MHz;
    STATEID: (NORMAL);
    STATIONTYPE: BASIC;
    INTERFACE Line
         DRIVER: IO
         TRANSFER: INOUT
         TRANSFERRATE: 20971520 BPS;
STAEND;
NET: S1.Line<->S2.Line; S1.Line2<->S2.
Line; NETEND;
SYSTEM:
   NAME: S1;
      S1.Line INOUT;
   NAME: S2;
      S2.Line INOUT;
SYSEND;
CONFIGURATION:
   COLLECTION C1 ! autopilot configuration
    PORT P1 : IN BYTE OUT BYTE;
    MODULES C1_M;
    TASKS C1_t (DEADLINE 50); TASKEND;
    MODEND;
   COLEND;
   COLLECTION C2 ! manual configuration
```

```
    PORT P2 : IN BYTE OUT BYTE;
    MODULES C2_M;
    TASKS C2_t (DEADLINE 100); TASKEND;
    MODEND;
   COLEND;
   COLLECTION C3 ! voter/controller con-
figuration
      PORT P : IN BYTE OUT BYTE;
    MODULES C3_M;
    TASKS C3_t (DEADLINE 50); TASKEND;
    MODEND;
   COLEND;
   LOAD C1 TO S1; ! initial configuration
   LOAD C3 TO S2; ! (autopilot+voter)
   CONNECT C1.P1<->C3.P PREFER S1.Line;
   STATE (MANUAL) ! re-configuration to
manual configuration
      BEGIN
         DISCONNECT C1.P1<->C3.P;
         REMOVE C1 FROM S1;
         CONNECT C2.P2<->C3.P VIA
S1.Line2; ! manual configuration
         LOAD C2 TO S1;
      END;
CONFEND;
ARCHEND;
```

A plain-text explanation of the above example reads as follows: collections (e.g., *C1, C2,* and *C3*) are units of software, which are loaded to stations (e.g., *S1* and *S2*) and selectively activated based on the current station state. Stations have the specified component's properties and are foreseen to be in one of the prescribed states (e.g., *NORMAL* being the initial state).

The hardware/software specifications, as described above, are used in S-PEARL when parameterising the configuration managers, being the primary executive programs at each station. During execution or co-simulation of a system (model), this architecture information is taken into account when task activities and CM operations are executed.

Collections are the units of *dynamic re-*

configuration. At any time there is exactly one collection of tasks being ready to run on a station. Execution scenarios are expressed by *configurations* of collections, and by their connections associating them with operational modes (states) of host stations and their connection lines. Re-configuration management is defined in S-PEARL by the specification of re-configuration conditions and actions as given by the S-PEARL mapping specifications. The initial mapping of collections to stations is determined by the *initial LOAD statements*, whereas subsequent re-loads are prescribed by the *re-configuration LOAD statements*. The latter are station-state-dependent (*STATE statement*). Hence, they are executed when a station's state changes accordingly. Due to a change in a software configuration, also the existing connections between the collections, as established by *CONNECT statements* for the initial/previous software configuration, may become invalid. Prior to changing the configuration, they have, hence, to be closed by *DISCONNECT statements* and, after the new configuration is established, (re-) opened with *CONNECT statements*. The stations' lines, used to connect collection PORTs can be

selected with preference (*PREFER* attribute) or exclusively (*VIA* attribute).

The graphical form of the hardware model for station *S1* in the example can be seen in Figure 11. The lines between *S1* and *S2* are represented by a single connection. At station *S1* there are two interfaces, however, each serving its line (cp. Figure 12). The representation of *S2* is similar, although there is only one interface there representing the connection. The graphical form of the software model can be seen on the right hand side of Figure 11. Note that the PORT-to-PORT connections between *C1, C2,* and *C3* are represented separately.

The properties of hardware/software model entities can be entered in corresponding pop-up dialogues by right-clicking on them, and are saved in the model repository. They correspond to the properties shown in the textual S-PEARL model description, which can automatically be generated from the co-design environment.

So far only the system architecture has been laid out. Behavioural modeling is carried through by constructing the timed state transition diagrams for the collections' tasks. In our case we have just

Figure 11. Top-level hardware and software models for the example

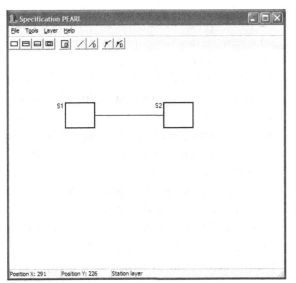
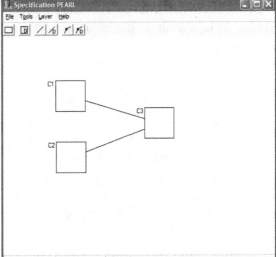

Figure 12. S1 detailed description (component level)

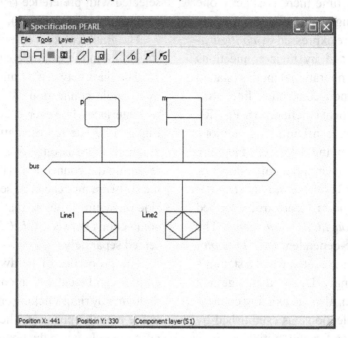

three tasks – one in each collection. This means that there is no task-switching, so we do not need to introduce a RTOS in any station, although we still wish to dynamically re-configure our system and communicate among tasks located at different stations. In the course of this, CM-API functions are invoked from the task states as shown below.

In Figure 13, the timed state transition diagram and C code for *NORMAL* mode processing of data at station *S1* is laid out. In this mode, collection *C1* is active and its task communicates through the port *P1* with collection *C3* from *S2*. If an operation times out, it is assumed that the autopilot has a malfunction or the connection with the control system has been broken. Hence, a signal is raised, which switches the state of *S1* to *MANUAL*, triggering switching scenarios from normal (*C1*) to manual mode processing (*C2*). Correspondingly, also the connection to *C3* could be re-connected through a slower yet (possibly) more reliable *Line2* for hard-wired FGS control.

FUTURE WORK

The S-PEARL development environment, that originally did not support full code generation from the designed models, is being improved to support this feature for both target platforms as well as co-simulation environments. Our small RTOS kernel, which was designed and used to verify the concepts, was written in C to support the widest range of target platforms. It is being enhanced in functionality (e.g., by alternative, possibly custom, scheduling methods) as well as with support for off-the-shelf real-time operating systems that have gained the status of industrial standards in the field (e.g., OSEK). Also we found that, if supplemented by a library of standard components (e.g., EDDL descriptions), the development environment could represent a very useful design tool to build networked embedded systems (for, e.g., fieldbus applications) as well.

The UML profile and pattern described in (Gumzej, Colnarič & Halang 2007) were introduced not only to demonstrate the expressive

Figure 13. C1_t TSTD and C code for the simulation model.

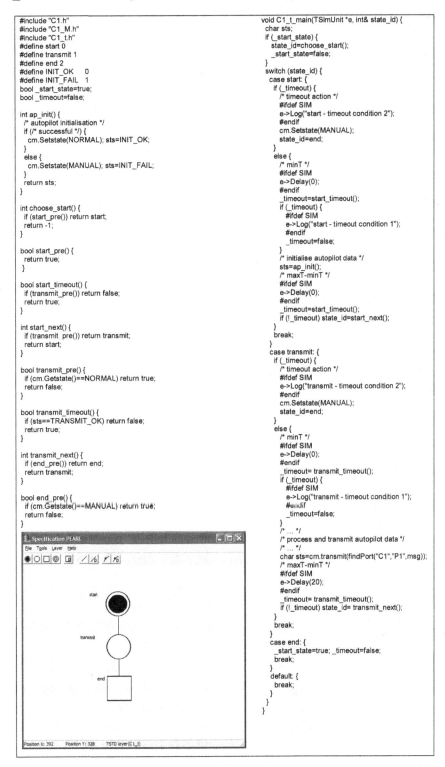

```
#include "C1.h"
#include "C1_M.h"
#include "C1_t.h"
#define start 0
#define transmit 1
#define end 2
#define INIT_OK     0
#define INIT_FAIL   1
bool _start_state=true;
bool _timeout=false;

int ap_init() {
  /* autopilot initialisation */
  if (/* successful */) {
    cm.Setstate(NORMAL); sts=INIT_OK;
  }
  else {
    cm.Setstate(MANUAL); sts=INIT_FAIL;
  }
  return sts;
}

int choose_start() {
  if (start_pre()) return start;
  return -1;
}

bool start_pre() {
  return true;
}

bool start_timeout() {
  if (transmit_pre()) return false;
  return true;
}

int start_next() {
  if (transmit_pre()) return transmit;
  return start;
}

bool transmit_pre() {
  if (cm.Getstate()==NORMAL) return true;
  return false;
}

bool transmit_timeout() {
  if (sts==TRANSMIT_OK) return false;
  return true;
}

int transmit_next() {
  if (end_pre()) return end;
  return transmit;
}

bool end_pre() {
  if (cm.Getstate()==MANUAL) return true;
  return false;
}
```

```
void C1_t_main(TSimUnit *e, int& state_id) {
  char sts;
  if (_start_state) {
    state_id=choose_start();
    _start_state=false;
  }
  switch (state_id) {
    case start: {
      if (_timeout) {
        /* timeout action */
        #ifdef SIM
        e->Log("start - timeout condition 2");
        #endif
        cm.Setstate(MANUAL);
        state_id=end;
      }
      else {
        /* minT */
        #ifdef SIM
        e->Delay(0);
        #endif
        _timeout=start_timeout();
        if (_timeout) {
          #ifdef SIM
          e->Log("start - timeout condition 1");
          #endif
          _timeout=false;
        }
        /* initialise autopilot data */
        sts=ap_init();
        /* maxT-minT */
        #ifdef SIM
        e->Delay(0);
        #endif
        _timeout=start_timeout();
        if (!_timeout) state_id=start_next();
      }
      break;
    }
    case transmit: {
      if (_timeout) {
        /* timeout action */
        #ifdef SIM
        e->Log("transmit - timeout condition 2");
        #endif
        cm.Setstate(MANUAL);
        state_id=end;
      }
      else {
        /* minT */
        #ifdef SIM
        e->Delay(0);
        #endif
        _timeout= transmit_timeout();
        if (_timeout) {
          #ifdef SIM
          e->Log("transmit - timeout condition 1");
          #endif
          _timeout=false;
        }
        /* ... */
        /* process and transmit autopilot data */
        /* ... */
        char sts=cm.transmit(findPort("C1","P1",msg));
        /* maxT-minT */
        #ifdef SIM
        e->Delay(20);
        #endif
        _timeout= transmit_timeout();
        if (!_timeout) state_id= transmit_next();
      }
      break;
    }
    case end: {
      _start_state=true; _timeout=false;
      break;
    }
    default: {
      break;
    }
  }
}
```

329

power of the language and methodology to the UML community, but also to enable the construction of S-PEARL models in UML. Since UML has become the de facto standard also for designing embedded control applications, this feature has become very important, too. Although the mentioned profile and pattern were originally designed for UML-RT, they are being converted to UML 2.

CONCLUSION

In this chapter the S-PEARL methodology has been presented, featuring holistic co-design and co-simulation of models of embedded systems. It demonstrates the early introduction of the real-time application programming language PEARL, which soon outgrew its framework and was, hence, extended to program distributed applications in Multiprocessor PEARL. Already at the time of introduction, the concepts of PEARL were very advanced – and to the present day they are still unmatched by other languages. Unfortunately, the concepts were not used due to lacking support from industry, which only a decade ago became aware of the importance of time-aware execution.

The possibilities of the language were enhanced by a methodology to co-design embedded applications – Specification PEARL. Although still lacking industrial support, this research project rendered the listed results and revealed its possibilities to the academic community. Hence, we are looking at a re-juvenation of the language PEARL, which is expected to evolve in one of two ways: (1) as a scripting language with high-level constructs and library support, or (2) as a template in the sense of aspect-oriented programming where its rich features could provide also C programmers with better insight and overview of their program code. Due to methodological support also by UML patterns, it is expected to comprise safety and security features for embedded applications while at the same time facilitating their timeliness.

REFERENCES

DIN 66253-2 (1998): *Programmiersprache PEARL90*. Berlin-Köln: Beuth Verlag.

DIN 66253 Teil 3 (1989): *Mehrrechner-PEARL*. Berlin-Köln: Beuth Verlag.

Douglass, B. P. (2002). *Real-Time UML*. Reading, MA: Addison Wesley.

Gumzej, R. (2004). *Overview of the Project Z2-3493: Holistic Embedded Control Systems Design*. Retrieved from http://www.rts.uni-mb.si/misc/projekti/SPEARL

Gumzej, R., Colnarič, M., & Halang, W. A. (2009). A reconfiguration pattern for distributed embedded systems. In: *Software & Systems Modeling, 8*(1), 145–161.

Gumzej, R., & Lu, S. (2007). Modeling distributed real-time applications with Specification PEARL. *Real-Time Systems, 35*(3), 181–208. doi:10.1007/s11241-006-9007-9

Halang, W. A., Pereira, C. E., & Frigeri, A. H. (2002). Safe object-oriented programming of distributed real-time Systems in PEARL. *Comput. Syst. Sci. Eng., 17*(2), 85–94.

Kappatsch, A., Mittendorf, H., & Rieder, P. (1979). *PEARL: Systematische Darstellung für den Anwender*. München-Wien, Germany: R. Oldenbourg.

Miller, S. P. (1998). Specifying the Mode Logic of a Flight Guidance System in CORE and SCR. In *Proceedings of the Second Workshop on Formal Methods in Software Practice (FMSP '98)* (pp. 44–53). New York: ACM.

Mok, A. K. (1991). Towards mechanization of real-time system design. In A.M. van Tilborg & G.M. Koob (Eds.), *Foundations of Real-time Computing: Formal Specification and Methods* (pp. 1–37). New York: McGraw-Hill.

OMG (2005). *Unified Modeling Language: Superstructure. Version 2.0.* OMG document formal/2005-07-04.

Selić, B., Gullekson, G., & Ward, P. T. (1994). *Real-Time Object-Oriented Modeling.* Hoboken, NJ: John Wiley & Sons.

Selić, B., & Rumbaugh, J. (1998). *Using UML for Modeling Complex Real-Time Systems.* White Paper, Rational Software Corporation. Retrieved from http://www.rational.com/media/whitepapers/ umlrt.pdf

Verber, D. (1999). *Object Orientation in Hard Real-Time Systems Development.* Unpublished doctoral dissertation, University of Maribor, Slovenia.

Compilation of References

Abdulkadir, S. (2001). *Daily Operational Aircraft Maintenance Routing Problem*. PhD Thesis. State University of New York at Buffalo, Buffalo, NY.

Adeli, H. (2001). Neural Networks in civil engineering: 1989-2000. *Computer-Aided Civil and Infrastructure Engineering, 16*, 126–142. doi:10.1111/0885-9507.00219

Adeli, H., & Hung, S. L. (1995). *Machine learning: neural networks, genetic algorithms, and fuzzy systems*. New York: Wiley Inc.

Adolph, S. (1999). Whatever Happened to Software Reuse? *Software Development*. Retrieved in July, 2008, from http://steveadolph.com/articles%20and%20papers/articles%20and%20papers.htm

Ahlvin, R. G., Ulery, H. H., Hutchinson, R. L., & Rice, J. L. (1971). *Multiple-Wheel Heavy Gear Load Pavement Tests, Vol. 1: Basic Report*. Technical Report No. AFWL-TR-70-113, U.S. Army Engineer Waterways Experiment Station, Vicksburg, MI.

Almeida, E. S., Alvaro, A., Garcia, V. C., Mascena, J. C. C. P., Burégio, V. A. A., Nascimento, L. M., et al. (2007). *C.R.U.I.S.E. – Component Reuse in Software Engineering*. C.E.S.A.R e-books Brazil. Retrieved March, 2009, from http://cruise.cesar.org.br/.

Al-Sultan, K. S., & Al-Fawzan, M. A. (1997). A Tabu Search Hooke and Jeeves Algorithm for Unconstrained Optimization. *European Journal of Operational Research, 103*, 198–208. doi:10.1016/S0377-2217(96)00282-2

Alur, R., & Henzinger, T. A. (1996). Reactive Modules. In *Logic in Computer Science, 1996, LICS '96, Proceed-*ings Eleventh Annual IEEE Symposium (pp.207-218), New Brunswick, NJ.

Alur, R., & Wang, B.-Y. (1999). "Next" heuristic for on-the-fly model checking. In *Proceedings 10th CONCUR*, (LNCS 1664, pp. 98–113). Berlin: Springer.

Alur, R., de Alfaro, L., Grosuz, R., Henzinger, T. A., Kangy, M., Majumdar, R., et al. (2001). MOCHA: A Model Checking Tool that Exploits Design Structure. *23rd International Conference on Software Engineering*, (pp. 835-836).

Alur, R., Henzinger, T. A., & Kupferman, O. (1997). Alternating-time temporal logic. *Proceedings of the 38th Annual Symposium on Foundations of Computer Science*, (pp.100-109).

Alves, D. P. (2006). *Modelagem usando Aprendizagem por Reforço em Sistemas Multi-agentes para um Ambiente Controlado em Nível Meta*. Master dissertation, Universidade de Brasília, Brasilia, DF.

Ambühl, C. (2007). *Introduction to Spark. Seminar of the Complexity Theory and Algorithmics Group*, University of Liverpool. Retrieved in March 01, 2009, from http://www.csc.liv.ac.uk/~ctag/

Andreatta, G., & Romanin-Jacur, G. (1987). Aircraft flow management under congestion. *Transportation Science, 21*, 249–253. doi:10.1287/trsc.21.4.249

Andreatta, G., Brunetta, L., Odoni, A. R., Righi, L., Stamatopoulos, M. A., & Zografos, G. (1998). *A set of approximate and compatible models for airport strategic planning on airside and on landside*. 2nd USA/Europe ATM R&D Seminar, Orlando.

Arbuckle, D., et al. (2006). U.S. Vision for 2025 Air Transportation. *ATCA Journal of Air Traffic Control, January-March 2006 quarterly issue.* Retrieved July 12, 2008, from http://www.jpdo.gov/library/vision_2025_air_trans.pdf

Aschauer, D. (1989). Is Public Expenditure Productive? *Journal of Monetary Economics, 23,* 177–200. doi:10.1016/0304-3932(89)90047-0

Aschauer, D. (1990). Why Infrastructure is Important? In A. Munnell (ed), *Is there a Shortfall in Public Capital Investment? Conference Series No 34,* Boston, Federal Reserve Bank of Boston.

Ashford, N., & Wright, P. H. (1984). *Airport Engineering (3rd Ed.).* New York: Wiley-Interscience.

ATECH. (2007). *Gerenciador de fluxo de tráfego aéreo - SYNCROMAX.* Retrieved December 2008 from http://www.atech.br/new/site/negocios/produtos.php?id=126

Atkins, S. (1998). *A Unified Methodology for the Management of Time-Dependent Information in Aeronautical Systems.* PhD Thesis, Massachusetts Institute of Technology, Cambridge, MA.

Ball, M. O., Chen, C., & Hoffman, R. (2001). New Concepts and Methods in Air Traffic Management. In Lucio Bianco (Ed.), *Collaborative Decision Making in Air Traffic Management: Current and Future Research Directions* (pp. 17-30). Berlin: Transportation Analysis.

Ball, M. O., Hoffman, R., Odoni, A., & Rifkin, R. (2003). A stochastic integer program with dual network structure and its application to the ground holding problem. [INFORMS]. *Institute for Operations Research and the Management Sciences, 51,* 167–171.

Balzer, Y. (2004). *Improve your SOA project plans: Strong governance principles ensure a successful outcome.* Retrieved September 22, 2008, from http://www.ibm.com/developerworks/library/ws-improvesoa.

Barenberg, E. J., & Petros, K. A. (1991). *Evaluation of Concrete Pavements Using NDT Results.* Project IHR-512, University of Illinois at Urbana-Champaign and Illinois Department of Transportation, Report No. UILU-ENG-91-2006.

Barnes, J. (2003). *High Integrity Software: The Spark Approach to Safety and Security.* Reading, MA: Addison-Wesley.

Barros, C. (2008). Technical Efficiency of UK Airports. *Journal of Air Transport Management, 14,* 175–178. doi:10.1016/j.jairtraman.2008.04.002

Bartholomew-Biggs, M. C., Parkhurst, S. C., & Wilson, S. P. (2003). Global optimization approaches to an aircraft routing problem. *European Journal of Operational Research, 146,* 417–431. doi:10.1016/S0377-2217(02)00229-1

Bartholomew-Biggs, M. C., Parkhurst, S. C., & Wilson, S. P. (2003). Using DIRECT to Solve an Aircraft Routing Problem. *Computational Optimization and Applications, 21,* 311–323. doi:10.1023/A:1013729320435

Bell, M. (2008). *Service-Oriented Modeling: Service Analysis, Design, and Architecture.* Hoboken, NJ: Wiley.

Bellman, R. (1957). *Applied Dynamic Programming.* Princeton, NJ: Princeton University Press.

Ben-Or, M. (1983). Another Advantage of Free Choice: Completely Asynchronous Agreement Protocols. In *Proceedings of the 2nd ACM Symposium on Principles of Distributed Computing,* (pp. 27-30).

Benson, T., & Aspin, C. (2008). *Latam airlines still buoyant even as fuel soars.* Retrieved April 2008 from http://uk.reuters.com/article/basicIndustries/idUKN2548662620080425.

Berbers, Y., Rigole, P., Vandewoude, Y., & Van Baelen, S. (2005). COCONES: An Approach for Components and Contracts in Embedded Systems. In *Component-Based Software Development of Embedded Systems,* (LNCS 3778). Berlin: Springer.

Bertsekas, D. P. (2000). *Dynamic Programming and Optimal Control,* (Vol. I, 2nd Ed.). Belmont, MA: Athena Scientific.

Bilegan, I. C. (2003). *Contribution à la conception de systèmes réactifs daide à la décision pour maximiser les recettes dune compagnie aérienne.* PhD Thesis,

Polytechnic National Institute in Toulouse and LARA/ ENAC.

Bilegan, I. C., El Moudani, W., Achaibou, A., & Mora-Camino, F. (2001). A new approach to update probability distributions estimates of air travel demand. *Smart Engineering System Design, 11,* 853–856.

Blake, A., & Sinclair, M. T. (2003). Tourism Crisis Management – US Response to September 11. *Annals of Tourism Research, 30,* 813–832. doi:10.1016/S0160-7383(03)00056-2

Borgstrom, R. E. (1974). Air travel: Toward a behavioral geography of discretionary travel. In M.E. Eliot-Hurst (Ed.), *Transportation geography: Comments and readings* (pp. 314-326). New York: McGraw-Hill.

Bowen, J. (2000). Airline hubs in Southeast Asia: National economic development and nodal accessibility. *Journal of Transport Geography, 8,* 25–41. doi:10.1016/S0966-6923(99)00030-7

Bradley, M. A. (1998). Behavioural models or airport choice and air route choice. In J. de Dios Ortuzar, D. Hensher, & S. Jara-Diaz (Eds.), *Travel behaviour research: Updating the state of play* (pp. 141-159). Amsterdam: Elsevier.

Brom, L., & Pilon, N. (2008). *Challenges of Air Tranport 2030, survey of expert views.* EUROCONTROL Experimental Centre, Report n° 09/07/15-20.

Brown, S. F., & Pappin, J. W. (1981). Analysis of pavements with granular bases. *Transportation Research Record, 810,* 17–23.

Brunetta, L., Righi, L., & Andreatta, G. (1999). An operations research model for the evaluation of an airport terminal: SLAM (simple landside aggregate model). *Journal of Air Transport Management, 5,* 161–175. doi:10.1016/S0969-6997(99)00010-1

Bryan, D. L., & O'Kelly, M. E. (1999). Hub-and-spoke networks in air transportation: An analytical review. *Journal of Regional Science, 39*(2), 275–295. doi:10.1111/1467-9787.00134

Bush, A. J. III, & Baladi, G. Y. (1989). Nondestructive testing of pavements and backcalculation of moduli. [STP]. *ASTM Special Technical Publication,* 1026.

Butler, S. E., & Kiernan, L. J. (1987). Measuring the regional transportation benefits and economic impacts of airports. In Transportation Research Board, National Research Council (Ed.), *Transportation economics: Issues and impacts* (pp. 63-69). Washington, DC: Transportation Research Board.

Button, K., & Taylor, S. (2000). International Air Transportation and Economic Development. *Journal of Air Transport Management, 6,* 209–222. doi:10.1016/S0969-6997(00)00015-6

Camelier, I., Lourenço, L., & da Saúde, J. (2008). Aircraft Sustaining: A Holistic And Systemic Approach Establishing The Various Support Components. *Aircraft Engineering and Aerospace Technology, 55,* 3.

Carlyle, W. M., Royset, J. O., & Wood, R. K. (2007). Routing military aircraft with a constrained shortest-path algorithm. Retrieved from http://www.nps.navy.mil/orfacpag/resumePages/papers/woodrkpa/Carlyle-RoysetWoodAircraftRouting.pdf

Carr, F. (2000). *Stochastic modelling and control of airport surface traffic.* SM Thesis Electrical Engineering and Computer Science, MIT, Cambridge, MA.

C-ATM Consortium. (2005). *Cooperative Air Traffic Management - Phase 1: C-ATM High-Level Operational Concept: Deployable from 2012* (Tech. Rep). Retrieved July 13, 2008, from http://www.eurocontrol.fr/Newsletter/2005/March/SVC/CATM_HLOC.doc

Census and Statistics Department (CSD), Hong Kong Special Administration Region (SAR) Government. (2001). *2001 population census: Basic tables for district council districts.* Hong Kong: Printing Department.

Census and Statistics Department (CSD), Hong Kong Special Administration Region (SAR) Government. (2002). *Hong Kong monthly digest of statistics.* Hong Kong: Printing Department.

CERMAS. (2003). *ACARE CERMAS Report.* Advisory Council for Aeronautic Research in Europe.

Ceylan, H., Tutumluer, E., Thompson, M. R., & Gomez-Ramirez, F. (2004). Neural Network-Based Structural Models for Rapid Analysis of Flexible Pavements with Unbound Aggregate Layers. *Proceedings of the 6th International Symposium on Pavements Unbound (UNBAR6)*, Nottingham, UK.

CGNA. (2005). *Relatório Geral*. Departamento de Controle do Espaço Aéreo, Rio de Janeiro, RJ.

Chandra, T. D., & Toueg, S. (1996). Unreliable Failure Detectors for Reliable Distributed Systems. *Journal of the ACM, 43*(2), 225–267. doi:10.1145/226643.226647

Chelouah, R., & Siarry, P. (2000). Tabu Search applied to global optimization. *European Journal of Operational Research, 123*, 256–270. doi:10.1016/S0377-2217(99)00255-6

Chen, D.-H., & Hugo, F. (1998). Full-Scale Accelerated Pavement Testing of Texas Mobile Load Simulator. *Journal of Transportation Engineering, 124*(5), 479–490. doi:10.1061/(ASCE)0733-947X(1998)124:5(479)

Cheng-Ying, M., & Yan-Sheng, L. (2005) Improving the Robustness and Reliability of Object-Oriented Programs through Exception Analysis and Testing. In *Proceedings 10th IEEE International Conference on Engineering of Complex Computer Systems, (ICECCS 2005)*.

Chin, A., Hooper, P., & Oum, T. H. (1999). The Impacts of the Asian Economic Crises on Asian Airlines: A hort-Run Responses and Long-Run Effects. *Journal of Air Transport Management, 5*, 87–96. doi:10.1016/S0969-6997(99)00003-4

Chinainfobank (2002). Retrieved April 19, 2002, from http://www.chinainfobank.com/IrisBin/ (in Chinese).

Chockler, G., Demirbas, M., Gilbert, S., Newport, C., & Nolte, T. (2005). Consensus and Collision Detectors in Wireless Ad-hoc Networks. In *Proceedings of the Twenty-fourth Annual ACM Symposium on Principles of Distributed Computing*, (pp. 197-206).

Civil Aviation Administration of China (CAAC). (2002). Retrieved April 19, 2002, from www.caac.cn.net.

Civil Aviation Department (CAD), Hong Kong Special Administration Region (SAR) Government. (2002). *CAD annual report 2000/2001*. Retrieved April 19, 2002, from http://www.info.gov.hk/cad/english/annualreport00.htm.

Clothier, R. A., & Walker, R. A. (2006). Determination and Evaluation of UAV Safety Objectives. *In Proceedings 21st International Unmanned Air Vehicle Systems Conference*, (pp. 18.1-18.16), Bristol, United Kingdom.

Coldren, G. M., & Koppelman, F. S. (2005). Modeling the Competition Among Air-Travel Itinerary Shares: GEV Model Development. *Transportation Research Part A, Policy and Practice, 39*(4), 345–365.

Coldren, G. M., Koppelman, F. S., Kasturirangan, K., & Mukherjee, A. (2003). Modeling Aggregate Air Travel Itinerary Shares: Logit Model Development at a Major US Airline. *Journal of Air Transport Management, 9*(6), 361–369. doi:10.1016/S0969-6997(03)00042-5

Cole, S. (1998). Applied Transport Economics. In *Policy Management and Decision Making* (2nd Edition). London: Kogan Page Limited.

Cook, A. (2007). *European Air Traffic Management*. Aldershot, UK: Ashgate Publishing.

Cooper, A. *(2005)*. The Economic Catalytic Effects of Air Transport in Europe, EUROCONTROL Experimental Centre, EEC/SEE/2005/004.

Cooper, J. P. (1973). Time-varying regression coefficients: a mixed estimation approach and operational Limitations of general Markov structure. *Annuals of Economic and Social Measurement, 2*, 525–530.

Cormen, T. H., Leiserson, C. E., & Rivest, R. L. (1998). *Introduction to Algorithms*. New York: McGraw-Hill Book Company.

Correia, M., Neves, N. F., & Verissimo, P. (2006). From Consensus to Atomic Broadcast: Time-Free Byzantine-Resistant Protocols without Signatures. *The Computer Journal, 49*(1), 82–96. doi:10.1093/comjnl/bxh145

Correia, M., Verissimo, P., & Neves, N. F. (2006). Byzantine Consensus in Asynchronous Message-Passing

Systems: a Survey. In *Resilience-building Technologies: State of Knowledge, RESIST Network of Excellence Deliverable D12.*

Crespo, A. M. F., Aquino, C. V. D., Souza, B. B., Weigang, L., Melo, A. C. M. A., & Alves, D. P. (2007). Sistema Distribuído de Apoio a Decisão Aplicado ao Gerenciamento Tático do Fluxo de Tráfego: Caso CINDACTA I. In *VI Simpósio de Transporte Aéreo (VISITRAER 2007)*, (Vol. 1, pp. 317–327).

Cristian, F. (1991). Understanding Fault-Tolerant Distributed Systems. *Communications of the ACM, 34*(2), 56–78. doi:10.1145/102792.102801

Crovetti, J. A. (2002). Deflection-Based Analysis Techniques for Jointed Concrete Pavement Systems. *Transportation Research Record, 1809*, 3–11. doi:10.3141/1809-01

Cunningham, S. W., & De Haan, A. R. C. (2006). Long-Term Forecasting for Sustainable Development: Air Travel Demand Forecast for 2050. *International Journal of Environment and Sustainable Development, 5*(3), 297–314. doi:10.1504/IJESD.2006.010899

Dajani-Brown, S., Cofer, D., & Bouali, A. (2004). *Formal Verification of an Avionics Sensor Voter Using SCADE.* (LNCS 3253). Berlin: Springer.

de Neufville, R. (1976). *Airport Systems Planning: A Critical Look at Methods and Experience.* Cambridge, MA: Macmillan and MIT Press.

DECEA, Departamento de Controle de Espaço Aéreo, Divisão de Informações Aeronáuticas (2006). *Regras do ar e serviços de tráfego aéreo.* ICA 100-12.

Dennis, F., Mathaisel, X., & Idris, H. (1998). Aircraft ground movement simulation. In G. Yu, (Ed.) *Operations research in the airline industry*, (pp. 189-227). Amsterdam: Kluwer.

Dib, M. V. P. (2004). *Sistema Multi-agentes para Sincronização e Gerenciamento de Fluxo de Tráfego Aéreo em Tempo Real.* Master dissertation, Universidade de Brasília, Brasilia, DF.

Dimarogonas, D. V., & Kyriakopoulos, K. J. (2002). Inventory of Decentralized Conflict Detection and Resolution System in Air Traffic. *Technical Report HYBRIDGE, Deliverable D6.1.*

DIN 66253 Teil 3 (1989): *Mehrrechner-PEARL.* Berlin-Köln: Beuth Verlag.

DIN 66253-2 (1998): *Programmiersprache PEARL90.* Berlin-Köln: Beuth Verlag.

Douglass, B. P. (2002). *Real-Time UML.* Reading, MA: Addison Wesley.

Drabkin, V., Friedman, R., & Segal, M. (2005). Efficient Byzantine Broadcast in Wireless Ad-hoc Networks. In *Proceedings of the 35th IEEE/IFIP International Conference on Dependable Systems and Networks*, (pp. 160-169).

Durvasula, S., Guttmann, M., Kumar, A., Lamb, J., Mitchell, T., Oral, B., et al. (2006). *SOA Practitioners' Guide Part 2: SOA Reference Architecture* (Tech. Rep.). Retrieved July, 14 from http://www.soablueprint.com/practitioners_guide.

EASA CS 25. (2003) *European Aviation Safety Agency.* Decision nr 2003/2/RM, October 17.

EASA OPS. (2006). *Commission Regulation (EC) No 1899/2006 of the European Parliament and of the Council*, Annex I.

EASA PART 145, (2003). *Commission Regulation (EC) No 2042/2003 of November 20*, Annex II.

EFE. (2008). A crise nos EUA não reduzirá o tráfego aéreo de passageiros, diz AIRBUS. Retrieved April 2008 from http://www1.folha.uol.com.br/folha/dinheiro/ult91u394334.shtml

Erl, T. (2005). *Service-oriented Architecture: Concepts, Technology, and Design.* Upper Saddle River, NJ: Prentice Hall PTR.

EU FP6 (2008, February). *Potential transfer of passeenger demand to personal aviation by 2020.* European Personal Air Transportation System -D2.1.

Eurocontrol. (1999). *1999 Annual Report.*

European Commission (2001, September). *European transport policy for 2010: time to decide.* Brussels, Belgium.

European Commission. (2001b). *European Aeronautics - A Vision for 2020, Report of the Group of Personalities.* Brussels, Belgium.

European Commission. (2002). *STAR 21- Strategic Aerospace Review for the 21st Century, July 2002.* Brussels, Belgium.

European Commission. (2004). *Regulation (EC) 549/2004, Single European Sky - The Framework Regulation.* Brussels, Belgium.

European Commission. (2007). *Proposal for a council regulation on the establishment of a Joint Undertaking to develop the new generation European air traffic management system (SESAR).* Brussels, Belgium.

European Organization for the Safety of Air Navigation. (2004). *EUROCONTROL Operational Concept Document (OCD) Volume 1 (The Vision)* (Tech. Rep. FCO.ET1.ST07. DEL01). Retrieved July 12, 2008, from http://www.euro-control.int/oca/gallery/content/public/docs/op_concept/OCD_2_1_Released.pdf

European Organization for the Safety of Air Navigation. (2006). *Airport CDM Operational Concept Document, 3th ed.* (Tech. Rep. 05/04/05-1). Retrieved June 23, 2008, from http://www.euro-cdm.org/library/cdm_ocd.pdf

European Organization for the Safety of Air Navigation. (2008a). *Digital AIM.* Retrieved September 10, 2008, from http://www.eurocontrol.int/aim/public/standard_page/interoperability.html

European Organization for the Safety of Air Navigation. (2008b). *Airport CDM Implementation: The Manual* (rev. 3). Retrieved January 13, 2009, from http://www.euro-cdm.org/library/cdm_implementation_manual.pdf

FAA PART 25. (n.d.) *Airworthiness standards: transport category airplanes.* Federal Aviation Administration. Code of Federal Regulations.

FAA. (2004). *Reusable Software Components.* Advisory Circular (AC) 20-148.

FAA. (2004). *Use of Nondestructive Testing in the Evaluation of Airport Pavements.* FAA Advisory Circular No. 150/5730-11A, Office of Airport Safety and Standards, Federal Aviation Administration, U.S. Department of Transportation, Washington, DC.

FAA. (2008). *Current TSOs by Number.* Retrieved July, 2008, from http://www.airweb.faa.gov/Regulatory_and_Guidance_Library/rgTSO.nsf/MainFrame?OpenFrameSet

FAA/Eurocontrol. (2001). Principles of Operation for the use of ASAS. *FAA/EUROCONTROL Cooperative R&D Report for Action Plan 1.*

Fabrycky, W. J., & Torgersen, P. E. (1966). *Operations Economy – Industrial Applications of Operations Research.* Englewood Cliffs, NJ: Prentice-Hall, Inc.

FAR PART 145. (n.d.) *Repair Stations. Federal Aviation Administration. Code of Federal Regulations.*

Fischer, M. J. (1983). The Consensus Problem in Unreliable Distributed Systems (A Brief Survey). In *Proceedings of the International FCT-Conference on Fundamentals of Computation Theory,* (pp. 127-140).

Fischer, M. J., Lynch, N. A., & Paterson, M. S. (1985). Impossibility of Distributed Consensus with One Faulty Process. *Journal of the ACM, 32*(2), 374–382. doi:10.1145/3149.214121

Fisher, W. (1983). *Cannibalisation Policies In An Aircraft Maintenance System With Spares, Repair And Resources Constraint.* PhD Thesis. The University of Texas Austin, USA.

Flintsch, G. W. (2003). Soft Computing Applications in Pavement and Infrastructure Management: State-of-the-Art. *CD-ROM Proceedings of the 2003 Annual Meeting of the Transportation Research Board,* National Research Council, Washington DC.

Foxworthy, P. T., & Darter, M. I. (1989). ILLI-SLAB and FWD Deflection Basins for Characterization of Rigid Pavements. In A. J. Bush III & Y. Baladi (Eds.), *Nondestructive Testing of Pavements and Backcalculation of Moduli,* (pp. 368-386). West Conshohocken, PA: American Society for Testing and Materials.

Frangolho, A. P., & Zerkowitz, E. (2006). *Aeronautical Information Management Strategy* (Tech. Rep. 4th ed.). Retrieved September 10, 2008 from http://www.euro-control.int/aim/gallery/content/public/pdf/aim_strategy_vol1_ed4.pdf

Garcia-Formieles, J. (2003). A Work Breakdown Structure that Integrates Different View in Aircraft Modification Projects. *Concurrent Engineering-Research And Applications, 11*, 47–54. doi:10.1177/1063293X03011001005

Garg, N., & Marsey, W. H. (2002). *Comparison Between Falling Weight Deflectometer and Static Deflection Measurements on Flexible Pavement at the National Airport Pavement Facility (NAPTF)*. CD-ROM Proceedings of the 2002 Federal Aviation Administration Airport Technology Conference, Chicago, IL.

Garg, N., Tutumluer, E., & Thompson, M. R. (1998). Structural Modeling Concepts for the Design of Airport Pavements for Heavy Aircraft. *Proceedings of the Fifth International Conference on the Bearing Capacity of Roads and Airfields*, Trondheim, Norway.

Gervais, E. L., Hayhoe, G. F., & Garg, N. (2003). Towards a permanent ACN solution for 6-wheel landing gear aircraft. *Proceedings of the 2003 ASCE Airfield Pavement Specialty Conference*, Las Vegas, NV.

Gervais, E. L., Hayhoe, G. F., & Garg, N. (2003). Towards a Permanent Solution for 6-Wheel Landing Gear Aircraft. *Proceedings of the 2003 ASCE Airfield Specialty Conference*, Las Vegas, Nevada.

Ghaboussi, J., & Sidarta, D. E. (1998). New nested adaptive neural networks (NANN) for constitutive modeling. *Computers and Geotechnics, 22*(1), 29–52. doi:10.1016/S0266-352X(97)00034-7

Gilbo, E. P. (1993, September). Airport capacity: representation, estimation, optimisation. *IEEE Transactions on Control Systems Technology, 1*(3). doi:10.1109/87.251882

Gillen, D., & Lall, A. (2003). International Transmission of Shocks in the Airline Industry. *Journal of Air Transport Management, 9*, 37–49. doi:10.1016/S0969-6997(02)00068-6

Givoni, M. (2007). Environmental benefits from mode substitution: Comparison of the environmental impact from aircraft and high-speed train operations. *International Journal of Sustainable Transportation, 1*(4), 209–230. doi:10.1080/15568310601060044

Goh, C., & Law, R. (2002). Modeling and Forecasting Tourism Demand for Arrivals with Stochastic Non-Stationary Seasonality and Intervention. *Tourism Management, 23*, 499–510. doi:10.1016/S0261-5177(02)00009-2

Goktepe, A. B., Agar, E., & Lav, A. H. (2005). Comparison of Multilayer Perceptron and Adaptive Neuro-Fuzzy System on Backcalculating the Mechanical Properties of Flexible Pavements. *ARI: The Bulletin of the Istanbul Technical University, 54*(3), 1–6.

Goldberg, D.E. *Genetic Algorithms in Search, Optimization and Machine Learning.* Reading, MA: Addison-Wesley.

Gomez-Ramirez, F. M., & Thompson, M. R. (2002). *Characterizing Aircraft Multiple Wheel Load Interaction for Airport Flexible Pavement Design.* Civil Eng Studies, COE Report, University of Illinois at Urbana-Champaign, IL.

Gonzaga da Silva, A. M. (2001). *Sistema de simulação acelerado para análise de fluxo de tráfego aéreo.* Master dissertation, Instituto Nacional de Pesquisas Espaciais - INPE, São José dos Campos, SP.

Gopalakrishnan, K., & Thompson, M. R. (2003). Rutting Study of NAPTF Flexible Pavement Test Sections. In *Proceedings of the 2003 ASCE Airfield Specialty Conference,* Las Vegas, NV, Sep. 21-24, 2003.

Gopalakrishnan, K., & Thompson, M. R. (2004). Comparative Effect of B777 and B747 Trafficking on Elastic Layer Moduli of NAPTF Flexible Pavements. In *Proceedings of the 2004 FAA Worldwide Airport Technology Transfer Conference*, Atlantic City, New Jersey, April, 2004.

Gopalakrishnan, K., & Thompson, M. R. (2004). *Backcalculation of Airport Flexible Pavement Non-Linear Moduli Using Artificial Neural Networks.* CD-ROM Proceedings of the 17th International FLAIRS Conference.

FLAIRS-2004, Florida Artificial Intelligence Research Symposium, Miami Beach, FL, May 17-19, 2004.

Gopalakrishnan, K., Thompson, M. R., & Manik, A. (2006). Rapid Finite-Element Based Airport Pavement Moduli Solutions Using Neural Networks. *Int. J. of Computational Intelligence, 3*(1), 63–71.

Gopalan, R. (1998). The Aircraft Maintenance Routing Problem. *Operations Research, 46*(2). doi:10.1287/opre.46.2.260

Government Electronics and Information Technology Association. (2008). *FAA SWIM Program: SOA Best Practices – Industry Input* (Doc. Version 7). Retrieved September 9, 2008 from U.S. FAA website http://www.faa.gov/about/office_org/headquarters_offices/ato/service_units/techops/atc_comms_services/swim/documentation/media/best_practices/ATC FAA SWIM Program SOA Best Practices.pdf

Gramlich, E. (1994). Infrastructure Investment: a Review Essay. *Journal of Economic Literature, 32*, 1176–1196.

Guangdong tongjiju (Ed.) (2001). *Guangdong tonji nianian (Guangdong statistical yearbook)*. Guangzhou: Guangdong sheng tongjiju (in Chinese).

Gucunski, N., & Kristic, V. (1996). Backcalculation of Pavement Profiles from Spectral Analysis of Surface Waves test Using Neural Networks using Individual Receiver Spacing Approach. *Transportation Research Record, 1526*, 6–13. doi:10.3141/1526-02

Guerraoui, R., & Schiper, A. (1997). Consensus: The Big Misunderstanding. In *Proceedings of the 6th IEEE Workshop on Future Trends of Distributed Computing Systems*, (pp. 183-188).

Gumzej, R. (2004). *Overview of the Project Z2-3493: Holistic Embedded Control Systems Design*. Retrieved from http://www.rts.uni-mb.si/misc/projekti/SPEARL

Gumzej, R., & Lu, S. (2007). Modeling distributed real-time applications with Specification PEARL. *Real-Time Systems, 35*(3), 181–208. doi:10.1007/s11241-006-9007-9

Gumzej, R., Colnarič, M., & Halang, W. A. (2009). A reconfiguration pattern for distributed embedded systems. In: *Software & Systems Modeling, 8*(1), 145–161.

Haas, R., Hudson, R. W., & Zaniewski, J. P. (1994). *Modern Pavement Management*. Malabar, FL: Krieger Publishing Co.

Halang, W. A., Pereira, C. E., & Frigeri, A. H. (2002). Safe object-oriented programming of distributed real-time Systems in PEARL. *Comput. Syst. Sci. Eng., 17*(2), 85–94.

Hall, K. T. (1992). *Backcalculation Solutions for Concrete Pavements*. Technical Memo Prepared for SHRP Contract P-020, Long-Term Pavement Performance Data Analysis.

Hall, K. T., Darter, M. I., Hoerner, T., & Khazanovich, L. (1996). *LTPP Data Analysis – Phase I: Validation of Guidelines for K Value Selection and Concrete Pavement Performance Prediction*, Interim Report prepared for FHWA, ERES Consultants, Champaign, IL.

Halpern, N., & Pagliary, R. (2007). Governance Structures and the Market Orientation of Airports in Europe's Peripheral Areas. *Journal of Air Transport Management, 13*, 376–382. doi:10.1016/j.jairtraman.2007.07.003

Harmatuck, D. (1996). The influence of Transportation Infrastructure on Economic Development. *Logistics and Transportation Review, 32*, 63–76.

Hayhoe, G. F. (2002). LEAF – A new layered elastic computational program for FAA pavement design and evaluation procedures. *CD-ROM Proceedings of the 2002 Federal Aviation Administration Technology Transfer Conference*, Chicago, IL.

Haykin, S. (1994). *Neural Networks: A Comprehensive Foundation*. New York: Macmillan College Publishing Company, Inc.

He, J., Watson, L. T., Ramakrishnan, N., Shaffer, C. A., Verstak, A., & Jiang, J. (2002). Dynamic Data Structures for a Direct Search Algorithm. *Computational Optimization and Applications, 23*(1), 5–25. doi:10.1023/A:1019992822938

Hessburg, J. (2000). *Air Carrier MRO Handbook*. New York: McGraw-Hill.

Hewitt, C., & Broatch, S. A. (1992). *A Tactical Navigation and Routeing System for Low Level Flight*. [Tech. Rep]. Rochester, UK: BAE SYSTEMS Avionics Ltd.

Hewitt, C., & Martin, P. (1998). *Advanced Mission Management*. [Tech. Rep]. Rochester, UK: BAE SYSTEMS Avionics Ltd. Chen, Z., Holle, A.T., Moret, B.M.E., Saia, J. & Boroujerdi, A. (1995). Network routing models applied to aircraft routing problems. *Simulation Conference Proceedings*, Winter, 1200-1206

Heymann, M., Meyer, G., & Resmerita, S. (2003). A framework for conflict resolution in air traffic management. *In Proceedings of 42nd IEEE Conference on Decision and Control*, (Vol. 2, pp. 2035–2040), Maui, Hawaii.

Hicks, R. G. (1970). *Factors Influencing the Resilient Properties of Granular Materials*. Ph. D. dissertation, University of California, Berkeley.

Hicok, D. S., & Lee, D. (1998). Application of ADS-B for airport surface surveillance. In *Proceedings of the AIAA/IEEE/SAE 17th Digital Avionics Systems Conference, 2*, 34/1-34/8.

Hillier, F. S., & Lieberman, G. J. (1967). *Introduction to Operations Research*. San Francisco: Holden-Day, Inc.

Ho, H. W., Wong, S. C., & Loo, B. P. Y. (2004). Sequential optimization approach for the multi-class user equilibrium problem in a continuous transportation system. *Journal of Advanced Transportation, 38*, 323–345.

Ho, H. W., Wong, S. C., & Loo, B. P. Y. (2006). Combined distribution and assignment model for a continuum traffic equilibrium problem with multiple user classes. *Transportation Research Part B: Methodological, 40*, 633–650. doi:10.1016/j.trb.2005.09.003

Holzmann, G. J. (2006). *The SPIN Model-Checker: Primer and Reference Manual*. Boston: Addison-Welsey.

Hong Kong Tourism Board. (2001). *Visitor profile report 2000*. Hong Kong: Hong Kong Tourism Board.

Hossain, S. M., & Zaniewski, J. P. (1991). Characterization of Falling Weight Deflectometer Deflection Basin. *Transportation Research Record, 1293*, 1–11.

Howden, W. E. (1986). A Functional Approach to Program Testing and Analysis. *IEEE Transactions on Software Engineering, SE-12*(10), 997–1005.

Hudak, J., & Feiler, P. (2007). *Developing AADL Models for Control Systems: A Practitioner's Guide*. Technical Report. CMU/SEI-2007-TR-014, ESC-TR-2007-014.

Hutchinson, B. G. (1993). Analyses of Canadian Air Travel Demands. *Journal of Transportation Engineering, 119*, 301–316. doi:10.1061/(ASCE)0733-947X(1993)119:2(301)

Huth, W. L., & Eriksen, S. E. (1987). Airline Traffic Forecasting Using Deterministic and Stochastic Time Series Decomposition. *Logistics and Transportation Review, 23*(4), 401–409.

INCOSE-TP-2003-016-02 (2004). *Systems Engineering Handbook, Version 2a*. International Council on Systems Engineering, Bristol.

Information Services Department, Hong Kong SAR Government (2002). Press release on May 8, 2002.

Internatfional Civil Aviation Organization. (2003). *ATM Operational Concept Document (AN-Conf/11-WP/4 - Annex)*. International Civil Aviation Organization, Eleventh Air Navigation Conference, Montreal, Canadá. Quebec, Canada.

International Civil Aviation Organization. (2005). *Global Air Traffic Management Operational Concept*. (Doc 9854-AN/458, 1st Ed.). Montreal, Canada: ICAO.

International Civil Aviation Organization. (2004). *Global Air Traffic Management Operational Concept [Doc 9854]*. Quebec, Canada.

Ioannides, A. M. (1990). Dimensional Analysis in NDT Rigid Pavement Evaluation. *ASCE J. Transp. Engrg., 116*(1), 23–36. doi:10.1061/(ASCE)0733-947X(1990)116:1(23)

Ioannides, A. M. (1994). Concrete Pavement Backcalculation Using ILLI-BACK 3.0. In A. J. Bush III &Y. Baladi (Eds.), *Nondestructive Testing of Pavements and Backcalculation of Moduli*, (Vol. 2, pp. 103-124). West Conshohocken, PA: American Society for Testing and Materials.

Ioannides, A. M., Alexender, D. R., Hammons, M. I., & Davis, C. M. (1996). Application of artificial neural networks to concrete pavement joint evaluation. *Transportation Research Record, 1540*, 56–64. doi:10.3141/1540-08

Ioannides, A. M., Barenberg, E. J., & Lary, J. A. (1989). Interpretation of Falling Weight Deflectometer Results Using Principals of Dimensional Analysis. *Proceedings of the 4th International Conference on Concrete Pavement Design and Rehabilitation*, Purdue University, West Lafayette, IN.

IPCC (2007, May). *Aviation and the Global Atmosphere*. Report of the Intergovernmental Panel on Climate Change Working Groups III.

ISO 15288. (n.d.). *Systems Life Cycle Processes*. International Standard Organisation.

Iyer, P. (1999). *The Effect of Maintenance Policy on System Maintenance and Life Cycle Cost*. MSc Thesis, Faculty of the Virginia Polytechnic Institute and State University, USA.

Izquierdo, R. (1997). *Gestión y Financiación de las Infraestructuras del Transporte Terrestre*. Madrid: Asociación Española de la Carretera.

Izquierdo, R. (2003). *Economic Impacts of Infrastructure Investment: the Spanish Infrastructure Plan 2000-2001*. In ECMT (ed), 16th International Symposium on Theory and Practice in Transport Economics. Budapest, ECMT.

JAA JAR-OPS Part 1 (2005). *Commercial Air Transportation (Aeroplanes) Amendment 9*, September.

Jantsch, E. (1972). *Technological planning and social features*. New York, NY: John Wiley and Sons.

Johnson, A. M., & Baus, R. L. (1993). Simplified direct calculation of subgrade modulus from nondestructive pavement deflection testing. *Transportation Research Record*, (1406): 133–141.

Johnson, F., Hill, J., Archibald, J., Frost, R., & Stirling, W. (2005). A Satisficing Approach to Free Flight. In *Proceedings of the 2005 IEEE International Conference on Networking, Sensing and Control*, (pp. 123-128).

Joint Planning & Development Office. (2007). *Concept of Operations for the Next Generation Air Transportation System* (Tech. Rep.). Retrieved September 10, 2008 from http://www.jpdo.gov/library.asp

Jones, D. R. (2001). The DIRECT Global Optimization Algorithm. *Encyclopedia of Optimization*, (vol. 1, pp. 431-440).

Jones, D. R., Perttunen, C. D., & Stuckman, B. E. (1993). Lipschitzian Optimization without the Lipschitz Constant. *Journal of Optimization Theory and Applications, 79*, 157–181. doi:10.1007/BF00941892

Kanafani, A. (1974). *Demand Analysis for North Atlantic Air Travel* (Research Rep., Vol. 1). Berkeley, CA: Institute of Transportation Studies.

Kanafani, A. (1981). *Transportation Demand Analysis*. New York: John Wiley and Sons.

Kappatsch, A., Mittendorf, H., & Rieder, P. (1979). *PEARL: Systematische Darstellung für den Anwender*. München-Wien, Germany: R. Oldenbourg.

Karczewski, N. J., III. (2007). Optimal Aircraft Routing in a Constrained Path-Dependent Environment. Master's thesis, Naval Postgraduate School, Monterey, CA.

Karlaftis, M. G., Zografos, K. G., Papastavrou, J. D., & Charnes, J. D. (1996). Methodological Framework for Air Travel Demand Forecasting. *Journal of Transportation Engineering, 122*(2), 96–104. doi:10.1061/(ASCE)0733-947X(1996)122:2(96)

Kazda, A., & Caves, R. E. (2007). *Airport Design and Operation* (2nd. ed., pp. 188-190). Oxford, UK: Elsevier.

Khadem, M. (1992). Short-term load forecasting using Neural Networks. In Sobajic (Ed.), *1992 INNS Summer Workshop.*

Khazanovich, L., & Roesler, J. (1997). DIPLOBACK: A neural networks-based backcalculation program for composite pavements. *CD-ROM Proceedings of the 1997 Annual Meeting of Transportation Research Board*, Washington, DC.

Kikuchi, S., et al. (1994). *Estimation of trip generation using Fuzzy Regression Method.* Paper presented at 73rd Transportation Research Board Meeting in Washington, DC.

Kim, Y., & Kim, Y. R. (1998). Prediction of layer moduli from FWD and surface wave measurements using artificial neural network. *CD-ROM Proceedings of the 1998 Annual Meeting of Transportation Research Board*, Washington, DC.

King, F. (1986). *Aviation Maintenance Management.* Carbondale, IL: Southern Illinois University Press.

Koo, C.-Y., Bhandari, V., Katz, J., & Vaidya, N. (2006). Reliable Broadcast in Radio Networks: the Bounded Collision Case. In *Proceedings of the Twenty-fifth Annual ACM Symposium on Principles of Distributed Computing*, (pp. 258-264).

Kowloon-Canton Railway Corporation. (2002). Retrieved April 20, 2002, from http://www.kcrc.com/eng/service/erdfc.html.

Krafzig, D., Banke, K., & Slama, D. (2004). *Enterprise SOA: Service-Oriented Architecture Best Practices.* Upper Saddle River, NJ: Prentice Hall PTR.

Kuchar, L., & Yang, L. (2000). A Review of Conflict Detection and Resolution Modeling Methods. *IEEE Transactions on Intelligent Transportation Systems, 1*(4), 179–189. doi:10.1109/6979.898217

Ky, P., & Miaillier, B. (2006). SESAR: Towards the New Generation of Air Traffic Management Systems in Europe. *ATCA Journal of Air Traffic Control.*

Lai, S. L., & Lu, S. L. (2005). Impact Analysis of September 11 on Air Travel Demand in the USA. *Journal of Air Transport Management, 11*, 455–458. doi:10.1016/j.jairtraman.2005.06.001

Lee, D., Nelson, C., & Shapiro, G. (1998). The aviation system analysis capability airport capacity and delay models. *NASA, C*, R-1998–R-207659.

Lee, T. C., & Hersh, M. (1993). A Model for Dynamic Airline Seat Inventory Control with Multiple Seat Bookings. *Transportation Science, 27*, 252–265. doi:10.1287/trsc.27.3.252

Lenz, R. C. (1962). *Technological Forecasting.* ASD-TDR-62-414. Ohio: Wright-Patterson AFB.

Levenbach, H., & Schultz, W. (1987). Econometric Methods for Managerial Applications. In Makridakis & Wheelwright (Eds.), *Handbook of forecasting.* New York: Wiley Intersience.

Leveson, N. (1995). *Safeware: System Safety and Computers.* Boston: Addison-Wesley.

Li, R. (2007). *D-AIM Deliverable 2: D-AIM Architecture Description,* (Tech. Rep. D-LFV 2006-37208). Retrieved December 20, 2008, from http://www.d-aim.aero//output/D-AIM Deliverable 2_ D-AIM Architecture Description.pdf

Loo, B. P. Y. (1999). Formation of a regional transport network: Some lessons from the Zhujiang Delta. *Journal of Transport Geography, 7*, 43–63. doi:10.1016/S0966-6923(98)00037-4

Loo, B. P. Y. (2000). An application of canonical correlation analysis in regional science: The interrelationships between transport and development in China's Zhujiang Delta. *Journal of Regional Science, 40*(1), 141–169. doi:10.1111/0022-4146.00168

Loo, B. P. Y. (2008). Passengers' airport choice within multi-airport regions (MARs): Some insights from a stated preference survey at Hong Kong International Airport. *Journal of Transport Geography, 16*, 117–125. doi:10.1016/j.jtrangeo.2007.05.003

Ma, Z., Cui, D., & Cheng, P. (2004). Dynamic network flow model for short-term air traffic flow management. *IEEE Transactions on Systems, Man, and Cybernetics,*

Part A, Systems and Humans, 34(3), 351–358. doi:10.1109/TSMCA.2003.822969

Maestas, J. M., & Mamlouk, M. S. (1992). Comparison of pavement deflection analysis methods using overlay design. [Washington, DC: Transportation Research Board.]. *Transportation Research Record, 1377,* 17–25.

Maier, M. W. (2006). *Architecting Principles for Systems-of-Systems.* Retrieved September 06, 2008, from http://www.infoed.com/Open/PAPERS/systems.htm

Martino, J. (1972). *Technological Forecasting for Decision Making.* New York: American Elsevier Publishing.

Mathworks. (2008). Verification, Validation (V and V) and Test in Model-Based Design. *The Mathworks website.* Retrieved in June, 2008 from http://www.mathworks.com/products/featured/vv/.

McDonnell-Douglas. (1972). *Measuring the Seventies.* Market Research Report CI-804-2752. Long Beach, California.

McGill, J. I., & van Ryzin, G. J. (1999). Revenue Management: Research Overview and Prospects. *Transportation Science, 33*(2), 233–256. doi:10.1287/trsc.33.2.233

McQueen, R. D., Marsey, W., & Arze, J. M. (2001a). Analysis of Nondestructive Data on Flexible Pavement Acquired at the National Airport Pavement Test Facility. In *Proceedings of the 2001 Airfield Pavement Specialty Conference, ASCE,* Chicago, IL.

Meserole, J. S., & Moore, J. W. (2006). What is System Wide Information Management (SWIM)? In *25ᵗʰ Digital Avionics Systems Conference.* Retrieved September 08, 2008, from http://ieeexplore.ieee.org/iel5/4106227/4106228/04106233.pdf

Miaillier, B. (2007). *The SESAR Vision* [PowerPoint slides]. Retrieved September 07, 2008, from 26ᵗʰ DASC – Digital Avionics Systems Conference, Plenary Session Presentation http://www.dasconline.org/26dasc/plenary/bm.pps

Miller, S. P. (1998). Specifying the Mode Logic of a Flight Guidance System in CORE and SCR. In *Proceedings of*

the Second Workshop on Formal Methods in Software Practice (FMSP '98)* (pp. 44–53). New York: ACM.

Mirghani, M. (1996). Aircraft Maintenance Budgetary and Costing Systems at the Saudi Arabian Airlines: An Integrated Business Approach. *Journal of Quality in Maintenance Engineering, 2,* 4. doi:10.1108/13552519610153580

Mok, A. K. (1991). Towards mechanization of real-time system design. In A.M. van Tilborg & G.M. Koob (Eds.), *Foundations of Real-time Computing: Formal Specification and Methods* (pp. 1–37). New York: McGraw-Hill.

Moniz, H., Neves, N. F., Casimiro, A., & Veríssimo, P. (2007). Intrusion-Tolerance in Wireless Environments: An Experimental Evaluation. In *Proceedings of the 13th IEEE Pacific Rim International Symposium on Dependable Computing,* (pp. 357-364).

Moniz, H., Neves, N. F., Correia, M., & Veríssimo, P. (2006). Randomized Intrusion-Tolerant Asynchronous Services. In *Proceedings of the 36th IEEE/IFIP International Conference on Dependable Systems and Networks,* (pp. 568-577).

Moore, H. L., III. (1973). *Forecasting Demand at Airports.* Civil Engineering Thesis, Department of Civil Engineering, MIT.

Mora-Camino, F. (1978). *Introduction à la Programmation Géométrique.* Rio de Janeiro, Brazil: COPPE Edition.

Moschoyiannis, S., & Shields, M. W. (2004). A Set-Theoretic Framework for Component Composition. *Fundamenta Informaticae, 59*(1), 1–24.

Moschoyiannis, S., Shields, M. W., & Krause, P. J. (2005). Modelling Component Behaviour with Concurrent Automata. *Electronic Notes in Theoretical Computer Science, 141,* 199–220. doi:10.1016/j.entcs.2005.04.035

Mukherjee, A. (2004). *Dynamic Stochastic Optimization Models for Air Traffic Flow Management.* PhD thesis, University of California, Berkeley, CA.

Munnell, A. (1992). Infrastructure Investment and Economic Growth. *The Journal of Economic Perspectives, 6*, 189–198.

NASA SP-610S (1995). *Systems Engineering Handbook.* Washington, DC: National Aeronautics and Space Administration.

NCHRP 1-26 (1990). *Calibrated Mechanistic Structural Analysis Procedures for Pavements.* Final Report, National Cooperative Highway Research Program Project 1-26, TRB. Washington, DC: National Research Council.

Ndoh, N. N., Pitfieldand, D. E., & Caves, R. E. (1990). Air transportation passenger route choice: A nested multinomial logit analysis. In M. M. Fischer, P. Nijkamp, & Y. Y. Papageorgiou (Eds.), *Spatial choices and process* (pp. 349-365). Amsterdam: North-Holland.

Neter, Wesserman, & Kutner (1989). *Applied Linear Regression models (2nd Ed.).* Irwin, Homewood, III.

Newcomer, E., & Lomow, G. (2005). *Understanding SOA with Web Services.* Upper Saddle River, NJ: Addison Wesley Professional.

Nordwall, B. D. (1995, July 31). Free Flight: ATC Model for the next 50 years. *Aviation Week & Space Technology, 143*(5), 38–39.

O'Connor, K., & Scott, A. (1992). Airline services and metropolitan areas in the Asia-Pacific region 1970-1990. *Review of Urban and Regional Development Studies, 4*, 240–253. doi:10.1111/j.1467-940X.1992.tb00045.x

Omega. (2008). Definition of a development methodology in UML for embedded and real-time systems based on formal techniques. *Correct Development of Real-Time Embedded Systems.* Retrieved in June, 2008, from http://www-omega.imag.fr/.

OMG (2005). *Unified Modeling Language: Superstructure. Version 2.0.* OMG document formal/2005-07-04.

Ortuzar, J. D., & Simonetti, C. (2008). Modelling the Demand for Medium Distance Air Travel with Mixed Data Estimation Method. *Journal of Air Transport Management, 14*, 297–303. doi:10.1016/j.jairtraman.2008.08.002

Pack, J. (1987). A Practical Overview of Arima Models for Time Series Forecasting. In Makridakis & Wheelwright (Eds.), *Handbook of forecasting.* New York: Wiley Intersience.

Pasareanu, C., & Giannakopolou, D. (2006). *Towards a Compositional SPIN* (LNCS 3925). Berlin: Springer.

Paulussen, T. O., Jennings, N. R., Decker, K. S., & Heinzl, A. (2003). Distributed patient scheduling in hospitals. In *IJCA-03* (pp. 1224-1232). San Francisco: Morgan Kaufman. Hallenborg K. (2007). *Decentralized scheduling of baggage handling using multi-agent technologies.* In E. Levner, (Ed.), *Multiprocessor Scheduling: Theory and Applications*, (pp.381-403). Vienna, Austria: I-Tech Education and Publishing.

Perry, T. S. (1997, August). In Search of the Future of Air Traffic Control. *IEEE Spectrum, 34*(8), 18–35. doi:10.1109/6.609472

Plumpton, D. (2002) *Planning to Maintain an Advantage: an Aircraft View. An Industry Research Document to Effectively Plan Aircraft Maintenance.* MBA thesis, University of Bath, England.

Polak, F. R. (1996). *Airport modelling: capacity analysis of Schiphol airport in 2015.* 1st USA/Europe ATM R&D Seminar. Blondel, V.D., Hendrickx, J.H., Olshevsky A., & Tsitsiklis, J.N. (2005). *Convergence in multi-agent coordination, consensus and flocking.* 44th IEEE European Conference on Decision and Control-ECC.

Portwood, B. E. (1998). Current government and industry developments in the area of system safety assessment. *Proceedings of the 17th DASC Digital Avionics Systems Conference*, (vol.1, pp.B31-1-6). The AIAA/IEEE/SAE.

Profillidis, V. A. (2000). Econometric and Fuzzy Models for the Forecast of Demand in the Airport of Rhodes. *Journal of Air Transport Management, 6*, 95–100. doi:10.1016/S0969-6997(99)00026-5

Raad, L., & Figueroa, J. L. (1980). Load response of transportation support systems. *ASCE J. Transp. Engrg., 106*(TE1), 111–128.

Rabin, M. O. (1983). Randomized Byzantine Generals. In *Proceedings of the 24th Annual IEEE Symposium on Foundations of Computer Science*, (pp. 403-409).

Rada, G. R., Richter, C. A., & Stephanos, P. J. (1992). Layer moduli from deflection measurements: software selection and development of Strategic Highway Research Program procedure for flexible pavements. *Transportation Research Record, 1377*, 77–87.

Rada, G., & Witczak, M. W. (1981). Comprehensive Evaluation of Laboratory Resilient Moduli Results for Granular Material. *Transportation Research Record, 810*, 23–33.

Raja, A., & Lesser, V. (2004). Meta-level reasoning in deliberative agents. In *Proceedings of the Intelligent Agent Technology, IEEE/WIC/ACM International Conference on (IAT'04)*, (Vol. 00, pp. 141–147).

Rauhut, B. J., & Jordahl, P. R. (1992). Variability in measured deflections and backcalculated moduli for the Strategic Highway Research Program - Southern Region. *Transportation Research Record, 1377*, 45–56.

Rierson, L. (2000). *Software Reuse in Safety-Critical Systems*. Master's Thesis, Rochester Institute of Technology.

Rix, G. J., Baker, N. C., Jacobs, L. J., Vanegas, J., & Zureick, A. H. (1995). Infrastructure Assessment, Rehabilitation, and Reconstruction. *Proceedings of ASEE-IEEE Frontiers in Education Conference*, Atlanta, GA.

Rizzi, J. A. (2003). *Um modelo matemático de auxílio para o problema de controle do tráfego aéreo*. Master dissertation, Instituto Tecnológico de Aeronáutica - ITA, São José dos Campos, SP.

Rolim, T. H. L., Portela, T. A. A., & Alves, T. R. A. (2004). *O controle do espaço aéreo*. Technical report, DECEA, Departamento de Controle do Espaço Aéreo.

Roque, R., Romero, P., Shen, X., & Ruth, B. (1992). Prediction by asphalt pavement structural layer moduli using optimized FWD configuration. *J. Assoc. Asphalt Paving Technol., 64*, 278–305.

RTCA Incorporated (1992). Software Considerations in Airborne Systems and Equipment Certification. *RTCA document number RTCA/DO-178B.*

RTCA Task Force 3. (1995). *Final Report.*

Rubin, D., & Fagan, L. N. (1976). Forecasting air passengers in a multiairport region. In Transportation Research Board, National Research Council (Ed.), *Airport and air transport planning* (pp. 1-5). Washington, DC: Transportation Research Board.

Rumelhart, D. E., Hinton, G. E., & Williams, R. J. (1986). Learning internal representation by error propogation. D.E. Rumelhart, (ed.), *Parallel Distributed Processing*, (pp. 318-362). Cambridge, MA: MIT Press.

Saaty, T. L. (1990). *The Analytic Hierarchy Process*. Pittsburgh, PA: RWS Publications.

Saaty, T. L., & Vargas, L. G. (1991). *Prediction, Projection and Forecasting*. Boston, MA: Kluwer Academic Publishers.

SAE. (1996a). Certification Considerations for Highly Integrated or Complex Aircraft Systems, Aerospace. *Recommended Practice (ARP) 4754.*

SAE. (1996b). Guidelines and Methods for Conducting the Safety Assessment Process on Civil Airborne Systems and Equipment, Aerospace. *Recommended Practice (ARP), 4761(12).*

Samaranayake, P. (2002). Development to Engineering Structures for Scheduling and Control ff Aircraft Maintenance. *International Journal of Operations & Production Management, 22*, 8. doi:10.1108/01443570210436172

Santoro, N., & Widmeyer, P. (1989). Time is not a Healer. In *Proceedings of the 6th Annual Symposium on Theoretical Aspects of Computer Science, 349*, 304-313.

Sarris, A. H. (1973). A Bayesian approach to estimation of time varying regression coefficients. *Annuals of Economic and Social Measurement, 2*, 501–523.

Sasaki, T., Iida, Y., & Yang, H. (1990). User equilibrium traffic assignment by continuum approximation of network flow. In *Proceedings of the 11th International*

Symposium on Transportation and Traffic Theory (pp. 233-252). Japan, Yokohama.

Satishan, S. (1989). *Airline Safety Posture: A Study ff Aircraft Maintenance-Related Indicators*. PhD Thesis, University of California-Berkeley, USA.

Sayadian, L., & Weill, E. (2003). *System-Wide Information Management (SWIM) Concept in the ATN Architecture* (Tech. Rep. WGN02-WP05). Retrieved September 22, 2008 from ICAO http://www.icao.int/anb/panels/acp/wg/n/wgn2/wgn02-wp05.doc

Selić, B., & Rumbaugh, J. (1998). *Using UML for Modeling Complex Real-Time Systems*. White Paper, Rational Software Corporation. Retrieved from http://www.rational.com/media/whitepapers/ umlrt.pdf

Selić, B., Gullekson, G., & Ward, P. T. (1994). *Real-Time Object-Oriented Modeling*. Hoboken, NJ: John Wiley & Sons.

Senge, P. (1990) *The Fifth Discipline*. Currency Press.

Smith, D. E., Frank, J., & Jonsson, A. K. (2000). Bridging the gap between planning and scheduling. *The Knowledge Engineering Review, 15*(1), 47–83. doi:10.1017/S0269888900001089

Smith, K. D., Wade, M. J., Peshkin, D. G., Khazanovich, L., Yu, H. T., & Dater, M. I. (1996). *Performance of Concrete Pavements, Volume II – Evaluation of In-Service Concrete Pavements*, Report No. FHWA-RD-95-110, ERES Consultants, Champaign, IL.

Sodano, M., et al. (2008). *SWIM-SUIT: System Wide Information Management Supported by Innovative Solutions - Overall SWIM Users Requirements version 01* (Tech. Rep. D1.5.1). Retrieved August 13, 2008 from http://www.swim-suit.aero/swimsuit/projdoc.php

Sodhi, J., & Sodhi, P. (1999). *Software Reuse: Domain Analysis and Design Process*. New York: McGraw-Hill.

Souza, B. B. (2008). *Modelo de Balanceamento com Multi-Fluxos para Aplicação em Gerenciamento de Tráfego Aéreo*. Master dissertation, Universidade de Brasilia, Brasilia, DF.

Souza, B. B., Weigang, L., Crespo, A. M. F., & Celestino, V. R. R. (2008). Flow balancing model for air traffic flow management. *In Proceedings of Twentieth International Conference on Software Engineering and Knowledge Engineering (SEKE'08)*, California, CA.

Spies, G., et al. (2008). *Operational Concept for an AirPort Operations Center to enable Total Airport Management*. Paper presented at ICAS 2008 - 26th Congress of International Council of the Aeronautical Sciences, Anchorage, Alaska, USA.

Staniscia, G. F., & Dalmolin Filho, L. (2008). ATM modernisation: Air traffic control facilities in brazil have undergone a huge modernization and increase in service capacity. *Air Traffic Technology International*, (pp. 74–76).

Stirling, W. (2005). Social Utility Functions - Part I: Theory. *IEEE Transactions on Systems, Man and Cybernetics. Part C, Applications and Reviews, 35*(4), 522–532. doi:10.1109/TSMCC.2004.843198

Stricht, S. V. (2008). *Digital Aeronautical Information Management (D-AIM)*. Retrieved October 10, 2008, from EUROCONTROL, http://www.eurocontrol.int/aim/public/standard_page/daim_principles.html

Stubstad, R. N., Jiang, Y. J., Celvenson, M. L., & Lukanen, E. O. (2006). *Review of the Long-Term Pavement Performance Backcalculation Results – Final Report*. Report No. FHWA-HRT-05-150, Federal Highway Administration, McLean, VA, (p. 97).

Subramanian, J. (1995) *Airline Yield Management and Computer Memory Management via Dynamic Programming*. Ph.D. Dissertation, University of North Carolina, Dept. of Operations Research, Chapel Hill, NC.

Sultanik, E. A., Modi, P. J., & Regli, W. C. (2007). On modelling multi-agent task scheduling as a distributed constraint optimization problem. In *IJCAI*, (pp. 1531-1536).

Sun, W., Zhang, K., Chen, S., Zhang, X., & Liang, H. (2007). Service-Oriented Computing – ICSOC 2007. In *Software as a Service: An Integration Perspective* (pp. 558-569). Berlin: Springer.

Swenson, H., Barhydt, R., & Landis, M. (2006). *Next Generation Air Transportation System (NGATS)*. Air Traffic Management (ATM) Airspace project. Technical report, National Aeronautics and Space Administration.

Taguchi, A., & Iri, M. (1982). Continuum approximation to dense networks and its application to the analysis of urban road networks. *Mathematical Programming Study, 20*, 178–217.

Talluri, K., & van Ryzin, G. J. (1998). An Analysis of Bid-Price Controls for Network Revenue Management. *Management Science, 44*, 1577–1593. doi:10.1287/mnsc.44.11.1577

Tam, M. L., Lam, W. H. K., & Lo, H. P. (2008). Modeling air passenger travel behavior on airport ground access mode choices. *Transportmetrica, 4*(2), 135–153. doi:10.1080/18128600808685685

Tanaka, H. (1980). Fuzzy Linear Regression Model. *IEEE Transaction Systems, Man, Machine . Cybernetics, 10*(4), 2933–2938.

Taneja, N. K. (1978). *Airline Traffic Forecasting*. Lexington, MA: Lexington Books.

Tapiador, F., Mateos, A., & Martí-Henneberg, J. (2008). The Geographical Efficiency of Spain's Regional Airports: a Quantitative Analysis. *Journal of Air Transport Management, 14*, 205–212. doi:10.1016/j.jairtraman.2008.04.007

Tayabji, S. D., & Lukanen, E. O. (2000). Nondestructive Testing of Pavements and Backcalculation of Moduli [STP]. *ASTM Special Technical Publication, 1375*.

The Asphalt Institute. (1982). *Research and Development of The Asphalt Institute's Thickness Design Manual (MS-1) Ninth Edition*. Research Report No. 82-2, The Asphalt Institute, College Park, MD, USA.

Theunissen, E., Koeners, G. J. M., Roefs, F. D., Rademaker, R. M., & Bleeker, O. F. (2005, August). *Evaluation of an EFB Airport Map with Integrated Routing in a Distributed Simulation Environment*. Paper presented at the AIAA Modeling and Simulation Technologies Conference and Exhibit, San Francisco, CA.

Thompson, M. R. (1992). Report on the discussion group on backcalculation limitations and further improvements. [Transportation Research Board, Washington, DC.]. *Transportation Research Record, 1377*.

Thompson, M. R., & Elliott, R. P. (1985). ILLI PAVE based response algorithms for design of conventional flexible pavements. *Transportation Research Record, 1043*, 50–57.

Thompson, M. R., & Robnett, Q. L. (1979). Resilient Properties of Subgrade Soils. *Transportation Engineering Journal, 105*(1), 71–89.

Thompson, M. R., Tutumluer, E., & Bejarano, M. (1998). *Granular Material and Soil Moduli Review of the Literature*. Final Report, Center of Excellence for Airport Pavement Research COE Report No. 1, University of Illinois at Urbana-Champaign, February.

TRB. (1997). *Macroeconomic Analysis of the Linkages between Transportations Investments and Economic Performance*. NCHRP Report No 389. Washington DC: National Academy Press.

TRB. (1999). *Use of Artificial Neural Networks in Geomechanical and Pavement Systems. Transportation Research Circular No. E-C012*, TRB. Washington, DC: National Research Council.

Trip.com Travel (2002). Retrieved April 22, 2002, from www.trip.com.

Turek, J., & Shasha, D. (1992). The Many Faces of Consensus in Distributed Systems. *Computer, 25*(6), 8–17. doi:10.1109/2.153253

Tutumluer, E., Little, D. N., & Kim, S.-H. (2003). Validated Model for Predicting Field Performance of Aggregate Base Courses. *Transportation Research Record, 1837*, 41–49. doi:10.3141/1837-05

U.S. Federal Aviation Administration. (2007). *System Wide Information Management (SWIM) - Final Program Requirements - Segment 1* (Tech. Rep. rev. ed. 7.3). Retrieved September 5, 2008 from http://www.faa.gov/about/office_org/headquarters_offices/ato/service_units/techops/atc_comms_services/swim/documentation/media/requirements/20070523_swim_fpr.pdf

Ullidtz, P. (2000). Will nonlinear backcalculation help? *NDT of Pavements and Backcalculation of Moduli*, ASTM STP 1375, PA.

US COE. (2001). *O & M: PAVER, Asphalt Surfaced Airfields Pavement Condition Index (PCI)*. Unified Facilities Criteria (UFC). UFC 3-270-06, U.S. Army Corps of Engineers (Preparing Activity), Naval Facilities Engineering Command, Air Force Civil Engineering Support Agency.

Uzan, J. (1994). Advanced backcalculation techniques. *NDT of Pavements and Backcalculation of Moduli*, ASTM STP 1198, PA.

van Ommering, R. (1998). *Koala, a Component Model for Consumer Electronics Product Software* (LNCS 1429). Berlin: Springer.

Verber, D. (1999). *Object Orientation in Hard Real-Time Systems Development*. Unpublished doctoral dissertation, University of Maribor, Slovenia.

Vickerman, R. (1996). Location, Accessibility and Regional Development: the Appraisal of Trans-European Networks. *Transport Policy, 2*(4), 225–234. doi:10.1016/S0967-070X(95)00013-G

Vickerman, R. (2000). Transport and Economic Growth. *In Regional Science Association International (ed), 6th World Congress of the RSAI*. Lugano, Switzerland: RSAI.

Vora, A., Nesterenko, M., Tixeuil, S., & Delaet, S. (2008). Universe Detectors for Sybil Defense in Ad Hoc Networks. *INRIA Technical Report* (6529).

Walters, J. M., & Sumwalt, R. L. (2000). *Aircraft Accident Analysis: Final Reports, an Aviation Week Book*. New York: McGraw-Hill Professional Book Group.

Wambsganss, M. C. (2001). New Concepts and Methods in Air Traffic Management. In L. Bianco (Ed.), *Collaborative Decision Making in Air Traffic Management* (pp. 1-16). Berlin: Transportation Analysis.

Wardrop, J. G. (1952). Some theoretical aspects of road traffic research. In *Proceedings of the Institute of Civil Engineers, Part II*, 1, (pp. 325-378).

Washington, S. M., Karlaftis, M. G., & Mannering, F. L. (2003). *Statistical and Econometric Methods for Transportation Data Analysis*. Boca Raton, FL: Chapman & Hall / CRC Press.

Watson, L. T., & Baker, C. A. (2001). A fully distributed parallel global search algorithm. *Engineering Computations, 18*, 155–169. doi:10.1108/02644400110365851

Weigang, L., Alves, C. J. P., & Omar, N. (1997). An expert system for Air Traffic Flow Management. *Journal of Advanced Transportation, 31*(3), 343–361.

Wheelwright, S. C., & Makridakis, S. (1987). Introduction to Management Forecasting. In Makridakis & Wheelwright (Eds.), *Handbook of Forecasting*. New York: Wiley Interscience.

Widrow, B., & Beaufays, F. (1992). Neural Control Systems. In Sobajic (Ed.), *1992 INNS Summer Workshop*.

Wilson, S. P. (2003). *Aircraft Routing Using Nonlinear Global Optimization*. Unpublished PhD thesis, University of Hertfordshire.

Wing On Travel. (2002). Retrieved April 22, 2002, from http://202.181.172.71/v6/3tic/A_Ticket2.asp.

Wing, D. J. (2005). A Potentially Useful Role for Airborne Separation in 4D-Trajectory ATM Operations. In *Proceedings of AIAA 5th Aviation, Technology, Integration, and Operations Conference*.

Winkler, R. (1987). Judgmental and Bayesian Forecasting. In Makridakis & Wheelwright (Eds.), *Handbook of Forecasting*. New York: Wiley Interscience.

Winston, W. L. (1994). *Operations Research – Applications and Algorithms,* (3rd Ed). Belmont, CA: Duxbury Press.

Wolfowitz, P. (2004). *Guidance for Implementing Net-Centric Data Sharing* (DoD Directive 8320.2-G). Retrieved August 15, 2008, from http://www.dtic.mil/whs/directives/corres/pdf/832002p.pdf

Wong, S. C. (1998). Multi-commodity traffic assignment by continuum approximation of network flow with variable demand. *Transportation Research Part*

B: Methodological, 32, 567–581. doi:10.1016/S0191-2615(98)00018-6

Wong, S. C., & Sun, S. H. (2001). A combined distribution and assignment model for continuous facility location problem. *The Annals of Regional Science, 35*, 267–281. doi:10.1007/s001680100042

Wong, S. C., & Yang, H. (1999). Determining market areas captured by competitive facilities: A continuous equilibrium modeling approach. *Journal of Regional Science, 39*, 51–72. doi:10.1111/1467-9787.00123

Wong, S. C., Lee, C. K., & Tong, C. O. (1998). Finite element solution for the continuum traffic equilibrium problems. *International Journal for Numerical Methods in Engineering, 43*, 1253–1273. doi:10.1002/(SICI)1097-0207(19981215)43:7<1253::AID-NME468>3.0.CO;2-B

Wong, S. C., Zhou, C. W., Lo, H. K., & Yang, H. (2004). An improved solution algorithm for the multi-commodity continuous distribution and assignment model. *Journal of Urban Planning and Development, 130*, 14–23. doi:10.1061/(ASCE)0733-9488(2004)130:1(14)

EUROCONTROL (2005, September). ATM R&D Activities in Europe – Overview 2004. *Green Book 2004, R&D.ARDEP-2004*. Brussels, Belgium.

EUROCONTROL. (2006, May). *Performance Review Commission Performance Review Report* (PRR 2005). Brussels, Belgium.

EUROCONTROL. (2008). *Challenges of Growth 2008 Report*. Brussels, Belgium.

OSATE. (2008). *Open Source AADL Tool Environment*. Retrieved in July, 2008, from http://la.sei.cmu.edu.

SESAR Consortium (2006, July). *Air Transport framework, the current situation, D1* (DLM-0606-001).

SESAR Consortium (2008, April). *SESAR Master Plan D5* (DLM-0710-001-02-00).

Xu, B., Ranjithan, S. R., & Kim, Y. R. (2001). Development of Relationships between FWD Deflections and Asphalt Pavement Layer Condition Indicators. *CD-ROM Proceedings of the 81st Annual Meeting of the Transportation Research Board*, Washington, D.C.

Yang, H., & Wong, S. C. (2000). A continuous equilibrium model for estimating market areas by competitive facilities with elastic demand and market externality. *Transportation Science, 34*, 216–227. doi:10.1287/trsc.34.2.216.12307

York Aviation, L. P. P. (2007). *Social Benefits of Low Fares Airlines in Europe*. Leeds: York Aviation.

Zabarankin, M., Uryasev, S., & Murphey, R. (2006). Aircraft Routing under the risk of detection. *Naval Research Logistics, 53*(8), 728–747. doi:10.1002/nav.20165

Zhang, Z., Gao, W., & Wang, L. (2005). Short-term flow management based on dynamic flow programming network. *Journal of the Eastern Asia Society for Transportation Studies, 6*, 640–647

Zhongguo jiaotong nianjianshe (Ed.) (2000). *Zhongguo jiaotong nianjian 2000 (China transport yearbook)*. Beijing: Zhongguo jiaotong nianjianshe (in Chinese).

Zienkiewicz, O. C., & Taylor, R. L. (1989). *The finite element method*. New York: McGraw-Hill International Edition.

About the Contributors

Li Weigang has a Doctor in Science degree in Computer Engineering from Institute of Aeronautic Technology (ITA). Currently he is an associate professor and coordinator of graduate program at the Department of Computer Science of the University of Brasilia. He is the vice-president of Brazilian Air Transportation Society (SBTA) and with the fellowship from the National Council for Scientific and Technological Development (CNPq). His research interests include Computation in Finance and Air Transportation.

Alexandre de Barros is a Civil Engineering by the Campinas State University (1991), Master in Transportation and Operations Research by the Technology INstitute of Aeronautics ITA (1994), and Doctor in Transportation Engineering by the University of Calgary (2001). Currently he is Director of the Brazilian National Civil Aviation Agency and (Licensed) Lecturer of Transportation Engineering at the University of Calgary, and member of the Editorial Board of the Journal of Advanced Transportation. He has experience in the Transportation Engineering Field, with emphasis in airports, air transportation system planning, and intelligent air transportation systems, having participated in several internation airport projects, such as Toronto/Pearson, Montreal/Trudeau, Atlanda, New York/JFK, Seattle/Tacoma, Boston/LOgan, Leeds(UK), Hong Kong and Seoul/Incheon.

Ítalo Romani de Oliveira is Expert Engineer in Atech Tecnologias Críticas, a Brazilian Company of Systems Engineering with great specialization in air transportation and critical systems. He has experience in safety analysis of aeronautical applications, having received his PhD degree from the School of Engineering of the University of São Paulo, and participated as temporary collaborator in the Dutch National Aerospace Laboratory NLR, and in the Rolls-Royce University Technological Centre in Systems Engineering at York, UK. He participated of safety analysis projects also in the fields of radar and railway systems. He has been director member of the Brazilian Air Transportation Research Society since 2006.

* * *

Jorge Rady de Almeida Jr. is a professor in the Computing and Digital Systems Engineering Department, School of Engineering, at the University of São Paulo. He is also a coordinator of the school's Safety Analysis Group, where he has extensively performed research in dependable and safety-critical systems applied to critical applications. He has also investigated real time issues in the Software Engineering area, especially in the database, data-warehouse and data-mining subareas. He has substantial experience in safety analysis of urban-railway systems, database systems and air traffic systems. He received his doctorate degree in computer engineering from the School of Engineering, and is currently supervising doctorate students over the main theme of Dependability in Air Traffic Control Systems

G.J (Bert) Bakker received his Masters in Applied Mathematics from Twente University in 1989. Since joining NLR in 1992, his research has focussed on the area of collision risk modelling and stochastic analysis of advances in air traffic management. His results have found application in probabilistic conflict detection algorithms, in the development of the accident risk assessment methodology TOPAZ (Traffic Organization and Perturbation AnalyZer), supporting TOPAZ toolsets, and applications of TOPAZ to various air traffic operations. He has published many of these developments as co-author of over thirty peer reviewed scientific articles in journals, books and conference proceedings.

Michael Bartholomew-Biggs obtained his PhD from London University in 1974. He has worked as an applied comptational mathematician in many aerospace applications, first in the aircraft industry and subsequently through consultancy work with the Numerical Optimization Centre which included a series of trajectory optimization projects for the European Space Agency. He has also been active in the development of algorithms for continuous optimization - particularly sequential quadratic programming methods for tackling problems with nonlinear constraints. In the last ten years or so he has been engaged on solving global optimization problems in a wide range of application areas, from engineering to finance. He is currently Reader Emeritus in Computational Mathematics at the University of Hertfordshire.

Henk Blom is Principal Scientist at National Aerospace Laboratory NLR in Amsterdam, The Netherlands. He received his Masters from Twente University in 1978. Subsequently he performed research in forward looking infra-red picture processing at TNO Physics Laboratory, The Hague. In 1980 he joined NLR to work on research in Air Traffic Management. In 1988 he was visiting scholar at the University of Connecticut, Storrs, USA. In 1990 he received PhD from Delft University of Technology on the thesis "Bayesian estimation for decision-directed stochastic control". In 2004 he received NLR's Dr.Ir. B.M. Spee Award. Dr. Blom is Fellow IEEE since 2007. Dr. Blom has over twenty five years experience in the theory of stochastic modeling and analysis and its application to signal processing, data fusion and safety risk analysis. He is the scientific leader of innovative developments such as the widely known IMM (Interacting Multiple Model) filter algorithm, Eurocontrol's Bayesian multi-sensor multi-target tracking system ARTAS (ATM Radar Tracking And Server) and NLR's safety risk analysis methodology TOPAZ (Traffic Organization and Perturbation AnalyZer) and supporting TOPAZ tool sets. He is author of over hundred articles in scientific journals, books and conference proceedings, and of the volume "Stochastic Hybrid Systems, Theory and Safety Critical Systems", Springer, 2006. Currently he is coordinator of the European research project iFly, and at the same time he enjoys the fun and challenge of continuing his own research.

Lawrence Brom. In April 2007 Lawrence enrolled in the Strategy & Business planning Unit of the EUROCONTROL Experimental Centre where he contributed to strategic studies. He started his career in 1991 as junior consultant in ergonomics and human engineering. He passed through the banking sector from 1994 to 1997 before joining EUROCONTROL were he performed successive management responsibilities in the HR domain where he recently returned. Lawrence studied Psychology at the University of Brussels, Belgium, with a particular interest for industrial and commercial psychology.

He completed his main education with a bachelor's degree in management informatics and later with the one year management induction program of Bank Brussels Lambert now ING.

João Batista Camargo Jr. is an Electronic Engineer (1981) by the School of Engineering of the University of São Paulo (Poli-USP, Brazil), MSc by Poli-USP (1989), and PhD by Poli-USP (1996). Currently he is Associate Professor of the Computer and Digital Systems Engineering Department at the Polytechnic School, University of São Paulo, Brazil. As leader of the Safety Analysis Group in that department, he has been researching on reliable and safe computational system for critical applications, and advising several Master and Ph.D. alumni.

Félix Mora-Camino is a civil aeronautical engineer with Dr.Ing. and DSc degrees from the university of Toulouse. He was for several years, a professor of Control and Computer Science at the Royal Airforce Academy in Marrakech, Marrocco, and at the Federal University of Rio de Janeiro (titular professor of the COPPE institute) in Brazil where he has his permanent residence. He has been, for the last ten years, responsible for the Automation and Operations Research Laboratory (LARA) at the Air Transportation Department of ENAC (French Civil Aviation Institute) in Toulouse where he teaches Control theory and Operations Research. He is an associate senior researcher at LAAS (Laboratoire d'Architecture et d'Analyse des Systèmes) du CNRS (Centre National de la Recherche Scientifique) in Toulouse. Mr. Mora-Camino is the author of many communications in the fields of Aeronautics and air transportation operations.

Victor R. R. Celestino holds a BSc in Aeronautical Engineering and a MSc in Operations Research from Institute of Aeronautic Technology (ITA), a MBA in Corporate Strategy from Getulio Vargas Foundation (FGV), and ongoing PhD in Transports at University of Brasilia (UnB). More than 25 years experience in civil and military aviation at Brazilian and multinational organizations, such as EADS. His research interest includes Planning Strategies and Methodologies in Air Transport.

Miguel Correia is an Assistant Professor of the Department of Informatics, University of Lisboa Faculty of Sciences. He received a PhD in Computer Science at the University of Lisboa in 2003. Miguel Correia is a member of the LASIGE research unit and the Navigators research team. He has been involved in several international and national research projects related to intrusion tolerance and security, including the MAFTIA and CRUTIAL EC-IST projects, and the ReSIST NoE. He is currently the coordinator of University of Lisboa's degree on Informatics Engineering and an instructor at the joint Carnegie Mellon University and University of Lisboa MSc in Information Technology - Information Security. His main research interests are: intrusion tolerance, security, distributed systems, distributed algorithms.

Antonio Márcio Ferreira Crespo is Bachelor of Aeronautical Science by the Air Force Academy (1994) and Bachelor of Social Science at Federal University of Santa Catarina (2003), with specialization in Electronic Engineering by the Technological Institute of Aeronautics (ITA-2004). He is a Brazilian Air Force Officer working at CINDACTA I and currently a Masters student at the University of Brasilia. He has experience in the fields of sociology, with emphasis on social indicators, Electronic Engineering, with emphasis on antennas applied to military systems and Control and Air Traffic Management, acting mainly in the following areas: management of air traffic flow, electronic warfare programs and operational safety and quality assurance in air traffic services.

Luis Gustavo Zelaya Cruz is a Civil Engineer from the National Autonomous University of Honduras, where was graduated in 1983, has a MSc. in Transportation Engineering (1986) and a PhD in Production Engineering (2006) from the Federal University of Rio de Janeiro, COPPE Institute, and also undergone a specialization course on Port Management from the Brazilian Merchant Marine in 2000. Currently he is Lecturer at the Federal Fluminense University, teaching in the courses of Petroleum and Gas Industry Management, Enterprise Logistics and Petroleum Logistics.

Paulo Sérgio Cugnasca is an Electronic Engineer (1987) by the School of Engineering of the University of São Paulo (Poli-USP, Brazil), MSc by Poli-USP (1993), and PhD by Poli-USP (1999). Currently he is Assistant Professor of the Computer Engineering and Digital Systems Department at Poli-USP. As member of the Safety Analysis Group in that department, he has been researching on reliable and safe computational system for critical applications, and advising several Master and Ph.D. alumni.

Adilson Marques da Cunha, DSc, is an associate professor in the Brazilian Aeronautical Institute of Technology at the Computer Science Division. He holds MSc from the United States Air Force Institute of Technology – AFIT (1983-84), and DSc from the George Washington University – GWU (1985-87). He is the coordinator of the Software Engineering Research Group (GPES) at ITA. Professor Cunha has experience in Information Systems, Software Engineering, and Artificial Intelligence. In the last 15 years, he has advised more than 30 master and doctoral degree students in the areas of computer science, and has written more than 50 different papers for international conferences, symposiums, and congresses. He also has been developing and coordinating more than 20 R&D successful projects in the ITA. As a former full colonel from the Brazilian Air Force, and a pilot, he had more than 5,000 hours in flight on 26 different types of aircrafts. He is the ITA coordinator of the on-going exchange project, called Cooperative Air Traffic Management – C-ATM, between the German Berlin Institute of Technology (TU-Berlin) and the Brazilian Aeronautics Institute of Technology – ITA (2008-2011).

Felipe M. G. França is an Associate Professor at the Systems Engineering and Computer Science Program, COPPE, Universidade Federal do Rio de Janeiro (UFRJ). He received his BEE (Electronics Engineering, 1981) and his MSc (Computer Science, 1987) from UFRJ, and his PhD (Neural Systems Engineering, 1994) from Imperial College London. His research and teaching interests includes computer architecture, computational intelligence models and all aspects of parallel and distributed computing.

Ricardo Alexandre Veiga Gimenes is a researcher in the School of Engineering at the University of São Paulo, where he is a member of Safety Analysis Group. He is also member of Brazilian Air Transport Research Society. Since 2002, he has been gathering substantial experience in safety analysis of dependable systems controlling critical applications as Air Traffic Control and Railway Systems. He received his master's degree in Computer Engineering from School of Engineering and now, the main focus of his doctoral research is the development of a methodology to integrate Unmanned Aircraft Vehicles in non-segregated airspace under supervision of Air Traffic Control.

Kasthurirangan Gopalakrishnan is a Research Assistant Professor of Civil Engineering at Iowa State University, Ames and has over 10 years of experience in transportation infrastructure systems. Dr. Gopalakrishnan received his PhD in Civil Engineering from the University of Illinois at Urbana-Champaign and a Masters from Louisiana State University at Baton Rouge. Dr. Gopalakrishnan is also a recipient of *Dwight D. Eisenhower Transportation Research Fellowship* which gave him the opportunity to work at the Turner-Fairbanks Highway Research Centre (TFHRC), Washington DC on a research project entitled "Simulation, Imaging, and Mechanics of Asphalt Pavements". His current research interests include soft computing applications in pavement analysis, mechanistic-empirical pavement design concepts, image analysis, and non-destructive evaluation of pavements and he has published over 50 peer-reviewed journal articles in these areas.

Roman Gumzej, born 1970 in Maribor, Slovenia, received a doctorate in computer science and informatics from University of Maribor in 1999. He worked both in industry (Institute of Information Science, IZUM Maribor) and academia (University of Maribor), before he was elected assistant professor at the Faculty of electrical engineering and computer science at University of Maribor in 2004. He was a visiting researcher at ifak e.V. Magdeburg, Germany in 2002 and at the Chair of Computer Engineering at Fernuniversität in Hagen, Germany in 2007. Currently he is assistant professor at the Faculty of logistics at the same university. His research interests comprise all major areas of hard real-time computing with special emphasis on operating systems, co-design and quality-of-service. He has conducted a national and co-operated in several national and international research projects. He has authored or co-authored several refereed book chapters, and about 40 journal publications and conference contributions, and is involved in various professional organisations and programme committees of several conferences.

Wolfgang A. Halang, born 1951 in Essen, Germany, received a doctorate in mathematics from Ruhr-Universität Bochum in 1976, and a second one in computer science from Universität Dortmund in 1980. He worked both in industry (Coca-Cola GmbH and Bayer AG) and academia (University of Petroleum and Minerals, Saudi Arabia, and University of Illinois at Urbana-Champaign), before he was appointed to the Chair of Applications-Oriented Computing Science and head of the Department of Computing Science at the University of Groningen in the Netherlands. Since 1992 he holds the Chair of Computer Engineering in the Faculty of Electrical and Computer Engineering at Fernuniversität in Hagen, Germany, whose dean he was from 2002 to 2006. He was a visiting professor at the University of Maribor, Slovenia, 1997, and the University of Rome II in 1999. His research interests comprise all major areas of hard real-time computing with special emphasis on safety-related systems. He is the founder and was European editor-in-chief of the journal Real-Time Systems, member of the editorial boards of 4 further journals, co-director of the 1992 NATO Advanced Study Institute on Real-Time Computing, has authored 12 books and some 350 refereed book chapters, journal publications and conference contributions, has edited 16 books, holds 12 patents, has given some 80 guest lectures in more than 20 countries, and is active in various professional organisations and technical committees as well as involved in the programme committees of some 180 conferences. In the International Federation of Automatic Control he chaired the Technical Committee on Real-Time Software Engineering before he became member of the Technical Board in 2002 chairing the Co-ordinating Committee on Computers, Cognition and Communication for Control until 2008.

H.W. Ho is a Research Associate at the Department of Civil & Structural Engineering of The Hong Kong Polytechnic University. He received his B.Eng. and Ph.D. degrees from the University of Hong Kong. His research interests includes congestion pricing studies, land-use and transport modeling, macroscopic facility choice studies, and continuum modeling approach for traffic equilibrium problems.

Matthew G. Karlaftis is an associate professor in the department of transportation planning and engineering at the National Technical University of Athens, in Greece. He holds a bachelor's and a master's degree in civil engineering from the University of Miami and a Ph.D. from Purdue University. His interests include public transport operations, transit economics, and transportation data analysis.

Becky P.Y. Loo is Associate Dean of the Faculty of Social Sciences and an Associate Professor of the Department of Geography at the University of Hong Kong. Her research interests are transportation, spatial analysis, and economic geography. Her research uses surveys, quantitative techniques and spatial modelling to analyze transport and development phenomena. She published very high-quality and substantial articles in top-ranking internationally-refereed journals. In recognition of her research achievements, she was awarded the Outstanding Young Researcher 2006. Becky Loo is on the Editorial Board of ten academic journals, including the *International Journal of Sustainable Transportation, NETCOM, Transportation and Transportmetrica*. Moreover, she was invited to serve as a reviewer for important grant councils and for 18 different academic journals in geography and transportation. From 2005 to 2009, she was the chairperson of the Hong Kong Section of the International Geographical Union.

Denis Silva Loubach received the BS degree in Computer Engineering from the University of Mogi das Cruzes – UMC, Sao Paulo, Brazil, in 2004; and the MSc degree in Electronics and Computer Engineering, Computer Science area, from the Aeronautics Institute of Technology – ITA, Sao Jose dos Campos, Sao Paulo, Brazil in 2007. Currently, he is a PhD student at ITA in the computer science area, working mainly with real-time systems, embedded systems, scheduling, fault tolerance, and microcontrollers. He also integrates the Software Engineering Research Group – GPES at ITA. Its main projects in Brazil have been the Student Satellite from 2005-07, the Unmanned Aerial Vehicle from 2006-08, and the On-Board Data Handling Computer since 2008. He is an IEEE student member.

Osvandre Alves Martins is a Brazilian computer science researcher and professional who started his career in 1989 after finishing a technician course about data processing. He received the BS degree in Computer Science from the Faculty of Informatics of Presidente Prudente (Brazil) in 1994 and Information Systems Specialist title in 1997 from Federal University of São Carlos. In 2003 he received the MS degree from the Brazilian Aeronautics Institute of Technology (ITA) and his studies and works comprised software systems interoperability for project management. His professional experience includes information technology management and software engineering in some companies in Brazil, and Research & Development activities considering software engineering, software development process and support tools, mainly performed in projects that involve the ITA and public and private companies, since 2001. He is now a doctoral student and member of the Software Engineering Research Group (GPES) at ITA.

Giovani Volnei Meinerz is a Computer Science doctorate student at the Brazilian Aeronautics Institute of Technology (ITA), advised by Professor Dr. Adilson Marques da Cunha. He integrates the Software Engineering Research Group (GPES) at ITA. He has experience in Computer Science, focusing on Software Engineering, acting mainly on the following topics: integrated development environment and software development process, applied on research and development projects since 2002. Currently, he is a researcher in the on-going exchange project between the German Berlin Institute of Technology

(TU-Berlin) and ITA which aims to investigate and propose the main requirements and recommendations for future cooperative ATM concepts, using collaborative technologies and procedures to enhance process efficiency.

Henrique Moniz is a Ph.D. student at the Department of Informatics, University of Lisbon. He is a member of the LASIGE laboratory and the Navigators research group. He is also a teaching assistant at the University of Lisbon. His research interests are concerned with distributed algorithms in hostile environments. He is involved in several research projects related to intrusion tolerance and security, including the RITAS (FCT), the CRUTIAL and HIDENETS (EC-IST) projects, and the ReSIST NoE.

Nuno Ferreira Neves is an assistant professor of the Department of Informatics, University of Lisboa, and also an adjunct faculty at the Information Network Institute, Carnegie Mellon University, for activities related to the MSc in Information Technology - Information Security. He received a Ph.D in Computer Science from the University of Illinois at Urbana-Champaign (1998). His main research interests are in dependable and secure parallel and distributed systems, and in the recent years, he has participated in several European and National research projects in this area, namely CRUTIAL, Resist, AJECT, RITAS and MAFTIA. His work has been recognized with the IBM Scientific Prize in 2004 and the William C. Carter award at the IEEE FTCS in 1998. Currently, he is member of the editorial board of the International Journal of Critical Computer-Based Systems.

Stephen Parkhurst obtained his PhD at the University of Hertfordshire based on research into the application of nonlinear optimization to problems of reservoir management in the oil and gas industry. Subsequently he worked with the Numerical Optimization Centre on the development of trajectory optimzation software (in both Fortran and Ada) for the European Space Operations Centre in Darmstadt. He then joined the Mathematics department at the University of Hertfordshire, taking particular responsibility for teaching mathematics to engineers and to other non-specialist students, while retaining a research interest in conjugate-gradient methods for optimization. He has now left the university sector to pursue a career as a school mathematics teacher.

Nadine Pilon. Responsible for Strategic studies in the Strategy unit at the European Organization for the Safety of Air Navigation, Dr Nadine Pilon joined EUROCONTROL in 1994 where she initiated and managed the Safety Research Area at the Experimental Centre. She then set-up Society research as Deputy Manager of the Society-Environment-Economy Research Area. She holds a PhD in modeling sciences at Paris VI University and several years in software and system engineering in European industry. She is now also responsible for the Influence modeling in the context of the Performance Framework of the European project EP3, a contributor to SESAR.

Walter N. Pizzo currently works as Defense Systems Manager at Atech – Tecnologias Críticas (www.atech.br), with activities in defense programs management and proposals coordination related to critical systems engineering for the Brazilian MOD and military organizations. His experience includes contract management, specifications and design of air defense systems. Recent projects include simulation systems for military air operations training, airborne mission systems, command and control systems, air to ground datalink solutions and reliability assessment studies of critical systems. He holds a Bachelor's Degree in Electronics Engineering from the Polytechnic School of the University of Sao Paulo (1984), specialization in Education at Sao Paulo Catholic University (2000) and a Masters of Science Degree in Electrical Engineering by Polytechnic School of the University of Sao Paulo (2008).

José Lourenço da Saúde graduated in 1985 from the State University of Coimbra (Portugal) as Chartered Mechanical Engineer. In 1986 finalised his MSc at the von Karman Institute for Fluid Dynamics, Belgium. In 1981 made a post graduation course in the management of aeronautical programmes (Airbus Industries, Cranfield University and Pisa Univerity). Joined the Portuguese Air Force in 1987, being assigned for almost 15 years to the aeronautical industry where he held various senior positions, ranging from maintenance, production and project engineering to logistics. In 2007 received is PhD in Aeronautics Sciences, being invited at the State university of Beira Interior in Portugal (www.ubi.pt) to be Assistant Professor in the domain of aircraft Manufacturing and Maintenance. He is member of the Portuguese Society of Professional Engineers.

Eno Siewerdt was born in the city of Jaragua do Sul, Brazil, 1952, started his professional career as an Air Navigation Instructor with the Brazilian Air Force and Air Traffic Controller. Chief Air Traffic Controllers' Training Officer, and Head of Air Traffic Management R&D in Brazil from 1980 to 1998. Member, Brazilian CNS/ATM (Communications, Navigation, Surveillance/Air Traffic Management) Commission. Advisor on the Future Air Navigation System Special Committee, Member of the Obstacle Clearance Panel (OCP), Air Traffic Management Operational Concept Panel (ATMCP), and the Human Resource Planning and Training Study Group (HRPTSG), of the International Civil Aviation Organization (ICAO). Air Navigation Expert and international coordinator of technical cooperation projects. Instructor at the Brazilian Civil Aviation Institute, and guest lecturer at several major Universities, focusing on Navigation, Traffic Management and Air Transport subjects. Currently, Air Navigation and Traffic Management Consultant with ATECH and the Polytechnical School of the University of São Paulo.

Jorge Miguel Reis Silva, Merchant Marine Officer, SOPONATA (Sociedade Portuguesa de Navios Tanque, Lisbon, Portugal), 1979-1987. Aeronautical Telecommunications Technician, ANA,ep (Aeroportos e Navegação Aérea, Lisbon, Portugal), 1988 1995. Marine Systems Engineer for Electrical and Telecommunications, Escola Náutica Infante D. Henrique, (Oeiras, Portugal), 1993. Lecturer and (since 2005) Assistant Professor, State University of Beira Interior (Covilhã, Portugal), 1995-2007. MSc on Operational Research and Systems Engineering, Instituto Superior Técnico (Lisbon, Portugal), 1996. PhD on Transports, Instituto Superior Técnico (Lisbon, Portugal), 2007. Main interests: Air Transport Systems, Aircraft Operations, Air Transport Safety and Security, Operational Research. AIAA (American Institute of Aeronautics and Astronautics) Member.

Giacomo F. Staniscia currently works as Defense Systems Director at Atech – Tecnologias Críticas (www.atech.br) and as Director of Innovation at the same company. Develop activities in national defense programs for the Brazilian government and military organizations. His experience includes contract management, specifications and design of aerospace, air defense systems and air traffic systems. Worked as technical manager on Brazilian Amazon surveillance system (SIVAM), recent projects include simulation systems for military air operations training, airborne mission systems, command and control systems, air to ground datalink solutions and reliability assessment studies of critical systems. Mr. Giacomo holds a Bachelor's Degree in Electronics Engineering from Federal University of Parana (UFPR) and post-graduation in electronics systems from University of Sao Paulo.

Alessandra Tedeschi is an employee at Deep Blue Srl. She has a PhD in Applied Mathematics from the University of L'Aquila and Rome La Sapienza. Her research interests are agent based models and game theory applied to the optimization and control of complex and safety critical systems.

Antonio Pedro Timoszczuk received a BS degree in Electronic Engineering in 1984 from Industrial Engineering Faculty - FEI-SBC, received MSc and PhD degrees in Electronic Systems in 1998 and 2004 respectively, from Politechnic School University of Sao Paulo. He has experience as university researcher and worked on industry in R&D Projects involving military systems, air traffic control, telecommunications and location based services. On faculty his research interests concentrate on intelligent systems and artificial neural networks applications. Currently he works as a R&D and Innovation Coordinator at Atech and as a collaborate researcher at Sao Paulo University where he develops advanced research on biologically plausible neural networks. Dr.Timoszczuk is a member of IEEE Society, Brazilian Society for Science Progress-SBPC and Brazilian Computer Society.

Lúcio F. Vismari has Diploma (2001) and Masters Degree (2007) in Electrical Engineering, with emphasis on Telecommunications and Digital Systems, respectively, both by the School of Engineering at the University of Sao Paulo (USP), Brazil. In 2008, he began the studies to receive his Doctor of Engineering degree at same university. After receiving his degree in Electrical Engineering in 2001, he joined to the Safety Analysis Group (GAS) of Escola Politécnica at USP (GAS/EPUSP), doing researching on themes related to the area of computer-based dependable systems (mainly the aspects of Reliability, Availability and Safety), with specific focus on risk assessment methodologies applied to transportation systems. Concomitant with his research, he acts as a system safety analyst in computer-based dependable systems projects, as railway signaling and control systems, air traffic control systems, defense equipments and others.

Simon Wilson currently works as a Researcher and Software Engineer in the fields of Traffic Modelling and Applications for a research establishment in the UK. He gained his PhD in 2003 from the University of Hertfordshire carrying out research into the application of Global Optimization algorithms to solving Aircraft Routing problems. The research programme was funded by BAE SYSTEMS whom he worked for as a Software Engineer prior to starting his PhD.

S.C. Wong is a Professor at the Department of Civil Engineering and Director of the Institute of Transport Studies of the University of Hong Kong. He received his B.Sc.(Eng.) and M.Phil. degrees from the University of Hong Kong, and Ph.D. degree in Transport Studies from University College London. His research interests include the optimization of traffic signal settings, continuum modeling for traffic equilibrium problems, traffic flow theory, traffic management and control, transportation planning and network modeling, and road safety. He is currently Editor-in-Chief of *International Journal of Sustainable Transportation*, and *Transportmetrica*; Associate Editor of *IEEE Transactions on Intelligent Transportation Systems*, and *Journal of Advanced Transportation*; and Editorial Board Member of *Transportation Research Part B, Transport Reviews, ASCE Journal of Urban Planning and Development, Journal of Intelligent Transportation Systems, Journal of Transportation Systems Engineering and Information Technology, International Journal of Shipping and Transport Logistics*, etc.

Dave Young. Head of Strategy and Stakeholder Relations Management at the European Organization for the Safety of Air Navigation, Mr. Dave Young has been a member of EUROCONTROL since 1980. Early in his career he led many HMI research and operational validation activities, which were instrumental in the introduction of windowing techniques and colour for today's Air Traffic Control. Later, he led a pioneering application of distributed technology for Air Traffic Management, managing the introduction of open system architectures and technologies, including the development of very large scale CORBA based air traffic management simulation facilities. More recently, together with the European Commission and the ATM supply industry, he was a key actor in the developments leading to the establishment of the European ATM Master Plan and SESAR.

Peng Zhang is a Professor at the Shanghai Institute of Applied Mathematics and Mechanics, Shanghai University, Shanghai, China. He received his B.Sc. degree from Sichuan University, Sichuan, China, and M.Sc. and Ph.D. degrees from the University of Science and Technology of China, Hefei, China. His research interests include traffic flow theory and computational methods.

Index